A PRISON ANTHOLOGY
Brushy Mountain 2005-2007

By Garry W. Johnson

Covenant Concepts
CovenantConcepts.org

Covenant Concepts
Post Office Box 12, Eidson, TN 37731
CovenantConcepts47@gmail.com
CovenantConcepts.org

All Covenant Concepts titles, imprints, and distributed lines
are available at special quantity discounts for bulk purchases
for sales promotions, premiums, fundraising,
educational, or institutional use.

ISBN: 978-1-7354507-0-4
ISBN: 978-1-7354507-1-1

Printed in the United States of America

The *Mountain Review* was produced as a free government document written by inmates at Brushy Mountain State Penitentiary and Morgan County Regional Correctional Facility. It was sponsored by the Education Department at those facilities and was a censored publication. Permission to reprint was granted on the back page of each edition. The views expressed are those of individual authors and do not necessarily reflect the Tennessee Department of Correction's policy at the time, nor the views of the editors, staff, sponsors, administration, or those of Covenant Concepts.
Photos of Brushy Mountain contributed by Mrs. Sonya Newport.

Preface

In 2005, I was transferred from the Sevier County jail to begin serving a fresh 48 in the Tennessee Department of Correction. My first stop: Brushy Mountain. The archaic castle was quite a site for a newbie to the penal system. I had spent the previous five years in 23 and 1 lockdown, fighting off a double homicide charge, and Brushy was my first taste of what this new existence would hold. Despite my familiarity with the correctional mentality, the old guard at Brushy still had some surprises for me.

You'll learn more about me as these pages unfurl and new editions are released, but these anthologies aren't entirely my own. These pages hold the writings of the prisoners who walked these sally ports and breezeways, and a chronicle of the events that affected them, the staff, and at times the country, over this three-year period. Through the pages of *Mountain Review*, the prisoner-written newspaper, you will see what they saw and read what they read, and at times get a taste of what they thought.

iii

Proceeds from the sale of this book go directly to Covenant Concepts, a 501(c)3 non-profit organization dedicated to providing prisoners with free educational resources.

Covenant Concepts
P.O. Box 12
Eidson, TN 37731
CovenantConcepts.org
covenantconcepts47@gmail.com
Facebook@CovenantConcepts47

Table of Contents

The BMCX
Mountain Review

Inmate News Items   For the Compound

Spring 2003 Edition   ►◄   A Brushy Mountain Correctional Complex Publication   ►◄   Volume 17, Number 1

Introduction

I began working at *Mountain Review* shortly after being classified at site one (the Castle) to Brushy Mountain site two, Morgan County. The Morgan County Regional Correctional Facility (MCRCF) was situated on the other side of the mountain that skirted the rear of the Castle, and in the summer of 1997 the two were combined administratively to form BMCX, the Brushy Mountain Correctional Complex. *Mountain Review* served as the official publication for the entire complex (though I quickly put the Morgan County moniker on the drop head, see page 23.) Two years after the last issue covered here, Brushy, which opened in 1896, closed its doors forever.

This compilation starts with the first issue I was part of, though the history of the paper far exceeds me. Unfortunately, the papers I once held, dating back to about 1992, were lost during a remodel of the school where our offices were originally located. In an effort to trace some of that history I interviewed one of Brushy's oldest residents, Jim Slagle, in 2014 (Jim, along with the remainder of Brushy's residents were moved to Morgan County in 2009, when the facility closed. According to state records, Jim made parole in February 2018, at the age of 81. He had been incarcerated since June 24, 1968.)

Jim was best known for mailing himself out of the Brushy Mountain mailroom – a story he's not too fond of perpetuating, though nonetheless true (sorry, Jim). The package was unfortunately "returned to sender" before getting too far down the road. At the time of our interview, Jim had been in for 46 years and was 78 years old. He didn't remember the prison having a paper before 1981. That year Brushy's warden, Otie Jones, allowed Jim to start a publication called *Cabbages and Kings*, a name Slagle said he took from the walrus' dialogue in Alice in Wonderland (if you know Jim, you believe him). Jim Slagle's paper ran for two years before a new warden

shut it down, not caring much for Jim's uncensored style. He said at least four more years would go by before the facility produced another publication, around 1987.

Jim's account is indicative of the paper's more modern history as well. Over the nine years I was involved with this publication various officials and entities confiscated materials or obstructed and maligned the process, but somehow the work went on (despite losing two sets of computers, countless files and man-hours of work). And thanks to the digital process, the publications here survived – escaping prison the same way Jim tried to.

In October of 2003, the Golden Bears Veterans Association (a prisoner club at site two) donated two computers to the News department, and in April of 2004 the first digital file was created of the 10.25" x 11.5" newsprint publication *Mountain Review* was at that time. (The original Review, prior to 2003, was a magazine-size publication with 16-20 pages. Its camera-ready proofs were made by hand with a typewriter, layout paper, Exacto knives and paste.) Since the introduction of those machines, a digital history has been kept. In these pages are part of what I was able to preserve.

Brushy Mountain's Mark

As is true with many of the prisoners and staff of MCCX, Brushy Mountain has left its mark on me – and in my case, quite literally.

By Garry W. Johnson
MOUNTAIN REVIEW

On April 19, 2005, I pulled up to the ominous-looking prison in the back of a Sevier County transport van. Having spent the previous 4 years and 7 months in a maximum-security cell, Brushy was a new and exciting taste of freedom for me (yes, I said freedom).

Unfortunately, my enthusiasm wasn't too well received by my new overseers. After spending so much time with the staff of Sevier County Jail, I had become way too comfortable with incarceration, and Brushy security was ready and willing to remind me of my current lot in life.

One morning I found myself quietly whistling a tune as I strolled through the chow hall unfettered by the cuffs and chains to which I had formerly been accustomed. As the Captain hollered for my joyous tune to cease, I heard myself do the whistling equivalent of "WHAAAA, Whaaaa, whaaaaaa." Hoping that I had adequately blended into the cloud of blue uniforms, I hung my head and hurried into the chow line – but it was too late, I was busted.

I soon found myself in the 113-year-old stairwell adjacent to the cafeteria – where there weren't any cameras (as my cohorts pointed out to me later). Two astute-looking officers had escorted me there, neither seeming too happy with their current assignment.

One stood face-to-face with me and proceeded to inform me of the rich history of BMCC and the likelihood of my becoming a casualty of its traditions – if my "attitude" didn't improve. The other officer stood somewhere in my blind spot, an observer of the class, likely there to insure the material was well-received.

For generations Brushy Mountain has had an emotional attachment for many of the residents of Morgan County, nicknamed by some the "Alcatraz of the South." As Tennessee's oldest operating penitentiary closed its doors on Thursday, June 4, 2009, over a century of service came to an end. "When the last group was going out, it was emotional," said Jim Worthington, Brushy Mountain's last Warden. "We never thought (the prison) would close."

Opened in 1896, Brushy was known throughout the country, even listed in the Guinness Book of World Records as the only prison in the United States with a natural bluff for a prison wall. In 1977, part of that wall received national media attention as James Earl Ray and six other prisoners made a short-lived dash for freedom using a ladder made from 20 pieces of conduit pipe. That sparked a widespread manhunt, which apprehended Ray's accomplices within two days. Bloodhounds took another 48 hours to locate the convicted killer of civil rights leader Martin Luther King Jr. Ray, now deceased, was serving a life sentence for the 1968 Memphis murder.

The enclosure wall and some of the buildings that make up BMCC were constructed entirely of hand-carved stone, collected by inmates from the nearby rock quarry. Brushy itself was designed in the shape of the Greek cross, because at that time it was understood the penitentiary's purpose was to convert inmates to Christianity. After its opening, Brushy and other prisons of the day participated in the notorious convict-lease system, a relic of the post-Reconstruction South. Even for several years prior to the building of BMCC, convicts in the lease system worked the area coal mines and lived in tents until Brushy came online.

TDOC Commissioner George Little recently noted that BMCC was "the end of the line for some inmates." The facility held some of the most violent prisoners in the state, including some on death row. Others, then, even as now, came into the system and never left. The only prisoner from Morgan County to be executed by the state, killed a guard while trying to escape from Brushy. For that he was sentenced to death and electrocuted in 1939.

Commissioner Little also told reporters about "the hole," as it existed prior to 1960. "The hole was an empty room with a mattress and two buckets in it, one for water and one to use the bathroom," he said. "It wasn't heated or cooled, and there was no light." Up until about 50 years ago corporal punishment was also a regular exercise at BMCC, a fact eluded to in my impromptu seminar. My instructors never made it clear that they understood the practice had ended, but they did stop short of using it.

So as I said at the beginning, Brushy did literally leave a mark on me, but not from anything physically inflicted on me by the staff or other prisoners. My mark came in the form of a spider bite, which became infected with STAPH just before I left BMCC. The tan whelp surrounding the little red mark on my leg always reminds me to keep check on my attitude with prison employees, because in a 113-year-old prison – as well as a brand-new institution – there is always a blind spot, where the cameras don't see! *MR*

Editor's note: This article was rejected for publication at a time when violence within the Brushy Mountain Correctional Complex was experiencing a spike. Labeled as "inflammatory," the article was only shared among prisoners.

2

Mountain Review

BMCC

Volume 18, Number 3 A Brushy Mountain Correctional Complex Publication **DEC. 2005**

BMCC Varsity Club

"Producing Productive Citizens Through Education."

By Jeremy Ingram,
MOUNTAIN REVIEW Staff

The Varsity Club was established in 1992 to address the needs of the incarcerated student. Since its inception, the Varsity Club has done a great deal to further rehabilitative programs here at BMCC and create community awareness and promote public support for these programs. The results of the efforts by the Varsity Club are evident—the ideas that constitute good citizenship have been instilled, dignity and self worth have been nurtured, and the motivation to further one's education has been fostered. Ultimately, the efforts of the Varsity Club have helped lower the recidivism rate and provided a foundation for success for inmates once they are released.

There are many programs and classes here at BMCC that the Varsity Club directly aids. Because of the monthly dues by its members and donations by inmates, the Varsity Club is able to purchase supplies and provide certificates for many classes offered to inmates. Through the cooperation of the Varsity Club, the administration, and free-world volunteers, many programs that inmates have access to were created. Inmates

The 2005 Varsity Club Banquet

from the Varsity Club facilitate many of these programs.

Current Projects

● Alternative to Violence Project (AVP)—The Varsity Club helps pay for supplies and certificates needed for this program.

● Parenting class—The Parenting class follows the philosophy of the Cline and Fay Institute. It utilizes the materials from *Love and Logic Parenting* and *Nurturing Parenting*.

● Domestic Violence Prevention class—The Domestic Violence Prevention class uses material from Paul Kivel's *Men's Work* publications and selected exercises from the AVP manual. As part of the class, the Avalon Domestic Violence Response Center comes in to teach a section. Chaplain Dean Yancey also speaks to the class on the subject of battery.

● Anger Management—The Anger Management class, facilitated by current facilitators and AVP facilitators, utilizes material from *Cage Your Rage*. The class will be observed by one of the A&D counselors. It will also use material

See VARSITY CLUB on page 10

What's Inside

CHRISTMAS MESSAGE 2005

By Jim Worthington, Acting Warden

Greetings! 2005 has been a very busy year for the Brushy Mountain Correctional Complex. There have been many changes going on all around us—changes within the department, staff, the Warden and the promise of new construction. The coming year is going to be busy as we begin the expansion project in full swing.

There is no time of the year more joyous than Christmas regardless of how you celebrate. We once again get an opportunity to reflect on our lives over the past twelve months. We get an opportunity to learn from the mistakes we've made throughout the year and try to improve ourselves. Times may be tough for us at times, but we can always find the answer within us.

I would like to express my appreciation to each of you for your support throughout the year. Without your efforts this year would not and could not have been as

productive and successful as it has been. Together we can accomplish a lot when we work together.

May you and your family have a most joyous Christmas season and a very healthy and happy New Year. Remember to give thanks for all you have been given throughout the year. ■

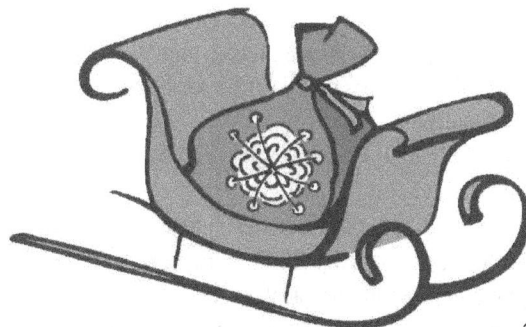

3

7th Step Foundation

Original Contribution,
By Luther Swallows

The 7th Step Foundation offers a program of self-help for those incarcerated persons who sincerely desire to stay out of prison once they are released. The philosophy of the program is based on informational "Steps", a "Pledge", and a "Motto" that guide us through our daily journeys. ❼

Three Points of the 7th Step Foundation Program

By Gregory Gregg—Parole Counselor/Project Director and J.R. Evans—Assistant Chapter Coordinator

What we try to offer the members of the 7th Step Group, here at Brushy Mountain Correctional Complex - Morgan Site, is a three-point application toward parole.

First, we offer counseling to those coming up for parole, based on what is best for the individual's need. We help with half-way houses (the starting point for entering parolees back into society) increasing their chances of successfully staying out of prison. Also, we help them with other outside agencies, such as NA, AA, treatment centers, and health-care services.

Second, we work with T.C.C. (Tennessee Career Center), a state agency that offers job listings for those who are in need of employment. T.C.C. has offices in all major cities in Tennessee.

Third, we help with a parole petition—this shows that staff members feel the inmate is ready to return to his community and has worked toward his freedom.

In conclusion, we try to do our best to offer inmates a plan for parole, as well as every possible solution to prepare them for the outside world. Our aim is for them to maintain their freedom in here, as well as out there. ❼

The 7th Step Foundation's Domestic Violence Prevention Program in January 2006

We are looking forward to our next Domestic Violence Prevention program starting in January 2006. Last year's class was a great success as all the men participated in learning how they affect themselves and others around them by their everyday actions.

We noticed when the men saw some aspect of their lives within a particular topic of discussion, their eyes lit up as if they'd come to some understanding of where they went wrong and how they could have better handled a past situation.

We want to thank everyone who participated in last year's Domestic Violence Prevention class and we look forward to the next class in 2006. We hope to see you there. The program is scheduled to last twelve weeks (one day a week for twelve weeks). There will be certificates given once the class has been completed, and you **must** attend all twelve meetings to receive a certificate.

Sign-up for this class will be in December. We hope you will visit us and find out more concerning this program. ❼

From the Editor of the 7th Step Foundation Program

We have seen several men go to the Annex in the recent past—regular members as well as board members. We will miss them as they continue their journey in preparation for their future on the outside. We hope they will remember the information that they received during the meetings in the 7th Step Program and use the information to help themselves and others as they endeavor to better themselves on a daily basis. ❼

7th Step Foundation Program Banquet for 2005

By Luther Swallows

The banquet for 2005 was excellent. Everyone had a good time and is looking forward to next year's banquet.

The 2005 banquet menu consisted of pizzas from Pizza Hut™, as well as a choice of B.B.Q. or deep-fried chicken wings, and a choice of cheese sauces (mild and hot) to dip your wings in. We also had pecan pie with a large quantity and variety of Mayfield™ ice cream.

There was one feller in particular who **REALLY** enjoyed the festivities because he just kept coming back up for more and more cheeseburger pizza, and every time he came up to get some more he had the biggest smile I have seen in a long time. I was exceedingly surprised to see him the next morning eating a **full** weekend breakfast. ☺

We want to thank all the people without whom this 2005 banquet could not have taken place:

Mr. Jack Morgan, previous warden; Mr. Jim Worthington, deputy warden (now acting warden); Mr. Rick Elmore, acting A.WO.; Mr. Dean Yancey, chaplain; Mr. Jeff Nance, inside sponsor; our outside sponsors, Mr. Bill Copeland, Mr. Bob Livesey, Mrs. Alice Hanks, and J.B. Mankin; the 7th Step Program board members and members alike. ❼

Chapter Sponsors and Board Members

Our Outside Sponsors are:
Bill Copeland, Bob Livesey, Alice Hanks, & J.B. Mankin.

Our Inside Sponsor is:
Jeff Nance
(Director of the Drug/Alcohol Program in unit 5).

Chapter Board Members:
Chapter Coordinator–Larry Cable, Unit 4.
Assistant Chapter Coordinator–J.R. Evans, Unit 3.
Parole Counselor–Gregory Gregg, Unit 3.
Project Director–Gregory Gregg, Unit 3.
Assistant Project Director–Joshua Davis, Unit 4.
Treasurer–John Lambert, Unit 4.
Secretary–Buddy Coward, Unit 3.
Assistant Secretary–Lance Winebrinner, Unit 3.
Legal Aide Counselor–"Chuck" Donohue, Unit 5.
Editor–Luther Swallows, Unit 6.
Sergeant-at-Arms–Kenneth Greene, Unit 9.
Assistant Sergeant-at-Arms–John Lambert, Unit 4 and Stacey Poole, Unit 5.

The 7th Step Foundation Program meets every Thursday at 7 o'clock, P. M., in the dining room. We hope you will join us to learn more about yourself and the world around you. ∎

Please Execute My Son

These are actual excuse notes from parents (including original spelling) collected by Nisheeth Parekh, University of Texas Medical Branch at Galveston.

My son is under a doctor's care and should not take P.E. today. Please execute him.

Please excuse Lisa for being absent. She was sick and I had her shot.

Dear School: Please ekscuse John being absent on Jan. 28, 29, 30, 31, 32, and also 33.

Please excuse Gloria from Jim today. She is administrating.

Please excuse Roland from P.E. for a few days. Yesterday he fell out of a tree and misplaced his hip.

John has been absent because he had two teeth taken out of his face.

Carlos was absent yesterday because he was playing football. He was hurt in the growing part.

Megan could not come to school today because she has been bothered by very close veins.

Chris will not be in school cus he has an acre in his side.

Please excuse Ray Friday from school. He has very loose vowels.

Please excuse Tommy for bing absent yesterday. He had diarrhea and his boots leak.

Irving was absent yesterday because he missed his bust.

Please excuse Jimmy for being. It was his father's fault. ∎

The Bottom Line

Correctional Education as an Alternative to Expansion
By Jeremy Ingram,
MOUNTAIN REVIEW Staff

Tennessee's newly elected Supreme Court chief justice recently expressed concerns over prison overcrowding. This prompted Hamilton County Attorney General Bill Cox to suggest that lengthening prison sentences would work as a deterrent and reduce recidivism. This attitude is not new. The past two decades have seen lawmakers cut educational and rehabilitative programs to fund prison expansion—expansion that is a necessary result of lengthening sentences.

It seems that correctional policy is not made based on considerations of the reduction of crime. Politicians recognize that cutting correctional education will result in higher recidivism rates and thus, a need for more prisons. In fact, cutting education in favor of expansion is not only more costly, it is also counterproductive. Criminals are locked up, expected to do their sentences, and then come out as law-abiding citizens. The adage, "You get out of it what you put into it," needs to be remembered. Without the impetus for change, Tennessee cannot expect its prisoners to "change" into better people without the needed education and vocational training that will allow them to live productive lives. "When [inmates] are released (as the majority will be) their chances for law-abiding behavior will not be enhanced if nothing is done to deal with their deficiencies while incarcerated." (American Correctional Association). More than 90% of Tennessee's prisoners will be released one day. It is good common sense to want to enable inmates to become productive members of society. Unfortunately, lawmakers do not seem to share this opinion.

Educating prisoners has many advantages. Foremost, it is less costly than lengthening sentences and expanding prisons. Research has shown that education is almost twice as cost effective as lengthened sentences and increased incarceration rates. Not surprising is the fact that an educated prisoner is 20% less likely to return to prison than one who was not afforded some type of education while incarcerated. The bottom line is that prison education works.

There are many reasons why correctional education works. One reason is that an educated prisoner has a choice between committing crimes and engaging in employment. Before incarceration, the individual did not have any marketable job skills. Choosing to commit crimes was easier for him or her. Nevertheless, when having a job pays more than committing crimes, criminal behavior will be a less attractive option. "Why commit a crime and risk imprisonment when I have the option of making more money in the labor market?" Studies have shown that increased income is associated with decreased crime. One way to increase income is to enable a prisoner to gain such employment by education and vocational training.

Other reasons why correctional education works are apparent. Besides learning how to live a crime-free life, a prisoner's behavior changes as their ability to think more clearly is improved. There is also a social aspect. With interaction between inmates and educators, prisoners learn how to respond and deal with free-world people normally. Prisoner's self-esteem is improved when they recognize that they can amount to more than a common thug.

It will be debated whether or not a prisoner "deserves" an education at the expense of the taxpayers. It is hard, from this author's point of view, to understand how taxpayers can afford *not* to educate prisoners. But the fact remains that more than just the prisoner benefits from correctional education—there is the potential employer. Beyond inflated unemployment figures and increased reliance on the foreign-labor market, there is still a demand for trained and educated people to enter the job market. Several years ago, the Director of the Office of Correctional Education remarked that, "No solution is more readily available, practical, and obvious than the restoration of prisoners to the status of workers and taxpayers."

To sum all this up, allow me to borrow an illustration I read. Years ago, the "Peanuts" comic strip had Charlie Brown and Lucy on the deck of a cruise ship. Lucy was looking back towards where they had come from and forward to where they were going. She asked Charlie Brown which direction he wanted the deck chairs facing—backward or forward. Charlie Brown replied, "You want *me* to decide that? I can't even figure out how to get these darned chairs set up." It is unfortunate that as the prison population and correctional budgets grow, educational opportunities suffer. Any change in the prison system must take into consideration the failures and successes of the past as well as a bright vision for the future. Historically, the lengthening of sentences and expansion has not had a significant impact on reducing recidivism. "It is illogical to expect an inmate to become a productive member of society after release from prison if that inmate has no education or training during incarceration. It is logical, however, to expect that inmate to go back to what he knows: crime." (Journal of Correctional Education). Instead of being like Charlie Brown who doesn't know how to set the chairs up, let's hope that prison administrators will explore better methods of reducing recidivism—methods that save taxpayers money while producing inmates that can stand the test of life outside the walls.

And that is the bottom line. ■

Pre-Release Class IV Graduates

By Jeremy Ingram,
MOUNTAIN REVIEW Staff

The fourth Pre-Release class graduated in September, 2005. Graduates included: Jimmy Averitt, Larry Burchfield, Jimmy Byrd, Scott Conibear, David Cutshall, Kenneth Duckett, Larry Dunnigan, William Eaton, Donald Flenniken, Larry Frasier, Jeff Fugate, Paul Harris, David Honey, Troy Johnson, John Lankford, Jared Love, Jamie Matthews, Tony McReynolds, Jimmy Miller, Brian Stedman, Bryan Veal, Jonathan Waddell, and Clarence Weaver, facilitators Melvin Lane and John Johnson, and aide Curtis Hudson. ■

5

A Change In Direction

Original Contribution,
By Garry W. Johnson

Being new to news writing, I wanted my first article to be particularly outstanding. Not only would it be an introduction to BMCC as a whole, but it would also serve as a sample of work by which to judge my qualifications as a writer. Up to this point, my writing experience has been limited to business letters and corny poems—save the long lost essays of high school. Consequently, I found the task before me somewhat daunting, and questioned what I could write about that anyone would find entertaining.

Looking back over my last five years of incarceration, it occurred to me that what many inmates/convicts find most entertaining is each other. Gossip permeates our closed society, and the most hardened criminals seem transformed into little old ladies when the object of their scorn is mentioned. However, this writing is not about the evils of slander. It is simply to give the gossips a solid basis for their musing, and everyone a general knowledge of the new guy.

In General

I was born Garry William Johnson, in the year 1970, in the city of Savannah, Georgia. My parents are Garry and Judy Johnson, and I have one sister, Misty Hurst. I grew up in the Savannah area and remained there until about the age of twenty-five. I then moved to Sevierville, Tennessee. I remained mostly in that area for a little less than five years before my arrest in September 2000. In early 2005, I pled guilty to two counts of Facilitation of First Degree Murder and one count of Aggravated Arson. I am currently serving two consecutive twenty-four-year sentences on the Facilitation charges. I also received a 20-year sentence for the Aggravated Arson, which is concurrent with my other judgements. I have been married twice and have one son, Joey, who was born in Savannah, in 1994.

Employment

During my life on the outside, I worked predominately in sign manufacturing and residential construction. I have more than seven years experience in industrial screen printing and about four in fabrications. I have also been self-employed as a residential painter. In the mid-90's, I built a small business doing turnkey work for apartment complexes, residential painting, home renovations, and custom interior graphics. I have worked several construction jobs from framing to finishing. Most of my life has been spent working with my hands.

Education

In high school, I took three classes in architectural drafting, and I have a working knowledge of blueprints. I attended school through the twelfth grade, but came a few credits short of graduating. Several years later, at the urging of my parents, I attained my GED, but never attempted to further my education beyond that level.

I have spent several years working with computers—mostly in graphics and business applications. Nevertheless, I never developed any literary interest until these last few years. That interest came through improved reading skills, which was a gift from God.

Yes, God

For the secular minded among us, this article is pretty well over. I thank you greatly for your interest, and I pray that each of you finds peace and happiness in your life.

Goodbye to the Old Man

After my incarceration in September of 2000, I found myself sitting in a maximum security cell in Sevierville, Tennessee. Like a rubber ball thrown into a concrete box, bouncing frantically from surface to surface, eventually you come to rest at the lowest point . . . very still (Psalm 46:10). I started to wonder exactly how I came to be here, and what faults in my character had ultimately led to my demise. Looking back over my life, my general understandings had seemed to be all right. Still, something was definitely wrong—I mean, I could not get out of this box (Proverbs 14:12).

At an attorney visit one day, I passed a guy in the hall who had worked for me in the past. He was locked up in a unit across from me, and later that night he sent me a Bible, via a guard (Romans 7:9-12). I thumbed through it now and then, reading a little bit here and there. I started questioning people about what they believed, and a myriad of responses came to me. People told me they were raised in such and such a church, or they married into such and such a religion. They would tell me, "We believe it is all right to . . ."or, "Scripture does not mean you shouldn't . . ." After awhile it occurred to me that most people I had spoken to had chosen their beliefs based on one of two worldly considerations: personal affiliations and/or permissible sins (Matthew 7:13-14).

I was not a stranger to religion. I'd been brought up going to church. Until junior high I had attended services regularly. I knew all the basic Bible stories and all the general concepts. I came away from my childhood indoctrinated, and I believed that I knew everything necessary to get into heaven. I mean, after all, the preacher said it, so it must be right (2 Corinthians 11:13-15). So I began reflecting on my past, my religion, and my understanding of God. I had heard all these ideas from those around me and compared them with my own. Then, I considered all the nastiness in some of this world's current "Christian" organizations. There seemed to be many conflicting ideas about what Christianity was all about and what I was supposed to be as a result. My childhood indoctrination had rightly taught me one thing, believe in Jesus. So, what did Jesus have to say (John 14:6)?

I had remembered from Sunday school that the New Testament was the part of the Bible for this modern time. So, I opened my Bible to Matthew and started reading. I did not get far before I ran into red letters, where Jesus speaks. In Matthew 4:4, Jesus begins quoting Scripture, and He repeats the same phrase often: "It is written." But where is it written? I was taught that this was the beginning of the book for me. By the twelfth chapter Jesus asks the Pharisees, "Have ye not read what David did. . . ?" Of course the Pharisees had—but I was not sure that I had (2 Timothy 3:16).

It was quite apparent early on that some reading was prerequisite if I was ever going to understand what Christ wanted me to know. After clearing my mind and resolving to put away my early teachings and the ideas of earthly men, I decided to read every word aloud, from Genesis to Revelation. It took me nine months to complete my first reading. During that time, the God of the Bible revealed Himself to me. I spent thirty years of my life believing that I knew all about God. It turned out that I only knew man's description of God. Christ admonishes us to become as little children, and as children we start out knowing nothing. Well-meaning men have millions of concepts about God, but only through Scripture and the Holy Spirit does the God of Abraham, Isaac, and Jacob speak (Matthew 11:25; 18:3; Luke 10:21; 18:17; 1 Corinthians 1:26-29).

Please do not misunderstand me, I am hardly suggesting that one complete reading of Scripture is going to alter your understanding of God—but it can. If you are willing to completely surrender your beliefs and trust God to teach you from His Word, through the power of His Holy Spirit, if you will accept what the Bible really says and not allow men to explain away its literal meaning, if you will obey the unchanging God—then you will learn, like little children, how to become like your Heavenly Father, the Father of our Lord, Jesus Christ. May His peace be with you always (Malachi 3:6; Hebrews 13:8). ∎

> Like a rubber ball thrown into a concrete box, bouncing frantically from surface to surface, eventually you come to rest at the lowest point . . . very still.

Happy Holidays From the MOUNTAIN REVIEW Staff

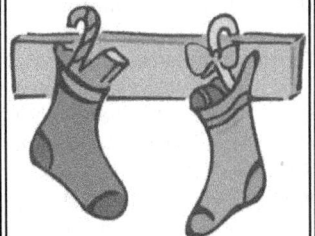

Tent Revival

By Roy Ridley,
MOUNTAIN REVIEW Staff

On September the fifth through the ninth, 2005, we were blessed once again with a Tent Revival here at BMCC-Morgan Site by Comfort Ministries. Their staple blue-and-white-striped tent was a clarion call to worship.

Comfort Ministries has been headed up by Hillus and Dottie Pardue from Scottsville Kentucky for fifteen years. Along with the Pardues, Marvey and Frances Wood plus Leland and Bernice Humphrey ministered in word and in song. The Chapel Band and Choir, led by Orlando Spratling, kicked off the meetings every night with vibrant praise and worship.

A special guest, former prison inmate George Barnes, was the designated speaker on Friday night. George was incarcerated in a federal reform school from 1960 to 1966 and at the Walls (TSP in Nashville) from 1970 to 1982. He was born-again when Jesus came into his life on February 1, 1975.

Inmates packed the tent night after night.

Since leaving prison, George Barnes has been the pastor of C-Team Church in Nashville for fifteen years, a volunteer chaplain at DeBerry and Turney Center, and twice named the Volunteer Chaplain of the Year for the state of Tennessee. For many years Brother Barnes was convinced he would die in prison, but Jesus Christ had other plans! Praise God for His amazing grace!

Inmates listen to the band during the tent revival.

On behalf of the men here at BMCC-Morgan Site, I would like to thank Chaplain Dean Yancey, the prison staff, Comfort Ministries, George Barnes, the Chapel Band and Choir, and especially the Lord and Savior Jesus Christ for a wonderful time of spiritual renewal. ∎

Are "All Things" Good For God's Children?

By Jeremy Ingram,
MOUNTAIN REVIEW Staff

The answer to this question will surprise most people. But those who know the God of the Bible will find it no surprise that all things that happen to God's people are for their good. God has promised in His word, "And we know that all things work together for good to them that love God, to them who are the called according to his purpose" (Romans 8:28). Therefore, let us draw our attention to how God is able and willing to work all things for our good.

God is able to work all things for our good because He is omnipotent. The word omnipotent means that God is all-powerful. He can do all things. There is nothing too heavy for Him to lift, nothing too high for Him to reach, nothing too difficult for Him to handle. As for our ability it is said, "Thou wilt surely wear away, both thou, and this people that is with thee: for this thing is too heavy for thee; thou art *not able* to perform it thyself alone" (Exod. 18:18). But God tells us to be ". . . fully persuaded that, what he had promised, he *was able* also to perform" (Rom 4:21).

If we believe that God is able to work all things for our good, then it still begs the question "Why would He work all things for our good?" The answer is simple—God is good. The Scripture is replete with examples of God's goodness. Moses wrote, "And the LORD commanded us to do all these statutes, to fear the LORD our God, *for our good always*, that he might preserve us alive, as it is at this day" (Deut. 6:24), and ". . . We are journeying unto the place of which the LORD said, I will give it you: come thou with us, and we will do thee good: *for the LORD hath spoken good concerning Israel*" (Num. 10:29). Once again, "If ye then, being evil, know how to give good gifts unto your children, how much more shall your Father which is in heaven give good things to them that ask him" (Matt 7:11).

Lastly, if God is able to work all things for our good and He will work all things for our good, then our attitude should be one of faith and contentment. Joseph, having been sold into slavery and falsely accused of trying to lie with his master's wife, later told his brothers, "But as for you, ye thought evil against me; *but God meant it unto good*, to bring to pass, as it is this day, to save much people alive" (Gen. 50:20).

Listen to how the Bible describes those who have faith in God's good will in their lives: "Yet I will rejoice in the LORD, I will joy in the God of my salvation. The LORD God is my strength, and he will make my feet like hinds' feet, and he will make me to walk upon mine high places" (Hab. 3:18-19), "In God have I put my trust: I will not be afraid what man can do unto me" (Ps. 56:11), "Happy is that people, that is in such a case: yea, happy is that people, whose God is the LORD" (Ps. 144:15), and "Be careful for nothing; but in every thing by prayer and supplication with thanksgiving let your requests be made known unto God" (Phil. 4:6).

Now for the reason that God is able, willing, and faithful to work all things for our good. On the cross Jesus Christ bore the wrath of God for us so that, through faith in Him, we would be objects of God's favor. "Much more then, being now justified by his blood, we shall be saved from wrath through him" (Rom. 5:9).

Charles Spurgeon says, "There are many common mercies that God gives freely to all sorts and conditions of men. 'He maketh his sun to rise on the evil and on the good, and sendeth rain on the just and on the unjust" (Mt. 5:45). But the pardon of sin is a special blessing reserved for his own peculiar people, those whose names He wrote in the Lamb's book of life, and whom He gave to his Son in the covenant of his grace, and whom Christ redeemed by his precious blood when he "loved the church, and gave himself for it" (Eph. 5:25). These are the people in whom God takes a peculiar delight, and these are they whose sins are forgiven them for Christ's sake." ∎

WHAT DO YOU GET WHEN YOU CROSS A GAZELLE WITH A ZEBRA?

By Roy Ridley,
MOUNTAIN REVIEW staff

A *gazebo*, (from the root word "*gazebra*"). The Building Trades Class, affectionately nicknamed "The Nail-Benders," built, or should I say genetically engineered, the gazebo pictured here. We think they did a fine job, in spite of the fact that some folks believe crossbreeding exotic animals like gazelles and zebras is, well, unnatural. ∎

Expansion Update

The expansion is getting off to a great start. Moving of the creek has begun and groundbreaking ceremonies will be Friday, December 16. Commissioner Little will be on hand to help shovel dirt along with Acting Warden Jim Worthington and several invited guests. The construction company has moved in trailers that will become their offices for the next three years and are busy getting electricity and telephones installed. We are anticipating a lot of activity within the next several months. Lots of dirt and gravel will need to be hauled to begin filling in low places. Hopefully we will not experience too many weather delays along the way. The Morgan Site will be a very busy place for the next several years! ∎

7

Bredesen Names New TDOC Commissioner

By Jeremy Ingram,
MOUNTAIN REVIEW Staff

On October 3, Governor Phil Bredesen appointed George Little the new Commissioner of the Tennessee Department of Correction. Commissioner Little has worked as a correctional administrator in the State of Tennessee for years. Previously employed by the Shelby County Division of Correction, he oversaw the department and its operations.

Governor Bredesen spoke highly of his new commissioner. "I am confident that the wealth of experience he brings to this role, along with his front line knowledge of our state's correctional system, makes him the ideal next leader of the Tennessee Department of Correction."

The "wealth of experience" that the governor speaks of includes a Bachelor's degree from Morehouse College in Atlanta and graduate work at the University of Texas at Austin.

Commissioner Little, originally from Pennsylvania, has a history of work in correctional administration that spans two decades. Before working for Shelby County, he was the Assistant to the Executive Director of Tennessee's Board of Pardon and Paroles. He also served as the Regional Director of the Delta Probation Region of the Tennessee Department of Correction.

Commissioner Little has served under two previous governors, first as an assistant to Governor Lamar Alexander and then as the Assistant Commissioner for the Tennessee Department of Correction under Ned McWherter. ■

George M. Little

What Happened On Christmas Day?

Feast day of the Martyrs of Nicomedia, St Eugenia, St Alburga, and St Anastasia of Sirmium.

Events

800: Charlemagne was crowned first Holy Roman Emperor in Rome by Pope Leo III.
1066: William the Conqueror was crowned king of England at Westminster Abbey.
1914: During World War I, British and German troops observed an unofficial truce, even playing football together on the Western Front's 'no man's land'.
1926: Hirohito succeeded his father Yoshihito as emperor of Japan.
1941: Hong Kong surrendered to the Japanese.
1972: The Nicaraguan capital Managua was devastated by an earthquake which killed over 10,000 people.
1979: The USSR invaded Afghanistan in a bid to halt civil war and protect USSR interests.
1989: Dissident playwright Vaclav Havel was elected president of Czechoslovakia.
1991: Unable to maintain control over a disintegrating Soviet Union, Mikhail Gorbachev announced his resignation as president.

Births

1642: Isaac Newton, English scientist
1883: Maurice Utrillo, French painter
1899: Humphrey Bogart, US film actor
1918: Anwar Sadat, Egyptian statesman
1949: Sissy Spacek, US film actress
1954: Annie Lennox, British pop singer

Deaths

1938: Karel Capek, Czech dramatist
1946: W. C. Fields, US actor and screenwriter
1977: Charlie Chaplin, English actor and director
1983: Joan Miró, Spanish artist
1989: Nicolae Ceauşcescu, Romanian politician, executed ■

The Player

Original Contribution,
By Richard Peters

The air was filled with the putrid smell of sulfur and the stench of death. Bombs whistled through the sky toward their targets, exploding with earthquake menace. People were running everywhere and nowhere. Screams and angry shouts amidst the sound of guns firing were loud and nerve racking with every bomb's explosion.

A lone boy scampered around the corner of a burned out building which still had a few fires burning. The heat was hot and intense against the boy's near naked body, searing his hands, arms, and any exposed flesh. His face was dirty and hair was matted. His once bright, exciting, blue eyes, now darted wearily in all directions as he worked to remain unseen.

He didn't know for sure if his parents were alive or not, it seemed a long time ago. He tried to remember them but for some reason he couldn't. Just then a tattered newspaper flew up against his left leg. He reached down and retrieved it straightening it out to the front page.

"JUNE 7, 2010," he whispered, "it's my birthday." A tear worked its way down his cheek. He brushed it away, only to have another take its place. Holding the paper open he read the headline: "WORLD WAR EMINENT — CHINA AND NORTH KOREA THREATEN WAR WITH THE U.S."

He shook his head as he tried to remember how it actually began, he couldn't.

Just then a shot was fired not far away. He turned to peer carefully around the corner. There were two Chinese officers over two kids not much older than himself. One lay dead with blood oozing out the back of his skull. The other knelt begging for his life.

"Please," the boy cried. "Please let me live! I'm only fourteen . . . please!"

"You know Mark Ripper? You tell me now!" yelled one of the officers.

"I don't know him, please. . ."
BANG. Silence.

Mark edged back against the wall. He couldn't figure out why they wanted him. He felt sorry for those boys. They were telling the truth; they didn't know him. Now, he wished he had. He'd seen them at school many times but had never met them.

Mark looked himself over. His Guns and Roses t-shirt was ripped and was barely hanging on his shoulders. His pants had so many holes he felt a bit embarrassed, but what could he do. Maybe he could sneak into the old Wal-Mart, if it wasn't bombed out yet, and get a new pair. However, it was his feet that worried him most. His shoes were about to fall apart but for some duct tape he came across not long before. He'd have to find another pair or his feet would get blistered and sore.

Rolling up the paper he worked his way deeper, back into the shadows, and began his arduous trek to Wal-Mart. Keeping to the shadows and avoiding a few garbage cans, he came to another corner where all four buildings lay in ruin. People milled about aimlessly, some pushing grocery carts full of their belongings. While most were silent, a few mumbled choice curses at their invaders, all the while oblivious to

Mark standing at the corner.

No one ventured to ask him who he was or where he was going, which in a way was good. He didn't want anyone else killed on his account. He slipped between the people as if he were invisible and made his way down the street.

A few blocks later an odd sight came into his view, a street that wasn't bombed out! Cars sat parked on the side of the road and people seemed to be hurrying everywhere without fear in their eyes. They seemed oblivious to the carnage he'd left behind. He turned back to see where he just came from only to find that the rest of the town looked normal now.

Mark turned back around and saw the Wal-Mart sign a block further down the road. No sooner had he spotted the sign than he heard someone call his name.

"Mark! Mark, wait up."

"Paul! You're alive, I can't believe it."

"Of course I'm alive. Are you all right? Why are you dressed in rags?"

"I uh. . .don't know."

See Player on page 18

Hurricane Katrina Donation

By Jeremy Ingram
MOUNTAIN REVIEW Staff

Amid the devastation and destruction of Hurricane Katrina, inmates from both Brushy and Morgan showed their support of the relief efforts. After inmates requested to be allowed to donate money from their personal trust fund accounts to the victims of Katrina, over 340 dollars was collected. Near the end of September, a check was mailed to the American Red Cross along with a letter explaining that the money was collected from inmates. Jim Worthington, Acting Warden, wrote, "We are very pleased with their interest and generosity and are proud to forward this check to you from them."

Don Cheatham, a Red Cross volunteer from Wetumpka, Alabama, took these pictures of the aftermath of the hurricane. ■

Beached charter boat, Bayou LaBatre, AL, about 75 miles east of eye of hurricane.

Demolished home site, ½ mile in from gulf. Long Beach, MS.

Demolished dwelling and one nearby with major damage four blocks in from gulf. "401" is the house number.

A church located three blocks from gulf. Pass Christian, MS.

An American Red Cross service center where those affected by the hurricane receive financial aid. Meals are served while people wait for assistance. Money from BMCC inmates helped provide this relief. Gulfport, MS.

A destroyed business (animal hospital) in Pass Christian, MS. Located four blocks in from gulf. The eye of the hurricane passed just to the west of Pass Christian.

Waveland, MS, submerged cars upside down in ditch, 1½ miles inland from gulf. The eye of the hurricane came ashore very near Waveland.

"Misplaced" house—blown from foundation and deposited on side of road by 140 mph winds. One mile in from gulf. Pass Christian, MS.

Scene along road leading to gulf two blocks from gulf. Destroyed wooden frame homes piled along each side of road. Long Beach, MS.

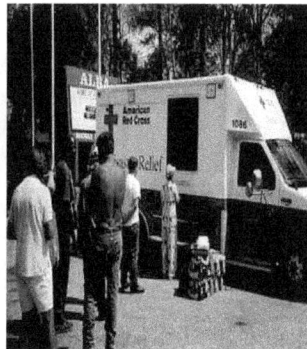

Hot meals are provided by the American Red Cross. Bayou La Batre, AL.

FEMA officials arrive in New Orleans.

9

Literary & Visual Arts

The Love of a Mom
Original Cotribution,
By Jerry Wright, Sr.

Mom, I want you to know I love you with all my heart,
Even though we are so many miles apart.
I know your love for me was there from the start,
Because I came from you in a whole part.

I know that I have been a lot of stress and strain,
Even from birth a whole lot of pain.
There's been many times I'm sure I drove you insane,
I look back to find that your love has stayed the same.

From childhood up and down,
Your love for me has always been there all around.
Even at times when you didn't mutter a sound,
Even when you were tightly wound,
You always stood your firm ground.
I know all of this holds true because that I have found.

When I look at you, Mom, I see me.
Everyone can tell you this is true, because they can see,
I know this, that you will agree.
You can't deny that you're my mother, Frances Louise,
This is true, I'm your son, Jerry.
All of you, you give to me,
Now together we will always be. ■

TSUNAMI
Original Contribution,
By Richard Peters

The earth trembled
The ground opened up
Buildings began to sway
Buildings began to tumble

People ran
People screamed
Many fell
Many died

Curses uttered softly on dying lips
Curses shouted with up lifted fists
Crying wives wept over husbands
Crying mothers wept over children lost

Then the water came
Then the Tsunami hit
Now, its quiet
Now, its calm

Who will bring us healing balm?
  A tourist
    Yes
  A friend

          Yes
    A friend afar
          Yes

Who about you

Will you come ■

Original Watercolor,
Patrick Stansberry

TRANQUIL
Original Contribution,
By Richard Peters

The sky is blue
  Green grass a-new
  Light of day making the heart happy and gay
  Tranquil . . . afield you lie at rest
Trees budding for spring
Birds sing in ecstasy
Eggs hatch with newness of life
  Tranquil . . . afield you lie at rest
People hurry to and fro
Women cry with glee
Babies are born in ecstacy
  Tranquil . . . afield you lie at rest
People age   people die
Women and children cry
Eternal rest   eternal cradle
  Tranquil . . . afield you lie at rest ■

LIFE
Original Contribution,
By Richard Peters

Chatter, Chatter, voices flow
  To and fro knowledge goes
  Though understanding oft doesn't show
So be quiet, lest it leads to blows.

Work, Work, what's done all day
Without much to anyone's say
Just to take home a meager pay
So slip off silently to the Oasis to play.

Drink, Drink, all night long
Often floundering, till the dregs are gone
Then thrown out into the dead of night
In silence smile, it was a wonderful night.
Sneak, Sneak, back into the house
Trying not to wake the spouse

Slide into bed, kiss her on the head
Best not to wake her, lest you sleep with the dead.

Loud, Loud, the world is shrill
Ringing ears, pounding still
Maybe you should go back to bed
Coffee gone, now in bed, close your eyes you sleepy head.

Silence, Silence, is the home
Awaking thus, to find you alone
A note you find says a final goodbye
She's taken the Vette, your only prize. ■

Forever With You
Original Contribution,
By M. Delano Jordan

If God spoke to me from Heaven
And told me my remaining days were few,
I could do nothing but thank Him
For blessing me with you.
Of course, I'd be disappointed
Because you'd be left on earth alone,
But you can bet we'd walk side by side
When our Maker called you home.
When I think of eternity in Heaven
I look at dying with a different point-of-view
Especially when death becomes life
Forever with you. ■

Original Watercolor,
Joshua Davis

Softball Season

Statistics Contributed By Recreation Department

Softball Season Statistical Leaders						
Name	**Home Runs**	**Name**	**RBI**	**Name**	**Batting Average**	
Charles Gaylor	26	Joshua Davis	71	Ricky Cox	.812	
Ricky Cox	26	Jesse Dabbs	70	Clayton Stipes	.789	
Jesse Dabbs	25	Kenneth Tucker	67	Kenneth Tucker	.775	
Joshua Davis	24	Ricky Cox	62	Brian Hartman	.732	
Kenneth Tucker	23	Charles Gaylor	54	Jared Love	.689	
David Presley	20	Jared Love	49	Michael Gay	.661	
Michael Gay	20	David Presley	45	Charles Gaylor	.655	
Billy Greenwood	18	Traco Wilhoite	43	Jesse Dabbs	.648	
Tim Harris	14	Billy Greenwood	42	Traco Wilhoite	.621	
Jared Love	14	Michael Gay	40	Kevin Moton	.619	

The Credibility Gap

By Judy Harmon

The "credibility gap" that once alienated the public from people in high places now seems to separate us from one another in all walks of life. Americans lie on their income tax returns to the tune of millions of dollars a year. Doctors fake reports in order to profit from Medicare patients. Prize athletes at great universities are kept eligible for competition through bogus credits and forged transcripts of academic records. Children soon acquire the cynical assumption that lying is the normal tack for TV advertisers. In the words of a Time magazine essay, ours is a "huckstering, show-bizzy world, jangling with hype, hullabaloo, and hooey, bull, baloney, and bamboozlement." After awhile, people tend to expect not to hear the truth anymore. In 1976, a national poll showed that 60% of Americans believed that the country's leaders had, over the last decade, consistently lied to the people. I wonder what the percentage would be today?!

In the book, *The Day America Told the Truth*, some statistics point to our apathy toward truth. Ninety-one percent said they lied regularly. Two out of three people said that they thought that lying was sometimes a good thing to do. Thirty-one percent said that they didn't believe the old adage, "Honesty is the best policy." The book concludes that falsehood has become the cultural trademark of our society.

Did you hear about the man who went to the National Liars Convention? He took third place! Of course, he went home and told his wife he won!

God tells us in the ninth commandment that we're not to lie! God wants us to reflect His holy nature. The Bible makes it clear that God doesn't lie! He is always true. Numbers 23:19 says: "God is not a man, that He should lie. He is not a human, that He should change His mind. Has He ever spoken and failed to act? Has He ever promised and not carried it through?"

It's often in the little things that we allow falsehood to erode our character and compromise our integrity. It hurts many others as well as ourselves when we make excuses for not getting a project done, when we lie about what someone else did or said because we know we'd be in trouble if the truth were really known, when we tell the kids to answer the phone and say that we're not there, when we lie on our driver's license concerning our height, weight, or age. And the list goes on and on.

We must reclaim something precious that we've lost. . .an unrelenting love for the truth and an abhorrence of falsehood.

God says, "Don't lie. Tell the truth. Love the truth. Embrace the truth." ∎

What "exactly" is 2+2?

An engineer, a physicist, and a lawyer were being interviewed for a position as chief executive officer of a large corporation. The engineer interviewed first and was asked a long list of questions ending with "How much is two plus two?" The engineer excused himself and made a series of measurements and calculations before returning to the boardroom and announcing, "Four."

The physicist was next interviewed, and was asked the same questions. Again, the last question was, "How much is two plus two?" Before answering the last question, he excused himself, made for the library, and did a great deal of research. After a consultation with the United States Bureau of Standards and many calculations, he also announced, "Four."

The lawyer was interviewed last, and again the final question was, "How much is two plus two?" The lawyer drew all the shades in the room, looked outside to see if anyone was there, checked the telephone for listening devices, and then whispered, "How much do you want it to be?" ∎

11

Varsity Club

Continued from page 1

from former Anger Management Instructor, Doug Roach.

● Sign Language class—The Sign Language class teaches American Sign Language. It is facilitated by Paul Rutherford, who was a graduate of the first Sign Language class. The class meets every Tuesday night from 6:00 P.M. till closing in the library classroom. Everyone is welcome to attend.

David Jackson, Jesse Coffey, Paul Smith, and Gene Twitty take a break from eating to pose for a picture.

● G.E.D. Tutoring—Tutoring is held Saturday in the library or as needed. William Barney and several others are available for tutoring.

● Writer's Workshop—Writer's Workshop meets every Thursday except the first Thursday of the month. Meeting in the library classroom at 6:00 P.M., everyone is welcome to attend. The workshop utilizes material from Long Ridge Writer's Group. The Writer's Workshop aids in editing, rewriting and critiquing any written material by its participants. They also facilitate in the participation in writing competitions and publication markets. This workshop is not facilitated by any individual—it is a group project. Caroline

The 2005 Varsity Club Banquet

Matthews, Dick and Marge Hettrick from Bethel assisted in setting up the Writer's Workshop.

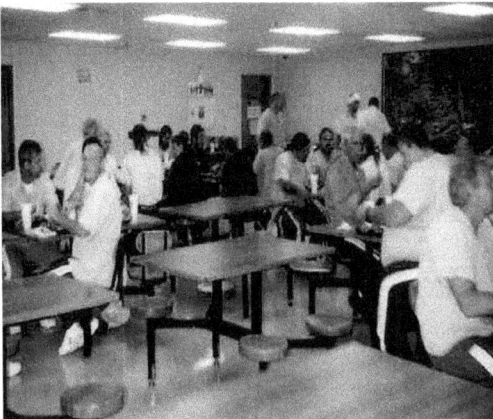

Additional Activities

Besides these programs, the Varsity Club is involved in other activities that benefit inmates. The club helps the enrollment of inmates in various correspondence courses and recording and tracking the participation in these studies. The Varsity Club has helped aid inmates in

paying for the EPA Certification Examination. It has also helped inmate students afford their academic needs.

Periodically, the Varsity Club will do special projects. Recently, the club donated money to Mr. K's Used Books in Oak Ridge to buy the library some different books. Other projects have included an Easter Egg Hunt and Christmas Stockings for children who come to visit on the holidays.

Although the Varsity Club is concerned with helping the inmate population, it also has a burden for those less fortunate outside these walls. For instance, in the recent past the Varsity Club has sponsored the collection of donations to be sent to the Red Cross for the victims of both the 9/11 terror attacks and the tsunami. Each month the club sends a donation to the Knoxville Area Rescue Ministry. During the Thanksgiving and Christmas season, the club donates money to the same ministry to pay for meals for the homeless.

Profiles

A word should be said about the effort of one of the club's most prestigious members. Dr. Myer Pettyjohn, along with several others, created the Parenting class, the Domestic Violence Prevention class, and the Anger Management class. Several free-world people aided P.J. in the formation of these programs. Dick and Marge Hettrick, from the Bethel volunteers, Veteran's for Peace, Linda Barbier, Chaplain Dean Yancey, Claudine Norris, and the prison administration worked together to bring these classes to inmates at BMCC. P.J. passed away several years ago, but his selfless efforts live on. If you are interested in more about Dr. Myer Pettyjohn, see the article on page twelve.

Many programs rely heavily on the efforts of inmate facilitators. That is what makes these programs unique. The current facilitators of the Parenting class and the Domestic Violence Prevention class are Paul Sharp, Melvin Lane, John Johnson, and Randall McPheeters. Acting with these facilitators are Rex Stedam, Jeff Nance and Lou Ann Roberts of the A&D program.

Ricky Bunch, Pre-Release Coordinator, also acts with the inmate facilitators. He has encouraged the refinement of the Parenting class so that it is more applicable to the needs of the incarcerated father. Because of his encouragement, inmate facilitators are in the

William Barney, Jerry Rollins, Gary Hall, David Jones, Johnny Davis, and Rick Johnson

process of creating a new parenting program.

The Varsity Club

The Varsity Club meets on the first Thursday of every month at 6:00 P.M. in the library classroom. Everyone is welcome to attend. Membership is open to anyone who is interested. Full membership is open to any person who meets any one of the following criteria: is currently enrolled in a G.E.D., vocational, or correspondence class; teacher's aid who helps further the education of others; or anyone who has achieved a four-year degree or better from a college or university. Associate membership (memberships without voting privileges) may be

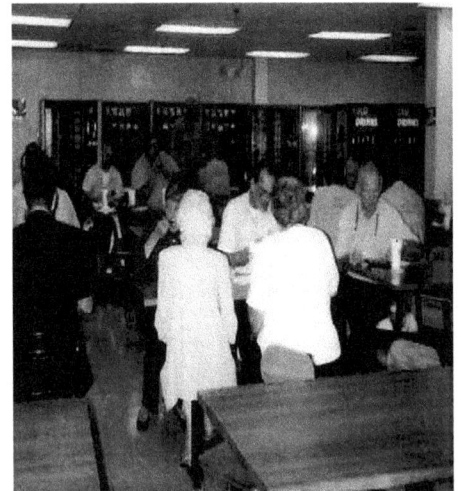

Claudine Norris, Dick and Marge Hettrick, Linda Barbier, and Randall McPheeters.

granted to persons who do not meet the above criteria as long as the individual wishing to be a member pays his dues and follows all rules of conduct.

As you can imagine, the Varsity Club depends

See Varsity Club on page 16

Music Corner

Techniques for Playing Lead Guitar Solos
By Charlie Brandler

Okay, aspiring guitarists! In the last lesson I gave you a basic explanation on how to read tablature, as well as two scales to learn. Hopefully, you have practiced the exercises that I gave you and you're ready for the next lesson. I want to talk about hammer-ons, pull-offs, slides, bends, and triplets.

A hammer-on is a technique where you pick a note and "hammer-on" the next note with another finger. For example, say you have your first finger on the fifth fret of the second string (B-string), which is an E note, then pick the string with the guitar pick in your right hand and "hammer-on" the G note at the eighth fret of the same string with your third finger. This is a hammer-on.

A pull-off is the opposite of a hammer-on. Say you have your third finger on the G note (eighth fret again) and you pick that note then "pull-off" your third finger (slightly downward in motion, instead of straight up and off of the string) so that you hear the E note that is fretted at the fifth fret with your first finger. This is a pull off.

With either the hammer-on or the pull-off, you are sounding two notes having only picked once—get it? With the hammer-on you are picking a note and "hammering" the second or higher note. You can't just put your finger on the next higher note. You have to hammer it to compensate for not picking it. And with the pull-off, you have to pull downward (kind of plucking the string, with the finger you are pulling off to compensate for not picking the string or note) "pulling-off" to a lower note that is already fretted with the first finger. Fig. 1 shows what both a hammer-on and a pull-off look like in tablature. They both show two numbers with an arch between them. If the arch goes from a lower number to a higher number, then it's a hammer-on. If it's from a higher number to a lower number, then it's a pull-off.

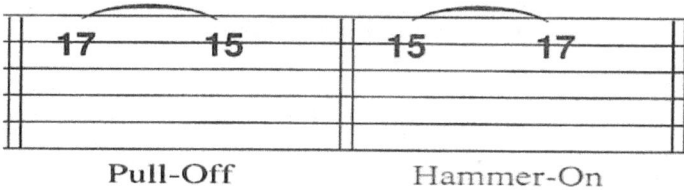

Figure 1

Now, I will explain a slide. A slide is a technique where you fret a note and "slide" to another note with the same finger. In tablature, a slide is signified by a slanted line. Fig. 2 shows two examples of slides.

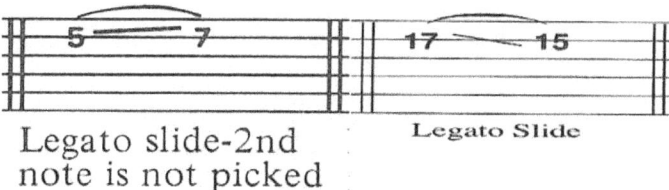

Figure 2

The first example shows you fretting the fifth fret and sliding that same finger up to the seventh fret. The slanted line, slanting up toward the higher number, shows that you are sliding up. The second example shows you fretting the seventeenth fret and sliding down to the fifteenth fret. The line slants down signifying a downward slide. Practicing sliding to different frets is a really good way to develop callouses on your finger tips, as well as eye-to-hand coordination. For example, practice sliding from fret five to seven, five to eight, five to nine, etc.

That takes us to "bends." Bends are techniques where you pick a note and bend it to the next desired note. But before I explain that, let me tell you that a "step" is the equivalent of two frets. Fig. 3 shows four examples of what bends will look like in tablature.

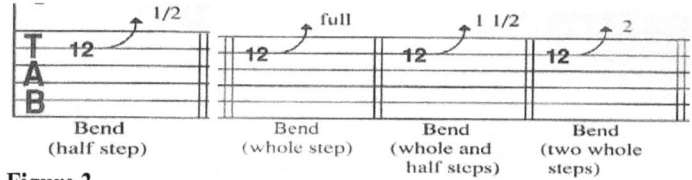

Figure 3

They are all played at the twelfth fret which is a B note. The first example shows a half-step bend which means one fret. So you will pick the string, sounding the B note, then bend the string up to a C note. The second example shows a whole-step (or one-step) bend which equals two frets. You are bending the B note up to a C# (C sharp) note. The third example show a one-and-one-half-step bend, meaning that you are bending the B note up to a D note. The fourth example shows a two-step bend, which is equal to four frets and bends the B note up to an Eb (E flat) note. (NOTE: One-and-one-half as well as two-step bends are difficult to perform. You can usually only do half-and whole-step bends on acoustic guitars since the strings are tighter than on electric guitars).

You can practice each of these four examples by fretting the note to hear it and then bending up to it. For instance, in the first example you are to bend the B note a half step (or one fret) to a C note. So you fret the C note at the thirteenth fret to hear what it sounds like. Then, go back to the twelfth fret, pick the note, and bend it up to a C note. Get it? Come and see me if you need help and I will show you. Most guys that have been here a while know who I am.

Let's move on to triplets, shall we? My definition of a triplet is: playing the notes of any scale in sets, or groups, of three. Fig. 4 shows the major scale in the key of C.

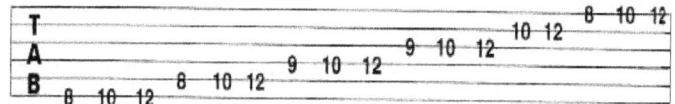

Figure 4

There are lots of ways to play triplets. The one I am about to show you is one that I also explain as "backtracking." You play the first three notes of the scale, then you start at the second note of the scale (or the middle note of the three notes) and play three more notes. Then, you back up to the second (middle note of the second triplet) and play three more notes. So, with each additional triplet (three notes) you are leaving off the first note and adding another note of the scale until you have completed the entire scale. It is much easier to execute if you already have the scale memorized. Also, doing this same triplet backwards is really cool—starting at the end of the scale and doing triplets until you've reached the beginning of the scale.

All of these techniques are very helpful in playing "lead" (or guitar solos). They will help you to play all sorts of variations of any scale. Slides and bends will give your guitar solos lots of "flavor," as well as make them sound sweet and smooth. Hammer-ons and pull-offs can really help you play faster, because they enable you not to have to pick each and every note that you are playing. The possibilities are endless.

Once you learn a scale, you can mix up the notes, play them in different variations, and create your own style. The key is to spend as much time practicing as possible.

It's so much easier to show someone than it is to tell them. So again, I don't mind showing anyone who is willing to put forth an effort to practice and learn, but I can only teach what I know. Guitar playing is like anything else—the more you put into it, the more you will get out of it. Peace! ■

13

How to File a Freedom of Information Act Request
Anonymous Contribution

The Freedom of Information Act is a federal law that states that except for specific exemptions, all records of agencies of the federal government are available for public use. This means that by law any person can request any records from any federal agency.

Like any process, particularly those involving bureaucracy, there is a right way and a wrong way to get things done. The following paragraphs are the recommended steps to successfully receive the records you request.

1) First you have to find which agency has the records you need. If you are not sure, contact each agency you think may have the records and consult with the "Freedom of Information Officer" to find out if they have them or where they can be found.

2) Once you are sure where the records you are seeking are located, write to the "Freedom of Information Officer" of that department. Each agency has a designated employee or department that handles FOIA requests.

3) Always make your request pursuant to the FOIA. Here is an example. Plainly state, "I am writing to request agency records pursuant to the Freedom of Information Act, 5 U.S.C. 552."

4) Find out what it costs. Ask what the agency charges to search for and copy records. Specify in writing that you will pay for search and copy fees. If there is a limit you are willing to spend, be sure to specify the maximum you are willing to pay, in writing. Request that the agency inform you if more funds than those you specified are required to comply with your request.

5) Be precise. Specific and detailed information will increase the likelihood that the agency will promptly locate and secure the records you seek. List such things as author, recipient, relevant time and dates, subject matter, etc. The more information you can supply with your request, the better.

6) Use qualifiers in your request. What this means is simply to use "or" and "and" a lot. For example, you know that you want information on Inquiry 7D; ask for all records that concern Inquiry 7D "or" that relate to Inquiry 7D "and" all records that have to do with both Inquiry 7D "and\or" that relate to Inquiry 7D. It's that old grammatical game that our government plays so well.

7) Exemptions. The agency might withhold a document just because a part of it is exempt. If you want the part of the document which isn't exempt, you must specifically request that the agency give you those portions. Be aware that some exemptions protect national security and intra-agency memoranda. Do not let claims by the agency that the records are exempt deter you. Seek legal counsel when faced with claims of exemption because the federal court generally favors disclosure over agency secrecy. The Freedom of Information Act provides that any portion of a record shall be disclosed to anyone requesting it after the exempted portions are deleted.

8) Request a written reply. There are statutory time limits in which the agency has to respond to your request: ten days for a normal request, twenty days for an abnormal request and thirty days for an appeal (these are working days; Saturdays, Sundays and holidays do not factor into the time limit). The agency must make a determination within the time frames mentioned.

9) If the agency does not answer your request within the time frame, appeal immediately. If the agency denies your request, appeal immediately. Find out from the agency to whom you should appeal. Appeal immediately. Attach copies of all relevant correspondence. Most agencies have a thirty-day limit on appealing. Did I mention that you should appeal immediately? Appeal immediately!

10) If your appeal is denied you can sue. Talk to an attorney and if the attorney advises that you have a good case, then consider suing. Bring your suit in Federal District Court asking that the court compel the agency to release the requested records. Don't forget to ask that attorney fees and court costs be awarded to you if you win!

On the state level, the library has ready-made forms that you need only fill out and submit. These forms are for records maintained at the Board of Paroles and any records held by the courts, court clerk or D.A. Knowledge is power and the Freedom of Information Act allows you to access that knowledge. Any job will become easier if you use the right tool; the FOIA is a very useful tool. ∎

Tribute to Myer "PJ" Pettyjohn, Leader and Healer

By Ed Hart with the Veterans for Peace

Myer "PJ" Pettyjohn, organizer and president of the only prison chapter of Veterans for Peace in recent years and the only member of such a chapter to serve on the national board of directors, died Tuesday, May 6, in Nashville, Tennessee. He succumbed to liver cancer after a short illness.

He grew up on a farm in northern Kentucky and went to war with the 101st Airborne in Vietnam as a recent high school graduate. Experiences there left him with PTSD and the effects of self-medication. The residue of those experiences led to a killing in which he was not a direct participant, but a jury found him guilty as an accomplice and he received a life sentence.

PJ was a remarkable man. He earned his bachelor's, master's and doctorate of divinity and counseling while in prison and used his education to benefit his fellow inmates. Many who lived in the free world also profited from their exposure to him over the years.

With assistance provided by Peter Shaw and Charlie Atkins, he developed Conflict Resolution and Alternatives to Violence programs and trained facilitators to run them at his institution. His prison's chaplain recommended to Tennessee authorities that the programs be replicated at the other prisons in the state and, in a presentation to a regional conference, that they be widely adopted in other states because of their great effectiveness and low cost. Chaplain Dean Yancey, a good Southern Baptist, said PJ was "the best Christian I've known, in or out of the free world."

He also designed and initiated programs and facilitated classes in Domestic Violence Prevention and in Parenting Skills. For nearly 15 years he had participated in his institution's Straight Talk Panels, which offer advice to children at risk of criminal activity, in an effort to reduce the likelihood that they might one day join the prison population.

In a final letter from the hospital, PJ apologized for leaving his fellow inmates in the lurch. His cellmate of 10 years, Johnny Wright, close friend Randall McPheeters and others with whom PJ had worked to make life at Wartburg a useful and healing experience have pledged to continue the work he commenced.

During his years at the helm of the Wartburg chapter [of the VFP], the group sent underprivileged children to summer camp, made donations to the children's hospital in Memphis, provided school supplies to low-income children and later, made monthly contributions to VFP's national office.

The members of the chapter nominated PJ to the board of directors in 1999 and the membership elected him to that high office.

Myer "PJ"Pettyjohn (center) with a few of his friends.

When a dispute arose in board positions that fall, PJ wrote in to suggest that it should be resolved by removing him in favor of another; his suggestion was rejected by the board.

He was always appreciative of support provided by his VFP comrades, including especially Phil Butler, the POW from Monterey, who understood what it meant to be confined. Alabama's General David M. Shoup Chapter adopted PJ and the Wartburg chapter when the latter group was formed. It's hard to know which group benefitted more from the arrangement. ∎

Where To Sit?

Original Contribution,
Name Withheld

Upon first entering prison despite the charade to the contrary, I was scared. Suddenly forced, I navigated through society's outcasts to discover my place. I had to answer basic questions: who to sit with while eating? who to speak with? and who to avoid? In answering these, I made a decision on the kind of inmate I was going to be. Imagine high school, the pressure you felt to sit at the "right" table and be associated with the "right" people. Multiply that by life or death, add the fact you might have to kill in here, and do not forget to carry the possibility of forced sex to form the equation. Each answer to the equation gives a different impression, which in turn produces it's own individual consequences. From my point of view there were three kinds of prisoners: type A, active criminals: type B, dormant criminals: and type C, "once in a lifetime criminals" and reforming criminals.

Active criminals are people that attempt to deeper embed themselves in unlawful acts. Gang members, drug dealers, robbers, and some murderers fall in this category. They strive to improve on their ill chosen trades. Prison, to them, serves as a school of higher learning. They form fraternity-like connections to increase their livelihood in violence and drugs both inside and outside the walls. If society happens to have the misfortune of this group graduating back to the general public, it will be but a short reunion. They will, with all probability, be back for their recidivism master's degree within the first year. The consequences of this lifestyle include a shortened life span, inability to trust and really love others, and staying imprisoned. Life for them consists of a strong love—but only for themselves.

Dormant criminals are mostly comprised of people in for rape, child abuse, child molestation, alcoholics, and drug addicts. The main distinction in this category appears to be that the behavior changes but the way of thinking does not. They refrain from criminal activities and are often model inmates. A few, unconsciously, hide in the chapel behind religion or in the library behind books. The drug addicts and alcoholics behave well because while incarcerated their access to or means of getting high or drunk is severely limited. A number brag about how much they have changed immediately preceding a war story in which they glorify past crimes or drug use. Prison is just a vacation from heinous behavior for these individuals until released back to repeating what they were doing before their incarceration. The drawbacks to this life include the self-delusion of rehabilitation just because they are removed from the catalysts that initiate their sickness. They may think of or help others, but only to impress people or appease their guilt and not out of an unconditional love.

People brought together from two previous areas of the prison populous make up the "once in a lifetime criminal" and reforming criminals. "Once in a lifetime criminals" are everyday people who are productive members of society but find themselves in a position where they commit a criminal act, mostly crimes of passion, or maybe an accident. They were never criminally minded, so they rejoin society most readily. Reforming criminals are people actually trying to make a change because it is right and not because it is mandatory. Most usually have an epiphany of some kind. Even while incarcerated they struggle with the conundrum of prison politics versus doing the right thing. An example, they, if on the street, faced with saving someone or dying, would give their life for another's or at least help. However in here if you see someone being stabbed not only are you expected not to interfere but also not to even get help which would be a criminal act in itself on the streets. These people show the best of the prison population. They will remain good ambassadors whether out there doing good deeds or in here helping to illuminate others. This class is definitely the minority because of the difficulties to do the right thing with so much negativity around you. These people help out of an unconditional love for others.

Whether you are in prison or not you still have to pick a table at which to sit, people with whom to speak, and whom to avoid. I have discussed different classes of prisoners in here; those only concerned with themselves, those that help others as long as it causes only mild discomfort, and those who sacrifice and serve others. The same divisions apply to people out there. I have picked what kind I will be. Now what kind of person will you be? ∎

Twas The Night Before Jesus Came

Anonymous

"Twas the night before Jesus came and all through the house,
Not a creature was praying, not one in the house.
Their Bibles were laid on the shelf without care,
In hopes that Christ Jesus would not show up there.

The children were dressing to crawl into bed,
Not once ever kneeling or bowing their head.
And Mom in her rocker with babe on her lap,
Was watching The Late Show while I took a nap.

When out of the East there arose such a clatter,
I sprang to my feet to see what was the matter.
Away to the window I flew like a flash,
Tore open the shutters and threw up the sash!

When what to my wondering eyes should appear,
But angels proclaiming that Jesus was here.
With a light like the sun sending forth a bright ray,
I knew in a moment this must be The Day!

The light of His face made me cover my head,
It was Jesus returning, just like He said.
And though I possessed worldly wisdom and wealth,
I cried when I saw Him in spite of myself.

In the great Book of Life which He held in His hand,
Was written the name of every saved man.
He spoke not a word as He searched for my name,
When He said, "It's not here, " my head hung in shame.

The people whose names had been written with love,
He gathered to take to His Father above.
With those who were ready, He rose without a sound,
While all the rest were left standing 'round.

I fell to my knees, but it was too late,
I had waited too long and thus sealed my fate.
I stood and I cried as they rose out of sight,
"If only I'd been ready when Christ came tonight."

In the words of this poem the meaning is clear,
The coming of Jesus is drawing quite near.
There's only one life, and when comes the Last Call,
We'll find that the Bible was true after all! ∎

Just Pray

Original Contribution,
By David Skipper

There are times when we feel abandoned and lost because of what we have done in our past and what we can be facing right now. In these moments and trying times, we may even believe we deserve to be corrected or punished for our sinful ways, because we are "bad" or have done so many bad things in our lifetime. There are times when we feel so abandoned and lost we begin to "convince" ourselves that our life doesn't matter, and neither does anyone nor anything else.

That is when we start thinking about God: Is there such a Divinity as God? Does God really care or love us? However, had we gone before Jesus in the first place, our life wouldn't be where it's at right now.

But no matter where we are in our lives or what we have done in our lifetime, Jesus' loyalty in His love for us is very real. We're in a mess in our life right now. So let's go to Jesus in prayer and ask for our forgiveness right now. Because, this will be a prime opportunity to make a new start, to begin again, and move on in your life with a spiritual relationship with our Savior, Jesus Christ, in your heart. ∎

15

Tricor Life Skills Class

**By Jeremy Ingram,
MOUNTAIN REVIEW Staff**

Tricor held its Life Skills Training class on August 1-2, 2005. A dozen inmates participated in the program, including eleven from the textile plant and one from the old refurbishing plant. This class is held twice a year. Molly McIntosh was the instructor for the class and she has been very helpful in assisting inmates in their search for a job once they are released. Because of Tricor's post-release program, out of the ninety-four inmates who were released from prison last fiscal year 84% of them became employed. Only five of them returned to prison.

Participants from the textile plant included John Berry, Jeff Bivens, Gregory Brewster, Quincy Goodine, Daniel Gunter, David Jones, Clifton Looper, Jamie Lavato, Gregory Oxendine, Ronald Rice, and David Tatham. Harry Conklin, a former refurbishing worker, also participated.

The Life Skills class is a part of Tricor's Free Enterprise Post-Release Placement System. To qualify for assistance, an inmate must have at least one year of training with Tricor within the past three years and be within six months of his parole or flat date. Also, a good work record is imperative.

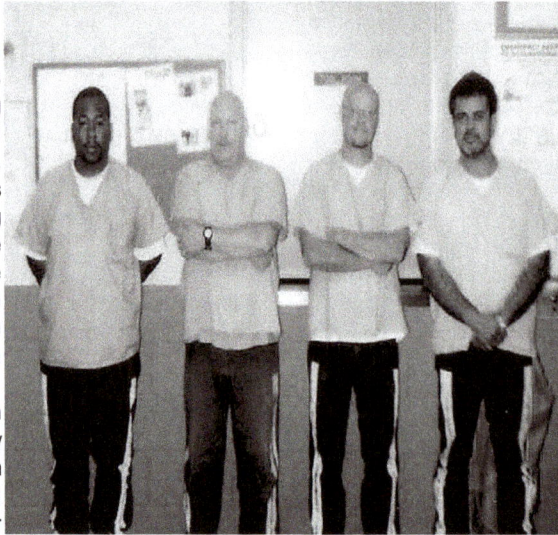

Pictured from left to right are: Quincy Goodine, David Tatham, David "Golden Boy" Jones, and Jamie Lavato.

Once an inmate qualifies for the program, Tricor will offer him a Certificate of Employment Assistance that qualifies him for a six-month job waiver. In addition, once released from prison, Tricor will help with the job search in an attempt to find the individual full-time employment.

The Life Skills class itself is very useful for inmates who will eventually be released from prison. The subjects that are taught in the class help prepare a person for release. Inmates are taught how to make a fresh start after prison. Topics such as self-esteem, anger management, personal hygiene, obtaining important personal documents, and setting goals are covered. As for obtaining a job, this class will teach a person where to look for a job, what employers are looking for, and using the internet for a job search. The class also covers important matters such as the job application, a resume, and the interview.

Tricor's Life Skills class, above all, teaches inmates that they can change. Instead of hanging onto our past behavior and way of life, we can make changes that will have a positive effect on our lives. Knowing what changes we need to make and having the courage to make those changes can be the biggest help in not coming back to prison. Don't be like the people of whom John Osborne said, "They spend their time mostly looking forward to the past." ∎

Kairos #8

**By Jeremy Ingram,
MOUNTAIN REVIEW Staff**

If you were to have walked into the visitation gallery Thursday, September 22nd, you would have found that a transformation had taken place. As you walked through the maze of tables and banners, you would have discovered the snack bar and met free-world men who had an interest in your life. If you stayed for the weekend, you would have found much more than words could describe.

Unless you are new to the compound, you will have at least some idea of what Kairos is—cookies, cookies, and more cookies. Yet Kairos is much more than that. The cookies (usually more than 15,000 to be exact) are symbolic of the agape love that the members of Kairos have for inmates. The Kairos weekend is ultimately a symbol of God's great love for this world and His expression of that love through the service of the free-world volunteers. The Kairos team consists of the free-world men who spend most of the weekend behind the walls, and several women who have set up camp down the road. The women constantly cook food that they haul into the prison to feed the participants of the Kairos weekend. Add to that the hundreds of people, literally across the world, who are praying for the inmates who are going through the weekend, and you have something that is much larger than it appears—spiritually and physically.

The word Kairos is derived from the Greek word meaning time. It is more particularly, God's special time. Although the free-world men are unashamedly Christian, the Kairos weekend is offered to anyone who wants to go through it with an open mind. The weekend itself, beginning with an orientation Thursday night, is filled with music, prayer, great food, fun activities, and (amazingly) more cookies. The Kairos motto, "Listen, Listen, Love, Love" is practiced by all the free-world men. Although inmates only have the weekend to spend with these men, once it is over there is the feeling that they have been friends much longer. That is what compels the free-world men to travel to prison once a month for a reunion of sorts.

The free-world participants of Kairos #8 include Robert Lambert, Terry Barr, Francis Gross, Charles Moore, Jim Muir, Spencer Hudson, Wally Moore, James Bauman, David Jackson, Bill Duffey, Joe Melia, Timothy Brown, Bob Nine, E. F. Gillooly, Harry Myer and J. B. Mankin. The inmates that graduated from Kairos #8 are Michael Coatney, Donald McCall, Michael Weist, Larry Smith, John Lambert, Rick Johnson, Michael Gay, Alfro Chambers, James Willis, Tyrone Bishop, Mike Roberts, Ricky Williams, Jessie Dabbs, James Thomas Davis, Greg Brewster, Seria Ward, Jackie Bowman, and Michael Gross. In support of Kairos #8 were Musicians Orlando Spratling, Charlie Brandler, Terry Turpin, John Johnson, and Bobby Tate; Kitchen Runners Corey Milliken and Allen Burch; and Servers Robert Clay, Ricky Bishop, Jeremy Ingram, Allen Bowers, and David Jones.

If you have not participated in the Kairos program and would like to, you will need to fill out an application in the Chapel. On behalf of the Kairos community, we hope to see you there! ∎

The Gift of Life

**Original Contribution,
By John R. Sweat**

Life isn't simple, no one ever said it would be either. We've been given the greatest gift on earth and most people mechanically become drones to the gift.

I am speaking of the gift of life, not just living, but the opportunity to live life fully. When is the last time you've taken the time to appreciate a beautiful sunset, or saw a bird soaring gracefully upon the gentle currents of the wind and felt a kindred spirit swell from within you?

Life is a celebration and if you have to ask "Where are the fireworks?" . . . you are off somewhere. I find my "fireworks" in the mystery of a clear night sky filled with a million dazzling stars. I find their beauty humbling. My oohs and ahhs come when I look into my family album, or when I hold my daughter's hand and see a smile come across her face.

Don't allow life to pass you by before you have the chance to figure it out. Life is so short when looked at from an overall point of view. Take the time to share it with your friends and loved ones. All involved will end up with cherished memories that will last a lifetime.

If I had to sum up my words, I would have to do so by saying *carpe diem* (a Latin adage meaning *seize the day*). If you don't live your life to the fullest, no one will do it for you.

Who am I to write these words? I am that little part within each of us that still feels like a kid in a candy store about life. I am also an inmate in the Tennessee Department of Correction that refuses to allow his situation to drain the life out of him.

Think about my words. Best wishes and bright blessings always! ∎

> **Rom 8:28
> "And we know that all things work together for good to them that love God, to them who are the called according to his purpose."**

To Spank or Not To Spank: An Argument

Original Contribution,
By Randall McPheeters

Throughout the history of the United States, various Old Testament Bible scriptures have been used to justify violence. Slave owners used many quotes from Proverbs not only to justify being a slave owner but also to justify beating their slaves. Parents quote many verses from the same scriptures to justify spanking their children.

It is my opinion (shared by many Biblical scholars and violence experts) that these scriptures are misused and misunderstood. Since the majority of society today agrees that slavery is wrong and that its violent practices are a moral embarrassment, my argument will focus on the misuse of these scriptures to support violent parenting.

First, let's look at some of the most popular Biblical quotes used to justify violent parenting.

> WITHHOLD NOT CHASTISEMENT FROM A BOY; IF YOU BEAT HIM WITH THE ROD, HE WILL NOT DIE. BEAT HIM WITH THE ROD, AND YOU WILL SAVE HIM FROM THE NETHERWORLD. (Prov. 23, 13&14)

and,

> THE ROD OF CORRECTION GIVES WISDOM, BUT A BOY LEFT TO HIS WHIMS DISGRACES HIS MOTHER. (Prov. 29, 15)

and,

> CORRECT YOUR SON, AND HE WILL BRING YOU COMFORT, AND GIVE DELIGHT TO YOUR SOUL. (Prov. 29, 17)

and,

> HE WHO SPARES HIS ROD HATES HIS SON, BUT HE WHO LOVES HIM TAKES CARE TO CHASTISE HIM. (Prov. 13, 24)

and,

> FOLLY IS CLOSE TO THE HEART OF A CHILD, BUT THE ROD OF DISCIPLINE WILL DRIVE IT FAR FROM HIM. (Prov. 22, 15)

All of these verses from the book of Proverbs are chain referenced and commonly used to justify spanking. From the words written, it is understandable that generations have believed God wants parents to strike their children in order to correct them. In fact, there is little doubt the people who preserved these writings understood them to be saying just that.

It is important here to note the context of these writings in Proverbs in order to contrast current understanding. Consider this quote:

> BY WORDS NO SERVANT CAN BE TRAINED; FOR HE UNDERSTANDS WHAT IS SAID BUT OBEYS NOT. (PROV. 29,19)

and,

> IF A MAN PAMPERS HIS SERVANT FROM CHILDHOOD, HE WILL TURN OUT TO BE STUBBORN. (PROV. 29, 21)

and,

> . . . BUT A ROD IS FOR THE BACK OF HIM WHO LACKS JUDGEMENT. (PROV. 10,14)

Current American thinking tells society it is wrong to possess a servant, and it would be reprehensible to beat a servant with a rod just as it would be to beat any person for practicing bad judgement. . .So, my question is — how can our society realize that either these quotes are period specific or they have some metaphoric meaning, yet hold to the idea the other quotes are for our time and literal?

In Proverbs 23, 13&14, the rod mentioned must be a metaphor. If it were literally a physical rod, there could be no guarantee that beating your son with it would not result in death. Proverbs 26,3 reads: A WHIP FOR THE HORSE, A HALTER FOR THE DONKEY, AND A ROD FOR THE BACKS OF FOOLS! and, Proverbs 14, 3 reads: A FOOL'S TALK BRINGS A ROD TO HIS BACK. . . . We know this rod is not literal but is a metaphoric rod symbolizing the bad life a fool's spoken deceptions will bring. No man can judge another to be a fool and then beat him in the streets. The rods spoken of in these verses are not physical anymore than a "tongue lashing" is actually given with the physical tongue. My argument is that this rod and the rod recommended for a son are equal in that they are both symbolic.

The "rod of correction" is obviously a symbol for discipline. However, discipline does not have to mean striking a child. Discipline can refer to counseling and from this point of view, Proverbs is telling parents to counsel their children and do so without waver.

Since modern society now knows that spanking children seldom has a desirable effect, it is doubtful the Bible would claim it is "THE" way to raise a good child. It is far more likely our understanding of what the Bible is teaching has been flawed.

I believe I have shown that the Bible does not advise us to beat (hit) our children, anymore than it advises us to beat our servants or to attack those fools on the streets and beat them. Once the Biblical support is removed, then our argument can focus on the affects of spanking and whether this form of punishment can achieve its intended goals.

Now, let's look at the message we are giving a child when we spank him or her. Even if the parent is a great communicator who spanks a child, there are subtle messages given which are usually unintended.

Most parents do not make it clear that the child isn't bad but his or her actions were bad. However, getting this message right doesn't negate the other unintended message. These other messages are subliminal and may include:

> If you're big enough, you make the rules and can enforce them with physical force.
> It's okay for someone who really loves you to hit you for your own good.

A parent may not mean to give these messages, but how can the child not get them? The child believes his parent loves him, and that parent is hitting him to teach him not to do something that he shouldn't do. It would be impossible, with a child's understanding, not to receive the message it's okay to hit someone you love. Let us be clear, spanking is hitting just like

slapping, whipping, and beating are hitting. The part of the body or target of the hit does not change the fact that it is hitting.

I knew a man who believed in spanking his children and would not change his mind, no matter how logically someone argued against it. He would begin with a biblical argument until someone punched holes in that argument, then he would fall back on, "It's how my father raised us and it was good enough." This is the hardest argument to break because it has no real logic. Nobody can argue against this mentality without insulting the person using it.

In the case of my friend, I was forced to point out that even though his father spanked him as he was growing up, he still became an alcoholic womanizer and didn't become a respectable man until God moved in his wretched life. He is the good person he is today not because of his father's spankings but because his life couldn't get any worse and God changed him. If spanking a child had the desired result, a man would remain a respectful and honorable person from childhood to manhood.

There is no biblical support for spanking and there is no real logic supporting it. Historically, spanking has been a failure and the learned violence has passed from father to son without variance. ■

BELIEVING IN US

Original Contribution,
By Jason Carroll

The odds are stacked against us,
    They have been all along.
    Nobody gives us much of a chance,
Thinking love can't be so strong.

Too many mountains stand in the way,
    Too much to overcome.
Years apart have hardened our hearts,
    Too much has been said and done.

The wounds have been cut too deep,
    This time the wounds can't heal.
Some say we'll never make it,
    This isn't how I feel.

Some people call us dreamers,
    Believing dreams come true.
I've never once given up on us,
    I believe in me and you. ■

17

heavily on donations and dues from inmates to be able to function. Years ago, when they took the fund-raising projects from the clubs, many projects were terminated due to the lack of funds. Even now, some current and future projects stand the risk of being dropped due to a shortage of money. As inmates, it is our responsibility—in fact, our privilege—to participate in the programs that can make us better people and enable us to live better lives. The Varsity Club implores anyone who is interested in helping the inmate community either to join the club or donate money to the club. Your generosity will help you and everyone around you have the means to learn how to become a productive person ready to overcome the obstacles of life.

The Varsity Club would like to thank our sponsor, Robin Marmon, for his hard work and dedication. Mr. Marmon has sponsored the club for many years. He selflessly gives up his time to attend meetings, handle paperwork, and support the overall affairs of the club. Without him, the club would not be where it is today.

On behalf of the Varsity Club, we hope to see you at our next meeting. We meet on the second Tuesday of every month at 6:00 P.M. in the library classroom. Come and be part of the solution as we help "Produce productive citizens through education." ■

2005 VARSITY CLUB BANQUET

Billy Grooms, Tommy Tate, Allen Bowers, Jeremy Ingram, and David Jones.

David Jones, Bryan Veal, Robert Martin, Tommy Tate, Billy Grooms, Travis Hancock, Allen Bowers, and Richard Vowell.

Jeff Nance, Paul Sharp, Rex Stedam, and Melvin Lane.

The Spider Cave

**Submitted By,
Judy Harmon**

During World War II, a U.S. marine was separated from his unit on a Pacific island. The fighting had been intense, and in the smoke and the crossfire he had lost touch with his comrades.

Alone in the jungle, he could hear enemy soldiers coming in his direction. Scrambling for cover, he found his way up a high ridge to several small caves in the rock. Quickly he crawled inside one of the caves. Although safe for the moment, he realized that once the enemy soldiers looking for him swept up the ridge, they would quickly search all the caves and he would be killed.

As he waited, he prayed, "Lord, if it be your will, please protect me. Whatever Your will though, I love You and trust You. Amen."

After praying, he lay quietly listening to the enemy begin to draw close. He thought, "Well, I guess the Lord isn't going to help me out of this one." Then he saw a spider begin to build a web over the front of his cave. As he watched, listening to the enemy searching for him all the while, the spider layered strand after strand of web across the opening of the cave.

"Hah", he thought. "What I need is a brick wall and what the Lord has sent me is a spider web. God does have a sense of humor."

As the enemy drew closer he watched from the darkness of his hideout and could see them searching one cave after another. As they came to his, he got ready to make his last stand. To his amazement, however, after glancing in the direction of his cave, they moved on. Suddenly, he realized that with the spider web over the entrance, his cave looked as if no one had entered for quite awhile. "Lord, forgive me", prayed the young man. "I had forgotten that in You a spider's web is stronger than a brick wall."

We all face times of great trouble. When we do, it's so easy to forget what God can work in our lives, sometimes in the most surprising ways. And remember with God, a mere spider's web becomes a brick wall of protection. ■

The Legal Library

Original Contribution,
By Thomas Reddick

Just about everyone on the compound knows where to find a good book, their favorite magazine, or catch up on their hometown newspaper. The library also has a legal department that can assist inmates with their legal affairs, both criminal and civil. Sometimes kiddingly referred to as the "Dream Team," the legal library is staffed by inmate legal aides Jeff Whitaker, Terry Kin Cannon, Ed Kendricks, and myself, Tom Reddick. The annex also has a legal library that is staffed by inmates Ronald Floyd and Alden Daniels.

The legal aides assist inmates with filling out legal forms and help put together their legal papers. They assist with legal research and supply legal books inmates request. The aides will also help find the right book for inmates after getting a little background information on a pending legal matter.

The segregation unit can request to see a legal aide on an appointment basis. They can also request to borrow books and policy papers for up to three days at a time. Cases and other legal material, not readily available in a book, can be copied as well. If the segregation inmates return the copies within three days, there is no charge for this service. Once returned, the legal copies will be placed in the case inventory so that the legal library can use them.

Although too many to mention, the legal library stocks many books used by inmates for legal research. Among these are *Tennessee Decisions S.W. 2d and S.W. 3d*, *Federal Reporter, Federal Practice Digest* and the *United States Code Annotated* series. Other selections that are widely used are the *Raybin's* series, *Tennessee Forms*, and the *Tennessee Code Annotated* series. The legal library also assists the annex with research, computer work, and the loaning of law books.

Through the generosity of inmate John Roe, who donates his *Tennessee Attorney Memo* to the law library, we can provide up-to-the-minute updates on all the new developments in Tennessee law. The *Tennessee Attorney Memo* is a weekly publication that is archived going back to 1990. It highlights the activities of the Tennessee Supreme Court, Court of Appeals, Court of Criminal Appeals, trial courts and recent attorney general decisions. The *Tennessee Attorney Memo* is an extremely popular and useful tool among the inmates working on their cases—both criminal and civil.

The legal aides also assist inmates with the Tennessee Department of Correction policies. This includes policy research, help with filling out information request forms, and if the need arises, grievance forms.

The law library also offers computer access to a variety of cases of which an inmate can do research. Most notably, it offers Tennessee's unpublished decisions dating back to 1985. Most of the time, if the library does not have it in book form, the case can be found on the computer.

In early 2005, the library installed a computer that helps cut down on the time it normally takes to Shepardize a case. Usually six to eight hours after a case has been handed down, the outcome of the case is available for research. It allows you to find out what case is the controlling one for the topic you are researching. It lists the strengths and weaknesses of your argument and what other cases have used those cases and citations to their advantage. Two of the computers are inmate accessible. Because of space constraints, the legal aides operate the third computer.

On a personal note, as I was writing this article, inmate Anthony Stokes, a longtime legal aide, was in the process of changing jobs to become an inmate advisor. I wanted to thank him for his patience, friendship, and legal knowledge that he passed on to me. He will be missed in the legal library, but I know that he will be just as big of an asset to inmates in his new position as he has been in the past. ∎

Law clerks Thomas Reddick, Jeffery Whitaker, Terry Kin Cannon, and Edward Kendricks

Library Book Donations

By Jeremy Ingram,
MOUNTAIN REVIEW Staff

Over the past several months, the library has received thousands of new books. Along with a new officer working in the library, this has been a busy time.

Several months ago, the Varsity Club collected donations from the inmate population to purchase books. Unfortunately, only twelve dollars was collected. The Varsity Club donated the rest and Mr. K's Used Books in Oak Ridge was contacted. They agreed to sell the club $50 worth of paperbacks. In addition to these books, Mr. K's was nice enough to throw in some freebies.

Recently, the library got a new officer. Her name is Pat Lynch. She has worked with the Department of Correction for five years. Since joining the library staff, she has already made a big contribution by facilitating the procurement of approximately 2,000 books.

The Unicorn Fund, in Wartburg, gave approximately 2,000 used books to the library here at BMCC. The library staff has worked hard to catalog these books and get them on the shelves for everyone.

We want to thank the Unicorn Fund for giving the books to us. As a result, the library was able to sort through the books and place several children's books in the visitation area and more were sent to the women's prison in Nashville. ∎

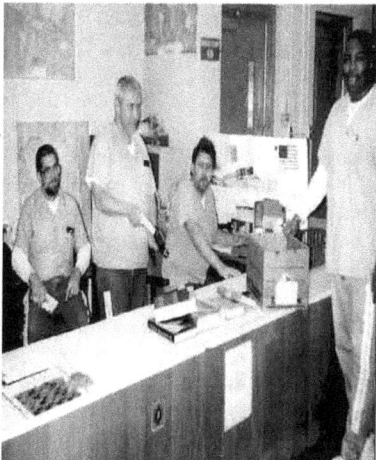

Richard Peters, Wallace Miller, Jimmy Green, and Robert Clay sort through a box of donated books.

Library clerks at work in the library.

Varsity Club President Randall McPheeters and Treasurer Jeremy Ingram stand in front of recently donated books.

19

Player

Continued from page 6

"Man, you look bad. Your ol' man's gonna kill you after payin' fifty bucks for that Guns and Roses shirt. What happened?"

"I don't know . . . wait, look at this paper." Mark unfolded the paper.

"Man, I heard war may be comin'. My dad says it's years away."

"But, but!"

"What's wrong, Mark?"

"Just a while ago this paper read JUNE 7, 2010. Now it reads JUNE 7, 2005. I don't get it . . . here, look, the headline's different too!"

"Oh?"

"Yes! Before it read 'WORLD WAR IMMINENT — CHINA AND NORTH KOREA THREATEN WAR WITH THE U.S.'"

"You're kidding, right? Mark, I think you are hallucinating. Maybe going to the beach was a bad idea."

"No, Paul, I'm not lying. I have a photographic memory! I remember what I saw. I just came from the north side of town and it was being bombed, buildings were burning. I even saw two guys from school, football jocks I think, get wasted by two Chinese soldiers."

"Impossible, Mark, look around you, the town's perfectly fine. Come on, I'll walk you home."

"Sure . . . whatever." Mark just shook his head.

"Hey, aren't you glad that things aren't like you're hallucinations?"

"I wasn't hallucinating, Paul."

"Right . . . if you say so. Come on."

As they walked Mark noticed everything appeared to be normal and the air smelled fresh with a summer breeze. It made him forget what he'd seen and reminded him that it was his birthday. Not just any birthday . . . his sixteenth. Tomorrow, his dad would take him to get his driver's license. He smiled.

"What now, Mark?"

"Just thinking . . . today's my birthday."

"Oh, yea, I forgot, sorry, buddy. Well, Happy Birthday!"

"Yea, thanks. Sorry about all that, guess my mind's been crazy, too many vid games."

"Yea, me too, I guess. Let's go see a movie later, that'll ease your mind."

"Sure, that would be cool."

"Hey, is someone supposed to be home?"

"No . . . why?"

"Your front door's open."

They bounded the steps quickly but quietly. Mark peered through the open door.

"Nothing," he whispered. "Let's have a look."

Paul nodded. They entered onto a plush white carpet and moved toward the living room.

"Hi boys!" called Mark's dad. The boys jumped back, their hearts began to race.

"Dad? You left the front door open."

"I did, huh? Close it, will ya, and come on in here. You're both in time for some good cooking."

"Hi, mom."

"Oh, hi dear," she answered with a kiss. "Where have you been and why are you dressed like a beggar?"

"I, uh . . ."

"Well, never mind, go get dressed. You can't eat naked, especially with a guest."

"Yes, mother. Come on, Paul. I'll show you my new video games."

"Sure," he answered as he followed Mark out of the kitchen and up the stairs. "You all right, man? You've got that funny look on your face again."

"Yea, I think . . . I don't know, it just doesn't' feel right somehow."

"What do you mean, doesn't feel right?"

"My dad's never that jovial and he didn't yell at me for the way I look. I mean I'm practically naked! Besides, he'd have beaten me to a pulp by now for wreaking this shirt."

"Right. At least you've still have your pants on," Paul laughed as they raced up the stairs and into Mark's room.

"Not for long," Mark replied as he slipped out of his pants.

"Ah! Warn me next time will you. Hey, these your new games?"

"Yea, cool, aren't they?"

"World War III; China verses the U.S. and Korea verses the U.S. Now I see why you're hallucinating. You've played these games too much, Mark!"

"I couldn't have, I just got them last night."

"Then you've played them all night long?"

"Nope, we went out to my grand-dad's farm for homemade ice cream. My grandparents had to go to some weird fair today so we celebrated my birthday early."

"They gave you these games?"

"Yep, Granddad fought in the Korean War so he must have thought those games would be cool to me."

"So, you've never tried them yet?"

"Nope, never seen them run yet."

"Weird."

"Yep, I agree, Paul. Now let's go get something to eat."

"Sure . . . I'm starving, too."

They raced each other back down the hall to the stairs. Mark headed down first laughing then stopped.

"Shh . . . something's not right, Paul. Paul? Paul? Damn! Where did he go?" He turned back up the stairs when a large BOOM, shook the house. Mark hit the wall then fell face first onto the steps knocking the wind out of him.

"Not again," he wheezed. His side hurt but he made himself sit up.

He peered down the steps and what he saw made his heart skip a beat.

"Mom," he whispered. "Mom . . ." He slid slowly down the stairs stopping three steps above her. She lay in a pool of blood, a hole the size of a thumb in her temple. Then he saw his dad slumped on the floor, blood dripping down his face.

Mark leaned over and threw up. *Not again*, he thought. *This can't be happening. Yet, it's different somehow.* Just then he remembered the newspaper.

Yanking it out and open he looked at the date. "JUNE 7, 2010 CHINA HELPS START CIVIL WAR!" he read aloud. He shook his head. "NO . . .! This has to STOP, it's not real!"

"What's not real?" asked a voice.

Mark stood up quickly making his head swim. Grabbing the handrail as he looked around for the object of the voice. "Who's there?"

"No one you need to be concerned about."

"Right and I'm the tooth fairy. Come out where I can see you."

"Sorry, Mark, I can't. I'm just here."

"Just here, what do you mean by that?"

"Not sure I can explain it to you. However, I can tell you should you ever need mo, just call out the name Jack."

"So, Jack, what's going on? One minute bombs are everywhere, the next everything's perfect. I came home in rags, my mom's cooking and my dad's watching T.V., which he rarely does, let alone on my birthday. He also never cussed me out for destroying the fifty dollar T-shirt he gave me the other day. Now . . . they are here, on the floor, dead. So tell me, what gives?"

"Calm down, Mark. It's like this . . . you're not really alive, and yet you are."

"That makes no sense. None whatsoever!"

"In a way, yes, you're right. However, I'm afraid you're in for a big surprise."

"Really, let's hear it."

"Okay . . . you're in a video game."

"A video game? You're crazy!"

"No, sorry, I'm not."

"Why the changes, huh?"

"When the user is viewing or playing the game you'll experience a world at war even if the user doesn't choose you as one of his or her characters."

"Now that's really crazy!"

"No, not really. See you'll experience the war on your own without being involved in the game, that is until the user wants you. But when the user isn't using the game, you'll return to this tranquil universe with your friend Paul, your mom and dad, and all your friends."

"I'm alive but in a made up world, so nothing's real?"

"Oh, I beg to differ, Mark. It's real to you and your family."

"Do they experience the war, too?"

"In a way, yes, but not the way you do. You're one of the ten characters that a user can choose."

"This isn't happening. I just can't believe it," he said sitting down on a step.

"Oops, guess I better go. You're about to be called, Mark. Have fun."

"Wait, wait! Ah . . . what's happening? I feel like I'm being pulled apart."

"Relax, Mark," came a distant voice. "You're a player now."

"AHHHHH . . . ."

Beep, beep.

"There's our man, Mark Ripper, the head of Kids Black Ops," laughed a young man.

"I've been hunting you down Mark Ripper," said another as a battle scene ensued on the screen. "You're a hard man to find. We'll get paid handsomely for this."

"Yea, we will," replied his partner who grinned menacingly.

Mark's last thoughts were, "I'm doomed!" and he was shot.

A few minutes later he awoke, finding himself looking at his executioners, who stood not far away. They were getting paid for the killing by two Chinese officers. *They think I'm dead*, he thought. *Hmm, how can I use this to my advan . . .*

All of a sudden he felt his muscles stiffen up and he became incapable of controlling his actions. He stood up rather quickly then flew into the air and did some martial arts on the two killers while grabbing their weapons as they fell. Then he turned the weapons on the Chinese soldiers who stood in shock at the action taking place. The two officers, now shot full of holes with blood gushing from them, fell over dead. He smiled as he viewed the carnage—but only for a moment.

A platoon of Chinese and Korean

See Player on page 19

Crock's Puzzle Fun

Across

1. Kindergarten supplies
8. Matter
14. Fast horse
15. Believe in
17. Hearing organ
18. "T" separates them
19. Quartermaster
21. Established (Abr.)
23. Type of music
25. Dandy
26. Worker's assn.
28. Popular medical drama
29. Limb
31. Hog feed
32. Executive officer, for short
34. With "phine," surgical instrument
35. Born as
36. Possibility
38. Ms. Landers
39. Nut
41. Deep track
42. Nasty
44. Ford flop
45. Postscriptum
46. Shoe width
48. Rises
49. Accomplish
50. Reading or B. & O.
51. Anchovy
56. AWOL hunter
58. Egyptian sun god
59. Stringed instrument
64. Turkish mountain
66. Who _____ you?
68. Simpler
69. Child
70. Arrest records
73. Opp. of SSW
74. Opal suffix
75. President (Abr.)
76. Not on time
77. Relatives
78. Receipt of goods (Abr.)
80. With "cial," anti-social
81. With "on," cool gas?
83. Absolutely not
84. Debtor's letters
86. Boob tube
87. Atop
88. Cool!
90. Must not (Archaic)
92. Estate house
94. Think over
95. Janus, perhaps

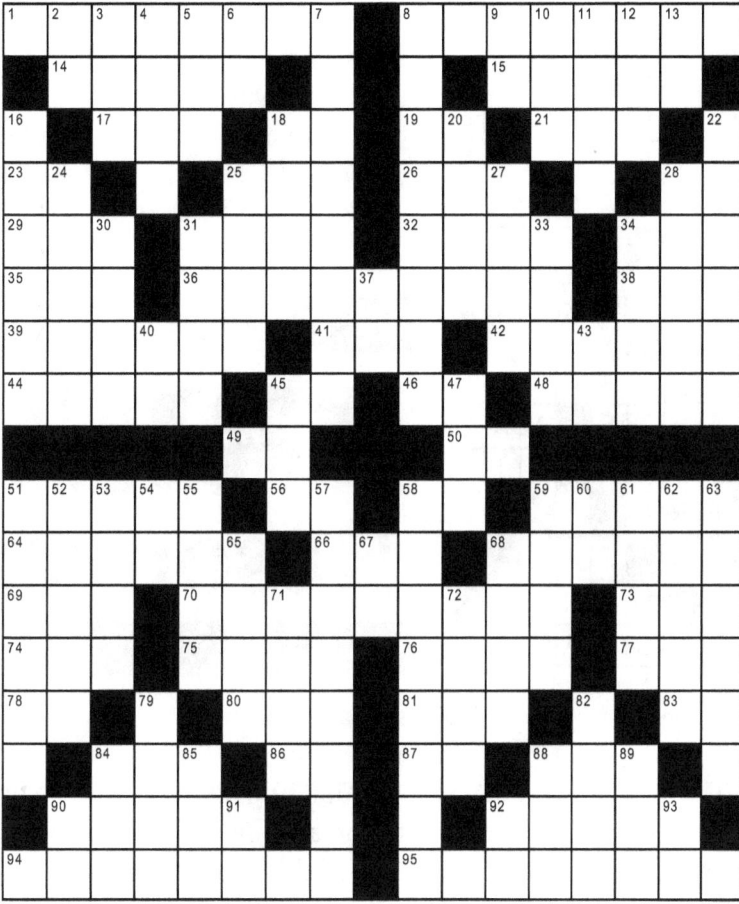

Down

2. Q and T separators
3. Dined
4. 12 months
5. Over, poetically
6. Load (Abr.)
7. Openings, like on a ship
8. Velvety carpet
9. Trust Territories (Abr.)
10. Before
11. Sit out in the rain
12. Follower
13. Where ___ ?
16. Suspended animation
18. Laundry problem for Santa
20. Type of skirt
22. Tendencies
24. Money (Slang)
25. Ebb and ___
27. Don
28. Bert's pal
30. Disarray
31. 19th, 16th, 5th, and 12th of 26
33. Talon
34. Small nail
37. Name unknown (Abr.)
40. That guy
43. Sha-na- ___
45. Small dog
47. Baseball stat
51. Irony
52. Tine
53. Speed
54. Clinton's st.
55. Cover
57. Pay no heed to
58. TN lake
59. Urn
60. As ___, no warranty
61. Babe's reply
62. Soviet leader
63. Reply to "is too"
65. Scarlette's pad
67. Type of factor
68. Diminutive suffix
71. Bother
72. Work for money
79. Diane or Betsy
82. Actress Turner
84. Author Flemming
85. Prefix with cycle or corn
88. Brit fliers
89. Mr. Holiday
90. ___ unto others . . .
91. Football score
92. ___ money
93. Symbol for rhenium

Player

Continued from page 18

solders were running toward him yelling and cursing. Mark turned and fired till both guns were empty. He began searching for more ammunition. Then his eyes fell on some new weapons that appeared out of nowhere and a female voice said, "Fifty bonus points . . . extra ammo given."

Mark laughed then turned on his fast approaching enemies and fired indiscriminately. They fell groaning as the blood splashed and gushed everywhere. Mark felt no fear or shame as he finished them off one by one.

The female voice returned, "One hundred bonus points and new weapons." The weapons appeared floating in the air.

He then spotted something new, a points board. It was high up in the air above him and presently read, 5676 - NEW HIGH SCORE. He groaned; "So, it is all true . . . I'm a player in a game. How do I get out of HERE?"

"You can't, Mark," came the now familiar voice of Jack. "There's no escape, not now or ever."

"So, I'm really stuck being a player killing off enemy troops?"

"Yes."

"What if I get shot and killed?"

"You'll live. You've done it already, just a few minutes ago."

"No! This can't be happening . . . there's got to be something better than this."

"Sorry, Mark. You need to face it, this is your reality."

Mark fought back a tear as he realized that he was back at home. The smell of cooking was once again in the air. Paul was at the top of the stairs grinning like a Cheshire cat. He could also hear the T.V. and his dad laughing at some comedy show.

"It's obvious I'm home. What's next, Jack?"

"Mark, things change a lot in games. However, I know that anytime someone plays the game, you're world will change. Get used to it."

"Great! . . . Jack, I'm going to find a way out of this game, you wait and see."

"That's the spirit! Now, go and have dinner with your parents and Paul. Oh, by the way; HAPPY BIRTHDAY, and good luck."

"Yea, I'll need it. Come on Paul, I'm hungry. Worked up an appetite killing the enemy."

"Sure, but what just happened? What enemies did you kill? I didn't see any enemies around here. You just disappeared for a while."

"Forget it, Paul. All I can say is that for now, I'm a **player**." ∎

> "My people and I have come to an agreement which satisfies us both. They are to say what they please, and I am to do what I please."
>
> — Frederick the Great

Answers to crossword puzzle on page 19.

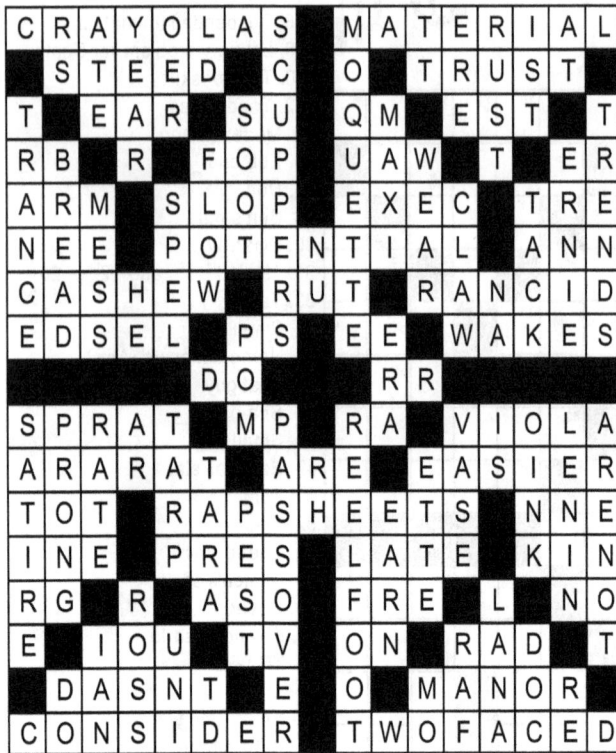

```
C R A Y O L A S   M A T E R I A L
  S T E E D   C   O   T R U S T
T   E A R   S U   Q M   E S T   T
R B   R   F O P   U A W   T   E R
A R M   S L O P   E X E C   T R E
N E E   P O T E N T I A L   A N N
C A S H E W   R U T   R A N C I D
E D S E L   P S   E E   W A K E S
      D O       R R
S P R A T   M P   R A   V I O L A
A R A R A T   A R E   E A S I E R
T O T   R A P S H E E T S   N N E
I N E   P R E S   L A T E   K I N
R G   R   A S O   F R E   L   N O
E   I O U   T V   O N   R A D   T
  D A S N T   E   O   M A N O R
C O N S I D E R   T W O F A C E D
```

MOUNTAIN REVIEW

The *Mountain Review* was produced as a free government document written by prisoners at Brushy Mountain State Penitentiary and Morgan County Correctional Complex. It was sponsored by the Education Department at those facilities and was a censored publication. Permission to reprint was granted in this section of each edition. The views expressed are those of individual authors and do not necessarily reflect the TDOC policy at that time, nor the views of the editors, staff, sponsors, or administration.

PRISONER Resource Guide

2021 Edition

Appalachian Prison Book Project
P.O. Box 601
Morgantown, WV 26507
appalachianpbp@gmail.com
aprisonbookproject.wordpress.com
Send SASE for full details. You may order one book plus a dictionary or sacred book, for a total of two books. Include a return address and DOC number and any forms necessary to send you a book.

The Beat Within
P.O. Box 34310
San Francisco, CA 94134
415.890.5641
thebeatwithin.org
Their purpose is to educate readers inside and outside of the system, of the convict's plight. Prisoners may send commentaries, artwork, and poetry directed toward teaching, inspiring, and giving hope. Contributors from death row, county jail, and youth facilities make up the content. Prisoners may receive a free subscription; donations are appreciated.

Discern Magazine
P.O. Box 3490
McKinney, TX 75070-8189
info@discernmag.com
A free, premium-quality, full-color, bimonthly Christian-living and world-news periodical. Additional free materials offered in every issue. Write for a print subscription or visit their website for more information.

College Guild
P.O. Box 696
Brunswick, ME 04011
info@collegeguild.org
Offers free non-accredited educational correspondence courses to prisoners. Write for an application.

Cornerstone Books
P.O. Box 28224
Santa Ana, CA 92799
714.668.1718
cornerstonebooks.org
A wide selection of new and used religious books at discount prices. Write for a free catalog.

Freebird Publishers
P.O. Box 541
North Dighton, MA 02764
888.712.1987; 774.406.8682
Diane@FreebirdPublishers.com
Exclusive publisher of *Inmate Shopper* and wide variety of entertaining and helpful books and publications. Assist prisoners in getting their books typed, edited, published, and publicized. Send for their packet of color brochures. Include an SASE for faster service.

Inside Books Project
ATTN: Resource Guide
12th Street Books
827 W 12th Street
Austin TX 78701
512.655.3121 (voice mail only)
insidebooksproject@gmail.com
Free national resource guide for people in prison, with listings of organizations that can send free books or information on finding legal help, pen pals, release planning, publications, and more.

The Mountain Review

Volume 19, Number 1   **A Morgan County Correctional Complex Publication**   Spring/Summer 2006

UT Football Comes To Spring Graduation

By Jeremy Ingram,
MOUNTAIN REVIEW Staff

On May 4, 2006, nineteen graduates marched into the gym under the admiring eyes of nearly three-hundred people including staff, peers, and special guests. After Principal David Pack welcomed everyone, Warden Mills congratulated the graduates on a job well done. He spoke about the difficulty involved in getting an education. But despite the obstacles, he was pleased the graduates had made the best use of their time.

Several special guests were in attendance. These included University of Tennessee offensive coordinator David Cucliffe (see sidebar on page 3), quarterbacks Bo Hardagree and Jonathan Crompton, and Associate Athletic Director Carmen Tegano. Also attending was Brent Hubbs, editor of VolQuest.com.

Mr. Hubbs, an outstanding sports radio personality, said about his visit to the prison, "Not only was it an educational experience and a positive one for two college athletes but it was also a great experience for me. I also was surprised at how up to date inmates were on things and surprised that several of them knew me. But I think what left the biggest impression on me is the effort the teachers and administrators make daily to try and help the inmates better themselves for what their life holds for them down the road. To me that is real service work and I am wiser for my Thursday trip with David Cutcliffe."

Joel Sampsel introduced some of the outstanding students. He remarked that Valedictorian Rain Chesher scored the highest score on a GED test that he had ever seen at MCCX. Class President, Martin Golden then gave a short address.

Next, David Pack introduced keynote speaker, David Cutcliffe. Mr. Cutcliffe has never said no when asked to participate in a graduation.

Coach Cutcliffe began his commencement speech by dividing the room and running a snap-count drill. After the drill was over, he mentioned he ran this drill many times and in many places but the student body at MCCX preformed it the best he had ever seen. Coach Cutcliffe spoke of his offense at Tennessee and listed three important factors in football that we can apply to our lives: say

Jonathan Crompton, David Cutcliffe, and Bo Hardagree answer questions from inmates

what you mean, mean what you say; get things done on time (tempo); and pressure—we can feel pressure and we can apply pressure. He also said if you don't like what you're getting out of life, then change what you're doing in life. We form our habits, then our habits form us. Commenting on how hot it was in the gym, he said people also needed to know when to be brief.

After his address was over, graduates received their diplomas and shook hands with Coach Cutcliffe. Then the students were able to ask the coach and his players questions about the UT football team.

Continued to page 03

In This Issue:

UNIT CHRISTMAS BANQUETS

By Jeremy Ingram,
MOUNTAIN REVIEW Staff

During the month of December, we are especially thankful for those churches who show God's love to us by hosting annual Christmas banquets for each unit. These churches sacrifice their time, money and energy to provide a special Christmas meal to everyone at MCCX. Together with music, preaching and fellowship, unit Christmas banquets are the highlight of the year for many of us.

River of Life Church held their banquet on December 9. Before they served the meal, Pastor Alan Crider shared his testimony of how God brought him to a saving knowledge of the Lord, Jesus Christ. Pastor Crider is not unlike many of us who have lived disobedient and unlawful lives. In his past, Pastor Crider was not unfamiliar with alcohol, bars and jail. Describing his mind set before God saved him, he remarked, "When you figure you're God, you don't need anything else." By the time he was 28, Pastor Crider was despondent and miserable. But in a Louisville, Kentucky convention center, God used the destituteness of Pastor Crider's spirit to convert him from darkness to the light of Jesus Christ. "God touched me from the top of my head to the soles of my feet," he said.

On December 8, United Christian Church held their

Providence Baptist Church

banquet. Ms. Rhonda Hart spoke about walking away from Jesus early in her life. As a result, she became miserable without Him. Ms. Hart implored her hearers to give their lives to Jesus. She also sang, "Just a Closer Walk With Thee."

Anton Burnette spoke on the exclusivity of Jesus Christ. He explained that there is one way for man to gain eternal life—Jesus and Him alone. The world tells us that there are many ways that are right, not just one. But the Bible says, "There is a way which seemeth right unto a man, but the end thereof are the ways of death" (Proverbs 16:25). Mr. Burnette explained that salvation is according to the will of God. Man does not seek after God, he seeks after his own ways. Therefore, it is God alone who saves sinners according to His good pleasure.

Continued to page 12

23

Pre-Release Class GRADUATION

By Jeremy Ingram,
MOUNTAIN REVIEW Staff

On March 23, 2006, thirty-eight students, inmate facilitators, and free-world staff assembled in the visitation gallery to celebrate the commencement of Pre-Release classes five and six. Pre-Release Instructor Rickey Bunch spoke to the assembled guests about the inmate facilitated Domestic Violence segment and the general Pre-Release curriculum, but focused on the most fundamental part of the program, Thinking For A Change. He explained that if a person leaves prison thinking the same way they did when they entered prison, their chances at success would be slim. Mr. Bunch remarked that it was not his job to get the students out of prison; it was his job to keep them out of prison.

On the subject of Thinking For A Change, Mr. Bunch mentioned the way inmates used to think is characterized as criminal, and he challenged everyone to begin thinking more about freedom than about crime. Concerning a change in thinking, students were equipped with the tools to be better able to ask for help when they need it. Mr. Bunch also taught them to be better judges with whom to associate.

As class five and class six were called name by name to receive their certificates, Mr. Bunch remarked about each individual's participation and progress toward remaining free once released. The students were given the opportunity to speak and several expressed their thankfulness toward Mr. Bunch.

Addressing the two classes, Mr. Bunch remarked on the many changes they had gone through, but congratulated them on getting through it. The students had learned many things, including to be better able to choose right over wrong and, therefore, better able to succeed at remaining free. In the words of Mr. Bunch, "The question is, will you?"

After the commencement, pizza, ice cream and cake were served. Everyone was thankful for the cooperation and work of the Commercial Food Service class and Instructor John Cross for preparing the pizza and cake. Everyone was also thankful for the help from the kitchen and Cory Milliken, who served the food during graduation. ∎

Class five graduates are: Greg Brewster, Randy Carter, John Carter, Jimmy Cline, Walter Donahue, Ronald Grimmett, Cedric Harris, Paul Jones, Derrick McDaniel, Aric Moses, Avery Smith, Larry Smith, Shane Snyder, Bobby Thompson, Jonathan Upchurch, Bobby Wallace, and Jason Watson.

Class six graduates are: Donald Smith, Ricky West, Charles Hamilton, Frank Cates, Robert Trosch, Matthew Taylor, Walter Johnson, Bertrum Hay, Kenneth Griffin, Jason Munsey, Rodney Johnson, Michael Hogan, Larry Vaughn, Avery Jones, Aaron Foskey, James Davis, Josh Phillips, Kenneth Seay, Michael Harrison, Jason Docktor, and Terry Heffner.

AVP

Original Contribution,
By Randall McPheeters

The Prisoner's Aid Society of Tennessee (PAST), located in Oak Ridge, was founded in 1917, as a nonprofit organization. It was developed in response to a request from staff at Brushy Mountain Prison. The staff wanted a fund to purchase recreational equipment for inmates but needed a citizen's group to manage the fund.

The organization's goals were to assist in the rehabilitation of inmates by collecting funds and supplying needed services to inmates. They also planned to inform the community of ways in which it could contribute to the rehabilitation of inmates.

Recently, several officials of the Anderson County Court System asked for a community or church to assist in providing a program for inmates at their new facility. PAST selected the Alternatives to Violence Project (AVP) as a project they were willing to help implement there. They formed a steering committee with Avery Johnson, Facility Administrator, Reverend Larry Davidson, Facility Chaplain, Jan Hicks and Jim Ramsey from the District Attorney's office and PAST members Charles Barton, Joe Crichton and Margaret Burns. This committee worked with the PAST Board to start AVP. At the request of inmate Myer Pettyjohn, AVP was brought to Morgan County by Elsie Farmer, Claudine Norris, Margaret Burns and Doug Roach.

AVP is a nonviolence peace project begun in New York State in 1975 in response to an inmate request for such a program. The program is built on a spiritual base of respect and caring for self and others. It was founded on the belief that there is a power for peace and goodness in everyone. This power has the ability to transform potentially violent situations into peaceful, mutually beneficial, situations. All participation in AVP is voluntary.

AVP is an experiential program that helps inmates learn new skills and attitudes that lead to fulfilling and crime-free lives. Being led by the AVP manuals and inmate and free-world facilitators, participants share personal experiences that help each other find new ways to deal with violence. AVP is a local project that presents four three-day workshops: Basic, Advanced, Train the Trainer and Apprenticeship of facilitators.

The first workshop (Basic) introduces participants to the basic principles of nonviolence and the methods of the AVP workshop and begins the building of the nonviolence community. The second workshop (Advanced) continues the principles of nonviolence and further builds the community. This workshop demonstrates the method of working by consensus rather than by majority rule and introduces the benefits of empowerment. The third workshop (Training for Trainers) teaches participants to be facilitators of AVP. This workshop introduces participants to the manuals and allows participants to practice public speaking skills and practice leading AVP exercises. Finally, for the Apprenticeship stage, they may ask Training for Trainer graduates to apprentice as facilitators with an experienced leadership team. This places each individual graduate in the role of a facilitator and allows other facilitators to evaluate his potential and commitment to AVP.

If you would like to sign-up for AVP, please contact Psychiatric Examiner Linda Barbier. Ms. Barbier and Chaplain Dean Yancey try to schedule one AVP workshop each month. ∎

THE WINTER 2006 GRADUATION

By Garry W. Johnson,
MOUNTAIN REVIEW Staff

At 1:15p.m. on January 19, 2006, a sea of blue poured into the gymnasium at the Morgan County Correctional Complex. The students of the MCCX School were gathering to pay honors to twenty-four individuals who had achieved the academic and vocational goals of their respective studies. The winter 2006 GED graduating class was as follows: **Marvin Branner, Donnie Bryant, Timothy Canaday, Timothy Coffey, Brandon Compton, Eddie Crippen, Michael Fitzgerald, Michael Harrison, Tony Hicks, Chris Jeffers, Jackie Johnson, Teri Kelly, Steven King, Brian Snodderly** and **Reynaldo Villasenor**. Two classes of vocational instruction also had graduates. **Randy Hicks** graduated from his training in Upholstery. Eight students earned certificates in Industrial Cleaning Apprenticeship: **Frank Cates** and **Dennis Harmon** earned Federal Certificates, and State Certificates were awarded to **Gregory Brewster, Michael Drennon, Avery Green, Kerry Mickler, James Parks** and **Clarence Porter**.

The twenty-four students clad in black robes marched into the gym to a hail of applause and the melody of Pomp and Circumstance. Jeff Hughes headed the procession and offered up the opening prayer. At 1:37 David Pack welcomed the students and staff. He gave recognition to the instructors, CCO's and the administrative and secretarial staffs for their hard work and devotion. Joel Sampsel was next to the podium to introduce Valedictorian Michael Harrison. Mr. Harrison gave an encouraging address, quoting from Scripture Proverbs 24:16, "For a just man falleth seven times and riseth up again: but the wicked shall fall into mischief."

Mr. Pack again took the microphone to introduce a most impressive orator, Leonard Adams. Mr. Adams was the keynote speaker for the event and was the TDOC Assistant Director of Education. His job history also included positions with the State as Instructor at the Tennessee Correction Academy, Counselor at Riverbend Maximum Security Institution, Charles Bass Correctional Complex and DeBerry Special Needs Facility, and Director of the Nashville Transition Center.

Leonard Adams

Mr. Adams delivered a stirring ten minute speech about challenges, positive attitude and accomplishment. He reflected on his own abusive upbringing and drew distinctions between positive and negative choices. Mr. Adams told his audience they would be either thermometers (reflecting their environment), or thermostats (controlling their environment). He also used one of my favorite quotations by Frank Covey, "We cannot go back and make a new start, but we can start now to make a new ending."

After the speech, Mr. Adams presented the General Educational Development (GED) diplomas and vocational graduation certificates. Jack Mcinnis took photos of each student receiving their degree. Once he passed out the parchments, Mr. Adams opened the floor to questions. He spoke of several projects the TDOC Education Department has in the works. Mr. Adams said that ex-cons reentering the workforce should have computer skills and that they have already purchased 400 computers to meet that goal. He has proposed that GED students receive thirty days good time upon graduation and that programs be initiated for students with learning disabilities, such as dyslexia. Mr. Adams then turned the conversation to a pilot program called the "Transition Accountability Program" (TAP). Should the TAP be instituted at MCCX, it would be set up at an inmate's intake and outline an education program and specific job training throughout the term of his incarceration. According to Mr. Adams, all the inmates who have gone through the TAP at other institutions have made parole. At 2:20 the ceremony closed with a benediction by Jeff Hughes. Afterward there was a reception for the graduates and guests. ∎

Spring Graduation,
Continued from page 01

Continued from page 01

Jonathan Crompton remarked, "The thing I will remember is the question and answer part, it's not every day that you do that with inmates to get their perspective on what they knew about us. I did not know how much information they got on us."

After the question and answer session, the graduates were dismissed and a reception was held in the visitation area. Commercial Food Service class and instructor John Cross prepared the refreshments. On behalf of everyone, I wish to thank the administration for allowing us to hold graduations as well as the school staff for the hard work in bringing it all to pass. I also wish to thank the school staff for the preparations required. And a special thanks should be given to the University of Tennessee football team for taking the time to attend graduation and sign autographs at the end. The last time Coach Cutcliffe spoke here was in the spring of 1997. That season the Vols won the National Championship. Who knows, this may be the year. ∎

2006 Graduating Class

GED Graduates: Rain Chesher, Ricky Dotson, Nicholas Godrefy, Martin Golden, Danny Hill, Kevin Harris, Ryan Martinec, Robert Morton, and Jeffrey Smith.

Commercial Food Service Graduates: Robert White and Jeff Wilder.

Industrial Cleaning Apprenticeship Graduates: Wiltha Brown, Michael Collier, Jeremy Brown, Scott Deam, and Christopher Green.

Residential Construction Technology II Graduates: Jerome Deveruaux, Brian Hartman, and Roy Jenkins.

UT Offensive Coordinator
David Cutcliffe

Cutcliffe was a member of UT's staff for seventeen years, including six years as offensive coordinator. After the 1998 season he left UT to become head coach at Mississippi. Coach Cutcliffe compiled a 44-29 win-loss record with the Rebels from 1999-2004 and coached Ole Miss to four bowl victories. He was the only head coach in Rebel history to win at least seven games in each of his first five seasons. He was selected SEC Coach of the Year in 2003 by his fellow league coaches and shared the Associated Press honor while leading the Rebels to a share of the SEC Western Division crown.

Under Coach Cutcliffe's tutelage as offensive coordinator (1993-1998), UT twice led the SEC in total offense and three times was the league's rushing leader. The Vols finished no worse than fifth in scoring offense, including leading the SEC in 1993 and placing second nationally with an average of 42.8 points per game. The Vols were 63-11 during that span with three SEC Eastern Division crowns, two league championships, and the 1998 national title.

Born September 16, 1954, in Birmingham, Alabama, David Nelson Cutcliffe attended the University of Alabama and received his bachelor's degree in health, physical education and recreation in 1976. He returned to his alma mater, Banks High School in Alabama, as an assistant coach for four years before being named head coach in 1980. His teams reached the Alabama state playoffs three times as an assistant and in both his seasons as a head coach. Coach Cutcliffe's workload at Tennessee, his first collegiate coaching position, documented the trust placed in him by Coach Fulmer. Cutcliffe served as assistant head coach, offensive coordinator and quarterbacks coach, filling all three positions capably and enthusiastically.

In the latter position of quarterbacks coach, Mr. Cutcliffe supervised the development of future NFL first-round picks Heath Shuler and Peyton Manning as they rewrote the Tennessee record book. Before then, Coach Cutcliffe mentored Andy Kelly, who has gone on to a long and noteworthy career in arena football. Overall, Mr. Cutcliffe has coached eight first-round draft picks, including recent first pick Eli Manning. ∎

25

Prison Expansion Begins

By Jeremy Ingram,
MOUNTAIN REVIEW Staff

Although we, on the compound, have not felt the force of the expansion, it has begun. In the distance, we hear the roar of the heavy equipment and see the hills changing shape. What is involved in the expansion and how it will affect us remains to be seen. Here are some facts from TDOC's web site and a local newspaper that may help us understand the immensity and impact of the expansion.

Currently there are 1,603 existing beds in Morgan County. This number includes beds from both BMSP and MCCX. When the expansion is complete, the total number of beds will be 2,441—an addition of 838 beds. After the construction is finished, Brushy Mountain State Prison in Petros (built in the 1800's) is planned to be shut down. The expansion will absorb the beds lost due to that closure.

Reports of the cost of the expansion range from $102 million to $180.5 million.

Because of the rising costs of building materials due to the reconstruction of the hurricane damaged areas in Mississippi and Louisiana, expansion cost may increase. The federal government is supplying $61 million of the funding. Commissioner George Little explains that the decision to expand is, "a sound business decision." The reason the expansion is good for the economy is twofold. First, the expansion creates 138 new jobs. When the expansion is complete, the total employee force will be nearly 700. Second, the state will save money by the closure of BMSP.

The Brushy Mountain prison currently has a $13 million operating budget. When this budget is transferred to the completed expansion project, $17 a day per inmate will be saved. This adds up to $10,030 a day or $3.6 million a year. The total operating cost of the expanded prison will be about $45 million a year.

It is reported that the expansion will be complete in the Spring of 2009. ∎

2006-SOUTHEASTERN CONFERENCE-FOOTBALL SCHEDULE

Dates and sites subject to change. SEC Championship Game—December 2, 2006 in Atlanta. Source: secsports.com

SEC-2006	Sept. 2	Sept. 9	Sept. 16	Sept. 23	Sept. 30	Oct. 7	Oct. 14	Oct. 21	Oct. 28	Nov. 4	Nov. 11	Nov. 18	Nov. 25
Alabama	Hawaii TUSCALOOSA	Vanderbilt TUSCALOOSA	Louisiana-Monroe TUSCALOOSA	Arkansas FAYETTEVILLE	Florida GAINESVILLE	Duke TUSCALOOSA	Ole Miss TUSCALOOSA	Tennessee KNOXVILLE	Florida International TUSCALOOSA	Mississippi State TUSCALOOSA	LSU BATON ROUGE	Auburn TUSCALOOSA	
Arkansas	South Carolina FAYETTEVILLE	Utah State FAYETTEVILLE	Vanderbilt NASHVILLE	Alabama FAYETTEVILLE		Auburn AUBURN	SE Missouri State FAYETTEVILLE	Ole Miss FAYETTEVILLE	Louisiana-Monroe LITTLE ROCK	South Carolina COLUMBIA	Tennessee FAYETTEVILLE	Mississippi State STARKVILLE	LSU LITTLE ROCK
Auburn	Washington State AUBURN	Mississippi State STARKVILLE	LSU AUBURN	Buffalo AUBURN	South Carolina COLUMBIA (9/28)	Arkansas AUBURN	Florida AUBURN	Tulane AUBURN	Ole Miss OXFORD	Arkansas State AUBURN	Georgia AUBURN	Alabama TUSCALOOSA	
Florida	Southern Miss GAINESVILLE	Central Florida GAINESVILLE	Tennessee KNOXVILLE	Kentucky GAINESVILLE	Alabama GAINESVILLE	LSU GAINESVILLE	Auburn AUBURN		Georgia JACKSONVILLE	Vanderbilt NASHVILLE	South Carolina GAINEVILLE	Western Carolina GAINESVILLE	Florida State TALLAHASSEE
Georgia	Western Kentucky ATHENS	South Carolina COLUMBIA	UAB ATHENS	Colorado ATHENS	Ole Miss OXFORD	Tennessee ATHENS	Vanderbilt ATHENS	Mississippi State ATHENS	Florida JACKSONVILLE	Kentucky LEXINGTON	Auburn AUBURN		Georgia Tech ATHENS
Kentucky	Louisville LOUISVILLE	Texas State LEXINGTON	Ole Miss LEXINGTON	Florida GAINESVILLE	Central Michigan LEXINGTON	South Carolina LEXINGTON	LSU BATON ROUGE		Mississippi State STARKVILLE	Georgia LEXINGTON	Vanderbilt LEXINGTON	Louisiana-Monroe LEXINGTON	Tennessee KNOXVILLE
LSU	Louisiana-Lafayette BATON ROUGE	Arizona AUBURN	Auburn BATON ROUGE	Tulane BATON ROUGE	Mississippi State BATON ROUGE	Florida GAINESVILLE	Kentucky BATON ROUGE	Fresno State BATON ROUGE		Tennessee KNOXVILLE	Alabama BATON ROUGE	Ole Miss BATON ROUGE	Arkansas LITTLE ROCK
Ole Miss	Memphis OXFORD	Missouri COLUMBIA	Kentucky LEXINGTON	Wake Forest OXFORD	Georgia OXFORD	Vanderbilt OXFORD	Alabama TUSCALOOSA	Arkansas FAYETTEVILLE	Auburn OXFORD	Northwestern State OXFORD		LSU BATON ROUGE	Mississippi State OXFORD
Mississippi State	South Carolina STARKVILLE (8/31)	Auburn STARKVILLE	Tulane STARKVILLE	UAB BIRMINGHAM	LSU BATON ROUGE	West Virginia STARKVILLE	Jacksonville State STARKVILLE	Georgia ATHENS	Kentucky STARKVILLE	Alabama TUSCALOOSA		Arkansas STARKVILLE	Ole Miss OXFORD
South Carolina	Mississippi State COLUMBIA (8/31)	Georgia COLUMBIA	Wofford COLUMBIA	Florida Atlantic COLUMBIA	Auburn COLUMBIA (9/28)	Kentucky LEXINGTON		Vanderbilt NASHVILLE	Tennessee COLUMBIA	Arkansas COLUMBIA	Florida GAINESVILLE	Middle Tennessee COLUMBIA	Clemson CLEMSON
Tennessee	California KNOXVILLE	Air Force KNOXVILLE	Florida KNOXVILLE	Marshall KNOXVILLE	Memphis MEMPHIS	Georgia ATHENS		Alabama KNOXVILLE	South Carolina COLUMBIA	LSU KNOXVILLE	Arkansas FAYETTEVILLE	Vanderbilt NASHVILLE	Kentucky KNOXVILLE
Vanderbilt	Michigan ANN ARBOR	Alabama TUSCALOOSA	Arkansas NASHVILLE	Tennessee State NASHVILLE	Kent State NASHVILLE	Ole Miss OXFORD	Georgia ATHENS	South Carolina NASHVILLE	Duke DURHAM	Florida NASHVILLE	Kentucky LEXINGTON	Tennessee NASHVILLE	

SOME GOOD ADVICE FROM CYBERSPACE
Contributed By Judy Johnson,
Anonymous E-mail

1. God wants spiritual fruit, not religious nuts.
2. Dear God, I have a problem. . .it's me.
3. Growing old is inevitable, growing up is optional.
4. There is no key to happiness. The door is always open.
5. Silence is often misinterpreted, but never misquoted.
6. Do the math. . .count your blessings.
7. Faith is the ability to not panic.
8. Laugh every day, it's like inner jogging.
9. If you worry, you didn't pray. If you pray, don't worry.
10. As a child of God, prayer is kind of like calling home everyday.
11. Blessed are the flexible, for they shall not be bent out of shape.
12. The most important things in your house are people.
13. When we get tangled up in our problems, be still.
14. A grudge is a heavy thing to carry.
15. He who dies with the most toys is still dead. ∎

26

6666666666

Straight Talk

Original Contribution,
By Howard G. Humphrey

We sit daily in our cells, watching our windows on the world (televisions) and wonder what positive effects we could have on our communities if we could only be freed. What if we were back in the community being positive mentors to our children rather than wasting away with time and watching helplessly as our children become progressively more violent with each passing generation. Oh how we wish we could somehow employ some super meta-physical force to go out there and make things better for our children than what we had. We all know that God is the answer for all troubles and it is through God's divine inspiration and intervention that programs such as "Straight Talk" and/or "Scared Straight" were created.

These programs allow us to effect positive change on society without even being there. While "Scared Straight" is more popular and preferred nationally, Morgan County decided long ago that the "Straight Talk" format was much more effective. The powers that be conducted all of the necessary scientific research and consulted with leading child-psychologists to reach their conclusions.

While some may disagree and think this approach is too soft and compromising, I beg to differ. As an 11 year veteran member of our panel, I see the look in the childrens' eyes up close and personal when they're being shot straight to as opposed to solely attempting to scare the daylights out of them.

While that technique may have been workable years ago, today's kids are much more intelligent, sophisticated, and technical than at any time in our history. How can this generation be scared of things unseen and unknown, when they've seen and done almost everything from violence, drugs, and sex? The adolescent naivety of past generations is no longer applicable. We had no idea about the consequences of our actions due to a lack of knowledge. By contrast, this generation is well aware due to a more sophisticated media.

So, what we try to do on our panel is awaken their natural instincts and habitual reactive behavioral tendencies. In other words, we are all creatures of our own chosen habits and the development of positive habits can only result in positive conclusions and vice-versa, negative habits can result in negative conclusions.

In simpler terms, imagine this scenario. You're in your 'hood and come up on two groups of kids. One group is busy smoking blunts, throwing back 40s, and getting money through illegal drug sells. Another group is busy doing homework and getting good grades, participating in sports or working after-school jobs, and doing their household chores. What do you think the incarceration percentages are for either group? The answer should be easy. About 88% for the first group verses 10% for the second group.

Today's more worldly and intelligent kids can be trusted to make the right choices when confronted on the real and not shot a bunch of the same old recycled penitentiary mumbo-jumbo over and over. So in conclusion, it shouldn't take a rocket scientist to figure out that its better to take the advice of college PHDs on this one. ∎

Straight Talk panel: Marcus Thomas, Melvin "St. Louis" Lane, Jeremy Ingram, Paul Sharp, and Tony Rackler. Not Pictured: Howard "Popcorn" Humphrey.

Amachi
By Jeremy Ingram,
MOUNTAIN REVIEW Staff

More than eight-hundred children in the Knoxville area have a parent in prison. Consequently, these children have a 70 percent chance of being incarcerated later in life. It is not surprising that most of the children and teenagers in juvenile facilities have a parent who is in prison. Without intervention, this pattern will continue. Without physical, mental, and spiritual help, these children face a challenge in life that may seem insurmountable.

Amachi Knoxville is an organization bent on helping children realize their best potential. The word Amachi means, "who knows what God has brought us with this child." Amachi helps these children by partnering with area organizations so these children will have a positive mentor relationship in their lives. Organizations such as Big Brothers Big Sisters, University of Tennessee College of Social Work, Project Grad, and local churches and schools have bonded together to offer continuing support to children in need.

Mentoring is simply putting a caring and responsible adult in the life of a child to help them in many areas of life. A mentor is a person who will help a children with their homework, take children to church, and spend time talking and playing with children. Children desperately need these types of relationships in their lives. When one or both parents are incarcerated, the children are prone to miss an important part of their upbringing.

The mentoring relationship that Amachi hopes to foster does not assume something that needs fixing is wrong with the child. They realize that life is hard, and when children do not have a normal family environment, life is even more difficult. The results of the effort of Amachi are evident—children in mentoring relationships get better grades in school, get along better with their families and friends, and are less likely to imitate the same behavior that led to their parents' imprisonment.

For children to be eligible for the mentoring program, it is advisable that they are between the ages of six and fourteen and live in the inner city area of Knoxville. If the child does not meet these criteria, they may still be accepted into the program. Inmates may sign up their own children by contacting the Mountain Review newspaper office. An Amachi volunteer will contact the care giver of the child to discuss the child's needs and what type of person would be best suited as a mentor. All mentors are rigorously checked, trained and monitored. When arrangements are made with the child's care giver, the child will begin meeting once a week for at least a year (probably longer) with his/her mentor.

If anyone has any questions, contact the Mountain Review newspaper office. If anyone in the free-world would like to be a mentor or volunteer in another way, Amachi can be contacted at 901 E. Summit Hill Drive Suite 300, Knoxville, TN, 37915, tel. 865-524-2774. ∎

AMACHI Knoxville
KNOXVILLE **LEADERSHIP** FOUNDATION

Victim Impact

By Jeremy Ingram,
MOUNTAIN REVIEW Staff

On February 27, Sheryl Demott, Director of Victim's Service for TDOC, presented the Victim Impact program to a group of inmates in the visitation gallery. This program was designed to educate prisoners on the impact they have had on the lives of victims. Before Ms. Demott began her presentation, she explained that she had a message to deliver to us from our victims. That message was, "No more victims." This article will highlight some of the points Ms. Demott made during her presentation.

Cindi

Cindi and her daughter, who was five months old, took a drive one day. Unexpectedly, a drunk-driver swerved into Cindi's lane and hit her car head-on. As a result, her daughter was paralyzed. After the wreck, Cindi remembered she felt an intense rage toward the man who was driving drunk. In fact, her rage was so intense she admitted having the desire to kill the driver. For years Cindi took care of her daughter until her daughter died at the age of seven. Because Cindi carried these feelings of rage with her, she described the man who wrecked her as a burden.

Cindi's feeling toward the culprit of the crime is common. Many victims harbor feelings of rage toward those who commit crimes against them. Often, this hatred is expressed through alcoholism, drug addiction, and other harmful activities. For most of these people, communication is the most therapeutic way of dealing with the anger. Unfortunately, victims seldom have anyone they can talk with about these issues.

Who is a Victim?

What is meant when the term "victim" is used? Without much thought, someone will answer, "A victim is a person who was raped, murdered, robbed, etc. . . " As Ms. Demott showed, this definition is not realistic. When a person is murdered, there are more victims than just the person killed. For instance, there are the co-victims. The co-victims are the close relatives of the person killed. When a son is killed, the family suffers far longer than their son did. The family must live with the pain of their loss for the rest of their lives. As noted earlier, the feelings produced because of the crime often lead to self-destructive behavior.

Beyond the victim's family, there are other groups of people affected by the commission of a crime. The friends, neighbors, and co-workers of the person (here, the person killed) suffer loss and anguish. Even this one crime affects society at-large in that they must pay, via taxes, for criminal prosecution and the many years of incarceration. When a second crime is committed, the number of victims increases exponentially. It is an understatement, although very true, that there are no victimless crimes.

This may all seem far removed from the life of us doing time. "Why should I care?" is an attitude reflected by many inmates behind bars. The reason offenders should care is that this "community of pain" we have created because of our choices is the same community to which we are trying to go back. The question Ms. Demott asked is relevant, "Why should this community of pain you've caused want you back?"

Another way to look at the result of crime is to see it as a tear in society. On one side of the gap is the free-word and on the other side is the offender. The gap seems irreparable. Often, society does not want to repair the gap. The offender must take the initiative to fix the tear they have made. What is left to do is to bridge the gap created by the offenders. Ms. Demott noted that the bridging of the gap is not done all at once, it starts with little steps. What is the first step? It is to ask and understand what the victims need from the offender.

The Making of a Peanut Butter Sandwich

When someone commits a crime, they rarely realize the choices involved that led to the actual commission of the crime. Ms. Demott likened this to making a peanut buffer sandwich. She asked how to make a sandwich. Someone would answer, "You take two pieces of bread. . . " Ms. Demott would ask, "Where do you get the bread?"

"From the store." "How do I get to the store?" " By a car." "How do I get to the car?" The questions she asked revealed that when we act, seldom do we think about the choices that precede our actions.

The point is when a victim suffers loss due to a crime, the criminal's explanation that they "didn't mean to do it" is meaningless. As the peanut butter illustration shows, we made conscious choices that led to the crime being committed. The drunk driver in Cindi 's case may say that he did not mean to do it, but the decision to drink and drive preceded and caused the fatal accident.

The problem of the consequence of our choices is a problem that needs to be accepted and reckoned with by the offender. When we analyze our crimes and break them down, in stages, we realize that the decisions we made are important, no matter how seemingly "innocent" they may be.

General Crime Statistics

Every 33 minutes a murder is committed.
Every two minutes a rape happens.
Every 50 seconds someone is robbed.
Every 19 seconds a violent crime is committed against someone at work or on duty.
Every 6.5 seconds someone is assaulted.
Every 5.5 seconds a violent crime occurs.

Stress and Victims of Crime

When a person is a victim of crime they are exposed to stress which throws them off balance. What was once normal fare for them—working, eating, family—is now overshadowed by the crime committed against them. When a person is the victim of violent crime, the stress level increases drastically. Because of the stress of being a victim, a person usually enters a crisis in their life. Shock and disbelief are common emotions felt by victims. These emotions are often strong and confusing. Even after the victim has regained their sense of balance, life may be different from what it was before.

Four Injuries

Injuries to victims are not one-dimensional. There are many aspects of the nature of injury inflicted upon a victim. Noting four of these is worthy. The first is the most common injury. Physical injury can be minor, moderate, or severe depending on the nature of the crime. The second type of injury is financial. Of course, when a person is robbed, they suffer the loss of property. Still, other financial losses are incurred by the commission of crimes. A few of the potential losses are evident: hospital bills, time off from work, legal bills, and the cost of professional counseling. A third type of injury is emotional. There are both short-term and long-term emotional injuries suffered by victims. Remember Cindi? At first, she felt an intense rage toward the drunk-driver. She characterized this rage as intense, uncontrollable, and instantaneous. Yet the long-term emotion that Cindi described was an overbearing sense of the offender being a burden on her life. The last injury is of a social nature. When a person is victimized, they are often the stigma of society. This is no fault of their own. Nevertheless, society often blames the victim (in part) for the crime committed against them. Because of these injuries, many victims need financial, emotional, and physical help from society. Victims are further injured when they cannot receive the help they need.

Emotions Related to Crime Victims

There are many emotions felt by the victims of crime. Anger and rage are common. However, this anger is not always directed solely toward the offender. Often, the victim is angry with God, the family members of the criminal, and even the criminal justice system. Many victims suffer from fear or panic attacks because of their victimization. If a person was raped when walking alone in a park at night, then years later the same environment might trigger a panic attack. These overpowering emotions lead to frustration that leads to a feeling of helplessness. In this state of helplessness, the victim is confused. They cannot understand or receive an answer to the question "why?" As often happens, the victim may begin to blame themselves. This can lead to shame where the victim may retreat into feeling they deserved what happened to them; this is common with rape victims. Eventually the feelings of grief and sorrow set in. The victim is left with an intense sadness. Consequently, depression is a familiar result of this cycle.

One emotion, in particular, experienced by many victims is a reawakened memory of the crime.

Continued to page 22

NATURE'S NASTY NATURE?

By Garry W. Johnson,
MOUNTAIN REVIEW Staff

As I put pen to paper today, the news services are replete with stories reflecting the one year anniversary of the Indian Ocean tsunami. Associated Press (AP) writer Chris Brummitt recounts, "a magnitude-9 earthquake ripped apart the ocean floor off Indonesia's coast and sent 30-foot-high waves crashing onto shores." WBIR (an NBC affiliate) confirmed that 216,000 souls perished in the December 26, 2004 disaster that ravaged twelve countries from Malaysia to East Africa. CNN Headline News reported the death toll would top 230,000 should those still considered missing be declared dead. CNN covered several memorial services and reported that the area still experiences small quakes 2-3 times a week. Out of the 1.8 million people displaced by the disaster, 80 percent still live in tents, plywood barracks or the homes of family and friends according to the aid group Oxfam International. Despite $13 million in donations world-wide—75 percent of which have already been secured—the area still has not fully recovered.

Just a year before the Indian Ocean tsunami, an earthquake in Bam, Iran killed more than 30,000 people. *USA Today* reported that on March 28, 2005, an 8.7 magnitude quake again shook Sumatra and killed another 647 people, most on the island of Nias. On October 8, 2005, a 7.6 quake caused 80,000 more deaths in Pakistan.

Anyone who regularly watches the evening news or reads the newspapers knows that earthquakes of varying degrees have become a staple of our news digest. In their November-December 2005 issue, *The Good News* magazine reported that geological activity in the new Madrid fault zone had caused considerable concern for the United States. The fault runs from southern Illinois to northeastern Arkansas and includes the St. Louis and Memphis areas.

"Major quakes occurred in that area during the early 1800's, at one point even causing the Mississippi River to flow backwards for a time. Officials stated that 'a repeat today would cause wide spread loss of life and billions of dollars in property damage'" (*The Good News* magazine p.15, citing *USA Today*).

In this satellite photo, Hurricane Katrina covers much of the Gulf of Mexico. Katrina was the most expensive natural disaster in U.S. history and killed over 1,200 people.

WHAT DOES IT MEAN?

My dad had a collection of Bill Cosby records that I loved to listen to as a child. A bit from one of Mr. Cosby's monologues always comes to mind when the subject of earthquakes is mentioned. Paraphrasing Mr. Cosby, he said, "You can say that you don't believe in a Higher Power. You can call yourself an atheist and say you don't believe there is a God. But I'm telling you right now, when that ground shakes, you're going to look up!" There are several of us looking up now.

THE TEMPEST

Those who are awaiting the coming Kingdom of God look to the Bible to understand the signs of the times. In order to fully grasp the depth of Scripture it is often beneficial to examine the text in its original language. Most English translations have much to say about future earthquakes (i.e., Matthew 24:7; Mark 13:8; Luke 21:11; Revelation 6:12; 8:5; 11:13, 19; 16:18). The Greek word translated "earthquake(s)" in each of these prophecies is "seismos." However, this same Greek word can also be translated "tempest," as in Matthew 8:24, "And, behold, there arose a great *tempest* in the sea, insomuch that the ship was covered with the waves. . ." *Strong's Lexicon* defines *seismos* as "a commotion, i.e., (of the air) a gale, (of the ground) an earthquake—earthquake, tempest" (Strong's No. 4578).

Hurricane Katrina was the most costly natural disaster Americans have ever experienced, and it occurred only eight months after the Indian Ocean tsunami. In the human toll 1,200 lives were lost. Katrina caused an estimated $200 billion in damage, not counting the economic hit from losses to shipping, oil and gas production, fishing and agriculture.

Science magazine, in its September 16, 2005 issue, reported on research by scientists at the National Center for Atomospheric Research. They concluded that while the number of hurricanes and cyclones had not increased, there has been "a sharp increase during the past 35 years in the number of category 4 and 5 tropical cyclones, the most intense storms that cause most of the damage on landfall" (Richard Kerr, "Is Katrina a Harbinger of Still More Powerful Hurricanes?", p. 1807). Specifically, the most dangerous storms—those rated category 4 and 5—have increased by 80 percent from the 1970's to the last decade.

Last year so many violent storms occurred that the National Oceanic and Atmospheric Administration (NOAA) ran out of names and had to resort to using characters from the Greek alphabet. Now, one month after hurricane season officially ended, "Zeta" is forming in the Atlantic Ocean. Zeta is the 6th letter in the Greek alphabet and the 27th-named storm of 2005.

Even the secular media cannot help but draw parallels between Biblical pronouncements and modern headlines. On my desk is a drawing by Jonathan Brown, a cartoonist for the *Desert Morning News*, which depicts a weatherman in thigh-high water holding a microphone. In the dialog box he says, "As bizarre weather continues across the world, we can expect more floods, earthquakes, disease, pestilence, fire, brimstone . . . your garden variety Wrath of God in Biblical Proportions." Ironically, he penned this cartoon in early 2005, long before hurricanes Katrina, Rita, and Wilma ever came about. At that time parts of California and the Northeast were experiencing unprecedented flooding, while central California and the Midwest battled wildfires. At the time of this writing the Midwest is again on fire and parts of California are under water. Seventy-three wildfires swept across 30,000 acres in Texas and Oklahoma as a result of that region's worst drought in fifty years (AP). California, our country's most liberal state, is experiencing wide-spread flooding and mud slides as another new storm front settles in.

Even Biblical history shows similarities with the degenerating morals of today's society. The debased state of man before the global deluge (Genesis 6), or more pointedly, the account of Sodom and Gomorrah (Genesis 19) should serve as sobering indications as to the direction we are headed. The Indian Ocean tsunami wiped out the portion of the Thai coast infamous for its child-sex trade. Hurricane Katrina devastated New Orleans just five days before 100,000 invited gays and lesbians were to gather there for their annual "Southern Decadence" festival.

Is a loving God beginning to force humanity to consider its ways, beliefs and practices, or were these just random acts of nature out of control? If God is indeed trying to get our attention, are we listening? The Mississippi barge casinos are already being rebuilt inland, and Bourbon Street is open for business. New Orleans Mayor C. Ray Nagin (D) recently lifted the ban on 24-hour-a-day liquor sales just weeks after informing still homeless citizens that funds were being set aside for the 2006 Mardi Gras celebration.

America can recover from these "natural" disasters, from 911 and (hopefully) from the war on terror. Nevertheless, if these are just "the beginning of sorrows" (Matthew 24:8), then what will God have to do to really get our attention? I hope that we are all prepared to find out. ∎   29

Art Shop Makes Gifts for UT Football

Quarterbacks Bo Hardagree and Jason Crompton, Art Shop employees Allen Bowers, Travis Hancock, Stephen Malham, and Coach David Cutcliffe. UT players and coach stand with the matted art presented to them by Warden Mills. Art shop employees matted the art for the guests who attended graduation.

Art Shop employees Stephen Malham, Travis Hancock, and Allen Bowers stand with Newspaper Worker Jeremy Ingram in front of the art gallery inside the art shop. Art shop workers create matted and framed prints as gifts given to various guest to the institution.

Don't Worry, Be Happy

By Jeremy Ingram,
MOUNTAIN REVIEW Staff

Remember the song "Don't Worry, Be Happy" by Bobby McFerrin? You may have forgotten it, but in 1988 it was a sort of minor national anthem. Not only did it win a Grammy for the year's best song, but it was also George Bush's unofficial campaign theme in the 1988 presidential election. In fact, this song brought back the smiley face of the 60's.

The idea that worry is a bad thing is not something new; it is a teaching found in the Bible. Scripture teaches that worry is sin. The Apostle Paul says not to be anxious for anything (Phil. 4:6) and Peter leads us to cast all our cares on God because He cares for us (1 Pet. 5:7). Jesus repeatedly expresses, in His famous Sermon on the Mount (Matt. 6), not to be anxious. The logic is simple: why worry about something you can do nothing about?

Worrying has many effects. Physically, worrying can cause ulcers. Mentally, it saps the energy out of life causing a person to become depressed. It commonly causes a person to become incapable of dealing with life's problems. Sometimes, worrying can lead to an early death.

What is worry?

In the New Testament, the Greek word denoting worry is usually translated as anxiety or care. It carries the idea of ripping something apart, dividing, or tearing. In fact, these ideas relate to the effects of worry. Worrying will tear a person apart. This should not surprise us. What else would a person expect when he exerts all kinds of energy toward the purpose of fixing a problem he is incapable of fixing?

In Jesus' sermon mentioned earlier, He tells his listeners not to worry about "tomorrow." Why tomorrow? Jesus implies that tomorrow will always be outside the control of man. Tomorrow will always be tomorrow. Our concern should be directed toward today because today a person can direct their energy toward a definite purpose (even planning for tomorrow). So, as Jesus said, " . . . do not be anxious for tomorrow; for tomorrow will care for itself" (Matt. 6:34).

Worrying about tomorrow is essentially trying to usurp the authority of God. God has told us that He is in charge of history. Tomorrow is in His hands (as is today). He is working out His plan according to His purpose. It is not ours to worry about.

Does it follow that God does not want us to be concerned about anything? Does He condone laziness, irresponsibility, and neglect? Does He forbid us from planning for tomorrow? Never! Instead of worrying, we are told to redirect our concerns. Do not worry about tomorrow—be concerned about today. You see, we are able to do something about today. Our energies can be directed toward a purpose that is within our reach. When we focus on today, our attention is targeted toward a concrete reality. Instead of worry (and the negative effects associated with it), we find fulfillment as our concerns are guided by the will of God revealed in Scripture.

Physiological Nature of Worry

What happens to us when we worry? First, it must be noted that the emotions we have as human beings have been put inside us by God. Each emotion has its proper place in our lives. They are an important part of the constitution of our nature. However, when these emotions are not used according to the Word of God, they cease to benefit a person and instead become detrimental to a person's well-being.

God has planted inside each of us the ability to focus our energy on a problem. In one sense, this ability to focus our energy on a problem can be called "Biblical concern." This is what Jesus referred to as He told us to seek first His kingdom. We are promised that if we direct out concern toward His kingdom then everything will be taken care of.

However, when our attention and energies are directed toward "tomorrow," our ability to solve a problem is frustrated and the energy (meant to be used) remains unused. Physically, the chemical produced from worrying builds up and can cause ulcers. The reason is that the chemicals are not being used. They cannot be used because worrying is useless. We cannot act on tomorrow.

When we worry, this cycle is repeated. Energy (both mentally and physically) is produced. Since we cannot dissipate that energy, our purpose is thwarted. The energy is built up like air in a balloon. Eventually the balloon will burst. Only when energies are directed by a Biblical concern toward a problem within our sphere of influence will this energy be used.

Does This Apply to You?

Worry is a problem common to most men. However, only certain people are able to apply Biblical principles to their lives and cease to worry. Those people are Christians. Because their faith is in Jesus Christ, they can rest assured that God works all things for their own good (Rom. 8:28). There is no reason to worry. Worrying goes against the very principle by which they live their lives.

If you would like to be in the position where all things work on your favor, then put your faith in Jesus Christ. When you repent and believe in Jesus Christ then you are one who can truly say, "Don't worry, Be Happy." ∎

2005 Basketball Championship

2005 Winter Intramural Basketball Champions
UnderDogs

UNDERDOGS
RECORD 8-1
Brian Janeway
William Elben
Billy Greenwood
Ryan Willis
Scott Gardner
Jimmy Cline
Sammy West
Michael Cal
Marlon Ellis

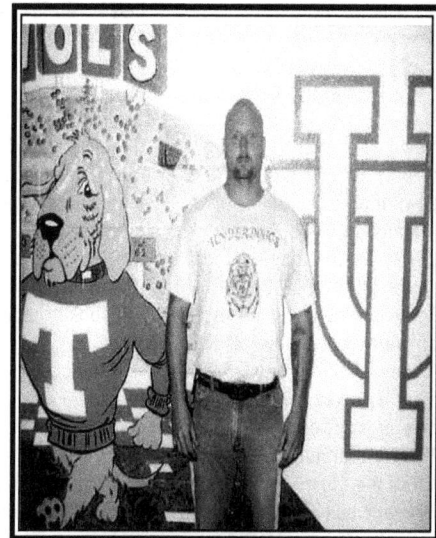

2005 Intramural Basketball Coach of the Year
William "Billy E" Elben

Fifteen Years in Industry: Rick Johnson
By Jeremy Ingram,
MOUNTAIN REVIEW Staff

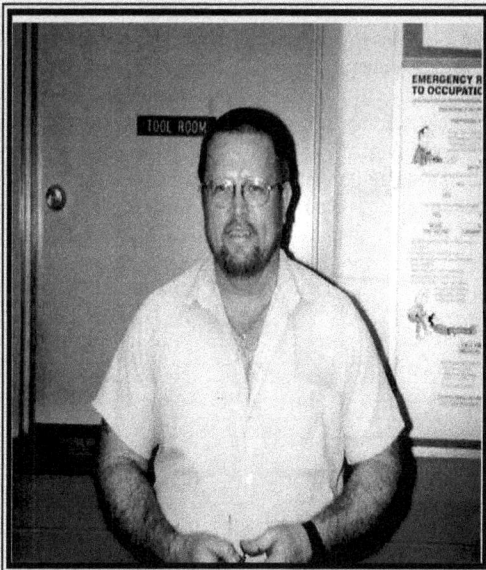

When Rick Johnson started work at the sewing plant in 1991 about twenty inmates worked there. The most a sewing machine operator could make was fifty cents an hour. Fifteen years and five plant managers later Rick has seen the sewing plant increase its size both with respect to the workforce and physical size. There are currently three times the number of inmates employed, three times the number of sewing machines, and instead of using half the industry building, the sewing plant now takes up the whole building. Inmates now average well over a dollar an hour.

Rick Johnson started working at the plant on April 25, 1991, as a sewing machine operator. A month later, they offered him the job he currently holds as maintenance. Rick had no experience with sewing machines except the month they trained him to sew. Yet his responsibility as maintenance required him to fix all the machines in the plant. Rick called upon his knowledge of tools and motors from his past when he worked on truck motors. Besides having mastered the mechanics of the sewing machines, Rick also does electrical work, helps load and unload trucks, operates the tow motor, and many other jobs required of him.

I asked Rick how working at industry has helped him get through the life sentence he is serving for first degree murder. He replied, "Working for industry for the past fifteen years has helped the time go by faster because I stay so busy. I have learned a lot about sewing machine maintenance and I look forward to learning more every day." Rick also commented on how working at industry will help him if he is ever released. According to him, "Industry has instilled in me a work ethic that I believe employers are

> **"Industry has instilled a work ethic in me that I believe employers are looking for in a person."**

looking for in a person. I've never missed a day of work. In fact, I've worked overtime and even an occasional Saturday."

Finally, Rick had a word of advice for someone new to this institution, "Sign up for Tricor to better yourself, learn new job skills, and help your time go by quicker. Plus, you can earn money so that you will not need to rely on your family." Despite tough circumstances, Rick Johnson has used his time wisely and in the process has prepared himself for success if released. For many inmates, his work ethic and progress are examples to be followed. ∎

31

Music Corner

**Playing Lead Guitar
Original Contribution,
By Charlie Brandler**

In my last article, I showed you some bends and slides that are very helpful in soloing. Now I want to show you how to play in any key up and down the neck.

Many guitarists know how to play an A minor pentatonic scale (shown in box 1 of figure one), but I do not know of many who know all five "boxes." Figure one shows all five boxes with the root note of A circled in each box. The Roman numerals to the left of the boxes show which fret each box starts on. Box 1 is the best known of the five. It starts on the fifth fret. Each new box starts with one scale tone higher up the neck. In other words, you will notice that the second note on the top string in box 1 is a C note on the eighth fret. That is also the first note on the top string in box 2.

If you look closely, you will notice that the bottom half of each box is the same as the top half of the next box. This shows how all five boxes are connected. The bottom of box 5 is the same as the top of box 1—only an octave higher at the seventeenth fret, which shows how it starts all over. Box 5 can also be played in the second position, with the first note of G being played at the third fret instead of the fifteenth. Memorizing all of the different shapes or patterns that each box has is very important before you can transpose them to other keys.

Transposing the boxes to any other key is simple. You shift box 1 to the desired key and the other four boxes will follow suit. For example, to play in the key of B you would move box 1 to the seventh position (seventh fret) and box 2 would start in the ninth position. Another easy example would be to shift all five boxes down two frets so that box 1 starts at the third fret (or third position). Doing this will put you in the key of G. That's easy enough, isn't it?

When I first started playing lead, I only knew box 1. So if I were soloing in the key of A, I would play different variations of box 1 beginning

Figure 1

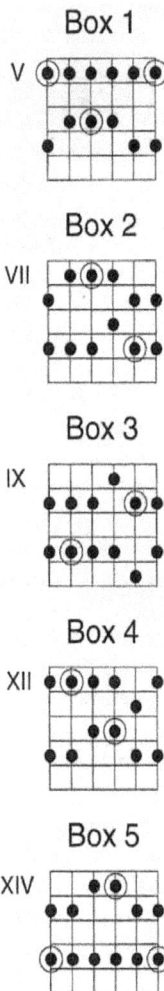

at the fifth fret. If the song changed keys during my lead solo (say to the key of E), I would simply play box 1. I would play it beginning at the twelfth fret. Now that I know all five boxes, I can still move up to the twelfth fret, but this time I am playing box 4. This enables me to play in the E position while still in the key of A. This really helps my soloing capabilities.

You can see that boxes 1 and 5 have three root notes of A in them, while boxes 2, 3, and 4 have two root notes in them. Each box provides a different sound or flavor. So using a particular box can give you a certain sound for any type of song—according to the mood of the song. Learning where your root note in each box is will help you learn all the notes on the neck (every note on every string).

I really like using box 5 as an ending to a song. I simply go through the scale backwards, starting with the root note of A at either the fifth or seventeenth fret on the bottom string. I also like to use box 4 quite a lot because it has the root on

the A and G strings for a different sound than the traditional box 1 sound.

The main thing is to practice playing each box forward and backward until you have each box's shape or pattern memorized. Unless you do that, you will have a much harder time transposing the boxes to other keys. Play through each of the five boxes and then play them backward, so that you go up the neck and back down to where you started.

Now try the rising six-note triplet pattern shown in figure two. Don't forget to practice it backwards. Then you can try the "ascending while descending" approach in figure three.

Of course you will want to practice the exercises in figures two and three with the patterns in the other four boxes. You want to develop fret board visualization. The most important thing when you are improvising is being able to see the entire neck as a whole. After you commit all five boxes to memory, they will seem more like one giant box. ■

Figure 2

Figure 3

WHAT IS THE GUITAR?

By Garry W. Johnson,
MOUNTAIN REVIEW Staff

As we know it today, the guitar is a musical instrument with a wooden, "waisted" body, flat back, fretted neck, and four-to-six strings which are plucked (usually by the fingers, fingernails, or a guitar "pick") or strummed. Prior to the late 1700's, most guitars had four or five courses. A course is one or more strings tuned to a single pitch.

The guitar was originally associated with folk and popular music, especially Spanish flamenco. With the advent of guitarist-composers such as Mauro Giuliani (1781-1829) and Fernando Sor (1778-1839), the 19th century six-course instrument attracted an extensive printed repertory. Andrés Segovia's example and influence was also instrumental in the elevation of the classical guitar to the status of a recital and concerto instrument.

There are two types of electric guitar: the semi-acoustic, with a hollow body, and the more common type with a solid body acting not as a resonator but as an anchor for the strings, and a panel to which the electronic pickups and tone and volume controls are attached. The sound from these guitars are amplified and fed through a loudspeaker.

The standard instrument, or lead guitar, has six strings, played with plectrum (i.e. a pick) or fingers. The bass guitar has four strings, and is tuned one octave below the four lowest strings of the standard instrument. Both of these instruments are widely used in all types of modern popular music. (Source: Webster's World Encyclopedia 2002.) ■

Kitchen Prepares Holiday Meals

By Jeremy Ingram,
MOUNTAIN REVIEW Staff

The hard work put into the holiday meals added the flavor of home for many inmates. Many hours of preparation and hard work by both staff and inmates yielded two holiday meals that far surpassed any other meal during the year. During a time that can be hard for inmates, these meals provide something to look forward to and enjoy.

Just how much food is involved in each meal? For the Thanksgiving meal, seventy twenty-five-pound turkeys and thirty-five pork loins were cooked. Each inmate received twelve ounces of meat on his tray. Unlike the rest of our meals, the holiday meals were not pre-prepared. They cooked the entire meal from scratch. Because the holiday meals are more expensive than normal meals, the kitchen chose to cut back on a few meals to cover the cost. In the weeks preceding Thanksgiving and Christmas, occasionally an extra vegetable plate was served.

Preparation begins in the beginning of November for the Christmas meal. Two stages are involved in preparing these meals. The first stage takes place in the days leading up to the holiday. A special crew works for three days preparing the meals. This crew works double shifts during these days, often working all night. On the day they serve the meal, much preparation is involved. For instance, the yams have to be prepared on the day that they serve them, as opposed to sausage balls, which are prepared in the days leading up to the meal. Not only do inmates work long hours, but the kitchen staff, led by food Service Manager Carey Newberry, works hard and long hours to ensure that the meals were cooked and served.

It is well known that MCCX has the reputation of serving the best meals on the holidays in the entire Tennessee prison system. For the inmate population, I would like to thank Mr. Newberry, staff, and inmate workers whose tireless efforts make these meals possible. We look forrard to more holiday meals this winter season. ■

Harold Sharkley gets ready to dig in to his Christmas dinner.

Serving line workers await the first unit to be called.

Kitchen workers prepare a tray of banana splits.

A single Christmas dinner complete with beverages, deserts, and entree.

Continued from page 01

nited Christian Church invites all inmates to attend their service on the second and fourth Sunday each month beginning at seven o'clock in the chapel.

St. John Baptist Church hosted their banquet on December 20. Pastor Joe Colquitt preached on Isaiah 9:6-7. He said that Christmas is about the greatest gift God could give to the world—Jesus Christ. Christ is the fulfillment of Isaiah's prophecy, "For unto us a child is born, unto us a son is given: and the government shall be upon his shoulder: and his name shall be called Wonderful, Counselor, The mighty God, The everlasting Father, The Prince of Peace."

The same evening, everyone listened to the incredible story of Kathy Romero, a nurse who is the head of surgery at Blount Memorial Hospital. At one point in her life, doctors gave her a two percent chance of living. But her husband believed God could heal her. He put his faith in God and prayed for a miracle. Not only did her husband pray, but many other Christians also prayed for her. Miraculously, she was healed. The experience taught her the power of prayer. Today, she talks to people in her

hospital and prays for them. Commenting on her experience she said, "Miracles really do happen in this day and age." She exhorted everyone to bring everything to God, no matter how small it is.

On behalf of inmates at MCCX, I would like to thank all the churches and volunteers who made these evenings possible: United Christian Church, St. John Baptist Church, Faith Promise Church, Focus Prison Ministry, Covenant Ministry Center, River of Life Church, and Providence Baptist Church. In addition to these church groups, there were many other people who supported these banquets. Although not mentioned, we thank them as well. Without the cooperation of MCCX's administration and the hard work of Chaplain Yancey, these banquets would not have been possible.

Starting from the top of page twelve and proceeding clockwise, the photographs show: St. John's Baptist Church group, River of Life Church group, St. John's singing, United Christian serving, United Christian Church group, Al Bowers, David Jones and Josh Davis (and look closely—a chapel musician is squeezed in between) Chaplain Dean Yancey and Doc Harmon, Providence serving and River of Life singing. ∎

TOUR OF AN AMERICAN PRISON

Original Contribution,
By Stephen Malham

Tour of an American Prison was written with the sole purpose of showing that other alternatives need to be sought in the rehabilitation of human beings. It is not intended to discredit any particular institution.

Rehabilitation can only come from within oneself. It is a decision that is based on the realization of one's wrongdoing. By becoming "penitent," or sorry, one tries to restore oneself to a good reputation; therefore, the name "penitentiary" is fitting. For the purpose of incarceration is to cause a person to think about what he has done wrong and make a change for the better. Having but a taste—a bitter taste at that—has caused this writer to make many valuable changes in his pursuit of life, liberty and happiness.

If a person commits a crime and knows the penalty for getting caught, and if their rights are protected, they have no choice but to hope for the best plea their attorney can bargain for. If convicted and sentenced in accordance with the law, that individual can harbor no animosity toward society, the courts or his attorney. His anger must be directed inward, toward himself, not for just getting caught, but for the wrongdoing itself. Rehabilitation can come quickly for a person who can humble himself and admit that he or she is wrong. But for the person who is only sorry for getting caught, rehabilitation may never come. May God grant wisdom to the men and women who have to stand in judgement in these situations.

The content of this is written in such a manner—bluntly—to hopefully help someone else in the same situation, or prevent someone from getting this far. It is not meant to glorify or justify any criminal acts, but possibly as a learning tool to prevent others from making the same mistakes in their life.

THE TWILIGHT ZONE

You are entering another dimension, a dimension void of love or happiness. It's a dimension of time, where even that stands still. Sit back—but don't relax, you are about to take a "Tour of an American prison!"

Last time it was the local softball team, before that it was the Youths for Christ, today students from all around are taking the tour. Well people, would you like to see the school, library or mess hall? They are all cleaned and polished right before each tour, and staffed only with model convicts selected not to offend your dignity. Each wearing cleaned pressed clothes, shaved, showered and groomed, all with well-rehearsed speeches about the errors of their ways. They'll tell you how they have seen the light, learned their lesson, and promised never to do it again—cross their hearts and hope to die.

Or maybe you came to see the new construction, while 37 men are turned down for college programs because more prison cells are needed. Perhaps you're interested in the factory where license plates are mass-produced, accounting for hundreds of millions in state revenue every year. But they won't tell you that inmates are forced to work for 17¢ an hour, 12 hours a day, in 100 degree temperatures in the summer, and 30 degree temperatures in the winter. Is that what you came to see? How the jails are run like country clubs, where criminals are given luxuries that most others can't afford, free college educations, extravagant recreational facilities and living conditions. Is that it?

No. You're not interested in any of that. You can watch it on T.V., hear it on the radio or read it in the newspapers. But you came to see something, didn't you? Something society sweeps under concrete carpets, something nightmares are made of. Yeah, that's what you came to see, animals in their cages, beasts in captivity, creatures in a zoo—the outcasts and killers and thieves, the junkies and queers, rapists and robbers, misfits and morons, all of them here year after year.

All of them are human, regardless of race, sex, age or creed. These people are the boy next door, your husbands and brothers and friends, the man down the street, the drunk in the bar, the druggist, the butcher, the milkman, the grocer, the doctor, the priest. Not just freaks and perverts collected from around the world. They are men and boys, sons and lovers—right out of America's own backyard—regardless of race, sex, age, or creed.

You'll hear how much good your tax dollars are doing, how better citizens are programmed, how important it is to reform the underprivileged, how society benefits and justice is served, how the law is blindly obeyed, all in the American tradition, all in the name of the Lord. But they'll never tell you what prison does to people. They'll never show you what you really want to see, what you came here for. They'll never show you the man huddled in the corner of his cell, or the one found hung from his belt, hands mysteriously tied behind his back, unexplained bruises all over his body. They'll not show you the one who loses control and kills everything that moves, while his original crime was just possession of a controlled substance, or the one who eats broken glass, steel wool and cleanser just for attention. You won't see the one who's been raped so many times he no longer has fantasies of women or freedom of life, or the one who writes daily letters to his wife and son, who were killed three years ago by police while arresting him for stealing some lunch meat and trying to get away. They'll never show you any of that. It's too real, too disgusting. It might cause embarrassment, outrage and maybe even shame.

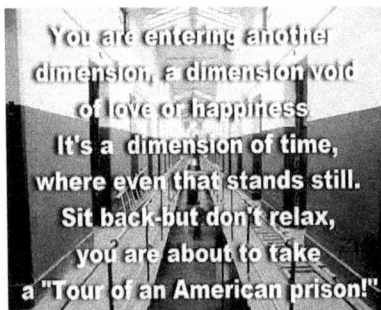

As you are leaving, they might point out an old inmate, crippled with age and disease, and tell you he's served 27 years and now is fit to work outside the walls among decent folks. Looking at this pathetic remnant of a man, you wonder about his crime, all the sordid details: his method of attack, was it summer or winter, day or night, did he wear a mask, have a gun, was the barrel long or short? As your body tingles with excitement and your blood begins to heat, waiting for them to tell you what your imagination wants to hear most, you find out he only stole a bicycle from a bank owner's son at the age of 13. He got six years to life under the old juvenile act, and no one thought to release him when the law was removed from the books. Because you never consider that people go to prison for things like that. Then you sigh with disappointment. Nor did you ever consider that he once had a mother or father, made good grades in school, wanted to be a veterinarian, was never kissed by a girl. Still, he knows enough about love to dream, though now he can't even remember how to laugh.

Tonight, after all your curiosities have been satisfied, after all this is as distant from you as the other side of the moon, after you're safe and secure in your snug little worlds, you'll never consider as you kiss your husbands and lovers and children goodnight, that there are numbers waiting for everyone, regardless of race, sex, age or creed. While most crimes are only mistakes, accidents or just victimless, they're going to need several million new license plates next year—and they will get them! Regardless of race, sex, age or creed—DON'T LET IT BE YOU!!

THERE IS HOPE

As I have been writing this story, I have noticed there is a harshness or bitterness in my words. Has all thoughts of love, kindness and gentleness faded away? Thank God, not completely! The fire has only a trace of warmth left. Maybe it is just a way of self preservation, to keep the hurt from hurting so much. The hope of knowing that one day I can love again, to have someone to hold and care for that will return the same. I see the hurt and pain in the eyes of other inmates that don't have anyone outside these gates. I might be a little better off because I have the chance to see my life and who my friends really are. What keeps me going is knowing there is someone out there waiting and praying for me. I will pull through this because of them. Right now they are mostly a part of my thoughts and dreams. One day—one day I will be able to share my love and life with them. All this will be behind me, and we will build a life together.

A tour of an American prison has been a life changing experience for me. But I'm one of the lucky ones. For others, well, this will be their life. The lucky ones are the ones that can admit they were wrong and will hang onto their dreams. So this is the end of the tour: I hope you haven't enjoyed yourself, and please, don't ever come again. ∎

THIS JUST IN : SMOKING IS OUT

By Garry W. Johnson,
MOUNTAIN REVIEW Staff

The Air Resource Board of California ruled January 26, 2006, that secondhand smoke causes breast cancer in younger women. Why should this matter to you? It matters because this powerful board is also known nationally for its groundbreaking rules limiting auto and diesel pollution [remember the advent of the catalytic converter?].

California Environmental Protection Agency scientists unanimously approved a 1,200-page report that is the strongest indictment yet of secondhand smoke. The Air Resources Board accepted CalEPA's findings, and officially listed secondhand smoke as a "toxic air contaminant" under state law. As a result, new restrictions are possible in the state with the nation's current toughest anti-smoking laws. Those restrictions could include reducing exposure in rental buildings where smoke drifts from smokers' apartments to nonsmokers' units, or in vehicles carrying children. If history is any indicator, as goes California, so goes the U.S. ("Calif. links passive smoke, breast cancer," John Ritter, *USA Today*, January 27, 2005).

Being a former smoker of nearly twenty years, I find it astonishing how the public perception of smoking has changed. In 2005, six states banned indoor smoking, more than any previous year. According to Americans for Nonsmokers' Rights, statewide or local laws limiting smoking cover 39 percent of Americans. In the United States in 1985, there were fewer than 200 such state or local laws. Now there are more than 2,000, with 118 state or local governments banning all smoking in restaurants, bars and other workplaces ("39% live in areas limiting smoking," *USA Today*, December 29, 2006).

Some businesses are even getting ahead of the government regulations. Last January, Westin Hotels & Resorts became the first big chain to go completely smoke-free. In its 77 U.S., Canadian and Caribbean lodgings, they ban smoking throughout the entire property. Other chains are considering the move, according to Joe McInerney, president of the trade group American Hotel & Lodging Association. He believes this move by Westin is the start of a nationwide

trend. According to a survey of major hotel chains and analysis of media reports by *USA Today*, at least 200 North American hotels now prohibit smoking in rooms and other indoor areas ("Westin touches match to smoke-free trend," Gary Stoller, *USA Today*, January 31, 2006). Disneyland Resort in Anaheim, Calif. made the announcement in February that they also will be banning smoking in their 2,224 room property by March 1 ("Disneyland Resort plans to ban smoking in hotels," Gary Stoller, *USA Today*, February 8, 2006).

After my incarceration in 2000, I gave up the smoking habit. This however, was no great feat of will power on my part. The county jail I was housed in for four years and seven months was a nonsmoking facility. This came as a result of the local sheriff's own bout with lung cancer. Cigarettes become very expensive when peoples' good time credits are on the line. I thank God that I am no longer a slave to cigarettes.

These days there is no shortage of information on smoking. The following are some statistics compiled by writer Noel Hornor in a publication titled *Making Life Work*. Quoting Carl Sagan on page 26, he writes, "'The global proliferation of cigarettes leads to an estimated 3 million deaths a year. . .By 2020, the number is estimated by the World Health Organization, to reach 10 million a year' (Carl Sagan, *Billions & Billions*, 1997, p. 205).

"The number of premature deaths from tobacco use is staggering in comparison to other causes of premature death. '. . .Take a random sample of a thousand young men who smoke; on the basis of actuarial data it can confidently be predicted that one of these young men will eventually be murdered, six will be killed on the roads and two hundred and fifty will die prematurely from the effects of smoking' ([Paul] Martin [M.D., *The Wellness Encyclopedia*], p.59).

"Tobacco is a deadly substance. Its smoke 'contains more than 4,000 chemicals including trace amounts of such known poisons as cyanide, arsenic, and formaldehyde. There are 43 known cancer-causing chemicals (carcinogens) in tobacco smoke' (*Mayo Clinic Family Health Book*, 1996, p. 317).

"Tobacco users raise their

susceptibility to numerous diseases, including a variety of cancers, cardiovascular ailments, sexual dysfunction and lung diseases, including emphysema. 'Each year smoking kills more than 400,000 Americans, more than died in battle in World War II and Vietnam combined' (ibid., p. 316).

"Smoking not only shortens life, but its detrimental effects often deprive smokers of the opportunity to live an active life to the full. This is ironic because cigarette advertising typically associates smoking with vigorous outdoor activities. Smokers are shown skiing, hiking, swimming, playing ball games and the like. The reality is that continued tobacco use damages the heart and lungs, eventually reducing the smoker's activities and bringing on premature aging.

"The smoker's body looks older too, especially in facial appearance. 'Compared to nonsmokers, smokers are more likely to appear at least five years older than their stated age' (*Wellness Letter*, April 1994). The term 'smoker's face' was coined a few years ago to refer to certain physical features that accompany smoking. These include increased wrinkling, facial discoloration, stained teeth and a tendency toward gauntness. All of these make smokers appear older than they are.

"Reducing or eliminating tobacco use is the only proven way to reduce the health hazards of smoking. If you are a smoker you should quit. Those who don't smoke should never start. Smoking is a losing gamble, and you are not the only one who will suffer from the habit. Secondhand smoke puts others at risk and increases the chance of respiratory disease in children who are exposed.

"Some think they are better off switching to cigars, pipes or smokeless tobacco. Although these products lower the amount of toxins and carcinogens taken into the body through tobacco use, they do not eliminate the health risk. Any form and amount of tobacco used is ultimately harmful to our bodies" (© 1999, 2001 United Church of God, P.O. Box 541027, Cincinnati, OH, 45254, reprinted by permission).

On January 27, 2006, WVLT (a CBS affiliate) aired a short segment on smoking. They reported that people who spontaneously quit smoking are far more successful than those who plan their quitting.

They advised that those who want to quit should just do it, and not try to cut back slowly. The benefits are great, as Mr. Hornor tells us, "One item of good news related to tobacco use is that when you quit your body will begin to recover. For example, even long-term smokers can reduce their risk of stroke to the same level as nonsmokers within five years (*Wellness Letter*, September 1988). By the end of five years your risk of heart attack will be almost the same as that of lifetime nonsmokers. Over several years the risk of various types of cancer decreases significantly as your body slowly repairs the damage caused by smoking (*Mayo Clinic Health Book*, p. 324)" (ibid.).

Smoking is on the decline in the United States. In 1970, 37.4 percent of Americans 18 or older smoked. By the early 90's, that figure was down to 26.5 percent. The latest figures out by the Centers for Disease Control and Prevention has the number down to 20.9 percent for 2004. Attributed to this decrease, and the improved detection and treatment of tumors, is the recent drop in overall cancer deaths. An Associated Press report by Mike Stobbe reported in February that the number of total cancer deaths in the U.S. is down from 557,271 in 2002, to 556,902 in 2003—a decline of 369 deaths. Statistically, lung cancer death rates for men have drooped about 2 percent a year since 1991, due to the reductions in smoking ("Cancer deaths dip for 1st time in 70 years," *News Sentinel*).

"From a biblical standpoint, smoking is wrong because God tells us we should not inflict harm on the bodies He gave us. We are told, 'Honor God with your body' (1 Corinthians 6:20, NIV). To mistreat our bodies by subjecting them to the harmful effects of tobacco violates this command."

"God also tells us, in the first of the Ten Commandments, that we are to have no other gods before Him (Exodus 20:3). We are to let nothing come between us and Him to adversely affect that relationship. When we allow ourselves to become addicted to tobacco (or any other substance), we have become enslaved (Romans 6:16) to a harmful, wasteful, destructive habit that hinders us from wholeheartedly serving Him (Matthew 4:10)" (Hornor, p.27). ∎

37

DO YOU HAVE A HEALTHY HEART?

By Garry W. Johnson,
MOUNTAIN REVIEW Staff

With the $400 billion in annual cost of heart treatment and lost productivity; the 900,000 heart attacks and strokes; the 1.2 million angioplasties; the 500,000 bypass operations; and the one million hospitalizations for heart failure, it is time to take a close look at heart disease and its main causes. Ninety percent of heart disease is attributable to nine risk factors, according to Salim Yusuf, a global heart specialist at McMaster University in Toronto. The risk factors are nothing new. What is new is the overwhelming evidence of the toll they take. Yusuf's Interheart study examined risk factors for heart disease involving more than 26,000 volunteers in fifty-two countries. In a *USA Today* article Mr. Yusuf says, "we know virtually all of the risk factors in every population." Surprisingly, the study shows that family history—long believed to be the biggest risk factor of all—accounts for only 10 percent of the remaining risk ("9 factors that affect your heart's health," Steve Sternberg, January 9, 2006, p. 7D). In this article we plan to look at these factors and how they affect the body.

OBESITY

The Interheart study focused on abdominal obesity which more than doubles a person's risk of heart attack. Abdominal fat is hormonally active, according to Richard Milani, director of preventive cardiology at the Ochsner Institute in New Orleans (ibid.). Because of this activity, abdominal fat begets diabetes, high blood pressure and high cholesterol—three other risk factors for heart disease. "It's not the big butt that will get you in trouble; it's a big belly," Milani says. Despite the placement of body fat, other studies show obesity alone puts stress on the heart. Dr. Julie Gerberding, director of the Centers for Disease Control, said in a March 2, 2005, Associated Press report, "It is not OK to be overweight. People need to be fit, they need to have a healthy diet, they need to exercise." The comment came as acknowledgment of a flawed study that suggested people slightly overweight might be healthier than people who were not. "I'm very sorry for the confusion that these scientific discussions have had." Of those people who are not of a healthy weight, 65 percent are considered "overweight," 30 percent are considered "obese," while 5 percent are considered "extremely obese" (Center for Disease Control and Prevention). *The Guardian* [London] reported in 2002 that one in four American adults are obese, doubling the rate from 1980. Age may also be a factor in the effect obesity has on the heart.

In the January 11, 2006 *USA Today*, Nanci Hellmich writes "A study in today's *Journal of the American Medical Association* shows that people who are obese in their middle years are at greater risk of dying from heart disease when they're older than those at a healthy weight." She continues, "The study finds that this holds true even for those who do not have other risk factors in midlife" ("Obesity alone puts heart in jeopardy," p. D4; [See also: Psalm 78:18-31; Numbers 11; Psalm 106:14-15; 1 Corinthians 10:5-6; Proverbs 23:1-3, 20-21; Philippians 3:19]).

DIABETES

Diabetes doubles the risk in men of having a heart attack. One and one-half million new cases of diabetes were diagnosed in 2005, part of the 20.8 million cases worldwide. Eleven percent of the male population age twenty and older have diabetes, as 6.2 million cases remain undiagnosed (National Diabetes Information Clearinghouse). Similar to the effects of smoking, diabetes causes platelets to stick together, producing scores of tiny clots. These clots destroy circulation by clogging the microscopic blood vessels that feed the nerves and arteries. Harmful fats in the blood are also raised by diabetes (See also: Leviticus 11:1-30; Exodus 15:26; 23:25; Proverbs 24:13; 25:16, 27; Ecclesiastes 10:17; Hebrews 12:16).

SMOKING

Those who smoke are two to three times more likely to have a heart attack than those who do not. Paving the way for inflammation and cholesterol build up, cigarette smoking narrows the arteries and damages the artery walls. This damage activates platelets. As cholesterol deposits burst inside the arteries, clots form. If a clot tears loose from the artery wall, it will cause a heart attack (See article on page 15; also: Psalm 40:1-5, 11-7; 116:1-7; Proverbs 23:29-35; 2 Corinthians 5:16-21; Ephesians 4:22-24; 1 Peter 2:11).

PSYCHOSOCIAL STRESS

Stressful life events (such as being put in prison), behavioral disorders and depression nearly triple the risk of a heart attack. Depression may be the worst factor, as 20 percent of people in the United States with heart disease suffer from it. These people are four times more likely to have a heart attack or die (See also: Matthew 10:26-31; 11:25-30; John 4:1-30; Isaiah 55:1-9; Proverbs 18:14; 2 Corinthians 6:3-10; Revelation 22:17).

HIGH BLOOD PRESSURE

High blood pressure nearly triples a man's risk of having a heart attack. The heart is forced to work harder as blood is forced through narrowed blood vessels. A heart attack can also result from the rupture of plaques as blood creates friction against artery walls (See also: Deuteronomy 14:3-21; 32:14; Isaiah 55:2; 65:4; Proverbs 17:1; Psalm 81:16; Ecclesiastes 2:24).

BAD CHOLESTEROL / GOOD CHOLESTEROL

High cholesterol nearly quadruples heart attack risk. Bad cholesterol (LDL) carries fats into the artery wall, while good cholesterol (HDL) carries it away. A fatty diet and sedentary lifestyle increases bad cholesterol and lowers good cholesterol. A healthy diet and exercise have the opposite effect and keep the arteries clean (See also: Leviticus 3:17; 7:23-24; Isaiah 66:15-17; Ecclesiastes 9:7; Acts 10:14, 28; 2 Corinthians 6:17; Revelation 18:2).

ALCOHOL

This should not be a big issue for us, but alcohol is a platelet blocker (platelets are the sticky cells that cling together and promote clotting). Modest amounts of alcohol reduce a man's risk of heart attack by 12 percent. All forms of alcohol help in small amounts—but do not break out the julep yet. Too much drinking, more than one drink a day, can promote heart disease, cancer and alcoholism (See also: Psalm 104:15; Proverbs 20:1; Isaiah 5:11; John 2:1-11; Ephesians 5:18; 1 Timothy 5:23; 1 Peter 4:1-7).

EXERCISE

The risk of heart attack drops by 23 percent with only moderate exercise. Just walking an hour every day promotes blood vessel growth, improves cholesterol and staves off diabetes by improving blood sugar (See also: Genesis 2:15; Exodus 20:9; Proverbs 15:19; 21:25; Ecclesiastes 10:18; 1 Timothy 4:8; Hebrews 6:12).

EATING FRUITS AND VEGETABLES

Daily consumption of fruits and vegetables will cut your heart disease risk by 30 to 40 percent. They lower bad cholesterol, improve blood sugar and offset foods that might not be as healthy (See also: Genesis 1:29-30; 3:18-19; 2 Samuel 17:27-29; Psalm 104:14; Proverbs 15:17; Isaiah 65:8; Daniel 1:12-15). ■

Nursing News : Hepatitis C—"The Silent Killer"

Original Contribution,
By Jennifer Anderson, R.N.

WHAT IS HEPATITIS C?

Hepatitis C is a viral, blood-borne infection caused by the Hepatitis C virus (HCV). The virus causes an infection of the liver, which initiates swelling. The swelling then causes scarring of the liver, liver failure or liver cancer.

IS HEPATITIS C COMMON?

Hepatitis C is the leading cause for liver transplants in the United States. More than four million Americans have been exposed to the virus and more than 170 million worldwide. HCV causes approximately 10,000 to 20,000 deaths each year in the U.S. Of every 100 persons infected with HCV, about 55% to 85% develop long-term infection. About seventy of 100 might develop chronic liver disease. One to five persons out of 100 may die as a consequence of long-term infection.

HOW IS HEPATITIS C TRANSMITTED?

Transmission of Hepatitis C happens when a person comes in contact with blood of an infected individual. This can happen through blood transfusion, organ transplant, contaminated needles, sexual contact or from mother to baby during pregnancy.

WHAT ARE THE SYMPTOMS OF HEPATITIS C?

Symptoms of Hepatitis C include flu-like symptoms such a fatigue, loss of appetite and nausea. Jaundice (yellowing of the skin) abdominal pain and dark urine may also occur. Other, less common symptoms are muscle and joint pain, tenderness in the liver area and a low-grade fever.

HOW CAN HEPATITIS C BE DIAGNOSED?

Hepatitis C can be detected through blood tests and is usually detectable as early as 1-2 weeks following exposure. Eighty percent of infected persons will have no symptoms and do not receive treatment until it is too late. A person can remain asymptomatic for ten to twenty years after being exposed to the virus.

HOW IS HEPATITIS TREATED?

One treatment is Alpha Interferon. Interferon is a host protein made to attack viruses and protect the body from the viral infection. The body naturally produces interferon to ward off infection, but additional injections of interferon three to four times a week gives added protection. A newer treatment is called the Pegylated Interferon. This is taken with Ribavin, an oral medicine that fights certain viruses. This combination creates a constant level of interferon in the blood that causes protective proteins to remain in the blood stream longer and helps keep the virus away for greater periods of time. Some have faith in the herbal treatment known as "milk thistle" which aides in healing and rebuilding the liver. It also increases the production of new liver cells and may even reduce the sever scarring of cirrhosis.

There is no vaccine for the prevention of Hepatitis C, but if the virus is detected and treated early enough, it can be curable. Russia is currently using a new HCV treatment that has now become available in the U.S. It is able to repair injured liver cells. Although treatment has come a long way, researchers still have a long way to go. ∎

> Editor's Note: Jennifer Anderson is a Registered Nurse at Parkridge Hospital in Chattanooga TN. Jennifer will be a regular contributor to the MOUNTAIN REVIEW in coming issues. ∎

Smile, It's Good For You!

"A merry heart doeth good like a medicine: but a broken spirit drieth the bones." Proverbs 17:22

By Garry W. Johnson,
MOUNTAIN REVIEW Staff

Two studies at the University of Maryland have confirmed the Biblical prescription: happiness is good medicine.

Dr. Michael Miller and colleagues tested the function of blood vessels of twenty healthy volunteers as they viewed two movies, one humorous and one stressful. They focused primarily on the lining of the blood vessels where hardening of the arteries begins. Fourteen of the twenty subjects had diminished blood flow after watching the stressful movie clips. During those stressful periods blood flow was decreased by an average of 35 percent. The humorous movies had the opposite effect. Nineteen of the twenty subjects had increased blood flow while laughing at the funnier movie clips, an average increase of 22 percent.

In a report on the study Dr. Miller said, "the magnitude of change we saw in the endothelium [the lining of the blood vessels] is similar to the benefit we might see with aerobic activity, but without the aches, pains and muscle tension associated with exercise." However, he warns, "We don't recommend that you laugh and not exercise, but we do recommend that you try to laugh on a regular basis." Dr. Miller believes, "Thirty minutes of exercise three times a week, and fifteen minutes of laughter on a daily basis is probably good for the vascular system." He also explained, "Laughing may be important to maintain a healthy endothelium, and reduce the risk of cardiovascular disease."

In the second study, Dr. Wei Jiang and colleagues at North Carolina's Duke University, tracked 1,005 heart failure patients and tested them for depression. Excluding other factors such as age, marital status and original cause of the patients' heart failure, Dr. Jiang reported that patients with mild depression were at 44 percent greater risk of dying. He noted that patients experiencing depression were more likely not to exercise or not take medication properly and make unhealthy lifestyle choices in diet and smoking (*The Good News* magazine, p.15, July/August 2005).

Other medical studies featured in *The Philadelphia Trumpet* (August 2005, p.25), show that laughter actually boost endorphin levels (the body's natural pain killers) and increases the production of T-cells, which help to ward off viruses. Laughter also suppresses the body's level of epinephrine, the "stress" hormone.

The immune system also gets a boost as humor increases levels of antibody immunoglobulin, which fights upper respiratory tract infections. Laughter helps antibodies penetrate infected cells and helps lower dopamine levels (which are associated with high blood pressure).

As implied by Dr. Miller's study, laughter is considered a great cardiovascular workout. It lowers your heart rate, blood pressure and improves coordination of the brain (stimulating alertness and memory). It is actually possible for all 400 muscles of the body to move during a good hard belly-laugh!

So remember that laughter is good medicine and smile, because God loves you! (Sources: *The Good News, The Philadelphia Trumpet.*) ∎

Slow Metabolizers Of Caffeine Risk Heart Health

By Garry W. Johnson,
MOUNTAIN REVIEW Staff

A recent study suggest that coffee drinkers with a common genetic trait might experience a higher risk of heart attacks. The study was conducted in Costa Rica, where more than 4,000 people were tested and about half were found to carry the trait. The genetic trait allowed the caffeine to linger longer in their bodies, which made them "slow caffeine metabolizers." The rest of the test subjects had the opposite trait, which caused their bodies to rapidly break down the caffeine. In this group coffee drinking seemed to reduce heart attack risk. In the first group however, those who drank two or more cups of coffee daily were at least 36% more likely to have a nonfatal heart attack than those who drank little or no coffee. Slow metabolizers under 50 were at an even higher risk, being four times more likely than the others in their age group who drank little or no coffee. University of Toronto researcher Ahmed El-Sohemy said the findings might explain why there have been such mixed results in studies investigating caffeine's effect's on the cardiovascular system. El-Sohemy co-authored the study in the March 8, 2006 *Journal of the American Medical Association.* ∎

THINK ABOUT THIS

Original Contribution,
By Stephen Malham

With all the talk in political campaigns about crime and punishment, I wonder how many politicians have visited prison. Not many, judging by the way some politicians on the campaign stump make prison life sound like a breeze.

I spent some time in prison (past and present), and trust me, it's not a nice place, not even to visit. Don't get me wrong, I think people who have committed serious crimes should be behind bars. Prison should not be like a vacation or a country club. Nor should it be like a torture chamber. Prison doesn't look like the" Big House" in those Jimmy Cagney movies. To me, it looks more like a military base with treeless acres of low-sprawling buildings surrounded by miles of razorwire fences.

When you walk through the yard and cellblocks, the atmosphere of fear, anger and resentment is so thick that you could cut it like a block of cheese. What some people might not realize is that most of the corrections officers mingle with prisoners. If something goes wrong, the CO's would be in a world of hurt. They have no firearms, no nightsticks, no nothing. We hear a lot of politicians talking about getting rid of the televisions, the basketballs and the weightlifting equipment in the prisons and jails. Most CO's I talked to, though, don't care for these notions because they would make prisons more dangerous. Idle time and unspent energy spell trouble behind bars. Removing the equipment also deprives CO's of privileges they can take away to punish inmates.

Contrary to what you may hear, most inmates don't spend the day watching Geraldo. More than 80%. of them work. That labor includes working on highway crews, building prisons and doing most of the maintenance chores inside the prisons. That makes sense. Making prisoners do hard labor is not a big problem. Most are young and fit. They relish the exercise.

Brutal treatment does little good because that's how life was for many before they were sent to prison.

An old guy who raised a lot of dogs once told me that the best way to make a dog mean is to keep kicking it. Seems to me that brutal treatment would have the same effect on humans. If you really want to cause prisoners some pain, make each one read aloud a paragraph from a book while standing in front of a class. The overwhelming majority of inmates would be humiliated because they can't read.

That's the nut of the problem. Most of the people in our prisons are functionally illiterate, lack job skills and have drug and alcohol problems. Let's also remember that most of them eventually will be set free.

If you make them address their weaknesses while there in prison, there is convincing scientific evidence that most convicts won't get involved in crime again after they are released. That is not coddling prisoners. The point is to prepare them to be responsible and productive when they get out. I think back to a circuit court judge who told me that he has asked victims, "Would you rather get even, or do you wish that you had not been the victim of a crime?" The answer to that is simple.

Wouldn't it be wiser in the long run for our elected officials to spend less time trying to make prisons more brutal and instead spend more time figuring out how to work constructively with prisoners and young people so there will be fewer crime victims in the future? Open your eye's America, there is a way to work things out without violence or hatred.■

In Memoriam
Original Contribution,
By Randall McPheeters

I met Bill Anderson in 1992 when he came to work as a teacher's aide for Fay Butturini. We worked together as teachers' aides for many years until I moved on to the newspaper and Bill moved on to TRICOR. During that time, I found Bill to be a loyal friend and a very easy-going person. We made a good team in the classroom, first under Mrs. Butturini and then for David Pack.

Bill and I even celled together for a while during that time. We were good friends who counted on each other when it really mattered. He stayed out of trouble, keeping to himself a lot. He never got too far into debt and he would help almost anyone who asked whenever he could. Bill's biggest failing was that he didn't take care of his health very well.

He smoked a lot, and he didn't eat right. If you ever saw him on the lower yard, you are a part of a very small group. Bill hated to leave his cell and the television. On the few occasions when someone was able to convince him he needed to exercise, he would start walking the track only to stop due to the terrible pain in his hip or leg.

Early in his sentence, Bill became depressed over the crime he committed for reasons he could not fathom. I don't believe he ever came to a clear understanding of the events which led to his crime, but he mourned the lives lost that day. He learned to work through the depression and function, but I don't believe he ever shook it.

I spent many hours talking with Bill about his family. I witnessed his sadness over the death of his mother and his joys and frustrations over his daughter. I met his brother and his nieces through visitation. He was always eager to tell me about his family and how they were doing, and I enjoyed hearing about them. I, no doubt, don't know everything about his family but I appreciated what he shared with me. Bill seemed to sense that I missed having news of my own family and his news always helped.

There are few people in this world who love to argue like Bill did. There was always someone in the unit getting riled up about something just to hear him rant. In fact, if no one teased him into a rant on any given day, he would go out and start an argument of his own. There was no malice in his arguments, but there was definitely fire.

Bill Anderson was my friend and I will miss him greatly. I am sorry he did not survive his incarceration. I am sorry he will never get the chance to spend time with his daughter like he wanted. I am sorry he didn't get to hang out with his brothers the way he wanted. Most of all, I am sorry I have lost yet another good friend. ■

LIFE SAVED

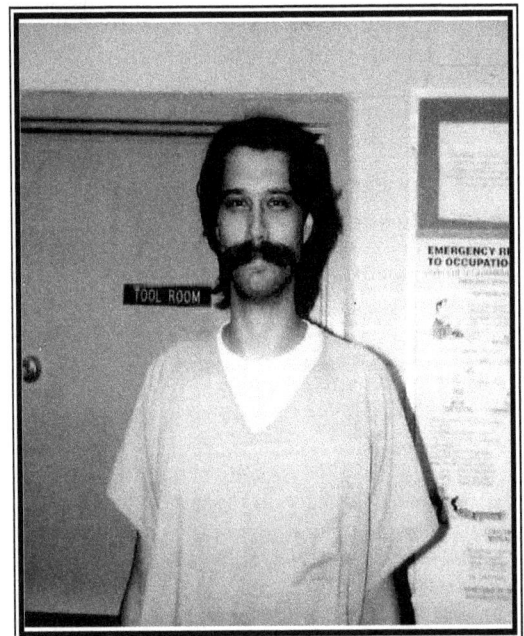

By Jeremy Ingram,
MOUNTAIN REVIEW Staff

It was just like every other night for Jonah Mainwaring. As he sat in the chow hall eating his meal, Jonah would have never imagined that he would become a hero. When one of his friends started choking on a piece of food Jonah jumped into action. Relying on his superb Heimlich maneuver skills, Jonah successfully dislodged the piece of food from his friend's throat, thus saving his life. ■

Club News:
Veteran's Club

Original Contribution by,
Grant Henderson

The Golden Bear Veteran's Club is an organization for veterans of any branch of the military. We have a Veterans Administration Representative at every meeting to help with the needs of our veterans (you do not have to be a member to talk to the representative). If you are disabled or were hurt while in the service, you may be eligible for benefits (you could even receive a check while you are incarcerated). The representative will also help you get any or all of your military records.

We recently held our annual elections. The results were:
President—Grant Henderson
Vice President—David Presley
Secretary—Terrill Turpin
Treasurer—Jeff Bivens
Sergeant-at-arms—Howard Humphrey
Chaplain—Randall McPheeters

We also have a banquet once a year. Last year's was a great success. We had a lot of food and a wonderful time.

The Golden Bear Veteran's Club would like to invite any and all veterans to join our club. If you have any veteran's business with the V.A. Rep., feel free to come and talk to him. God bless you! Thanks for your service. ∎

Varsity Club

By Jeremy Ingram,
MOUNTAIN REVIEW Staff

The Varsity Club held elections in January. The membership unanimously voted the incumbent board for another term. The following is a list of the Board of the Varsity Club:
Randall McPheeters—President
David Jackson—Vice President
Jeremy Ingram—Treasurer
William Barney—Secretary
Gene Twitty—Sergeant-at-Arms
Paul Rutherford—Chaplain

The Varsity Club continues to push ahead with the many programs and classes it supports. In addition to the Parenting class and Domestic Violence class (taught in the A&D and Pre-Release programs), the Anger Management class started in January. Due to the number of inmates interested in participating in the program, two classes were begun simultaneously. This program is open to anyone interested in learning more about anger management. The Varsity Club also offers a Sign Language class (every Tuesday at 6:00), G.E.D. tutoring (Saturday as needed), and Writer's Workshop (every Thursday of the month at 6:00) in the library classroom.

The Varsity Club meets on the second Tuesday of the month in the library classroom at 6:00 p.m. Anyone interested in joining the club is invited to attend a meeting. ∎

The 7ᵗʰ Step Foundation Program

Original Contribution,
By Luther Swallows, 7th Step Editor

The 7th Step Foundation Program is a program that offers self-help for the incarcerated who sincerely want to stay out of the prison system once they are released through normal channels.

WHAT WILL YOU DO WHEN YOU GET OUT?

When you get out of prison, will you be prepared for the jobs that are out there today? Do you have skills in a particular job or vocation? How ready are you when you step beyond the confines of the prison system? In the 7th Step Foundation Program, we recently completed the topic of a study entitled "My readiness for work," where we learned just how ready (or ill-prepared) we are to jump back into the workforce.

One thing we will try to do to put ourselves back into the employment world is to fill out an employment application, or send possible employers a resume containing our accomplishments and work history. What education do you have and what were your grades while in school? What are you skilled in? Where have you worked before? Do you have exact dates written down for all this history in you life?

Many do not write all this information down and keep an accurate record of their life's history. Often they will forget dates and past employment,

something many employers are looking for to verify whether potential employees are qualified for a particular job.

When you go for an interview to a company, try not to show things that might hurt your chances of being hired. For example, dress appropriately for the job position you are applying for. If you are looking for a desk job, dress neatly in nice clothes or a suit. If you are looking for a job in a garage, you can dress in nice clothes or a clean uniform. Future employers look at how well groomed an individual is. Is his or her hair combed or brushed, or is it a mess? Does the individual smell clean, or does he or she have an offensive odor?

Do not say things that might hurt your chances of being hired. Negative statements might be something like, "I do not want to do that kind of job."

If times are hard when you get out, you may have to take a job you really do not like to gain some work experience. Once you acquire that work experience and show you are a team worker, finding a better paying job with better working conditions should not be too difficult.

Some positive statements might include something like, "I am looking forward to becoming an asset to the company, and I am willing to learn whatever you want me to do." Showing confidence that you can and are willing to learn from the company is a "BIG PLUS" to a possible employer.

Be honest on your application, even if it means you might not get a particular job.

Many employers will hire you because you were honest enough to put on the employment form your incarceration time or that you have some kind of physical limitation that will keep you from doing certain tasks. It may keep you from being put in some positions, but it could put you in a working environment that is better for you. Put down the job you did while locked up, whether it was a teacher's aide, TRICOR worker, maintenance crew, electrician, plumber, newspaper editor, cleaner, or a library worker. It all counts as having previous employment experience—even in prison.

Mention what your responsibilities were in some detail to give your future employer some idea of what you can and cannot handle. An employment application is your chance to BRAG about yourself and your accomplishments, so tell everything you can about what you have accomplished in your life that could be beneficial to your future employer.

Join us every Thursday night at 7:00 in the inmate dining room to learn more about how you can help yourself and how to better yourself before you get out. When you learn to help yourself, then you can help others better themselves. See you there. ∎

We're Looking For Qualified Writers

Do you have a way with words? Do you have something to say? Want to see your work in print? The Mountain Review is an inmate newspaper. We are looking for original material for publication. News articles, original poems, comics, songs—whatever you would like to share with the inmates, staff and administration of Morgan County Correctional Complex. All submission information can be found on page twenty-four of this publication, or the back page of any Mountain Review issue. So let us know what's on your mind, and we'll share it with our readers.—The Editors ✍

Is It Just An Issue Of Blood?

By Garry W. Johnson,
MOUNTAIN REVIEW Staff

There is a case before the state Supreme Court questioning the constitutionality of the Tennessee law allowing blood samples to be drawn from inmates and their DNA profiles stored in a database. Assistant Public Defender John R. Halstead of Knox County is representing the alleged "UT rapist," Bruce Warren Scarborough in the landmark case. Scarborough is charged with attacking five University of Tennessee female students in 1997. The state's high court has chosen his case to test whether the profiling and storing of inmates' blood constitute an "unreasonable" search and seizure that would violate the Fourth Amendment.

By 2002, the Knoxville police department still had no clue who committed the series of rapes in 1997, when a random run through the DNA database linked Scarborough to the crimes. He had been imprisoned in 1999, for an unrelated attack on a Blount County woman, and had his blood drawn as mandated by the Tennessee law. Based solely on that link a search warrant was issued and a second blood sample drawn. That sample was matched to semen recovered from some of the rapes. Authorities then constructed a case against him for the remaining crimes.

The state Court of Criminal Appeals ruled against Scarborough last year. They opined that prisoners are not afforded the same privacy rights as ordinary citizens. In a hearing February 1, 2006, before the Supreme Court, Halstead argued that the appellate court was only half right. He said, "Prisoners do have a reduced expectation of privacy in those things that have legitimate penal purposes." He conceded that prisoners needed to have their cells and even their bodies searched to ensure the safety of prison guards and other inmates. However, he points out that prison officials do not use blood drawn from inmates for security purposes. Those samples instead are sent to a laboratory for profiling. "This (taking of blood) has absolutely nothing to do with the normal course of a prison," he said. He argued that the only purpose for taking an inmate's blood is, "to solve crimes, taking your blood with absolutely no suspicion." Probable cause must be shown in most every other situation before police can search a person or their possessions, and certainly so before blood can be drawn.

Halstead also argued that coercion is applied to force inmates to sign a form giving permission for blood to be drawn. Good-time credits and parole are withheld from anyone refusing to sign. Assistant Attorney General Brent Cherry rebutted that the drawing of blood is no different from the taking of fingerprints. He pointed out that fingerprints are also held in a data bank. Cherry asserted that if inmates have any privacy rights at all, those rights should be weighted against what he called, "great government interest" in solving crimes. He went on to add that good-behavior credits and parole are "privileges," not rights, and can be taken at will by the state.

Justice Adolpho A. Birch Jr. wondered aloud, "Why are we moving so far away from probable cause in this case?" He went on to say, "We're not talking about crime prevention. We're talking about crime solution." Chief Justice William M. Barker questioned both sides that if the state could show "a legitimate medical purpose" would the taking of inmates' blood then be considered constitutional. Justice E. Riley Anderson brought up the possibility of wrongly convicted persons being cleared of crimes by the DNA database. Anderson, who along with Birch is retiring this year, asked, "Wouldn't that DNA sample then serve another purpose—to exonerate someone else?" Justice Cornelia A. Clark asked, "If (authorities) are not concerned they're conducting a search, why do they ask for consent?" Cherry responded, "They're going above and beyond."

The Scarborough cases are on hold pending the outcome of the Supreme Court review. The court should hand down a ruling on this case later this year. (Source: "Justices ponder inmate rights," Jamie Satterfield, February 2, 2006, Knoxville *News Sentinel*.) ∎

$500,000-Drug-Sniffing Dogs, Coming To A Camp Near You.

By Garry W. Johnson,
MOUNTAIN REVIEW Staff

Correction Commissioner George Little told lawmakers March 13, that the nearly $500,000 they appropriated last session to train dog units was money well spent. Appearing before the Oversight Committee on Corrections, he said that drug-sniffing dogs are helping to keep drugs out of state prisons and upcoming drug testing of employees should also help.

The dog units have already investigated all of the state's prison facilities. Marijuana and cocaine were the primary drugs found. Drug dogs also sniffed out visitors trying to bring in prescription drugs. Participating in a massive search of West Tennessee State Penitentiary last year, the dog units uncovered drugs, alcohol, weapons, cell phones and other banned items. Little said that the investment was worthwhile.

"We've gotten feedback through the inmate population and staff that it is having an effect, and they are having to govern themselves accordingly." He also said, "We think it is a deterrent."

Little said there were some cases of staff members having marijuana and they are facing disciplinary action. "The standard recommendation is termination," he said. The department should have a program in place shortly after July 1 that will randomly drug test employees, according to Little. Currently, only prisoners are randomly tested for drugs.

House Speaker Pro Tem Lois DeBerry [D], a member of the committee, said that she was pleased to know the money was spent wisely. "The program right now is a success," she added. "If we continue to invest in that kind of program, I think we will eventually rid our prisons of drugs and other contraband."

There are fifteen prisons under the supervision of the Correction Department, employing more than 5,000 people. More than 20,000 inmates are under TDOC jurisdiction in thirteen male populated facilities and two female facilities. One of the women's prisons is in Nashville, and the other is in Memphis. (Source: "Drug-sniffing dogs cleaning up prisons," Lucas L. Johnson II, Associated Press, March 14, 2006.) ∎

Just One More Right, Slipping Away . . .

By Garry W. Johnson,
MOUNTAIN REVIEW Staff

Most of us will never run for public office, but a new bill sponsored by Senator Jamie Woodson, R-Knoxville, seeks to make it a fact of law. A Senate Committee voted February 28, to permanently ban convicted felons from ever seeking elective office, no matter how long ago the offence was committed and regardless if a judge had restored all their rights. Woodson tried to pass the same legislation through in 1999, as a state representative, but was blocked by opponents who believed that voters should have the right to choose, regardless of a candidate's past. "This is a different time," says Woodson. "The time for this bill is now. . .A person who has breached the public trust should be forever banned from running for office."

As the bill was presented to the committee, it would have only applied to those committing a crime after July 1 of this year. However, with Woodson's consent, the committee amended the bill to cover past crimes as well. Out of concern that the amendment to include past crimes would be ruled unconstitutional if challenged in court, another amendment was added stating that if one part of the bill was declared unconstitutional, the rest of the bill would remain in effect. (Source: "Proposed law keeps felons out of office," Tom Humphrey, *News Sentinel*, March 1, 2006.) ∎

A quick look at our religious activities schedule will show that our compound is abounding with various ideas about who and what God is. Those of us ascribing to a Christian understanding claim to derive our notion of God from the Bible. Yet even under the banner of Christendom, hundreds of denominations differ in their worship of the living God. The Scripture says, "to whom ye yield yourselves servants to obey, his servants ye are to whom ye obey . . ." (Romans 6:16). So, just who do you obey? Who is God?

THE FATHER AND THE WORD

"In the beginning was the Word, and the Word was with God, and the Word was God. The same was in the beginning with God" (John 1:1-2). In these opening verses of John's Gospel, we find that the Word (Greek: *logos*) was God. We also learn that the Word was with God. The Word and God were together in the beginning, and the Word was on the same plane of existence as God.

"All things were made by him; and without him was not any thing made that was made" (John 1:3). "And the Word was made flesh, and dwelt among us . . ." (John 1:14). Many seem to overlook the plain teaching of the New Testament that Jesus Christ, in His preexistent state as the Word, was the agent through whom God the Father created all things (Ephesians 3:9; Hebrews 1:1-3).

Let me give an example of what I mean. In 1979, my mom and dad started a sign business in southern Georgia. My dad was a screen printer and had a friend who did hand lettering. With my mom handling the books and the phone, they began a business called Savannah Sign and Screen.

By the time I went to work there in 1988, the company was incorporated and my dad was president of a twelve-man operation. He wore decent cloths to work, met with clients, and quoted prices. The rest of us painted, printed, designed and built the signs. My dad was still a sign maker, although he was seldom involved with the manufacturing of the product. His employees, working with tools and computers—and the *power* of electricity—were the agents by which he produced signs.

In the same sense, God the Father is Creator. He "created all things by Jesus Christ" (Ephesians 3:9). Jesus was the Word. "He spake, and it was done; he commanded, and it stood fast" (Psalms 33:9). God tells Christ what to do (John 8:28-29). As the workman, Jesus speaks, and the

power of God's Spirit does what Jesus commands (Psalms 104:30; Genesis 1:2).

In the account of Genesis 1:1, we learn that "In the beginning God created the heaven and the earth." In the original Hebrew text, the word translated "God" in this verse is *Elohim*. Elohim is the plural form of the Hebrew word for God, *Eloah* (Strong's) or *El* (Nelson's), depending on the source you consult. Elohim is plural in form, but usually translated in the singular. An example in English would be words like "family" or "United States." Both words are plural in meaning, but singular in usage. The plurality of this word is more easily understood in the context of verses like Genesis 1:26, 3:22, and 11:7, where God and the Word confer about the activities and fate of man.

Both the Old Testament and New Testament contain references to more than one personage in the Godhead (Psalm 110:1, for example, which is quoted in Acts 2:29-36). In the New Testament they are identified as God the Father and Jesus Christ the Son (1 Corinthians 8:6). The Son is also called God (Hebrews 1:8-9). Through the power of the Holy Spirit, God *fathered* Jesus Christ in the womb of a virgin named Mary (Matthew 1:18, 20; Luke 1:27, 31-35). By this conception in the flesh, the Word *physically* became the "only begotten" Son of the Father (John 1:14; 3:16) and "the Son of man" (Matthew 9:6). Paul tells us, ". . . although He existed in the form of God, did not regard equality with God a thing to be grasped, but *emptied Himself*, taking the form of a bond-servant, and being made in the likeness of men. And being found in appearance as a man, He humbled Himself by becoming obedient to the point of death, even death on a cross" (Philippians 2:6-8 NAS, emphasis mine throughout). Jesus never sinned (Hebrews 4:15; 1 Peter 2:22). He never transgressed God's law (1 John 3:4). It was by living this sinless life in the flesh that Jesus qualified to be the only perfect sacrifice and offering for the sins of the world (Ephesians 5:2; Hebrews 10:10). John 1:12 tells us, ". . . as many as received him, to them gave he power to become the sons of God, even to them that believe on his name."

In Exodus 3:14-15, God identifies Himself to Moses as "I AM" and "The LORD God of your fathers, the

God of Abraham, the God of Isaac, and the God of Jacob" (The word LORD here is derived from the Hebrew YHWH). In John 8:58, Jesus Christ revels Himself as the "I am" of the Old Testament. It was this same "I am" who delivered the Israelites out of Egypt, accompanied them in the wilderness, and who was later known in the New Testament as Jesus Christ (1 Corinthians 10:4, 9). This same "I am" codified His spiritual law to the children of Israel in the Ten Commandments (Exodus 20), and spoke to Moses "face to face" (Numbers 12:8). Adam and Eve walked and talked with God in the Garden of Eden; however, Christ said concerning His Father, "Ye have neither heard his voice at any time, nor seen his shape" (John 5:37). John tells us in the opening chapters of his gospel, "No man hath seen God at any time . . ." (John 1:18). This thought is reiterated in verse 6:46, 1 Timothy 6:16, and 1 John 4:12. Yet God testified of Moses in Numbers 12:8 that "He sees the form of the Lord." In Exodus 33:18-23, Moses, under protective measures, was even allowed to see the back parts of God in His glorified form. These Old Testament encounters with God are more precisely encounters with the Word, who became Jesus Christ.

The New Testament emphasizes the harmony between the Father and the Son, yet in numerous scriptures, makes the distinction between the two clear (e.g., John 20:17; Romans 15:6). Jesus Christ revealed His Father to His disciples (Matthew 11:25-27). He asked the Father to give them the same purpose and singleness of mind that He and the Father share (John 17:20-23). The relationship between the Father and the Son demonstrates God's perfect and eternal way of life. The Father has always loved the Son, and the Son has always loved the Father (John 17:4, 20-26). "Father" and "Son" constitute a *family* relationship.

"For this cause I bow my knees unto the Father of our Lord Jesus Christ, Of whom the whole family in heaven and earth is named" (Ephesians 3:14-15). God the Father is head of the family, He is greater than the Son (John 14:28), and He is greater than all (John 10:29). God is now adding to His family by begetting sons and daughters through the Holy Spirit. "For as many as are led by the Spirit of God, they are the sons of God" (Romans 8:14). "And because

ye are sons, God hath sent forth the Spirit of his Son into your hearts, crying, Abba, Father" (Galatians 4:6). "The Spirit itself beareth witness with our spirit, that we are the children of God" (Romans 8:16).

By His resurrection, Jesus Christ became, "the *firstborn* from the dead" (Colossians 1:18). He is also "the *firstborn* among many brethren" (Romans 8:29). When Christ returns, those spiritually begotten sons and daughters will be born of the Spirit into God's family. "That which is born of the flesh is flesh; and that which is born of the Spirit is spirit. Marvel not that I said unto thee, Ye must be born again. The wind bloweth where it listeth, and thou hearest the sound thereof, but canst not tell whence it cometh, and whither it goeth: *so is every one that is born of the Spirit*" (John 3:6-8). "Behold, what manner of love the Father hath bestowed upon us, that we should be called the sons of God: therefore the world knoweth us not, because it knew him not. Beloved, now are we the sons of God, and *it doth not yet appear what we shall be*: but we know that, when he shall appear, *we shall be like him*; for we shall see him as he is" (1 John 3:1-2). "For the earnest expectation of the creature waiteth for the *manifestation of the sons of God*" (Romans 8:19). "And as we have borne the image of the earthy, *we shall also bear the image of the heavenly*. Now this I say, brethren, that *flesh and blood cannot inherit the kingdom of God*; neither doth corruption inherit incorruption. Behold, I shew you a mystery; We shall not all sleep, but *we shall all be changed*, In a moment, in the twinkling of an eye, *at the last trump*: for the trumpet shall sound, and the dead shall be raised incorruptible, and we shall be changed. For this corruptible must put on incorruption, and *this mortal must put on immortality*" (1 Corinthians 15:49-53).

This is just a small taste of what Scripture reveals about the God family. God wants you to know Him, He wants you to trust Him. Do not allow men to talk you out of what the Bible actually says about God the Father, and our Lord Jesus Christ. Do not take my word for it either. If you are truly seeking God, then you must diligently search the Scriptures for yourself. No one can offer you salvation but Christ alone. "Jesus saith unto him, I am the way, the truth, and the life: no man cometh unto the Father, but by me" (John 14:6). Take that step today. Wipe the dust off that old Bible of yours and start reading it for yourself, you might be surprised at what it says. ■ 43

Who Is God?

By Garry W. Johnson,
MOUNTAIN REVIEW Staff

Black History Week Deemed A Success

Original Contribution,
By William Barney

Although off to a rocky start when the opening night speaker had to cancel, those who attended the black history week-long event proclaimed it a success. "I think this is the best one we've had," commented inmate Brandon Patrick. This was just one of the many positive feedbacks heard by this reporter.

The week was filled with a variety of educational, entertainment, and worship experiences—from the Jamaican flavor of the reggae songs performed by inmate George Stewart to the exuberant sounds of the gospel medley of Men of Praise from Knoxville. . .from the old-time spirituals sung by Sister Marilyn to the dynamic preaching of Pastor Wilma Walden. . .from thought-provoking def poetry recited by inmate Devon Fowler to the dramatic reading of Martin Luther King's I Have a Dream speech by Daryl Lowery.

Many people were responsible for the success of this week-long event. These include inmate speakers: William Barney, Antonio Williams, Anthony Stokes, Devon Fowler, George Stewart, Thomas Cummings, and Lewis Grimes; the guest speakers: Billy Morrison (filling in for an ailing Joe Colquitt), David Upton, Gerald Williams, Edward Thrasher, and Thurman Kinnebrew; inmates Orlando Spartling, John Johnson, and Donald Coleman who provided special songs; the back-up singers; band members; and those individuals who gave the invocation each night.

David Upton showed up wearing a t-shirt depicting a collage of well-known black faces on the front and back with the message, "Without black history, there is no history" running across the shoulders of the shirt. He echoed this message when he said that blacks need to study their history and culture on a daily basis and not just one week or one month out of the year.

In her message, Pastor Walden deplored the conditions of modern blacks, but said they had brought it on themselves. "You blame some white woman for taking prayer out of the schools, but," she inquired, "who took prayer out of the home?" These same ideas were also expressed by the other guest speakers during the week.

Behind the scenes thanks need to be given to Travis Hancock for designing the program covers, Garry Johnson for printing the inside of the programs, and the Varsity Club for providing the programs and the certificates for the black history quiz. Varsity Club Sponsor Robin Marmon garners special thanks for providing the prizes for the quiz. The event was put together by a three-man committee consisting of Howard Humphrey, William Barney, and chairman Bobby Tate.

The one area of disappointment was the lack of participation in the black history quiz. "I am deeply saddened," said inmate Robert Clay, "by the lack of participation in the black history quiz and the black history program with so many young black men who are noticeably very knowledgeable of their black history. In the future, I hope and pray that these young black men will make a better effort in their participation."

Only three people handed in quizzes; however, all three people scored 100% on the quiz. The results necessitated a runoff on Thursday night. Robert Clay was unable to attend that night and therefore took third place. Second place went to Devon Fowler, while the top honor went to Travis Sharp, who's knowledge of black history proved superior.

All in all, the week was a huge success. Even those who did not have a chance to attend heard of the success of the event and commented on it. We hope to make next year's event even better, with more participation from the compound. ■

Making Amends

Original Contribution,
By Melvin E. Lane Jr.

Some people may think that saying "I am sorry" is enough to make up for their past actions. I would like to challenge that way of thinking and share my thoughts on the subject.

It has been said that actions speak louder than words. I would like to use this forum to call everyone to action. We all have the ability and the resources to better ourselves. We can acquire the tools needed to make ourselves better men, family members, and citizens now and once released. We probably cannot change the pain and suffering that our past actions have caused our victims, our families or ourselves. Nevertheless, I believe we owe it to everyone to make sure we do everything we can to ensure we never offend again.

Following is a list of some programs provided here at Morgan County that can teach you the tools needed to make these changes: Alcohol and Drug Treatment program, Alternative to Violence Project, Pre-Release class, Anger Management, Domestic Violence, and Parenting Skills. I would also suggest that everyone get at least a GED and learn a vocational trade.

I know that many of you have completed these courses. I believe those of you who have completed these courses are on the path to making amends. Still, you can do more. Now is the time to pass on what you have learned to other people. This will help build and strengthen a better community. If you think about it, I am sure you will agree helping someone else learn the tools preventing them from re-offending is a great step toward making amends.

Now, for those of you that have completed these courses and are passing on the information to other inmates, you can take it a step further. Once you are released, you can continue to reach out to people on the streets. Can you imagine what it will mean to victims everywhere if you kept just one person from offending someone? As a man doing a life-sentence for first degree murder, I know I may never get out. Until I get out, I will continue on my path of making amends. ■

Now is the time to pass on what you have learned to other people

Victim Impact, Continued from page 06

Many triggers lead to a victim "re-living" the crime including a parole hearing. Imagine what a victim must go through at a parole hearing, seeing their offender face-to-face years after they were sentenced. The last time they saw their offender was at the sentencing phase of the criminal proceedings. At that time, they were being sentenced to prison, away from society and the people they victimized. The victim did not have to deal with the eventuality of the offender being released. Now the offender is up for parole. The victim attends the parole hearing and sees their offender for the first time in years. This shocking event usually causes the victims to resort back to the same feelings they encountered when the crime first happened. Seeing the offender again was a trigger. It should not be surprising when inmates at parole hearings experience an outburst of angry feelings from their victims.

Other triggers may include news stories of the crime, the anniversary of the crime, holidays, and even mention of the criminal justice system. Similar events in and around the victims may trigger them to remember the crime. It is a fair conclusion to say that the victims are serving a life-sentence. Even when the offender is released from prison, the victim must live with the effects of the crime for the rest of their lives.

Long Term Reactions

The long-term effects of a crime a victim may experience can be devastating. Health problems are common to victims of crime due to the stress discussed earlier in this article. The statistics are staggering. Of those victims suffering from the effects of stress, many will battle a serious illness within two years of the commission of the crime. Many other physical problems continue to affect the life of the victim long after the crime. This is one reason the victim never returns to a normal state of life. Eating problems are not uncommon. Increased weight and weight loss are also problems suffered by victims. Victims may also encounter sleeping problems as they battle insomnia, depression, and nightmares.

A major problem not adequately covered so far are the problems victims suffer in their relationships. Apparently, victims of crime are more prone to divorce, substance abuse, and familial separation. Many reasons can be offered to explain why this is so. Now it is sufficient to note that victims must deal with these realities; not because of anything they have done but because of something done to them.

The presentation by Ms. Demott was both informative and humbling. In the future, the Victim Impact program will be offered to inmates at MCCX. If you are interested in learning how your choices affected your victims and ways to deal with the damage to society, I highly recommend this program. ■

CROCK'S PUZZLE FUN

Across
1. Moved forward
8. Daddy Warbucks, e.g.
14. Sleeping bag stuffer
15. Ebon
17. Digs
18. Bachelor of Science (Abr.)
19. Arisen
21. ___ ___ sec, soon
23. Medicine dose
25. Who ___ you?
26. Teacher's assoc.
28. Plutonium's symbol
29. Music genre
31. Vicinity
32. Office helper
34. Sable or ermine
35. Jackie's second
36. Washington Post, e.g.
38. Electromotive energy, (Abr.)
39. Pity
41. Prefix for center or tome
42. ___, Ohio Fox sitcom
44. Amer. Patriot Allen
45. Not Miss or Mrs.
46. Opp. Of SW
48. Untidy
49. Negative
50. Do not pass ___, . . .
51. Begin
56. Air rifle ammo
58. Movie rating
59. Devil Fish
64. Isn't able to
66. Atmosphere
68. Westerns
69. ___ Tin Tin
70. Between thirteens and fifteens
73. Nopes
74. Opp. Of WSW
75. Goad
76. Large African antelope
77. Eastern Carolina University (Abr.)
78. Poundage (Abr.)
80. TV alien
81. Refusals
83. Dorothy's aunt
84. Noise
86. Hey
87. ___ / DC
88. ___ shucks!
90. Italian, perhaps
92. Heavenly hunter
94. Glutton for punishment?
95. Flat-out refuse

Down
2. Football pos.
3. Gig-wig
4. Leading man
5. Homer's neighbor Flanders
6. Chromium's symbol
7. Illnesses
8. Big hill
9. New Brunswick (Abr.)
10. Samuel's keeper
11. Pull sharply
12. Record company
13. Alaska (Abr.)
16. Scuff
18. Witch's potion
20. Bird's sound
22. ___ you jest!
24. Jeweler's weight
25. God of war
27. Prayer closer
28. Cougars
30. To kill by severing the spinal cord
31. Soon
32. School dance
34. Girls
37. Pages
40. That's a laugh!
43. Prefix with pay or possess
45. Crowd
47. Early bird?
51. Something ___ is going on!
52. Make impure
53. Author Rice
54. Nurse
55. Bean curd
57. ___ and in the kitchen
58. See 57 down
59. Church service
60. ___ once!
61. Hawaiian goose
62. Without a ___
63. Take for granted
65. Wrestler Tanaka
67. Stephen King novel
68. Responsibility
71. ___ duckling
72. Methuselah's father
79. Peru's capitol
82. Domestic help
84. Canine
85. South East Asian Country (Abr.)
88. Wrestler Anderson
89. Ric Flair's comment
90. Small St.
91. Nickel's symbol
92. Truth ___ Consequences, NM
93. Opp. Of SE ■

Dave's Cryptograms

Dave's Cryptograms are created from Biblical quotes. Each letter in the puzzle stands for another letter.

Clue for puzzle #1: R equals O

GDDAJFH CKL DFMTPD URP K FJHWN,

YTN BRL SRCDNW JF NWD CRPFJFH.

Clue for puzzle #2: X equals W

FJ AKD BJHJREJB; IKB RC AKD WKHGJB: TKP XLMDCKJEJP

M WMA CKXJDL, DLMD CLMSS LJ MSCK PJMU.

By: David Pendleton

45

Answers to crossword puzzle on page 23.

A	D	V	A	N	C	E	D		M	O	N	E	Y	M	A	N
	E	I	D	E	R		I		O		B	L	A	C	K	
S		P	A	D		B	S		U	P		I	N	A		S
C	C		M		A	R	E		N	E	A		K		P	U
R	A	P		A	R	E	A		T	E	M	P		F	U	R
A	R	I		N	E	W	S	P	A	P	E	R		E	M	E
P	A	T	H	O	S		E	P	I		N	O	R	M	A	L
E	T	H	A	N		M	S		N	E		M	E	S	S	Y
			N	O				G	O							
S	T	A	R	T		B	B		P	G		M	A	N	T	A
C	A	N	N	O	T		A	I	R		O	A	T	E	R	S
R	I	N		F	O	U	R	T	E	E	N	S		N	A	S
E	N	E		U	R	G	E		G	N	U	S		E	C	U
W	T		L		A	L	F		N	O	S		M		E	M
Y		D	I	N		Y	O		A	C		A	A	W		E
	R	O	M	A	N		O		N		O	R	I	O	N	
B	I	G	A	M	I	S	T		T	U	R	N	D	O	W	N

MOUNTAIN REVIEW

The *Mountain Review* was produced as a free government document written by prisoners at Brushy Mountain State Penitentiary and Morgan County Correctional Complex. Permission to reprint was granted in this section of each edition. The views expressed are those of individual authors and do not necessarily reflect the TDOC policy at that time, nor the views of the editors, staff, sponsors, or administration.

PRISONER Resource Guide
2021 Edition

Books to Prisoners
% Left Bank Bookstore
92 Pike Street, Box A
Seattle, WA 98101
206.527.3339; 206.442.2013
206.622.0195
bookstoprisoners.net

Employee-owned bookstore. Provides up to three free books at a time to prisoners. They do not offer religious or legal books, and specific titles are rarely available. Please send them three areas of interest to work from. They also sells books from small publishers.

The Great Courses
The Teaching Company
4151 Lafayette Center Drive
Suite 100
Chantilly, VA 20151-1232
800.TEACH.12
thegreatcourses.com

Sells a huge assortment of non-credit, college-level lecture courses at discount prices. Formats include DVD, CD and cassette, most of which come with a course guidebook in print.

Beyond Today
P.O. Box 541027
Cincinnati, OH 45254-1027
BTmagazine.org

A free magazine, published bi-monthly, as an educational service in the public interest. Each full-color issue offers Christian literature (booklets on numerous subjects), books, and Bible studies – all free. The publication features articles on current events, human interest, health, the environment, and world news, presented in clear and concise terms.

Ways to Wealth Publications
P.O. Box 751352
Memphis, TN 38175
731.671.5531

Publishes and sells volumes of self-help and educational documents, focusing on wealth-accumulating programs. Several free brochures for the cost of postage. Subjects include: "Fifty Money-Making Online Businesses," "How to Start a Credit File" and "Money-Making Secrets of the Rich." Send SASE for a free brochure.

World College
Cleveland Institute of Electronics
1776 East 17th Street
Cleveland, OH 44114-3679
800.243.6446; Fax: 216.776.6331
cie-wc.edu

Distance education programs in electronics: print, CD, DVD, and online. Financing and individual print lesson also available.

Youth Law Center
832 Folsom Street, #700
San Francisco, CA 94107
415.543.3379
info@ylc.org

Handles major institutional and class-action cases on behalf of juveniles only: conditions of confinement, special education and treatment of juveniles in adult correctional facilities.

Zenni Optical
zenni.com

Although Zenni does not have a mail-order business, they are listed here because their prices are extremely low. It is worth the effort to check-out their site or have it done for you.

Fall 2006 Edition Volume 19 Number 2

MOUNTAIN REVIEW

A Morgan County Correctional Complex Publication

Field Day Photos

Special Sports Coverage: Field day stats from the compound and annex with a report by Brian Hartman on this year's Softball season — plus the Tennessee Basketball Schedule 10-13

We Focus On:

SPECIAL PHOTO EDITION

Bruce Pearl Coming to MCCX

By Jeremy Ingram,
MOUNTAIN REVIEW Staff

University of Tennessee Head Basketball Coach Bruce Pearl has led his teams to 13 20-win seasons, won 19 games in the NCAA tournament, has a .785 career winning percentage, and has reached the 300-win mark faster than all but one active coach. Next year, Coach Pearl will be the guest speaker at the MCCX 2007 Spring Graduation.

Coach Pearl had been a head coach for 13 years before coming to Tennessee in 2005. Before coming to Tennessee, the Vols were picked to finish fifth out of six teams in the SEC's Eastern Division. After Coach Pearl's first season, the Vols won 22 games and were crowned the Eastern Division champions. In just one year, Coach Pearl turned Tennessee's basketball program around. Attendance rose to the fifth-highest in the nation.

Coach Pearl previously coached at Southern Indiana where he led the Screaming Eagles to nine NCAA Division II Tournaments. He won the championship in 1995 and was runner-up in 1994. After his stint at Southern Indiana, he moved to UW-Milwaukee, where he led the team to a sweet 16 berth at the 2005 NCAA tournament. After winning the national championship in 1995, Coach Pearl was named the National Association of Basketball Coaches (NABC) Division II Coach of the year.

After the 2005 season-opener, Coach Pearl instructed his players to go into the stands and thank the fans for their support.

Coach Pearl has succeeded through hard work, dedication, and a high expectation of his staff and players. From humbler beginnings to national coaching honors, Coach Pearl represents an example we all look forward to seeing. ∎

Volunteer Banquet

By Jeremy Ingram,
MOUNTAIN REVIEW Staff

On August 24, 2006, administration, guests and VIPs gathered in the outside visitation area to celebrate the annual volunteer appreciation banquet. This was a special night for everyone attending. TDOC Commissioner George Little not only attended the banquet but also delivered a positive message about the priority the administration places on the services of the volunteers. Kitchen Manager Carey Newberry and others prepared an exceptional dinner, the Fellowship Chapel Band entertained the guests, and the art shop decorated the area in a state park theme. With great weather, good food, and lively guests, this night lived up to expectations.

*See **Photo Layout** on page 3*

47

Prison Life

By Garry W. Johnson,
MOUNTAIN REVIEW Staff

What happens in prison affects society—whether you believe it or not. Ninety-five percent of the 13.5 million people who spend time in jail or prison over the course of a year are eventually released back onto the streets. They carry their experiences with them (whether good or bad) and attempt to build a new life or simply reestablish the old one. What they have learned while in prison determines the effect they will have on society.

BY THE NUMBERS

The U.S. Justice Department reported that nearly 2.2 million people—one in every 136 U.S. residents—were serving time in 2005. From June 2004 to June 2005, the number of people in the nation's

becoming overcrowded and the construction of new prisons simply cannot keep up.

RELIEF IN SIGHT?

In another 19-24 years there could be some relief in overcrowding. Since the passing of a law in Tennessee giving judges more discretion in sentencing, the sentences for Class A felonies have dropped by an average of fifteen months. The law took effect June 7, 2005, and was a direct result of the U.S. Supreme Court decision in *Blakely v. Washington*. The state of Washington had similar laws to those in Tennessee, and in the 2004 decision the court said a judge could not increase a defendant's sentence unless a jury found aggravating factors. Governor Phil Bredesen assembled a panel shortly after the decision to study the law's effects.

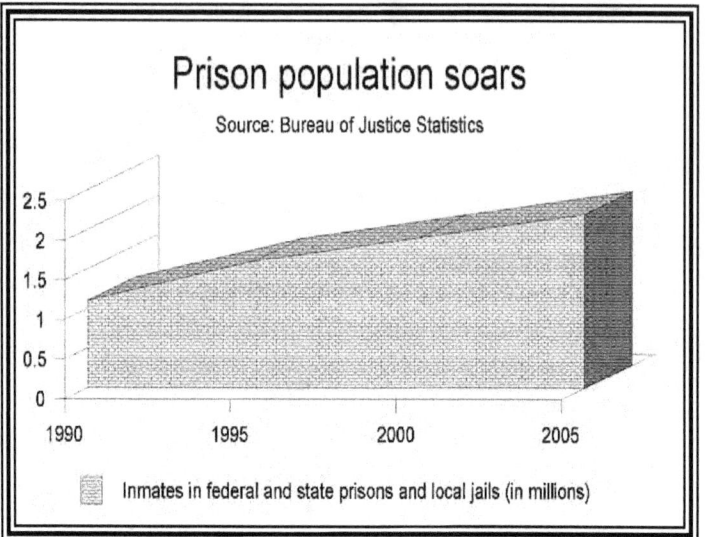

Prison population soars

Source: Bureau of Justice Statistics

Inmates in federal and state prisons and local jails (in millions)

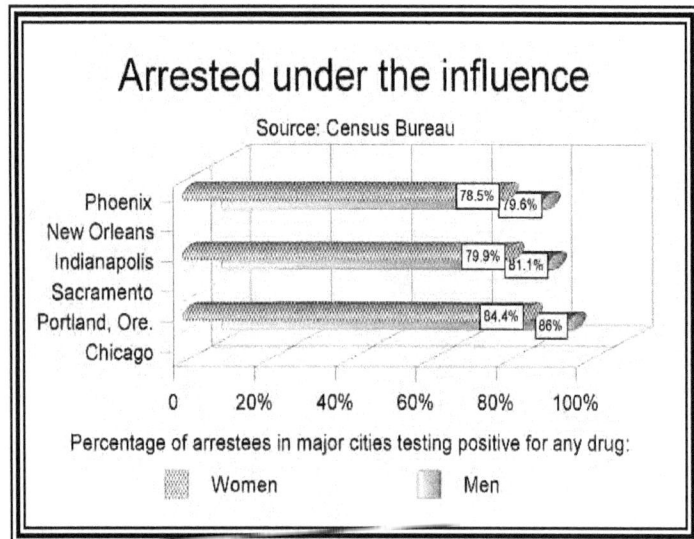

Arrested under the influence

Source: Census Bureau

Percentage of arrestees in major cities testing positive for any drug:
Women   Men

Phoenix 78.5% / 79.6%
Indianapolis 79.9% / 81.1%
Portland, Ore. 84.4% / 86%

prisons and jails grew 2.6 percent according to Bureau of Justice Statistics. Over twelve percent of the jail population are women, up from 10.2 percent a decade ago. Women also account for seven percent of all federal and state prisoners, up from 6.1 percent. Marc Mauer, executive director of The Sentencing Project (a Washington, D.C.-based group that promotes alternatives to prison) said, "Crime rates have been going down for a decade now, so it's somewhat disturbing that the prison population continues to rise." Tom McMahon of the *News Sentinel* reported that nearly seven million people in the United States were in prison, in jail, on probation or parole in 2004. That figures out to one out of every 31 adults. With the steady increase in population, more jails and prisons are

The task force released a study in June showing that the sentences had dropped from more than 256 months to about 241 months.

The study showed that the average sentence for second-degree murder dropped from about 274 months under the old law to 262 months. Child rape sentences also dropped from 240 months to an average of 229 months. Especially aggravated kidnaping was the only sentence to increase, going up from 263 months to more than 275 months.

REDUCING RECIDIVISM

According to a report released in June by the independent blue ribbon Commission on Safety and Abuse in America's Prisons, recidivism rates could be cut by half with increased education programs. The commission, established by the

nonprofit Vera Institute of Justice in New York, reports that while the prison population has doubled since 1990, funding for education and vocational training has not kept pace. The report further found that educational programs increase an inmate's compliance with the established rules of their institution.

HEALTH MATTERS

As the Tennessee Department of Correction takes steps this year to improve the health of its inmate population, the blue ribbon report said that 1.5 million inmates nationwide are released each year carrying life-threatening contagious diseases. The commission also found that some prisons with as many as 5,000 inmates have only two or three doctors. An editorial on the report in *USA Today* commented that, "Prisons must do more to test and treat infectious diseases, and they should partner with medical personnel in the

community to deliver care."

MENTAL HEALTH MATTERS TOO

Another article in *USA Today*, this one by Kevin Johnson, continues the reporting on the commission's findings. According to the commission, which took testimony from prison advocates and corrections officials in several states over a year-long period, 300,000 to 400,000 mentally ill offenders suffer from disease and neglect. Co-chair to the commission and former attorney general to President Lyndon Johnson, Nicholas Katzenbach said the number of mentally ill prisoners was "particularly shocking." The report goes on to say, "the need for mental health care is enormous."

Reginald Wilkinson, former director of the Ohio Department of Rehabilitation and Correction said in the report that prisons have become

See **Prison** *on page 22*

Citizenship of Prison Population

Source: Bureau of Federal Prisons

Federal inmate population by citizenship

United States 72.5%
Cuba .9%
Dominican Republic 1.8%
Colombia 1.8%
Other/Unknown 6.1%
Mexico 16.9%

Volunteer Banquet Photo Gallery

Pre-Release Graduation

By Jeremy Ingram,
MOUNTAIN REVIEW Staff

On June 16, twenty-two students, inmate helpers, and free-world staff assembled in the outside visitation gallery to celebrate the commencement of Pre-Release class seven. Pre-Release Instructor Rickey Bunch spoke to the assembled guests about the great potential class seven class has. He said that he believed everyone in this class has the ability to "make it." In fact, he remarked that this class was the best so far. They *knew* all the answers, but did they *believe* them? Mr. Bunch asked everyone to look around them. Beyond the chain-link fence and razor wire was the free world. He told the class they had a choice between here and there. After thanking Mrs. Palmer for her help, he recognized that the staff could only go so far. The students needed to make the final decision.

During this class, four students met the parole board. In each case, the board asked the student about his involvement in the class. In the end, the parole board recommended all four students for parole. Mr. Bunch fought hard for this to happen. He has been pushing for the state to recognize the rehabilitative efforts of inmates and consider their efforts when deliberating the possibility of release. Mr. Bunch concluded that now the blame falls back on the inmate, since the State of Tennessee is doing more every day to rehabilitate its inmates and give them the opportunity for success.

At this point in the graduation, Mr. Bunch had his aide read a story written by Max Lucado in his book, *Tell Me the Secrets*. The name of the story is "The Secret of Love" and is reprinted on this page. It tells the story of a jewel trader who would trade all the finest gems in the world for the one jewel he never had. The story is an analogy of love. The man in the story found true love, but because he did not recognize it, he passed it by. Only later did he realize that true love and beauty is found within.

Mr. Bunch used this story to illustrate the characteristics of criminal thinking regarding their relationships. Criminals are never satisfied because they seek only what is on the outside. As a result, they do not trust, are not satisfied with one woman, and therefore use drugs and women as an escape from reality. Mr. Bunch gave this bit of advice after reading Lucado's story, "If you put that same value into all you do, you will never see these fences again." The decision is essentially the difference between being satisfied and not being satisfied. According to Mr. Bunch, people should be content within themselves.

As class seven was called name by name to receive their certificates, Mr. Bunch remarked about each individual's participation and progress toward remaining free once released. He gave the students the opportunity to speak and several expressed their thankfulness to him and the class. Addressing the class, Mr. Bunch told everyone this was the first Pre-Release class to receive the Victim Impact certificate. He also said that he enjoyed the class and thanked each student for their dedication. He went on to say there was a significant crowd on the compound who is changing. "You do not have to be like everyone else when so many people are doing right."

After the commencement, pizza and cake were served. Pre-Release class seven is Bobby Greer, John Lambert, Gene Twitty, Lorenzo Porter, Jasper Talford, Robert Taylor, Marvin Branner, Darrol Davis, Joseph Mains, Sherman Mason, Robert Johnikin, Charles Clevenger, Wade Alan Greer, Michael Bromley, Jeff Womack, Tommy Flanagan, Dominic Brown, Larry Covington, Richard Van Pelt, Victor Pearson, Justin Jenkins, and Bradley Neal. Also attending the graduation was Curtis Hudson, George Killingsworth, Jeff Durham, Melvin Lane and Jeremy Ingram. ■

The Secret of Love

By Max Lucado

Seek beauty and miss love. But seek love and find both.

I am a seller of stones. I travel from city to city. I buy jewels from the diggers in one land and sell them to the buyers in another. I have weathered nights on stormy waters. I have walked days through desert heat. I have dined with kings. I have drunk with paupers. My hands have held the finest rubies and stroked the deepest furs. But I would trade it all for the one jewel I never knew. It was not for lack of opportunity that I never held it. There was a chance in Madrid when I was young. No, it was not for lack of opportunity. It was for lack of wisdom. The jewel was in my hand, but I exchanged it for an imitation. And now I fear my days will end without my ever knowing the beauty of the precious stone. I have never known true love. I have known embraces. I have seen beauty. But I have never known love. If only I'd learned to recognize love as I have learned to recognize stones. My father taught me about stones. He was a jewel cutter. He would seat me at a table before a dozen emeralds. "One is true," he would tell me. "The others are false. Find the true jewel." I would ponder—studying one after the other. Finally I would choose. I was always wrong. "The secret," he would say, "is not on the surface of the stone; it is inside the stone. A true jewel has a glow. Deep within the gem there is a flame. The surface can always be polished to shine, but with time the sparkle fades. However, the stone that shines from within will never fade." With the years, my eyes learned to spot true stones. I am never fooled. The stones I purchase are authentic. The gems I sell are true. I have learned to see the light within. If only I'd learned the same about love. But I've been foolish, dear reader, and I've been fooled. I've spent my life in places I shouldn't have been, looking only for someone with sparkling eyes, beautiful hair, a dazzling smile, and fancy clothes. I've searched for a woman with outer beauty, but no true value. And now I am left with emptiness. Once I almost found her. Many years ago in Madrid, I met the daughter of a farmer. Her ways were simple. Her love was pure. Her eyes were honest. But her looks were plain. She would have loved me. She would have held me through every season. Within her was a glow of devotion the like of which I've never seen since. But I continued looking for someone whose beauty would outshine the rest. How many times since have I longed for that farm girl's kind heart, her sweet smile, her faithfulness? If only I'd known that true beauty is found inside, not outside. If only I'd known, how many tears would I have saved? I'd trade in a moment a thousand rare gems for the true heart of one who would have loved me. Dear reader, heed my warning. Look closely at the stones before you open your purse. True love glows from within and grows stronger with the passage of time. Heed my caution. Look for the purest gem. Look deep within the heart to find the greatest beauty of all. And when you find that gem, hold onto her and never let her go. For in her you have been granted treasure worth far more than rubies.

"A wife of noble character who can find? She is worth far more than rubies."

Proverbs 31:10 (NIV)

Taken from "Tell Me the Secrets" by Max Lucado, copyright © 1993, 2004, pp. 43-47. Used by permission of Crossway Books, a publishing ministry of Good News Publishers, Wheaton, IL 60187. For more information, visit www.crossway.com <http://www.crossway.com/>

Ten Popular Myths of the Pre-Release Program at MCCX

By Rickey Bunch, CC3,
Pre-Release Coordinator

(1) MYTH: Pre-Release Class (PRC) will help you make parole. REALITY: PRC does have a higher statistical probability for making parole but priority for the class is given for those who are expiring their sentence. PRC is **not** designed to *help* you get out of prison. It is designed to help you *stay* out of prison.

(2) MYTH: PRC is a class only for inmates who are going up for parole. REALITY: PRC is a class for all inmates who are preparing to go home. *Priority* for the class will be given to (a) inmates who have been granted parole contingent upon completion of the PRC, (b) inmates who are expiring their sentence, (c) inmates who have been granted a release date and have time to complete the program prior to their release, and finally (d) inmates who are going up for parole within nine (9) months at the start of the class.

(3) MYTH: The state will take 60 days off your sentence when you complete the PRC. REALITY: This policy does not include PRC. It is for completion of academic and vocational classes or accredited college degrees only.

(4) MYTH: Pre-Release services are available only to those in the PRC. REALITY: There are several services available to every inmate leaving the institution. Included in those are

*See **Myths** on page 22*

MUSIC CORNER

Movable Chords on the Guitar

**Original Contribution,
By Charlie Brandler**

Greetings fellow guitarists. This is my fourth installment of "Music Corner." If you have read and practiced my last three installments, then you should be making considerable progress. Of course, this depends on how often and how long you practice. If you need a copy of any of the first three articles, then see me and I will get them to you. Knowing the information in my first article concerning the notes of the neck and the corresponding fret numbers with note names or letters is important. That information will be very helpful in moving these chords to any desired key. I will also be discussing the construction of these chords—possibly in the next installment of this column. First, let us look at a few different chords, shall we?

These first two chords are very simple. They are used in innumerable rock and blues songs. They are the chords on which I started. They are called "power chords." Power chords are written with a five next to the chord name (for example: E5). But more on that later. Figure one shows an E5 power chord. It consists of only two notes played together or simultaneously—the open E string (the top or sixth string) and the B note on the second fret of the A or fifth string. Figure one also shows a A5 chord that consists of the open A or fifth string and the E note on the second fret of the D or fourth string. That is simple enough, right? If you will notice, you have the root note of either E or A and then the five note (or the fifth note in the major scale) two frets up on the string below the root string. Now I will show you how to move these chords anywhere on the neck of the guitar.

The diagram in figure two shows a power chord that can be played anywhere on the neck of the guitar. The "R" points to the root note of the chord. The letter name of this note will also be the letter name of the power chord. The numbers next to the black dots show which fingers to use when fretting the notes. The chart in figure two shows the names of

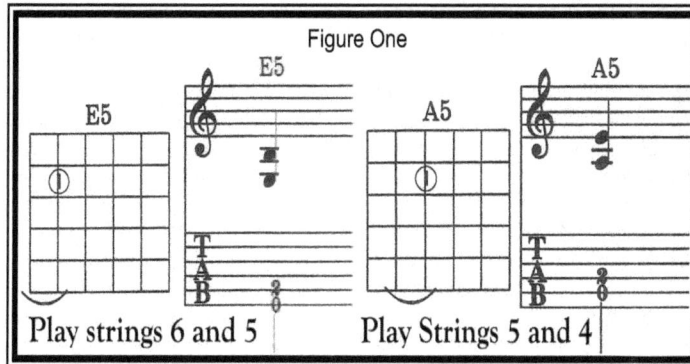

Figure One

E5 — Play strings 6 and 5

A5 — Play Strings 5 and 4

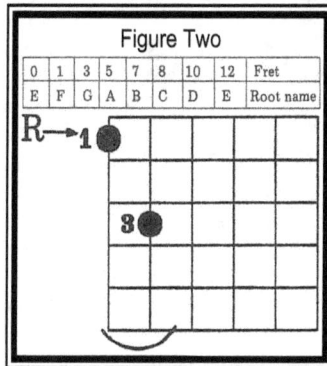

Figure Two

0	1	3	5	7	8	10	12	Fret
E	F	G	A	B	C	D	E	Root name

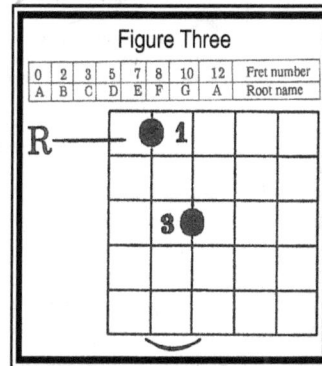

Figure Three

0	2	3	5	7	8	10	12	Fret number
A	B	C	D	E	F	G	A	Root name

the root notes on the sixth string of the guitar and the fret numbers in which they are played. So if you play this power chord with the root note on the seventh fret you will be playing a B5 or a B power chord.

Figure three shows the same thing. Only now we are on the fifth string of the guitar. The chart now shows the fret numbers for the root note names on the A string. So if you play with the root on the third fret you are playing a C power chord. You should be able to recognize how important it is to memorize which notes are at which

frets, starting on the top two strings and then going on to the bottom four strings. If you have not done so already, you really should.

Now let us check out some barre chords. When a chord has a finger that lies (bars) across all the strings, it is called a barre chord. The first category of barre chords I will show you has the root note/chord name on the sixth string. You can move these chords to any position on the neck of the guitar by using the chart shown in figure two. Figure four shows four chords that are very common in rock

and blues music (major, minor, seventh, and minor seventh). Again, the number next to the dots shows which finger to fret each chord with. As I mentioned earlier, I will talk about chord construction later. Right now I want to show you how you can play any of these four chords in any key on the neck of the guitar. By key I mean the root note of the chord that also gives the chord its name. For example, if I play the major barre chord with my first finger barring the fifth fret of the guitar, that would put me in the key of A. That would also make it an A major barre chord. Got it? So we will use this chord for our examples.

Now if you look at the minor chord, you will notice that all you have to do is lift up and remove your second finger and the chord now becomes an A minor. OK, now make the major chord again. Now lift up or remove your fourth finger and you have made an A7 chord. Working off the major chord, remove both your second and fourth fingers and you now have an Am7 chord.

It helps to know another group of barre chords to keep chord changes closer together and more convenient. This group of barre chords has its root on the fifth string and you can use the chart in figure three to know which fret to find the root or chord names. Figure five shows the same chords as figure four. Only the root note or chord is on the fifth string. Please note and keep in mind that on these four chords the top or sixth string is <u>not</u> to be played. In other words, only the bottom five strings will be played on these four chords. You will need to memorize these shapes as well as the shapes for the four chords in the first category on the sixth string. It will make it a lot easier to move them to any fret, and therefore any key. So in essence, I have just showed you how to play 96 chords—four different chords for frets zero through eleven on the sixth string, and the same on the fifth string. This is of course including all sharps (♯) and flats (♭) in which we will discuss in the next installment of music corner along with chord construction. Until then, practice, practice, practice! ∎

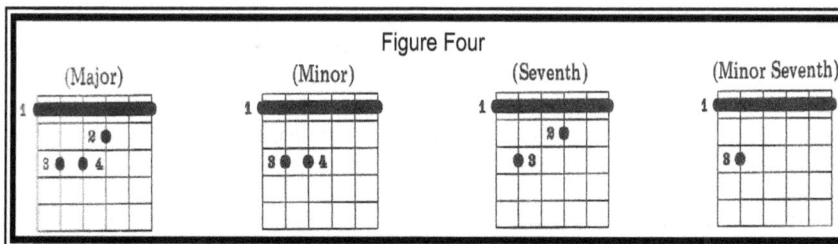

Figure Four

(Major) (Minor) (Seventh) (Minor Seventh)

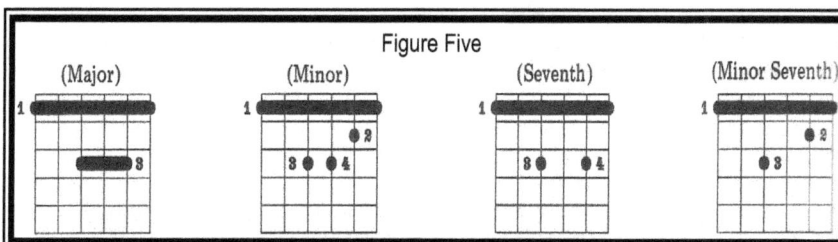

Figure Five

(Major) (Minor) (Seventh) (Minor Seventh)

Restoration of Voting Rights

By Garry W. Johnson,
MOUNTAIN REVIEW Staff

The 104th General Assembly passed a bill back in May that revises State law on when many convicted felons can restore their right to vote. The former law had varying standards on when felons could regain their voting rights, depending on the date of their conviction and the offense which they were convicted of. The new bill (HB1722/SB1678) made the standards more uniform and allowed for earlier petitioning of the courts.

Still banned from ever restoring their right to vote are those convicted of murder, rape, voter fraud, treason, and—if committed after July 2005—bribery and official misconduct by elected or appointed officials. Apart from these, those wishing to petition the court to reinstate their voting rights would have to be pardoned or serve their full sentence and make complete restitution.

Among the bill's opponents was Representative Gerald McCormick (R-Chattanooga) who sponsored legislation to ban anyone convicted of a felony on or after July 1, 2006, from ever voting. That bill died while this one proceeded forward. Representative McCormick was quoted by USA Today as saying, "I don't believe we need to have a voting bloc that comes out of prison angry at the sheriff's department . . . and angry at the prosecutor's office." He adds, "I don't think it's right to have them on the same level as people who've paid their taxes and played by the rules" ("R.I. to revisit felons' voting rights," Charisse Jones, June 1, 2006).

The original Senate bill (SB1678), sponsored by Senator Steve Cohen and Representative Larry Turner (both D-Memphis) was approved in May 2005, but failed to get House approval that year. After some changes, the House approved the bill 57-40, and returned it to the Senate. The Senate concurred with the House changes on Wednesday, May 17, 2006.

This new law is just one example of a nationwide push to restore felons to the voting roles. In March, Nebraska lawmakers passed legislation to automatically restore voting rights to felons two years after they complete their sentence. Last year Iowa Governor Tom Vilsack signed an executive order to automatically restore voting rights to felons two years after they complete their sentences (including probation or parole) or receive early release. In Kentucky, Rhode Island and other states, coalitions of former inmates, faith-based organizations and civil rights groups are registering voters and lobbying election officials and lawmakers.

"Once people start voting, they're quite a bit less likely to commit new crimes," says Christopher Uggen, a criminologist and sociology professor at the University of Minnesota. He goes on to say, "I think we can clearly say that there's no threat to the public safety by permitting prisoners and felons to vote" (Ibid.). ∎

Good Time Awarded to Graduates

By Garry W Johnson,
MOUNTAIN REVIEW Staff

House bill HB2554 passed the 104th General Assembly on March 30, 2006, and has been signed by the Governor. The new law makes prisoners who earn educational degrees while incarcerated eligible to be released two months early. The following degrees will be eligible for the 60-day credit: a high school diploma, graduate equivalency diploma (GED), vocational education diploma, or a two- or four-year college degree or certification in applied sciences.

The bill carried two amendments that read as follows: "Amendment #1 limits eligibility for the 60-day educational good time credit to a qualifying prisoner, and requires priority in enrollment in existing educational and vocational programs to prisoners who: (1) Are eligible for parole or release upon completion of their sentence and who can reasonably be expected to re-enter the workforce; and (2) Will be incarcerated by the department of correction for such period of time that they will receive full credit for sentence reduction pursuant to this bill.

Under this amendment prisoners would only be eligible for one 60-day educational good time credit regardless of the number of educational or vocational programs completed. Also, credit would only be given for completion of programs that have been approved by the department."

The second amendment specifies, "that any prisoner who is convicted of any of the following offenses would not be eligible for the 60-day educational good time credit: (1) Murder in the first degree; (2) Murder in the second degree; (3) Especially aggravated kidnapping; (4) Aggravated kidnapping; (5) Especially aggravated robbery; (6) Aggravated rape; (7) Rape; (8) Aggravated sexual battery; (9) Rape of a child; (10) Aggravated arson; (11) Aggravated child abuse; or (12) Any person convicted as a multiple rapist." ∎

God vs. State

Original Contribution,
By Randall McPheeters

In the past 25 years the world has gone through many changes. One such change has had a major effect on our schools and our youth. Of course, I'm speaking of the removal of God, moral teachings, and spirituality from our public schools. The next time you see one of our chaplains in the visitation gallery, call him over and have a prayer with him. While you do this look around at the reactions of the officers and other visitors. In most cases, you will find this is not a problem with them. If your child tried that at school, he or she would be threatened with suspension and/or expulsion. Currently, children in public schools are not allowed to bring Bibles to class or to hold prayer groups on school property. This is in the United States where religious freedom was one of our main founding points. We used to be the world leader in religious freedom, but now, we are surpassed by even the formerly atheistic Russia.

Even U.S. prisoners have more religious freedom than U.S. school children. We are able to carry a Bible or a Quran with us to work or school without problems. We can stop a chaplain on the upper or lower yard and have a word of prayer with him and nobody will sue us. We open each graduation celebration with a prayer and we close it with one as well. There are a couple of Quran study groups on this state property and no one is offended by them. It could be argued that inmates need the moral teachings of religion more than free-world people. However, it is my belief that if society would give their children this training while they are in grade school, they wouldn't have so many inmates in need of the training while in prison.

According to a Pat Robertson broadcast from the Nineties, the new Russian government has formed a committee whose sole purpose is to integrate the Ten Commandments into their law. In addition to this, Russia is adding Creationism to their school curriculum. The Christians in Russia now have more freedom to worship and learn about their religion than Christians in the United States. While this is a joyful time for Russian Christians, it is a very sad time for U.S. Christians.

In the United States Christmas season nativity scenes came under attack about five years ago. A group of people calling themselves Citizens United for the Separation of Church and State objected to Christian scenes of the birth of Christ being on government property. In addition to that argument, an atheist parent sued his local school system on behalf of his daughter because her grade school recited the Pledge of Allegiance including the phrase, ". . . one nation under God . . ." His daughter wasn't required to say the pledge or to use the phrase in question if she chose to recite the pledge, but—according to the father—she was embarrassed by her objections to the phrase. The Nativity Scenes were removed from government property, but the Pledge remains the same.

In recent years, we have all seen the battle over the Ten Commandments being displayed in courtrooms. It is ironic that a nation which governs under a system of Judeo-Christian laws would have that legal system used against them to force the removal of the foundation of those laws from open display in their courtrooms. Some local government officials and/or judges resisted the order of the courts to remove the Ten Commandments from their courtrooms. Some even lost their jobs and were fined, but in the end, the Ten Commandments were removed from the courts and our legal system suffers for their removal.

Some time in the Sixties, the constitutional right to freedom of religion became the right to be free from religion. The U.S. Constitution actually says, "Congress will make no law respecting any religion or abridging the free practice thereof." In the time of the writing of the Constitution, the term, ". . . law respecting any . . ." meant in today's language, . . . law **having to do with** any . . . So, I have to wonder how making a law which bans prayer from school is not a violation of that law. Our forefathers came to this country for the express purpose of being free to practice their religions as they saw fit. Somewhere along the line, our citizens began being offended by the free practice of various religions and our intolerance has become a ban of the free expression of any religion in certain places. HOW SAD FOR US. ∎

Supreme Court Limits Police Searches, Defines Admissible Statements

By Garry W. Johnson,
MOUNTAIN REVIEW Staff

On March 22, 2006, the Supreme Court ruled that police cannot search a home when one resident invites them in but another tells them "no". In a 5-3 decision the court put new limits on officers who want to search for evidence without first obtaining a warrant. The court ruled that searches over the objection of just one of the residents is unconstitutional.

In the ruling on *Georgia v. Randolph*, the court decided that an officer responding to a domestic dispute did not have the authority to enter and search the home of a Georgia lawyer in 2001, even after the man's wife invited him in. Janet Randolph called police to the home in the small town of Americus, Ga. Over her husband's objections, Mrs. Randolph invited the officer in and led him to evidence used to charge Scott Randolph with cocaine possession. That charge was put on hold while the courts considered whether the search was constitutional.

The case turned on the Constitution's ban on unreasonable searches. Because there was no evidence of wrongdoing, Janet Randolph's invitation to enter the residence did not overrule her husband's refusal to let police conduct a search. Justice John Paul Stevens wrote in a side opinion, "assuming that both spouses are competent, neither one is a master possessing the power to override the other's constitutional right to deny entry to their castle."

Justice John Roberts in his first written dissent said the ruling could hurt investigations of domestic abuse. Justice David H. Souter, who wrote the majority opinion said, "This case has no bearing on the capacity of police to protect domestic victims." Souter went on to say, "the question whether the police might lawfully enter over the objection in order to provide any protection that might be reasonable is easily answered yes."

In June the court made two, more unified, decisions concerning the admissibility of statements. In a unanimous ruling the court found that an alleged crime victim's emergency 911 call could be used at trial, even if he or she does not testify and undergo cross-examination.

In a separate case, and by an 8-1 vote, the court ruled that if an alleged victim recounts an incident to police at the scene after it occurs, the account cannot be used at trial unless the defendant is allowed to cross-examine the accuser.

The two cases originated from the Washington and Indiana state courts respectively, and address the Sixth Amendment right of confrontation. The right insures that a defendant is permitted to closely question witnesses against him or her. The court had barred the use of "testimonial" statements at trial in 2004, unless the witness was unavailable or had been previously cross-examined.

In the Washington case Michelle McCottry had told a 911 operator that her boyfriend, Adrian Martell Davis, was attacking her. She described the incident and named her attacker. At Davis' trail the prosecutor offered McCottry's statement as evidence. Since McCottry did not testify, Davis claimed the admission of the 911 recording violated his constitutional rights. The court disagreed.

In the Indiana case, police questioned Amy Hammon after responding to a domestic disturbance call at her home. The court found a trial judge erred when he allowed a report she signed to be admitted as evidence in her husband's domestic battery trail. Justice Antonin Scalia said the report, given when there was no immediate threat, was "testimonial." ■

Law Prohibits Smoking in Tennessee Prisons

By Garry W. Johnson,
MOUNTAIN REVIEW Staff

The 104th General Assembly has approved legislation to ban smoking in 528 state-owned or state-operated buildings, as well as tobacco use throughout the Tennessee Department of Correction. The TDOC requested and received an amendment to the bill allowing for an extension of one year to create a smoke-free environment throughout the prison system. The TDOC asked for the time in order to help assist staff and inmates with smoking cessation classes.

The law went into effect July 1, 2006, and gave the TDOC until July 1, 2007, to eradicate smoking within the prison system. The bill (SB3368/HB3269) was unanimously approved by the Senate on May 23. The House approved the bill on May 27, and Governor Phil Bredesen (who describes himself as an "avid nonsmoker") signed it into law the week of June 12. The bill was sponsored by Senator Roy Herron, (D-Dresden) and Representative Craig Fitzhugh, (D-Ripley). Commenting on the Department of Correction amendment, Mr. Herron said, "The Department of Correction has a special situation where their people are there involuntarily, and violence and unrest is always a concern."

Before the passing of the legislation, Tennessee Correction Commissioner George Little announced

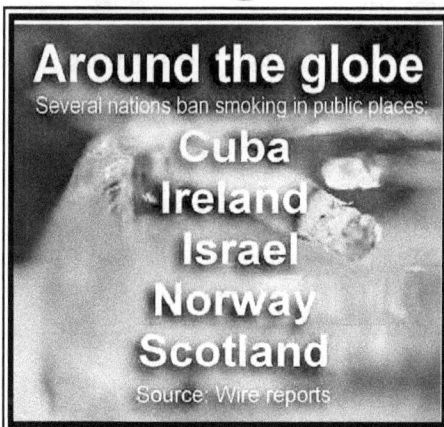

Around the globe
Several nations ban smoking in public places:
Cuba
Ireland
Israel
Norway
Scotland
Source: Wire reports

that he intended to ban smoking at Lois M. DeBerry Special Needs Facility (DSNF) and Turney Center Industrial Prison (TCIP) within the next year, regardless of the laws implementation. Little cited the governor's speech earlier this year urging Tennesseans to take "personal responsibility" for their health, and said that it is hoped the ban will curtail healthcare cost, especially at the special-needs prison where many already suffer from cancer and heart disease. Little was quoted by the Associated Press as saying, "It's about health care in the prison system." After a meeting before the Oversight Committee on Correction he said, "Why should we enable an inmate to get sick just so we can pay for the cost of his or her health care?" Commenting on these pilot programs, Little said that they had been in the talking stages for quite a while. He decided it was time to take action after witnessing the effects smoking had on one of the walls in a housing unit. "Where it hadn't been painted, it was yellow from the tar and nicotine," the Commissioner said, adding that employees will also not be allowed to smoke. According to the TDOC press release of June 12, 2006, Little told staff at

DSNF, "we will have incentives to help you stop smoking if that's what you choose to do. No one is telling you to stop smoking. For your health we wish you would. This law says you can't smoke at our facilities and we want to make the transition easier for everyone." He also said that, "not only will tobacco products come out of our facilities but so will lighters and that means the fire hazard will go down."

Tennessee is just the latest in a growing list of prison systems to implement full or partial bans on tobacco. The Federal Bureau of Prisons banned smoking in the majority of its facilities in 2004. A ban on all forms of tobacco went into effect the week of May 1, at the Kentucky State Reformatory. The KSR houses one thousand of Kentucky's most medically fragile prisoners. In North Carolina a ban on all indoor smoking started on January 1, even though most of the state's wardens had already prohibited it before the measure became law. Both staff and prisoners are still allowed to smoke in designated areas outside in that state's 76 prisons. ■

Strange Bedfellows

Turns out that anti-smoking laws in Australia have paired smoking advocates with Australian brothel owners. The Australian Adult Entertainment Industry is seeking an exemption to laws that ban smoking in the workplace. The Australian Associated Press quoted the industry group's William Albon as saying, "people smoke when they drink, and people smoke when they fornicate." The group claims that the smoking ban will drive prostitutes back onto the streets. Albon added that prostitutes could become targets for violence if they have to go outside to smoke. ■

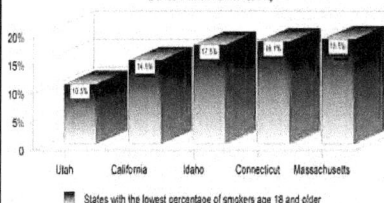

Where smoking is not cool
Source: American Cancer Society

10.5% Utah   14.5% California   17.5% Idaho   18.9% Connecticut   19.0% Massachusetts
■ States with the lowest percentage of smokers age 18 and older

Smoking Cessation Marks Beginning of Better Health

By Garry W. Johnson,
MOUNTAIN REVIEW Staff

We all know that smoking is not the best health care choice. Since everyone will soon be required to quit, I thought it would be good to take a final look at what we are leaving behind.

THE STATISTICS

The health risks involved with the use of tobacco have been well known for several decades. It has been more than forty years since smoking was identified as the most preventable cause of premature death and disability in the United States. One general estimate puts a twenty-five-year-old nonsmoker living an average of 25 percent longer than his smoking counterpart. The U.S. Surgeon General reported in 1990, that smoking cessation has immediate and major health benefits for people of all ages, and that former smokers live longer than those who continue to smoke. The ex-smoker reduces his risk of lung and other cancers, stroke, heart attacks, and chronic lung disease. In fact, those who stop smoking before the age of fifty have only half the risk of dying in the next 15 years of their life as those who continue to smoke. "Smoking cessation represents the single most important step that smokers can take to enhance the length and quality of their lives."—U.S. Surgeon General

While the media focuses a great deal on lung cancer, the risks of other cancers are indisputably higher for smokers. Smokers increase their risk of cancers of the mouth, throat, esophagus, stomach, pancreas, kidney, bladder, and in women, cancer of the cervix. The chances of acquiring acute leukemia are also higher in both sexes. Although the magnitude of the increased risk of these malignancies is not as dramatic as that seen in lung cancer, none need be overlooked. Patients with cancer of the esophagus or pancreas are highly unlikely to survive, and acute myeloid leukemia has only a 25-30 percent cure rate. For the fraction that are fortunate enough to beat their first cancer, a second cancer of the lungs, mouth, throat or esophagus is a major cause of death. However, with any of these cancers, once it spreads away from the main tumor there are no known cures.

THE CAUSE OF ADDICTION: NICOTINE

Nicotine is a drug found naturally in tobacco and is as addictive as heroin or cocaine. It makes the smoker feel good and their body becomes both physically and psychologically addicted to it. As with many other drugs, as the nervous system becomes accustomed to the nicotine, users need more to get the same level of satisfaction until they reach a maintenance level. When a person takes a draw off a cigarette, the nicotine enters their lungs with the smoke (and at least forty other known carcinogens), is absorbed in the blood stream, and travels through the entire body.

SECONDHAND SMOKE

"Have you ever breathed the smoke that curls up from the tip of someone else's cigarette? Or the smoke exhaled by a smoker? If so, then you have breathed most of the same harmful, cancer-causing parts of smoke inhaled by smokers. This is called secondhand smoke or environmental tobacco smoke (ETS). As a nonsmoker breathing the smoke from others, you are at risk for the same illnesses as smokers.

"If you are around others who smoke, you are at risk. Ventilation (airing out a room or opening a window) does not eliminate the health problems of secondhand smoke." This quote was taken from a 2003 pamphlet produced by the American Cancer Society. Richard Carmona, the U.S. Surgeon General, released a report in June that is the government's most detailed statement ever on secondhand smoke. Among other things, the report found that secondhand smoke increases the risk of heart disease and lung cancer by 25 percent in nonsmokers and can be especially dangerous for children living with smokers. "The health effects of secondhand smoke exposures are more pervasive than we previously thought," says Carmona, vice admiral of the U.S. Public Health Service. "The scientific evidence is now indisputable: secondhand smoke is not a mere annoyance. It is a serious health hazard that can lead to disease and premature death in children and nonsmoking adults." It is estimated by the American Lung Association that secondhand smoke caused roughly 3,000 lung cancer deaths and 35,000-62,000 heart disease deaths in adult nonsmokers in the US every year. The Vanderbilt Institute for Smoking Prevention and Cessation puts the cardiovascular death toll at 50,000.

Living with a smoker increases an adult nonsmoker's risk of lung cancer and heart disease by up to 30 percent; However, children are the most susceptible to the deadly effects of tobacco use. The Centers for Disease Control and Prevention estimates that 43 percent of children from age two months to eleven years live in a home with at least one person who smokes. In a recent study scientist found cancer-causing tobacco chemicals in the urine of nearly half the babies they tested of smoking parents. Out of 144 infants tested, 67 were fond to have a "substantial uptake" of nicotine and the chemical NNAL. That equates to 47 percent of the total test group. The levels were directly related to how much their parents smoked around them in the home or car. NNAL is a by-product of a tobacco toxin known to cause lung cancer. The children

See **Smoker** *on page 22*

With Quitting, Sooner is Always Better

"Quitting smoking is easy. I've done it a thousand times."—Mark Twain

By Garry W. Johnson,
MOUNTAIN REVIEW Staff

To quit smoking is a battle for many people, both inside and outside of prison. With the recent implementation of the statewide smoking ban, many of us are being faced with a struggle that we probably would not have chosen for ourselves. As we have thoroughly covered the new law, the physical effects of smoking and the benefits of cessation, this article will focus on stresses and strategies of quitting.

Because of the nicotine withdrawal the body goes through, many people will suffer some unpleasant physical and psychological symptoms. Depression, anger and irritability, frustration, dizziness, rest-lessness, headaches, sleep problems and trouble with concentration, fatigue, and increased appetite are among the effects some smokers may experience. These problems can last for several days or even weeks.

A PLAN FOR SUCCESS

No single strategy will work for everyone, but there are several key elements to becoming a successful nonsmoker. First you need to set a date to quit and stick to it. Once a person gives up smoking they may go through a period of six months to five years during which there is a high risk of a relapse, so the sooner you commit the better.

Once the date you have set to quit arrives you should get rid of all your cigarettes, matches and ashtrays—anything related to smoking. Next, be sure to stay busy doing things you enjoy, drink lots of water and avoid situations associated with smoking. The biggest challenge facing most trying to quit will be psychological rather than physical. Those who have smoked for many years will have developed several activities they associate with smoking, like eating, drinking coffee and watching television. Breaking these associations will not be easy, but those trying to quit can do the following: (1) Stay away from places and people who tempt you to smoke. (2) Use candies, mints or healthy low-calorie snacks for an oral substitute. It may also help to stretch out your meals; eat slowly and pause between bites. (3) Change those habits that tempt you to smoke (watch less T.V., drink less coffee, etc.). (4) Exercise or take up hobbies that keep your mind occupied and your hands busy. Exercise also helps relieve tension which reduces the urge to smoke. (5) Take deep breaths when the urge to smoke strikes and exhale slowly; remember, the desire to smoke will pass. (6) Use delay tactics such as postponing smoking for 15 minutes and then another 15 minutes until the urge to smoke goes away. (7) Use the money you save from not buying tobacco to reward yourself for not smoking.

STAYING THE COURSE

To remain tobacco-free is the most important part of the quitting process. You can use the same strategies you used in quitting to remain a nonsmoker. Even armed with this information you may experience strong and unexpected urges to smoke for months or even years after you quit. Remember, even one cigarette can cause a relapse. Stay strong. ∎

Nursing News: MRSA Being Under Reported in Prisons?

Original Contribution,
By Jennifer Anderson, RN

What is MRSA and how is it affecting inmates? MRSA stands for Methicillin Resistant Staphylococcus Aureus, also referred to as "staph" infection. It is a type of infection caused by bacteria that normally live on the skin or in a person's nose. Staph infections usually cause boils or other skin infections. Staph skin infections usually start as a pimple or a painful, swollen patch of skin. They then can develop into boils or draining sores. The only way to tell if the sore is indeed staph, is to have the fluid collected and a culture done. The process takes two to four days.

MRSA has been around for a long time, but recently we have started to see an increase of staph infections within the prison system. An MRSA infection is usually passed by direct physical contact with someone who has an open, infected sore. MRSA bacteria from the infected sore can spread to the person's hands or other parts of the skin. Sometimes a person can be infected with MRSA through direct physical contact with a contaminated personal item such as a towel, washcloth, clothing, sheets, soap, or razors. MRSA can even be passed by direct physical contact with a contaminated surface such as shared sports equipment. People who share the same bathroom are at a high risk of spreading MRSA if the appropriate cleaning solution is not used. A diluted bleach solution should be used to kill the MRSA bacteria. MRSA is not spread through food or water and is not contracted through animals or insects, even though MRSA can look like a spider bite to begin with. MRSA can, however, be spread by an inmate to a visitor through direct physical contact. Therefore all open sores suspected of being MRSA positive should be cleaned thoroughly and covered at all times. Strict hand washing should also be observed.

Because MRSA normally lives on the skin or in a person's nose, once a person heals it is possible to be infected with another boil. Draining pus from a boil can also spread boils to other parts of the body by direct touch. That is why washing your hands often when you have a boil is extremely important. Anytime the immune system does not work just right any infection is easier to get. Advanced stages of HIV, cancer, or liver disease make it easier to get a boil, but these diseases do not cause the boil.

Treatment for MRSA infections includes carefully cleaning and covering any open sores. An antibiotic ointment may also be used to treat open sores. Some MRSA infections must be "lanced" in order to remove the pus. If antibiotics are needed, there are a number that treat MRSA including Bactrim and doxycycline. In most serious MRSA infections, IV antibiotics, such as vancomycin must be used.

Several steps can be taken to avoid spreading MRSA to other people including covering all sores with clean bandages, washing hands often, taking frequent showers, practicing good personal hygiene, not sharing towels or other personal items, and routinely cleaning bathroom surfaces and any exercise equipment used by others.

Because MRSA has emerged recently as a more frequent cause of skin and soft tissue infections in correctional facilities, one may wonder what the department of correction is doing to take care of these prisoners and to keep the MRSA from spreading. Inmates infected with MRSA should receive care at their prison infirmary. At some local prisons, doctors and nurses have received training in managing MRSA infections. The Arkansas Department of Correction has even gone as far as to provide education material on how to keep from getting infected with MRSA. In some cases, infected inmates are "isolated" or restricted from certain activities until their infections have cleared up.

Statistics on the occurrence of MRSA in one Georgia Correctional facility amounted to eleven cases in a two hundred bed prison. In a Los Angeles prison 921 MRSA infections were accounted for in the year 2002. In 2003, 776 inmates were diagnosed with an MRSA infection. Out of 105 Texas facilities that house a total of 145,000 inmates, a total of 10,942 cases of MRSA were reported from 1996 to 2002.

These investigations identified four factors that contributed to the spread of MRSA among inmates. First, there were barriers to routine inmate hygiene. Second, there was a lack of proper access to medical care. Third, frequent medical staff turnover was a challenge to providing education on infectious control. Finally, MRSA might have been an unrecognized cause of skin infections among inmates. MRSA infections were often misdiagnosed as spider bites. A strategy to improve hygiene and infection-control practices in correctional facilities will likely be the most effective approach for long term success.

In conclusion, the most important way to protect yourself from MRSA is to practice cleanliness and wash your hands often. It may sound elementary but is proven effective. ∎

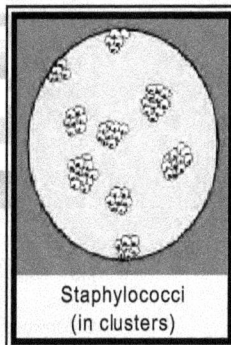

Staphylococci
(in clusters)

MRSA Prevention at MCCX?

By Jeremy Ingram,
MOUNTAIN REVIEW Staff

Studies have found that MRSA infections are unexpectantly high in prisons. This is surprising because MRSA is more often found in healthcare settings. These same studies concluded that correctional facilities can reduce the prevalence of MRSA by identifying those infected and instituting prevention methods. What is this prison doing to detect, treat, and prevent MRSA infections?

Doctors and nurses normally receive education and training at the schools where they earned their degrees. In addition to this education, nurses at MCCX have received specialized training in managing and treating MRSA infections. Nurse Practitioner Dale Hadden and Karen Massey (Continuous Quality Improvement) work with local health departments and other agencies to bring back what they have learned. Hadden has been to seminars and carries back the information she learned. In this way, the clinic staff at MCCX is able to keep up with the latest changes in medicine and treatment options.

The clinic provides educational material in the clinic lobby on how to keep from getting infected with MRSA. According to Nurse Deloris Hohman, the key to preventing infection is proper hand washing. Close contact among inmates increases the likelihood of the transmission of MRSA. Therefore, inmates should practice good personal hygiene including regular hand washing, daily showers, and regular laundry.

When an inmate is suspected of being infected with MRSA, several steps are taken to prevent further spread of MRSA. Since MRSA is often misdiagnosed as a spider bite, the clinic will take a culture from any infection thought possibly to be MRSA. They send off the culture to a lab and normally the results are back within five days. During this waiting period, inmates are placed on an AVO and confined to their cell. They are required to take daily showers and wash their own cloths in bleach once a day to prevent spread of the suspected infection.

If the test results come back negative, the inmate is released from AVO. However, if results are positive, antibiotics will be administered based on the lab results. Every day a nurse will check the inmate until the infection is dry and ceases to drain. Nurses have gone as far as making the inmate wash his hands in front of them. Bandages and dressings, if changed by the inmate, are required to be brought to the clinic and disposed of in the proper receptacle.

MRSA is becoming more common in prison settings. We should all take notice of this threat and respond with proper hygienic practices. For more information on MRSA and prevention methods you should visit the clinic. ∎

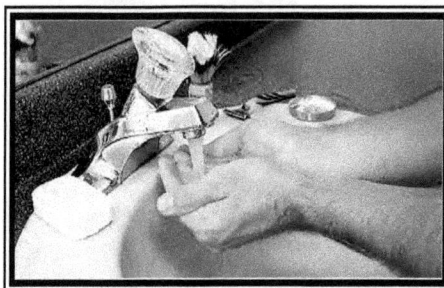

2006 INTRAMURAL SOFTBALL SEASON

**Original Contribution,
By Brian Hartman**

2006 was a great year for softball. No, let me rephrase, in my opinion, 2006 was the best softball season I have seen in the eight years I have been at this camp. I have played with several teams in my time here, but this year, with only four teams, it still has been a hotly contested championship race. Mainly due to the fact that there was no real dominant team.

The Outlaws, A-Game, and the Mean Machine all have fought tooth and nail for first place and the right to strut around atop the mountain, with the A-Game winning the championship in the end. The top three teams have traded wins and losses all year long. Every team has proven that when they come to play ball, any team can win the game. Even Down and Dirty has shown that if you count them out, they will sneak in and get a win.

The Recreation Director (Jimbo Godwin) even tried to throw us a curve ball this year by buying a .44 core softball instead of the usual .47 core ball (a softer, restricted flight ball). But we adapted and still hit several home runs, (with Tim Russell the home run champion). There are so many other great players, that I cannot list them all due to lack of room. Thanks for a great year of softball guys. ∎

A-GAME

Name	Hits	At-Bats	Average	Walks	Home Runs	R.B.I.'s
Russell	57	79	0.72152	23	29	68
Roden	52	104	0.51	02	22	54
Williams	34	86	0.35802	02	01	18
Tatrow	34	66	0.51515	00	01	05
Cravens	41	88	0.46429	06	06	26
Stinnett	31	60	0.5	05	16	32
Galen	54	97	0.56522	11	06	39
Davis	49	84	0.58228	21	13	34
Adams	28	53	0.54	10	00	10
Buckner	33	43	0.76923	05	08	24
Team Average			**0.55257**			

MEAN MACHINE

Name	Hits	At-Bats	Average	Walks	Home Runs	R.B.I.'s
Hartman	54	75	0.72	13	13	45
Bivens	20	43	0.46512	03	01	10
Bates	30	62	0.48387	06	02	14
Flenniken	31	90	0.34444	04	00	17
Gay	42	74	0.56757	04	21	55
McMillian	42	77	0.54545	12	01	19
Wilhoite	33	57	0.57895	06	08	31
Welch	38	72	0.52778	10	02	21
Harris	17	42	0.40476	05	00	08
Team Average			**0.51533**			

DOWN & DIRTY

Name	Hits	At-Bats	Average	Walks	Home Runs	R.B.I.'s
Johnson	14	31	0.45161	01	00	07
Pollard	14	38	0.36842	03	00	03
Key	05	16	0.3125	01	00	01
Janeway	23	57	0.40351	01	04	15
Fox	17	45	0.37778	01	02	09
Robert	12	24	0.5	00	00	02
Hyder	15	46	0.32609	02	00	04
Heady	04	13	0.30769	00	00	03
Clayton	04	20	0.2	00	00	01
Eblen	13	54	0.24074	05	00	09
Monholland	10	34	0.29412	03	00	05
Team Average			**0.34386**			

OUTLAWS

Name	Hits	At-Bats	Average	Walks	Home Runs	R.B.I.'s
Mike Ward	50	85	0.6125	05	00	28
Tucker	55	95	0.59551	08	06	29
Greenwood	47	88	0.56098	06	14	43
West	35	85	0.425	09	04	22
Presley	62	101	0.61702	00	18	55
Hardrick	55	94	0.5977	09	24	60
Bishop	43	86	0.51852	04	01	25
McGlone	22	58	0.38462	06	01	13
Love	38	72	0.56061	04	15	34
Meadows	21	43	0.47368	01	02	07
Cox	65	89	0.75	08	25	54
Team Average			**0.55419**			

AVERAGE LEADERS

Ricky Cox	0.73
T. Russell	0.721
Hartman	0.72
D. Presley	0.613
Ward	0.588
Hardrick	0.585
Davis	0.583
Wilhoite	0.578
Tucker	0.578
M. Gay	0.567

HOME RUN LEADERS

T. Russell	29
Ricky Cox	25
Hardrick	24
T. Roden	22
M. Gay	21
Presley	18
Stinnett	16
Love	15
Greenwood	14
Davis	13
Hartman	13

R.B.I. LEADERS

T. Russell	68
Hardrick	60
Presley	55
Roden	54
Rick Cox	54
Hartman	45
Greenwood	43
Galen	39
Love	34
Davis	34

2006-07 Tennessee Basketball Schedule

Date	Opponent	Site	Time
Dec. 1	Murray Sate	Knoxville	7:00 p.m.
Dec. 6	Memphis	Knoxville	9:00 p.m.
Dec. 16	Western Kentucky	Knoxville	4:00 p.m.
Dec. 18	Oklahoma Sate	Nasville, TN	7:00 p.m.
Dec. 23	Texas	Knoxville	Noon
Dec. 28	Tennessee Tech	Knoxville	7:00 p.m.
Dec. 30	East Tennessee State	Knoxville	8:00 p.m.
Jan. 7	Mississippi Sate	Knoxville	1:30 or 4:00 p.m.
Jan. 10	Vanderbilt	Nashville, TN	8:00 p.m.
Jan. 13	Ohio Sate	Columbus, Ohio	1:00 p.m.
Jan. 17	Auburn	Auburn, AL	8:00 p.m.
Jan. 20	South Carolina	Knoxville	6:00 p.m.
Jan. 24	Ole Miss	Oxford, MS	8:00 p.m.
Jan. 28	Kentucky	Lexington, KY	1:00 p.m.
Feb. 31	Georgia	Knoxville	7:30 p.m.
Feb. 3	Florida	Gainsville, FL	3:00 p.m.
Feb. 6	LSU	Knoxville	9:00 p.m.
Feb. 10	Vanderbilt	Knoxville	3:00 p.m.
Feb. 13	Kentucky	Knoxville	7:00 p.m.
Feb. 17	South Carolina	Columbus, SC	3:30 p.m.
Feb. 21	Alabama	Knoxville	8:00 p.m.
Feb. 24	Arkansas	Fayettesville, AR	1:00 p.m.
Feb. 27	Florida	Knoxville	9:00 p.m.
Mar. 3	Georgia	Athens, GA	4:00 p.m.
Mar. 8-11	SEC Tournament	Atlanta, GA	TBD

Event	Place	Name
Horseshoes	1st	York & Carroll
	2nd	Blalock & Rittenberry
Free Throw	1st	Cooper
	2nd	Eremity
Three Point	1st	Cooper
	2nd	Rucker
Football Toss	1st	Francis
	2nd	Noble
Three-Leg Race	1st	Henderson & Harris
	2nd	Rucker & Cooper
Fat Man Race	1st	Carson
	2nd	Thomas
100 Yard Dash	1st	Cooper
	2nd	Officer
220 Yard Run	1st	Ball
	2nd	Cooper
440 Yard Run	1st	Bingham
	2nd	Rucker
Shuffleboard	1st	Robinson & Davis
	2nd	Cooper & Carson
Tug of War	1st	Unit 18

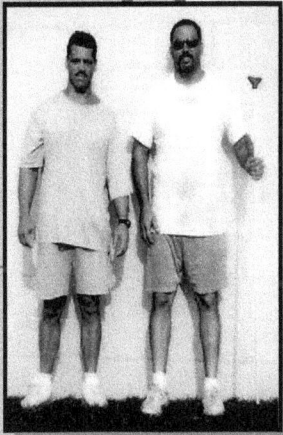

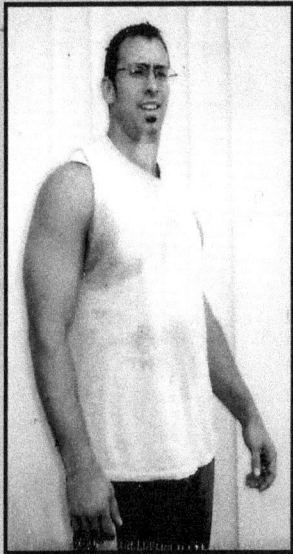

Name	Weight	Bench	Squat	Dead	Total
Shellhouse	120-135	160	230	0	390
Barker	136-151	280	320	320	920
Workman	136-151	180	230	280	690
Tindell	152-166	250	230	0	480
King	152-166	0	330	0	330
Farmer	167-183	340	630	470	1,440
Bahh	167-183	300	0	400	700
Rucker	184-199	350	410	410	1,170
Williams	184-199	140	230	320	690
Oliver	200-214	370	320	320	1,010
Harrs	200-214	230	0	0	230
Cooper	215-231	0	230	0	230
Moore	215-231	0	140	0	140
Hughs	232-over	480	822	660	1,962
Hoffman	232-over	290	370	320	980

Event	Place	Name
Horseshoes	1st	Vann & Gaylor
	2nd	Jeff & Mathis
	2nd	Wade & Greer
Free Throw	1st	Waddell
	2nd	Stewart
Three Point	1st	Hutchins
	2nd	Anglio
Football Toss	1st	Jones
	2nd	Hutchins
Three-Leg Race	1st	Davis & Welch
	2nd	Clayton & Covington
Fat Man Race	1st	Stodghill
	2nd	Presley
100 Yard Dash	1st	Knight
	2nd	Simpkins
220 Yard Run	1st	Buckner
	2nd	Cal
440 Yard Run	1st	Abrams
	2nd	Davis
Shuffleboard	1st	Broom & Neman
	2nd	Rogers & Bruce
Old Man Race	1st	Beamer
	2nd	Price
Tug of War	1st	Roe, Cogburn, Johnson, Moses, Thomas, Kilgore, Brown, Hartman, Margrum, Cummings

Name	Weight	Bench	Squat	Dead	Total
Hyder	120-135	145	315	295	755
Hunt	136-151	305	315	375	995
Bunch	136-151	305	315	345	965
Darnell	152-166	305	405	425	1,135
Coller	152-166	305	405	365	1,075
Henderson	167-183	345	495	295	1,335
Burchfield	167-183	375	435	405	1,215
Gardner	184-199	425	525	525	1,475
Gay	184-199	275	405	475	1,155
Hunley	200-214	435	725	705	1,865
Key	200-214	275	365	405	1,045
Eblen	215-231	335	495	455	1,285
Roden	215-231	355	405	455	1,215
Patrick	232-over	505	505	585	1,595
Gann	232-over	465	585	495	1,545

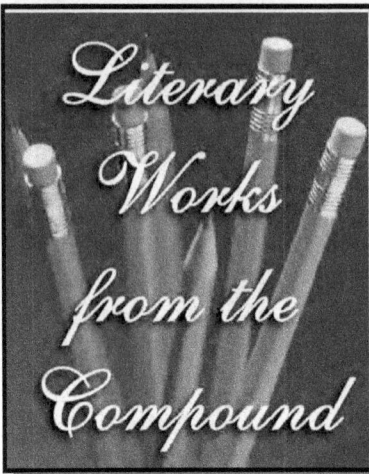

Literary Works from the Compound

Just when I thought life was over
By Danny Jay Johnson

There was a time down in my heart when I thought life was over.

I prayed and prayed that God would end this time down here.

I cried all night and wept all day, just to get the pain to go away.

It seemed like there was no hope in sight; Until I heard a man say on one dark and lonely night,

"It's not over my son, It's not over- for your time has just begun.

I am here with you in your time of need, for life is not over- I will save you indeed.

For roads are rocky, the mountains are high and the rivers are wide.

The ways of this life are rough. Now you put your hand in my hand

and this life is not so tough. Be of good cheer and listen to the Spirit here,

lean on Me and that pain will go away.

Trust in Me and I will make your dark nights into a bright day."

Now just listen to what the Spirit had to say, "He will turn your night into day."

Now who is this man, this man with a brighter day?

Who is this man that can make your pain go away?

Why this man is Jesus, our Lord and Savior.

Put your heart in His hand and He will pick you out of the miry clay.

He will put your feet on solid ground and brake the chains that have you bound.

And when you think life is over, just call on Jesus and He will come down.

Amen.

60

Try Love
By Jeff Durham

Try love, it will make you happy.
Try love, it will make you smile.
Try love, it will improve your health.
Try love, it will give you peace.
Let us all remember daily that even though we all are convicted criminals we are loved by God, no matter what we have done in our lives. "For God so **loved** the world, that he gave his only begotten Son, that whosoever believeth in him should not perish, but have everlasting life" (John 3:16, emphasis mine). If God who created all things loves us that much, why can't we love each other?

Things I see in You
By Henry Laurence Nix

In your voice I hear happiness,
when you speak there is joy;
to me that's a blessing,
that God put deep inside your heart . . .

In your eyes I see wisdom,
your eyes have that special glow;
you have seen the words of God,
because, your eyes tell me so . . .

In your arms I feel strength,
strong, yet gentle is your touch;
yours is a feeling I love around me,
your hugs do mean so much . . .

In you I see gifts of life,
qualities, that we all will need;
in your heart I see compassion,
in you, I see God is well pleased.

When I Cried Out to the Lord
By Terry Myers

When I cried out to the Lord
The response was so great
He gave me love and salvation
Then took away all my hate

When I cried out to the Lord
I realized not even death can do us part
I will always be in His hands
And His love will never leave my heart

When I cried out to the Lord
I sat there in agony and pain
But when He answered my prayers
I could see His love very plain

When I cried out to the Lord
His love was a surprise
He forgave me of my sins
Then opened my eyes

When I cried out to the Lord
He changed my wants and needs
I started to see miracles
And many good deeds

When I cried out to the Lord
I knew I would go to heaven and not to hell
I thank Him for His love
And dying for my sins as well

When I cried out to the Lord
My life started to change indeed
I am here to tell you, brother
It is the Lord that you need!

Number 13
By Richard Peters

A tall, rundown manor stood at the end of Dropsy Lane. I stood, knees knocking, staring up at the dilapidated structure. Out of curiosity, I had come because of a dare a friend had taken forty years ago while drunk at a bachelor party. It felt like deja vu as my mind began recalling Marty's story . . .

Marty approached the front door, pulled out a pencil flashlight, and found the house number stenciled on the doorframe — thirteen. A shiver ran down his spine, *Nothing good ever came from the number thirteen*, he thought.

When he reached for the doorknob, the door had suddenly swung open, creaked loudly until it stopped, revealing utter darkness. Cautiously, Marty stepped over the threshold flashing his pencil flashlight about. No sooner had he entered when the door closed behind him with an ominous 'click.'

Marty turned and tried the door to no avail, his face drenched in sweaty fear. He turned back around and headed for a sitting room where he was told he must go. As he entered the room, he found that he couldn't see anything; the darkness being so thick, even his flashlight couldn't penetrate it. He moved slowly forward into the room, feeling the tendrils of the darkness move across his face, then crawl up his arms, until his whole body prickled with horrific fear.

His left foot stubbed against a hard object and at that precise moment the fireplace roared to life with high bright flames but without any noticeable heat. As the room brightened, he turned to find a family of corpses who stared up at him with empty eye sockets.

Marty opened his mouth but no sound escaped. As he observed the corpse family, he realized they were also in a state of horror. Marty turned to see what could possibly have frightened these people and his heart stopped when he saw a pair of large, yellow eyes.

Marty froze, unable to move and soon he was high, near the ceiling. He turned to look back down on himself when a voice startled him out of the darkness, "Not you also, Martin?"

He swung around and saw the ghosts of the family floating next to him. Marty let out a scream, turned tail and flew back into his body, reignited his heart and ran pell-mell from the room. Somehow the front door opened and out Marty ran, never once did he look back.

It's been two days since I saw Marty lying on his death bed. It was then that I was able to coax this story out of him. I even leaned toward Marty and asked about the big yellow eyes — "Was it a basilisk?"

He said, "No." That made me curious, but before I could ask again, he died. So, I decided to take it upon myself to go see what it was, only I was going during the day.

So, here I presently stand, staring up at the old manor, its windows dark and eerie. Approaching the front door with shaking hands, it opens for me. I had thought this a joke; however, now that I see it, I shiver and hesitantly go into the manor.

I flip on the electric lantern in hopes of seeing more than Marty did — I don't. The darkness is so thick and overwhelming, it feels like I will choke to death.

Inside the sitting room, I find the family of corpses sitting, the fireplace blazing brightly. I move to stand behind them; however, before I turn to see what horror lay in front of them, I put on a pair of sunglasses.

I turn to see big, bulbous, yellow eyes — not round eyes, but shaped in a number 13. At first I am horror-stricken, but now I think, "HA! It's just two globes glowing, each with the number 13, what's so scary about that?"

Then a voice calls out to me, "Junior! You're late, we've been waiting for you."

"Why?" I ask.

"You're the thirteenth person to visit — now, the curse is broken."

While watching the five corpses, they stand up, dust themselves off and turn to face me. With a salute, they disappear. Now I am horrified, again. What can this mean?

I sit down on the couch — the realization hits me, I am now stiff as a corpse. Glancing around in horror, I also realize, I must now wait until thirteen people enter this manor before I, too, am to be released forever.

"Please, save me!"

Who Made These Things
By Michael Coatney

One day a little boy was riding down a country road with his parents when all of a sudden he asked his mom, "Who made the trees?" His mom responded, "God did." And he said, "Who made the mountains?" She said, "God did." "Mom, who made the cows and horses?" "God did." And the last question he asked, "Mom, who made God?" His mom was quiet for a moment, and then answered, "Son . . . God has always been and always will be." Love mom to her son.

Perseverance of the Saints

By Jeremy Ingram,
MOUNTAIN REVIEW Staff

After a Christian has been saved, can he totally and finally fall away from the faith and become apostate? Several different answers have been posited regarding this question. This article will expound the doctrine of the saint's perseverance. The perseverance of the saints is the doctrine that those who have truly been saved cannot totally and finally fall away from the faith.

First, the Bible says that those who persevere to the end are those who hold fast to their salvation. Three verses in the gospels state that ". . . he who stands firm to the end will be saved" (Matt. 24:13, 10:22, Mark 13:13). It is by this standing firm that the Christian enters eternal life. "By standing firm you will gain life" (Luke 21:19). The writer of Hebrews encourages his readers by telling them that they ". . . are not of those who shrink back and are destroyed, but of those who believe and are saved" (10:39).

Many ideas of salvation compete for acceptance in the church. Some teach that all there is to salvation is simply walking an aisle, praying a prayer, or making a decision. Some modern evangelists seem more concerned with having a person come forward and decide for Christ than with the regenerating work of the Holy Spirit on a person's soul. C. H. Spurgeon, responding to those who would seek a room to pray or make a decision says, ". . . we are not willing to pander to popular superstition. We fear that in those rooms men are warmed into a fictitious confidence. Very few of the supposed converts of enquiry-rooms turn out well. Go to your God at once, even where you now are. Cast yourself on Christ, at once, ere you stir an inch!"

The problem with those who teach that making a decision for Christ is all there is to salvation is that the biblical proof of salvation is not simply a decision but continuance in Jesus Christ ". . . Jesus said, 'If you hold to my teaching, you are really my disciples'" (John 8:31). The apostle Paul says that true saving faith is characterized by "persistence in doing good" (Rom. 2:7). In the end, only those who evidence true salvation by overcoming will be given the "right to eat from the tree of life, which is in the paradise of God" (Rev. 2:7). Nowhere does the Bible say that those who only make a decision have the right to insist on their eternal security.

How then does one share in the promises of Christ? It is by steadily maintaining his confession of faith: "We want each of you to show this same diligence to the very end, in order to make your hope sure" (Heb. 6:11). "And we are his house, if we hold on to our courage and the hope of which we boast" (Heb. 3:6). "We have come to share in Christ if we hold firmly till the end the confidence we had at first" (Heb. 3:14).

So then, the perseverance of the saints is a characteristic of those whom God has truly saved. Yet Scripture does not leave anyone in doubt what this perseverance in true faith looks like. Several things characterize perseverance:

1. **Holiness** "For those God foreknew he also predestined to be conformed to the likeness of his Son" (Rom. 8:29). ". . . from the beginning God chose you to be saved through the sanctifying work of the Spirit and through belief in the truth" (2 Thess. 2:13). ". . . who have been chosen according to the foreknowledge of God the Father, through the sanctifying work of the Spirit, for obedience to Jesus Christ and sprinkling by his blood" (1 Pet. 1:2).

2. **Knowledge of God, Christian conduct, and fruitfulness** "And we pray this in order that you may live a life worthy of the Lord and may please him in every way: bearing fruit in every good work, growing in the knowledge of God" (Col. 1:10).

3. **Faith** "if you continue in your faith, established and firm, not moved from the hope held out in the gospel. This is the gospel that you heard . . ." (Col. 1:23).

4. **Loyalty to Christ and obedience** "This calls for patient endurance on the part of the saints who obey God's commandments and remain faithful to Jesus" (Rev. 14:12).

5. **Running the race and good works** "Therefore, since we are surrounded by such a great cloud of witnesses, let us throw off everything that hinders and the sin that so easily entangles, and let us run with perseverance the race marked out for us. Let us fix our eyes on Jesus, the author and perfecter of our faith, who for the joy set before him endured the cross, scorning its shame, and sat down at the right hand of the throne of God" (Heb. 12:1,2). "Let us not become weary in doing good, for at the proper time we will reap a harvest if we do not give up" (Gal. 6:9), "For we are God's workmanship, created in Christ Jesus to do good works, which God prepared in advance for us to do" (Eph. 2:10). "We continually remember before our God and Father your work produced by faith, your labor prompted by love, and your endurance inspired by hope in our Lord Jesus Christ" (1 Thess. 1:3).

Second, given the scriptures quoted above, someone might argue that a person remains a Christian as long as he does these things. However, Scripture does not present these fruits of faith as something optional to salvation. Instead, Scripture declares that a true Christian *will* do them. Jesus Christ has begun the good work in the Christian's life and he will bring it to completion (Phil 1:6). He will be the one who "will keep you strong to the end, so that you will be blameless on the day of our Lord Jesus Christ" (1 Cor. 1:8). With this strong motivation the true Christian will make every effort to enter eternal life so that he will "receive a rich welcome into the eternal kingdom of our Lord and Savior Jesus Christ" (2 Pet. 1:11).

Contrary to much popular preaching, the Christian faith is not a bed of roses. The true believer will persevere only through trials, spiritual warfare, and afflictions. In fact, the Bible says that these things are the tools God uses to prove those who are his.

"Because you know that the testing of your faith develops perseverance" (Jam. 1:3), "Not only so, but we also rejoice in our sufferings, because we know that suffering produces perseverance; perseverance, character; and character, hope." (Rom. 5:3). "Therefore, among God's churches we boast about your perseverance and faith in all the persecutions and trials you are enduring" (2 Thess. 1:4). "You need to persevere so that when you have done the will of God, you will receive what he has promised" (Heb. 10:36). "If anyone is to go into captivity, into captivity he will go. If anyone is to be killed with the sword, with the sword he will be killed. This calls for patient endurance and faithfulness on the part of the saints" (Rev. 13:10).

In John Bunyan's classic book, *Pilgrim's Progress*, the main character, Christian, is shown the sight of a vast company of men desiring to go into a beautiful palace. They were prohibited from entering because many armed men stood at the door of the palace to prevent them. Then a man approached the door, drew his sword, put his helmet on, and rushed toward the group of armed men. The man laid into them with deadly force until at last, having received many wounds, he pressed forward into the palace. This is an analogy of the Christian life. There will be a fight but to those who accept the fight, there will be perseverance. "Therefore put on the full armor of God, so that when the day of evil comes, you may be able to stand your ground, and after you have done everything, to stand" (Eph. 6:13).

Another reason the Christian can be sure that he will endure to the end is that it is the Father's will that the Son will not lose any of them given to him, "And this is the will of him who sent me, that I shall lose none of all that he has given me, but raise them up at the last day" (John 6:39). "My sheep listen to my voice; I know them, and they follow me. I give them eternal life, and they shall never perish; no one can snatch them out of my hand. My Father, who has given them to me, is greater than all; no one can snatch them out of my Father's hand" (John 10:27-29).

Third, the reason a person holds fast to his faith is that he is held fast by the Lord. This is the crux of the argument. A Christian's perseverance is made sure by the almighty hand of God. A Christian does not keep himself nor does he save himself. God keeps the Christian from falling through faith. "Who through faith are shielded by God's power until the coming of the salvation that is ready to be revealed in the last time" (1 Pet. 1:5). "And he will stand, for the Lord is able to make him stand" (Rom. 14:4). Because God is just and faithful he will not forsake his people, "For the LORD loves the just and will not forsake his faithful ones. They will be protected forever, but the offspring of the wicked will be cut off" (Ps. 37:28). "But the Lord is faithful, and he will strengthen and protect you from the evil one" (2 Thess. 3:3). None of God's purposes will ever fail. Because he has purposed to save to the uttermost all who put their trust in him, Scripture says "The LORD will fulfill [his purpose] for me; your love, O LORD, endures forever" (Ps. 138:8). According to his faithfulness and his calling "He will keep you strong to the end, so that you will be blameless on the day of our Lord Jesus Christ. God, who has called you into fellowship with his Son Jesus Christ our Lord, is faithful" (1 Cor. 1:8-9).

Therefore, perseverance is a result of the mighty work of God in the lives of those who believe in him, "being strengthened with all power according to his glorious might so that you may have great endurance and patience, and joyfully" (Col. 1:11).

Finally, some will object to the doctrine of eternal security by citing a case when someone professed to be a Christian and later apostatized. However, when Scripture rightfully judges experience (instead of the Scripture being interpreted by experience) one learns that those who apostatize were never saved, "They went out from us, but they did not really belong to us. For if they had belonged to us, they would have remained with us; but their going showed that none of them belonged to us" (1 Jn. 2:19), "Not everyone who says to me, 'Lord, Lord,' will enter the kingdom of heaven, but only he who does the will of my Father who is in heaven" (Matt. 7:21).

This doctrine flows from other doctrines in the Bible. God's purpose in election prompted the apostle Paul to thank God for the Thessalonian believers because he knew that God had chosen them "For we know, brothers loved by God, that he has chosen you" (1 Thess. 1:4). It flows from God's covenant to redeem for himself a people, "I will make an everlasting covenant with them: I will never stop doing good to them, and I will inspire them to fear me, so that they will never turn away from me (Jer. 32:40). It flows from the great atonement Christ made on the cross. Despite some preacher's tendencies to reduce the efficacy of the death of Christ the writer of Hebrews declares that ". . . by one sacrifice he has made perfect forever those who are being made holy" (Heb. 10:14). Christ, in dying for all those who would believe in him did not merely make salvation possible. Christ's death actually perfected those who would believe in him. Thus, the saint's perseverance hinges on the efficient death of Christ on the cross.

There is another fact from which the saint's perseverance flows: the heavenly ministry of Jesus Christ. Because Christ rose from the dead and has gone before those who will be saved, he is able to intercede for them at the right hand of the Father, "Therefore he is able to save completely those who come to God through him, because he always lives to intercede for them" (Heb. 7:25).

The doctrine of the perseverance of the saints should be a comfort to true believers and a warning to those who merely profess faith but who lack the evidence of a relationship with Jesus Christ. To those who do not believe in Christ, what an encouragement it is to know that Christ is able to save forever those who trust in him. In the end, it is for God's glory that anyone is brought through this wilderness into heaven "The Lord will rescue me from every evil attack and will bring me safely to his heavenly kingdom. To him be glory for ever and ever. Amen" (2 Tim. 4:18). ∎

Alcohol & Drug Treatment Program Graduation

By Jeremy Ingram,
MOUNTAIN REVIEW Staff

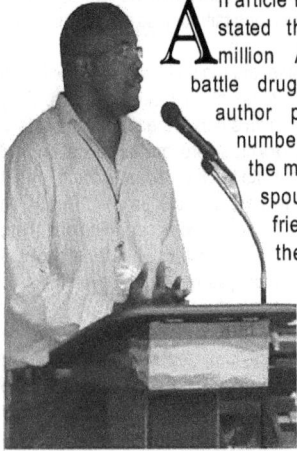

An article in the *USA Today* stated that roughly forty million American adults battle drug addiction. The author pointed out this number did not include the millions of parents, spouses, children and friends affected by the addictions of these people. What is alarming is that many professionals believe this number is too low. Since over half of adults drink alcohol, professionals

Mr. Dixon, Director of Rehabilitative Services

believe the number of addicts is realistically much higher. Considering this epidemic, it is remarkable to find in prison those who have sought help for their problems.

On July 6, 2006, students, instructors, and special guests gathered in the visitation area for the Alcohol and Drug Treatment Program graduation. After Chaplain Yancey offered the invocation, A&D class instructor Jeff Nance noted his appreciation for the hard work and perseverance of the students. He remarked that it had been a long six months. Instructor Louann Roberts then introduced the keynote speaker, Richard Dixon.

Mr. Dixon is the Director of Volunteer Services for the State of Tennessee. He began by saying the accomplishments of the A&D class graduates were noble. For many students, a major accomplishment during this six-month program has been staying clean. He compared this clean streak to the title of the material used in class, *A New freedom*. Mr. Dixon said that substance abuse is the same as bondage. When a person is addicted to drugs or alcohol, he is in bondage to his addictions. Through the change of thinking taught in the A&D program, freedom is possible from the bondage to these substances. However, Mr. Dixon warned of the temptations on the outside. Inmates are used to the temptation in prison—they can avoid the people and situations that may tempt them. Yet, on the street, temptations come in different shapes and size.

The statistics concerning the relation of substance abuse and crime are staggering. Eighty percent of offenders were abusers at the time they committed their crime. Mr. Dixon noted that when an abuser uses drugs or alcohol for an extended period, it becomes normal for them. This is one reason why the A&D program is built on a therapeutic community design. The accountability the therapeutic community provides is a key to the program's effectiveness.

Mr. Dixon told the assembly that his boss Jim Crosby, Assistant Commissioner over Rehabilitation for TDOC, has a perspective: there are two reasons that people reoffend. One is that drug and alcohol abuse complicate their home. Two is unemployment. He believes that only when a person is free from drug and alcohol addictions will that person have control over his life.

After Mr. Dixon spoke, all three A&D class instructors handed out certificates to their students. When time came for Rex Stedam to pass out certificates to the annex graduates, he brought to attention the fact that annex students went through the program voluntarily and without pay. After certificates were passed out, a reception was held that included sandwiches and eclairs, courtesy of John Cross's cooking class. Congratulations to the graduates of the A&D program. We wish them success on their road to recovery. ∎

The Experiential Method

Original Contribution,
By Randall McPheeters

An exciting method of training is sweeping our nation. It is called the **EXPERIENTIAL** method, and it teaches participants through interactive exercises and discussions rather than using lectures. Correctional departments in several states have adopted it for training their officers and many treatment programs have been using it to treat inmates in other states. Tennessee Corrections has begun using the experiential method in some of the institutions, and the Alternatives to Violence Project has been employing this method since its beginning. The experiential method of training is superior to the lecture method because the lessons learned through experience remain with the learner longer and more strongly than the lessons learned by sitting through a lecture.

Have you ever played the game where you whisper something to one person and that person whispers it to another person, and so on, and so on? At the end of the line, whatever was whispered has become something totally different. Playing this game is an experience which teaches us the folly of repeating rumors and it is remembered well after the game has ended. You could learn that repeating rumors or listening to repeated rumors is inaccurate by being told that it is, but would you believe it and apply it to your life as strongly if you learned it that way? Experiencing the game embeds the lesson into your life knowledge. Another exercise demonstrates to participants the many things we all have in common. For some exercises, role plays are used to allow participants to experience conflict from another persons point of view.

You could listen to a person talking about the damage done to his life by hurting others and perhaps you would be convinced by his tale. However, if there were a game like the whispering game that would allow you to experience some damage from hurting others, you would be more easily convinced and the lesson would stay with you much longer. Most of us grew up hearing lectures from our fathers and grandfathers or mothers and grandmothers about how to stay out of trouble, yet here we are. Those lectures may have helped, but they would have been much more memorable if there were a life lesson reinforcing them. You can spend years telling a person how to resolve conflict without violence, but the lesson isn't truly learned until a real conflict is resolved using a nonviolent technique. In experiential workshops like AVP, group exercises are designed to give the participants practice with such techniques.

Another benefit of the experiential method for prisoners is they are usually facilitated by other prisoners. This has the double effect of giving the participating prisoners an empathetic leader as well as empowering prisoners who can see the facilitator doing something worthwhile with his or her life. The group experience will usually result in a feeling of community amongst the participants and create a support system for practicing these new behaviors. Participants who wish to continue learning about and practicing new behaviors may do so by becoming facilitators.

The experiential method of training is more effective than the lecture method because techniques learned through experience are remembered longer, practiced more readily, and are more empowering. The confidence of trying something new after experiencing its capability is much higher than trying something you have only heard about and never tried. One might think of experiential training like a vocational skills class where the book and lecture training play a role but the key to learning is in the hands-on training. ∎

For those of you who watch what they eat, here's the final word on nutrition and health.
1. The Japanese eat very little fat and suffer fewer heart attacks than Americans.
2. The Mexicans eat a lot of fat and suffer fewer heart attacks than Americans.
3. The Chinese drink very little red wine and suffer fewer heart attacks than Americans.
5. The Germans drink a lot of bear and eat lots of sausages and fats and suffer fewer heart attacks than Americans.
Conclusion: Eat and drink whatever you like. Speaking English is apparently what kills you. ∎

Varsity Club Banquet

The Varsity Club is an organization designed to address the educational and rehabilitative needs of inmates and to promote the growth and support of such programs. The Varsity Club meets on the second Tuesday of every month at 6:00 p.m. in the library classroom. For more information on the club contact Randall McPheeters in the chapel office or Jeremy Ingram in the newspaper office. ∎

63

Seventh Step Foundation Banquet

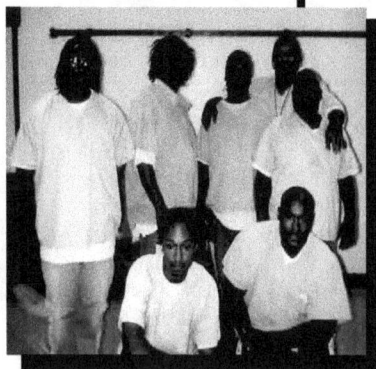

The Seventh Step Foundation is a program whose purpose is to prepare the offender for a successful life once released. Seventh Step does this in three ways. First, they offer counseling for those coming up for parole including providing information on halfway houses. Second, they work with the Tennessee Career Center to provide help employing released inmates. Third, they help with the parole petition. Seventh Step meets every Thursday night at 7:00 in the inmate dining room. ■

Gospel Tent Revival

**By Jeremy Ingram,
MOUNTAIN REVIEW Staff**

Monday morning, May 22, a truck unloaded the gear that would be assembled into a large tent. All morning inmates and free-world men worked on assembling the canvas, lines, and metal structure. That night, under the fluorescent lights, United Christian Prison Ministry kicked off a week long gospel tent revival.

Monday night, Charles Poteat preached on John 14:6. "I am the way and the truth and the life. No one comes to the Father except through me." Poteat stressed the importance of having a personal relationship with Jesus Christ. He is the former senior pastor at United Christian and has been a pastor for 33 years.

Tuesday night, Adrian Varlack Jr. preached a sermon on the death and raising of Lazarus found in John 11. Varlack spoke in detail about the condition of Lazarus as he emerged from the cave, "his hands and feet wrapped with strips of linen, and a cloth around his face." The man who God calls and restores to life comes out from the awful, dark cave of sin in which he had been buried into the brightness and newness of life.

Wednesday night, Pat Hayes preached from several texts including Luke 4:18 and Luke 15. Luke 15 records three parables of Jesus—the parables of the lost sheep, the lost coin, and the prodigal son. Luke 4:18 is a quotation from Psalm 51. "The Spirit of the Lord is on me, because he has anointed me to preach good news to the poor. He has sent me to proclaim freedom for the prisoners and recovery of sight for the blind, to release the oppressed." Hayes' sermon focused on the recovery of something lost and the subsequent joy that resulted. In each case, the something lost is a picture of the sinner who is lost. The good news that Hayes preached was the recovery of life in Jesus Christ. The result of life in Christ is much rejoicing and joy.

Thursday night, Mike Shreve preached on 2 Chronicles 14:11. Before he began, the men assembled under the tent were treated to a song sung by Rita Burnette. During Shreve's sermon, he spoke about the circumstances and victory Asa encountered in this text. Asa was the king of a small force of soldiers. As they encountered a large army, Asa committed his cause to the Lord and God gave him the victory. We, as well, will experience victory in this life and the life to come as we place our trust and confidence in Jesus Christ alone.

On the last night, Anton Burnette preached. Burnette is the new senior pastor of United Christian Church. He preached from Ephesians 4:1-16.

We would like to thank the men and woman who spent their time and efforts to bring the gospel to MCCX. United Christian Prison Ministry holds their services Sunday nights in the chapel. Please check the schedule for particular dates. ■

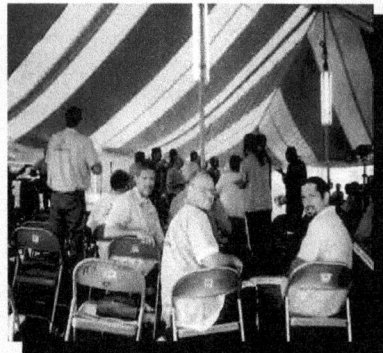

Golden Bear Veterans Club

I have learned from many conversations and common observances that the majority of Christians have absolutely no idea how to study the Bible. Disputes among Christians about the meaning of certain Scriptures are commonly heard. One says it means this, while another says it means something else. How can this be? Does a God who is so specific about what He wants from us—and has taken so much care to lay out and perform His plan of salvation from the foundation of the world—leave it to us to interpret the meaning of His Word?

Paul wrote in his first epistle to the Church at Corinth, "Now I beseech you, brethren, by the name of our Lord Jesus Christ, that ye all speak the same thing, and that there be no divisions among you; but that ye be perfectly joined together in the same mind and in the same judgment" (I Corinthians 1:10). This passage of Scripture suggest that this type of unity is possible among believers. So how do we achieve such unity? It can only be done through the Word of God. If we are told in Scripture to do something, not only is it possible, but we're also empowered by God to do the very thing His Word says.

We must first understand the Word of God (commonly known as the Holy Bible) is a self-interpreting book, and that God our Creator does not leave it up to us to interpret it's meaning. So why is the Bible so hard to understand? Let's begin our journey to understanding by looking at the supreme example given us in Christ Jesus. In an examination of the Gospels, you'll find that Jesus almost always taught the people in parables. In the fourth chapter of Mark, Jesus is telling the people the parable of the sower. After finishing the parable, Jesus makes this statement in verse 9, "He that hath ears to hear, let him hear." We'll get back to this statement shortly. Verse 10 tells us that, "when He was alone, they that were about Him with the twelve (disciples) asked of Him the parable." Before expounding on the parable itself, He explains why He speaks to the people in parables. He tells them in verse 11, "Unto you it is given to know the mystery of the kingdom of God: but unto them that are without, all these things are done in parables." Now in verse 12, He addresses the statement He earlier closes the parable with in verse 9, "That seeing they may see, and not perceive; and hearing they may hear, and not understand; lest at any time they should be converted, and their sins should be forgiven them." Jesus explains to His followers

that to those who are His it is given to understand the mysteries of the kingdom of God, but to those that are not His understanding is withheld.

Now the very basis of our faith is that we accept Jesus Christ is the Son of God—that he was crucified for our sins, died, was buried, and was resurrected on the third day for the justification of our sins. The Bible tells us if we believe this in our hearts and confess it with our mouths, we shall be saved (Romans 10:9,10). This is the first step to coming into a clear understanding of the Bible. The second step is to develop a relationship with this same Jesus who died for you. JESUS CHRIST IS THE WORD OF GOD (John 1:1,14, Revelation 19:13). So in order to get to know Him you must develop a relationship with Him through His Word, the Bible. We're told to "Study to shew thyself approved unto God, a workman that needeth not to be ashamed, rightly dividing the WORD OF TRUTH" (2 Timothy 2:15, emphasis mine). The only way for the believer to effectively do this is by the Spirit of God, which is rightly called the "SPIRIT OF TRUTH."

In the Gospel of John chapters 14, 15 and 16, Jesus explains the responsibility and characteristics of the Holy Spirit. He says the Holy Spirit will "teach you all things, and bring all things to your remembrance" (John 14:26). Christ calls His Spirit "the Comforter" and the "Spirit of truth" (John 15:26). God will send the Comforter unto us, and by the Spirit of truth "He will reprove the world of sin, of righteousness, and of judgment." The Holy Spirit will convey to us only that which Jesus reveals. Jesus will give the Holy Spirit that which He receives from the Father (John 16:7-15). It is by the Holy Spirit that we obtain "the mind of Christ" (1 Corinthians 2:16).

Paul, in his first epistle to the Church at Corinth, gives insight to the believer concerning what is required for him to receive understanding of God's Word. Paul states, "And I was with you in weakness, and in fear, and in much trembling. And my speech and my preaching was not with enticing words of man's wisdom,

The Principles of Bible Study

Original Contribution, By Roland Matlock

but in demonstration of the Spirit and of power: That your faith should not stand in the wisdom of men, but in the power of God. Howbeit we speak wisdom among them that are perfect: yet not the wisdom of this world, nor of the princes of this world, that come to nought: But we speak the wisdom of God in a mystery, even the hidden wisdom, which God ordained before the world unto our glory" (1 Corinthians 2:3-7). Note, Paul reminds the Corinthians that when he spoke to them he did not use the persuasive words of man's wisdom. This was the custom of the time among Greek philosophers, which they used to draw crowds in the public squares. Instead Paul spoke in demonstration of the power of the Spirit of God. He also tells us that the wisdom of God's Word was given for us who are His before the very foundation of the world, given that we might understand its mystery. But why is it not given to all? Paul continues, "Which none of the princes of this world knew: for had they known it, they would not have crucified the Lord of glory. . . . But God hath revealed them unto us by His Spirit: for the Spirit searcheth all things, yea, the deep things of God. For what man knoweth the things of a man, save the spirit of man which is in him? Even so the things of God knoweth no man, but the Spirit of God. Now we have received, not the spirit of the world, but the Spirit which is of God; that we might know the things that are freely given to us of God. Which things also we speak, not in the words which man's wisdom teacheth, but which the Holy Spirit teacheth; comparing spiritual things with spiritual. But the natural man receiveth not the things of the Spirit of God: for they are foolishness unto him: neither can he know them, because they are spiritually discerned (v.8, 10-14).

As Paul speaks to the people at Corinth he gives insight to the believer, explaining why not just anyone is given the wisdom and understanding of God's Holy Word. Paul explains the things of God are spiritual and can only be discerned

spiritually by the Spirit of God, which compares spiritual things with spiritual. And since His Word is spiritual, it must be discerned by His Spirit.

Isaiah 28:9-10 gives explanation to the believer on what it means to compare spiritual things with spiritual and shows just how the Bible interprets itself. This passage begins with a question, "Whom shall He teach knowledge, and whom shall he make to understand doctrine? Them that are weaned from milk, and drawn from the breast." Verse 9 of this passage shows us that for us to be taught the mysteries (the deeper things), we must be coming into spiritual maturity. Hebrews 6:1 tells us, "Therefore leaving the principles of the doctrine of Christ, let us go on to perfection (maturity), not laying again the foundation of repentance from dead works, and faith toward God." This passage of Scripture assures the believer there is more to the Word of God than the mere basics of the faith. In fact, the believer is told that once his foundation is laid through repentance and the building of their faith towards God, that they are to go on to maturity (to seek and implement the deeper elements of our faith).

Now back to Isaiah 28. Verse ten expounds to the believer a specific principle we've briefly touched on, but must be understood and applied for a clear understanding of the Scriptures. This principle is comparing spiritual things with spiritual, which allows the Bible to interpret itself. The Scripture states, "For precept must be upon precept, precept upon precept; line upon line, line upon line; hear a little, and there a little."

The word translated "precept" in verse ten is taken from the Hebrew word "tsavah" (pronounced tsaw—vaw). This word can be found in the Strong's Hebrew lexicon under the number 6680. The word is defined as a command or commandment. In the context of the Scripture it can be defined as a subject.

Now the word translated in the text as "line" comes from the Hebrew word "qavah" (pronounced kaw—vaw). This word can also be found in Strong's under number 6960. Strong defines it as a cord (as connecting), or to bind together (perhaps by twisting).

So when this information is applied in the context of this Scripture it's found to say, "Subject must be connected to subject, because it is dispersed here a little and there a

Continue to next page >

little." The only way all the lines can be connected is by diligent study through the help of the Holy Spirit. Remember the responsibility of the Holy Spirit is to teach you all truth and recall all things to your remembrance that God has taught you. As you study you will begin to notice while studying one subject, you will run across a Scripture that reminds you of another from a different study. Upon your examination of both passages, suddenly your understanding will be enlightened. However, without study this will not happen.

Now when it comes to the study of the Bible, a reverent attitude is indispensable to the believer. We must regard the knowledge the Bible offers as vital principles for life. The believer must always regard the Bible as God's Word and never as some ordinary work of literature. Nor can it be regarded the same as you would some historical work. It surely will be found both interesting and profitable. But, no matter how scholarly and persistent the believer is, he will never discover the Bible's choicest treasures with this method alone. We should study the Bible as eagerly as a hungry man seeks for food.

The formal reading of a portion of God's Word each day will have some value as a religious exercise. But, for full value to be received from God's truths, these truths must be appropriated to the believer's personal needs. For instance, a baker may handle a thousand loaves of bread a day and yet go home hungry at night; so the Bible reader may peruse large portions of the Word of God each day with little profit, unless

the believer makes it his very own by personal appropriation and feeds on it.

The believer must accept that first-hand knowledge is best. Many Christians are satisfied to receive the majority or all of their truth filtered through the mind of a teacher, minister, or commentator—seldom, if ever, going to the Book of Books for independent study. They inevitably become mere echoes of others' opinions. They are not "grounded in the truth," and are liable to be "carried about by every wind of doctrine."

It is a great day for a child when he learns to feed himself; and so it becomes a new era in the believers life when he's formed the habit of going daily to the original source of spiritual truth for his own personal nourishment.

Study the Bible as a traveler who seeks to obtain a thorough knowledge of a new country. Go over its vast fields of truth; descend into its valleys of decision; climb its mountains of vision; follow its streams of inspiration; enter its halls of instruction; and visit its wondrous portrait galleries. Seek all the wonders the Bible has to offer, but most of all learn to hold them as invaluable. Jesus spoke a series of parables in Matthew 13. All of them deal with the kingdom of God and His Word. They can be found between verses I & 52. In one of them found in verse 44, He says, "Again the kingdom of heaven is like unto a treasure hid in a field; the which when a man hath found, he hiddeth and for joy thereof goeth and selleth all that he had, and buyeth that field." In this

parable Jesus shows us just how valuable the knowledge of the Word should be viewed by the believer. This man found a treasure, and went to sell all that he possessed to buy the field he found the treasure in so the treasure would belong to him.

Meditation is a major part of Bible study. Just like eating, food must be chewed before being swallowed and so must be the Word of God. Remember it is the Holy Spirit that reveals all truth and recalls all things to your memory whatsoever you have been taught. By not meditating on the Word of God, you take away opportunity for the Spirit of God to work with you.

The believer must always remember that many doctrinal errors have grown from a lack of spiritual perspective, or a narrow view of spiritual truth. Jesus said to the Sadducees when they came to Him with a question about the resurrection, ". . .Ye do err, not knowing the Scriptures, nor the power of God. . ." (Matthew 22:23-33). In other words, no doctrine should be formed on speculation, but solely on the instruction of the Word of God.

The believer must seek to know and understand the deep things of God. Study the Word of God as a miner digs for gold, or a diver plunges into the depths of the sea for pearls. Most great truths do not lie on the surface. They must be brought into the light by patient toil.

The believer must adopt a systematic method of study. Haphazard reading of a few verses of Scripture each day is better than nothing, but is not real Bible study. It is simply nibbling at the truth and does not tend to build strong Christians. The following are four different types of study methods the believer can use. Remember, these are not the only methods available, just my suggestions to help you create good and productive study habits.

1. THE TOPICAL METHOD: This consists of the selection of a subject and tracing it thoroughly through the Scriptures. For the novice using this method I suggest using a topical Bible, such as Nave's Topical Bible or some sort of chain reference Bible, like the Thompson Chain Reference Bible. Either type of Bible will help the young believer to learn to trace their way through the Bible until they build up their knowledge of the Scriptures and they can do it on their own.

2. THE BIOGRAPHICAL METHOD: This is a study of various characters of the Scriptures, such as Jesus, David or Paul. A study of any character of the Bible will reveal things such as time

and place of birth, their relationship to and with God, lessons they may have learned in service to God and even their advice to you, and so much more. I suggest for the novice some sort of inductive study Bible. These types of Bibles usually have character studies that entail the life, travels, and accomplishments of the main characters of the Bible.

3. THE STUDY OF BOOKS: This study entails the selection of a certain book in the Bible. The believer will endeavor to master the book by ascertaining its authorship, to whom it is addressed, the circumstances under which it was written, its purpose, its message, etc. This can be done with any Bible.

4. THE STUDY OF CHAPTERS AND IMPORTANT PASSAGES: This familiarizes the believer with the gems of scriptural literature. This especially becomes important to the believer as they grow into spiritual maturity. The believer will learn to look to them for guidance, help and encouragement for himself and others.

Last but not least, the believer should memorize verses of Scripture that really have had some impact on their spiritual growth. This way they're available for any sudden need or emergency that may arise. A ready passage of Scripture is invaluable to the believer. He needs to have passages so arranged in his memory that they are available for instant use. Memorization of Bible truths puts both defensive and offensive weapons into the hand of the believer. By having these verses memorized, they can be exercised during times of trial and attack. Remember, Jesus Christ is the Word of God, and when He was raised from the dead He was raised with all power in heaven and earth. There is nothing more powerful than the Word of God. So learn it, live by it, and practice it in every instance of your life. By doing so you will fulfill the Scripture, "Be strong in the Lord and in the power of His might."

May God our Father bless you with an abundant knowledge and understanding of His Word as you diligently seek Him, Amen. ■

Can You Really Believe the Bible?

By Garry W. Johnson
MOUNTAIN REVIEW Staff

Many people today assume modern scholarship has discredited the Bible. Even some who consider themselves "religious" reduce the Scriptures to mere myth or allegory. Then others simply scoff at the idea that God exist—or that if He does, He is personally interested in them. Fortunately, the truth is the same for anyone falling into any of these categories: some things are true, whether you believe them or not.

Bible prophecy is unfolding with increasing speed in today's headlines. Anyone who regularly watches the Discovery channel can see scientist struggling to explain away the current natural phenomenons predicted in the Biblical text. Earthquakes, hurricanes, floods, droughts (the subsequent wildfires), and volcanic activities are growing in strength and regularity. Even the evolution of politics is racing toward the predicted end-time scenario.

The overwhelming scientific, archeological and historical evidence—not to mention fulfillment of countless prophecies—confirm the Divine origin of the Bible. If you have never determined to prove for yourself the validity of the Bible, I strongly recommend the publications Is the Bible True? and Does God Exist? Both are available to you free by writing the United Church of God, P.O. Box 541027, Cincinnati, OH 45254-1027. All UCOG publications are provided free as an educational service in the public interest. You may also want to request their 12 Lesson Bible Study Course and a one year subscription to The Good News magazine, also free of charge. ■

Editor's Note: Roland Matlock is a inmate minister here at MCCX. He and several other inmate ministers conduct a Saturday chapel service from 11:00am-1:00pm. Sponsor Bill Joo says the question-and-answer format has been ongoing for the past two years, and the services are continuing to grow. All are welcome to attend.

Prison
from page 02

the "new asylums."

HOMICIDES DOWN

Since 1980, state prison homicide rates have dropped dramatically. In 1980 there were 54 murders for every 100,000 prisoners in state custody. That number had dropped to four per 100,000 in 2002. The commission found that some data on violence was not reliable. Arkansas, North Dakota and South Dakota each erroneously reported to the U.S. Justice Department that there were zero assaults statewide among prisoners in 2002.

"Perhaps the biggest blind spot," the report went on to say, is that "there are no national measures of physical violence and excessive use of force by staff against prisoners, including the inappropriate use of restraints and non-lethal weapons."

THEN THERE IS "THE HOLE"

According to the group, from 1995 to 2000, the number of offenders assigned to solitary confinement increased by 40%, surpassing the 28% rise in overall prison population growth. The rapidly expanding use of segregation to control problem inmates "concerned the commission," said Alexander Busansky, the commission's executive director. Case in point is the Texas prison system. In 2005, nearly 10,000 of Texas's 150,000 inmates were in some form of solitary confinement in which offenders are kept in small cells for up to 23 hours a day with little or no contact with other inmates. Texas Department of Criminal Justice spokesperson Michelle Lyons said isolating inmates has become necessary to protect both prisoners and staff from particularly violent offenders. Lyons said, "these (isolated) inmates are those who have proven to be a problem."

The commission found that even the most difficult offenders needed some human contact to guard against extreme conditions "that cause lasting harm."

The USA Today editorial concluded by saying, "None of this means coddling criminals. But failing to deal with prisoners effectively only ensures more problems for society when they are released."

The Tennessee Department of Corrections currently supervises more than 20,000 inmates and employs more than 5,000 people at 15 prisons.

A CHANGE OF ADMINISTRATION

The prison system is not perfect, and neither is the justice system; however, in this country we have been blessed by the best *human government* has to offer. Though you are on the bottom-side of this human system now, you can change your lot in this life—and secure your place in the next. Jesus Christ came to this world with a message of hope and love, a message of a new government and a new way of life. His message was "the gospel of the Kingdom of God" (Mark 1:14; Luke 4:43). If you will completely and obediently submit to His royal sovereignty now (Matthew 5:19-20; James 2:8-12), you will be added to the cadre of saints being trained as "kings and priests" (Revelation 1:6, 5:10) to administer that government on earth (Daniel 7:27; Revelation 11:15). Put your past behind you (Romans 3:23-31, 2 Corinthians 5:17-20) and look now to the glorious future ahead (Revelation 21-22). ∎

Stomach Cancer Linked to Certain Meats

By Garry W. Johnson
MOUNTAIN REVIEW Staff

In a recent study reported on by *USA Today*, Swedish researchers found that eating more processed meats such as bacon, sausage and smoked ham may increase the risk of stomach cancer (August 3, 2006). The research, published in *The Journal of the National Cancer Institute* reviewed 15 studies involving 4,704 people from 1966 to 2006. These studies collated by researchers at the Karolinska Institute found that stomach cancer rose by 15 to 38 percent if the consumption of processed meats increased by one once a day.

The study says the increased risk is possibly connected to the meats being salted or smoked or having nitrates added to them to extend their shelf life. ∎

Myths
from page 04

help in preparing to take the driver's license test and *The Release Resource Manual* designed to inform the inmate of services available. This is practically a condensed version of the PRC.

(5) MYTH: PRC is a life skills program. **REALITY**: PRC does include life skills. But it also includes a cognitive behavior modification program called "Thinking For A Change" that will help you learn how to change your criminal behavior. Also included in the class is a program called "Victim Impact" where you address the effects your crimes have had on your victims.

(6) MYTH: PRC will give you certificates that will help you make parole. **REALITY**: The parole board is not interested in how many certificates an inmate has collected. They are looking for a working knowledge of the programs you have taken and a noticeable change in your way of thinking.

(7) MYTH: PRC is taught by inmates. **REALITY**: PRC is supervised and taught by the Pre-Release Coordinator, other staff and outside volunteers.

(8) MYTH: PRC will boost your pay for the rest of your time in prison. **REALITY**: Students who complete PRC will be given the top of the pay scale for whatever job they are assigned to after graduation. The exceptions to that rule are for (a) those who are expiring their sentence within nine months (their pay will remain at 50 cents per hour) and (b) those who have been granted parole and are awaiting their release (their pay will remain at 50 cents per hour).

(9) MYTH: Pre-Release services can only be provided by the Pre-Release Coordinator. **REALITY**: Pre-Release services *can* be given by *any* counselor, IRC, IPPO, or other member of a Unit Management or treatment team.

(10) MYTH: PRC will cause the Parole Board to put my parole off. **REALITY**: If you are granted parole during the PRC then more than likely the Parole Board will require that you finish the class before you are sent home and you will have plenty of time to get the PRC class finished. ∎

Smoker
from page 08

aged from 3-12 months and tested higher levels of NNAL than those seen in adults exposed to secondhand smoke in the home. Apart from the risk of cancer and the above-mentioned diseases, these children are at risk for many other illnesses too. Children of smokers can expect higher incidents of ear infections (up to two million each year), bronchitis and pneumonia (150,000 to 300,000 each year in those less than 18 months of age), as well as colds and asthma. The Surgeon General also reports that secondhand smoke is known to cause sudden infant death syndrome.

With all the ill effects associated with smoking and secondhand smoke, it is good to know that quitting now has immediate and long-term health benefits.

LET THE HEALING BEGIN

According to the US Surgeon General's Report, the body begins healing within twenty minutes after a smoker has his last cigarette. His blood pressure and pulse rate begins to come down and the temperature of his hand and feet warm back up to normal levels. Approximately eight hours after that last smoke the carbon monoxide level in the blood drops and the oxygen level increases to normal. Twenty-four hours later the chance of a heart attack starts decreasing. After only forty-eight hours nerve endings start regrowing and the ability to smell and taste is enhanced. Depending on the smoker, the next phases of healing will vary. Somewhere between two weeks and three months time, the ex-smoker's circulation improves and his lung function increases up to 30 percent. From a month to nine months later he can expect his coughing, sinus congestion, fatigue, and shortness of breath to decrease. During this time his lungs will begin to regain normal function; cilia in the lungs begin regrowing and moving mucus again which clean the lungs and reduce the risk of infections. One year after his last smoke, his risk of heart disease drops to half of that of a smoker. His risk of a stroke drops five to fifteen years after quitting, and around the ten year mark his chance of dying from lung cancer becomes half of what it would have been if he had continued to smoke. Around this same time the risk of cancer of the mouth, throat, esophagus, bladder, kidneys, and pancreas also decreases. It takes fifteen years before the risk of coronary heart disease lowers to the level of a nonsmoker.

There are many other benefits to kicking the smoking habit as well. The risk of gum disease, premature wrinkling of the skin, bad breath, and stained teeth are all reduced when one quits using tobacco. One's sense of smell also improves causing food to tastes better and strenuous physical activity causes less shortness of breath. Pulse rate and blood pressure may also improve.

Health wise, smoking cessation is a win-win for everyone. ∎

CROCK'S PUZZLE FUN

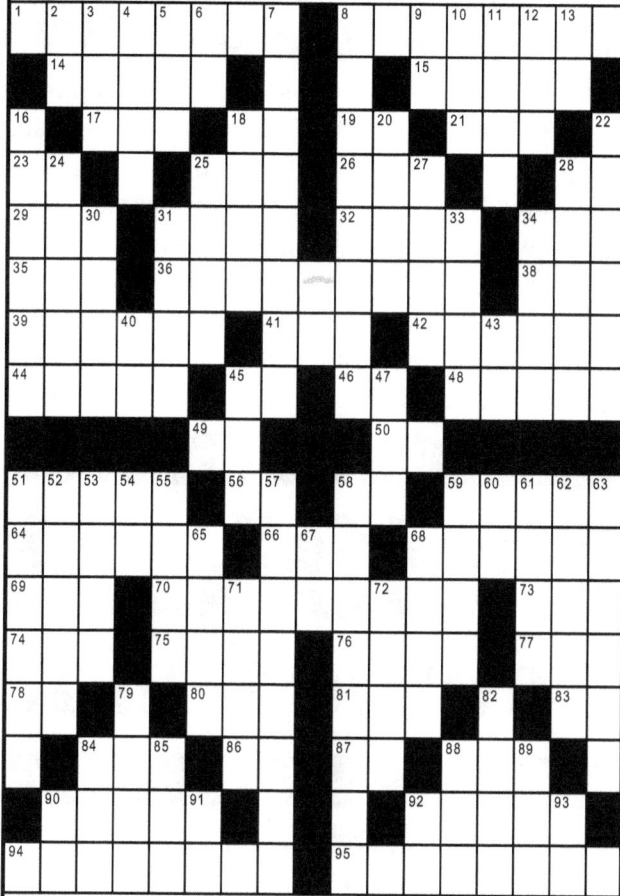

Across

1. Walks all over
8. Soft shelled clam
14. Silly
15. Demand, as in payment
17. Sharp bark
18. Thallium's symbol
19. For Example
21. Shade tree
23. _ _ Hooker
25. Bark
26. Tiny ____
28. St. Paul's St.
29. 3 men in a ____
31. U.S.A. citizen
32. Lawyer's exam
34. Big ____
35. Dr.'s Org.
36. Gives it a whirl
38. Man-mouse connector
39. Humpbacks
41. Actor Chaney
42. Swaps
44. Uniform color
45. Belonging to me
46. ____ you hear what I hear?
48. Fat
49. The Shaggy _ _
50. Sun god
51. White wash
56. East Carolina (abbr.)
58. Physical Education, for short
59. Headliners
64. Type of goat or rabbit
66. Western Indian
68. ____ Dream, Nugent album
69. B-I-_-_-_ was his name-o
70. Spur of the moment
73. Movie studio abbr.
74. With "wa," all wet?
75. Dock
76. Mined
77. Above, poetically
78. Hit medical drama
80. Dr. ____
81. Had a salty wife
83. Opp. Of N.W.
84. ____ Paulo
86. Prefix with "dive" or "case"
87. Psyche part
88. Synthetic gemstone
90. Late
92. Ms. Ross
94. Ancestry
95. Pachyderm

Down

2. N.E. St.
3. Indefinite amount
4. Central
5. Promissory Note payment (abbr.)
6. French article
7. Depend on one's self
8. Island N Scotland
9. Shoe width
10. Fire
11. Fellow
12. European Common Market (abbr.)
13. Separated by "s"
16. Jump on
18. Star ____
20. Main point
22. Enclose
24. Muslim prayer service
25. Pearl divers
27. Store
28. Female horses
30. Crimson Tide
31. Legendary Hun King
33. Novice
34. Method
37. ____ what?
40. With "E," scratch out
43. Workout target
45. Ms. West
47. Raw material
51. Gasped
52. Ire
53. Lab assistant
54. Absolutely not!
55. Voyage
57. Money
58. Memory drug
59. Type of missile
60. Translator (abbr.)
61. Designed for aerial use
62. Neatens, as with leaves
63. Gooey treats
65. In the middle of
67. ____ be, or not . . .
68. Editor's word
71. French father
72. Poke
79. Peel
82. Saturday night event
84. With "asota," Florida city
85. Strange
88. Opposite of nope
89. Youth org.
90. Football pos.
91. With "P," see 17 across
92. To ____, or not to . . .
93. 25th and 14th of the 26

DAVE'S CRYPTOGRAMS

Dave's Cryptograms are created from Biblical quotes. Each letter in the puzzle stands for another letter.

Clue for puzzle #1: S equals A

ZP FZSF FCGIADPFZ ZKN GBT ZGINP NZSDD KTZPCKF FZP BKTH.

Clue for puzzle #2: J equals K

NS FLBMC HCEMFG SB GLIOO JTRK FLBV.

Anonymous Email,
Contributed by Judy Johnson

The Funeral

As a young minister, I was asked by a funeral director to hold a grave side service for a homeless man, with no family or friends, who had died while traveling through the area. The funeral was to be held at a cemetery way back in the country, and this man would be the first to be laid to rest there.

As I was not familiar with the backwoods area, I became lost and being a typical man did not stop for directions. I finally arrived almost an hour late. I saw the backhoe and the crew, who was eating lunch, but the hearse was nowhere in sight.

I apologized to the workers for my tardiness, and stepped to the side of the open grave, where I saw the vault lid already in place. I assured the workers I would not hold them long, but this was the proper thing to do. The workers gathered around, still eating their lunch.

I poured out my heart and soul. As I preached the workers began to say, "Amen," "Praise the Lord," and "Hallelujah." I preached, and I preached, like I'd never preached before - from Genesis to Revelation! I closed the lengthy service with a prayer and walked to my car. I felt I had done my duty for the homeless man and that the crew would leave with a renewed sense of purpose and dedication, in spite of my tardiness.

As I was opening the door and taking off my coat, I overheard one of the workers saying to another, "I ain't never seen anything like this before . . . and I've been putting in septic tanks for twenty years."

69

Answers to crossword puzzle on page 23.

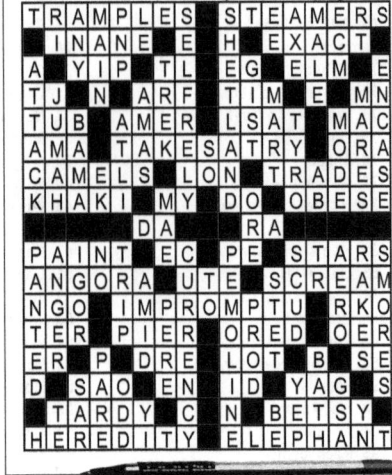

T	R	A	M	P	L	E	S		S	T	E	A	M	E	R	S
I	N	A	N	E		E		H		E	X	A	C	T		
A		Y	I	P		T	L		E	G		E	L	M		E
T	J		N		A	R	F		T	I	M		E		M	N
T	U	B		A	M	E	R		L	S	A	T		M	A	C
A	M	A		T	A	K	E	S	A	T	R	Y		O	R	A
C	A	M	E	L	S		L	O	N		T	R	A	D	E	S
K	H	A	K	I		M	Y		D	O		O	B	E	S	E
		D	A					R	A							
P	A	I	N	T		E	C		P	E		S	T	A	R	S
A	N	G	O	R	A		U	T	E		S	C	R	E	A	M
N	G	O		I	M	P	R	O	M	P	T	U		R	K	O
T	E	R		P	I	E	R		O	R	E	D		O	E	R
E	R		P		D	R	E		L	O	T		B		S	E
D		S	A	O		E	N		I	D		Y	A	G		S
	T	A	R	D	Y		C		N		B	E	T	S	Y	
H	E	R	E	D	I	T	Y		E	L	E	P	H	A	N	T

Answers to cryptograms on page 23.

HE THAT TROUBLETH HIS OWN HOUSE SHALL INHERIT THE WIND
ZP FZSF FCGIADPFZ ZKN GBT ZG INP NZSDD KTZPCKF FZP BKTH

BY THEIR FRUITS YE SHALL KNOW THEM
NS FLBMC HCEMFG SB GLIOO JT RK FLBV

MOUNTAIN REVIEW

The *Mountain Review* was produced as a free government document written by prisoners at Brushy Mountain State Penitentiary and Morgan County Correctional Complex. It was sponsored by the Education Department at those facilities and was a censored publication. Permission to reprint was granted in this section of each edition. The views expressed are those of individual authors and do not necessarily reflect the TDOC policy at that time, nor the views of the editors, staff, sponsors, or administration.

PRISONER Resource Guide

2021 Edition

Bound Together Bookstore
Attn: Prisoners Literature Project
1369 Haight Street
San Francisco, CA 94117
415.431.8355; 415.672.7858
prisonlit.org
Prisonlit@yahoo.com

Sends free books to prisoners upon request. Please include three areas of interest. No thrillers, westerns or romantic novels available. Cannot send books to county jails or prisons in Texas and Michigan. One request per year; 1-4 month wait.

Coalition for Prisoner Rights Newsletter
P.O. Box 1911
Santa Fe, NM 87504

A monthly newsletter sent free to prisoners, family members, and ex-prisoners who request them themselves. Also publishes several resource guides and a small yearly calendar, which they send to there subscribers free of charge. Send an SASE for their latest edition.

The Intercontinental Church of God
P.O. Box 1117
Tyler, TX 75710

Free literature available to prisoners. Request a copy of *The Answer to Unanswered Prayer* and *Here's the Best News You Could Ever Hear*. Sermons available to prisoners on cassette and CD; DVDs available to Chaplains. Ask for a list of their free literature, and request the free quarterly news magazine, *Twenty-first Century Watch.*

The Prison Mirror
970 Pickett Street North
Bayport, MN 55003-1490
615.779.2700

America's oldest, continually-printed prison newspaper. Established August 10, 1887. Published monthly by and for the men of the Minnesota Stillwater Correctional Facility. Two-colors, 16-pages, with correctional news, writings, art, and puzzles. A one-year subscription is $24.

Tightwad Magazines
% Julie Sanders
P.O. Box 1941
Buford, GA 30515-8941

A discount magazine subscription service. Offers special deals on multiple subscriptions, books and CDs from Amazon.com, and gifts for family and friends. Write for free information on current sales and offers. Send an SASE for their catalog.

U.S. Mennonite Office of Criminal Justice
Box 500
Akron, PA 17501-0500
717.859.3889; 717.859.1151
mcc.org
mailbox@mcc.org

Offers many publications and resources on issues of criminal justice and religion, as well as educational programs on criminal justice issues. Most of their programs are free to prisoners and their families, and they have a large archive online. A resource list available upon request.

Winter 2007 Edition
Volume 20
Number 1

MOUNTAIN REVIEW

A Morgan County Correctional Complex Publication

Prison Life

With the largest incarcerated population on the planet, prisons in the United States have become big business. **Garry Johnson** continues his series on the situation with America's prisons, shifts in criminal trends and the effect they have on society . . . . . . pages 8-11

Compound News In Brief

Robin Marmon

☞ Teacher and Varsity Club sponsor **ROBIN MARMON** retired February 16, 2007.

☞ Psychological Examiner **LINDA PALMER** also retired.

☞ Inmate **JESSE COFFEY** and Kairos volunteer **JIM MUIR** both passed away.

☞ AVP volunteer **CLAUDINE NORRIS** has taken ill.

☞ AW/O **JIM MARROW** has been promoted to warden of Bledsoe.

This Issue Focuses On

Feature Articles

Criminal Trends

Federal drug arrest holding steady

Number of DEA domestic arrest:

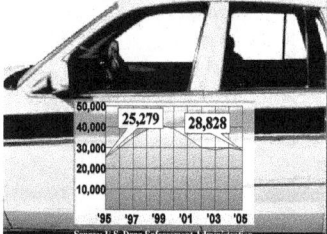

25,279   28,828

'95 '97 '99 '01 '03 '05

Source: U.S. Drug Enforcement Administration

Graphic by Garry W. Johnson, Mountain Review Staff

2006 Christmas Banquets

By Jeremy Ingram
MOUNTAIN REVIEW Staff

Thanksgiving and Christmas are the favorite times of the year for many people in the free-world. Family gatherings, food, and presents often mark the holiday seasons. For many at Morgan County, the holidays are just as special in many of the same ways. Just as family traditions abound in the free-world, Morgan County has its own traditions. Among all the Christmas packages, treat bags, and holiday meals, the unit Christmas banquets stand out. Local churches and Christian ministries celebrate the spirit of Christmas by providing home-cooked meals to the population at MCCX.

The 2006 Christmas banquets kicked off when United Christian Church celebrated Christmas at Morgan County with a meal and a service in the visitation gallery. Anton Burnette, pastor of United Christian Church in Cleveland, Tennessee, spoke about the story of Christmas and the birth of Jesus. United Christian has been involved in prison ministry for many years and has been a part of the Christmas banquets for many years. They hold a service in the chapel on select Sunday nights. Check your unit bulletin board for exact dates. The inmates from units 2, 3, and 4 extend their sincere gratitude to the church and its members for their time and compassion.

The following Monday, December 11, several churches united to celebrate Christmas. The churches present were Chaplain Dean Yancey's church, Providence Baptist, Covenant Presbyterian Church in Oak Ridge, First Christian Church, and Lighthouse Baptist Church. These churches, together with Dot's Catering Service, provided a delicious meal for units 5, 6, and 7. Dr. Duncan Rankin delivered a short sermon and Chaplain Yancey asked all the volunteers to introduce themselves. While the food was being served, free-world volunteers helped the inmates carry their plates of food back to their table. Because of the massive amount of food and desert, their help was needed and was appreciated. Inmates from these units enjoyed the food and company of all the church members. They wish to extend their gratitude for a wonderful evening.

Volunteer Chaplain David Upton

River of Life Church

had been talking since last Christmas about the banquet his church, Covenant Ministry Center, was going to sponsor. About midsummer men's mouths began watering. Chaplain Upton's words did not fail as they brought in enough food to feed an army. So much food was brought in that close to half of it was left uneaten. Also attending the banquet was Kathy Benn and Jackie White from St. Joseph Family Church, David and Almeda Thompson, and Harold "Gator" Evans and his wife Sarah. Some remember Gator from his years as an inmate at MCCX. One of the few that is true to their word, Gator did not forget us when they released him from prison. To prepare for the banquet, Gator went to several businesses and asked for donations for this year's banquet (he did the same in 2005). Great American Buffet in Knoxville, Kentucky Fried Chicken in Oak Ridge and the District Office, Ryan's Restaurant in Oak Ridge, Food Lion, Food City, and Save-a-Lot all pitched in and donated items for the banquet. They donated more than 1,000 pieces of

See **Christmas** *on pages 12-13*

Winner of the 2006 MCCX Arts Contest:

James White

This year's Arts Contest had a grand total of 11 entries submitted by seven contestants; six poems, three songs and two drawings. The winning entry (right) received six votes from the teaching staff at the MCCX school. The runner-ups and vote tallies are published on page 16.

71

Christmas in the Kitchen

By Jeremy Ingram
MOUNTAIN REVIEW Staff

Every year inmates at MCCX are treated to an outstanding Christmas meal. Kitchen workers, under the direction of Kitchen Manager Carey Newberry, spend long hours preparing the meal. Preparation normally begins a month in advance when orders and arrangements are made for the Christmas meal. In the days leading to Christmas, kitchen workers spend extra hours and sometimes extra shifts ensuring that all the food is prepared.

Christmas in prison can be a depressing time for many. Knowing the kitchen staff went the extra mile to make Christmas a special time deserves the utmost gratitude. Not only was the food prepared well, but also the ambiance was seasonal. Christmas tree, decorations, and festive dress enlivened the evening. Even with most inmates carrying their trays back to their units to eat with their friends, the Christmas meal turned the sometimes dispiriting holiday into a cheerful time.

Many people have commented that the holiday meals at MCCX—both Christmas and Thanksgiving—are the best meals in the state. How does the kitchen here prepare a better meal than most other places? In part, Carey Newberry is responsible for the preeminence of these meals. In the month or so preceding each meal, he substitutes ceratin foods for others in order to reduce the overall cost of food service. In this way, he is able to save a few dollars that in turn helps pay for the holiday meals. Recognition should also go to the free-world staff and inmate workers who put pride into these meals. One example is on Christmas—many kitchen workers worked all day without complaint. Their dedication is greatly appreciated by everyone who enjoyed the meal.

Inmates at MCCX would like to thank the whole kitchen crew for their hard work and dedication. We also would like to thank the administration who allows this meal to be prepared and enjoyed

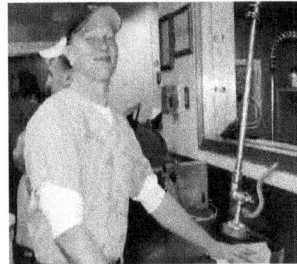

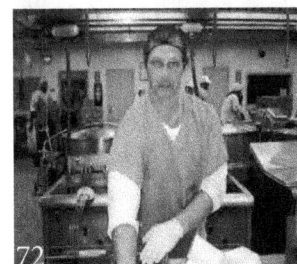

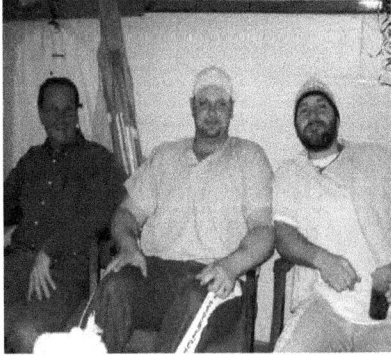

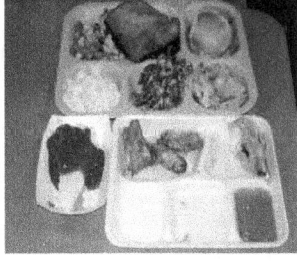

Pre-Release Graduation

By Jeremy Ingram
MOUNTAIN REVIEW Staff

PRE-RELEASE CLASS EIGHT

Pre-Release class eight graduated on September 21, 2006. Students and staff assembled in the outside visitation area to celebrate the completion of the Pre-Release program. Instructor Rickey Bunch, Unit Manager Charlene Walls, and Bearle Hensley were present. Mr. Bunch began the graduation by noting that most of the students worked hard during the class. This amounted to some improvement in most and a dramatic improvement in others. One request Mr. Bunch asked of the class at the beginning of the program is to keep the same enthusiasm throughout the program. Mr. Bunch remarked that the class did what he asked.

"We must become the change we want to be," remarked Mr. Bunch, following with "A mistake is only a mistake if you don't learn from it." He challenged everyone in the class to learn from their mistakes so that they do not repeat them. The old adage was impressed upon the class. If a person does not learn from his past mistakes, then he is doomed to repeat them. In Mr. Bunch's words, "If you keep reliving the past, you will have the same results." The purpose of the Pre-Release program is change. Old, criminal thinking needs to be replaced with a new way of thinking that leads to responsible, law-abiding behavior.

Success in life is not measured by how much money a person makes or how many major accomplishments a person totals. Real success is measured by the small things: respect for others, taking care of one's family, etc. Mr. Bunch challenged everyone to strive for the respect of others. This includes not only a person's family, but also society-at-large.

Mrs. Walls congratulated everyone on a job well done. She said that the men were lucky they were in this particular class. Most staff members think of their positions as mere "jobs." Yet Mr. Bunch was not like that. She ended by saying that she wishes every inmate would come into the system through Mr. Bunch and leave through him.

Several inmates offered comments on the program. One inmate commented on Mr. Bunch's dedication to the program. In his words he "felt Mr. Bunch took this class as more than a job." Another inmate talked about meeting Mr. Bunch during classification at Brushy Mountain. At the time he had a "certain opinion" of Mr. Bunch. But, after completing his program, he had a newfound respect for him.

Special thanks should be given to Food Service Instructor John Cross. Because of a fog count the morning of graduation, he volunteered to make all the refreshments by himself. ✍

PRE-RELEASE CLASS NINE

Pre-Release class nine graduated on December 15, 2006. Pre-Release Instructor Rickey Bunch opened the graduation by asking the class if they felt any different now than when they started. The answer he hoped for was a feeling of confusion. He explained that hopefully the class felt confused because confusion was a sign that the class was thinking. If the students have begun thinking, then things will become more clear. Mr. Bunch warned if the students thought that things were clear when they started then they have learned nothing.

Mr. Bunch commented on the mock job interviews everyone in the class had to go through. Mr. Bunch remarked that out of all the men who were interviewing for a job, not one of them simply said that he had a strong back, good health, and was willing to work. For Mr. Bunch, that would have made all the difference in the world. Many inmates getting out of prison need to have this humble attitude. An employer, knowing an inmate's past history, is looking for someone who will work hard for him. Opposed to this attitude were many inmates' responses. Mr. Bunch gave the example of an inmate who demanded a high pay. Someone fresh out of prison has no right to demand his pay without first proving himself.

The job interviews were designed to give released felons tools they can use in job interviews. Mr. Bunch, knowing the various questions that will inevitably arise in a job interview, prepares men to handle these questions and respond in the right way. Several examples were given. Felons will need to justify and explain why they were incarcerated. In addition to this question, felons must be prepared to answer the other questions that employers will ask. The Pre-Release class offers instructions and tools so that the potential employee will be able to succeed in a job interview. In the end, when the felon gets the job, he will need to work hard day in and day out to prove them wrong who said he will never make it. The last bit of advice Mr. Bunch gave was that the job field and workplace was "their field" so felons are expected to play by their rules.

Mrs. Walls, also attending the graduation, commented on Mr. Bunch's dedication to his job. She said that in her position at MCCX she has many opportunities to interview people for various jobs. Thus, she knew what a potential employer was looking for. She suggested that the felon "tell them the good and explain the bad." Afterward, she congratulated the class.

The main thing stressed at this graduation was that with hard work, honest money, and straightforward decisions, nothing was impossible. In reference to this dedication to success, Mr. Bunch and Mrs. Walls warned those people who were not ready to get out and stay out. They said that for some men, their parents, friends, family, etc ... could see that they are not ready. "Everyone knows you are not ready; everyone but you ... can you stand not seeing it?"

Refreshments were provided by the Food Service class. Special thanks to them. ✍

CLASS NINE GRADUATES

Jeff Pritchard
John Fortson
Richard Luallen
Ladonis Sanders
Chad Jennings
Timothy England
Chris Williams
Ronnie Hart
Jody Stout
James Cushman
Troy Rutledge
Timothy Moore
Michael Parks
Robert Milsap
Gary Hilley
Carl Jeremy Stout
Wesley Hammock
Jeff Meadows
Jeffrey Mathis

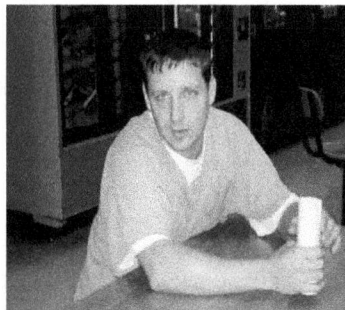

Table of Luke

Table of Mark

Table of Matthew

Table of John

airos is an interdenominational Christian ministry whose purpose is to bring the love and forgiveness of Christ into correctional facilities nationwide. Kairos is presented in state and federal, men and women, American and international facilities. Although the ministry's headquarters is in Winter Park, Florida, Kairos is conducted by selected, trained, and governed teams of individuals. These teams are composed of both clergy and laity and work in cooperation with the prisons' chaplains.

Kairos prison ministry is nondenominational. It is drawn from a vast range of denominational churches. Among those represented are the Baptists, Presbyterians, Catholics, Episcopalians, Methodists, and Pentecostals. Kairos volunteers usually have experience with groups within their churches that focus on small prayer and share groups. Kairos is also a continuing ministry. The introductory, three-day "short course" is not intended to be an end in itself. It is designed to foster a life of ongoing Christian ministry for the individual within the larger context of the Christian community.

Kairos originated in an attempt to launch a program in prison similar to that of the three-day movements within Christian churches on the street. Precipitated by a movement at the Raiford institute in Florida in 1976, a model was developed that could be presented in prison. They called it "Kairos."

There are two Greek words for time. One of them, with which we are all familiar, is "kronos,"

God's Special Time

By Jeremy Ingram
MOUNTAIN REVIEW Staff

meaning linear time ... hours, days, weeks, etc. The other is "kairos," used in the sense of a time set by God for a particular occurrence. "KAIROS" was found to be a word of very special significance in the environment of prison where the word "time" carries so many special connotations.

The idea behind Kairos is that after the three-day short course, small three-to-five person share groups are formed. These groups are encouraged to meet weekly to share their lives on a deep, spiritual level and pray for one another and for other residents and staff in the institution. An outline is given each group that will aid in the time that the groups spend together. Presently, these small groups meet in housing units, on the yard (when it is open), and in the chapel.

"Kairos is a ministry of the church ... a ministry of the apostles whom Jesus, the Christ, has called into community and sent forth into the environment of the correctional institution. Kairos has been called the best example of the early church in existence today."

Inmates interested in attending Kairos may sign up in the chapel. Spaces available for each Kairos weekend are limited. For inmates who have completed the Kairos weekend, a reunion is held on the fourth Saturday of every month at 7:00 P.M. in the chapel. Everyone is welcome to attend. Everyone in Kairos would like to thank the administration and free-world volunteers who make this special time possible. ✍

"Table Family"

David, Bill, & Jeremy

Gorge Smith & John Stone

John Stone at Closing Ceremony

Kairos #9 Team & Particiapnts

Free World					
David Jackson					Dwike McMiller
Bill Duffey					Jeremy Ingram
Joe Pace	Thurman Kinnebrew Jr.	Gary Johnson	Jerry McGaha	Donald Blair	Corey Milliken
Bob Lambertt	James Carmichael	Leonard Turner	Darrell Hamilton	Earnest Collier	Benjamin Moss
Alf Jones	Spenser Hudson	Bill Wolff	Aric Moses	Pail Smith	Orlando Spratling
Jamie Jordan	Bob Nine	Mark Tisch	Scott Metcalf	David Presley	Travis Sharp
Arch Jones	Pat Moore	Inmates	Kevin Smith	Michael Gay	Ricky Johnson
Wally Moore	Ron McKean	Larry Dunnigan	Thomas Hollowell	Jarvis Shropshire	Ricky Williams
Joe Melia	George Smith	Jerome Devereaux	Grover Hunter	Samuel Minton	John Johnson
Russ Neil	Jason Taylor	John Stone	Rickey Beamon	Gene Twitty	Bobby Tate
Thurman Kinnebrew Sr.	Chuck Dugger	Marcus Thomas	Thomas Cummings	Kenneth Green	Robert Bruce

Kairos Free-World Team

Kairos Number Nine

Kairos Servers

MCCX Leather Shop

The History and Art of Leather Craft

By Cecil "Bo" Smith

Leather making is an ancient art that has been practiced for more than 7,000 years. Primitive man dried fresh skins in the sun and softened them by salting and smoking. During the Middle Ages the Arabs preserved the art of leather making and so improved it that morocco and cordovan (from Córdoba, Spain), became highly prized leathers. By the 15th century, leather tanning was widespread in Europe and by the mid-19th century, power-driven machines were introduced. Toward the end of the 19th century, chemical tanning—in particular, the use of chrome salts—was introduced. The tanning process derives its name from tannin (tannic acid), the agent that displaces water from the interstices of the hide's protein fibers and cements these fibers together.

Cecil "Bo" Smith

After the basic tanning process is completed, the leather is ready to be fashioned into any multitude of products. These include shoes and boots, outer apparel, belts, upholstery materials, suede products, saddles, gloves, luggage, purses, and recreational equipment, as well as such industrial items as buffing wheels and machine belts.

Today at MCCX, the men in the leather shop practice one of the oldest and most useful crafts known to man. (See figure 1.) Many of the techniques and processes that are used by them daily have been handed down for generations.

Although there are many instructional books to learn from, an old craftsman once said he'd learned most of his skills of the craft from those who'd came before him, and he's most happy whenever given a chance to pass it on to the next man."

Practicing leather craft is one of the best things to happen to me since I've been locked up. It has taught me self-discipline, patience, and many other life skills, making me a more productive person. It has allowed me to make sense out of an otherwise senseless existence. For all those behind the walls everywhere—we have hands, minds and hearts—use them in a positive manner to better yourself and those around you. ✍

Figure 1
Inmate leather worker prepares to work on leather project.

Leather Carving and the Tanning Process

By Jeremy Ingram
MOUNTAIN REVIEW Staff

Leather has been an important part of life since the early days of mankind. It's uses in the ancient past were manifold—shields, weapons and clothing were made from leather to provide safety and protection. Dwellings used leather to shield man from the elements, and leather products have always been considered a work of art, pleasing to the eye. During the Middle Ages, explorers spread their leather working knowledge through Europe. The Spaniards were particularly gifted with the ability to make beautiful leather goods such as belts, boots, and saddles. Until the 15th century, leather carving was basically confined to geometric shapes. But when Cortez found the New World, dwellers forsook geometric designs in favor of more bold and nature-inspired designs. The art of leather carving was officially born.

Leather carving is the art of carving or "tooling" picturers into leather. The leather is prepared by tanning the hide to the exact specification needed by leather carvers. (See next article on leather tanning.) The leather is then wet to make it soft and malleable. A design is cut into the leather with a tool known as a swivel knife. Finally, different stamping tools are used to carve the design. (See figure 2.) When the leather dries, the pattern is permanent.

The art of carving leather was a top-secret knowledge, closely guarded by those in the trade. For the past 500 years the leather trade was passed on from father to son. No one else was ever allowed to learn the family trade. In today's world, the demand for leather goods has increased the number of people who desire to learn this trade. Although many good books are written on the subject, they are no substitute for being an apprentice for a skilled leather worker.

Even for a beginner, the leather hobby is both practical and beneficial. With only a few tools

Figure 2
A rack of leather tools used for stamping/tooling designs into leather.

and small pieces of leather, the beginner can make small leather products. Yet years are required for the serious enthusiast to develop skills required for carving beautiful pictures fit to be framed.

A HISTORY OF LEATHER TANNING

Much of the leather purchased in prison is Vegetable Tanned leather. This type of leather is tanned with a process that is very old. Hundreds of years ago, before the industrial age, the leather tanner had only oak and pine bark that he gathered from neighboring trees. In fact, many tanners cultivated their own groves of oak trees that they stripped in order to use their bark for tanning. From these minimal materials expert tanners could make leather that was as firm as a shoe's sole, to leather as soft as garments. Individual tanners specialized in different kinds of leather for specific purposes. Eventually, these tanners organized themselves into leather guilds. These organized guilds developed rules regulating where each tanner would work, how many apprentices he was allowed to have and for how long. Most of these tanners were located along rivers so that traveling hunters could sell them the skins of recently killed animals.

When the skins were procured, salt was used to cure them so that they would be preserved until the time of tanning. Leather was separated according to its use by its thickness. Also, leather hides were skived to ensure uniform thickness. Because the hides had hair on them, they were "sweated" to remove the hair. Hides were hung in a humid room and eventually, through the process of fermentation in which bacteria would attack the hair cells, the hair would be loosened enough so removing it would be easy. Later, hides were immersed in a solution made with lime. The lime would aid in the loosening of the hair. The entire process of unhairing a skin usually lasted from five to seven days.

Interestingly, some of the same tools used hundreds of years ago in the tanning business are still used today. These tools include the beam on which the unhairing, shaving, and fleshing were carried out, the various knives used for fleshing and shaving, the shaving beam, and the whetstone and steel needed for sharpening the knives and other tools.

After the skins had been dehaired, they were normally carried to the river to be rinsed and cleaned. The next several processes prepared the leather hide for the actual tanning process. These processes included "fleshing," where the un

wanted flesh and fat were removed using a shaving and fleshing knife. This produced a consistent thickness over the entire hide. An additional process is called "deliming." Due to the liming process, the leather needs to be delimed to neutralize the basicity. The next process, called "bating" was intended to soften the skin. Interestingly, pigeon dung was commonly used as a bating agent. Lastly, three processes known as "pickling," "drenching," and "souring" brought the skins to a proper chemical level required for the tanning process. At this time the skins could be either tanned or stored. The pickling of the skins allowed them to be stored for extended periods of time.

After the tanning process was begun, two containers were used. The containers were called dusters and layaways. The tanning was usually begun in the dusters and finished in the layaways. These huge vats were made of wood and normally built into the ground to prevent damage. The ground also provided insulation, and frequently clay was packed around them for added insulation. Layer by layer, hides were added to the vats. Because of the great weight produced by the large number of hides, liquor was added. The liquor would cause the hides on the bottom of the vat to float, thus reducing the pressure from the weight of the hides. Although skins could be carried off from the layaways after four to six weeks, skins were left in the dusters for months.

The actual materials used in the tanning processes were varied according to tanner and location. Some tanners had access to more oak trees and others to more pine trees. In Russia, sometimes in the open plains, the only trees available were the birch and willow tree. The Russian tanners would use the bark from these trees to tan their hides. This type of leather became known as Russian Leather. The bark from the various trees, coming into contact with the hides, would produce the desired result. A few other processes were involved in the tanning process. These were "oiling," where the leather itself would be made flexible and color would be added to the leather, "stuffing," or impregnating with oil so as to make waterproof, and "rolling" to make the skins flat.

Old shop manuals exist that give insight into the way these processes were preformed. These books show the great care the tanners put into their work. These books also give a glimpse of the habit of apprentices who would travel long distances to become acquainted with the various methods of different tanners. With the arrival of the steam engine, this old way of tanning was made obsolete. Guilds were gone and steam boilers would replace the vats. Eventually large factories would replace small, family owned tanneries. Many small businesses had to close because they could not compete with the factories. Eventually, technological advancements in chemistry allowed tanneries to utilize better methods of tanning. ✍

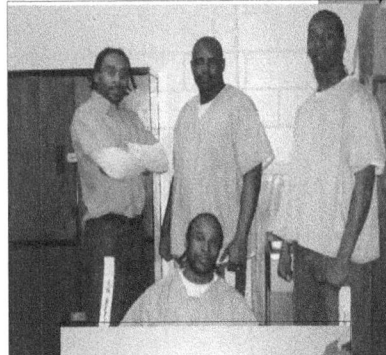

As salaamu Alaikum Wa Rahmantulillahi Wa barakatuhu
(May peace be to you and mercy of Allah and His blessings.)
By Travis Barton

Inside the Holy Bible it's relayed that Ishmael is the firstborn son of Abraham, and that Isaac is the second born (Gen. 16).

By Islamic belief, Allah (God) demanded that Abraham offer his firstborn son as a sacrifice to him which would have been Ishmael, by Islamic belief. Being the obedient servant of Allah he (Abraham) was, he headed to the mountains with Ishmael to make this divine sacrifice to his Rabb (Lord). Which even Ishmael was in acceptance of this divine decree.

Yet Allah only had intentions on showing the followers of them both just how greatly imbedded their faith was. Once they approached the destination point, as Ishmael finally lay still on a bed of stone. A revelation was revealed right before Abraham attempted to slay Ishmael. A voice spoke against it, and in the bushes lay a lamb which was to be a replacement for the sacrifice of the firstborn son (Ishmael).

This day or event became an all time Islamic Holy day in which the Muslims offer a two Rakat prayer in congregation and give a sermon to the congregation of gathers'. As well on this blessed occasion we congregate and eat Halal foods of sacrifice with one another, and simply enjoy each others company this is the purpose of the second EID feast which all Muslims celebrate yearly all across the globe. Masha Allah (It is as Allah wills)!

I pray you receive (as a whole) a great over sight to the purpose of this beautiful celebration. Thank you for acknowledging this message that I have supplied by way of Allah The Almighty, The Allah which is worthy of all praises!

The Sunni Islamic Community would also like to "Thank" this administration for all their support through the kitchen and food service. For making all our Islamic functions a great success.

Sincerely yours: Kaliim Bayyinah Shahid or you may be more familiar with Phoenix # 327834

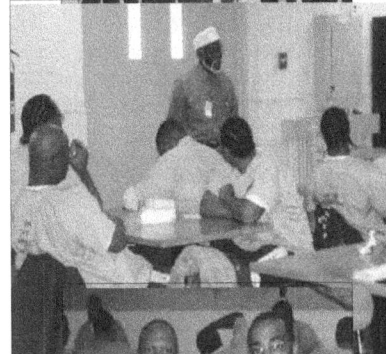

Amazing Facts About Your Heart

By Jeff Durham

We all know how to steal hearts, win hearts, break hearts, and have a deceitful heart. But how much do you really know about your heart and how it works? Read on until your heart is content. Put your hand on your heart. Did you place your hand on the left side of your chest? Many people do, but the heart is actually located almost in the center of the chest, between the lungs. It is tipped slightly so that a part of it sticks out and taps against the left side of the chest, which is what makes it seem as though it is located there.

Hold your hand out and make a fist. An adult heart is about the same size as one adult fist. Your heart beats about 100,000 times in one day and about 35 million times in a year. During an average lifetime the human heart will beat 2.5 billion times, which is amazing in itself.

If you give a tennis ball a good hard squeeze, you are using the same amount of force your heart uses to pump blood out to the body. Even at rest the muscles of the heart work hard, twice as hard as the leg muscles of a person sprinting. Feel your pulse by placing two fingers at the pulse point on your neck or wrist. The pulse you feel is blood stopping and starting as it moves through your arteries. As a kid, your resting pulse might range from 90 to 120 beats per minute. As an adult, your pulse rate slows to an average of 72 beats per minute. Your body has about 5.6 liters (6 quarts) of blood that circulate through it three times every minute. In a day the blood travels a total of 19,000 km (12,000 miles). That is four times the distance across the United States, from coast to coast. The heart pumps about one million barrels of blood during an average lifetime, enough to fill three super tankers. Your heart starts beating at around day

21, while you are being formed by God in your mother's uterus, and your heart will keep pounding away until you die.

Exercise protects the heart. Studies have shown that lack of regular physical activity may be an even more important heart risk factor than smoking or high blood pressure. The physically fit live longer. A 20-year study showed that physically active men live an average of 2.1

years longer that men who love to loaf and lounge around. Fitness walking is America's second most popular sport. Fifty-eight percent of Americans walk for fitness, and the number is growing fast. A regular exercise program of at least 30 minutes a day, three times a week will help you lose weight faster and more consistently than if you only cut back on food calories. But be aware that the more pounds you lose the

more efficient your body becomes and hence the fewer calories you burn during a workout. What an amazing gift God has given to us for free, and it is all up to each one of us as to how we use it or abuse it.

In my previous field of employment, I worked for a company that my sister and her husband own. Our duties were to train individuals who desired to become accredited in the field of ultrasound to become technicians and work for hospitals or other companies. In my past experience in scanning patients, each individual heart basically is the same—no matter what color the skin, what country they are from or what sex they may be. A heart is a heart. Also, the blood we humans have is the same in each man, woman and child. It serves the same purpose in all of us and that is it gives us life. Since we

have all of these things in common, have you ever wondered why we cannot get along? Why do some people have so much hate in their hearts? I believe there is another aspect about the heart that some of us overlook and that is the spiritual side of our heart. The spiritual side of our hearts need to be taken care of and maintained daily. In God's Word (the Bible), Jeremiah 17:9 tells us that without the Word of God abiding in our heart it is desperately wicked. Have you had the spiritual side of your heart checked recently? If not, find a quiet place to pray and talk with God about the condition your heart is in.

These are a few ways that Satan will attack our hearts: Genesis 6:5 tells us about an evil heart, Exodus 8:18 about a hardened heart, Proverbs 15:7 about a foolish heart, Romans 1:21 about a vain heart and Jeremiah 48:29 about a prideful and haughty heart. In Mark 7:21 God's word tells us, "For from within, out of the heart of men, proceed evil thoughts, adulteries, fornications, murders." Our hearts are the true source of sin and righteousness. When our heart is corrupt our life and conduct will be corrupt. When we decide to make our heart clean, our whole life will become clean. It is a life-long process, so why not start today? It is never too late. Always remember Gods penetrating eyes see all the hidden motives within each of our hearts. We cannot hide one single thing from the Almighty God of the universe. If you are having problems with sin corrupting your heart, turn to Jesus Christ right now and ask Him to come into your life. Accept Him as your Lord and Savior and He will show you through His Spirit and by His Word how to have your heart clean and sin-free before His eyes. Ask Him to forgive you of all your sins and you will receive a brand-new Spiritual heart. ✍

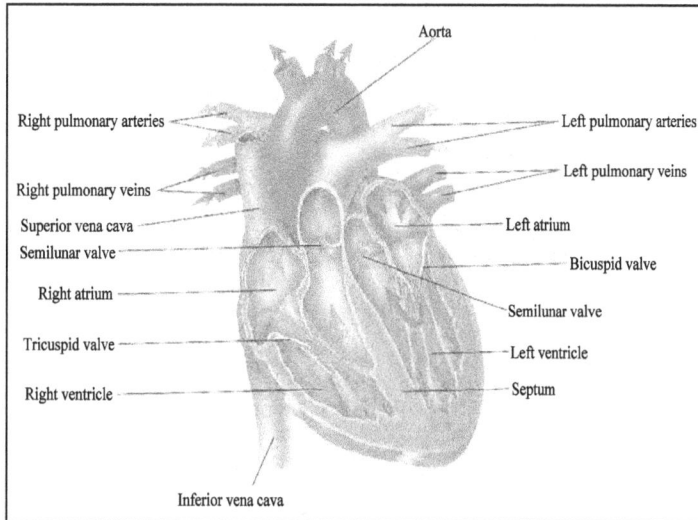

Nursing News

By Jennifer Anderson, R.N.

Tuberculosis: A Major Public Health Concern in Correctional Facilities

Tuberculosis is an infection that can affect the lungs and other organs of the body and can be extremely contagious. Tuberculosis, also known as TB, is common among people who have been or are currently imprisoned. Each year about 1.7 million people die of this curable disease. Someone in the world is newly infected with the TB bacteria every second. Overall, one third of the world's population is currently infected with the TB bacteria. Five to 10% of people who are infected with the TB bacteria become sick or infected at some time during their life. People with HIV and TB infections are much more likely to develop TB. Length of stay in prison is significantly associated with an increased risk of TB infections and disease. One year of jail time doubles the odds of developing TB. A 1991 outbreak of TB among New York state prison

inmates resulted in the transmission of TB to prison workers. In turn, the state then instituted a program of mandatory TB skin testing. A report on a 1994 outbreak in a Texas prison found a clustering of cases of active TB, including 15 cases in inmates and one case in a prison worker. The report did not include any information about mandatory skin testing. A recent outbreak of TB in a South Carolina state prison is still being investigated, but investigators have indicated that a medical student exposed to infectious inmates developed active TB. TB is present in most all correctional facilities, but the states mentioned in multiple studies were New York, Texas, South Carolina, Oklahoma, Hawaii, Minnesota, and Tennessee.

Only people who are sick with TB in their lungs are infectious. When infectious people cough, sneeze, talk, or spit, they propel TB germs (known as bacilli) into the air. A person only needs to inhale a small number of germs to become infected. Left untreated, each person with active TB disease will infect, on average, between 10-15 people every year. However,

people infected with TB bacilli will not necessarily become "sick" with the disease. The immune system "walls off" the TB bacilli which, protected with a thick waxy coat, can lie dormant for years. When someone's immune system is weakened, the chances of becoming sick are greater.

Risk factors for TB include: elderly people and young children, HIV, Diabetes, malnutrition, alcoholism, exposure to someone with TB, injection drug use, overcrowded conditions, homeless shelters, prisons, nursing homes, contaminated beef, and contaminated milk. Symptoms of TB depend on where in the body the TB bacterium is growing. The TB bacteria usually grow in the lungs. TB in the lungs could include symptoms such as: a bad cough that lasts longer than two weeks, pain in the chest, coughing up blood or sputum, weakness or fatigue, weight loss, no appetite, chills, fever, and night sweats. But keep in mind, there may be no symptoms during the early stages of TB.

If you suspect you have been exposed to TB you should be tested immediately. The current

method for testing is a skin test called the Mantoux/PPD TB test. If a person has been exposed to the TB bacteria, reddening and raising of the skin will occur within 48-72 hours in the area where the skin test was performed.

If diagnosed, the main thing is to begin the treatment of tuberculosis as soon as possible. TB can be successfully treated with specific antibiotics that have to be taken for at least six months, medications such as Isoniazid, Rifampin, Pyrazinamide, and Ethambutol.

In conclusion, it should be remembered that tuberculosis is as easily spread as the common cold, and the infection can remain "hidden" when first contracted. So if you come in contact with someone with any of the symptoms mentioned in the article, have a skin test as soon as possible. The only way to decrease the breakout of TB among prisoners is to be informed and aware. Anyone can get tuberculosis, so protect yourself and reduce the outbreak of correctional facility tuberculosis. ✍

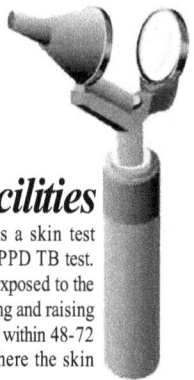

77

Prison Life

AN OVERVIEW OF PRISON NEWS AND CRIME STATISTICS FROM AROUND THE USA — BY GARRY W. JOHNSON

Incarcerated America

The United States maintains the largest prison and jail population on Earth. At the end of 2005 a staggering seven million people—one in every 32 U.S. adults—were on probation or parole or locked behind bars according to U.S. Justice Department Statistics. Of that total 2.2 million were in jail or prison, a 3% increase over 2004. The U. S. figures constitute "an incarceration rate more than five times that of England, six times that of Canada, and seven times that of Germany," according to Sasha Abramsky, author of *Hard Times Blues*.

Women now account for 7% of the total prison population, and their numbers are accumulating even faster than men. While the male prison population increased by 1.9% in 2005, female prisoners saw an increase of 2.6%. ✍

Fifty-seven felons flee TDOC

On the run for decades, many of Tennessee's 57 escaped convicts have eluded capture by managing to blend back into society, according to authorities.

"Some people have a very good ability just to blend in," said Steve Katz, supervising producer of the television show *America's Most Wanted*. "The way they are successful is that they seem normal, not like a crazy fugitive."

The Department of Correction reports that most of Tennessee's fugitives have been on the lam 30 years or more and are in their 50's and 60's.

Billy Wayne Hayes was one such individual. Convicted for murder, Hayes bolted from a work release program in Nashville in 1972 and was on the run almost 34 years. After receiving a tip, authorities re-arrested him near Dothan, Alabama on December 1.

In the mid-1970's Hayes' arrest warrant was mysteriously canceled, allowing him to stay at large despite being arrested several times. State authorities are still investigating how Hayes' warrant was voided.

Another fugitive, Margo Freshwater, was on the run for 32 years. She scaled a fence in 1970 and fled the Tennessee Prison for Women where she had served two years of a 99-year sentence for killing a Memphis store clerk.

Freshwater was found by the Tennessee Bureau of Investigation in 2002 in Columbus, Ohio, where she had established her own family. She was working for an insurance company and living under a false name.

According to the State's web site, Freshwater, now 58 and back in prison, will be eligible for parole in 2029.

Katz says many fugitives like Freshwater change their names, while others take more drastic steps, like plastic surgery or leaving the country to elude authorities.

Law enforcement officials acknowledge the longer someone stays on the run and assumes another identity, the harder it becomes to find them.

Katz adds, "unless they are really geniuses, they are going to leave traces of who they are. The longer time goes on, those traces get fewer and fewer." ✍

Terrorist recruiting from U.S. prison population

Prisons have long been fertile grounds for gang recruiting, but recent studies show that Islamic terrorists are increasingly drawing members from the prison population. One such report, a joint study by George Washington University and the University of Virginia, concluded state and local authorities are too cash-strapped to prevent or track recruiting.

The report released in September asserts there are not enough trained Muslim religious leaders to counsel the estimated 9,000 U.S. prison inmates who want Islamic services. Islamist extremists are thus able to target their vulnerable fellow inmates with distorted versions of the Quran and other Muslim readings that urge violence and radicalization.

"Radicalized prisoners are a potential pool of recruits by terrorist groups," concludes the report, which was released at a Senate Homeland Security and Governmental Affairs Committee hearing. "The U.S., with its large prison population, is at risk of facing the sort of home-grown terrorism currently plaguing other countries."

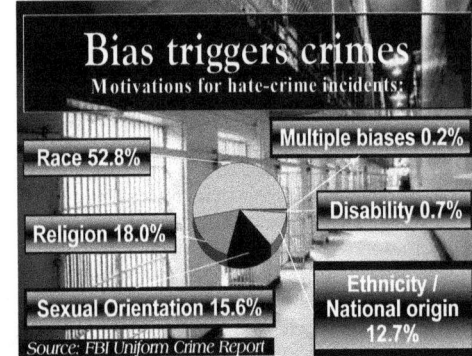

State and local prison officials struggle to track behavior changes of inmates or religious counselors. The report found these prisons have largely relied on contractors and volunteers to lead Islamic services due to the lack of well-trained Muslim chaplains.

While state and local officials deal with staff and funding shortages, the federal prisons are having problems of their own. In October the Justice Department issued a damning account of the federal prison system's failure to monitor potentially criminal communications of convicted terrorists and other inmates. The 100 page report focused on some of the nations most secure government facilities and found the federal Bureau of Prisons (BOP) fails to adequately monitor prisoners' mail, telephone calls, visitor communications and cellblock conversations.

In the report Justice Department Inspector General Glenn Fine found the bureau also lacks the staffing and expertise to translate communications conducted in foreign languages or to assess possible threats.

The report states that "the BOP incarcerates international terrorist inmates who require sophisticated monitoring and analyses of their communications and activities."

"The BOP's monitoring procedures, intelligence analysis and foreign language capabilities have not evolved to that level."

The investigation launched by Fine followed news reports last year that three terrorists convicted in the 1993 World Trade Center bombing wrote more than 90 letters to Islamic extremists outside the prison walls, despite being imprisoned at the government's most secure facility in Florence, Colorado.

The report was founded on reviews of 10 high-security facilities where many of the system's 146 convicted international terrorists are imprisoned and hundreds of the estimated 19,720 high-risk inmates are detained.

The report also estimated a 60% increase in high-risk inmates over the past 10 years —including gang leaders and international and domestic terrorists. The BOP staff increased by a mire 14% during the same period.

As a result of these findings the FBI and Homeland Security has begun working with prisons in dozens of states to improve intelligence gathering and monitoring of prisoners.

They are urging prison officials to do more extensive background checks on workers and volunteers who meet with inmates. Congress may even consider reforms in prison security as a way to combat the spread of extremist Islamic beliefs.

The government's foremost priority is preventing radical Muslim clerics from gaining access to prisoners and coercing them with terrorist literature. "It's a concern because we know that violent extremist groups will target people in prison," said the FBI's counterterrorism director, Donald Van Duyn. "We're working to improve monitoring, improve training and increase awareness."

Homeland Security officials are sending investigators to prisons around the country to gather intelligence on inmate radicalization. They are worried that plots similar to the one to blowup U.S. airliners in-route from the U.K. with liquid explosives maybe developing in U.S. prisons.

The British conspiracy involved people alleged to be home-grown terrorists in London and Canada and has heightened concerns that the U.S. maybe vulnerable to attacks by its own citizens. Further concerns were realized in June when Canadian officials charged 17 people in an al-Qaeda-inspired plot to possess bomb-making materials.

The FBI and Homeland Security are also urging prisons to develop more informants and set up their own intelligence units. They are asking prisons to work with local agents to share information, but would not say whether they already had agents in the prison system.

Although not addressing the issue of funding, federal officials are urging states to train more prison staff to recognize signs of radicalization among prisoners—extremist propaganda, sharing radical views and attempting to convert other inmates. They also want prisons to conduct background checks on volunteers and employees to ensure extremist Muslim clerics do not gain access to prisoners.

"Our concern is not with prison inmates converting to Islam," says chairman of the Senate Homeland Security Committee, Senator Susan Collins (R-Main). "For many converts, this religion brings direction and purpose their lives previously lacked."

Of the estimated two million people imprisoned in the United States, 6% of them are Muslim, according to the Federal Bureau of Prisons.

A California case may shed light on what is happening in some U.S. prisons. In 2005 a group of extremist robbed 12 Los Angeles gas stations to raise money for terrorist attacks against the United States. The FBI says the group's founder Kevin James recruited members from prison. Currently four of those members are awaiting trial for conspiracy to levy war against the U.S. government, among other charges.

Collins goes on to say, "We have to wonder how many other such conspiracies are taking shape under the radar in other prisons." ✍

> "The U.S., with its large prison population, is at risk of facing the sort of home-grown terrorism currently plaguing other countries."

Bias triggers crimes

Motivations for hate-crime incidents:

- Race 52.8%
- Religion 18.0%
- Sexual Orientation 15.6%
- Multiple biases 0.2%
- Disability 0.7%
- Ethnicity / National origin 12.7%

Source: FBI Uniform Crime Report

One in eight death-row inmates halt appeals

Of the 1,041 executions carried out from the time capital punishment resumed in 1977 until August 2006, 123 "volunteered" to die by abandoning their legal appeals. That is a rate of about 12% according to the Death Penalty Information Center, a Washington, D.C. group that opposes the death penalty.

"Why do they do it? And how should the legal system regard someone who just doesn't want to participate? It raises real questions," says J.C. Oleson, author of a 2006 law journal article about the phenomenon.

Although some of the so-called volunteers give no reason for their decision, Michael Ross—convicted of killing four Connecticut women —said his appeals risked the "living hell" of reliving his "absolute worst deed." Ross was executed in 2005.

Robert Nave, a death-penalty opponent says the isolation on death row and anxieties caused by years of appeals produce mental instability that causes volunteers to make an "essentially irrational" choice.

To the contrary, Oleson says that choosing death is "not necessarily an unreasonable or unprincipled thing to do." He believes lawyers should ask, "What's in my client's best interest at the end of the day?" ✍

Overall crime at 32-year low, while violent crimes surge

The government has released multiple reports over the past several months indicating a rise in violent crimes throughout the United States.

The Justice Department reported September 10, that Americans were robbed and victimized by gun violence at a greater pace in 2005 than the year before, even though overall crime rates hit a 32-year low.

In 2005 there were two violent gun crimes for every 1,000 individuals, compared with 1.4 in 2004, according to the department's Bureau of Justice Statistics. There were 2.6 robberies for every 1,000 people, compared with 2.1 the year before.

Criminal justice professor James Alan Fox of Northeastern University says, "this report tells us more of the serious events—robbery and gun crimes—increased and the FBI already told us homicides increased."

Fox continues, "so while the report shows the more numerous but least serious violence—simple assaults, which is pushing and shoving—went down, the mix got worse in terms of severity. That wasn't a very good trade off."

In June a preliminary FBI report showed a 4.8% increase in the number of murders and 4.5% increase in the number of robberies reported to police in 2005.

The overall violent crime rate was unchanged in 2005 from the year before, at just more than 21 crimes for every 1,000 individuals older than 12, according to the statistics bureau's victimization report. The FBI reported in December a 2.2% increase nationally, the first increase since 2001.

Because of a drop in household thefts, the property crime rate fell in 2005 from 161 crimes to 154 for every 1,000 people. Both rates are the lowest since the survey began in 1973.

The statistic bureau makes estimates based on interviews with 134,000 people. It counts not only reported crime but also crimes the police never hear about, unlike the FBI reports which are culled from police blotters. According to Michael Sniffen of the Associated Press, 53% of violent crimes and 60% of property crimes are never reported to the authorities.

An additional FBI report released September 18, adjusted the rising murder rate to 1.8% for the year 2005—3% lower than the June figure. The nation's murder rate hit a two-decade low in 2004. The report raised questions about whether violent crime rates will continue to rise after years of decline.

As for the most violent of crimes—murder, rape, robbery, and aggravated assault—they were up 1.3% in 2005. However, the 2005 figures remain far below the high set in 1991, when homicide rates in many cities soared amid gang wars and a sluggish economy. In fact, 2005's rate for rapes alone fell 2.2% and was the lowest it had been in more than 20 years.

Deputy Attorney General Paul McNulty said the recent increase in violent offenses could reflect a convergence of factors: a rise in gang membership, the spread of highly addictive methamphetamine and the increasing number of young people 18 to 24, the age group that generally commits the most crimes.

Chuck Wexler, executive director of the Police Executive Research Forum, said the FBI report was "not all gloom and doom," noting the decline in property crime.

Nevertheless, Wexler said the members of his group are concerned about increasing violence across the nation. In September, *USA Today* quoted Wexler as saying, "We believe we're on the front end of a tipping point on violent crime."

In October the group released its own report which showed a substantial increase in murder, robbery and assault in a cross-section of cities during the first six months of 2006.

The combination of these reports prompted a federal initiative by the Justice Department which will visit several cities to look at possible causes of increased violence. The teams will also visit communities where crime has declined to determine which crime-prevention tactics have been most effective.

Preliminary FBI data released in December seems to support the findings of the Police Executive Research Forum. The FBI found that violent crime rose by 3.7% from January 2006 to June of last year, compared with the first six months of 2005.

The new report also gave a break down on the crime statistics for that period, showing that murder rose by 1.4%, felony assaults by 1.2%, robberies by 9.7% and arson by 6.8%.

This new report, combined with the numbers for 2005, shows that violent crimes are likely headed for a second straight year of increases.

The new numbers also portend the downward trend in nonviolent crimes continuing, with a 2.6% drop in property crime over the same period. ✍

Counties seeking more funds for housing felons

Tennessee counties are requesting an increase in state payments to local jails for the state prisoners they maintain.

A recent survey concluded the cost to local jails at $47 per day per prisoner. The state generally caps reimbursements at $35 per day and has not increased that amount in at least a decade. As for housing thousands of felons awaiting probation revocation hearings, the counties receive no funds from the state.

An estimated 1,685 felons sentenced to serve time in state facilities were housed in local jails across the state in 2006, according to a Department of Correction report in September. Currently $124.1 million of the state budget is earmarked for prosecutions. That money is suppose to cover local jail reimbursements but also other expenses, like witness fees and jury boarding.

The Tennessee Advisory Commission on Intergovernmental Relations drafted a report saying state inmates are contributing to county jail overcrowding. At a recent commission meeting the commission's chair, Cleveland Mayor Tom Rowland said, "It seems to me that the State's acting very unfairly to county governments."

Tennessee's two largest counties, Shelby and Davidson, both have contracts with the state which permits them to be paid above the $35 cap. Although some counties' actual costs are well below the cap, the estimated cost vary throughout the 24 counties holding state contracts.

Hamilton County estimates state prisoners cost them $59 per prisoner daily. Hamilton County Auditor Bill McGriff estimates his county lost $700,000 in the last fiscal year due to the gap in state reimbursements. ✍

The Governator tries to ship felons to Tennessee

Two California employee unions sued in October to block Governor Arnold Schwarzenegger from shipping more than 2,000 inmates to other states, including facilities operated by Nashville-based Corrections Corporation of America (CCA).

Private prisons in four states signed contracts with California Department of Corrections and Rehabilitation to house 2,260 medium-security inmates at an estimated cost of $51 million a year.

Sending inmates out of state to private prisons violates the state Constitution, according to the Cal. Correctional Peace Officers Association who represents prison guards and Service Employees International Union Local 1000 who represent other prison employees.

Their lawsuit stated that Schwarzenegger overstepped his powers when he declared an emergency in October to speed up no-bid contracts with the GEO Group Incorporated of Florida and CCA. Chuck Alexander, executive vice president of the guards' union says that such emergency declarations should be reserved for unforeseeable disasters.

Schwarzenegger countered that the 174,000 inmates crowded into space designed for about 100,000 puts inmates, guards and the public in danger. Some inmates have been forced to sleep in gymnasiums and auditoriums, but even makeshift beds are projected to run out by August.

A California judge ruled in February that the Governor's plan was illegal. Schwarzenegger vowed to appeal, saying that some convicts might have to be released early otherwise. The transfer of prisoners to Arizona, Indiana, Oklahoma and Tennessee was expected to free up space until June 2008.

The nonpartisan Legislative Counsel issued a legal opinion in October saying the practice of using private companies for public safety services is illegal and should be provided by the state employees. Tennessee has had private prisons since 1992, California since the 1980's. ✍

Death-row population down for 5th straight year

"DNA testing, questions about the effectiveness of public defenders and other factors have raised issues about whether the death penalty is being applied fairly."

According to a federal study by the Bureau of Justice Statistics, 2005 saw fewer prisoners moved to death row and only one more execution than 2004.

Half of the 3,254 inmates awaiting execution in U.S. prisons at the end of 2005 were held in four states—California, Texas, Florida and Pennsylvania; another 37 were held in federal prison.

A total of 60 prisoners were executed in 2005 by 16 states, one more inmate than 2004. The overall number of inmates on death row on December 31, 2005, however, and the number of inmates moved there throughout the year dropped.

DNA testing, questions about the effectiveness of public defenders and other factors have raised issues about whether the death penalty is being applied fairly. As a result, the number of prisoners sentenced to death has dropped in recent years.

In 2005—the third consecutive year with a decline in year-long totals—128 inmates were moved to death row. That was the lowest number moved there since 1973. There were sixty-six fewer inmates on death row at the end of that year than the year before—the fifth straight year a decline occurred. There were also 10% fewer death row inmates at the end of 2005 than on December 31, 2000, when there were 3,601 death row prisoners nationwide.

As of the first of December, 2006 saw 52 executions according to data provided by the Death Penalty Information Center, a nonprofit research group.

Juries are allowed to consider the death penalty in federal and 38 state courts. All of those states except Nebraska allow lethal injection in executions. Nebraska allows electrocution, along with eight other states. Four states permit lethal gas, three death by hanging, and another three death by firing squad.

The Justice Department study reported at the close of 2005, 56% of death row inmates were white and 42% were black. Of those facing execution, 2% are women. Tennessee housed 101 death row inmates on January 3, 2007. ✍

Maryland short on prison guards

The *Baltimore Sun* reported in November that the state of Maryland spent more than $28 million on overtime pay in 2005—"nearly twice as much as the year before"—because it cannot find enough people to work in its prisons.

Hiring has been difficult because the prisons have been "racked by violence and other problems," leaving 630 vacancies in a system that is suppose to have 6,325 officers. "In some of the prisons, vacancy rates were as high as 30%" as of August.

Acting prison chief John Rowley says, "We're not exactly a vocation that people wake up ... when they are young and say, 'I can't wait to become a corrections officer.'"

—Garry W. Johnson, MOUNTAIN REVIEW Staff

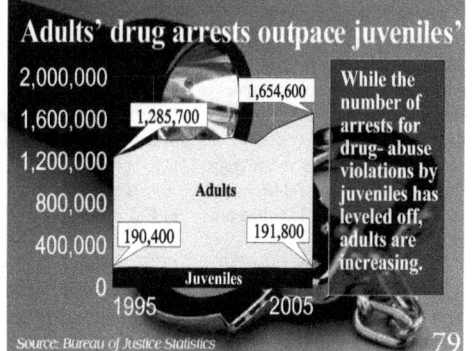

Adults' drug arrests outpace juveniles'

While the number of arrests for drug-abuse violations by juveniles has leveled off, adults are increasing.

2,000,000
1,654,600
1,600,000 1,285,700
1,200,000 Adults
800,000
400,000 190,400   191,800
Juveniles
0   1995   2005
Source: Bureau of Justice Statistics

A federal panel wants to experiment on you

At Philadelphia's Holmesburg Prison and other correctional facilities across the country, inmates were treated as human guinea pigs in gruesome medical experiments from the late 1940's to the mid-1970's. The prisoners were payed a few hundred dollars a month to be "volunteers" but were not told they had signed up for exposure to chemical warfare agents and radioactive, hallucinogenic and cancer-causing chemicals.

In Washington and Oregon more than 100 prisoners were paid $10 a month to have their testicles irradiated by government researchers. Prisoners in Pennsylvania were among those given LSD and other hallucinogens by military scientist and had dioxin rubbed into their skin. These abuses continued until Congress passed a law in 1978 limiting testing on inmates to research involving only the most minimal risk. Private companies in Arkansas and Arizona continued to use prisoners as plasma donors until the early 1990's.

The Institute of Medicine now wants the government to loosen the prohibitions on federally funded medical experimentation on prisoners. They propose a new tough oversight regime to prevent the abuses of the past and limit experiments to those that have a direct potential benefit to prisoners.

Given that prisoners are a convenient source of test subjects and prison is an inherently coercive environment—not to mention the long, sordid and well documented history of prison research—this issue is bound for a long debate. ✍

Civilian mortality rate higher than prisoners'

The Justice Department's Bureau of Justice Statistics reported January 21, that state prison inmates, particularly blacks, have lower mortality rates on average than people on the outside.

The overall population of free-world people between ages 15 and 64 die at a yearly rate of 308 per 100,000, compared with 250 per 100,000 for state inmates. The overall black free-world population has a death rate 57% higher than black inmates: 484 per 100,000 vs. 206.

White and Hispanic free-worlders both have death rates slightly below their prisoner counterparts.

From 2001 through 2004 the report found that 12,129 state prisoners died. Of those, 89% were due to medical reasons, two-thirds of which already had the medical problem they died of before being admitted to prison. Of the remainder, 8% were killed or committed suicide, 2% died due to alcohol, drugs or accidental injuries, and 1% of the deaths could not be explained. ✍

Recidivism prevalent among criminal immigrants

Justice Department Inspector General Glenn Fine reported in January that illegal immigrants caught and released back into the USA may have been rearrested as many as six times.

Fine reviewed the most recent completed data available—that of 2002—and sampled 100 arrested illegal immigrants. He found that 73 of the 100 illegals were collectively rearrested 429 times, on charges ranging from traffic tickets to weapons and drug violations.

Precisely how many of the illegal immigrants charged with criminal histories had been rearrested the audit did not conclude. It did note that if the results are "indicative of the full population of 262,105 criminal histories, the rate at which released criminal aliens are rearrested is extremely high."

Congress ordered the audit in 2005 to examine how local and state authorities which received federal funding to help catch and detain illegal immigrants are working with Homeland Security. Michael Chertoff, Secretary of Homeland Security declared in September an end to the "catch and release" policy that helped many illegal immigrants stay in the USA unhindered for years. ✍

Repeat violent offenders concentrated in urban areas

The Department of Justice released a study in August showing that half of all reported violent crimes from 1990 to 2002 occurred in the nation's 75 most populous counties. More than half of those convicted of violent felonies in these areas had previous convictions—38% had felony convictions and 15% of those were violent crimes such as murder, rape, robbery or assault. The remaining 18% had prior misdemeanors.

Of the violent urban felons, 91% were male; 88% pleaded guilty; and 81% came to prison. From 1990-2002 there were 180,298 reported crimes in these areas. Of that total, 38% were drug crimes; 32.7% were property crimes; and 18.2% were violent crimes.

In June of 2002 the Bureau of Justice Statistics released a report saying that recidivism overall was lowest among those arrested for homicide (41%), sexual assault (41%), and rape (46%). The highest recidivism rates were for stealing cars (79%), stealing or possessing other stolen property (77%) and larceny (75%). Of released convicts, younger people and those with longer criminal records were the most likely to be arrested again. ✍

Several states suspend executions, Tennessee to rewrite procedures

Tennessee added its name to the list of states suspending the death penalty in February, when Governor Phil Bredesen postponed four pending executions citing the state's outdated and jumbled procedure for lethal injection (see side bar, right).

In March the state Medical Board of North Carolina effectively halted that state's death penalty by threatening to discipline any doctor who takes part in an execution. Questions over whether lethal injection is unconstitutionally painful have halted executions in Florida, California and Missouri and are likely to curb the use of the death penalty across the USA, according to analysts.

It is unclear whether the increasing focus represents a significant and lasting turn against the death penalty or a temporary slowdown in executions that will end once procedures for injections are improved.

Deborah Denno, a professor at Fordham University Law School says, "I think we're headed towards fewer executions." Denno, who was on the U.S. Sentencing Commission from 1994 to 1997, says a range of problems in the nation's death penalty system—unqualified public defenders, the need for more DNA testing and questions about lethal injections, for example—have prevented capital punishment from being applied fairly.

Kent Scheidegger calls the controversy over lethal injection "a significant but temporary setback" for capital punishment that will lead to fewer executions only until problems with injections are resolved. Scheidegger, legal director of the Criminal Justice Legal Foundation which supports the death penalty, notes that public opinion surveys consistently show two-thirds of Americans support the death penalty.

Former Governor Jeb Bush suspended executions in Florida in December and appointed a panel to examine whether lethal injection represents an unconstitutional "cruel and unusual punishment" under the Eighth Amendment. Bush's decision came after the December 13th execution of Angel Nieves Diaz, which took a state execution team two injections and 34 minutes —more than twice the usual time. Needles used to administer the three-chemical mix were not inserted directly into Diaz's veins, according to a state medical examiner. In February the panel concluded that conflicting information from witnesses, prison staff and medical experts made it impossible to make findings on Diaz's execution. "The findings we really couldn't make—was did this man suffer," said Circuit Judge Stan Morris, one of four panelists who was drafting the commission's final report.

California's lethal injection was ruled in violation of the Eight Amendment by federal Judge Jeremy Fogel in San Jose shortly after Bush's announcement. Fogel left open the possibility that the state could come up with an acceptable protocol for executions.

Bredesen expects Tennessee to resume executing inmates after state officials complete a "comprehensive review" and reworking of the execution guidelines by the May 2nd deadline. ✍

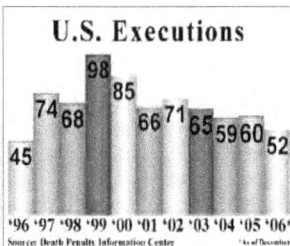

U.S. Executions

Bar chart values by year: '96: 45, '97: 74, '98: 68, '98: 98, '99: 85, '00: 66, '01: 71, '02: 65, '03: 59, '04: 60, '05: 52, '06.

Source: Death Penalty Information Center * As of December

Who's watching me?

Percentage of male and female stalking victims who know their stalker:

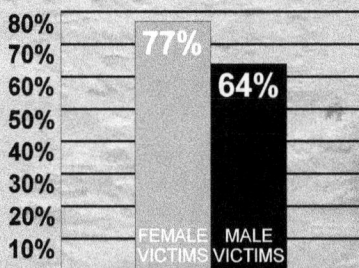

FEMALE VICTIMS: 77%
MALE VICTIMS: 64%

(Graphics and reporting by Garry W. Johnson, Mountain Review Staff)

Source: The National Center for Victims of Crimes

Excerpts from Tennessee's "Manual of Execution"

Governor Phil Bredesen calls the document a "cut-and-paste job" that mingles instructions for lethal injection with those for electrocution. The manual list the following steps for executing prisoners:

1. The warden shall contact the commissioner to insure that no last-minute stay has been granted.

2. The warden will permit the condemned inmate to make a last statement.

3. The extraction team will secure the head set.

4. The facility manager will check the electrodes to insure they are properly attached.

5. The assistant facility manager will proceed to electrical control panel and activate for execution.

6. The warden will give the signal to proceed, and the executioner will engage the automatic rheostat. The administrative assistant or designate will record the time the process began. When the current has been on for the required time, the rheostat will disengage automatically.

7. Once the cycle runs its course, the facility manager will indicate the current is off. The administrative assistant or designate will record the time the current is disengaged.

8. The Facility manager will disconnect electrical cables in rear of chair.

9. Following the completion of the lethal injection process, and a five-minute waiting period, with the blinds to the official witness room closed, closed-circuit TV camera disengaged, and privacy curtain closed, the warden will ask the physician to enter the room to conduct an examination. If the inmate is not dead, the physician will return to the designated waiting area. The curtain will be opened, blinds raised, camera activated, and the warden shall give the command to repeat the lethal injection procedure. After this procedure is completed, the blinds once again will be closed, closed circuit TV camera disengaged, and the privacy curtain closed. The warden once again will ask the physician to enter the room and check for signs of life. The physician shall then report his findings to the warden or designee.

10. The inmate is pronounced dead. The administrative assistant or designate records the time that death is pronounced.

Source: "Manual of Execution," Tennessee Department of Execution; Associated Press

Should juveniles be in the joint?

Get-tough legislation in the early 90's put more teenagers in adult prison, but a wave of new research suggests that line of reasoning was in error.

Young convicts

Number of inmates younger than 18 in adult jails and prisons:

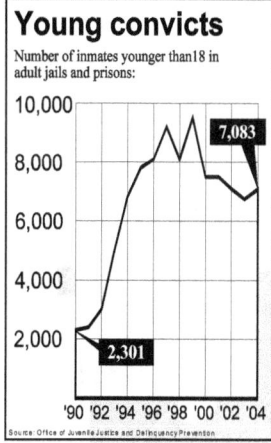

In September leading researchers met with directors of state juvenile justice systems, judges, prosecutors and attorneys in a two-day summit. They met to discuss how the new evidence should affect treatment of teen offenders.

Psychologist Laurence Steinberg says, "We know so much more about the adolescent brain and behavior than we used to, and we want to get these facts into the hands of people who can make a difference." Steinberg heads a network of researchers and juvenile-justice workers financed by the MacArthur Foundation, which sponsored the meeting.

Beginning in 1992, every state except Nebraska made it easier to try juveniles as adults, and most states have legalized harsher sentences as well. A judge's discretion is also limited by several states which send all teens who commit serious offenses directly to adult court, or allowing prosecutors to opt for adult prosecution.

Although that may sound reasonable, it can be unfair, according to Kimberly O' Donnell, chief judge of the Juvenile and Domestic Relations District Court in Richmond, Virginia. As an example, she points to a group of 14-year-olds tried as adults for "assault by a mob"—essentially ganging up on and hurting a child in school.

O' Donnell notes that "once you're tried as an adult, you're always an adult, which can have awful consequences." She says if any of these teens are ever arrested again, prosecutors can use the threat of lengthy prison sentences as leverage to gain a plea agreement that might not be in the child's best interest.

Shay Bilchik, president and CEO of the Child Welfare League of America, says there is firm evidence that teens prosecuted as adults are much more likely to commit crimes when they get out than comparable young people tried as juveniles.

He attributes these facts to juvenile facilities having better educational, job training, drug abuse and mental health treatment programs than adult prisons. Bilchik, former head of the federal Office of Juvenile Justice and Delinquency Prevention, also notes that teens in juvenile facilities are not learning from adults how to be career criminals.

That is not to say kids do not commit serious crimes before landing in adult jails, says psychologist Elizabeth Cauffman of the University of California-Irvine. She says some even score in the psychopathic range on written tests that predict which adults are likely to commit future crimes. These tests are sometimes used in deciding whether young people should get severe punishments or be tried as adults.

Cauffman says it is a dubious practice. Her studies show while adult scores are usually stable, adolescents tend to move away from this psychopath profile when they are tracked for a couple of years.

She points out that parents of most teenagers are all too familiar with some of the hallmarks of psychopathy, such as thrill-seeking, impulsivity and failure to accept responsibility. In effect, behaviors most youth grow out of.

Thomas Grisso, a psychologist at the University of Massachusetts Medical School in Worcester says many younger children are not even competent to stand trial because they do not understand the trial process or can not make decisions about pleas. He is training U.S. juvenile court workers to determine juvenile competence using guidelines he developed.

Other MacArthur network scientists challenge common assumptions about teenage criminals with their new findings. One study, for example, tracked 1,355 serious offenders for three years. It found that less than 10% of those heavily involved in criminal activites at the outset continued that level of involvement over the years. The study leader Edward Mulvey of the University of Pittsburgh Medical School says, "A lot of policy is driven by the view that if a kid does a felony assault, he must be a bad actor from here on forward."

Even so, 57% had at least one more arrest within two years. "Plus, we know arrests represent only the tip of the iceberg," says Adrian Raine, a psychologist at the University of Southern California who studies criminal behavior. "Who really knows how much else they did that they weren't caught for?"

He says that long-term studies of highly aggressive children suggest that some are headed for a life of violent crime and should be locked up early because they are dangerous. Raine recognizes that brain damage or family qualities may cause their behavior, "But it's naive to think many of these very violent kids are going to stop, and we don't need to be protected from them."

In the study headed by Mulvey, researchers found that better parenting and long-term treatment for drug or alcohol abuse directly correlated with less criminal behavior.

Teen crime

Percentage of arrests for selected crimes in 2003 by age:

■ Under 18   ☐ Over 18

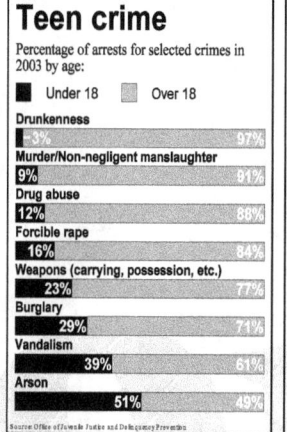

Bilchik, a former prosecutor of Juvenile cases in Miami for 16 years, understands why research has been slow to translate into action. He explains, "When you've got a kid in front of you who's done a vicious armed robbery with a beating, it's different than an intellectual argument about what works. Prosecutors think, 'Can I really make myself try him as a juvenile? Can I even get permission from my boss?'"

In some cases prosecutors know a particular juvenile system has scant mental health treatment or rehabilitation and would rather lock up a dangerous teen with adults than risk a slap on the wrist, according to Bilchik. And when troubled young people are let out there is often little follow-up monitoring by youth workers. Still, despite the short-term appeal of adult prison, he says they are not usually the long-term answer. "We have the research that tells us what to do. The tragedy is, we're not capitalizing on it."

As Rain and Mulvey both noted, better parenting can turn a child around. In the U.S. it is estimated that more than 7.3 million children have one or more parent in jail or prison. Without intervention 70% of those children are likely to follow in their parent's footsteps. ✍

Claims of sexual-attack rise in prison

The Justice Department reported in July that the federal government recorded 6,241 allegations of sexual violence by federal, state and local inmates in 2005—that is about 2.8 allegations per 1,000 inmates, up from 2.5 allegations per 1,000 inmates in 2004. Allen Beck and Paige Harrison of the Bureau of Justice Statistics say there may be more sexual violence in prison than reported because inmates fear reprisal, adhere to a code of silence, do not trust the staff or are embarrassed. The federal Prison Rape Elimination Act of 2003 allowed for the information to be collected. About 45% of the allegations were against other inmates; 55% were made against guards and other staff. ✍

Convicted killer sells effects on Internet

Nathaniel Bar-Jonah, serving 130 years in Montana State Prison for kidnaping, sexually assaulting and hanging a teen neighbor from his ceiling, is selling his letters, court documents, shoes and other paraphernalia on the Internet.

The Great Falls Tribune reported thirty items said to belong to Bar-Jonah "ranging in price from $5 for a signed letter and envelope to $3,000 for police reports" are available at the website murderauction.com. "Bar-Jonah is mailing his belongings to a woman in Saint George, Utah, who sells (them) on his behalf."

According to the Tribune, Montana has no law against what Bar-Jonah is doing, although prison policy does forbid convicts from running a business. Bob Anez, spokesman for the Montana Department of Correction, told the paper that his agency will investigate. ✍

Solitary confinement linked to inmate suicides

"... solitary confinement units counted for 69% of 2005's inmate suicides. Roughly half of last year's suicides were also in solitary units."

The nation's two largest state prison systems are reporting increasing suicides among their inmates. Authorities in California and Texas say increased use of solitary confinement is to blame.

California, the largest of the state systems with an inmate population of about 170,000, reported 41 suicides by December 27, 2006. That figure constitutes a 17% increase from 2005 and is the most suicides in at least six years.

Known as "administrative segregation," where inmates are isolated for 23 hours a day, solitary confinement units counted for 69% of 2005's inmate suicides. Roughly half of last year's suicides were also in solitary units.

The Texas system has 169,000 inmates and reported 24 suicides over the same period in 2006 and 22 in 2005. John Moriarty, inspector general for the prison system, says most inmates who killed themselves in Texas were in some form of solitary confinement.

Although California statistics on attempted suicides were not immediately available, Texas reported at least a 17% increase last year. By the December report there were 652 attempted suicides in 2006, up from 559 in 2005. According to prison records, those are the most attempted suicides in nearly a decade.

Of the 1.5 million inmates in state and federal prison, more than 70,000 are kept in isolation. These inmates typically have significant restrictions on visitors and get little help in dealing with the psychological effects of their confinement. Most are allowed out of their cells for no more than an hour a day to exercise alone; their exposure to TV and reading material is also limited.

There is a growing debate over the use of solitary confinement to control or punish violent or dangerous inmates, especially those who are mentally ill. Moriarty, whose office investigates every inmate death in Texas ask, "are we housing the mentally ill in prison facilities? I think the answer is yes. But I don't know if that's the best place for them to be." He goes on to say stress from isolation and increasing numbers of inmates with long sentences have contributed to the increased number of inmate suicides. "Length of sentence is a big factor. There is despair about not getting out."

In the federal prison system there were 13 suicides by December 27 of last year. The federal system houses 188,000 inmates and they reported the same total number of suicides in 2005. The third largest state system, Florida, reported nine prison suicides in its 90,000 inmate population—up one from the eight suicides reported in 2005. The *Mountain Review* was unable to obtain the TDOC suicide numbers for 2006. The annual report for the fiscal year 2003-2004 shows only one inmate suicide. ✍

Reporting by,
—Garry W. Johnson

Christmas
from page 01

chicken in addition to other items. Inmates from units 14, 15, and 16 pass on their warmest gratitude for the generosity of all those involved in making this night possible. Timothy Winegar, an inmate worker said, "Being around loving people has warmed my heart and opened my mind."

Tuesday, December 19, St. John's Baptist Church brought homemade food and deserts for units 11, 12, and 13. Individuals from several other churches also helped St. Johns. These were members of Mother Love Church, Lenoir City Church of God, Pilgrim Temple Church, and St. Peter Primitive

Christmas Banquet Participants
Faith Promise Baptist Church
United Christian Church
Providence Baptist Church
Covenant Presbyterian Church
First Christian Church
Lighthouse Baptist Church
St. John's Baptist Church
Covenant Ministry Center
River of Life Church
Focus Prison Ministries

Baptist Church. Pastor Colquitt entertained the inmates as the volunteers cheerfully served food. Muh's legendary tea was one of the highlights as usual. Inmates from these units wish to thank St. John's and others for the hard work and dedication evidenced in the meal and fellowship. St. John's holds services monthly in the chapel. Check the unit bulletin boards for exact date and time.

Last, but not least, River of Life Church anchored the Christmas banquets. River of Life, near Chattanooga, has been ministering at MCCX since 1994. Pastor Alan Crider, 24 volunteers, and special guest Sam Gooden brought the inmates an evening of ministry, fellowship, and love.

They also brought a delicious traditional turkey and dressing dinner. Sam Gooden was a founding member of the music group, The Impressions. He is also a member of the Rock and Roll Hall of Fame. Pastor Crider explained, during his sermon, that more than 30 years ago he was in jail. During the night, he was faced with the futility of his ways and decided that he did not want to continue living life the same way he had been living. He recognized his need of salvation and trusted in Jesus Christ. Today he looks back on his life with gratitude for what Jesus has done for him. He knows that Jesus can do it for others as well. After praying, they served dinner. Volunteers from River of life graciously served tea and desert while inmates ate. Near the end of the night, inmates and guests alike were treated with the singing of Sam Gooden accompanied by the chapel band. Inmates from units 8, 9, and 10 thank all those who made this night possible. River of Life holds a service on the first, second, third, and fifth Saturday night in the chapel (7:00) and at the Annex (5:30). All are invited to attend.

Treat Bags
Big Emory Baptist Association

Special Thanks To
Unit Manager Craig Williams for access to the newspaper camera, and Knox County Commissioner Diane Jordan for her support.

The *Mountain Review* would like to thank Unit Manager Craig Williams for allowing the use of the camera during the banquets his team supervised. Mr. Williams graciously picked the camera up from school and returned it each time his team had a banquet. We also would like to thank Unit Team Four and the rest of the administration for allowing these Christmas banquets to continue. We all look forward to this Christmas and the blessings we will receive. ✍

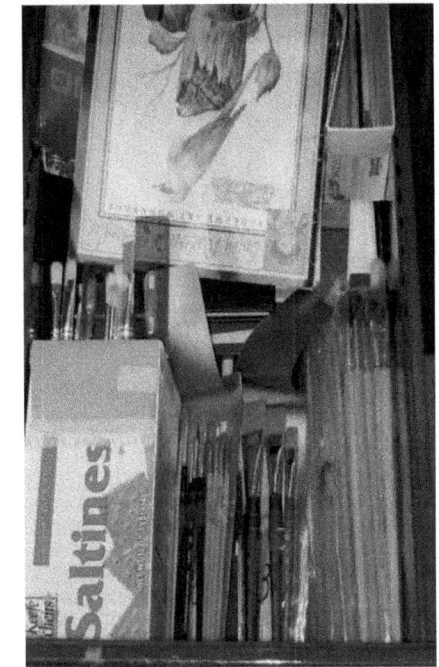

VARSITY CLUB ART CLASS

By Randall McPheeters

The Varsity Club is hosting an Arts and Crafts Workshop in the library classroom on Sunday mornings from 8:00 a.m. to 10:00 a.m. Some very nice local people donated various materials for painting with acrylic and/or water color paints and color-pencil art work. The workshop is overseen by the Varsity Club Sponsor, Librarian Pat Lynch and facilitated by Inmate Patrick Stansberry.

Anyone can attend the Sunday morning workshops and participate in the crafts. We try to keep it from becoming a classroom atmosphere, so people will feel more free to create. However, when someone needs help, we try to be sure someone is available to answer questions and help out. We paint, and or draw all morning and the people who know how to work with certain materials help show the other guys how to use them as well. The Varsity Club is very proud to be a part of this project and very grateful to our free-world patrons and the administrative staff who have been so helpful. ✍

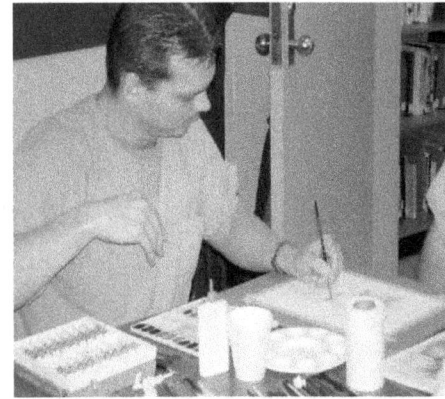

The Journey

By Cecil "Bo" Smith

Cursed are those who bare false witness against others.

We must go on with our lives now, without hate in our hearts and without resentment in our eyes. For money or position will play no part on our day of judgment. I have confessed my sins to God and man and that is more than many will ever do.

For those who cannot obey the laws in which they make for themselves, will surely never obey the laws of God. Many believe that man must sometimes suffer torment on earth in order to be better prepared to walk in the presence of God.

For my name is written in the book of life as I ask forgiveness for my worldly sins, I will prepare my soul with love for the days of atonement.

'The world is merely a small part of our journey. Soon we will all rest high upon the mountain, where we will reunite with our loved ones and walk hand in hand in the garden of Eden and feast from the tree of life.

What a joyous time it will be to rejoice in the very presence of God. That is what we have to look forward to, so let your hearts fill with joy.

I have lose nothing, but gained everything in the love of friends, family and the love of God. ✍

No Mail For Me

By Sammy Goff

I get my hopes up each day at two,
That's shift change and mail call you see,
Now I go back to my cell all down and blue,
No words of love on paper today for me.

Dear God help me make it this night,
Let me dream of loved ones so dear,
Visions of the past please bring to light,
As I sleep in peace without hurt or fear. ✍

MUSIC CORNER

In this installment I am going to discuss chord theory. I will explain the construction of the four chords I showed you in my last installment of *Music Corner*. Those four chords are the major, minor, seventh, and minor seventh.

Chord Construction
By Charlie Brandler

Before I can explain how the different chords are built, I must first explain a little about music and how to play or make a major scale. It would be very helpful for you to have and understand a copy of my first installment entitled *Reading Tablature and Playing Scales*. In it a chart shows all the notes on the neck of the guitar and how to play a C major scale. I will be using the C major scale for my examples since it is the only major scale without any sharps (♯) or flats (♭) in it.

For those of you who do not have a copy of my first article, Figure 1 is the chart with all the notes on each of the six strings of the guitar. It is important for you to see and know there are no sharps (♯) or flats (♭) between the notes E and F, and the notes B and C. There are many uses for this information including chord construction, playing scales, and finding chords and/or notes on different strings.

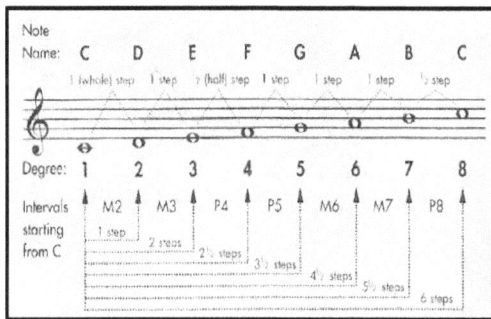

GUITAR FINGERBOARD CHART

Figure 1

If you play any note on the guitar, and then play a note one fret in either direction, the distance between these two notes is called a half step. Now play another note followed by a note two frets in either direction. The distance between these two notes is a whole step or the equivalent of two half steps. Of course three frets apart would be a step and a half or one and a half steps. A whole step (two frets) is also referred to as one step. Therefore four frets apart would be two steps, and so on. The distance between any two notes is called an interval. The chart in Figure 2 is very simple to read. It shows a C major scale. The note names are above the music staff. Below it are the degree numbers and the interval chart. I will use the degree numbers to explain the construction of the chords.

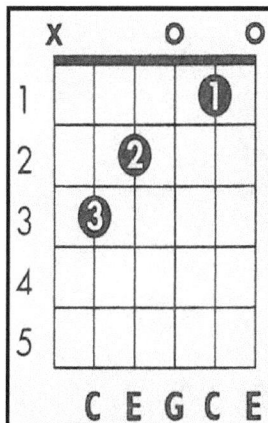

Figure 2

the chords.

Now that you know what steps are, you should remember that to make a major scale in any key (starting at any note) you have to use the formula of whole step, whole step, half step, whole step, whole step, whole step, half step as shown below the note names in Figure 2. In other words, there are two frets (or one step) from C to D, and from D to E. There is only one fret (half step) from E to F. There is a whole step from F to G, G to A, and A to B. Of course, from B to C is only one fret, or a half step.

Using the scale degrees as a guide, I will show you how to make the four chords mentioned at the beginning of this article.

All major chords are made up of the first, third, and fifth notes of the major scale. Looking at the degree chart you can see that C is the first note, E is the third, and G is the fifth. Figure three shows an open C major chord. You can see that it has the notes in order. The C note is on the third

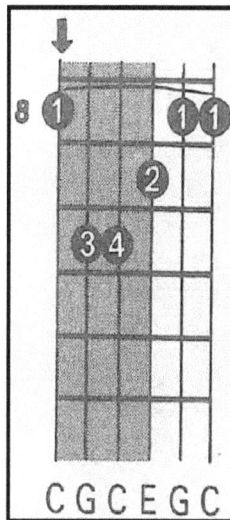

Figure 4

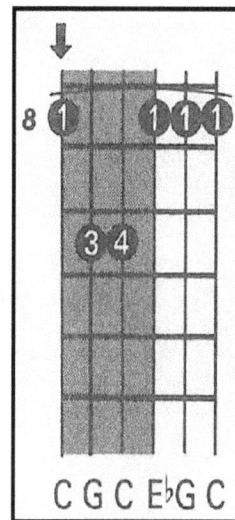

Figure 5

fret of the A string, the E note is on the second fret of the D string, and the G note is on the open G string. Those three notes played together form a C chord. The other two notes of C on the first fret of the B string and the open E string on the bottom are just extra to make the chord sound more full. You can see that the chord is made up of only the notes C, E, and G. Figure 4 shows the same chord played as a Barre chord at the eighth fret. Now there are three C notes, two G notes, and the one E note on the ninth fret of the G string (third string). Again, see that though some notes are repeated to make the chord sound more full, there are still just the three notes of C, E, and G.

To make a minor chord, you simply take the third note in the scale, in this case the E note, and make it smaller by one fret (or a half step) so that it is now an E♭ (E flat) note. Figure 5 shows a C minor (Cm) chord. Notice that the one E note that is at the ninth fret in the C major chord has now been moved down a half step to an E♭ note at the eighth fret. I call this flattening the third. Any time you reduce a note by lowering it one fret (half step), you have flattened that note.

Figure 6 shows a C7 chord. All you do is use the three notes that comprise the C major chord, C, E, and G, and add a minor seven note. To find that note simply find the seventh note in the scale (in this case it is a B note) and flatten that note to make it a minor seven. Now it becomes a B♭ note. If you compare the C major chord in Figure 4 with the C7 chord in Figure 6, you can see that all you have to do is remove your fourth finger from the tenth fret of the D string, so that it is now barred at the eighth fret with your first finger. That C note just became a B♭ note, and that B♭ added to the other notes—C, E, and G—form a C7 chord. If you do not flatten the seventh note in the scale (B), then it would be a C major seven chord.

Figure 7 shows a C minor seven (Cm7) chord. Understanding it is just as easy. By comparing the Cm in Figure 5 with the C in Figure 4 you can see that I flattened the third (E) by removing my second finger from the ninth fret of the third string. It is now barred at the eighth fret making it an E♭ note. I just explained how to add the minor seventh note of B♭ by removing your fourth finger from the tenth fret of the D or fourth string. Comparing Figure 7 with Figure 4 you can see that to make a Cm7 chord from a C major chord all you have to do is remove your second and fourth fingers

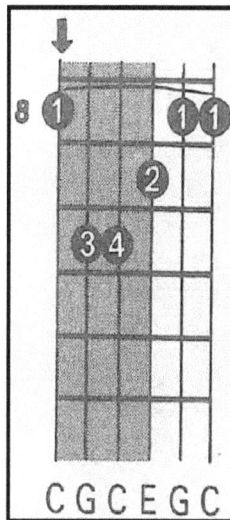

(Figure 3 — open C major chord)

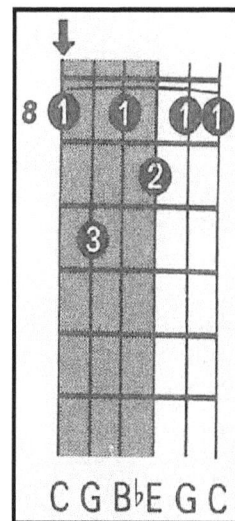

Figure 6

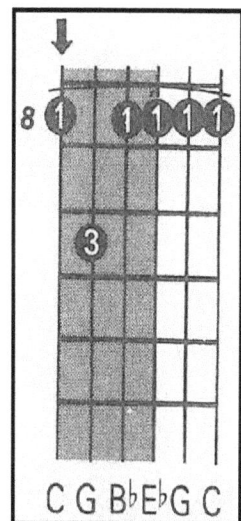

Figure 7

so that you are barring all the strings at the eighth fret with your first finger and fretting the G note at the tenth fret with your third finger. As I said in my last installment, these fingering positions or shapes will work in any key by using the charts in my last installment of *Music Corner*.

Knowing how these chords are made up will help you to reference them quicker, especially when making them in other keys. Hopefully I have helped expand your knowledge of scales, chords, and of course, the notes on the neck. That is all I have for now. Feel free to see me for further details or questions you may have. Until next time, keep practicing. ✍

Nothing Belongs to Me
By Michael Coatney

Received 3 votes

I used to think that everything I had belonged to me—
my family, all my possessions.
I knew God, my Father and that He loved me.
But one day I turned my back
away from Him and let sin enter in.
Then I realized that I was so wrong
because nothing belongs to me.

Friend are you tired and weary—
are your burdens too heavy to bear?
Listen to me, I've been there before—
everything that I had, it was gone.
I lost my home and my family,
then Jesus reminded me, nothing belongs to me.

Chorus:

Oh nothing belongs to me.
Jesus bought it all with His precious
blood He shed on Calvary.
There He suffered for all the world to see,
as He did on that tree.
But praise God, on the third day He arose
and now I know, nothing belongs to me.
Jesus bought us with a price—
the supreme sacrifice, and nothing belongs to me.

A Path Well Chosen
By Chester E. Williams

Received 1 vote

While traveling down the path of life
A road once lonely walked
A backward glance I often took
To see where I had been

I saw that rest was not often taken
A brief stop here and there
But not enough to brush away
The clouds that filled my mind

The hearts desire was for companionship
That I never seemed to find
Once there was a ring to wear
Somehow it did not measure

One day along the path
A choice came to be made
The direction not marked by sign
I took a turn I did not know

Traveling lonely an unused way
A still voice came to me
I walked a step real lightly
Pain I did not seek

I passed a weary traveler
By the path he had lain
I could not go any further
Stopped to hear what he had to say

Love comes to those who do not seek
A path they have known
In walking with eyes closed
Love finds them all alone

I walked a little further
And in time his words came true
The love I sought was before me
On a path that led to you.

Seconds of a Summer Hour
By Ellis Coleman

Received 2 votes

Fleeting like a wind driven leaf
That lost its grip on a tree;
Were the seconds of a summer hour,
So I lived them sacredly.

Nature allotted me precious jewels:
A breeze, the flowers, and sunshine;
I took a moment to notice them all;
They do deserve my time.

Synchronized, yet distinctively proud,
Right by my barefoot feet;
Two dandelions torn in the breeze
Performing for God and me.

The seconds of a summer hour;
Easy days and simple fun;
Green grass, smiles, a sun charmed child
Whose time had just begun.

By Jonathan A. Upchurch, *Received 1 vote*

Three Dog Town
By Charles E. Jackson

Received 1 vote

It's Friday evening with a steady downpour,
The storm is coming so close the door.
The night is calling, it itches my heart,
So tell me baby why don't we start,
a new beginning in a place far away,
I've got to leave here, I don't want to stay.
Two weeks pay and a full tank of gas,
We'll ride my Harley, she sure goes fast.
So hold on tight and be by my side,
The storm is above us on this one way ride.
There's no turning back and there's no giving in,
Our love is forever, your my best friend.
I don't want to loose you, but I don't want to stay,
Cause this three dog town is fading away!

From My Window
By Chester E. Williams

Received 1 vote

From my window there is no view
Day is present only from the shadow of light
Clouds roll by but are out of sight
Trees sway in the breeze not seen
Birds rest on the window sill
But only their shadow do I see
I listen for the song they sing
No sound do I hear, it's there I know
Locked in the recesses of my memory

Night falls so darkly without view
Does the moon glow or the stars shine
I search for the visions from my mind
Can I wish on what I don't see
Surely it's there I must believe
Time passes from shadows in front of my eyes
The fragrance of night is beyond my sense
I long to feel it's cool embrace
If only it could change glass to lace

Blue skies and moonlight recreated from heart
Raindrops and snowflakes do not touch my face
Reach for the life beyond this space
Drawn from my memory the place to begin
All that I see comes from the light within
For out of my window there is no view.

Window Prayers
By Ellis Coleman

Received 1 vote

Looking through my window
Solemnly praying for you
Spring is exhaling
Oh what a view
The colors are reminders
Of how life can be renewed
And like this bright expression
Love again with you could too.

Chorus

So you are the subject
Of all my window prayers
A thousand prayers in this window
I hope Heaven cares.

Suddenly clouds grow dark
So hard it begins to pour
That the raindrops deceive me
As someone knocking at my door
Inclining me to believe
It was you like before.

The rain finally ends
Clear skies return
I wonder if you got wet
is my only concern.

Chorus

So you are the subject
Of all my window prayers
A thousand prayers in this window
I hope Heaven cares.

War & Suffering:
A Christian Perspective
By Jeremy Ingram
MOUNTAIN REVIEW Staff

In the mid-1800's a young missionary traveled to the South Pacific with his wife and infant son. In a few months, both his wife and son were dead. How can a Christian, who believes in a good God, explain something like this? If God is truly in control of all things, then why does He allow bad things to happen? This article will explore several areas of suffering. The idea that permeates this discussion on suffering is that only when a person believes that God has ordained suffering can one make sense of it.

GOD'S CONTROL DOES NOT CONFLICT WITH HUMAN RESPONSIBILITY

The first point is that God's control of all things does not do violence to human will. The Bible certainly affirms that God controls all things and at the same time the Bible affirms that man is morally responsible for his own choices, "See, I have set before you today life and prosperity, and death and adversity ... I call heaven and earth to witness against you today, that I have set before you life and death, the blessing and the curse. So choose life in order that you may live" (Deut 30: 15, 19). God is unchangeable. He is also holy and righteous. Therefore, it is impossible that God would do anything that goes against His character, "Far be it from You to do such a thing, to slay the righteous with the wicked, so that the righteous and the wicked are treated alike. Far be it from You! Shall not the Judge of all the earth deal justly?" (Gen 18:25). This implies that God is internally self-consistent. All His works are perfectly consistent with His nature, "For I, the LORD, do not change; therefore you, O sons of Jacob, are not consumed" (Mal 3:6). These verses just mentioned go to show that the blame for sin, evil, and the suffering in the world belong completely to the sinner, "For indeed, the Son of Man is going as it has been determined; but woe to that man by whom He is betrayed!" (Lk. 22:22); "this Man delivered over by the predetermined plan and foreknowledge of God, you nailed to a cross by the hands of godless men and put Him to death" (Acts 2:23).

GOD'S CONTROL IN RELATION TO WARS

The Bible presents war as a necessary human experience in this present evil world, "Now these are the nations which the LORD left, to test Israel by them (that is all who had not experienced any of the wars of Canaan; only in order that the generations of the sons of Israel might be taught war, those who had not experienced it formerly)" (Judges 3:1-2); "When you hear of wars and disturbances, do not be terrified; for these things must take place first, but the end does not follow immediately" (Luke 21:9); and, "You will be hearing of wars and rumors of wars. See that you are not frightened, for those things must take place, but that is not yet the end" (Matt. 24:6). The cause of war is attributed to men who forsake the Lord to pursue false gods, "New gods were chosen; then war was in the gates. Not a shield or a spear was seen among forty thousand in Israel" (Judges 5:8). In the history of mankind, there have been and are nations that profit the world nothing. These nations toil and produce nothing. Other nations are much worse. They are a hindrance to mankind and some are downright evil. The Bible says that God allows these nations to continue according to His purpose at which time they will fall, "For the vision is yet for the appointed time; it hastens toward the goal and it will not fail. Though it tarries, wait for it; for it will certainly come, it will not delay" (Hab. 2:3). Wars, then, are not a hindrance to God's plan but a part of it. The Bible says that God uses wars for a variety of reasons—to call men to repentance and as punishment for unbelievers, "And He will judge between the nations, and will render decisions for many peoples; and they will hammer their swords into plowshares and their spears into pruning hooks. Nation will not lift up sword against nation, and never again will they learn war" (Is. 2:4).

GOD'S CONTROL IN RELATION TO SUFFERING

One perennial question that mankind has faced over the millennia is: If God is in control, why do the righteous suffer while the evil apparently prosper? The Scripture does not deny that the righteous do suffer. The Bible declares about suffering that "It is the same for all. There is one fate for the righteous and for the wicked; for the good, for the clean and for the unclean; for the man who offers a sacrifice and for the one who does not sacrifice. As the good man is, so is the sinner; as the swearer is, so is the one who is afraid to swear" (Eccl 9:2). In

fact, the Scripture explains that behind the suffering of the righteous God's mysterious purposes are worked out. Job is an excellent book on suffering. Although Job never knew why God allowed him to suffer, in the end his faith was strengthened as he learned to trust in God's unchanging plan.

According to some erroneous theology prevalent in the church today, sickness and suffering are assumed to be a direct result of someone's sin. However, the Bible explains that in many cases, this isn't true, "And Jesus said to them, 'Do you suppose that these Galileans were greater sinners than all other Galileans because they suffered this fate? ... Or do you suppose that those eighteen on whom the tower in Siloam fell and killed them were worse culprits than all the men who live in Jerusalem?'" (Luke 13:2, 4); "And His disciples asked Him, 'Rabbi, who sinned, this man or his parents, that he would be born blind?' Jesus answered, 'It was neither that this man sinned, nor his parents; but it was so that the works of God might be displayed in him'" (John 9:2-3).

For the believer, suffering turns out to be a good thing for it frequently is a tool that God uses in the process of sanctification, "for I will show him how much he must suffer for My name's sake" (Acts 9:16); "I, John, your brother and fellow partaker in the tribulation and kingdom and perseverance which are in Jesus, was on the island called Patmos because of the word of God and the testimony of Jesus" (Rev 1:9). Since sanctification involves the putting off of sin and the putting on of holiness, it pleases God to use sufferings as a form of fatherly discipline, "My son, do not reject the discipline of the LORD or loathe His reproof, for whom the LORD loves He reproves, even as a father corrects the son in whom he delights" (Prov 3:11-12). However, the ungodly do not profit from such suffering. Still, suffering is used by God in some cases to restore a straying sinner, "Before I was afflicted I went astray, but now I keep your word" (Ps 119:67).

Therefore, suffering should be patiently endured by every Christian with the unyielding belief that God is in complete control and has very good reasons for what He does. He is working all things for the believers good, even through suffering and trials, "But if we are afflicted, it is for your comfort and salvation; or if we are comforted, it is for your comfort, which is effective in the patient enduring of the same sufferings which we also suffer" (2 Cor 1:6). There are five reasons the Bible gives for patiently enduring suffering.

1. Patiently enduring suffering brings glory to God, "He said, 'Naked I came from my mother's womb, and naked I shall return there. The LORD gave and the LORD has taken away. Blessed be the name of the LORD.' Through all this Job did not sin nor did he blame God" (Job 1:21-22); "But he said to her, 'You speak as one of the foolish women speaks. Shall we indeed accept good from God and not accept adversity?' In all this Job did not sin with his lips" (Job 2:10); "Then Job answered the LORD and said, 'I know that You can do all things, and that no purpose of yours can be thwarted. 'Who is this that hides counsel without knowledge?' Therefore I have declared that which I did not understand, things too wonderful for me, which I did not know. Hear, now, and I will speak; I will ask you, and you instruct me.' I have heard of you by the hearing of the ear; but now my eye sees you; Therefore I retract, and I repent in dust and ashes. The LORD restored the fortunes of Job when he prayed for his friends, and the LORD increased all that Job had twofold." (Job 42:1-6, 10).

2. Because Christ has been through what we are going through He is able to help us in our suffering, "For since He Himself was tempted in that which He has suffered, He is able to come to the aid of those who are tempted" (Heb 2:18).

3. Suffering is only temporary. Furthermore, the suffering of believers is always seasoned with the mercy of the Lord, "For the Lord will not reject forever, For if He causes grief, then He will have compassion according to His abundant lovingkindness. For He does not afflict willingly or grieve the sons of men" (Lam 3:31-33).

4. The believer is assured that God will not allow too much suffering to come upon him, "No temptation has overtaken you but such as is common to man; and God is faithful, who will not allow you to be tempted beyond what you are able, but with the temptation will provide the way of escape also, so that you will be able to endure it" (1 Cor 10:13). God knows how much His children can handle. He only allows what is beneficial to His children's good.

5. Despite how much or what kind of suffering comes upon him, the believer will never be separated from the love of God,

"Who will separate us from the love of Christ? Will tribulation, or distress, or persecution, or famine, or nakedness, or peril, or sword? Just as it is written, *for your sake we are being put to death all day long; we were considered as sheep to be slaughtered*. But in all these things we overwhelmingly conquer through Him who loved us. For I am convinced that neither death, nor life, nor angels, nor principalities, nor things present, nor things to come, nor powers, nor height, nor depth, nor any other created thing, will be able to separate us from the love of God, which is in Christ Jesus our Lord" (Rom 8:35-39).

Not only should the believer patiently endure sufferings, but he should also rejoice in them because of the benefits which come through these trials, "And not only this, but we also exult in our tribulations, knowing that tribulation brings about perseverance; and perseverance, proven character; and proven character, hope; and hope does not disappoint, because the love of God has been poured out within our hearts through the Holy Spirit who was given to us" (Rom 5:3-5). There are eight reasons why the believer should rejoice in sufferings.

1. Rejoicing in suffering is proof of the genuineness of faith, "so that the proof of your faith, being more precious than gold which is perishable, even though tested by fire, may be found to result in praise and glory and honor at the revelation of Jesus Christ" (1 Pet 1:7).

2. Suffering produces better Christian character, "Consider it all joy, my brethren, when you encounter various trials, knowing that the testing of your faith produces endurance. And let endurance have its perfect result, so that you may be perfect and complete, lacking in nothing" (James 1:2-4).

3. The greatest possession the believer has is knowledge that he is in fellowship with his God, "For I have been stricken all day long and chastened every morning. Nevertheless I am continually with you; you have taken hold of my right hand. With your counsel you will guide me, and afterward receive me to glory. Whom have I in heaven but you? And besides you, I desire nothing on earth. My flesh and my heart may fail, but God is the strength of my heart and my portion forever" (Ps 73: 14, 23-26); "Though the fig tree should not blossom and there be no fruit on the vines, though the yield of the olive should fail and the fields produce no food, though the flock should be cut off from the fold and there be no cattle in the stalls, Yet I will exult in the LORD, I will rejoice in the God of my salvation. The Lord GOD is my strength, and He has made my feet like hinds' feet and makes me walk on my high places." (Hab 3:17-19).

4. Through suffering the believer discovers God's comfort, "and our hope for you is firmly grounded, knowing that as you are sharers of our sufferings, so also you are sharers of our comfort" (2 Cor 1:7).

5. When the believer endures suffering, he can rejoice that he is more fit to encourage others through their suffering. Thus, suffering enables Christians to fulfill the law of love, "who comforts us in all our affliction so that we will be able to comfort those who are in any affliction with the comfort with which we ourselves are comforted by God" (2 Cor 1:4).

6. The believer can rejoice that he has learned a deeper meaning of life through suffering, "Sorrow is better than laughter, for when a face is sad a heart may be happy" (Eccl 7:3).

7. Rejoice because suffering is a preparation for heaven and a time of training, "but to the degree that you share the sufferings of Christ, keep on rejoicing, so that also at the revelation of His glory you may rejoice with exultation" (1 Pet. 4:13).

8. Suffering has a way of bringing good to others, "Now I want you to know, brethren, that my circumstances have turned out for the greater progress of the gospel, so that my imprisonment in the cause of Christ has become well known throughout the whole praetorian guard and to everyone else, and that most of the brethren, trusting in the Lord because of my imprisonment, have far more courage to speak the word of God without fear" (Phil 1:12-14); "but you know that it was because of a bodily illness that I preached the gospel to you the first time" (Gal 4:13).

Even though suffering can seem hard for a time, God can so use suffering in a believer's life so that the believer will look back on it with tremendous thanksgiving, "It is good for me that I was afflicted, that I may learn your statutes" (Ps 119:71).

In conclusion, only when a person is confident in the sovereignty of God and His complete control of all things can suffering and war make sense. Even though things may seem hard to understand, one can still look to God confidently and say, "Even so, Father, for so it seemeth good in thy sight." ✍

The Scripture presents the Lord Jesus Christ as at the same time being perfectly human and perfectly divine. Jesus is shown as eternally preexistent. He has no beginning because He was from all eternity. Isaiah 9:6 states, "For unto us a child is born, unto us a son is given."

The eternity and deity of Jesus Christ are shown extensively in Scripture which affirms His infinite person and His eternal existence, coequal with the other persons of the Godhead. John 1:1-2 states, "In the beginning was the Word, and the Word was with God, and the Word was God. The same was in the beginning with God." In Micah 5:2 it states, "But thou, Bethlehem Ephratah, though thou be little among the thousands of Judah, yet out of thee shall he come forth unto me that is to be ruler in Israel; whose goings forth have been from of old, from everlasting." Isaiah 7:14 affirms His virgin birth and gives the name Immanuel, which means "God with us." In Isaiah 9:6-7 Jesus is called "Mighty God." Jesus states in John 8:58, "Verily, verily, I say unto you, Before Abraham was, I am." The Jews understood this to be a claim for deity and eternity. Isaiah 43:13 states, "Yea, before the day was I am he; and there is none that can deliver out of my hand: I will work, and who shall let it? (turn it back)." In John 17:5 Christ in His prayer stated, "And now, O Father, glorify thou me with thine own self with the glory which I had with thee before the world was." Paul tells us in Phillipians 2:6 that Christ "being in the form of God, thought it not robbery to be equal with God." We see in many other Scripture verses that Jesus is God the Son and is part of the Trinity.

In 1 Timothy 3:16 it is stated, "And without controversy great is the mystery of godliness: God was manifest in the flesh, justified in the Spirit, seen of angels, preached unto the Gentiles, believed on in the world, received up into glory."

In Hebrews 1:2-3 the fact that the Son is the Creator and the express image of God is again stated, and His eternity is affirmed in Hebrew 13:8 (cf. Eph. 1:4; Rev. 1:11).

Those who accept the Bible as authoritative overwhelmingly affirm the eternity and deity of Christ. The Son of God is eternal and ever lasting. He was before all things and will be forever in existence.

To further show that Jesus is God the Son, we see the works of creation ascribed to Christ. In John 1:3 it states, "All things were made by him; and without him was not any thing made that was made." Him meaning the Word which is

Jesus Christ. In Colossians 1:15-16 God's Word tells us, "(Jesus) is the image of the invisible God, the firstborn of every creature: For by him were all things created, that are in heaven, and that are in earth, visible and invisible, whether they be thrones, or dominions, or principalities, or powers: all things were created by him, and for him." We see it stated in Hebrews 1:10 that Jesus was in the beginning and laid the FOUNDATION of the earth. "And, Thou, Lord (Jesus), in the beginning hast laid the foundation of the earth; and the heavens are the works of thine hands." Again, this shows that Christ proceeded in time all creations.

In John 12:45 we see that Jesus Himself said, "he that seeth me seeth him that sent me." Jesus is saying here that if you see Him, you see the Father, God. Also, in John 14:7-9 Jesus said, "he that hath seen me hath seen the Father." These statements by Jesus are stating that He is God.

The preexistence and eternity of the Son of God are implied in the fact that He has the attributes of God: life (Jn. 1:4), Self-existence (Jn. 5:26), immutability (Heb. 13:8), truth (Jn. 14:6), love (1 Jn. 3:16), holiness (Heb. 7:26), eternity (Col. 1:17; Heb. 1:11), omnipresence (Mt. 28:20), omniscience (1 Cor. 4:5; Col. 2:3), and omnipotence (Mt. 28:18; Rev. 1:8).

In like manner the preexistence and eternity of Christ are implied in the fact that He is worshiped as God (Jn. 20:28; Acts 7:59-60; Heb. 1:6). It follows that since the Lord Jesus Christ is God, He is from everlasting to everlasting.

The theme of the deity and eternity of the Son of God should be closely connected with the humanity of Christ through the Incarnation.

To further show that Jesus is God the Son we see him appear in the Old Testament as "The Angel of the Lord" (Jehovah). The appearance of Jesus in the Old Testament is called a Theophany, or a self-manifestation of God. Even though He appears at times as an angel or even as a man, He still bears the unmistakable marks of deity. He appears to Hagar (Gen. 16:7) and to Abraham (Gen. 18:1; 22:11-12). Again, Jesus appears to Jacob (Gen. 48:15-16). He appears to Moses (Ex. 3:2,14), to Joshua (Josh. 5:13-14) and to Manoah (Judg. 13:19-22). There are

many more appearances of Jesus in the Old Testament. Because the angel of the Lord ceases to appear after the incarnation, it is often inferred that the angel in the Old Testament is a preincarnate appearance of the second person of the Trinity.

Christ's appearances in the Old Testament shows that He fought for his own. In 2 Kings 19:35 God's words tells us, "And it came to pass that night, that the angel of the LORD went out, and smote in the camp of the Assyrians an hundred fourscore and five thousand: and when they arose early in the morning, behold, they were all dead corpses." We see this also in 1 Chronicles 21:15-16 and Zech. 14: 1-4.

In Psalm 34:7 God's word shows, "The angel of the LORD encampeth round about them that fear him, and delivereth them."

The deity of Jesus Christ is declared in Scripture: (1) In the intimations and explicit predictions of the Old Testament. (a)- The theophanies intimate the appearance of God in human form, and His ministry thus to man (Gen. 16:7-13; 18:2-23, especially v. 17; 32:28 with Hosea 12:3-5; Exodus 3:2-14). (b) The Messiah is expressly declared to be the Son of God (Ps. 2:2-9) and God (Ps. 45:67 with Hebrews 1:8 and 9; Ps. 110:1 with Mt. 22:44; Acts 2:34 and Heb. 1:13; Ps. 110:4 with Heb. 5:6; 6:20; 7:17-21 and Zech. 6:13). (c) His virgin birth was foretold as the means through which God could be "Immanuel," God with us (Isa. 7:13-14 with Mt. 1:22-23). (d) The Messiah is expressly invested with the divine names (Isa. 9:6-7). (e) In a prophecy of His death He is called Jehovah's "fellow" (Zech 13:7 with Mt. 26:32). (f) His eternal being is declared (Mic. 5:2 with Mt. 2:6; Jn. 7:42). (2) Christ Himself affirmed His deity. (a) He applied to Himself the Jehovistic I Am. (The pronoun "he" is not in the Greek; cf. Jn. 8:24; Jn. 8:56-58. The Jews correctly understood this to be our Lord's claim to full deity [vs.59]. See also, Jn. 10:33; 18:4-6, where also, "he" is not in the original). (b) He claimed to be Adonai of the Old Testament. (Mt. 22:42-45). (c) He asserted His identity with the Father (Mt. 28:19; Mk. 14:62; Jn. 10:30; that the Jews so understood Him is shown by vs. 31 and 32; Jn. 14:8-9; 17:5). (d) He exercised the

chief prerogative of God (Mk. 2:5-7; Lk. 7:48-50). (e) He asserted omnipresence (Mt. 18:20; Jn. 3:13); omniscience (Jn. 11:11-14, when Jesus was fifty miles away; Mk. 11:6-8); omnipotence (Mt. 28:18; Lk. 7:14; Jn. 5:21-23; 6:19); mastery over nature, and creative power (Lk. 9:16-17; Jn. 2:9; 10:28). (f) He received and approved human worship (Mt. 14:33; 28:9; Jn. 20:28-29).

The New Testament writers ascribe divine titles to Christ. John 1:1 shows us that "the Word was with God, and the Word was God." In John 20:28 Thomas said, "My Lord and my God." In Acts 20:28 God's Word tells us, "Take heed therefore unto yourselves, and to all the flock, over the which the Holy (Spirit) hath made you overseers, to feed the church of God, which he hath purchased with his own blood." In Romans 9:5 God's word tells us that Jesus was over all things. "Whose are the fathers, and of whom as concerning the flesh Christ came, who is over all, God blessed for ever. Amen." In 1 Timothy 3:16, Jesus is described as "God ... manifest in the flesh." This is a statement showing that God came in the flesh as Jesus, but He was still God. Other verses that shows how the New Testament writers ascribe divine titles to Christ are: 2 Thes. 1:12, Tit. 2:13, Heb. 1:8 and 1 Jn. 5:20.

The Lord Jesus Christ has titles which indicate His eternal being. Apostle Paul wrote giving Jesus all Deity and Honor. He is precisely what His names imply. He is, "The Son of God," "The only Begotten Son," "The First and the Last," "The Alpha and Omega," "The Lord," "Lord of all," "Lord of Glory," "The Christ," "Wonderful," "Counselor," "The mighty God," "The Father of eternity," "God," "God with us," "Our Great God," and "God blessed forever."

These titles relate Him to the Old Testament revelation of Jehovah-God, as in Matthew 1:23. "Behold, a virgin shall be with child, and shall bring forth a son, and they shall call his name Emmanuel, which being interpreted is, God with us" (See Isa. 7:14). In Matthew 4:7 God's word tells us, "Jesus said unto him, It is written again, Thou shalt not tempt the Lord thy God" (See Deut. 6:16). Also, Jesus has the titles of God or Lord in Mark 5:19 with Ps. 66:16; and Matthew 22:42-45 with Ps. 110:1.

The deity of Jesus is shown all through God's Word and we who believe that God's word is without error and was written by the inspiration of the Holy Spirit can see that Jesus was God and was part of the Trinity.
HE IS GOD THE SON. ✍

God the Son
By George Killingsworth

How often do you pray or meditate outside of religious services:

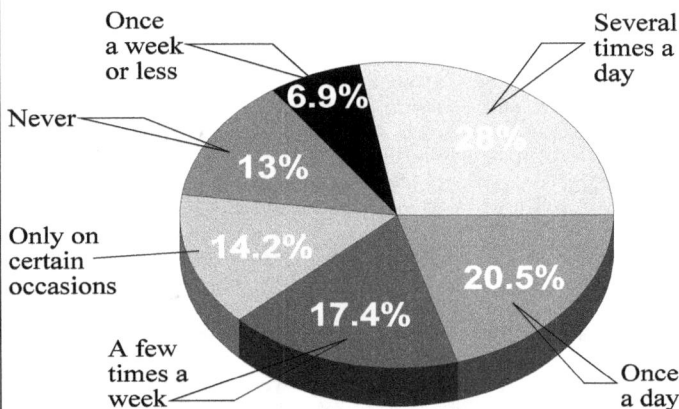

Once a week or less

Several times a day

6.9%

28%

Never

13%

20.5%

Only on certain occasions

14.2%

17.4%

A few times a week

Once a day

Source: Institute for Studies of Religion, Baylor University survey of 1,721 Americans, fall 2005; margin of error +/- 4 percentage points; *For more information see article on page 20*

How Can You Make Sense of the News?
By Garry W. Johnson
MOUNTAIN REVIEW Staff

So much is happening in the world, and so quickly. Where are today's dramatic and dangerous trends taking us? What does Bible prophecy reveal about our future? Is prophecy coming to pass before our eyes? How can you know the answers?

If you are concerned with the direction the world is headed, then *World News and Prophecy (WNP)* was created for you. This monthly newsletter is designed to help you understand world news in light of Bible prophecy. *WNP* provides interested persons with commentary and analysis of selected world news topics and helps you make the Scriptural connections. Its purpose is to help readers discern the times and increase their awareness and understanding of the answers Christ gave to His disciples' questions: "Tell us, when will these things be? And what will be the sign of Your coming, and the end of the age?" (Matthew 24:3).

This eye-opening newsletter offers you a perspective you will not find in any other news source—the perspective of God's Word. *WNP* is provided <u>absolutely free</u> as an educational service in the public interest. You may subscribe for as long as you would like and cancel at any time. So write for your free subscription today!

World News & Prophecy
P.O. Box 541027
Cincinnati, OH 45254-1027

My Testimony of Christ

By Gary Hall

On November 5, 1990, my fiancé broke it off with me after two years. We had a date set for July 13, 1991. My world came crashing down around me. This woman, whom I loved, ended our relationship without ever giving me a reason. She kept telling me she had to.

Several months had gone by since she broke up with me, and I was over at our mutual friend's house. She called and we ended up talking a few minutes in which she convinced me to meet her in North Carolina.

The next night, before I went to North Carolina, my friends and I had a little party. I shared with them what had happened and where I was going. Although none of us went to church, we all on numerous occasions had talked about wanting to get saved. Yet we knew we were not ready to quit our drinking, drugs, sex, etc. We thought that we should not get saved and then the next day do the same old things and be nothing more than hypocrites. We wanted to clean ourselves up first, then give our lives to the Lord. Boy, what little did we know about the Lord. We are to come just as we are and it is the Lord who will change us, not we ourselves! Anyway, a few of us (about six) went into this little bathroom/utility room and got in a circle and held hands and began to pray, asking God to bring Deanna and me back together. We prayed, "Lord, please hear us and do this for Gary." I kid you not about what happened next. When we said "amen," we all opened our eyes and lying on the floor was a very small booklet. Written on the cover were the words, "Have Faith in Christ." To this day none of us know where it came from!

The next night I met her in North Carolina and gave her a video tape I had made for her. We talked all night then I drove back the next morning. Later that day we talked on the phone and a few times more over the next couple of weeks. Around the third week she broke it off with me again and would not tell me why, she just kept saying, "I do, I just do!"

Two to three months had gone by since I met her in North Carolina. Around the first of June 1991, I decided I had all I could take. I needed to get out of Tennessee. Although she lived in Greenville, SC, I still could not seem to escape the continual reminder of my broken heart. I never felt like it could heal as long as I lived in Tennessee. But where to go? I got the idea of Washington because of a woman I got to know over the phone through a personal ad. So I had a map of Washington blown up. I closed my eyes, spun it around a couple of times, and set my finger down on the map. When I opened my eyes, my finger was on Spokane. To me that was a bigger sign that I needed to leave because that is where Angie, the woman from the ad, lived. Now I could be far away from anyone I knew and have a chance to start all over (boy, how true that was).

Several days later I took my only $300 and spent $176 for a bus ticket and another $25 on some things I needed before I left. I was off with a little less than $100 to my name. Three days and $70 later, I was sitting on a bus in Cour De' Lane Beach, Idaho, at the bus station. It was two o'clock on a Saturday morning. The initial excitement of getting far away was wearing off and the realization was setting in. Here I was on a bus almost 3000 miles away from what I know as home with $30 left to my name. I had no place to live or to work when I arrived in Spokane. I knew no one there except some lady whom I had only spoken to on the phone over the past weeks. Even she did not know I was coming to Spokane.

I had no clue what I was going to do. I suddenly remembered from years ago, when my mom and dad used to take me to church, that the Bible said "that God would supply all my needs." So I began to speak to God and I said, "God, I cannot promise You I will live right and be a Christian. However, I remember somewhere in Your Word You said You would supply all our needs. I am here 30 minutes away from Spokane, I have no place to go, only $30 to my name, and I do not know anyone! Please God, provide me with food and shelter at least until I can get on my feet. I will try to do right. I cannot promise though."

I finally arrived in Spokane around 2:50 a.m. I took what baggage I had, locked it in a locker and within ten minutes was on my way walking around Spokane. I finally found this park called Riverfront. I sat there on a bench and just watched the river go by and listened to the sounds of the night.

Around nine o'clock that morning a young man in his 30's sat beside me on the bench. He had a little girl with him who was around nine years old. He said good morning and asked me how I was doing. I said, "Fine thanks." His name was Kevin and he went on to tell me that they (they being his church), came out there every Saturday morning to share the Gospel. He asked me if I had ever been saved? I told him when I was young I had, but in my mind I did not really know what saved was. I just knew it was associated with going to the altar. After we talked awhile, he asked me where I was staying. I told him I would probably find some mission to stay in. We talked for another 30 minutes and then he said something that shocked me! He said, "I tell you what, my wife is coming to pick me up at 2:00 p.m. Meet us out there and you can come and stay with us tonight. Also, I know a young man who I used to live with a little over a year ago that is looking for a roommate, and he is your age. I will talk with him tomorrow."

Two o'clock came and his wife was there to pick us up. We stopped by the bus station to pick up my baggage, and we were off to their apartment. When we arrived, Kevin told me to make myself at home. I was blessed with a hot shower and a home-cooked meal! Around 5:30 that evening, after we ate, Kevin told me they go back out to where they cruise and witness to those hanging around. He told me I could stay there and watch TV, get some rest, or I could come with them if I wanted to. It was up to me. They would be back in a few hours. I went with them though. I was really confused. First they invited me into their home, for all they knew I could have been an axe murderer. Second, they were going to leave me, a complete stranger, by myself in their apartment. What if I were a robber looking for a score? These things were going through my mind. Then I thought, what if they are trying to set me up, they seemed a little nice and trusting (little did I know it was not me they were trusting in, it was Jesus!). So I decided to go with them.

The next morning, being Sunday, they were going to church and they invited me. I had yet to remember my prayer on the bus! Anyway, I went to church and I met Shane, this 23-year-old guy who used to be Kevin's roommate before he got married. He said he had no problems with me moving in. I told him all I had was a few dollars to my name until I found a job. Then it will take a few weeks from there to get my first check. He told me not to worry about that yet. Then he asked if I had a licence. I said "Yeah, why?" He said, "You can use my extra truck for transportation to learn your way around and enjoy Spokane, since you have never been here." Then he told me to let him know what kind of work I was looking for and he would talk to people at church to see if they had any connections to help me get a job.

During that time I went to church every Sunday and Wednesday. About my third week there I was sitting in church on a Sunday morning in the very back. As the pastor was doing the altar call God spoke to my heart and brought back to memory the prayer I prayed on the bus, asking Him to supply my needs! He then let me see that from the very first day I had shelter, food, and even transportation and a job. He showed me that through all those things and His people He provided me with the most important thing of all, His love. It is like He instantly opened my eyes. These people who had invited me into their homes, fed me, and done all the things they did, they were not crazy! Actually they were sacrificing their time, money and most of all themselves, to win one soul for Jesus. I truly understood how Jesus gave His all for me. That day I received Jesus into my heart. Praise God! ✍

Gary Hall is an inmate minister here at Morgan County Correctional Complex. He and other inmate ministers gather every Saturday in the chapel at 11:00 to fellowship and share their knowledge of Scripture and love for God. The services are designed to allow all who attend the opportunity to question the service's presenter about the message and other Biblical subjects. All are welcomed and encouraged to attend and participate in the service and discussion.

A Stone's Throw

By Ricky D. Moore

My main text is Ephesians 5:25-26, specifically verse 26, "That he might sanctify and cleanse it (the Church) with the washing of water by the word."

One morning when I was just waking up and thanking the Lord for another day, the phrase, "The washing of water by the Word" came to my mind. I sought the Lord through the Holy Spirit and asked Him if there was an example in His word of the washing of water by the word? He directed me to the scripture in 1 Samuel 17:40, "And he (David) took his staff in his hand, and chose him five smooth stones out of the brook ..." Then the Lord brought my attention to smooth stones and asked me, "How did the stones get so smooth?" Then I answered Him and said, "it was by the continual washing of water." That's when the Lord made it real to me that all born-again Christians are like those smooth stones. Just like when the constantly rushing water of the brook knocks off the rough edges of the stones to make them smooth. When we get born-again through Christ Jesus, we still have a lot of rough edges. That's why it says in 2 Corinthians 5:17, "Therefore if any man (or woman) be in Christ, he (or she) is a new creature: old things are passed away; behold, all things are become new." But by the continual washing of water by His word the rough sinful edges and bad habits are knocked off, one by one, through His Holy Spirit that brings about a change in us. The Lord also brought my attention to the roundness of the stones in the brook. By the tumbling of the stones on the other stones they became well-rounded. He said to consider the tumbling, "The trials of this life." "My brethren, count it all joy when ye fall into divers temptations (various trials); Knowing this, that the trying of your faith worketh patience. But let patience have her perfect work, that ye may be perfect and entire, wanting nothing" (James 1:2-4). So the trials we endure through our Lord and Savior Jesus Christ help to make us well-rounded Christians.

Now we can get to the use of these smooth well-rounded stones. You're probably wondering why David picked up five smooth stones instead of just one. You might just say that it's because Goliath had four brothers, as mentioned in 2 Samuel 21:22. David probably didn't pick up the first five smooth and well-rounded stones that he saw. He more than likely had to search for the smoothest and best well-rounded stones for his sling. "For many are called, but few are chosen" (Matthew 22:14).

We are a lot like those stones, and prison is our brook where we tumble through trials and get smoothed-out by the washing of water by God's word.

When we continue reading from 1 Samuel 17:45 through verse 50, we see that David has no fear of Goliath at all. As a matter of fact David never calls Goliath a giant, he just calls him the "uncircumcised Philistine." David tells the Philistine in verse 46 that, "This day will the LORD deliver thee into mine hand; and I will smite thee ..." This statement by David lets us know that David knew the Lord was going to direct the throw of that stone straight into Goliath's forehead. David gave all the glory to the Lord in verse 47 by saying, " ... for the battle is the LORD'S, and he will give you into our hands." So, my brothers (and sisters) in Christ, our desire should be to become smoother and better rounded stones for the Lord to use, so that when He picks us up out of this brook we call prison, He can place us into His sling and throw us strait into the Giant's forehead (the free world).

The Lord is truly the one who has helped us up to today, through all the trials that makes us better rounded Christians. And along the way He will smooth us out by the washing of water by His word. So let's get prepared by getting more rooted and grounded in Him through His word, and be ready for that day when the Lord our God picks us up out of the brook that we're in, knowing that we are only, "A Stone's Throw" away.

Remember that it takes a long time for a rough rock to become a smooth well-rounded stone. ✍

Looking at religious affiliations across the USA

Baylor sociologists broke down religious affiliation by region, gender, race and age:

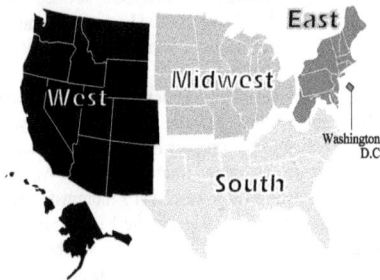

(Percentage)	West	Midwest	South	East	Total	Gender Male	Female	White	Black	Age 18-30	31-44	45-64	65+	Education High school or less	Some college or more
Black Protestant	1.3	5.6	7.2	5	5	2.8	6.9	0	62.5	3.8	5.4	3.9	7.3	5	3
Evangelical Protestant	31.7	33.7	50.3	13.1	33.6	30	36.7	35.4	9.5	39	34.9	31.3	33.1	45.4	23.5
Mainline Protestant	17.7	26	19.3	26	22.1	22.1	22.1	7.7	20.1	17.6	22.5	26.1	18	29
Catholic	19.2	22.1	11.5	35.1	21.2	23.8	18.9	22.8	5	10.1	23	23.7	19.9	22	21.4
Jewish	2.2	1.4	1.9	4.7	2.5	2.5	2.4	2.6	3.7	2.7	1.9	2.7	2.9	2.3	3.6
Other	10.3	3	2.7	4.6	4.9	6	3.9	4.3	6	5.7	5.8	4.8	3.5	2.1	6.7
Unaffiliated	17.6	8.3	7.1	11.6	10.8	12.8	9	10.8	5.7	18.6	11.4	11.1	5.4	5.2	12.8

Baylor survey finds: Americans worship four gods

By Garry W. Johnson
MOUNTAIN REVIEW Staff

In September Baylor University released preliminary findings from a survey of 1,721 Americans conducted by Gallup that highlights religious confusion in a whole new way.

The study, by far the most comprehensive national religion survey to date, was written and analyzed by sociologists from Baylor University's Institute for Studies on Religion, in Waco, Texas. The survey asked 77 questions with nearly 400 answer choices and found that Americans have widely divergent understandings of God.

Baylor's researchers avoided the more familiar divisions of denominational brands and doctrinal deviations and focused on the four dominate views of God that emerged from the study. As dubbed by the researchers, these 'four gods' are classified as: Authoritarian, Benevolent, Critical and Distant.

THE FOUR GODS OF AMERICA

Of the 91.8% of Americans that said they believe in God, a higher power or a cosmic force, 31.4% acknowledge the Authoritarian god (43.3% in the South). This god is angry at humanity's sins and engaged in every creature's life and world affairs. He is ready to throw the thunderbolt of judgement down on "the unfaithful or ungodly," says Baylor's Christopher Bader.

He describes these believers as "religiously and politically conservative people, most often black Protestants and white Evangelicals." He says they are the most inclined to say that abortion is always wrong (23.4% vs. 12.2% overall) and that God favors the USA in world affairs (32.1% vs. 18.6% overall).

Those that acknowledge the Benevolent god came in at 23% (28.8% in the Midwest) and believe that God still sets absolute standards for mankind in the Bible. This group draws more from mainline Protestants, Catholics and Jews, says Sociologist Paul Froese. He notes that this group is inclined (68.1%) to say caring for the sick and needy ranks highest on the list of what it means to be a good person.

The next group of believers claim a Critical god, 16% overall and 21.2% in the East. They see God as having a judgmental eye on the world, but not ever intervening to punish or to comfort. Bader says, "This group is more paradoxical. They have very traditional beliefs, picturing God as the classic bearded old man on high. Yet they're less inclined to go to church or affiliate seriously with religious groups. They are less inclined to see God as active in the world." These people are also significantly less inclined to draw absolute moral lines on hot-button issues such as abortion, gay marriage or embryonic stem cell research; only 54.7% of this group says gay marriage is always wrong, compared with 80.6% of the Authoritarian group, 65.8% of the Benevolent group and 57% of the overall sample.

The Distant god is "no bearded old man in the sky raining down his opinions on us," says Bader. Overall, 24.4% saw God this way (30.3% in the West)—as a cosmic force that launched the world, then left it spinning on its own. This has strongest appeal for Catholics, mainline Protestants and Jews, according to Bader. It is also popular among "moral relativists," those least likely to say any moral choice is always wrong, and among those who do not attend church. Of this group, only 3.8% believe embryonic stem cell research is always wrong, compared with 38.5% of the Authoritarians, 22.7% of the Benevolents and 13.2% of Criticals.

HOW THE STUDY WAS DONE

On behalf of Baylor University, the Gallup Organization contacted 3,702 potential respondents and asked them to complete a 16-page booklet on *The Values and Beliefs of the American Public—A National Study*. The English only survey asked respondents to agree or disagree with any of 10 descriptions of their "personal understanding of what God is like," including phrases such as "angered by my sins" or "removed from worldly affairs." When asked to describe God they could check off 16 adjectives, including words such as "absolute," "wrathful," "forgiving," "friendly" or "distant." More than 46% of the surveys were completed and returned and are a statistically representative sampling of the USA by age, gender and race.

Baylor's four visions of God as outlined in their research are not mutually exclusive, nor do they include the 5.2% of Americans who say they are atheists (the remaining 3% were not sure or did not answer).

Over the next two years Baylor's researchers will continue reviewing their findings and releasing reports on subtopics. In the fall of 2007 they intend to repeat the core questions to track trends. The John Templeton Foundation is funding the project.

RELIGION SALES

Mel Gibson's movie *The Passion of the Christ* was viewed by 44.3% of those polled; Dan Brown's book, *The Da Vinci Code* (the best selling book of 2004 and 2006) was read by 28.5%. Rick Warren's handbook, *The Purpose-Driven Life*, found its way into the hands of 25% of all U.S. women and 19% overall. Another 19% have read at least one of the novels in the apocalyptic fiction series, *Left Behind*. More than one in 10 of those surveyed say they spent $50 or more in the past month on items such as religious books, music and jewelry.

WHO MAKES THE CUT?

The Baylor Religion Survey finds that Americans are divided over who is eligible for salvation, the majority (58.3%) agreeing with the statement "many religions lead to salvation." Sociologist Kevin Dougherty says, "People clearly are not holding an exclusivist view." The survey found however, 61% of Evangelical Protestants and 46.4% of black Protestants say only Christians will "get into heaven." By contrast, the majority of Catholics (66.9%) say all or most non-Christians will. Overall, most people believe their family (75.3%) and friends (69.3%) will be saved. The survey did not ask people if they expect to receive salvation themselves.

Phyllis Tickle, author of books on religion in American life, sees problems in Baylor's survey because its questions rely on terms such as "heaven" and "salvation" in a multifaith society. "Heaven is not the only point," she says. "We may not share the same idea of where a religious path leads."

CONFUSION ABOUNDS

Paranormal beliefs are shared by millions of Americans, particularly women, the research found. Of those surveyed 52% overall say they believe in prophetic dreams. Four in 10 agree that places can be haunted and that ancient advanced civilizations such as Atlantis once existed.

When asked about alternative medical treatment, the response was so strong that Bader suspects the question's intent was not clear. "We asked whether 'Some alternative treatments are at least as effective as traditional medicine'" and 74.5% said yes. "We were thinking of crystals, aromatherapy. ... But people may have read the question to mean acupuncture, vitamins or herbs."

The survey found close to 25% use the Internet or books to research the prophecies of 16th-century astrologer Nostradamus, ghost, yoga, astrology and UFO's.

Baylor is a Baptist-affiliated university and is the information source for the charts on this page.

For more on the Baylor Survey and other religious statistics, please read the editorial article on page 21.

Paranormal beliefs popular in the U.S.

People who agree/strongly agree by gender: ▨= Women ☐=Men

	Women	Men
Dreams can sometimes foretell the future or reveal hidden truths.	58.9	49.9
Some alternative treatments are at least as effective as traditional medicine.	77.8	78.5
Ancient advanced civilizations such as Atlantis once existed.	44.9	41.8
Places can be haunted.	45.5	32.2
It is possible to influence the world through the mind alone.	31.0	28.3
Some UFO's are probably spaceships from other worlds.	23.2	29.1
It is possible to communicate with the dead.	27.2	14.0
Creatures such as Bigfoot and the Loch Ness Monster will be discovered by science.	19.8	17.6
Astrologers, palm readers, tarot card readers, fortunetellers, psychics can foresee the future.	18.2	8.0
Astrology affects one's life and personality.	19.7	10.1

How Americans see God

Americans' images of God vary by geography, gender and race:

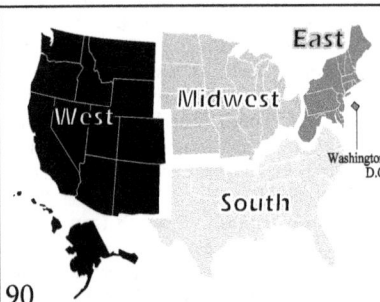

(Percentage)	West	Midwest	South	East	Total	Gender Male	Female	White	Black	Age 18-30	31-44	45-64	65+	Education High school or less	Some college or more
Authoritarian	20.8	32.5	43.5	25.2	31.4	28.9	33.6	29.6	52.8	40.2	33.3	27.4	28.8	40.4	23.9
Benevolent	27.4	28.8	16.6	19.9	23.0	15.4	30.4	24.5	13.5	13.4	20.9	27.2	25.6	24.0	22.2
Critical	13.6	13.8	15.9	21.2	16.0	19.9	12.3	15.3	30.3	14.9	13.9	16.0	20.0	18.6	14.7
Distant	30.3	21.2	21.5	25.8	24.4	28.0	21.0	25.1	3.4	25.3	26.4	24.3	21.4	14.7	32.5
Atheist	7.9	3.7	2.6	7.5	5.2	7.8	2.7	5.4	0.0	6.2	5.5	5.1	4.2	2.4	6.7

The religious politician, the declining superpower and the powerless church

By Garry W. Johnson
MOUNTAIN REVIEW Staff

Webster's dictionary defines religion as the service and worship of God or the supernatural. In order for one to be "religious," they must acknowledge something outside of the natural realm. Many scholars and scientists dismiss religion as primitive man's attempt to explain the world and his existence in it. Yet with all the advancements in technology and science, the religious still overwhelmingly outnumber the secular worldwide and throughout the world's current superpower nation.

Within the United States there is a growing divide over the country's direction, as evidenced by our most recent elections. Increasingly politicians are appealing to the religious sentiments of voters, and polls like the Baylor Religious Survey (page 20) help them to exploit those feelings. Studies of this nature also illustrate a growing stretch as to what passes for religion and our country's lack of biblical knowledge and/or understanding.

Reporting for *USA Today*, Cathy Lynn Grossman quotes Baylor sociologist Paul Froese in relaying that "the survey finds the stereotype that conservatives are religious and liberals are secular is 'simply not true. Political liberals and conservatives are both religious. They just have different religious views'" (September 12, 2006). Different views indeed. But does this outward profession of religion equate to godly conduct? It seems half our country's politicians proudly set policy reflecting unbiblical and degenerate beliefs, and the other half tout "family values" while personally committing shamefully immoral acts. How did our government become this way, and what does our current situation portend for the future?

THE DOWNSIDE OF DEMOCRACY

The United States has a relatively short history as a nation, this being the 231st year since its founding. From its inception our country was an altogether new experiment on the world scene—a nation for the people, ruled by the people, yet under God.

Recently there has been a movement in higher education to minimize the part religion—Christianity in particular—played in the establishing of this country. It is true that our founding fathers had diverse views on faith, yet they overwhelmingly recognized the hand of Providence in the establishing and sustaining of the young nation.

The early Americans were a deeply religious people. Although our nation had its share of brothels and womanizers (like any other nation of that period), those lewd and immoral practices were not nearly as prevalent or mainstream as they are today. Early Americans took biblical instruction more literally than modern churchgoers do. They had a character and code of ethics derived from *applying* biblical instruction. It was for these moral Americans that our government was designed. Our second U.S. President, John Adams, put it this way, "Our Constitution was made *only* for a moral and religious people. It is *wholly inadequate* to the government of any other" (emphases mine throughout). [You may also note that in those days "moral" and "religious" were nearly synonymous terms.]

Our Constitution established a democratic government. By definition a democracy is a "government by the people; *esp.*: rule of the majority" (*Webster's*). In essence a democratic government is representative of its citizens—our politicians reflect the attitudes and morals of the people they govern. President George Washington understood this form of government and how it would work. In his first Inaugural Address on April 30, 1789, he said, "The foundations of our national policy will be laid in the pure and immutable principles of private morality." As private morality declines, national policy suffers. An ancient king inspired by the Spirit of God once said, "Righteousness exalts a nation, but sin is a reproach to any people" (Proverbs 14:34).

THE REPROACH OF A NATION

As the character and values of the American people continue to decline, so will the quality and integrity of American leaders. "Somehow we Americans have let righteous conduct slip through our fingers, particularly in the recent decades since the end of World War II," writes John Ross Schroeder for *The Good News* magazine. "Our pioneer ancestors in America wouldn't understand our current behavior as a nation. Most of them would be appalled by our lack of morals. They would say we have turned our backs on God. *And they would be right*," (January-February 2007).

In the aftermath of 9/11, it seemed our country might awaken spiritually to a new direction. Memorial services from the National Cathedral, Yankee Stadium and the Pentagon sparked feelings of patriotism and religious platitudes, but no call for ***national repentance***.

Andrew Kohut, director of the Pew Research Center for People and the Press remarked, "Religion was in the air after September 11, in a way that hadn't been the case for a long time and may not be the case for a long time in the future." How right he was. Religious convictions in this country ebb and flow like the tide. By March 2002, Pew was reporting 52% of Americans thought religion's effect was in decline, though they still considered religion important. Of those polled, two-thirds believed the "terrorist attacks were the result of too little religion in the world rather than too much" (*San Diego Union-Tribune*, March 22, 2002).

TOO LITTLE RELIGION?

If the vast majority of this world's religious views were not false, this might be the case. Most religions obtained their foundation in the imagination, speculation and reasoning of certain human beings—with no basis in truth. The god (or gods) they produced were simply products of the human mind, much like what has become of mainstream Christianity in America. One of the articles *USA Today* published on the Baylor survey was titled, "*Americans define faith their way*."

"More than three-fourths of Americans call the nation's religious diversity a source of strength; fewer than a third think it makes it harder to keep the country united. ... Meanwhile, more than three in four Americans believe all religions have at least some elements of truth—even though few say they know much about religions other than their own. And nearly 70% think spiritual experiences are the most important part of religion. 'If one's religion is more about individual identity than doctrine or creed, it's a lot easier to be tolerant,' says Egon Mayer, a sociologist at the Graduate Center of the City University of New York. Gallup says that the high degree of religious tolerance reflects, in part, 'not only a lack of knowledge of other religions but an ignorance of one's own faith.' In some polls, he says, 'you have Christians saying, 'Yes, Jesus is the only way' and also, 'Yes, there are many paths to God.' It's not that Americans don't believe anything; they believe everything'" (*U.S. News & World Report*, May 6, 2002).

WHAT DO YOU BELIEVE?

From the first day man walked the earth, the Eternal God began to reveal to him His will. Almost as early, man's rebellion began. The devil's success was in his ability to twist God's revelation to man—to add a little error to the truth. Today he has all but mastered this technique and passed off many of his deceptions under the guise of religion.

Worldwide adherents to the Muslim faith outnumber Roman Catholics by more than 161 million. There are almost three times as many Catholics as there are Protestants, and Hindus outnumber Christian Orthodox, Anglicans and Independents combined (*The World Almanac*, 2005). If, as many Christian organizations claim, God is trying to "save the world" through their churches, why such a poor ratio?

True Christianity, indeed, true religion is ***a way of life***. Jesus Christ walked this earth for three and a half years teaching and clarifying God's expectations for mankind. True religion had become obscured by the traditions of men, and people clung blindly to the letter of the law without understanding its spiritual purpose and intent. Christ struck down their misconceptions and raised God's Law to a spiritual level. His perfect and sinless life was the model for all of His Apostles and all true Christians today. As John tells us in his first epistle, "He that saith he abideth in him ought himself also so to walk, even as he walked" (Ch. 2, verse 6).

Compare your church to the one described in the book of Acts. Compare your religious customs and observances to those *actually practiced* by God's True Church in the pages of your Bible. If you can see the difference, then God may be calling you into a more personal and intimate relationship with Himself through His Son, Jesus Christ. "Neither is there salvation in any other: for there is none other name under heaven given among men, whereby we must be saved" (Acts 4:12).

Please request your free booklets, *Restoring Apostolic Christianity* and *The Ten Commandments*, by writing to the Living Church of God, P.O. Box 3810, Charlotte, NC 28227-8010. You may also want to request a subscription to *Tomorrow's World* magazine and/or enroll in their *24 Lesson Bible Study Course*, both are also absolutely free. ✍

How images of God affect politics

The Baylor study finds that a person's image of God tells more about his or her social, moral and political views than religious denomination or other familiar measures.

	Authoritarian	Benevolent	Critical	Distant	Total
Supporting these policies is always wrong	(Percentage)				
Gay marriage	80.6	65.8	54.8	30.7	**57.0**
Research on embryonic stem cells	38.5	22.7	13.2	3.8	**20.3**
War	16.4	18.4	23.1	20.2	**19.2**
Abortion is always wrong even if ...					
The baby has/may have a serious defect	48.1	34.6	13.8	7.4	**27.1**
The woman's health is in danger	24.7	19.5	6.9	3.1	**14.1**
The pregnancy is the result of rape	41.5	31.7	12.6	4.6	**23.5**
The family cannot afford the child	80.8	69.2	41.7	22.9	**54.1**
The woman does not want the child	81.3	67.5	42.2	26.2	**55.2**
The federal government should ...					
Advocate Christian values	74.5	54.8	36.5	21.1	**45.6**
Fund faith-based organizations	47.2	24.6	32.3	12.7	**28.9**
Abolish the death penalty	12.1	17.3	14.2	27.3	**18.4**
Distribute wealth more evenly	56.8	53.2	58.7	62.5	**57.8**
Regulate businesses more closely	60.3	63.5	70.6	68.7	**65.1**
Do more to protect the environment	75.9	81.2	89.0	87.2	**82.9**
Expand its authority to fight terrorism	76.2	62.7	64.0	40.4	**59.5**
Allow prayer in public schools	90.9	79.0	69.4	46.5	**69.9**
God favors the United States in world affairs					
Agree	32.1	22.0	12.4	6.9	**18.6**

Source: Institute for Studies of Religion, Baylor University survey of 1,721 Americans, fall2005; margin of error +/- 4 percentage points

Top 10 religion stories of 2006

The top ten religious stories of 2006 as decided by the Religion Newswriters Association's poll:

1. Periodicals in Denmark and a few other European nations publish cartoons of the Prophet Muhammad which spark deadly violence.
2. By quoting an ancient text linking Islam and violence, Pope Benedict XVI angers Muslims.
3. Leaders of the Episcopal church elect a female presiding bishop who favors rites to bless same-sex unions and supports the consecration of a sexually active gay bishop.
4. President of the National Association of Evangelicals, Ted Haggard, resigns from his office and is dismissed as pastor of the New Life Church in Colorado Springs after allegations of gay sex and drug use.
5. Key election defeats are suffered by candidates backed by the Religious Right, while Democrats take steps to reach out to churchgoers, especially Catholics.
6. As sectarian conflicts between Sunni and Shiite Muslims increase, religious voices grow louder for peace in Iraq.
7. The murder of five Amish girls in a schoolhouse in Bart Township, Pa., focuses world-wide attention on Amish beliefs about grace and forgiveness.
8. (tie) The release of *The Da Vinci Code* movie sparks new interest in Dan Brown's novel, which claims Christianity is a fraud.
8. (tie) During midterm elections same-sex marriage bans pass in seven of eight states. The first state to defeat a ban is Arizona.
10. President Bush pleases religious conservatives and disappoints liberals by vetoing a bill calling for expanded stem-cell research.

Date / Team	Sept. 1	Sept. 8	Sept. 15	Sept. 22	Sept. 29	Oct. 6	Oct. 13	Oct. 20	Oct. 27	Nov. 3	Nov. 10	Nov. 17	Nov. 24
ALABAMA	WESTERN CAROLINA Tuscaloosa	VANDERBILT Nashville	ARKANSAS Tuscaloosa	GEORGIA Tuscaloosa	FLORIDA STATE Jacksonville	HOUSTON Tuscaloosa	OLE MISS Oxford	TENNESSEE Tuscaloosa		LSU Tuscaloosa	MISSISSIPPI STATE Starkville	LOUISIANA-MONROE Tuscaloosa	AUBURN Auburn
ARKANSAS	TROY Fayetteville		ALABAMA Tuscaloosa	NORTH TEXAS Fayetteville	KENTUCKY Fayetteville	CHATTANOOGA Little Rock	AUBURN Fayetteville	OLE MISS Oxford	FLORIDA INTERNATIONAL Fayetteville	SOUTH CAROLINA Fayetteville	TENNESSEE Knoxville	MISSISSIPPI STATE Little Rock	LSU Baton Rouge
AUBURN	KANSAS STATE Auburn	SOUTH FLORIDA Auburn	MISSISSIPPI STATE Auburn	NEW MEXICO STATE Auburn	FLORIDA Gainesville	VANDERBILT Auburn	ARKANSAS Fayetteville	LSU Baton Rouge	OLE MISS Auburn	TENNESSEE TECH Auburn	GEORGIA Athens		ALABAMA Auburn
FLORIDA	WESTERN KENTUCKY Gainesville	TROY Gainesville	TENNESSEE Gainesville	OLE MISS Oxford	AUBURN Gainesville	LSU Baton Rouge		KENTUCKY Lexington	GEORGIA Jacksonville	VANDERBILT Gainesville	SOUTH CAROLINA Columbia	FLORIDA ATLANTIC Gainesville	FLORIDA STATE Gainesville
GEORGIA	OKLAHOMA STATE Athens	SOUTH CAROLINA Athens	WESTERN CAROLINA Athens	ALABAMA Tuscaloosa	OLE MISS Athens	TENNESSEE Knoxville	VANDERBILT Nashville		FLORIDA Jacksonville	TROY Athens	AUBURN Athens	KENTUCKY Athens	GEORGIA TECH Atlanta
KENTUCKY	EASTERN KENTUCKY Lexington	TEMPLE Philadelphia	LOUISVILLE Lexington	FLORIDA ATLANTIC Lexington	ARKANSAS Fayetteville	SOUTH CAROLINA Columbia	LSU Lexington	FLORIDA Lexington	MISSISSIPPI STATE Lexington		VANDERBILT Nashville	GEORGIA Athens	TENNESSEE Lexington
LSU	MISS. STATE Starkville (Aug. 30)	VIRGINIA TECH Baton Rouge	MIDDLE TENNESSEE Baton Rouge	SOUTH CAROLINA Baton Rouge	TULANE New Orleans	FLORIDA Baton Rouge	KENTUCKY Lexington	AUBURN Baton Rouge		ALABAMA Tuscaloosa	LOUISIANA TECH Baton Rouge	OLE MISS Oxford	ARKANSAS Baton Rouge
OLE MISS	MEMPHIS Memphis	MISSOURI Oxford	VANDERBILT Nashville	FLORIDA Oxford	GEORGIA Athens	LOUISIANA TECH Oxford	ALABAMA Oxford	ARKANSAS Oxford	AUBURN Auburn	NORTHWESTERN STATE Oxford		LSU Oxford	MISSISSIPPI STATE Starkville
MISS. STATE	LSU Starkville (Aug. 30)	TULANE New Orleans	AUBURN Auburn	JACKSONVILLE STATE Starkville	SOUTH CAROLINA Columbia	UAB Starkville	TENNESSEE Starkville	WEST VIRGINIA Morgantown	KENTUCKY Lexington		ALABAMA Starkville	ARKANSAS Little Rock	OLE MISS Starkville
SOUTH CAROLINA	LOUISIANA-LAFAYETTE Columbia	GEORGIA Athens	SO. CAROLINA STATE Columbia	LSU Baton Rouge	MISSISSIPPI STATE Columbia	KENTUCKY Columbia	NORTH CAROLINA Chapel Hill	VANDERBILT Columbia	TENNESSEE Knoxville	ARKANSAS Fayetteville	FLORIDA Columbia		CLEMSON Columbia
TENNESSEE	CALIFORNIA Berkeley	SOUTHERN MISS Knoxville	FLORIDA Gainesville	NORTHERN ILLINOIS Knoxville		GEORGIA Knoxville	MISSISSIPPI STATE Starkville	ALABAMA Tuscaloosa	SOUTH CAROLINA Knoxville	LOUISIANA-LAFAYETTE Knoxville	ARKANSAS Knoxville	VANDERBILT Knoxville	KENTUCKY Lexington
VANDERBILT	RICHMOND Nashville	ALABAMA Nashville	OLE MISS Nashville		EASTERN MICHIGAN Nashville	AUBURN Auburn	GEORGIA Nashville	SOUTH CAROLINA Columbia		FLORIDA Gainesville	KENTUCKY Nashville	TENNESSEE Knoxville	WAKE FOREST Nashville

BUNCH OF BOOKS BOUGHT FOR THE BIG HOUSE

By Jeremy Ingram
MOUNTAIN REVIEW Staff

Recently the state approved the funds for the library to buy a bunch of books. Eight hundred dollars was allotted for the new book purchase. Library CO's Pat Lynch and Dana Daniels graciously shopped around for the best deals. In the end, over two hundred new books were purchased with the money.

The new books included a variety of subject matter chosen in large part from the reader survey forms found at the library desk. These subjects included mystery, thriller, classics, non-fiction, and western. Most of the books that were purchased were brand new.

Fortunately, this will not be the last purchase for the library. Already $400 is allotted for another purchase. If anyone has suggestions concerning what books should be bought, please see a library clerk in the library for a survey form.

Thanks to both library CO's and the administration for allowing these new books to be purchased. Also, thanks to the library clerks who worked hard at cataloging all the books for our use. If you are interested in the new books, a shelf located close to the front office has all the new books. Tolle Lege. ✍

Library worker logs in new library books.

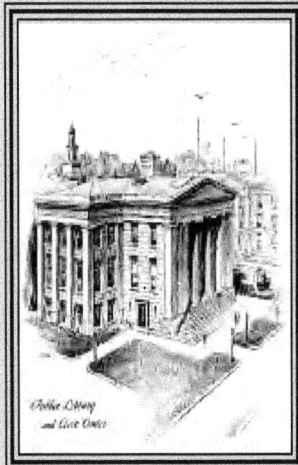

Stack of newly purchased books.

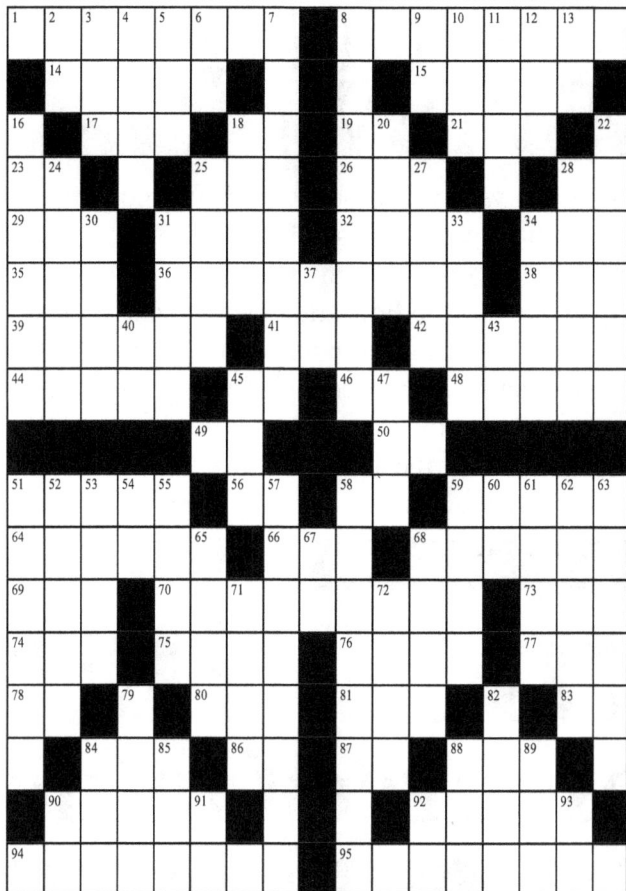

Crook's Puzzle Fun

ACROSS

1. _ _ _ _ _ as a _ _ _, like sandpaper
8. Exotic dancer
14. Daub
15. Beef
17. Crash or launch
18. Company, in short
19. _ _ VP
21. Reclined
23. Ocean (abr.)
25. Luau food
26. Dined
28. Savings and Loan (abr.)
29. 21st, 18th, 19th of 26
31. Bucket
32. Fish Catchers
34. Station (abr.)
35. Modern
36. National Cemetery
38. Erstwhile acorn
39. Vandalize
41. Born
42. Disposition
44. Sudden outburst
45. NCO
46. Egyptian sun god
48. North and South
49. All right
50. _ _ you feel like I do?
51. Blood type
56. Commercial
58. You might pass this
59. Banners
64. Sack material
66. _ _ _-Time Warner
68. Russians, Czechs, Bulgarians, e.g.
69. Mind over matter
70. Ancient country Euphrates-Tigris valley
73. Rower's need
74. Taste
75. Mild oath
76. _ _ _ _ and a prayer
77. Opposite of SSW
78. Symbol for Einsteinium
80. Slip up
81. Electrocardiogram
83. Bye
84. Fido's remark
86. Shoe width
87. Symbol for Rhenium
88. After Jrs
90. Gather
92. Dip brand
94. Den
95. Almost divine people

DOWN

2. Symbol for Osmium
3. Ref's Kin
4. Equipment
5. Owned
6. Symbol for Chromium
7. Cooking from above
8. Unknown person
9. Before TUV
10. _ _ _ not fair!
11. Fruit
12. Favorite
13. Popular medical drama
16. Pummels
18. Wrap
20. Editor's direction
22. Snow or frosted
24. Jerk
25. Skin
27. Town in Berkshire
28. Look intently
30. Couch
31. Walk to and fro
33. Fastener
34. Type of music
37. Opposite of SW
40. _ _ a glance
43. _ _ be, or not ...
45. Type of jazz
47. Din
51. Steaks
52. Andropov and Goremykin
53. Get ready
54. Elevated train
55. I got you _ _ _ _
57. Fantasy
58. Stared daggers
59. Banner
60. I love _ _
61. Shakespear's river
62. Huge
63. Yell
65. Turn the _ _ _ _
67. Good '_ _ boy
68. Chant
71. Naked
72. Shoe brand
79. Sad and gloomy
82. Pad hopper
84. Doc's org.
85. 6th, 19th, 18th of 26
88. Slide on snow
89. _ _ _ - Paulo
90. Mr. Bundy
91. _ _ what
92. Symbol for Samarium
93. Load (abr.)

DAVE'S CRYPTOGRAMS

Dave's Cryptograms are created from Biblical quotes. Each letter in the puzzle stands for another letter.

Clue for puzzle #1: V equals G

CON T BCX CO COVPF JLRP NLXO DALR EPCIPO, ECITOV HEP YPM LD HEP GLHHLRFPBB KTH

Clue for puzzle #2: F equals R

TCWPCOWBC JV AJWC, VOJDN DNC EHFI

Original cryptograms produced by David Pendleton

Search the Word

Word Search

```
R Z E B U N L G O D
I E P T H S A A N E
S N H R I J U D A H
S I R S L E T L P P
A M A N A S S E H E
C A I N W U I V T S
H J M H R S M I A O
A N U L U B E Z L J
R E U B E N O R I H
S B I B L E N O A H
```

Can you find ...
Israel's 12 sons
(Genesis 49)
Joseph's 2 sons
(Genesis 48)
Mary's firstborn Son
(Matthew 1:25)
Also included ...
God, Law
Noah, Bible
Cain

By Garry W. Johnson, MOUNTAIN REVIEW Staff

SHORT FUNNIES

Contributed by Judy Johnson

"The irony of life is that, by the time you're old enough to know your way around, you're not going anywhere."

"God made man before woman so as to give him time to think of an answer for her first question."

"I was always taught to respect my elders, but it keeps getting harder to find one."

"Aspire to inspire before you expire."

"My wife and I had words, but I did not get to use mine."

"Frustration is trying to find your glasses without your glasses."

"Blessed are those who can give without remembering and take without forgetting."

"Every morning is the dawn of a new error."

"Some people are like a Slinky ... not really good for anything, but you still can't help but smile when you see one tumble down the stairs."

"Life is sexually transmitted."

"Good health is merely the slowest possible rate at which one can die."

"All of us could take a lesson from the weather. It pays no attention to criticism."

"Health nuts are going to feel stupid someday, lying in hospitals dying of nothing."

"In the 60's people took acid to make the world weird. Now the world is weird and people take Prozac to make it normal."

Answers to crossword puzzle on page 23

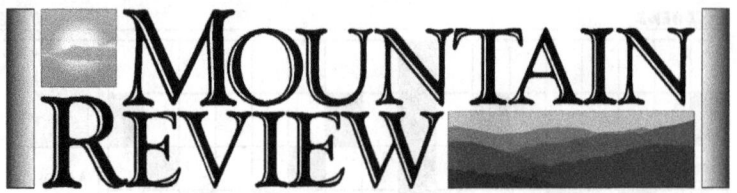

Crossword grid answers:

R O U G H C O B | S T R I P P E R
S M E A R | R | T | S T E E R
P | P A D | C O | R S | S A T | F
O C | R | P O I | A T E | R | S L
U R S | P A I L | N E T S | S T A
N E O | A R L I N G T O N | O A K
D E F A C E | N E E | N A T U R E
S P A T E | S G | R A | P O L E S
O K | D O
T Y P E B | A D | G O | F L A G S
B U R L A P | A O L | S L A V I C
O R E | B A B Y L O N I A | O A R
N I P | E G A D | W I N G | N N E
E S | G | E R R | E K G | F | T A
S | A R F | E E | R E | S R S | M
A M A S S | A | E | S K O A L
P L A Y R O O M | D E M I G O D S

Answers to cryptograms on page 23.

AND I SAW AN ANGEL COME DOWN FROM HEAVEN,
CON T BCX CO COVPF J L RP NL X O DAL R E PC IPO,

HAVING THE KEY OF THE BOTTOMLESS PIT.
ECITOV HEP YPM LD HEP GLHHLRFPBB KTH.

VENGEANCE IS MINE, SAITH THE LORD.
TCWPCOWBC JV AJWC, VOJDN DNC EH F I.

MOUNTAIN REVIEW

The *Mountain Review* was produced as a free government document written by prisoners at Brushy Mountain State Penitentiary and Morgan County Correctional Complex. It was sponsored by the Education Department at those facilities and was a censored publication. Permission to reprint was granted in this section of each edition. The views expressed are those of individual authors and do not necessarily reflect the TDOC policy at that time, nor the views of the editors, staff, sponsors, or administration.

PRISONER Resource Guide

2021 Edition

The Angolite
Cashier's Office
Louisiana State Penitentiary
Angola, LA 70712

A national prisoner publication produced by prisoners at Angola prison in Louisiana. Considered excellent prison journalism. Subscriptions are $20 a year, address is for orders only.

Books for Prisoners
℅ Groundwork Books
0323 Student Center
La Jolla, CA 92037
groundwork@libertad.uscd.edu
(858) 452-9625

A national program offering up to two books per person, free of charge. Send your request and specify your area of interests. They will send you a detailed booklet for that area of interest. Subjects include: politics, spirituality, feminism, dictionaries, culture, social criticism, and select novels. Please include a SASE for faster service. Stamp donations are appreciated, but not required.

Tomorrows World Magazine
P.O. Box 3810
Charlotte, NC 28227-8010
TomorrowsWorld.org

This full-color news and Christian-living magazine is offered completely free to anyone who requests it. Additional booklets, CDs, DVDs, and a 2-year Bible Study course are offered in each issue, also free of charge.

Edward R. Hamilton Bookseller Company
P.O. Box 15
5000 Oak Street
Falls, Village, CT 06031-0015
EdwardRHamilton.com

Sells all new books, CDs, DVDs and Blue-rays – publishers' closeouts, overstocks, remainders and current titles at special discounted prices. Write for details, give them your specific interest (Arts and Entertainment, Biographies, Science and Nature, etc.) and ask to be put on their *Bargain Books* catalog mailing list.

Triune Arts
Mail: 1804 Bedell Rd. RR #5
Kempville, Ontario
KOG 1JO, Canada
Website: triune.ca

A national educational resource for restorative justice programs; intended to raise public awareness of an alternatives to the existing justice system's approach, to provide training and to encourage citizens to participate in community justice programs. Send a SASE for information.

Channel Guide Magazine
1720 W. Florist Avenue, Suite 150
Glendale, WI 53209
414.352.8700
editor-tv@tribune.com
channelguidemag.com

Monthly magazine featuring daily program schedules for over 120 channels, weekly recommendations for the best bets on TV, starred ratings for over 3,000 movies showing this month, celebrity news and interviews, fun and TV crosswords.

Spring/
Summer
2007
Volume 20
Number 2

MOUNTAIN REVIEW

A Morgan County Correctional Complex Publication

Virginia Tech VT

The tragedy in Virginia shocked the nation. We look at the statistics of school shootings, federal and state reactions and the response of heros at the scene.

page 16

This Issue Focuses On

Feature Articles

Educational Trends

GED test-takers, by age

The average age of the 715,365 candidates for the high school diploma equivalency exam, in 2005 was 25.2 years. Age breakdown:

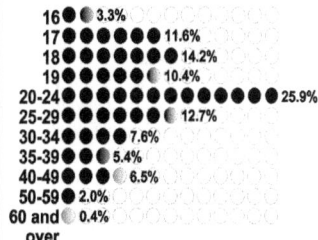

Age	%
16	3.3%
17	11.6%
18	14.2%
19	10.4%
20-24	25.9%
25-29	12.7%
30-34	7.6%
35-39	5.4%
40-49	6.5%
50-59	2.0%
60 and over	0.4%

Source: GED Testing Service; By Garry W. Johnson

UT Director of Broadcasting speaks at spring graduation

By Jeremy Ingram
MOUNTAIN REVIEW STAFF

Ronald Reagan once said, "This is not the end of anything, this is the beginning of everything." Likewise, the MCCX spring commencement exercise is not the end of anything, but the beginning of everything for the twenty-six students who graduated on May 30, 2007. Armed with GED diplomas and vocational certificates, these graduates embark on a new journey in life.

The commencement exercise began with an invocation by Chaplain Dean Yancey and the introduction of outstanding students by Instructor Jack McInnis. Among the outstanding students mentioned were Michael Gross, Theodore Smith, Patrick Stansberry, and Robert Houseal. Patrick Stansberry was singled out for his remarkable academic accomplishments. After struggling for years to pass the GED examination, Patrick finally prevailed. Upon completion of the GED, Patrick requested to be placed in the HVAC class, arguably the toughest vocational class at MCCX. Within a matter of months, Patrick had earned the Universal EPA Certificate—a feat that normally requires a much longer time to accomplish.

Another outstanding student was Theodore Smith. He was invited to give the graduates' address. Smith thanked Instructor Jack McInnis for helping prepare him for the GED. He remarked that an education was the best thing a person can

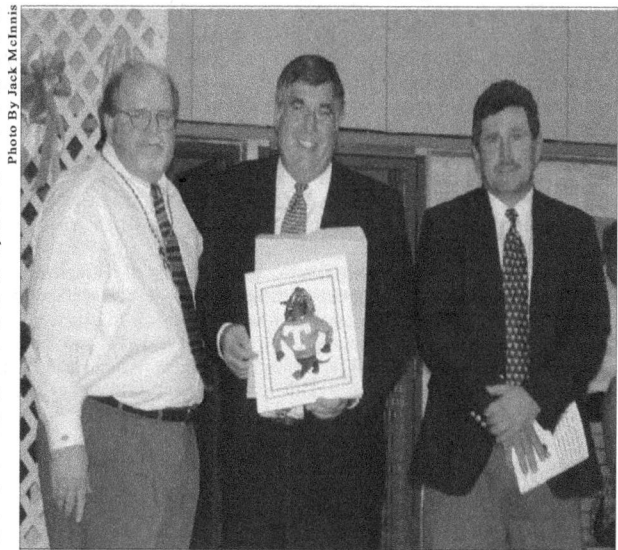

See **Grad** *on page 03*

Photo By Jack McInnis

From left to right—Warden David Mills, UT Director of Broadcasting Bob Kesling and MCCX School Principal David Pack.

The history of Straight Talk

By Jeremy Ingram
MOUNTAIN REVIEW Staff

Straight Talk is a program which reaches out to young people within our community who are constantly faced with crime, drug and alcohol abuse, peer pressure and family problems. Young people tour MCCX and at the end of the tour have an opportunity to participate in a panel discussion with inmates. These men share their stories including things in their past which contributed to their incarceration and then answer questions. This program was established by a former warden in the spring of 1986 for the purpose of reaching out to at-risk youth within the community and surrounding areas. These youth may be at-risk not only academically, but socially and psychologically as well. They may also come from abusive backgrounds which could include physical, mental, or sexual abuse.

HISTORY OF STRAIGHT TALK

Years ago, MCCX pioneered a new program within the TDOC specially designed to raise the public's awareness of what prison is like. The Straight Talk program involves tour groups of school kids who visit the prison. The idea for this program was created by the Lifer's Club and gained momentum when a group of students

See **Straight Talk** *on page 04*

Straight Talk ca. 1986

Religious books stripped from prison shelves

By Garry W. Johnson
MOUNTAIN REVIEW Staff

Part of a long-delayed post-September 11 federal directive has caused the removal of religious books from prison chapel shelves nationwide and triggered a lawsuit from federal inmates in Otisville, New York.

The inmates were stunned on Memorial Day to find hundreds of books missing from the chapel library. Although the federal directive was designed to keep radical religious text (specifically Islamic ones) out of the hands of violent inmates, the three Otisville prisoners say all religions are affected.

Inmate John Okon, speaking on behalf of the prison's Christian population, told a judge in June that "The set of books that have been taken out have been ones that we used to minister to new converts when they come in here."

Okon said the removal was unfortunate because "I have really seen religion turn around the life of some of these men, especially in the Christian community."

In April 2004, the Department of Justice reviewed how prisons chose Muslim religious service providers. The government was concerned that prisons "had been radicalized by inmates who were ... espousing various extreme forms of religion, which exposed security risk to the prisons and beyond the prisons to the public at large," according to Assistant U.S. Attorney Brian Feldman.

Feldman told U.S. District Judge Laura Taylor Swain that prison libraries limited the number of books for each religion to between 100 and 150 under new rules which stemmed from the study.

It is not exactly clear why it took until May of

See **Books** *on page 20*

Do our television choices effect what we say, do and think?

By Garry W. Johnson
MOUNTAIN REVIEW Staff

"It's a fact: Americans watched a record amount of television during the 2005-06 TV season: the average household had a television on for eight hours, 11 minutes per day, according to Nielsen Media Research. Individual viewers watched a record four hours and 35 minutes of television each day. Many media observers and critics had predicted that television viewing time would be eroded by time spent on new media. Since 1995-96, however, average household television viewing is up by nearly an hour per day, from seven hours and 15 minutes" (*The World Almanac, 2007*).

Media experts believed that new media – personal computers, PDAs, cell phones, and iPods, for example – would cut into people's television time. If the average American is still consuming more and more TV each year, just imagine how high those numbers are for prisoners who have no "new media" options. More importantly still, what is the effect on our mentality?

VIOLENT REACTIONS

Not long after Principal Mike Smajda learned in November of 2004 that one of his first-grade pupils had watched "The Texas Chainsaw Massacre," the little boy unexpectedly attacked a little girl. While playing in a leaf pile, the boy suddenly began kicking the girl in the head, and another little boy joined in. "They felt it was part of the game," said Smajda. "They both kicked her until her head was bleeding and she had to go to the hospital."

Of course, the principle could not prove the R-rated slasher movie provoked the child, but it did reinforce his commitment to an anti-violence program at his Escanaba, Michigan school. The program challenged students to do without TV and all other screen entertainment for 10 days, then limit themselves to just seven hours a week. Over the next year the district's other schools joined in. The short-term results were striking: Less aggressive behavior and, in some cases, better standardized test scores (they call it the "boob-tube" for a reason).

Designed for third and fourth grade students by health specialists at Stanford University, the program has been retooled for kindergarten through eighth grade. "I don't know of any other school district that has gone as far with this," said Lt. Col. David Grossman, a former West Point psychology professor and youth violence expert, who introduced the program called Student Media Awareness to Reduce Television.

The American Academy of Pediatrics sights more than 1,000 studies establishing a connection between violent entertainment and youthful aggression, but notes that family breakdown and peer influence also play a role.

The Stanford researchers also ran a trial of their program in San Jose, California schools, with promising results. The research team leader, Dr. Thomas Robinson told The Associated Press by e-mail, "I can't speculate on every individual violent act, but we do know that exposure to violent content does cause more aggressive behavior overall and that reducing screen time does reduce aggression overall."

When Smajda announced the TV turnoff during an assembly at Lemmer Elementary, he thought they might chase him out of the gym, judging from the boos and hisses. Even so, approximately 90% of the 400 plus students took part to some extent.

Immediately before and after the program, observers charted aggressive playground incidents – shoving, hitting, obscene gestures, name calling – at eight elementary schools. The totals dropped at every school but one. The overall average decline was 52%!

The district also compared standardized test scores of fourth-graders before and during the turnoff. Writing and math scores made double-digit leaps.

U.S. Census data suggest that parents are beginning to catch on. A 2003 national sample of 9,925 parents and their 18,413 children show that in 2003, 67% of parents with children ages 3-5 had rules about when, for how long, and the types of programs their kids watch. That compares with 54% in 1994. Parents with kids 6-11 reported 68.2% had such rules, up from 60.3% in 1994. The 12-17 age group received the least parental guidance with 43.7% having rules, up from 40.2% in 1994.

In January the Parents Television Council, a Los Angeles-based advocacy group, said violence on prime-time broadcast television has increased 75% since 1998. According to the group, the television season that began in the fall of 2005 was one of the most violent they ever recorded.

SEXUAL CONTENT

It is no secret that sex sells, and one commercial break without a shot of cleavage is rare, if it exists at all.

Network television has started down a bad road. Every major network today has a show, often in prime time, featuring a homosexual character and several more glamorizing extramarital sex. Partial nudity and graphically depicted sex scenes are also becoming more common place on non-paid channels (try watching FX after 10:00 p.m.).

Great Britain has already been where we are headed, and was recently labeled in the *Daily Mail* as, "the television porn capital of Europe." Britain now has 27 channels dedicated to pornography, compared to five in Germany, its closest rival. The channels air from 10:00 p.m. to 5:30 a.m., require a subscription and bring the total number of European porn stations to 84. Bel Mooney, a British commentator, lamented: "I'm tired of repellent, exploitative images being defended by privileged people who should know better – and who would sooner swallow razor blades than see their own daughters sell themselves for the gratification of strangers ... Now ask yourselves: 'What effect does it have on young boys to see women routinely treated like animals? What are the consequences of young women being brainwashed into thinking of themselves as mere sex objects?'"

The sad, joyless, demeaning display broadcast to millions is a far cry from the essential purpose of sex – to strengthen the marriage bond. Is it any wonder our divorce rate is 50%?

PROFUSE PROFANITY

Expletives are so common on television and in movies that many characters would have no lines at all if profanity was removed.

Since we know that TV influences life, it stands to reason that at some point life begins to reflect TV. An Associated Press-Ipsos poll last year showed 74% of Americans encounter profanity in public frequently or occasionally. I would guess the prison figure is closer to 100%.

Well over half of Americans (64%) said they use the "F-word" – ranging from several times a day (8%) to a few times a year (15%). It was especially a favorite among men, with 32% saying they use it at least a few times a week, compared to 23% of women.

Two-thirds believe people swear more than they did 20 years ago. Women are more likely than men to encounter people swearing – 75%, compared to 60%. They are also more likely to be bothered by it – 74%, compared to 60% for men. Men, however, admitted to swearing more: 54%, at least a few times a week, compared to 39% for women.

The AP poll, which questioned 1,001 adults between March 20-22, 2006, found that younger people use more bad language and are less bothered by it. Of 18 to 34-year-olds, 62% acknowledge swearing in conversation at least a few times a week, compared to 39% of those 35 and older.

In an AP interview, 67-year-old Irene Kramer says she gets her ears singed when passing the high school near her home. "What we hear, it's gross."

Kramer understands a major culprit to be television. "Do I have to be insulted right there in my own home?" she asks. "I'm not going to pay $54 a month for cable and listen to that garbage." Kramer's sentiments reflect a growing dissatisfaction with television among baby boomers.

DISSATISFACTION GROWING

More than 80% of people over 40 say they have a hard time finding TV shows that reflect their lives, according to a study conducted by Harris Interactive. A significant number of baby boomers – 37% – say they are dissatisfied with what is on television, and nearly two-thirds of Americans correctly believe most TV programs and advertising is targeted toward people under 40.

Advertisers target younger people with the hope of getting them hooked on certain products while their preferences are still forming, making them loyal customers for life. According to Nielsen Media Research, advertisers will pay $335 for every million people in the 18-to-24 age group a network delivers. Viewers ages 55 to 64 are only worth $119 for every million. That is why ABC and NBC conduct all of their business with advertisers in the 18-to-49 demographic. If you are 50 or older, you mean nothing to these network executives, at least from a financial standpoint. For FOX, the CW, MTV, BET, and countless others, even 40 is too old.

Surprisingly, even advertising itself has become alienating to boomers. The Harris Interactive study found half the group says they tune out commercials that are clearly aimed at young people. Another one-third said they go out of their way not to buy such products.

Still, a Schneider Associates/Stagnito survey of 1,001 consumers found TV commercials to be a major purchasing influence, with 67% of respondents watching the ads. The top five purchasing influences are: TV commercial (28%); store display (22%); product itself (15%); family or friend recommendation (13%); item needed (10%). (It is worth noting that people believe the TV over family and friends.)

It is the purpose of television to make money, not to build character. "Most television programming is insipid, illicit, and idiotic," said Douglas Groothuis, Ph.D., in a piece called *How the Bombarding Images of TV Culture Undermine the Power of Words,* in the January-February edition of *Modern Reformation.* And what about the power of words? In a 2002 survey conducted by the Census Bureau, only 38% of men said they read literature at least once in the previous 12 months (women reported 55%). Unfortunately, many newspapers and magazines use the same criteria as television networks, not to mention the ideological slant of the liberal media. If you are tired of killing brain cells on the television and would like to receive some quality, well-written media, there are several advertisement-free, no-cost publications you can receive on a monthly and bimonthly basis.

For quality world news coverage written from a Christian perspective, contact *World News and Prophecy, P.O. Box 541027, Cincinnati, OH, 45254-1027* (12 issues per year) and/or *The Philadelphia Trumpet, P.O. Box 3700, Edmond, OK 73083* (10 issues per year). For quality Christian living magazines with an eye for social issues, contact *The Good News, P.O. Box 54179, Cincinnati, OH, 45254-0179* (six issues per year) and/or *Tomorrow's World, P.O. Box 3810, Charlotte, NC, 28227-8010* (six issues per year). Each of these publications are provided absolutely free in the public interest. You may subscribe for as long as you would like and cancel at any time.

In *The Good News* March-April 2007 article, *Teaching Values to your Child: How to Make Wise Media Choices,* media analyst Marshall McLuhan remarked, "We become what we behold." The psalmist, addressing the Lord, says, "Turn away mine eye from beholding vanity; and quicken thou me in the way" (Psalm 119:37). So stop feeding your mind on the toxic influence of the television and look for godly, enriching ways to fill your time. ✍

Marketing the American dream

Television advertising expenditures in the United States, 2005

Network	**$23,635,000,000.00**
Spot	**$17,115,000,000.00**
Cable	**$16,453,000,000.00**
Spanish Lang.	**$3,072,000,000.00**
Syndicated	**$4,223,000,000.00**
Total	**$64,498,000,000.00**

Source: Reprinted in the *World Almanac, 2007,* with permission from Ad Age (www.adag.com) © 2006, Crain Communications Inc.

Do you really need it

Do you pretty much think of this as a necessity or pretty much think of this as a luxury you could do without?

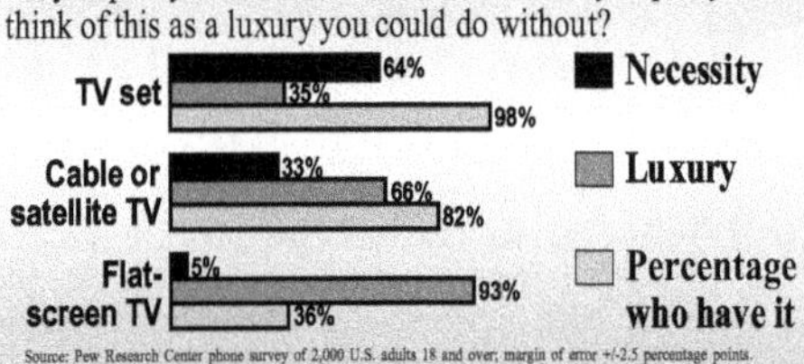
TV set
64%
35%
98%
Cable or satellite TV
33%
66%
82%
Flat-screen TV
5%
93%
36%
Necessity
Luxury
Percentage who have it

Source: Pew Research Center phone survey of 2,000 U.S. adults 18 and over; margin of error +/-2.5 percentage points. Additional sources: American Housing Survey for the U.S., 2005; Statistical Abstract for the U.S., 2006; *USA Today*

Grad

from page 01

do to better himself, "An education is not something they can take from you." Smith challenged the student body to study hard.

Warden Mills also welcomed the visitors and congratulated the students. He compared life with a toolbox and challenged everyone to get another tool for their toolbox. Mills remarked, "Education equips a person to better handle the challenges life throws at you." Thinking toward the future, Mills asked everyone to forget the mistakes they made in the past and instead think about what they will do in the future. Mills said he appreciated the time and effort of both the teachers and the students. He also thanked Bob Kesling for his long involvement in the MCCX educational programs.

To mark this event, Bob Kesling, UT's director of broadcasting was invited to be the keynote speaker for the spring graduation. Kesling graciously accepted and offered a speech he entitled, "Positives in Life."

You may know Kesling as the voice of Tennessee football, basketball and "Vol Calls." Kesling also serves as the television host of the Vol Network's "The Phillip Fulmer Show" and "The Bruce Pearl Show." He is three-time recipient of "Sportscaster of the Year" award for the state of Tennessee. In addition to his broadcasting duties, he represents the University at various events and functions throughout the year and works with UT student-athletes to develop communications and public relations skills.

Before joining UT, Kesling was known throughout the Southeast for his work with Jefferson Pilot Sports and the regional network's SEC football and basketball television package. He was a member of the SEC Radio Network and for twenty-three years served as the radio and television voice of the University of Tennessee women's basketball team. Kesling was also a popular sports director and anchor for Knoxville television station WBIR. A 1977 UT graduate, Kesling was born in Dallas, Texas, but grew up in Kettering, Ohio.

Kesling has served as the radio and television voice for the Lady Vols.

His experience also includes work with the SEC Radio Network, the Knoxville Cherokees (ice hockey) and the Knoxville Blue Jays (baseball). As a UT student, Kesling began his association with the Vol Network by helping edit film for the Bill Battle Show. He went on to serve as John Ward's football game spotter for fifteen seasons and became a fixture on Vol Radio and Television Network broadcasts and specials.

As Kesling prepared to speak, he congratulated the students, family, and staff for their dedication to education. He told a story about his attempts early in life to start a career in football. After having a door shut as a football player, another door was opened for him in broadcasting. Kesling remarked, "The problem isn't the problem, the problem is your attitude about the problem."

Kesling also spoke about setting the bar high. He used an illustration from UT's Head Basketball Coach Bruce Pearl. Upon coming to UT, Pearl set before the university the goal of winning the SEC championship. Kesling compared this with the goal the graduates had set for themselves—earning their diplomas.

Concluding his speech, Kesling told the student body the two most important words in the English language were "Thank you." He asked the students to tell their teachers "Thank you."

After the commencement address, Kesling fielded questions.

In an interview with Kesling following the graduation, he spoke about specific marks of character needed to succeed in life. Having a positive attitude is important. A person's outlook on life largely determines wether or not he will succeed. Above all, Kesling said the single most important trait is being a good listener. "Listen. Don't talk," was the advice he gave to the population at MCCX. He explained that good communication skills begins with being a good listener. In his years in the broadcasting business Kesling has learned to be a good listener and this skill had taught him to be a good broadcaster.

This is the third trip Kesling has made to MCCX to participate in the commencement exercises. We want to thank him for his long involvement and support of the educational pursuits of many inmates over the years. We look forward to seeing him visit again in the future.

After the commencement exercise, a reception was held in the visitation gallery. Refreshments were served compliments of John Cross's Commercial Food Service class. The State Art Shop also provided artwork. On behalf of the student body we would like to thank the administration, education staff, and special guests for making this graduation a success. ✍

Education behind bars

Percentage of adult prison population who have earned high school diplomas or general equivalency diplomas:

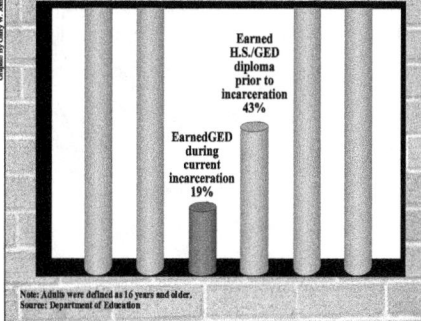

Earned H.S./GED diploma prior to incarceration 43%

EarnedGED during current incarceration 19%

Note: Adults were defined as 16 years and older.
Source: Department of Education

SPRING GRADUATION CLASS OF 2007

General Education Development Graduates

Jeffery Barnett
Chris Bieszec
Reginald Bost
Larry Covington
John Fine
Michael Gross
Michael Lyons
Kevin Moton

Justin Nielsen
James Ownby
Jockaree Phillips
Terry Polidoro
James Purkey
Shannon Russell
Charles Smith
Theodore Smith
Patrick Stansberry
Ricky Stults

Vocational Graduates

Michael Wiest
David Coronado
Michael McCroskey
James Parks
Clarence Porter
Roger Owen
William Voyles
Michael Gay, Jr.
Robert Houseal

97

Straight Talk

from page 01

from Hiawassee College visited. Four of the earliest inmates on the panel were William Forrest, Ricky Ward, Myer Pettyjohn and Tony Rackler. The students were given a chance to participate in a Q&A session with inmates. Their teacher, Dean William Bell, was so impressed with the response that he wrote the governor and asked that members of the prison be allowed to travel to Hiawassee College to address the school. The governor approved and two annex inmates made the trip.

The Straight Talk program has been compared with the New Jersey Scared Straight. However, there is one fundamental difference: the Straight Talk format employs the reality of prison life and the factors that contribute to the incarceration of its members. No scare tactics are used. The program is centered on positive reinforcement. Many inmates see it as a chance for their voices to be heard outside prison fences and perhaps influence law-makers of tomorrow.

DESCRIPTION OF THE STRAIGHT TALK PROGRAM

Guests tour the facility and then have an opportunity to learn what prison life is all about directly from several inmates on the Straight Talk panel. When these students and their teachers come to MCCX they are, of course, apprehensive about visiting a real prison. Their concept of prison life, like a lot of people in the free world, is that it is a place where guards walk around with big guns and the inmates look like something out of Alcatraz. But it does not take long after these young people have been given a brief history and background of MCCX and have taken a tour of our institution, that their preconceived ideas begin to change. The highlight of this life-changing day is when these young people meet with the Straight Talk panel and participate in a panel discussion that lasts up to two hours. One student wrote, "The most important thing to me about that field trip was

learning that you can't beat the system and not to get in with the wrong crowd because all that leads to is trouble. Like most of the prisoners said, they started out in the wrong crowd and look where it got them."

Inmates on the panel lead a discussion which

Straight Talk panel (from left to right): Brandon Patrick, Paul Sharp, Jeremy Ingram, Melvin Lane, Howard Humphrey, Rickey Beamon and Marcus Thomas

includes a brief description of their past and then questions are asked by the students and answered by the inmates. The dialogue focuses on crime, drug and alcohol abuse, peer pressure, and family interaction (especially from youth from dysfunctional family backgrounds). These inmates are able to share their past misguided thinking that resulted in their incarceration. These inmates are able to respond to the students and guests and to express their views without the use of threats, intimidation, or fear tactics which have historically been used in programs of this type.

During a typical session, the students sit silently as each inmate tells his story concerning the things in his past that contributed to his incarceration. Although profanity is not used, the intensity level in the room can be quite high. Jerry Carpenter, a former member of the panel, said what all of the inmate participants feel, "The reason we are talking so straight to you all is because we feel like we are looking into a mirror when we look at you guys. We were all at the same point you are at today, and we know what lies ahead for you if you don't take control of your life."

Often during these sessions, the staff leaves the room (except for one correctional officer) and things usually open up. The participants break it down on a more personal level. At times each inmate breaks into a smaller group and talks one-on-one with the students. As one

teenager put it, "You guys gave me a lot to think about tonight."

The founder of the program, a former warden, said to a group of students, "You can take advice today and take control of your lives or someone will take control of them for you." He was referring to the courts. Inmates believe that the program is a rewarding opportunity to talk to teenagers and give back to society.

RESPONSES TO STRAIGHT TALK

What has been the response of some of these young people who (in the past) have had the opportunity to participate in Straight Talk?

A young man named Steve wrote, "The first time I visited MCCX, I was close to getting sent to Taft; so when you told us about how uncool prison life is, I decided to turn my life around. Now I'm doing good in school and have a girl friend. I just want to say thanks a lot and I hope you get out soon!"

A little girl named Lynn wrote honestly, "I feel that I will benefit from the Straight Talk that I received. It was a disturbing visit for me and my remembrance of this will help keep me out of jail. I really appreciate the volunteering of your time and I believe it has given me a healthy anxiety. Thank you very, very, much."

Not only have the young people benefitted from this program, but the authorities and sponsors have spoken highly of their enthusiasm for Straight Talk.

Phil Keith, Chief of Police of the Knoxville Police Department, wrote, "I strongly believe and support this worthwhile program, and am proud the Police Department is able to work in conjunction with [MCCX] to make it available. I look forward to seeing the Straight Talk program in all middle schools in Knox County in the very near future."

Ms. Vicki Bennett, the "Just Say No" Coordinator of the Boys and Girls Clubs of America in Maryville, states in her letter, "Over the past couple of years I have brought 30—45 young men over to visit the prison to see just a little of what being free really means. Thank you once again for bringing the program to the Boys Club of Blount County." ✍

Highway to hell is life on drugs

When a person is living life on drugs or alcohol, it is like riding in a speeding car down a long stretch of open road, music blasting, everyone caught up in their own selfish thoughts. You tend not to be aware of what is going on outside the vehicle. You are too interested in smoking a cigarette and/or a joint, drinking alcohol, or taking some other type of drug to numb your conscious to what is really going on. Life is a big blur outside your car (life). You don't ever notice what kind of damage you have caused because of your drug use or your criminal behavior to obtain drugs until you reach a point in your life where the vehicle you are traveling in crashes and you start your journey back down the road you had traveled. That is when you start seeing all of the carnage that your actions have caused. You see some of the people that you used to ride down that highway to hell with still riding down it. They are oblivious to you standing on the side of the road because they look at you like you are trying to stop them from having fun or a good time. You are the enemy to them. You will even see some people who didn't make it as far down the road as you did before they changed. You will even see some who are no longer alive because of the life they chose to continue to live. The ditch will be full of broken lives, destroyed

marriages, jobless and homeless people. You may even see some of your family and friends there. These people are not as lucky as you; they didn't survive the ride down the highway to hell. The scene you are seeing is a scene that you rode through while you were oblivious to your surroundings (you were too high to see what tragedies were happening around you). Then you will meet some people that you have hurt very badly while you were living your life like there was no tomorrow. You will see that these people still care about you and want to see you change but will not put up with any of your old ways. The work you will have to put into repairing some of these relationships will be very painful, because you will come face to face with the pain that you have caused in the lives of those around you. If you are lucky you will be able to repair these broken relationships, but there will be some that are too late. That pain and regret will forever be a part of your life and a conscious reminder of who you were and the pain that you caused. So don't be one of those people that you've saw in the ditch who were too stubborn to change or thought that it wouldn't happen to them. Turn your life around and be accountable for your actions before you can only be answerable for them in front of your maker. From a changed man that hopes you change. ✍ —Anonymous submission

The creation and morphing of Straight Talk

By Howard Humphrey

After the prison building explosion of the late 70s and early 80s, the pertinent authorities, staff, and credible inmates, were exploring which programs and concepts that would have the best impact in steering our youth towards making more positive decisions in their lives. Several ideas were floated that were mostly along the traditional "Scared Straight" format.

After great consternation and perplexity about whether that particular format was still viable to the youth of the day, our Christian brother, Myer Pettyjohn, dug down into his deep Christian roots and turned to this verse which he felt was in direct correlation to the message they were trying to convey to youth: Galatians 6:8, which reads as follows, "For he that soweth to his flesh reaps corruption; but he that soweth to the Spirit reaps life

everlasting." In simpler terms, we are all creatures of habit and if we, individually or collectively, get into the habit of doing positive things, then we would get positive results. But on the other hand, if we form negative habits we can only expect negative results. However, as powerful as this message is, it would not mean a thing if the youth we are trying to engage do not respect and accept us in a positive manner. After researching the old and tried "Scared Straight" programs, they learned that it did scare the daylights out of the youth without question, but after the fear wore off, most of those same youth reverted back to their old criminally inspired ways. No system is perfect, but the research also revealed that when a person does something from the heart rather than fear, the results are ingrained, long-lasting, and profound. This is the quintessential difference between the two con-

cepts. Scared Straight gets its results through fear, intimidation, and temporary respect with temporary results, whereas, Straight Talk gets its results through trust, mutual respect, facing up to reality and responsibility, and being able to reach the hearts and minds of the youth of all eras.

These results have proven to be long-lasting and time-tested and in some cases, have changed lives for a lifetime. This brings to mind another biblical passage: "A house built upon the sand will soon come tumbling down, but a house built upon a rock will not fall, but will last forever." The Straight Talk program here at Morgan County was built upon the rock of Christianity. That is why after twenty years, it is still relevant and just as viable today as it was back in the day. Myer Pettyjohn lit the torch. All we have to do now is keep relaying it until the day when we hope and pray, it is no longer needed. ✍

MCCX continues black history tradition

By William Barney

Monday,
February 19, 2007
Mansa Musa
?—1337

Tuesday,
February 20, 2007
Richard Allen
1760—1831

Wednesday,
February 21, 2007
Frederick
Douglass
1817?—1895

Historian Carter G. Woodson was born in New Canton, Virginia. He attended Bere College, the University of Chicago, Harvard, and the Sorbonne in Paris. He became interested in preserving black history so that blacks and whites both would become aware of the contributions blacks have made to this country. In 1915 he established, with others, the Association for the Study of Negro Life and History. He also became editor of the "Journal of Negro History." In 1921 he established Associated Publishers to print textbooks and other supplementary materials on blacks. Books which Woodson wrote have become the foundation upon which more contemporary historians have based their research.

When Mr. Woodson initiated Negro History Week in 1926, he chose the month of February because it contained the birthdays of Abraham Lincoln and Frederick Douglass, the two people he considered to have had the most influence on the lives of blacks up to that time.

Since 1985, MCCX has had a Black History event during the month of February. This year the event was held February 19-24, from 6:00-8:30 p.m. in the chapel.

On Monday night we were treated to a couple of Gospel tunes sung by Lavinia Johnson of United Christian. Also, Adrian Varlack, the night's guest speaker, gave an overview of black history from the 1700's to the present. The one memorable quote from Mr. Varlack's presentation was: Art used to imitate life, now life imitates art.

Inmate Travis "Phoenix" Barton read his poem "The Culprit" on Tuesday night. The guest speaker was Charles Lawrence of St. John's Baptist Church. During his sermon, he reminded us that the only thing that keeps God from doing more for us is ourselves.

The highlight of Wednesday evening was the Gospel singing of the Benn brothers, Calvin and Varnell. Travis Barton treated us to another of his poems, "Hell Is Real." David Upton, our

guest speaker, told us about Cathy Williams who disguised herself as a man and joined the Buffalo Soldiers as William Cathy. He mentioned we cannot help how we were born or how we will die, but we can determine how we will live. He reminded us we cannot have a comeback without first having a setback, and that a winner never quits, and a quitter never wins.

Anointed Men of Praise from Knoxville entertained us on Thursday night with several Gospel songs. This was also the night of Final Jeopardy. Howard "Popcorn" Humphrey entered Final Jeopardy with 54,400 points. He wagered a modest 400 points, which he lost to end up with 54,000 points. Travis "TJ" Sharp came into Final Jeopardy with 40,200 points. In a gutsy move, Travis bet all the points he had. He got the question correct, thereby doubling his score.

On Friday the prizes for the Black History Jeopardy Game were awarded. Our guest speaker was Alvin Douglas, pastor of Anointed Praise and Worship Church in Harriman and brother of the Douglas Sisters singing group.

Trey Lee read his poem "Blessings of Color" on Saturday evening. The night's guest speaker was Anton Reece, Director of Student Activities at UT in Knoxville. Following his presentation, Ruth Hardin gave an interesting overview of the history of black music before she sang two Gospel songs for us.

We thank the *Mountain Review* and the Varsity Club for designing and printing the bulletins for each night's program, the Varsity Club for providing the prizes for the Black History quiz, Randall Vespie for purchasing those prizes, and Herb Judkins for coming in each night so we could get into the chapel by 6:00 p.m. We also wish to thank the many participants in the Black History event that made it a success. These include the inmate speakers, emcees, musicians (both singers and instrumentalists), and the coordinating committee. See you again next year.

Thursday,
February 22, 2007
Granville T.
Woods
1856—1910

Friday,
February 23, 2007
Daniel Hale
Williams
1858—1931

Saturday,
February 24, 2007
Mary McLeod
Bethune
1875—1955

Is juvenile justice black-and-white?

By Garry W. Johnson
MOUNTAIN REVIEW Staff

The discussion about juvenile justice in Tennessee "can't be race-driven," says Dennie Littlejohn in an article on page B1 of the April 21, *News Sentinel.* "People won't hear you" (*Black-and-White justice,* Jamie Satterfield).

But with the numbers in Tennessee showing black youths being incarcerated at a higher rate (compared to their percentage of the overall population) than white youths, race is a hard issue to avoid.

New research shows, however, that race is not necessarily—or even likely—the reason black youths are over represented in juvenile lockups. There is no evidence that judges single out black youths simply because they are black, according to a study that focused on seven Tennessee counties, including Knox.

The study uncovered some clear patterns of probable causes for the present situation. It found that young people coming up in single parent

Knox County Juvenile Justice 2005

	WHITE	BLACK
Total juvenile population	83%	12%
Sent to juvenile court	67%	18%
Sent to adult court	23%	77%
Locked up	57%	40%

Source: Tennessee Disproportionate Minority Confinement Task Force

homes, particularly single women, with little education are most vulnerable to being locked up. Another key factor is poverty, particularly arising from unemployment by a single parent. If the youth in front of a judge were selling dope and/or possessing a gun, harsher punishments are assured upon conviction, the study said.

The educational pursuits of a juvenile offender also play a predominate role in the figures. The academic, athletic or social student is far more likely to avoid lockup. Young people who either shun or are shut out of extracurricular activities are more likely to wind up in trouble.

White children account for 72% of

the total juvenile population in Tennessee; black children make up 21%. In Tennessee juvenile courts in 2005, 52,910 cases were filed against whites and 22,430 cases against blacks.

Of the juvenile offenders ordered locked up in that year, 50% were white and 47% were black. The gap in Knox County was not quite as wide, but still much higher than population totals suggest it should be— 57% white and 40% black.

When it comes to the percentage of youths deemed "unredeemable" in the juvenile system and ordered to stand trial as adults, the gap is even more startling. White youths account for 31% of transferred cases statewide;

blacks youths make up 67%. The disparity is greater in Knox County, with 23% of cases sent to adult court involving white youths, while 77% involved black youths.

Littlejohn, a black man raised by a single mother, chairs the state Disproportionate Minority Confinement Task Force. His group was established under a federal mandate several years ago to start compiling statistics and fixing whatever problems were discovered.

He spoke April 20 at an East Tennessee Council on Children and Youth meeting, held at the Knox County Public Defender's Office. "I know more about what a black child goes through—when the mother has to get up at 5 in the morning to work and you don't see her for the rest of the day," he told the council. "There's no dad, no big brother. All kinds of things go through their heads."

Littlejohn believes it is hard to get people to talk about the numbers because racial issues are too often polar-

izing. He said that even moderates feel uncomfortable with race-based discussions.

He also believes in spending money now to save lives later. "We want to saturate these communities with programs," Littlejohn said. He also realizes that children can be rescued for no money at all. "You can start by talking to the kid on the corner."

Littlejohn wants to see more adults in Knox County (where he lives) helping more children, regardless of race. "The really missing component in this country," he told the council, "is the advocacy, the parents, the ministers, the social workers."

Prison kids decrease

Number of inmates younger than 18 held in state prison:

2001 - 3,147
2002 - 3,038
2003 - 2,741
2004 - 2,485
2005 - 2,266

Source: U.S. Department of Justice

STUDYING THE BRAIN

Neuroscience and neurobiology are both names for the study of the brain. This remarkable field of science has made great strides in our understanding of how the brain works. Yet despite all the progress, there remains much to be learned and discovered.

PRECIOUS CARGO

The brain is very fragile and resembles a walnut made of jello. Brain cells are almost never replaced when damaged or destroyed, so care of the brain is very important.

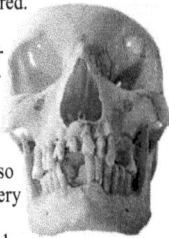

The human body is designed to give the brain three distinct layers of protection. First is a pool of jelly-like tissue, blood vessels and fluid which the brain floats in. This watery layer serves as a cushion to absorb shocks. Three tough membranes called meninges make up the next layer and also protect the spinal cord. The outermost and strongest of the membranes is called Dura mater, followed by the pia mater and the arachnoid. The last line of defense is the skull or cranium.

BIOLOGICAL HARD DRIVE

Powered by blood, oxygen, chemicals and electrical impulses, the complicated collection of cells that is the brain seems to work like a computer. Using less power than a hundred-watt light bulb, the brain consumes more than 25% of the body's required oxygen and 20% of the blood supply.

It would take just 15 seconds without blood flow to the brain to cause unconsciousness. Increase the time to four minutes and serious brain damage would occur. Permanent injury would also result from three to four minutes without oxygen.

Chemicals and drugs can also hurt the brain. Neurons that release serotonin are destroyed by the street drug Ecstacy, for example, and can result in mood swings, troubled thoughts, sleep and motivational difficulties and sometimes death. This is your brain on drugs ...

BRAIN DEVELOPMENT

According to medical experts, babies actually dream while in the womb. A baby's brain can grow incredibly quickly before it is born. There are periods of time during gestation when the brain increases its neurons by 250,000 every minute. At a child's birth its brain weighs less than 1 pound but has almost all the neurons it will ever have. The brain reaches its full weight of about 3.31 pounds (1.5 kg) by age 6, all but 10 ounces of which is water. The adult brain comprises roughly 2% of the bodies weight and is the second-heaviest organ in the human body (after the liver and ahead of the lungs and heart).

FOOD FOR THOUGHT

Eating fish can be important for the development of the brain. Decosahexaenoic acid is essential for the brain to develop and is found in oily fish. However, to keep the mind sharp, vegetables might be the key.

A recent study found that seniors who ate 2.8 servings of vegetables a day (about 1.5 cups) saw their rate of cognitive change slowed by 40%. The new study adds to scientific evidence suggesting a vegetable-laden diet might shore up the memory and protect against Alzheimer's. The Alzheimer's Association also recommends fish and dark-skinned vegetables thought to contain high levels of brain-protecting antioxidants.

THE BRAIN

By Garry W. Johnson
MOUNTAIN REVIEW Staff

This complicated collection of cells is the control center of the human body. Responsible for control of movement, sensory input and a wide range of physiological processes, this small, soft, pinkish-gray mass acts as the organ of thought and the housing of the mind. With all the facts scientists know about the brain, what they do not know is often just as interesting.

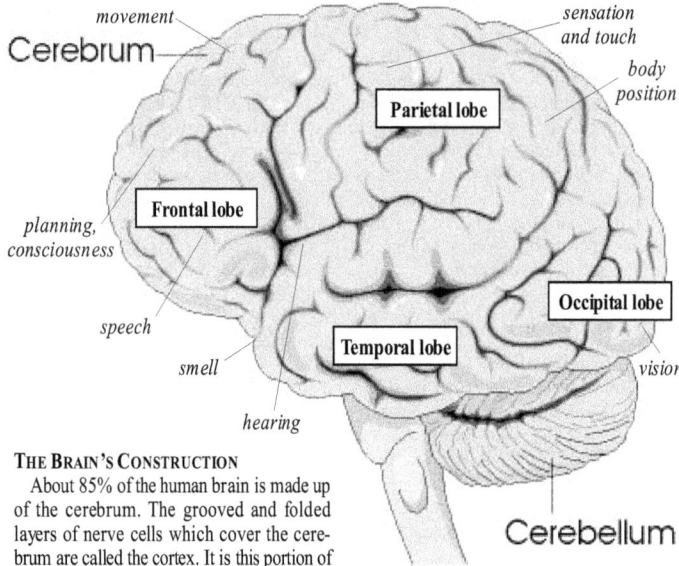

Cerebrum — movement; sensation and touch; body position; Parietal lobe; Frontal lobe; planning, consciousness; speech; smell; hearing; Temporal lobe; Occipital lobe; vision; Cerebellum

THE BRAIN'S CONSTRUCTION

About 85% of the human brain is made up of the cerebrum. The grooved and folded layers of nerve cells which cover the cerebrum are called the cortex. It is this portion of the brain, the cerebral cortex, which allows us to think, speak and remember.

By dividing the brain into halves, scientists have designated left and right hemispheres. Deep groves or fissures in the cortex divide each hemisphere into four lobes.

Anterior (front); Cerebrum; Olfactory bulb; Olfactory tract; Optic nerve; Oculomotor nerve; Trochlear nerve; Pons; Trigeminal nerve; Cerebellum; Spinal cord; Posterior (back)

One of the brain's primary functions is to coordinate all of the nervous activity in the body. The spinal cord and brain together make up the central nervous system. The functional unit of the nervous system is the nerve cell, or neuron. There are 46 miles of nerves in the adult human body, each made of many nerve fibers bound together. This nerve fiber called the axon, may range in length from only a fraction of an inch to many feet and may divide into many branches. The body's longest axon extends from the brain to the muscle controlling the big toe. When you stub your toe it takes 1/50 of a second for your brain to register the pain.

Neurons in the brain allow it to process information by transmitting chemical and electrical impulses. Sensitive fibers called dendrites transmit the signal to the cell body and along the axon. The axon has terminal branches specialized to carry the information to the dendrite of the next neuron.

Maintaining muscle tone, balance and coordinated movement are the primary functions of the cerebellum. Sometimes referred to as "the little brain," it contains a large mass of tightly knit nerve cells called folia, which look like leaves.

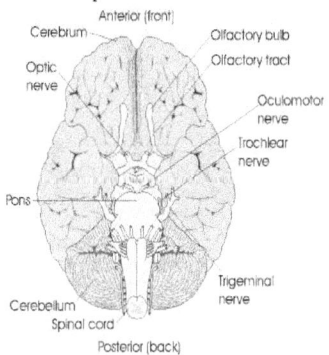

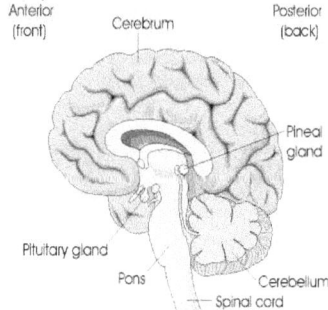

Anterior (front); Cerebrum; Posterior (back); Pineal gland; Pituitary gland; Pons; Cerebellum; Spinal cord

The lifeline between the cerebrum and the spinal cord is the brain stem. A set of nerves called the medulla—which controls breathing, heartbeat, and other essential functions—is located at the bottom of the brain stem. Connecting the brain stem to the cerebrum and cerebellum are the pons. The midbrain and the thalamus are located above the pons.

Cell bodies, dendrites, glia and axons compose the brain's grey matter. White matter is myelinated (coated) axons.

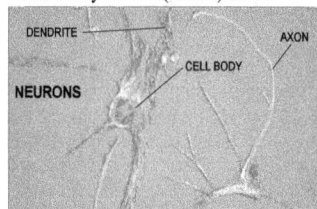

NEURONS — DENDRITE; AXON; CELL BODY

The brain alone has about 100 billion neurons. These cells, however, start to die daily after the age of 20. The brain will lose roughly 10% of it's neurons over a lifetime.

REMEMBERING SLEEP

Sleeping takes up about 2,920 hours or 122 days of the average person's year. Almost a third of our lives are spent asleep.

A new study shows people who are not getting enough sleep may be setting themselves up for attention lapses. The brain actively processes information during sleep, replaying memory during slow-wave sleep (often called deep sleep) in stages of non-rapid eye movement. The replay makes the memory stronger and people who do not get enough sleep (seven to eight hours) have more trouble retrieving the memory when they need the information. For long-term memory and good health sleep is essential. Lack of sleep causes anxiousness, irritability and an inability to concentrate. A person will actually die from a total lack of sleep more quickly than from starvation. About 10 days without sleep will kill you, starvation takes a few weeks longer.

THE ANIMAL BRAIN

Complex brains are not found in most invertebrates (animals without backbones). These animals use groups of nerve cells called ganglia to control their bodies. Two pairs of ganglia can be found in earthworms and three pairs in insects. The most complex brain of all the invertebrates belongs to the octopus.

Well-developed brains can be found in all vertebrates (animals with backbones). In simple vertebrates, the hindbrain or cerebellum is generally larger than the forebrain or cerebrum. In these animals the cerebrum is concerned with smell, the midbrain with vision and the cerebellum with balance and hearing.

Birds have the ability to learn new things. Their cerebrum is larger than those of fish, amphibians and reptiles. It is the bird's cerebellum, however, that controls flying and other motor skills. Comparatively speaking, the larger the cerebrum, the more advanced the design of the brain.

Mammals have the most complex brains. Highly-developed brains can be found in whales

and dolphins. Scientists recently discovered that humpback whales have a type of brain cell seen only in humans, the great apes, and other cetaceans such as dolphins. As in humans, the brain cell (called a spindle neuron) was located in the cortex area.

More than any other animal, the brains of chimpanzees are most like man's, only slightly smaller. That is likely due to the fact that 98% of their DNA is identical to humans.

THE HUMAN MIND

Elephants, whales and dolphins have much larger brains than humans do. The human brain is slightly superior in design, yet not enough to account for the vast difference in output. Although animals have a brain and are equipped with instinct, they have no intellect to understand and choose moral values or to develop godly character.

Could there be a *nonphysical* component in man that separates the human MIND from the animal BRAIN? To learn what scientists and psychologists do not know, please request a copy of *What Science Can't Discover About the Human Mind* and *The Incredible Human Potential*. Both books can be yours absolutely free by writing to the Philadelphia Church of God, P.O. Box 3700, Edmond, OK, 73083. ✍

Anticipating death?

By Jennifer Anderson, RN

As a stray from my usual information delivering column, this issue I am bringing an objective opinion on a different type of nursing issue. The following article is based on my views and opinions on death in a nursing setting and on a personal level. I believe in an afterlife of rewards and that every second of what we do on this earth matters even long after we are gone.

Does death mean the end of everything? Death is feared, dreaded, and avoided at all costs. Why do we loathe it so if such wonderful things await true believers? We shy away from wreckless behaviors, we don't walk down dark allies in the middle of the night—all for the fear of ending it all. The fear of the unknown is such a scary thought, because who really knows what awaits us when this life ends and our eternal life begins? Is it really death we fear or the unknown? I often hear people say in my profession "I'm ready to die." I believe one can be prepared for death, but still be afraid of it. We've all heard the "near death experience" stories—books have been written about this phenomenon and will continue to be until the end of time, but the reality is we never know until our number is called and our life on earth is finished.

In my year as a cancer floor nurse I watched life end on a weekly basis. I saw all of the grief and despair of families and loved ones. I'm not going to quote any books, or television shows, or studies—just my observation of how death has affected me and the patients and families for whom I have cared.

I became somewhat "fascinated" with death at an early age. I lived in Virginia at the time and my grandmother called and broke the news to me that one of my friends had been killed in a car accident along with her two younger siblings. Amanda was twelve, her younger sister was six, her younger brother was five. Their van veered off of a curvy stretch of road and plunged into the Ocoee River. It was reported that all the kids were in their seatbelts and despite frantic attempts to save them, their father was unable to undo the seatbelts. The thought sickened me. I could not imagine what thoughts were going through Amanda's head, if any. Did she realize she was going to take her last breath as the van plunged into the river? Was she aware that her dad loved her so much that he kept diving back under despite physical and mental exhaustion, to try to save her? My grandmother mailed me the obituary—it's been seventeen years since that happened and I still have it. Yellowed with years, I take it out from time to time and reflect. We never know when our time will be up, we never know how or why. I try to think that Amanda was happy on earth in the time that she was here. She always came to my pool parties, despite the fact that she couldn't swim. How ironic that she drowned to death.

I have read the obituaries ever since her death. Everyone thinks I'm strange for that. Maybe I am, maybe I'm possessed by morbidity. As strange as it sounds, I read the obituaries, in a sense, to answer questions about death. The things I absolutely know about death are—it's forever and there is no going back. It is the definite end to life as we know it. Another fact of death is it does not discriminate. It attacks any age, gender, color, and sexuality. The fact is our life will come to an end.

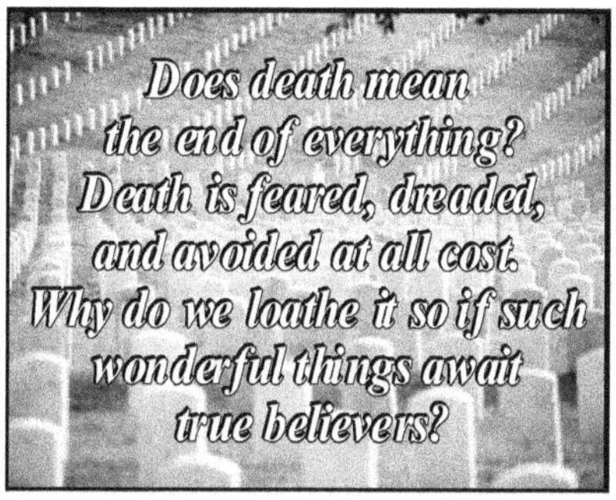

The second encounter I had with death was when my grandmother died. I was twelve and it happened within mouths of Amanda's death. I had been extremely close to my grandmother. She was my "safe-haven" when I felt the world was against me. She had a massive heart attack while sitting in the living room with my grandfather eating ice-cream and watching T.V. It was their nightly ritual. A lot of things happened on the day that my grandmother passed, but what stood out to me was it was the first time I had ever seen my father cry. The next couple of days were a blur and on May 7, 1991, she was buried. I knew she was going to heaven and I know she's there now smiling down on me. At twelve there was no way I grasped the "eternity" of death. I remember standing in front of her coffin looking at her. She looked as if she were sleeping—very peacefully. I looked at the wedding band that had not been off her hand for the past forty years. I cried and cried, but even at twelve, I knew she was going to a better place. The whole family went back to my grandparent's house following the funeral. My grandfather came up and hugged me and in my hand placed the wedding band that had never left my grandmother's hand. It was one of the many times in my life I felt such an immense love and hope that, though my grandmother was gone, life would go on.

I am such a sentimental person—almost to the point of insane. I held that wedding band in my hand on the morning of my wedding and prayed to be blessed with the happiness and longevity that my grandparents had known.

So years later, here I am still wondering and asking the same questions about death. Going into the nursing profession, I had this grand idea that I was going to save the world and make such an impact on so many people's lives. On the cancer floor in my first year of nursing, I felt like I was helping people die instead of helping people live. Out of the hundreds of patients that I cared for in my time on that cancer floor, two particularly stand out in my mind. Of course, many more than that tugged at my heart strings, but these two patients still bring tears to my eyes to this very day.

One very inspiring seventy-two year old lady dying of a terminal illness is the first I'll mention. Her husband was a minister, her family extremely supportive. I loved walking into her room. She was a breath of fresh air, because instead of the usual, "I'm gonna beat this, the doctor says there's a fifty percent chance," she had accepted the fact that she had only weeks, maybe even days left on this earth. Only a minimal amount of time to say all the things she wanted to say to her husband and her family. I never heard a negative word come out of her mouth. She talked as if her life was not ending. She told me stories of all the places that her and her husband had traveled. She truly believed that she had gotten the most out of her life. One of the last things she ever said was "I can't wait to see Jesus!" She died shortly afterward, surrounded by her family and me. At first I felt like an intruder, but she had wanted me there—she was holding my hand and I slowly felt her grip loosen and completely release as she breathed her last breath. And to everyone's amazement in the room that watched this, she died with a huge smile on her face! At first her husband and I just looked at each other—almost in disbelief and he said to me as if needing confirmation, "She's smiling, isn't she?" I responded, "Yes, she is". He said it again and again excited to tell his family. He almost shouted, "She saw Jesus, she saw Jesus!" He shed tears, but they weren't the familiar tears I usually saw, instead they were tears of joy. His beloved wife was going to receive her heavenly rewards. No more pain from her illness, no more suffering, no more tears, only infinite happiness. How inspiring to know that it can be that way—to celebrate instead of grieve. It truly amazed me.

My other touching story was a husband and wife of fifty-four years. Diagnosed with pancreatic cancer, the husband was given a maximum of three months to live. I cared for him for six weeks, right up until he succumbed to his cancer. He straddled the line between life and death for about four nights and his wife would not leave his side. She was exhausted, delirious, but determined that she was not leaving him. She wouldn't even sleep. She had requested that if she did fall asleep, I was to wake her up so she "wouldn't miss anything." I went into his room on the fourth night and his breathing was shallow, his oxygen level was dropping despite the non-rebreather mask covering his face. His wife looked at me and asked, "Is tonight the night?" Now, how does one answer that question? Dumbfounded, I stuttered, "We never know when." He died that night and she was right there beside him holding his hand with her head on his chest. I don't think she knew he was gone at first. I entered the room and went through the ritual of trying to find a pulse, listening with my stethoscope to the beatless heart. She looked at me and I told her that he was gone. She answered, "I know, but I'll see him again one day, and when I do it's going to be one heck of a reunion!"

I may wonder until the day I actually do die about what death really entails, but from this day forward I want to challenge everyone, including myself, to live life on this earth with the wonderful thought that a marvelous afterlife awaits me and that every second and every action that I make counts. I'm going to anticipate what the afterlife holds. I mean after all, death is just the moment that you take your last breath, your heart beats for the last time, and then it's done. It's the afterlife that goes on forever and ever. I may never have the answers, but I am content with never knowing because, what I do know is, there's something bigger and better and more indescribable than anything I can think of on the earth waiting for me. And in the words of my precious patients's wife, "It's going to be one heck of a reunion when we get there!" ✍

— The ageing process —

By Garry W. Johnson
Mountain Review Staff

Skin: Strength and elasticity of the skin are reduced by changes in the connective tissue. Wrinkles, creases, folds and furrows increase as collagen and elastin degenerate.

Muscles: They start to lose mass and shrink as the number and size of muscle fibers decrease.

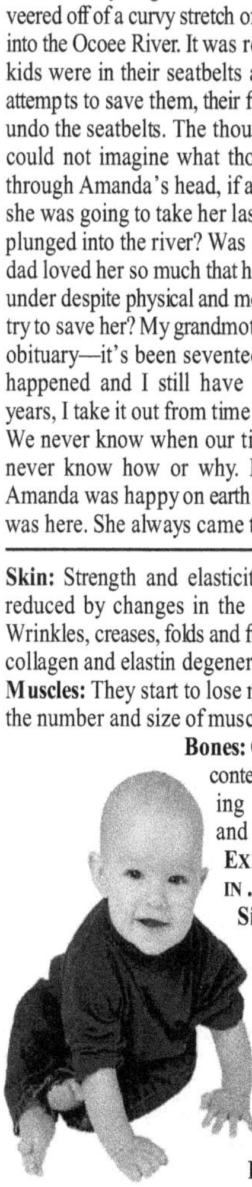

Bones: Over time mineral content decreases, making them less dense and more fragile.

EXPECT CHANGES IN ...

Sight: In your 40's visual acuity begins to decline.

Taste: At about 40 in women and starting at 50 in men the number of taste buds decreases.

Hearing: About 50 slight decline begins.

Smell: Around 70 decline is especially sensed.

OTHER AGING DECLINES ...

We tire more easily and take longer to recover as our heart becomes less able to pump large quantities of blood quickly throughout the body. We lose nerve cell mass. After 50 the stomach produces less acid which makes it more difficult to absorb vitamin B12 found naturally in food.

Because of changes in tendons and ligaments handgrip strength decreases, joint motion becomes more restricted and flexibility decreases. Cartilage begins to break down, which reduces cushioning between bones. And at a rate of about 0.4 inches for every 10 years after 40, height progressively decreases.

WHAT YOU CAN DO ...

Mental acuity: Physical activity and increased intake of vitamin B may help cut the risk of Alzheimer's disease.

Vision: Reduce risk of cataracts by wearing UV-shielded sunglasses. Macular degeneration can be combated by eating your vegetables, especially spinach. Also, smoking and caffeine can damage your eyesight.

Bones: To help preserve bone weight-bearing exercise like walking, jogging, and weight training can help. And do not forget to drink your milk, calcium and vitamin D are important.

Muscles: Weight training will help slow age-related muscle loss.

Digestive tract: Men should consume at least 38 grams of fiber daily, women need 25 grams.

Blood: To help prevent anemia, heart and neurological problems, foods rich in vitamin B12 are recommended.

Heart and blood vessels: Brisk physical activity—at least 30 minutes daily. Eat fiber-rich foods and two servings of fish weekly. Limit salt and skip or minimize as much trans fatty acids, saturated fat and cholesterol as possible.

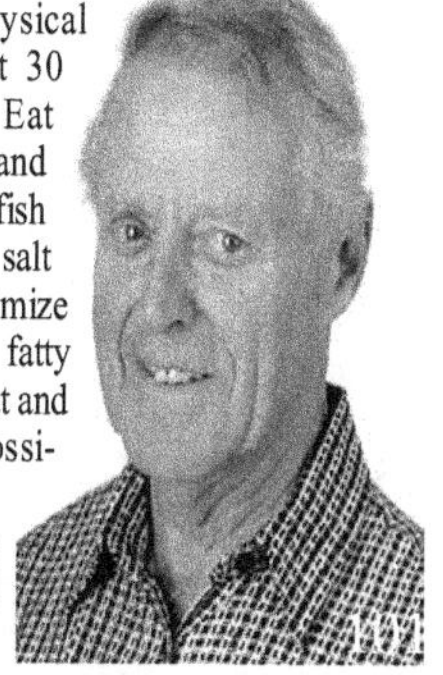

Skin: Use sunscreen and quit smoking. ✍

Prison Life

AN OVERVIEW OF PRISON NEWS AND CRIME STATISTICS FROM AROUND THE U.S.A.—BY GARRY W. JOHNSON

Inmate population to continue rising

In the next five years the U.S. prison population will likely rise nearly 13% and cost states up to $27.5 billion in new construction and operating expenses, according to new analysis by the Pew Charitable Trusts. The predicted cost increase is nearly half the amount now spent on American prisons each year.

Pew, a Philadelphia-based philanthropic organization that funds research on a variety of issues, projects the nation's inmate prison population will be about 1.72 million by 2011, up from last year's prediction of 1.53 million. The increase would be roughly equivalent to the current federal prison system population.

The Pew report, released in February, said the growth is being fueled by mandatory minimum sentences, declines in inmates granted parole and other policies states have passed in hopes of stemming crime. Also a factor in boosting prison populations are high rates of repeat offenders. Almost two-thirds of the more than 600,000 people admitted to prison each year have failed to satisfy terms of probation or parole.

As we reported in the last issue of the *Mountain Review,* female incarceration rates are now higher than males'. This new report predicts female incarceration will continue to rise at a rate of 16%, over males at 12%.

Researchers based their findings on population forecast gathered from the federal Bureau of Prisons and 42 states. For the eight states that did not provide projections, estimates were based on the states' most recent prison admission and release data.

"The projected growth is phenomenal," according to Sue Urahn, managing director of Pew's state policy programs. "But whether it comes to this is up to the states. They determine who goes to prison and for how long." ✎

Forecast: More people in prison

A study projects major growth in the U.S. prison population. The Pew Charitable Trust says more than 1.7 million adults will be in prison by 2011—an increase of nearly 200,000 from 2006. A look at the prison landscape:

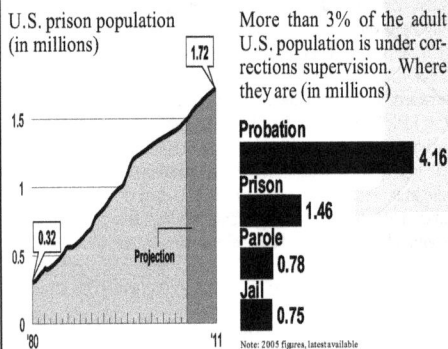

U.S. prison population (in millions)

More than 3% of the adult U.S. population is under corrections supervision. Where they are (in millions)

Probation	4.16
Prison	1.46
Parole	0.78
Jail	0.75

Note: 2005 figures, latest available

Projected increase of prison population in all 50 states

Mont.	41%	N.M.	21%	Okla.	13%	Ala.	7%
Ariz.	35%	Maine	21%	Kan.	13%	R.I.	7%
Alaska	34%	Ohio	20%	Ore.	13%	Mass.	6%
Idaho	34%	Fla.	18%	Neb.	12%	Mo.	6%
Vt.	33%	Pa.	17%	Va.	12%	Tenn.	5%
Colo.	31%	Ark.	17%	Mich.	11%	Wis.	5%
Wash.	28%	Iowa	16%	Ga.	11%	La.	4%
Wyo.	27%	N.H.	16%	Calf.	9%	Md.	1%
Nev.	27%	W.Va.	16%	Texas	9%	Conn.	0%
Utah	25%	S.C.	16%	N.C.	9%	N.Y.	0%
S.D.	23%	Indiana	15%	Ill.	8%	Del.	0%
Ky.	22%	N.D.	14%	N.J.	8%		
Hawaii	22%	Minn.	13%	Miss.	8%		

Sources: Pew Charitable Trust, Bureau of Justice Statistics

Politics play a prominent role in death-penalty cases

Recent decisions by the supreme Court and the 6th Circuit Court of Appeals highlight the political position of judges and show how their ideology affects the outcome of cases.

A sharply divided Supreme Court in June reinstated the death sentence of a Washington state murderer by a 5-4 vote. The ruling, which broke down sharp conservative-liberal lines, emphasizes that trial judges have wide latitude to decide when to cut potential jurors who object to capital punishment.

Tied closely to the facts of Cal Coburn Brown's appeal and statements of a potential juror, the decision could make it harder for other convicts to challenge a judge's decision during jury selection.

The conservative majority reversed a U.S. appeals court decision that said a judge erred during Brown's 1993 trial by removing a man who expressed ambiguity about the death penalty.

Justice Anthony Kennedy, writing for the majority, stressed that appeals court judges, "owe deference to the trial court, which is in a superior position to determine the demeanor and qualifications of a potential juror."

Justice John Paul Stevens, who took the rare step of reading portions of his dissent from the bench, said the level of deference given to the trial judge was "completely unwarranted." He went on to say millions of Americans oppose the death penalty but can serve as jurors in capital cases, as long as they set aside their personal beliefs.

The other dissenting justices, David Souter, Ruth Bader Ginsburg and Stephen Breyer all signed Stevens' statement.

As the usual practice of dissenters is to let their written statements speak for themselves, Stevens' comments from the bench are just the latest example of a growing pattern in the Supreme Court.

The four liberal justices are increasingly finding themselves on the losing side of cases after years of dominating the court and are objecting in unusually forceful terms. In two recent cases, Ginsburg has lashed out at the conservative majority in dissents from the bench.

The ideological divide is not confined to the high court either. A recent newspaper study found the fate of death penalty defendants before a federal appeals court often depends on the political party of the president who appointed the judges.

The study focused on the 6th U.S. circuit Court of Appeals —which handles cases from Ohio, Kentucky and Tennessee—and found that Republican appointed judges voted to deny death penalty appeals 85% of the time. Democratic appointees, on the other hand, voted to support at least part of the appeals 75% of the time.

The Enquirer in Cincinnati examined the 85 death penalty cases considered between January 2000 and April 7, 2007 by the 6th Circuit judges and found judges "consistently voted along partisan lines."

Inmates seeking appeals from the federal courts are first heard by a three-judge panel, which usually decide the inmate's fate. If the inmate loses with the panel he or she can request the full Circuit to consider the ruling, however, the full court rarely disagrees with the three-judge panels and fewer still are heard by the Supreme Court.

The court has 14 active judges and two semi-retired senior judges. Republican presidents appointed nine of the judges, the other seven by Democrats. Democrat Jimmy Carter's appointees vote, at least in part, in the inmates favor 89% of the time; Appointees of Republican Ronald Reagan voted in favor in 25% of cases; Republican George H. W. Bush's appointees, 7%; Democrat Bill Clinton's appointees 70%; and appointees of Republic President George W. Bush, 13% of the time.

"That means life-and-death decisions often hinge on the luck of the draw: A panel with a liberal majority gives the inmate a far greater chance of avoiding execution than one with a conservative majority," *The Enquirer* found.

Tom Fitton, president of the conservative group Judicial Watch said, "When you have the courts ... making such divergent rulings on similar facts and circumstances, it really throws off-kilter the administration of justice." ✎

Shower reveals feminine nature of inmate

People are not always who they appear to be. Investigators in Nashville learned that the hard way. In March, while awaiting a court appearance on an aggravated statutory rape charge, Alexander David Cross was discovered to be a woman as she showered in the county jail.

Chattanooga investigators were forced to reopen the case upon discovering Cross' correct gender and began by searching the house where she had been staying. They found among other things an original birth certificate for Elaine Ann Cross and an amended birth certificate from Pennsylvania dated 1997 changing the name to Alexander David Cross. A letter from Pennsylvania accompanied the amended certificate informing Cross that the gender of her birth could only be changed on the certificate upon proof of a successful sex change operation. It was not clear if she was actually pursuing a sex change.

The 42-year-old Cross pleaded guilty to an aggravated statutory rape charge stemming from a sexual relationship with a 15-year-old girl. As part of the deal, Cross will not serve any more jail time if she stays out of trouble for six years.

Hamilton County Assistant District Attorney General Boyd Patterson said, "The victim was completely in love with him." According to the charge, Cross performed oral sex on the teenager at least three times during June and July 2006. When she believed Cross was a man, the teenager had considered marrying him, Patterson said. "Now (the teenage victim) just wants it over with. I think the victim is going to have a lot to deal with."

Cross must register as a convicted sex offender, have no contact with the teen and change her gender designation on her driver's license to female as part of the plea deal. Authorities are still trying to determine how Cross obtained the licence with the fraudulent gender designation. ✎

For some, prison is a necessity

It is not every day that a defendant and prosecutor agree, but Kelly J. Gudger Jr. and Assistant U.S. Attorney Mike Winck both believe that Gudger is a dangerous guy and should remain behind bars.

Gudger had a second chance in March to convince Senior U.S. District Judge James H. Jarvis to cut him a break for a 2002 bank robbery and shootout with police, thanks to the landmark U.S. Supreme Court decision that struck down mandatory federal sentencing guidelines.

Winck reeled off for Jarvis Gudger's "career" of violent crime, ranging from an "ugly" kidnaping in Kentucky to the October 2002 Harrogate bank robbery for which Gudger wound up in federal court. In that case, Gudger opened fire on authorities, firing 19 shots before he was captured. "He emptied a .380 pistol on the police," said Winck. "He had a bulletproof vest on. He's dangerous."

"I agree with the prosecutor," Gudger added. He then asked Jarvis to reinstate the 248-month prison term he received three years ago under a sentencing scheme now deemed unconstitutional by the nation's high court. "If I get the regular sentence back, I guess I'll be happy," Gudger remarked. Jarvis reinstated his sentence.

Defense attorney Randall Reagan said a forensic examiner opined that Gudger hailed from "the most dysfunctional family the examiner has ever seen." At a hearing in U.S. District Court Gudger said he was literally "drinking in my momma's womb," noting that his mother was both drinking and smoking while pregnant with him. Reagan said Gudger's father taught him to fire a gun at age three, and that he "would shoot at him" as discipline.

Gudger began abusing alcohol at a young age and has a history of mental illness. He told judge Jarvis he was ready to go back to the medical prison in Butner, North Carolina, where he is currently he is being housed and treated. ✎

States resume executions with little change in method

On May 9, 2007, Tennessee resumed executing prisoners sentenced to death in state courts. The state halted executions in February to review procedures and rewrite the state's 100-page *Manual of Execution*. Governor Phil Bredesen's 90-day moratorium on the death penalty expired May 2, just seven days before the state executed Philip Workman for the 1981 shooting death of a Memphis police officer (see side bar on Workman).

On April 5, a public hearing was held seeking ideas on topics like changing the state's lethal drug formula and continued testing of the electric chair, last used for an execution in 1960. Few people showed up, and only four spoke at the hearing; two questioned the morality of the death penalty and the other two questioned the possibility of developing good protocols for lethal injection and electrocution in only 90 days. [Convicts who committed their capital crime before January 1999, can still opt for electrocution.] None of the participants addressed the topics at hand.

As reported in the last issue of *Mountain Review*, Tennessee's previous manual for executing prisoners was a jumble of conflicting instructions that mixed lethal injection instructions with those for the electric chair. Bredesen called the manual a "cut-and-paste job" that needed significant revision and said Tennessee's execution teams relied on an "oral tradition" and routine drills to ensure propriety.

The governor stayed the executions of four inmates scheduled to die between February and May. The reprieves came after a law suite brought against the state by death-row inmate Edward J. Harbison challenged an earlier version of the execution manual.

Harbison sued over the lack of specific guidelines, an absence of required professional standards for the execution team and the kinds of drugs used in the lethal cocktail which opponents say is needlessly cruel.

The revised rules, released April 30, still include the three-chemical method which Correction Commissioner George Little said "has been found to be humane when properly administered," in a letter to Bredesen. "We have significantly improved the documentation and procedures to support the three-chemical protocol."

Little would not comment on whom the commission has spoken to with regard to medical expertise, as the American Medical Association's code of ethics forbid its members to participate in executions.

A special commission in Florida studying lethal injection wrote in a final report that its ability to gather information was limited because "medical personnel are prohibited from participating in executions and rendering technical advice."

Nevertheless, Florida has also resumed executions that were suspended after the botched lethal injection of Angel Diaz, 55, on December 13, 2006. Diaz took 34 minutes to die, twice the usual time and had chemical burns on his arms after the lethal injection procedure.

Despite recommendations to explore other chemical mixes by a governor's panel, Florida officials "determined that the three-drug cocktail that currently is being used here ... was in fact the protocol we're going to stick with," according to Florida's prisons chief Jim McDonough.

A three-judge panel of the 8th U.S. Circuit Court of Appeals also has opened the way for Missouri to resume executing inmates. Their ruling stated that the lethal injection procedure used in that state is not cruel and unusual punishment. The court found no evidence that "the last six inmates executed suffered any unnecessary pain."

DNA usage expands to nonviolent crimes

Unsolved burglaries and other property crime cases are increasingly being subjected to the FBI database of DNA which was designed to help solve rapes and murders, according to an October 2006 review by *USA Today*.

The report indicated that Alabama, Florida, Indiana, Michigan, Missouri, New Mexico, Ohio, Oregon, Virginia and Wisconsin all have DNA matches in property-crime cases exceeding the number of matches in violent crimes. Other states are also following suit. In Georgia the first 171 matches contain only 13 DNA samples from unsolved burglaries. Of the next 300 matches, 79 were in burglary cases.

As DNA testing becomes more sophisticated analysts can draw genetic profiles from palm prints, cigarette butts, sweat stains on gloves and mask nearly as easily as they do from blood and semen, according to Oregon state police DNA analyst, Brian Ostrom. The wider scope allows for more effective use in property crime cases accompanied by government grants for that purpose, which use to be limited to violent crimes.

The states, the federal government and the military have collected DNA from felons since 1990 and stored the genetic profiles in computer databases. Several states even collect DNA in misdemeanor convictions (some have even proposed adding DNA of suspects in criminal cases, though that has yet to be approved). The profiles are compared with DNA from crimes using FBI software.

As of October 2006, the database contained about 3.5 million DNA profiles and had scored matches in about 38,000 cases, according to FBI scientist Thomas Callaghan. About 25,000 profiles are added to the system every month.

Critics say dramatically expanding the database to solve nonviolent crimes could raise privacy concerns. Some are concerned about spending millions of dollars to probe such crimes. University of Minnesota political science professor Jay Aronson says, "For what it does in terms of cost, and in threats to civil liberties, (the database) has to justify itself much better."

Proponents of expanding DNA testing say burglars often go on to commit more serious crimes. About 80% of rapes solved via DNA databasing in Alabama in the past five years were linked to criminals whose DNA was taken after a burglary conviction, state forensic biology chief Angelo Della Manna, says.

Colorado considers farming out inmates

An illegal-immigration crackdown has left private farmers in Colorado shorthanded and the state is considering letting prisoners take up the slack.

Corrections Department Executive Director Ari Zavaras said the program would probably start in Pueblo County and operate under the prison industry division that trains and employs about 1,200 inmates.

Joe Pisciotta and Phil Prutch, Pueblo County farmers say immigrant workers are afraid to come to Colorado due to tough immigration laws passed there last summer.

The laws require, among other things, people receiving state and federal benefits to prove they are legal U.S. residents.

Prison calls private ... kinda

A federal judge ruled last March that even though police and prosecutors can listen to recorded inmate telephone conversations, the tapes are not public-record and therefore cannot be subpoenaed by defense attorneys.

Prosecutors and law enforcement have increasingly made use of jail chats to bolster criminal cases, as in the high profile trail of Imperial Insane Vice Lords gang leader Walter "Heavy" Williams. In that trial jurors were played recordings of Williams' phone calls from state prison to show he was still running the street gang from behind bars. Those recordings helped lead to Williams' conviction in federal court.

In the case of alleged drug kingpin Vicente Corona, prosecutors charged that the illegal immigrant supplied a quarter-ton of cocaine and a half-ton of marijuana via mail delivery services to drug dealers in Knoxville and Georgia. Corona says he is being set up by alleged conspirators who told tales on him to get sentencing breaks.

Defense attorney Stephen Johnson used a subpoena to demand recordings of phone calls made by the six drug dealers while locked up in either Blount or Knox county jails, after both facilities opined that inmate phone calls are not public records. "I think there's an argument to be made that they are public under the Tennessee open Records Act," Johnson told U.S. District Magistrate Judge Bruce Guyton.

Assistant U.S. Attorney Mike Winck countered Johnson's argument with another set of recordings—the Nixon tapes. Winck said the court battle over a prosecutor's attempt to force the White House to turn over taped conversations between then-President Richard Nixon and his aides during the Watergate scandal laid out rules for when a defendant can subpoena information.

In his written opinion Guyton sided with Winck, saying that both the Nixon case and one involving dethroned Panama dictator Manuel Noriega are indeed the standard bears on the issue.

Noriega was overthrown in the late 1980's and later convicted of violating U.S. laws, including money laundering and drug trafficking statutes. It was the government in his case that sought to subpoena Noriega's jail calls.

Guyton wrote that in both cases the law required some proof that the information sought is "evidentiary and relevant." He opined that Corona failed that test.

On the issue of wether the jail tapes might fall under the Tennessee Open Records Act, Guyton said, "The general rule is that documents in an open criminal case ... are not subject to public inspection under the act."

The judge did order Winck to turn over any jailhouse recordings he or his agents might have of Corona's calls.

Federal rules allow Johnson to appeal Guyton's decision. Corona was set for trial in June.

Philip Workman

The May execution of 53-year-old Tennessee inmate Philip Workman was only the state's third execution by lethal injection and had been delayed by the courts five times. The 6th U.S. Court of Appeals lifted the final restraining order on May 7, which was filed over concerns about the state's revised execution method (see: *States resume executions with little change in method*).

In 1981 Workman was robbing a Wendy's restaurant when police showed up and a gun battle ensued. One officer was wounded and another, Lt. Ronald Oliver, was killed. Workman claimed another officer's bullet accidentally killed Oliver.

According to the state medical examiner Dr. Bruce Levy, Workman's autopsy "revealed no unexpected findings."

Workman had filed a petition before his death saying that an autopsy and embalming conflicted with his religious beliefs. A federal judge, however, cleared the way on May 18 for a "less-invasive" autopsy which showed Workman died of "acute intoxication" caused by "judicial execution by lethal injection."

Tennessee's two prior lethal injections were Robert Glen Coe in 2000 and Sedley Alley in June 2006. Before Coe, the state had not executed an inmate since 1960, and that was by electrocution.

The New Castle Riot

On April 24, 2007, inmates at a medium-security men's prison in Indiana staged a two-hour riot. Two staff members of the New Castle Correctional Facility were injured and helicopter video showed at least two fires burning in the courtyard. State Department of Correction spokeswomen Java Ahmed said more than one housing unit was involved in the disturbance at the facility located roughly 43 miles east of Indianapolis. According to State Police Sgt. Rod Russell, authorities secured the prison perimeter and no inmates escaped.

The riot began after a group of inmates from Arizona refused orders and removed their shirts in the prison's recreation area, said Correction Commissioner J. David Donahue. Built to house about 2,200 inmates, the prison has about 1,000 prisoners from Indiana and 630 from Arizona. In March, Indiana agreed to house up to 1,260 Arizona inmates.

By Garry W. Johnson, Staff writer

Communication captures

Number of people arrested because of intercepted wire or oral communication:

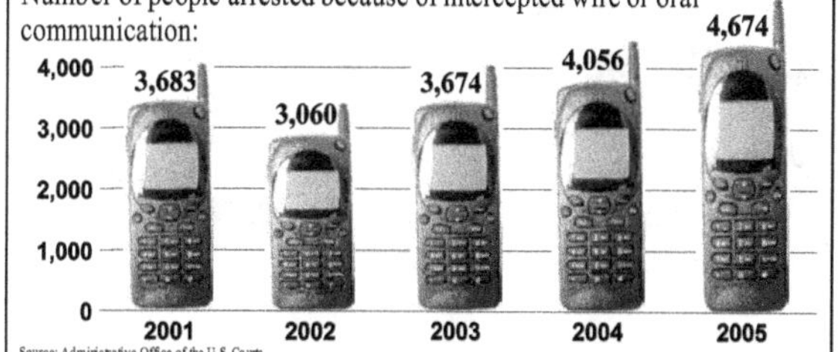
4,000
3,000
2,000
1,000
0
3,683
3,060
3,674
4,056
4,674
2001
2002
2003
2004
2005

Source: Administrative Office of the U.S. Courts

Nationwide DNA exonerations clear 200

By Garry W. Johnson
MOUNTAIN REVIEW Staff

Jerry Miller, who spent nearly 25 years in prison, was the 200th person to be cleared of a wrongful conviction by DNA evidence since the technology was first used for that purpose in 1989. On April 24, Judge Diane Cannon cleared Miller of all charges stemming from the September 1981 rape, robbery, assault and kidnaping of a Chicago office worker in a Near North Side parking lot. Miller, who was paroled from prison in March 2006, cheered after the judge made her decision.

"It was a high-profile case, and they basically had it in their minds to convict me from the start," Miller said of prosecutors in a USA Today interview. DNA testing had not yet been used in a criminal case when Miller was convicted.

The victim testified that she had been assaulted by a black man—whom she never got a good look at—robbed and raped in the back seat of her car before being thrown in the trunk. Miller was identified by two parking lot attendants, both black men, as the person who attempted to drive the car out of the parking lot, but fled when challenged. Miller's alibi, that he had been home watching the Sugar Ray Leonard-Thomas Hearns welterweight title bout, could only be confirmed by family members. To add to his appearance of guilt, he had been briefly detained by police a few days earlier for acting suspiciously near parked cars in the area.

Miller, a former Army cook, was convicted in 1982 of rape, robbery, kidnaping and aggravated battery.

After losing his appeal, serving 25 years in prison and being paroled, Miller still insisted on DNA testing to remove the "stigma" of the conviction and to be removed from Illinois' sex-offender registry. "I really need to hear from the judge—'your record is clear, we know you didn't do it'—before I feel truly free," Miller said before his exoneration hearing. "I'm waiting for this to be finally, truly over."

In March Miller got his wish when

DNA reversals

As of April 23, nine people this year have been exonerated of crimes due to DNA evidence. Yearly totals:

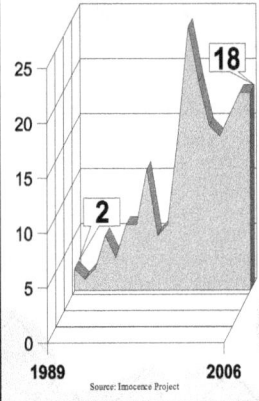

Source: Innocence Project

the genetic profile drawn from semen stains at the crime scene was shown not to match his DNA.

Continuing to insist you are innocent is the second-hardest part of living with a wrongful conviction says Miller, now 41-years-old. "Getting people to believe you" is the hardest part. "You know everybody (in prison) can't be innocent, but there's a lot of guys who say they are, and they've got pretty good cases," he believes. "But so many of them get discouraged, and they give up."

DNA exonerations have steadily picked up pace since the first case was overturned in 1989, according to the New York-based Innocence Project whose attorneys were instrumental in Miller's case. The legal group, which has 36 affiliates at law schools and law offices across the United States, says Miller's exoneration underscores the quickening pace of overturned convictions. Innocence Project records show that the 100th exoneration occurred in January 2002, 13 years after the first. In the little more than five years since then, that number has doubled. Miller expects the trend will continue because there are more innocent people in prison "than you would ever think."

Attorney Berry Scheck, cofounder of the Innocence Project says, "Five years ago, people said that the number (of exonerations) was going to dry up because there just weren't many wrongful convictions. ... But clearly, there are plenty of innocent persons still in prison. There's no way you can look at this data without believing that."

Improved testing technology and an increase in the number of lawyers who are willing to take on DNA cases should result in a continued increase in the number of wrongful convictions that are set aside, according to David Lazer, a Harvard University public policy professor who specializes in DNA issues.

Scheck notes that the "typical" DNA exoneration case has not changed much over the years. He says it often involves a sex crime allegedly committed by a black man in which the white victim is often the only witness.

According to the Federal Bureau of Justice Statistics, there were 1,051,000 felony convictions in state courts in 2002. That number is up from 829,300 in 1990. With this massive amount of activity in the courts, mistakes are bound to happen. Miller compares the criminal justice system to "a big assembly line," saying that "lots of products come off, and most of the time it's O.K." He notes however, "... then there's the defects, the one's that are messed up. ... You got an assembly line, you're always going to have some defects."

Since making parole in 2006, Miller has lived with his family in a town outside Chicago. He works as an attendant on a shuttle bus for disabled people and cooks part-time at a restaurant.

Before being exonerated Miller's parole required him to wear a Global Positioning System-based monitor that allowed parole officers to monitor his whereabouts and he was under an order forbidding him to interact with children. "It's like there's this weight I been carrying around for 25 years ..." Miller's weight has finally been lifted.

Overturned convictions

Number of overturned convictions per state[1]

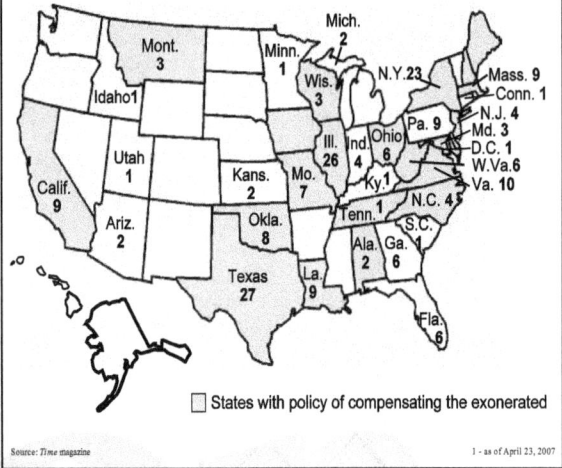

☐ States with policy of compensating the exonerated

Source: Time magazine

1 - as of April 23, 2007

Some states have no policy for compensating the exonerated

In 1981, three armed black men robbed five white occupants of an apartment in Tampa, Florida, and kidnaped and raped two of them —a woman, 38, and a 12-year-old girl. After the sexual assault, the perpetrators left their victims tied to a tree.

The woman later picked the photo of Alan Crotzer from a group of pictures shown to her by investigators. In 1982, Crotzer was sentenced to 130 years for his part in the gruesome crime. There was only one problem, he did not do it. Last year Crotzer was released after DNA testing proved him innocent.

Crotzer suffered greatly for someone else's horrid actions. While in jail awaiting his brief trail, he was slashed across the face by another inmate with an improvised knife. In an interview with DeWayne Wickham, Crotzer said his time in prison was even worse and relayed that rape and violent attacks were regular occurrences in the Florida penitentiary, sometimes at the hands of guards.

Crotzer, now 45, spent more than half his life behind bars. "I did 24 years, seven months, 13 days and four hours," he told Wickham, a weekly columnist for USA Today. Crotzer doubted he would ever get out of prison alive and credited his mother's faith for keeping him going. "She would tell me, 'Baby, don't give up 'cause God's gonna fix it. And when He fixes it, He's going to fix it right.'"

His mother died while he was in prison. Crotzer was not permitted to attend the funeral.

If his story was not heart-rending enough, Florida is one of 29 states that does not have a law prescribing how to compensate wrongfully imprisoned persons, according to the Innocence Project. Jenny Greenberg, executive director of the project's

Florida chapter says, "There has to be a process through the Legislature to pay people for the time they spend in prison for crimes they didn't do. The money and an apology are critical for their healing."

Though the Florida House passed a measure that would have given Crotzer $1.25 million, the state senate did not act on the bill. Without the legislation, Florida deals with these matters on a case-by-case basis—or in this case, not at all. In the 15 months since his release Crotzer, who has no useful job skills, has struggled to get his life on track. All this for a man whose only prior arrest was for stealing beer as a teenager.

Joshua Marquis, vice president of the National District Attorneys Association, says that convicting an innocent person is "every prosecutor's nightmare." Marquis is chief prosecutor in Clatsop County, Oregon (another state with no set policy for compensating the exonerated) and believes the "tiny number" of exonerations suggest the problem with bad convictions in the justice system is minimal.

Minimal as the problem maybe, the consequences for the individual can be permanent. Though Crotzer was robbed of more than half his life—what could have been his most productive years—some could have lost even more. Since the first exoneration in 1989, 14 death-penalty convictions have been overturned. Of the exoneration cases nationwide, most come from convictions in the 1980's and 1990's, before DNA testing was available or widely used. [The first American criminal court case to utilize DNA was in 1987.] According to the Innocence Project, its records show all but two of the exonerations occurred in convictions that happened before the year 2000. In 72 cases, DNA data revealed the real perpetrator. ✍

Inside exoneration cases

Race or ethnicity of those exonerated:

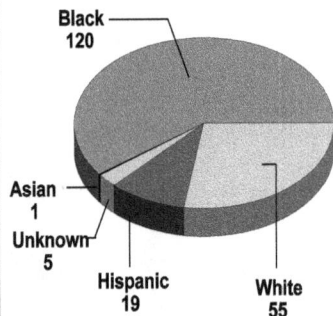

- Black 120
- Asian 1
- Unknown 5
- Hispanic 19
- White 55

Sources: Innocence Project and USA Today research

Leading types of crimes for which those exonerated were originally convicted:

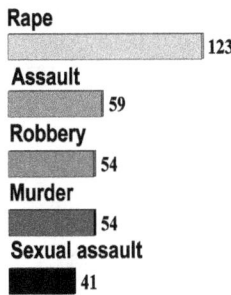

- Rape — 123
- Assault — 59
- Robbery — 54
- Murder — 54
- Sexual assault — 41

Note: Some were convicted of more than one offence

Leading reasons for wrongful convictions in exoneration cases:

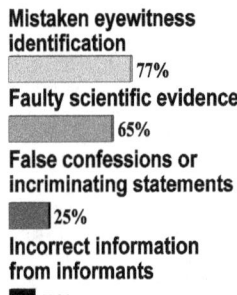

- Mistaken eyewitness identification — 77%
- Faulty scientific evidence — 65%
- False confessions or incriminating statements — 25%
- Incorrect information from informants — 15%

Note: Some convictions were based on more than one factor

Studies show violent crimes still going up

Two major studies—one released in March and the other in June—show violent crimes are continuing to rise for the second straight year.

The March report by the Police Executive Research Forum found that, overall, the number of homicides was up nearly 3% compared with 2005, while robberies were up 6.5%, and assaults involving guns rose 1.3%. Aggravated assault was the only decline, down 2.2% from 2005.

The forum's survey of 56 cities found that during the past two years, overall homicides in those cities were up 10%, robberies rose 12% and assaults involving firearms were up nearly 10%.

The forum began its surveys of violent crime in 2005, when the FBI recorded the first nationwide increases in rates of violent offenses in more than 10 years.

In June the FBI released new national numbers which also showed violent crime rose in 2006, fueled primarily by a 6% rise in robbery, which was the only category that increased in every region and in all eight city population groups. Even though murder decreased nationally 0.3%, overall violent crime rose 1.3%

The time for crime

Average sentence length by top offenses: (in months)

Murder 189.3
Kidnapping/hostage taking 149.3
Robbery 79.6
Drug trafficking 76.4
Sexual abuse 75.4

Source: U.S. Sentencing Commission

nationwide.

Brian Roehrkasse, spokesman for the Justice Department said that while the FBI report was "of concern," rape, assault and property crimes were declining. He believes "it is important to remember this data is preliminary and does not measure the crime rate (the number of crimes in proportion to the population), which is a better measure of public safety." Several cities reporting to the forum also indicated slight declines in violent crime.

Nashville, Milwaukee, and Norfolk, Va., for example, reversed double-digit percentage increases in homicide records in 2005 with double-digit declines in 2006. In Washington, D.C., where the number of murders had dropped slightly in 2005, the number of homicides fell 13% last year, to 169. Yet despite these inklings of improvement, most are reporting a much more dire situation.

In Boston, gangs and the increasing use of guns in crimes have contributed to a 23% jump in slayings during the past two years, according to Police Commissioner Ed Davis. "People are dying, and they are dying in significant numbers," he says. "We don't have the resources to deal with these problems."

In Los Angeles, Mayor Antonio Villaraigosa and Police Chief William Bratton identified 11 of the city's most violent gangs in February and vowed to use more officers to confront a surge in gang bloodshed. Police estimate the city has 400 gangs with 39,000 members. The "Most Wanted"-style list targeted gangs with histories of assaulting officers or targeting victims based on race.

In the March survey, Orlando, Atlanta and Miami recorded the largest increases in violent crime: In Orlando robberies rose 27% last year, and homicides jumped from 22 in 2005 to 49 in 2006—a 123% increase. Atlanta reported to the forum a 20% rise in homicides, from 89 in 2005 to 107 last year. And Miami reported 77 slayings in 2006, a 43% increase from the 54 reported in 2005.

The forum says the jumps in violence warrant the reconstitution of the Clinton administration's program that provided funding for 100,000 additional police officers across the nation. In February, the Bush administration proposed a $200 million grant program to help police agencies pay for overtime, equipment and other cost of responding to violent crime. ✍

Gun crime

Number of non-fatal firearm incidents in the USA:

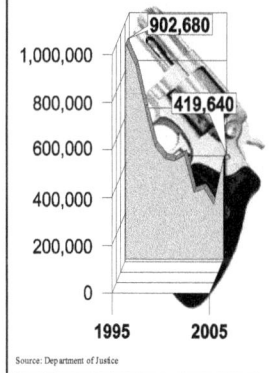

902,680 (1995)
419,640 (2005)

1,000,000
800,000
600,000
400,000
200,000
0

1995   2005

Source: Department of Justice

Homeless victims

Number of hate crimes and violent acts against homeless people, including deaths:

'02 '03 '04 '05 '06

Source: National Coalition of Homeless

Fake fax frees Kentucky inmate

Officials in Hickman, Kentucky released a prisoner from a state facility after receiving a phony fax from a local grocery store and did not catch the error for nearly two weeks.

Timothy Rouse, 19, was at Kentucky Correctional and Psychiatric Center for a mental evaluation after being charged with beating an elderly western Kentucky man. On April 6, he was released from the facility after officials received the fake court order.

The fax, which contained grammatical errors and was not typed on letterhead, falsely claimed that the Kentucky Supreme Court "demanded" that Rouse be released.

On the evening of April 19, Lexington police rearrested Rouse at his mothers home without further incident. ✍

Shortchanged Public Defenders

A study released in June by the Spangenberg Group showed Tennessee tax payers pay more than twice as much money to prosecute destitute people as they do to defend them.

The research and consulting firm specializes in the study of indigent defense and found Tennessee spends about $56.4 million representing its poor defendants each year. That is not a lot compared to the $140 million committed to prosecuting the same people.

The study said, "This extreme disparity in prosecution versus defense resources jeopardizes the fairness and accuracy of the Tennessee indigent defense system."

The study was commissioned by the Justice Project, a defense advocacy group based in Washington, D.C. and came under criticism for its methodology.

"I think that's ludicrous," said John Gill, special counsel to Knox County District Attorney General Randy Nichols.

Mark Stephens, Knox County's chief Public Defender does not believe the numbers are far enough apart. "I think a more accurate assessment is we spend four times as much money, five times as much even, when you consider local law enforcement."

Gill says all relevant evidence collected by police is turned over to the defense, thereby equaling out local law enforcement's effect.

Brad MacLean of the Justice Project's Tennessee branch said the study bears consideration by state legislators come budget time, regardless of how wide a disparity exists. "The basic premise of our judicial system is that the prosecution and the defense have equal jobs to do." ✍

State shuts down Bledsoe County Jail

Safety concerns caused the state to shut down Bledsoe County Jail in May.

The afternoon of May 23 Bledsoe County Mayor, Gregg Ridley told the Associated Press, "The fire marshal has visited Bledsoe County today and basically closed our jail and told us that we had until this afternoon to remove the prisoners." The jail, located in Pikeville, was built in the mid-1800's.

The 21 inmates were transported about 20 miles to the new Sequatchie County Jail in Dunlap. The Sequatchie facility can house 96 prisoners and averaged about 80 to 85 inmates per month from its opening in 2006 through May of this year. "With them (the Bledsoe prisoners) it put us with only two beds empty," said Sequatchie County Sheriff Ronnie Hitchcock.

Ridley and Sequatchie County Executive David Barker agreed on a 30-day contract to house Bledsoe's misdemeanor inmates at a charge of $17.50 per day, one-half of the rate the state pays counties to house felons. "We're not going to try and make money off them, they're our neighbors," Barker said.

The fees Ridley and Barker agreed on were assessed to cover each prisoner's food, clothes and daily hygiene. Any medical expenses the inmates generate will be charged directly to Bledsoe County by the medical provider. The Sequatchie County budget committee, Sheriff's department and other officials met during the 30-day contract to determine the actual cost of housing Bledsoe's prisoners.

Assistant director of Tennessee Corrections Institute Peggy Sawyer

said the jail closing is "very uncommon" and recalls only two similar cases—in Wayne and Lawrence counties. But Bledsoe County Sheriff Jimmy Morris was not surprised.

"When I first took office in September, the fire marshal came down and he discussed some issues with the jail." Morris said the fire marshal told him if the jail could meet safety standards, it could still only house nine inmates.

Ridley said the county will "immediately move forward" with plans for a new jail. The Bledsoe County Commission has reviewed two proposals to build a new $5 million jail in December, but did not commit to either plan.

By the end of the 30-day contract in June, Sequatchie County Commissioners had become a little less charitable and initiated a new 90-day contract designed to force Bledsoe County to expedite building a new jail facility. Bledsoe County Commissioners are expected to acquire an architect and approve the construction of a new jail within the time frame of the contract, or face a 10% increase in the $17.50 per-day-per-inmate charge levied by Sequatchie County.

Should Bledsoe fail to complete construction of the new facility within 24 months, the contract requires a 15% increase on the daily fees. It further states that Sequatchie County can terminate the agreement at any time, which would force Bledsoe to move its prisoners within two hours of notification.

Approval of the new contract was passed by the Sequatchie County Commission on June 18, by a 12-3-1 vote. ✍

Kidney worth 180 days good-time

In March, lawmakers in South Carolina began considering legislation that would let prisoners donate organs or bone marrow in exchange for time off their sentences.

Approved by the Senate Corrections and Penology Subcommittee, the proposal would set up a volunteer organ-and-tissue donor program in prisons to teach inmates about the need for donors. Debate on a measure to reduce the sentences of participating prisoners has been postponed, however, as federal law makes it illegal to give organ donors "valuable consideration." Lawmakers need to know if the term could apply to time off prison sentences.

"I think it's imperative that we go all out and see what we can do," said the bill's chief sponsor, Senator Ralph Anderson (D). "I would like to see us get enough donors that people are no longer dying."

Money for medical procedures and prison guard overtime would be paid by the organ recipient and charitable groups, according to the proposals. Which inmates could donate would be decided by the state. ✍

Felons freed due to overcrowding

The Seattle Times reported in February that "Eighty-three convicted criminals—including high-risk sex offenders and violent felons—have been released from two King County (Washington) jails because they exceeded the total that the state Department of Corrections was allowed to place."

Many had been jailed "because they were accused of violating the terms of their release from prison" and were awaiting hearings to determine punishment.

Each felon's case was reviewed by the correction's department before the release, according to department spokesman Gary Larson. "We didn't just say 'you, you and you are free.'"

The felons were told to check in with their community corrections officers by 5:00 p.m. the following Monday, according to Mindy Merrill, Chairwoman of the union that represents community corrections officers. The DOC did not know at that time how many had actually complied with the order. ✍

By Garry W. Johnson, Staff writer

MCCX gets new staff member

By Jeremy Ingram
MOUNTAIN REVIEW Staff

The Mountain Review would like to introduce to the compound of MCCX a new member of the mental health program. The TDOC recently hired Jeff Bemesderfer to fill the vacancies left by retired Psychological Counselor Linda Palmer and promoted Associate Warden Jennie Jobe. Mr. Bemesderfer is sixty-one years old and recently moved to Tennessee from Michigan, where he worked as a Marriage and Family Counselor. Mr. Bemesderfer's official job title is Psychiatric Social Worker 2.

Mr. Bemesderfer is a very likable person. Among his favorite hobbies is his love for Harley Davidson motorcycles as evidenced by the Harley Davidson clipboard he carries with him at times and the Harley Davidson calendar hanging in his office. Mr. Bemesderfer is well educated—he holds five college degrees. He earned his Bachelor of Arts in Biblical Literature and his Bachelor of Theology from Northeastern Bible College. He then pursued his graduate work at Eastern Michigan University where he pulled in a Master of Arts in Counseling and a Masters in Social Work. Later, he earned a Doctorate of Ministry in Marriage and Family Counseling from Eastern Baptist Seminary.

Mr. Bemesderfer has served in several vocations since graduating from college. At one time he was a youth pastor and at another time he was an associate pastor. Eventually, he began to work as a home health care social worker. As mentioned, before coming to MCCX, Mr. Bemesderfer worked as a private marriage counselor.

I asked Mr. Bemesderfer what made him decide to take a job at this prison. He explained that in the past he had worked with federal parolees but never in a prison setting. Several practical reasons prompted his applying for this job. He said that he wanted to move south and now that his kids were grown, this move would be easier. Mr. Bemesderfer has a true heart of compassion and explained that he really hoped to make a difference. His biggest regret would be knowing, at the end of his life, that he had not made a difference.

His view of counseling is very sensible. He prefaced his comments on his philosophy of counseling by saying that if every inmate had at least one good friend they could trust and talk to, then his job would be unnecessary. One, if not the most, important issue with Mr. Bemesderfer is confidentiality. He understands that if an inmate who comes to him cannot trust him, then he has failed. He also noted that he is not judgmental. He seeks no reprisals nor does he share what he is told.

If an inmate wishes to speak to Mr. Bemesderfer, he must go through the regular sick-call procedures. After signing up on sick call, a nurse will refer the inmate to Mr. Bemesderfer. Mr. Bemesderfer will schedule an

appointment on which the inmate will be allowed to speak with him. Presently, Mr. Bemesderfer is the acting coordinator of the mental health program at MCCX. Essentially, this means that he will evaluate all the cases referred to mental health and coordinate treatment accordingly. Two other staff members work with Mr. Bemesderfer as part of mental health. If prescription medication or other treatments are required, Mr. Bemesderfer will refer the inmate to one of these professionals.

Inmates have many reasons why they may want to talk to Mr. Bemesderfer. The list of problems includes

David Richards, Randall McPheeters, Jeff Bermesderfer, Jeremy Ingram, Seymore Hayes, Paul Sharp, Gary Hall, Joe Baker, & Curtis Hudson

stress, depression, anxiety, grief, sadness, and many other mental health concerns. Mr. Bemesderfer stated that he did not dispense medication. He was simply what they call a "level one provider."

Scheduling and length of visits varies based on issues. When an inmate is referred to Mr. Bemesderfer, how much time spent talking to him and the frequency of appointments vary. Depending on the issue, an inmate might spend 15-20 minutes talking to Mr. Bemesderfer or longer if there is a need for a more lengthy appointment. Inmates may visit once a week, once a month, or only once if they wish.

I asked Mr. Bemesderfer what changes we could expect in the future concerning the programs and classes offered to inmates. He said, "If it is not broken, there is no need to fix it." Mr. Bemesderfer plans to keep these programs going and has taken steps to ensure the availability of the programs for inmates.

Two programs in particular are being made available on a more consistent and frequent basis because of Mr. Bemesderfer's willingness to be involved. These are the Alternative to Violence Project and the Anger Management class. As many know, the AVP program used to occur on a monthly basis, but due to the lack of staff trained in AVP, the program grew more infrequent. Mr. Bemesderfer hopes to become trained in AVP material and become a facilitator so that he can help the program take place more often.

The Anger Management class that has met in the past during, afternoon count in the library, will be starting again. This program is based on material from the *Cage Your Rage* workbook and other material put together over the years. It is an excellent opportunity to learn and discuss anger management techniques so that you can be better equipped to handle your anger and other emotions.

Along with the hiring off Mr. Bemesderfer came the arrival of the Treatment Program Advisory panel. This panel is composed of nine inmates from the MCCX compound who meet weekly with Mr. Bemesderfer and discuss ways to improve the rehabilitative programs and opportunities for new programs here on the compound. The inmates on the committee are facilitators in most of these programs and many were instrumental in the founding of several programs in existence today. Already, several notable ideas have emerged that hopefully will be considered. Together with Mr. Bemesderfer, the panel hopes to make a difference not only on the compound but in society as well, by creating opportunities to produce productive citizens by equipping inmates with the tools needed for change. ✍

The MCCX Mountain Review Staff

Jeff Durham   Jeremy Ingram   Garry Johnson

Catholic community celebrates Easter

By Randall McPheeters

The Catholic community of Morgan County was blessed with the presence of Bishop Joseph Kurtz at their annual Easter celebration. Father Michael Sweeney greeted the parishioners and welcomed the Bishop of the Knoxville Diocese, Joseph Kurtz, who has been a staunch supporter of the Morgan County community since his assignment to the diocese.

Bishop Kurtz celebrated the Easter Mass with great reverence. He thanked Father Sweeney for his tireless work in this region on behalf of the church. Then he asked a prayer for a special intention with an excited gleam in his eye. On the very next day, we saw the Bishop named the Metropolitan Arch-Bishop of Louisville Kentucky. It was fitting that Bishop Kurtz celebrated his final Mass as Bishop of the Knoxville diocese here at Morgan County since his first Mass under the current Pope Benedict XVI was also here.

The gathering for the Easter Mass was small but pleasant. The Commercial Food Service class prepared an excellent meal for the banquet after the Mass, accented by a cake decorated with a Biblical scene. The class and their instructor, John Cross, served the meal and helped with the clean up afterward. The entire event was a grand success and a Holy celebration of the Lord's resurrection. The Gospel verse for the Mass was from the Holy Gospel according to Saint John featuring the finding of the empty tomb. It was a great honor to have Arch-Bishop Kurtz here for the Mass and the subsequent banquet. We are also thankful to Father Sweeney and volunteer Sean Driscoll for their steady support of our community.

We would also like to thank Chaplain Dean Yancey, Volunteer Chaplain Randall Vespie, The Warden and his staff and the security staff for working with the many helpers who made this event possible. The Catholic Community celebrates Mass every second and fourth Monday of each month. Everyone is welcome to attend. ✍

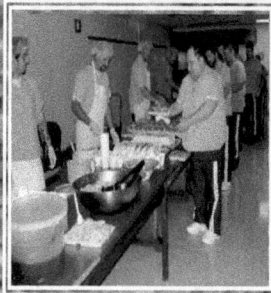

By Tom Reddick

Canada, Mexico, Ireland and New Zealand, next stop Wartburg, Tennessee. The Frozen Head Alcoholics Anonymous Group was proud to welcome Mr. Bill McNiff to Morgan County Correctional Complex on June 15, 2007 as he presented his dramatic one man play, *"Moments," An Evening with Bill W.* to a standing room only crowd in the gymnasium.

Bill McNiff, 72, a renowned speaker and actor, was born, raised and educated in New York City. After a successful sales and marketing career working for three Fortune 500 Companies in the New York, Boston, Washington D.C., Dallas and Philadelphia markets, he started his own successful marketing company in 1977. He spent the next twelve years traveling throughout the world representing United States firms to foreign markets and then foreign firms to U.S. opportunities. A serious illness forced him to close his firm in 1989. After a long convalescence and for personal reasons, he studied Drug and Alcohol Counseling at Villanova University in Pennsylvania. After completing his studies, he went to work for the Clare Center in York, Pennsylvania as a counselor. It was during his work there that he became aware of the fact that few, if any of his clients knew the history of Alcoholics Anonymous and the development of their Twelve Step Program of Recovery. He found that most people had heard of Alcoholics Anonymous, but few know of Bill Wilson, a.k.a. Bill W., one of the co-founders of this remarkable fellowship, and author of their Twelve Step Program of Recovery. Mr. McNiff put together a lecture on the subject that was informative but lacked any dramatic appeal. McNiff extended his lecture to include outside interests; jails, hospitals, schools and prisons. Building on the feedback from his "clients" in the first two years, the lecture finally developed into a ninety minute dramatic "Performance Piece".

His presentation eventually took on the title, "Moments", An Evening With Bill W. In "Moments", McNiff brings Bill Wilson to life on stage, in a one-man dramatic presentation, telling his story to a fictitious Alcoholics Anonymous group (the audience) drawing them into the mind of a man who figured he would die or go insane from alcohol, until he had a remarkable vision in a lonely hospital bed and Alcoholics Anonymous had its beginning.

In eighteen years, Mr. McNiff has performed his play more than one thousand times throughout the world. His extensive travel took him to New Zealand for vacation in May. He performed "Moments" for a regional A.A. convention there and has been invited back for their national convention in January 2008. Although he has performed for as many as 2000 people at a time, Mr. McNiff believes his greatest success was when he was privileged to perform the piece for four men in a locked jail cell ,in a prison at Owens Sound, Ontario, Canada. Two of them, native Canadians, were addicted to "huffing" gasoline and were trying to use the A.A. Twelve Steps to recover. One of the more interesting historical tidbits Mr. McNiff brought to the audience's attention was that early A.A. groups called their recovery plan "soul surgery" before coming up with the name, Twelve Steps. One of McNiff's guiding principles is, in the words of the Master, "I was in prison and you visited me."

As mentioned before in this article, Mr. McNiff has traveled around the world performing "Moments". He has traveled throughout the United States as well. Frozen Head Alcoholics Anonymous Group was glad he added Wartburg, Tennessee to his travel resume. McNiff's visit was hosted by the group's outside sponsors: Sean, Richard, Dave and John. Board president, Robert Cooper, on behalf of the group, presented Mr. McNiff with a Lifetime Membership Award to Frozen Head's A.A. Group. The group would also like to thank Jimbo, Trevor and their staff, for readying the gym for the program. Many thanks go out to Paul Rutherford, Randall McPheeters and Michael Gay Sr. for their audio and video technical support. The group would also like to thank the outside sponsors for their tremendous and unwavering support. In other A.A. news, long time board Vice president Ken Green resigned his position, citing rising commitments on the compound. He had a successful tenure and the group is grateful for his hard work. Larry Robinson was voted in as the new vice-president. He has big shoes to fill, but is very capable of the challenge. He is committed to his own sobriety as well as the rest of the group members. The art shop helped to make the program a success too. ✍

How to Read Music

Introduction: The History of Music
By Jeremy Ingram
MOUNTAIN REVIEW Staff

Before we undertake to explain the science of reading music, it will help to understand a little about the way sound itself works.

Most people are aware of the vibrations of a stereo speaker. The movement of the speaker produces vibrations that travel through the air. The slower the vibration of the speaker the lower the vibration will sound. Likewise, the faster the speaker vibrates the higher the vibration will sound. When these vibrations reach our ears, our eardrums themselves vibrate at the same rate as the speaker.

A complicated system of organs inside our ears turn these vibrations into electrical impulses which are carried to the brain. The idea of slow and fast vibrations is the same—a "slow" electrical impulse is interpreted by the brain as a low note and vice-versa. The brain can interpret a vibration as low as 20 vibrations per second and as high as 20,000 vibrations per second (vps). This encompasses the entire range of a standard piano keyboard with a large range left over.

The different sound that each vibration makes is called the pitch. The sound that is coordinated with a particular pitch is called a note. Thus at a vps of 260, a specific note is always produced. The difference between two notes is called a musical difference or an interval. Different people have a greater sensitivity to the differences between notes. Some people who are accustomed to discerning sound can tell the difference between a note vibrating at 260 vps and a note at 261 vps. Most people can hear a difference of 10 vps.

If a note vibrating at 260 vps is doubled, the resultant note sounds much like the original note. The second note will be higher than the first, but there is a similar quality between the two. This is referred to as an octave (Figure 1).

Figure 1

One octave is the distance between one note and its double. Interestingly, it has been shown that even dogs recognize the similarity between octave notes!

Since there is a great distance between two octave notes, the "scale" has been devised. A scale breaks up the space between octaves into smaller segments. In the history of music there is evidence to support the belief that almost every civilization not only recognized the similarity between octave notes, but also created a scale by breaking the octaves into smaller parts. These divisions were different for different civilizations, but the idea is the same.

One of the earliest musical instruments was

the bow. When hunters "plucked" the bowstring to fire an arrow, they realized that depending on the different pressure applied to the string, different sounds emanated from it. Some people in Australia still use the bow as a musical instrument. It wasn't until 2,500 years ago that the Greek mathematician Pythagoras reasoned that the distance between the two points on a bow string was directly related to the sound produced. He experimented with different lengths of string and made some remarkable discoveries. One discovery, was that a string half as long as another string produced a note that was exactly an octave above the longer

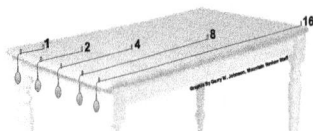

Figure 2

string. However, having only his ears and string to play with, Pythagoras only went so far. Since Pythagoras was preeminently a mathematician, it didn't take long for him to reason that if the ratio of 2:1 produces a similar sound, then other ratios may be related. He experimented by dividing the space between octaves notes into different divisions based on different ratios. Eventually, Pythagoras settled on a division of twelve pieces.

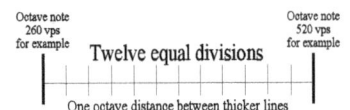

Figure 3

This division is still used today and is known as the chromatic scale. A chromatic scale is a division of an octave into twelve notes. (There are twelve keys on a piano keyboard in an octave).

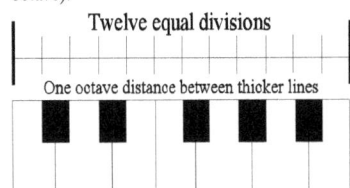

Figure 4

During the time Pythagoras lived, the notes he had identified remained unnamed. Several attempts were made to name the notes to make identification easier. One attempt was by Boethius in AD 500. He used the Roman alphabet. However, it was not until the 12th century that the familiar notes on a mucic staff was invented by a Benedictine Monk, Guido D'Arezzo. This system evolved into a seven-note format that is in use today. These seven notes (identified by the English letters A through G), are represented on a piano keyboard by the white keys.

Technically speaking, the note named C vibrates at 260 vps. An octave above C is another note named C that vibrates at double the vps, an so on. This is the gist of a piano keyboard; every seven white keys is an octave. Figure five shows a piano keyboard, the note

names of the white keys, and the corresponding vibrations per second.

Figure 5

Remember what was said about a chromatic division: there are twelve divisions or notes in an octave. However, there are only seven white keys on the keyboard. The need to represent all twelve notes makes it necessary to have the black keys in between the white keys. Therefore, the white keys and the black keys together form one octave.

This brings us to a confusing part of music theory, the "sharps" and the "flats." A simple way to understand the difference between a sharp and a flat is to remember that a sharp is "higher than" and a flat is "lower than." The sharp is represented by the symbol ♯ and the flat is represented by the symbol ♭.

Now, with that in mind, let us look at the black keys on a piano. Take one black key as an example. Compared with the white key before it, the black key is said to be sharp because it is "higher than" the white key. Compared with the white key after it, the black key is said to be flat because it is "lower than" the white key. Thus, each black key can be said to be both sharp and flat depending on which direction you are coming from!

Let's explain further: take as an example the two white keys (notes) A and B. Between the notes A and B there is one black key. If you think about that black key in relation to the A key beside it, then it is referred to as an A sharp (A♯) because it is higher than the note before it. If you think about that black key in relation to the B key beside it, then it is referred to as a B flat (B♭) because it is lower than the note before it.

Figure six is a handy way to visualize what has been said about sharps and flats. If you are having trouble understanding this concept, go back and study the previous section. This concept is fundamental in reading music.

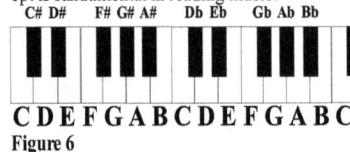

Figure 6

To sum it up, remember that an A sharp (A♯) is the same note as a B flat (B♭), and a C sharp (C♯) is the same note as a D flat (D♭). Fortunately, in the reading of music, it is traditional to use only one of these names. Thus, you rarely see a note referred to as an A sharp (A♯); it is much more common to see that note referred to as a B flat (B♭).

A chromatic scale is a scale that begins on one note and ends on the same note, either an octave higher or an octave lower. To play a chromatic scale on a piano, simply choose any note and play up or down 13 notes. The last note of the scale will be the same note you started on, only an octave different. Figure seven shows two different chromatic scales: the A sharp (A♯) and the E chromatic scale.

One principle of music theory is the concept

of "key." This is a fairly simple concept in context of our present discussion. In figure seven, the first or bottom chromatic scale begins with an E note. Therefore, it is in the key of E. The second or top chromatic scale begins with an A sharp (A♯), therefore it is in the key of A sharp (A♯).

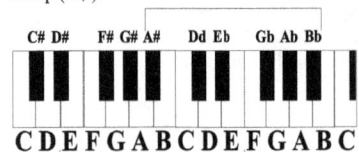

Figure 7

Previously, in this article, we mentioned that Pythagoras invented the chromatic scale. Because he did not name the notes of that scale many attempts were made afterward to name the notes. Eventually, the Benedictine monk Guido D'Arezzo used symbols placed on lines to name the notes. This, as was mentioned, is the method practiced today.

This method of using symbols placed on lines to name the notes is referred to as "standard notation." In passing, let it be remarked that the different shapes of the notes denote the length the notes should be held. However, this will be discussed in the future. For now, it should be learned that the position of the symbol (note) on the lines (staff) determines the note's pitch. The staff referred to is the music staff seen in any piece of music.

If you open a hymn book or any other piece of music written for the piano, you will see two staffs. The top staff is called the treble clef; it is for higher notes. The bottom staff is called the bass clef; it is for lower notes. There is one line in between the two staffs referred to as middle C. On a piano, middle C is the middle C note on the keyboard.

Figure eight will show a staff with various notes placed on it. Notice that a sharp or flat symbol next to a note corresponds to the black keys on the piano as discussed earlier. On the left side of the staff are the note names and on the right side of the staff are the note symbols. Study this example and try to relate it to the keys on a piano.

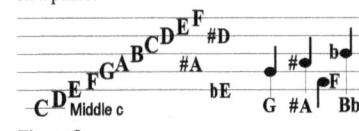

Figure 8

In summary, vibrations cause sound and as the vibration increases the sound becomes "higher." The highness or lowness of the sound is referred to as pitch and the particular speed of the vibration is labeled a note. Doubling the vps of a note results in an octave. Breaking the octave into smaller parts is a scale. The twelve notes in an octave are called a chromatic scale. The white notes on a piano have a letter name from A to G. Each black note has two names but only one of these names is used. When a specific note is chosen on which to begin a chromatic scale, that note is the key the scale is in.

Look for future lessons on reading music in upcoming editions of the Mountain Review.

Graphics and illustrations by
Garry W. Johnson.

Continuing Education

Myer Pettyjohn Memorial Grant

By Randall McPheeters,
President, Varsity Club

The Myer Pettyjohn Memorial Educational Grant was awarded to two inmates this year by the Bethel Presbyterian Prison Ministry. Inmates Dan Hunley and Chris Russell received the grant of $300.00 each toward their correspondence courses. These two were chosen from nine applicants by a board of five members of the Bethel volunteers. Chris' studies come from Ohio University and Dan's studies come from Blackstone School of Law.

The Myer Pettyjohn Memorial Educational Grant is named for Doctor Myer Pettyjohn, an inmate who got his doctorate in counseling while here. P.J., as he was known to his friends, believed in the power of education to help a man stay out of prison, so when he died in 2003, his friends set up this memorial in his name.

The Myer Pettyjohn Memorial Educational Grant will be awarded each year. Watch your bulletin boards each spring for announcements. ✍

Continuing Education important in prison

By Dan Hunley,
Myer Pettyjohn Memorial Grant Recipient

Scholarship Recipient Dan Hunley

When I first started doing my time over ten years ago, I didn't realize the value of education. Or if nothing else, occupying your mind with something other than the everyday prison life we face. I was a high school dropout (my senior year, of all things) and I could have graduated, only I didn't care. When I took and passed the GED in early '98, I did so without hardly even trying and still scored better than most. I didn't care then either, I just wanted out of school. Until recently, I was just doing time like a lot of us, watching the years go by with nothing to show for it. Then one day I asked myself, "What the hell are you doing, sitting on your butt all day?" I started looking into correspondence courses and what I could take for college credit and started saving my money and soliciting my family and friends. A degree from a university is going to run you thousands of dollars and as inmates we are not eligible for various government grants or student loans, as a normal student in the free world is entitled. So, if we decide to better ourselves and further our education, the burden is placed on us or our families to pay for it. A degree is where it is at. That is what is going to open doors for you.

The Varsity Club and Bethel Presbyterian Church sponsored a grant for inmates to use toward correspondence courses through the chapel. Inmates were encouraged to fill out an application stating what courses they are taking or planning to take. Also, they were asked why they are taking these courses and what their previous education was. The grant was in the name of Myer Pettyjohn, whom I never had the privilege of meeting. He received his doctorate in theology through correspondence while in prison, but unfortunately, died still in prison. He understood the value of education as I am just now beginning to understand. Luckily, I was chosen to be a recipient of the grant to help pay for a correspondence course I am currently taking. A "Thank You" is in order to Bethel Presbyterian Church, the Varsity Club, and Myer Pettyjohn. Thank you for your help. ✍

Two MCCX inmates awarded college degrees

On July 27, 2007, two inmates at MCCX were awarded college degrees. David "Golden Boy" Jones and Jeremy Ingram each received their college degrees from Covington Theological Seminary.

David Jones was awarded the Associate in Religious Education degree and Jeremy Ingram was awarded the Bachelor of Ministry. Jeremy was also graduated with the honor of Cum Laude for the third highest GPA in the graduating class.

David Jones has been studying at Covington for two years. After much time and effort, he completed his studies in Religious Education. David works at Tricor and did his studying in his spare time. He spent hundreds of hours meticulously preparing his lessons for submission. Jeremy Ingram has been taking college courses since the time he was a junior in high school, 16 years ago. Several years ago Jeremy earned his Associate's Degree and currently he is working on his Master's in Counseling.

Covington Theological Seminary was founded in 1977 as a chartered seminary and in 1985 moved to Fort Ogelthorpe, GA, which is only minutes from Downtown Chattanooga. The college is named after General Leonard Covington, an army officer and hero in the War of 1812. His bravery and character are examples for the many students who inspire to graduate from Covington. Since the 30 years Covington has existed, the college has seen considerable growth and recognition. Covington emphasizes a quality education in many areas intended to "Train Leaders and Impact Eternity," as their motto says.

Covington Theological Seminary is a licensed college under the licensure of the State Board of Independent Colleges and Universities. Covington is also a member of the Association of Christian Continuing Education Schools and Seminaries (ACCESS), Accrediting Commission International (ACI), and the National Association of Evangelicals of Washington, D.C. (NAE).

David "Golden Boy" Jones awarded Associate's degree

Jeremy Ingram awarded Bachelor's degree

Education vital to reduce recidivism

By Chris Russell,
Myer Pettyjohn memorial Grant Recipient

Education plays a pivotal role in recidivism rates. Several studies have shown that educating inmates substantially reduces crime. Once inmates who have been educated are released, they are about 10 to 20 percent less likely to re-offend than the average released prisoner. Therefore, as our level of education rises, our chance of coming back to prison falls. Even in here, many of us do not take education as serious as we should. The goals of many prison systems do not involve rehabilitation programs. Therefore, while we could still improve what we have in TDOC, we really need to take advantage of the opportunities that are available to us while we are here. Having no plan for when we get out is like having a plan to come back.

I am currently taking correspondence courses from Ohio University towards an Associate in Science degree. I plan to use the degree for a career in the medical field. I think working in the medical field would be a very fulfilling job. Just having the opportunity to support myself by helping others will be a huge blessing. At one point in my life, I did not know what I wanted to do. Now I know that this is my calling. I have a direction and I am working toward that. This is why I would like to thank Bethel Presbyterian Church in Kingston for helping me work towards my goal.

Bethel Presbyterian recently granted me a scholarship towards my education. The scholarship I received is one they

Scholarship Recipient Chris Russell

give every year in the name of Myer Pettyjohn. I did not know him personally, but I have heard that he really dedicated his life to helping others. I hope I can do the same. I am grateful to Myer Pettyjohn, and the Varsity Club for helping support the scholarship fund, and the church for setting this scholarship up to help inmates get an education. I sincerely hope that more organizations will get involved and more inmates can utilize this kind of assistance so we can eventually use it to benefit others. If you wish to help someone else get an education, you can donate to the Varsity Club Scholarship Fund. ✍

109

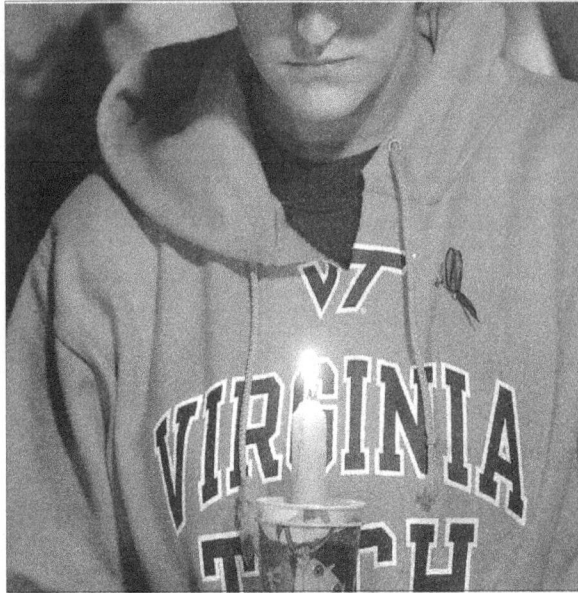

Virginia Tech Shootings

By Jeremy Ingram
MOUNTAIN REVIEW Staff

Time magazine reported that the wind was too strong that day. Nestled in the rolling foothills of the Blue Ridge Mountains the campus is left exposed to the cruelties of the Blue Ridge winters. Wind cuts through the layers of winter clothing and threatens to knock you down with its force. On that Monday morning the wind was at its cruelest. Students leaned forward into the biting wind as they tried to escape the volley of gunfire echoing through the streets. As if the elusive gunman was not bad enough, circling med-evac helicopters from area trauma centers were unable to land due to the fierceness of the winds. Even that night, as students stood in the quad trying to make sense of their enormous loss, the flames atop the candles they were holding were blown out as if to mimic the Hokie spirit that had been crushed earlier that day.

Watching the news a few months ago of a gunman loose on campus brought back old memories. When I was younger, my family lived a few miles north of the Virginia Tech campus. During that time Tech campus provided our high school with an indoor track and occasionally a place to play golf. After I moved to Tennessee I still visited friends on campus regularly. In fact, my last day of freedom I awoke on campus.

On April 16, 2007, students at Virginia Tech, a historic state university located in Southwest Virginia, went about their normal exercises. That is, everyone except 23-year-old Cho Seung-Hui. Described as a ticking time bomb that could explode at any minute, Cho apparently had little time left. By the time the ruins of the massacre were discovered, thirty-three people lay dead and many more wounded in the worst shooting in American history.

Cho's family legally emigrated to the United States in 1992. At the time Cho was eight and the family lived in Detroit but soon they moved to Centerville, Virginia, a Washington DC suburb. The family ran a dry-cleaning business and Cho himself attended Westfield High School in neighboring Chantilly. Although, Cho is remembered by almost everyone who had met him as withdrawn and strange, his family seemed normal; his sister in fact works under contract for the Sate Department.

After graduating from Westfield in 2003, Cho applied for admission at Virginia Polytechnical Institute and was accepted. His time at Virginia Tech was fairly uneventful; Cho was not known for any extracurricular activities or social activeness that characterizes much of the other 26,0-00 students. Interviews with Cho's former roommates revealed that he rarely talked, smiled, or showed emotion. Two events, in retrospect, stand out as a stark warning of things to come.

First, there were the morbidly violent writings. Lucinda Roy, VT's English department chair reported Cho to the campus administration and police after reading his writings that included vivid depictions of murder, suicide, revenge, and hate. In 2005, a court ordered Cho to undergo a mental evaluation in which he was found to be depressed with suicidal tendencies. State law did not require Cho to be hospitalized or subject to mandatory counseling, so he refused treatment and returned to his everyday life.

A second event (or series of events) were the harassing e-mails and phone calls from Cho to female students. One student in particular reported him to the campus police but later decided not to press charges. After another student complained about his harassing emails, the campus police investigated and this led to the afore mentioned court-ordered mental evaluation.

Following the tragic events of April 16, many wondered how the warning signs could have been left unresolved—warning signs to say the least. After the mental evaluation at Carilion St. Albans Behavioral Health Center in Radford, Virginia, a judge wrote that Cho "is mentally ill and in need of hospitalization, and presents an eminent danger to self or others as a result of mental illness, or is so seriously mentally ill as to be substantially unable to care for self, and is incapable of volunteering or unwilling to volunteer for treatment."

Many others parroted these findings. A long list of grievances followed Cho. Teachers reported they saw Cho's problems and tried to help him. One teacher in particular commented that Cho was not simply troubled, "Troubled kids get drunk and jump off buildings." According to her, Cho was just downright mean. Others said that Cho was intimidating. He would wear a hat and sunglasses into class, he would use the camera on his cell phone to take pictures of female students under their desk, and he would submit writings about sodomy, sexual abuse, and even horrifying scenes of murder. On account of his meanness, several students stopped coming to class.

"It was an unremarkable sale." said John Markell, proprietor of Roanoke Firearms, summing up the sale of a 9-mm Glock 19 and a box of 50 rounds. It is fairly easy to purchase a handgun in the state of Virginia. There are no licence, no waiting periods, no required classes. Nothing showed up on the instant background check. In similar fashion Cho purchased a Walther P22 in a Pawn Shop near the Virginia Tech campus.

It was later discovered that Cho had prepared a package that he sent to NBC on the day of the killings—between killings. The contents of the package would shock a bewildered nation. The insane rambling of a demented killer filled hours of video, haunted pages of handwritten letters and papers, and stacks of photographs revealed a depraved mind set on evil.

The first murders occurred in West Ambler Hall as early as 7:15 am. When police arrived at the scene they found VA Tech freshman Emily Hilscher and residential adviser Ryan Clark shot to death by Cho. Two hours later, campus officials issued a warning for all students to be aware that a shooting had taken place and to be on the lookout for any suspicious behavior. Meanwhile, Cho returned to his dorm room in Harper Hall, reloaded, mailed the package to NBC, and then walked across the campus to Norris Hall which housed the Engineering Science and Mechanics departments. In the words of Nancy Gibbs, Time correspondent, "Suddenly this was not over."

Methodically and cold-blooded, Cho walked quietly and purposefully into classroom after classroom, gunning down student and staff alike. During this brief rampage that left 30 dead, Cho had time to chain the doors shut to slow police down and post notes that informed potential intruders that the doors were booby trapped. This afforded Cho enough time to reload his guns and carry out his monstrous plan. In the end, a staggering couple hundred shots had been fired. One federal source said that Cho's effective, well-planned, cold, and methodical style of killing suggested someone who had been trained in the execution style of killing. What they found was that this was the work of a depraved, evil human with no formal training at all.

After that day stories of heroism emerged. Derek O'Dell, after being shot in the arm during an introductory class in German, moved to block the door in case Cho returned. In fact, Cho did return and fired several rounds through the door before leaving.

Unusually armed

Use of guns in crimes against college students:

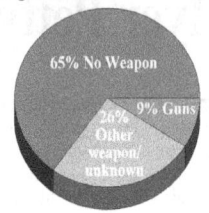

- 65% No Weapon
- 9% Guns
- 26% Other weapon/unknown

By Garry W. Johnson, MOUNTAIN REVIEW Staff; Source: *Time* magazine

Liviu Librescu was a 77-year-old holocaust survivor. At the time the shootings began he was teaching solid mechanics. He recognized the gunfire and braced himself in front of the door so his students would have time to escape through the window. Alec Calhoun, the last survivor out the window looked back just in time to see his teacher and two students shot to death. In one French class room two lone survivors, a male and female students, played dead while Cho emptied his weapons, reloaded several times, and emptied the guns into the lifeless and dying bodies of their classmates. When the police arrived the two students were the only ones alive. In another classroom one student had been shot through the femoral artery. The doctor that treated him said that the electrical cord the student had wrapped around his leg saved his life. Apparently the student was an Eagle Scout and knew that he was bleeding to death. The makeshift tourniquet worked.

Unusual killings

Nearly all homicides involve a single victim. Mass murders are less than one-quarter of 1% of U.S. homicides:

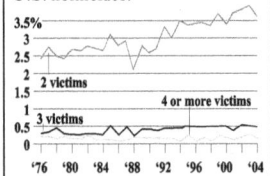

By Garry W. Johnson, MOUNTAIN REVIEW Staff; Source: *Time* magazine

As the nation turned its attention and prayers toward this quite campus in Virginia, somehow Hokie Pride outlasted the events on that fateful Monday morning. Some students left the campus, but most returned to finish the school year. That night, after the shootings, 10,000 Hokies filled the drill field arrayed in orange and maroon. On this night, the shrill, cold wind could not extinguish the orange glow of the candles kept alive by the solidarity of the Hokie Nation. ✍

PRE-RELEASE CLASS GRADUATION

Class 11

By Jeremy Ingram
MOUNTAIN REVIEW Staff

On Monday, July 2, 2007, Pre-Release class eleven held their graduation in the outside visitation area. Seventeen students, two staff members, and four helpers attended the graduation.

Pre-Release class Instructor Rickey Bunch opened the graduation by commenting on the uniqueness of this graduating class. One factor that made this class unique was the unique personalities of the students. Mr. Bunch stated that some of the students came into the class hard-headed, but all of them had made progress and improvement. Although, no one was where they needed to be, this is no different than anyone else. "None will be where he needs to be in this lifetime."

Mr. Bunch admitted that he listened to the students and understood their reasoning. He explained that, although the student's reasoning about life was not all the time correct, he did understand what they were saying. He also admitted that, at times, he has been called boring and full of crap, but the simple fact was that his way works.

Mr. Bunch said that he believed that most of the students in his class knew the right answers but sadly, experience has shown him that not all of them will follow these right ideas.

The same day that graduation was held was the deadline for his annual report. Upon completion of the annual report, Mr Bunch learned that parolees had a huge failure rate. Only a few parolees made it on parole. Men who expire their sentence have a lower failure rate than those released on parole. Bunch realized there were two ways of looking at these statistics. One side is the inmate's side. According to Bunch, inmates blame the parole officers. He said this was a cognitive distortion. The blame does not lie with the parole officer, but rather with the inmate. Inmates are required to sign a piece of paper stating that they know all the rules of parole. The problem is that they do not follow these rules. Their parole failure is due simply to breaking the rules.

A growing tide of realization is sweeping across the TDOC regarding the failures of parole. Already, Northeast prohibits inmates who are coming up for parole to take its Pre-Release class. In order to enroll in the Pre-Release class inmates must be expiring their sentences.

Bunch commented that he had a hard time believing that his students could not make it on parole. An old adage his father told him was "If one man could do it then anyone can do it." An example of a success was a former MCCX inmate, Kenneth Weston. Ken made parole and upon release, made an appointment with an office in Knoxville that helps released offenders find a job. Ken showed up early to the scheduled meeting and was directed to an interview that afternoon. He showed up early for that interview and was hired on the spot. Ken's promptness and willingness to work added to his success.

Bunch added that inmates have a lot to prove. Family, friends, and society in general, need to be convinced that you've changed.

Many of the students in Pre-Release class 11 will be released in the next three months. Bunch challenged those who will be released. He said he wanted to see what they will do. In fact, he will be able to see what each student will do. Bunch tracks each student that successfully completes his class.

Bunch noted that at the beginning of class each student came into class lying, but eventually came to tell the truth.

After Bunch finished speaking, certificates were awarded. In the envelope each graduate was given were several items: extra copies of their certificates, a resume, and two essays. The first essay was written by the students when they began the class. The second essay was the one written at the end of class. Bunch wanted each student to see how far they had come. Bunch finished by saying only a little could happen in ten weeks. He hoped the seeds he planted would fall on good soil.

Special thanks to John Cross and the Commercial Food Service class for preparing pizza and cake for the graduation.

In the future, the Pre-Release class will be offered to both inmates on the compound and inmates at the annex. Anyone who is within six months of their Release Eligibility Date may sign up for the program. For more information, please contact Rickey Bunch. The Pre-Release class meets in the library classroom, Monday through Friday. This is an unique opportunity to prepare oneself for successful living once released. ✍

Pre-Release Class 11 Graduates: Richie Cate, Robert Houseal, Jarvis Shropshire, Gary Evans, Scott Gardner, Terry Hudson, Clarence Kilgore, Mike Richardson, Kenny Stephens, Derrick Chitwood, Jonathan Sullivan, Kris Jackson, Larry Robinson, Jedediah Taylor, Denver Taylor, Michael Henderson, Steven Schimmel.

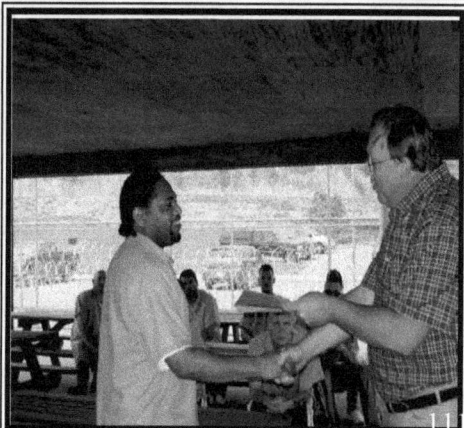

A Prisoner's Purpose

By Kenneth Hartman

Tear gas is more a presence then a smell. It clings to the back of your throat, a chemically induced feather that provokes a coughing fit after each attempt at a breath. It is one of the "less lethal" force options deployed in prison to quell a riot. On one windy, Southern California day, I could see that the last few wisps of tear gas blowing off the yard as the guards finally came back through the gates, the violence essentially over, the oppressive silence of stifled raw emotion pushing down over the several hundred men scattered about in segregated groups. My heart was beating so hard it caused my vision to throb.

The firestorm of riots that had been sweeping across the prison system in California had reached our relatively peaceful meadow. For several years, we had all read about, and heard tales of these conflagrations that had consumed one prison after another, a brush fire blown along by a hot wind of frustration and resentments un-addressed. A decade of "get tough" policies, which meant in practice, brutal conditions, and a systematic dehumanization of prisoners, was bearing its logical consequence. Prisoners, shot through with the reigning ethos of being tantamount to evil, condemned to de facto death sentences in ever worsening conditions, had become what had been projected onto them.

The United States has a legacy of relying on prisons to solve problems. We built the first penitentiaries, and instituted rules so repressive that insanity and suicide were common to the forced penitents. No less astute an observer of America than Alexis de Tocqueville commented, in 1833, "While society in the United States gives the example of the most extended liberty, the prisons of the same country offer the spectacle of the most complete despotism." His insight remains equally valid today. It is an American tradition to resort to bigger and more painful sticks to achieve the ever-elusive goal of a crime-free society.

More than two million people in this country are imprisoned, and several million are under some form of restraint by the government. (A higher proportion than any other country.) A mathematical extension of these numbers, using an average family, results in close to 10% of society with a connection to the prison system, the jails, and the county probation camps. No society in history has been able to sustain itself with such a massive and bitterly angry underclass. And make no mistake about it, no one who experiences this system, whether as a prisoner or the loved one or friend of a prisoner, is not angry and bitter. The system, which defines itself as society's protector, as the bulwark against chaos and anarchy, is sowing the seeds of society's destruction.

As the guards applied plastic riot handcuffs to me the morning I watched my world devolve into unmitigated and unrestrained violence, the most overwhelming emotion I felt was sadness. Since the age of 16 I had spent all but a few months of my life a prisoner of the state of California, "state-raised" as guys like me are called. A product of the concrete and steel womb of the criminal justice system, there were some expectations I held. Among these, a basic level of order, predictability, a certainty that chaos would be kept at bay. There were no Atticas, no New Mexico State Prison takeovers in our living memories. California, certainly no beacon of enlightenment, nevertheless, ran a relatively stable operation.

My journey through the adult system began when I killed a man in a drunken, drugged-up fistfight, one hazy night when I was 19 years old. I was sentenced to life without the possibility of parole and transferred into the legendary granite blocks of Folsom State Prison. Before long, I was deep in the mix of drugs and power politics, and the well-regulated violence that characterized the joint. Prisoners divided themselves, with the willing assistance of the system, into ethnically-based armies that engaged in largely ritualized combat, occasionally actually battering one another directly, while living a fantasy existence of ascribed significance.

Into this exceedingly simple life came the great disrupter, the most omnipresent of emotions, love. Through a series of happenstances, I met and fell in love with a beautifully complex and frustratingly passionate girl. One of the dark secrets of bad guys, one we all hate to acknowledge even to ourselves, is that our errant behavior is often motivated by a sneaking suspicion we just aren't lovable. All that studied posturing and smart [alec] indifference is really a mask. Coming to feel loved is nothing short of revelatory. Being a bad actor, when you believe at the heart of your being that you are bad, has certain logic. If you are lovable, then your rationale, your excuse, has vanished and you're diminished to [a detestable person].

In response to the challenge of love, I spent several years and most of my hair trying to make sense of my life in prison, society, and the world. The brutal conclusion to my search was that I was responsible for my actions, my actions were wrong, and I was obliged to suffer the consequences and seek atonement. Unfortunately, finding venues to perform expiating acts, while serving life without the possibility of parole has proven to be an exceedingly difficult task. I've counseled wayward youth, taught my illiterate peers how to read, and volunteered for every imaginable "good" work offered.

All along the way, I kept running into a stark reality: No matter how much I could accomplish it was but droplets in a sea of misery and failure, a sea that kept getting larger, deeper, and murkier. The very system I lived in, the ground under my feet, was slipping into a fundamental darkness. Butting up against this slide down, I developed a keen awareness, a sense of moral obligation, that coming to understand what was wrong, seeing it clearly and comprehensively and knowing how to reverse the decline, I had to act. To really affect the wider world I had to work to better my world, this world of confinement and failure, of programmatic and expected defeat.

The first ridge I had to scale was the ever-present prison mind-set, what is best described as "The Omnivorous Cult of the Lowest Common Denominator." It is, in effect, a surrendering to the worst elements, a way of thinking that devalues progress and optimism, a code of conduct that resents growth and glorifies violence. Prisoners and guards, both sides of the prison experience less adversaries than mirror images of one another, casting their self-loathing onto the other, practice it. I had learned, years before, this cult, like most cults, is based on fear and ignorance; once exposed to the light of reason, all but the most fear-filled and obstinate are willing to abandon it. While adherence to the cult is wide, it is not deep. In the face of a good idea, a better way, the cult quickly withers.

By 1998 as the California prison system was sinking ever deeper into chaos; I became convinced the only solution was to apply what I had learned to fundamentally change this world. A sympathetic lieutenant had promised me he would carry the water for the project, taking it directly to the warden. I began to cautiously discuss the idea of what became the "Honor Program" with both my fellow prisoners and other staff. I was pleasantly surprised to learn that many people, on both sides of the fence, also wanted to see change. There was a palpable sense of frustration, of powerlessness in the face of the onrushing fire of violence and disruption. Change was certainly desired, but no one seemed to grasp how to get it done.

I began to write a proposal that ultimately consumed me for months, during a time when my personal life was coming apart, and my environment was devolving steadily, growing uglier and more inhospitable to positive thinking. The basic principles were clear from the outset: exclusion of drugs and gangs, a voluntary commitment from each prisoner, a focus on a rewards-based system rather than a punitive, punishment-based system, and a need for a different relationship between staff and prisoners. My reading of prison reform material, studies of how other countries ran more effective and successful prisons, criminology texts, and my experience convinced me that the vast majority of prisoners desire to simply do their own time in as much a state of stability as possible. The remainders are so completely trapped in the negative cult as to be unreachable.

The deeper I traveled into the creation process, the more filled I became with a conviction that through this reform the prison system could be transformed. Instead of being a vast wasteland to which tens of thousands of damaged souls were deposited to rot, it could become a greenhouse, a place of productivity and growth. My conversations about the program became animated with a sense of opportunity and conviction; purpose, in other words.

Work of my campaign spread throughout the prison. Most of the powers-that-be derided the very idea that California maximum-security prisoners could ever act honorably. Sadly, many prisoners felt the same way, so inculcated by the reigning ethos, the dominant ideology of the cult of violence and failure. Like all good ideas that challenge the status quo, this one had a polarizing effect. Nevertheless, supporters appeared from out of the smoke, people I would not have expected, from some of the harshest guards to leaders within the various prison groupings. Ideas came pouring in along with connections to the right people.

The lieutenant who first agreed to support the plan, who had the courage to put his name on a good idea, took the completed proposal directly to the warden, bypassing the "chain of command." This act was a kind of career suicide for him, because it is looked on as a type of betrayal to go around the established order, regardless of whether the intent or the result is good. His peers never forgave him for this, but the program would have been stillborn if not for his belief in doing what is right. The Warden, another oddity, a product of this weakened "care and treatment" arm of the prison system, saw immediately the potential benefits of the Honor Program. There was an aligning of the planets, or perhaps the critical mass of concern necessary to motivate change had simply been reached; either way, the ball was put into play.

The howls from the "custody" arm, the uniforms, could be heard throughout the prison. When the Warden handed the task of developing the program off to a Catholic priest, there was an almost universal outrage from among the ranks of the guards. The campaign to flush the program began with a direct dismissing of the idea itself. The prisoners would never go for it; the omnivorous cult would burn it down and leave the program a pile of cinders. Of course, the guards who had utilized the cult of violence to maintain their dominance fully expected to simply unleash the angry horde. To their dismay and surprise, enough of the prisoners who had come to see the true nature of their world banded together to create a wall behind which they could stand.

Although the proposal went up to the Warden under the lieutenant's name, it quickly became common knowledge I was the author. I began to use all the contacts I had developed through my years to counter the forces in opposition. I talked to everyone who would listen. I recruited every strong, intelligent prisoner I could to keep our flock together. Over the couple of years between presenting the initial proposal and the start of implementation, the program and I became inextricably linked. Some people started to refer to me as The Founder. As much as I tried to protest and demur, the voice within me that demanded my continued, stubborn, single-minded pursuit of **real** change to this world of mine reveled in the recognition.

For too much of my life I had been known only for wrong, for playing a central role in the cult of violence's one-note act. My reputation revolved around savagery, around destruction and tearing down. I even came to the sad realization that the girl who fell in love with me, and through whom I had first found the impetus to grow out of the confines of this world, she too had been drawn to my negative energy. There is a species of power, illusory but compelling nonetheless, to the darkness of human nature. I bathed in this ugliness so much I reeked of it. When the time came to strive for something better, I still felt the taste for the malevolence, its siren call of primitive emotion and instant gratification. At a different level, deeper, I craved to stand in the light, to be known as one who had helped to bring peace into my world. Thankfully, the latter desires won out.

Implementation of the Honor Program required cleaning out a whole 600-bed facility, of those prisoners too caught up in the prison mind-set to seek the chance for a better life. The negative leadership amongst the prisoners quickly realized the program would disempower them. It is much easier to terrorize those who cannot see a way out, a route of escape. By focusing on gangs and drugs, the twin agitators, the program removed both the force and the grease of the motor driving the turmoil. The guards willingly participated in this stage of the process, enjoying exercising power, not fully cognizant of what they were creating. In a fairly rapid period of time, several months, the facility was transformed into a population of prisoners who wanted to do better, to be better, to live as normal a life as possible. Even though the negative leaders would continue to seek to undermine the program, all their efforts ultimately failed because the power of the idea was simply too great. As I believed, the vast majority of prisoners want to live like human beings to the degree possible in confinement.

Although it would seem only logical that the guards would also prefer to work in a safer and saner environment, for many of them the reverse proved true. The one great unforeseen development of the Honor Program project is how doggedly it has been resisted by so many of the guards;

See **Purpose** *on page 22*

Can a Christian Stop Sinning?
A Theological Essay by Jeremy Ingram

Can a Christian stop sinning? The answer to this question is not a barren theological curiosity nor a mere doctrinal debate. Rather, it penetrates to the very heart of the Christian life. Consider the countless Christians searching for that elusive "secret" of the Christian life where, once found, their struggles will cease and perfect happiness will ensue. Also consider the countless cases of defeat and despondency many of these Christians experience because they never find this "key" to the Christian life.

Is there a secret, a key that will unlock a higher life where the Christian can stop sinning and stop struggling with sin? Many people answer this question affirmatively. Weigh what Terry L. Johnson writes in his book *When Grace Comes Home*:

In the last 150 years there has been no shortage of people ready to supply that ingredient for them. Some have seen sanctification as happening through a special act of faith, whereby one might 'reckon' oneself 'dead to sin' (Rom. 6:11). Others imagine that through a passive act of yielding to God one may be sanctified. According to this scheme, the whole problem with most Christians is that they are striving. What they must do is stop striving. They must yield themselves to God, 'let go and let God'. Only as they do this will they reach a 'higher life', experience a 'victorious life', or an 'abundant life', as it has variously been called. Still others imagine a second work of the Spirit subsequent to conversion.

Johnson points out that these teachings, designed to eliminate the struggle with sin, give rise to a dangerous expectation that is neither attainable in this life nor is Biblical. Borrowing from Charles Hodge, the great Princeton theologian, the thesis of this article can be summed up in these words:

The doctrine of the Protestant church is that sanctification is never complete in this life, sin is never entirely removed, and even the most advanced believer has need to pray for forgiveness. The question is not what God's duty is, nor what his command is, nor the provisions of the gospel, nor God's promises. The question is rather: Are God's promises to make us perfectly happy, perfectly holy, and perfectly glorious all accomplished in this life or in the life to come? Of all the promises of God directed toward believers, only justification is perfectly fulfilled in this life. It is admitted that perfect happiness and gloriousness are not fulfilled in this life; why should sanctification be excepted?

The first proof that a Christian will not stop sinning is ***the perfection and immutability of God's law***. During Jesus' life, the Pharisees paraded around flaunting their self-righteousness. In their eyes they "kept the law" and were accustomed to lean on their own righteousness rather than the righteousness of God. This self-righteousness was exposed by Jesus many times during His public discourses. One point Jesus frequently pressed upon His hearers was that the law penetrated to the very core of a person's being. In other words, the law was spiritual. When asked which of the Ten Commandments was the greatest, Jesus summed up the whole law in these words, "Thou shalt love the Lord thy God with all thy heart, and with all thy soul, and with all thy mind and thou shalt love thy neighbor as thyself" (Mt. 22:37-39). One of the true intents of the law was to expose the sinful motives and affections of man's heart and thus drive him away from a trust in himself to a trust in Jesus. The demand that God places on our lives (Be ye therefore perfect, even as your Father which is in heaven is perfect) can only be fulfilled in Jesus' perfect life.

Therefore, the holy requirements of God that never change show man's own sin and need for a Savior. This is just as true for the believer as it is for the unbeliever. G.I. Williamson wrote, "The more light and understanding a believer has ... the more he will realize how great, or how high, the perfection required by God really is. Just as we see more clearly the spots on a garment when we bring it to greater light, so the Christian becomes more aware of his sin."

The second proof that a Christian will not stop sinning is ***the express declarations of Scripture that all men are sinners***.

The Bible is replete with verses that explicitly state that all men sin:

- "If we say that we have no sin, we deceive ourselves, and the truth is not in us" (1 Jn. 1:8).
- "For there is not a just man upon earth, that doeth good, and sinneth not" (Ecl. 7:20).
- "For there is no man that sinneth not" (1 Kin. 8:46).
- "For in many things we offend all" (Jam. 3:2).

These verses do not pertain only to the unconverted. The express declaration of the Bible is wholly that the sin remains in the life of a believer although sin will not have mastery over him. Charles Hodge says, "This does not mean simply that all men have sinned, that all are guilty, but that all have sin cleaving to them."

The third proof that a Christian will not stop sinning is ***the Biblical description of the conflict between Spirit and flesh***.

The Bible presents a clear picture of the life of every believer—it is a life of continual warfare. Perhaps one of the best illustrations of the conflict in the life of a believer is given in Romans 7. Paul describes the struggle between grace and sin in his own life as a Christian. There remains in him, indwelling corruption that daily manifests itself in sin. "That true grace strives against these sins and corruptions, does not allow of them, hates them, mourns over them, groans under them as a burden, is likewise certain" (Matthew Henry). The apostle here writes to encourage us to pursue a holy life amid the many battles we daily face and he designs to show that sinless perfection is not attainable in this life.

Some, who promote the possibility of sinless perfection, wish to evade the force of this passage by saying, Paul is describing his life before he was converted. However, as the old Southern theologian Robert Dabney put it, "And it is of no avail for the Wesleyan to attempt evading this picture of Romans 7, as the language of Paul convicted but not yet converted; for other similar passages remain, as Romans 8:7, Gal. 5:17, Phil. 3:13, 1 Tim. 6:12, etc, etc."

Let's look at the process of sanctification, whereby God continually grows those who believe in Christ.

Sanctification is the act of God in a Christian, whereby He purifies them from the pollution of sin and grows them in holiness. There are several aspects of sanctification that need to be noted.

First, sanctification is a work of God. The Bible presents our growth as Christians as a work that God does: "for without me you can do nothing" (Jn. 15:5) and "for it is God that works in you to will and to do" (Phil. 2:13).

Second, God uses His word as the means whereby He sanctifies the believer. "Sanctify them through Thy truth: Thy word is truth" (Jn. 17:17). It is in the Bible that mankind sees his sin as sin, it is in the Bible that sin is condemned in all its ugliness, it is the Bible that the Holy Spirit applies to the hearts of believers, and it is the Bible that ministers are called upon to preach.

Third, Christians are not all sanctified in the same measure. The Bible gives many illustrations of the progressiveness of the Christian life. In 1 John 2 the picture of a growing person is used—there is the child, the young man, and the father. Elsewhere, a tree is used to show the growth natural in all believers. However, just as every tree and every human being do not all grow at the same rate, sanctification is not at the same rate for all believers. It is the experience of all Christians that there are some who are weak and others who are strong. Just as there are degrees of holiness between members of the body of Christ, there are also degrees of holiness in each Christian's daily walk.

Fourth, sanctification has two purposes: in reference to sin, sanctification is the "putting off the old man" and in reference to holiness, it is the "putting on the new man."

This brings us to a subject that has seen its share of confusion. What is the relationship between the old man and the new man?

Before we answer this question, perhaps it would be wise to define what these terms mean. Wilhelmus á Brakel says, "The old man is the corruption of the human nature." In other words, the phrase "old man" refers to the sin nature that every person is born with. It is the natural disposition toward evil, the propensity toward sin. á Brakel points out, the phrase "old man" is used because this sin nature had its origin in the fall of man and it exists in a person prior to conversion—hence "old." This sin nature permeates the entire man so that his intellect, will, and emotions are affected by its power—hence "man." Many phrases are used interchangeably in Scripture to denote this sin nature: old man, flesh, the law of sin, the image of the first Adam, etc. By the law of opposites we can define the new man. It is that new nature that God implants into man subsequent to conversion which permeates all the faculties of the soul.

Therefore, only the old man exists and thus only sin issues forth from the unbeliever. After conversion, the new man exists and the believer has a new propensity for good. This new nature and the old nature coexist with one another even though God ensures that the believer has been set free from the power and dominion of the sin nature. Still, the two natures strive against one another.

There are many reasons why God has ordered things this way. By allowing this continuing strife in the life of a believer, God's free grace might shine forth all the more by preventing the old nature from winning. Christ's atoning work for the sins of those who believe in Him remains the believer's only source of comfort and hope. This continuing strife engenders a longing for heaven and rest from this spiritual warfare.

In conclusion, the old man and the new man coexist simultaneously and generate continual warfare in the Christian. However, if the Christian is diligent in this warfare, then the old man will decrease and the new man will increase.

The fourth proof that a Christian will not stop sinning is ***the fifth petition in the Lord's Prayer***.

Our Lord Jesus taught us to pray by saying ,"And forgive us our debts" (Mt. 6:12). If a Christian prays for God to forgive him of his sins, as he is shown to do, then he acknowledges that he is a sinner and therefore has not quit sinning. Charles Hodge says, "... the use of the Lord's prayer by all Christians, is an acknowledgment that no Christian in this life is perfect."

Among many things we can learn from this petition are the facts that man owes God, as his Creator, an obligation that he fails to perform every day. Therefore, man has incurred a debt and is liable to God's judgement. In praying for forgiveness, man acknowledges that he is a debtor and asks his Father to forgive him. Yet, because God is just and does not let sin go unpunished, man must have a surety who, on his behalf, satisfies God's justice. In praying this prayer rightly, the Christian must rest on the forgiveness found only in the person and work of Jesus Christ. Christians do not come before God as unconverted and in need of freedom from the divine wrath, but rather they come before God as their Father desiring to take refuge in the blood of Christ. Luther says, "unless God forgives without cessation we are lost."

Calvin commenting on the Libertines, who taught that perfection was attainable in this life, says that these teachers snatch followers away from Christ. They do this by denying what Christ has taught "that instructing all to confess their guilt, [Christ] admits none but sinners."

But if Christ, according to the authority given him by his Father, commands as throughout life to resort to prayer for the pardon of our guilt, who will tolerate these new doctors, who try to dazzle the eyes of the simple-minded with the specter of perfect innocence so as to assure them that they can rid themselves of all blame? This, according to John, is nothing else than to make God a liar [1 John 1:10]!

The fifth proof that a Christian will not stop sinning is ***the testimony of the universal church***.

B.B. Warfield, in his treatment on Perfectionism, calls attention to the universal teachings of Christianity since the Reformation. He says, "It belongs to the very essence of the type of Christianity propagated by the Reformation that the believer should feel himself continuously unworthy of the grace by which he lives." Warfield uses the term "miserable sinner" to describe the Christian—though blessed with every spiritual blessing, at the same time, deserving in ourselves nothing but God's everlasting wrath. "There is emphasized in this attitude the believer's continued sinfulness in fact and in act ... the Christian is conceived fundamentally in other words as a penitent sinner." Still, Warfield emphasizes that the miserable sinner is not prone to despair but quite the opposite, "The spirit of this Christianity is a spirit of penitent indeed, but overmastering exaltation."

It is said that Augustine brought this mood into the Christian church. Before, there was only an alternating feeling of fear and hope. Although lost in the Middle Ages due to the emphasis on human graces, it was rediscovered by Luther during the Reformation. Luther's own struggles with the conflict between the facts that he was a sinner and God hated sin was resolved in the person and work of Jesus Christ. Luther realized and taught that when a person is born again neither does he become sinless nor does he stop sinning. Yet in Christ, the just desert of his sins are no longer imputed to him. It was common to hear Luther say that the Christian is "at the same time a sinner and a saint."

This thought is confessed throughout the Protestant world— that Christians are not only hell-deserving sinners, in and of themselves, but also that in respect to the remaining sin nature, they continually transgress the law of God in thoughts, words, and deeds.

The sixth proof that a Christian will not stop sinning is ***the conscience of every believer***.

Anselm of Canterbury used to say "You have not yet considered how great the weight of sin is." There are some today who need to consider the weight of sin in their own lives. Those who claim they have reached a place in their spiritual lives where they have ceased to sin or those who teach it is possible to cease from sinning have not took seriously their own depravity.

It is no wonder the best of Christians exhibit some form of sin remaining in their life. Take for example the lives of the saints recorded in the pages of Scripture. Dabney says, "As if to refute the idea of their sinful perfection, Scripture in every case records of them some fault ..." Even our own daily lives, as believers testify to the point: "And if human experience can settle such a point it is wholly on our side; for those who are obviously most advanced in sanctification, both among inspired and uninspired saints, are most emphatic in their confessions of short coming; while those who arrogantly claim perfect sanctification, usually discredit their pretenses sooner or later, by shameful falls" (Dabney).

The seventh proof that a Christian will not stop sinning is ***the Biblical exhortations to strive after holiness***.

The bible is saturated with passages encouraging God's children to grow in holiness: "Not that I have already obtained all this, or have already been made perfect, but I press on to take hold of that for which Christ Jesus took hold of me. Brothers, I do not consider myself yet to have taken hold of it. But one thing I do: Forgetting what is behind and straining toward what is ahead, I press on toward the goal to win the prize for which God has called me heavenward in Christ Jesus" (Phil. 3:12-14).

To summarize, we have answered the question, "Can a Christian stop sinning?" by offering seven proofs why a Christian cannot stop sinning in this present life. Let it be remarked that if it so pleased God to completely remove sin from a Christian's life then it would immediately be gone. However, it rather pleases Him to leave the vestiges of sin in the Christian's life to further His divine plan. Let the reader be encouraged to pursue a life of holiness knowing that his life is not his own; he has been saved from the power of sin. Let the reader reflect on his relationship with God and consider His worthiness compared with the vanity of this world. God has called the Christian to a life characterized by a pursuit of holiness and attended to by great promises of peace of conscience, communion with God, growth in grace, and eternal blessedness. May God work in you both to will and to do according to His good pleasure. Amen. ✍

Testimony of Alonzo Felix Andres Juan

My dear friends, I wish to share with everyone the story of my life and how I came to know the Lord Jesus Christ through my sufferings in prison.

I am from a small village in Guatemala called Suntelah. I grew up very poor, but in church with my family. My mom and I used to walk to church which was about two hours away in San Miguel Acatan. I was of course very young but I remember the trips that my mother and I made to church.

We, as stated, were very poor and we lived way out in the country without cars or anything except horses and donkeys—as 90 percent of Guatemalans have done. We of course did not have much food nor clothing and we would leave each year to find jobs among the wealthy people wherein we would pick cotton, coffee and sugar all day long. We worked extremely hard, however, this was all that we felt we could do.

We would get paid only about three to five dollars per day and we would stay there to work for about three or four months before returning home. Of course we didn't bring much money back in that we had to buy the things that we needed while away.

I can remember the first pair of shoes that I ever had. I was eight or nine years old and my mother finally was able to sacrifice and buy them for me. It was truly one of the greatest days of my life. I found myself smiling big and never wanting to take my shoes off, even to sleep. Even though I have never driven a car, it was like driving one for sure.

Many of you have seen Guatemala on T.V., or even maybe have visited my country.

I started working at around age six or seven and had to work hard to care for my mother in that my father passed away when I was very young. I stayed in school for maybe a little over a year, but because of work I missed the opportunity to finish my schooling.

Our culture is Mayan Indian.

My mother never went to school nor can she read or write. So, with my having also not finished school, my mom in Guatemala and I cannot write letters back and forth. We can only send taped messages here and there in our language—Kanjobal.

It has been difficult to have to learn three languages; Kanjobal, Spanish, and English, but the Lord has blessed me to learn enough of each to share His word.

I have had a difficult and painful life in that I not only lost my dad to cancer but I likewise lost my sister to cancer as well. I was fortunate to be blessed, however, with five nieces and nephews which she had before she passed away.

During a certain period in my life I heard about the United States of America. I was told that I could come here, make some really good money working, and send this money back home to my family.

One day I made a decision to come to America; therefore, I informed my family of my intentions, but promised to return in about two years.

Upon coming to America I began working immediately, like the next day, with my uncle picking tomatoes and oranges in the fields in Florida. The money was great and I was earning about 40 to 45 dollars each day.

I truly started out doing great and was able to send money back home to Guatemala. I was living with my cousin at this time and my cousin's wife would always tell me not to drink or hang out with the wrong people and I would do well. Only if I had listened. Instead I was drinking and begin to hang out with the wrong people that I called friends. I know now that I had no friends, especially seeing that I haven't received any cards or letters from any of them.

At that dark time in my life, I never truly cared for anyone, not even myself. In fact, I actually should have been dead a long time ago. My life in fact was so sad that I used to wake up in the road or on a street somewhere, not even realizing it. I would have been better off had I stayed in poverty in Guatemala. At least I had my senses.

Furthermore, I truly never dreamed that I would be in prison. Even upon the beginning of my incarceration I was hit with the tragic news that my only son had been killed by killer bees back in Guatemala. I was both hopeless and helpless until the Lord intervened in my life.

When the Lord Jesus Christ came into my life, while incarcerated, my life changed completely for the good, even under the circumstances of being in prison. Of course, even though I have found love, joy, peace and happiness, I, as all do, still go through storms full of many hurts and pains. When I do, however, the Lord shows me that He allows such to strengthen me that I may be a help and comfort to others.

I have come to trust the Lord with all my heart. I do all to put Him first and my relationship with Him at the top of my list, even before family and friends. Of course, I fail sometimes, because certainly Satan is all around and doesn't wish for us to be happy and smiling. I had to let the Lord show me that Satan no longer can control my mind, will, or emotions.

As of right now I am in prison and many of you might say that's not good. For me, however, I must say that coming to prison actually saved my life. Certainly this would sound crazy to some, however, as I said earlier, I was clearly on a path to destruction before coming here.

Of course, being in the wrong place at the wrong time with the wrong person resulted in my being here, however, I made that wrong choice.

Whatever the circumstances, the Lord used this to cleanse me and to give me a new heart and life. I now realize that from my childhood the Lord was always there intervening and letting His presence be known. Instead of listening, I of course took it all for granted. Now my eyes have been fully opened.

I spend most of my time in prison attempting to be faithful in the ministry the Lord has blessed me with whereby I make crosses and other items out of potato chip bags and give them to other brothers, sisters, or individuals. It truly blesses me to see the smiles on their faces when I give them such in the name of Jesus. Even in prison I have likewise met some of the most wonderful people ever. With my Christian brothers here, we have truly had some great worship services, and without my brothers things would be even harder. The Lord, I must say, blesses us to comfort and strengthen each other continually.

Even in prison the Lord further blesses and meets my needs as well as blesses me to be able to send money home to my mother back in Guatemala. It is furthermore amazing how the Lord blessed me with a Christian cell mate. My cell mate and I have celled together for nearly ten years and we both love the Lord. Even though sometimes we have burdens of our own, we find it is okay to talk, cry and just pray together because the Lord, we know, has been good to us both and looks out for all that concerns us.

I would say to you, my friends, or whoever might be reading this, to please consider my Lord Jesus Christ in whatever you might be going through and receive His joy.

There is so much that I wish to say, however, the Spirit guides me to now just share Scriptures with you that I know, like me, will bless and touch your heart and maybe even change your life. Please, I ask you to pick up your Bible and study the following Scriptures: Matthew 6:25-34; 28:20; Psalms 34:14; 37:37; 94:12; Deuteronomy 8:5; Revelation 3:19; Job 5:17-18; Romans 1:7; 5:1; 8:6; 10:15; 12:18; Philippians 4:13, 19; Proverbs 3:11-12; Hebrews 10:38-39; 11:1; 12:6; Colossians 3:15; Hosea 4:6; Isaiah 42; Exodus 14:14; 1 Cor. 7:15; 13:13; 2 Cor. 13:11; Galatians 5:22; 2 Tim 1:2; Matthew 7:7-8; Luke 11:21; 2 Thes. 1:2; Eph. 6:25; Isaiah 26:3; Jeremiah 29:11; Mark 11:2-24, 37.

Thank you for allowing me to share my life with you and I pray the Lord's richest blessings in your life. God bless you. ✍

Who is this Man from Galilee?
By Jeff Durham

Who is this Man from Galilee

He walked beside the restless sea

This quiet man from Galilee

Words He spoke were meant for me

I was blind, He made me see

Who is this Man from Galilee

Whose voice has calmed the troubled sea

Some say He might the Prophet be

He is the Lord the Christ to me

I hear Him in the busy streets

He gives me directions to my feet

Once idle hands now make men whole

Heals their bodies, restores their souls

Who is this Man from Galilee

Who heals the world through you and me

Some say He might the Prophet be

He is the Lord the Christ to me

114

Books

from page 01

2007 to put the removal order into effect, but prison officials said they needed time to examine a long list of books.

Feldman said the review by the U.S. Bureau of Prisons (BOP) concluded that prison chapel libraries were not adequately supervised. The report went on to say, "The presence of extremist chaplains, contractors or volunteers in the BOP's correctional facilities can pose a threat to institutional security and could implicate national security if inmates are encouraged to commit terrorist acts against the United States."

Besides screening of religious service providers, the BOP report suggested audio and video monitoring of worship areas and chapel classrooms, as well as staff monitoring of inmate-led services.

Feldman told the court that officials would expand the libraries after choosing a new list of permitted books and that inmates are allowed to order books of their own and bypass the chapel libraries. "So, fundamentally, this is not a case about what books the inmates have the ability to read," he said.

By telephone, inmate Moshe Milstein testified that the chaplain at Otisville removed about 600 books from the chapel library on Memorial Day, including Harold Kushner's best seller *When Bad Things Happen to Good People*. Milstein told the court, "There is definitely irreparable harm done to us already, and we would like the court to issue the injunction to get the books back as soon as possible."

After complaining of "a denial of our First Amendment rights," inmate Douglas Kelly said books on Islam already were the least represented in the library's collection and were reduced by half in the Memorial Day removal. Describing himself as a representative of the prison's Muslim community, he said, "A lot of what we are missing were definitely prayer books or prayer guides and religious laws on the part of the Muslim faith."

The judge declined to block the removals and said the lawsuit may have been premature because the inmates had not yet followed prison administrative complaint procedures.

"A mass Memorial Day book burning," is how the book removal was described by Ron Kuby, a civil rights lawyer who has represented a former head Islamic chaplain banned from the state prison system after being accused of making extremist statements.

Kuby noted that there might be limits to the relief the prisoners can seek because prisoners' First Amendment rights are severely limited. ✍

I am nothing
By G. Frank Cavender

I am nothing ...

But a speck of dust on the earth,

Which is a speck of dust in the solar system,

Which is a speck of dust in the galaxy,

Which is a speck of dust in the universe,

Which is only a speck of dust in eternity;

But ... God knows my name

So ... I am something ... only because He knows me!

God bless you by the power of the name of Jesus. ✍

The Battle Over Origins

By Garry W. Johnson
MOUNTAIN REVIEW Staff

Many of you who came through Brushy Mountain might remember the close-circuit airing of a program by Ken Ham, the dinosaur guy; or perhaps you have read books by his publishing ministry Answers in Genesis. Even more likely, you may remember him from recent news stories about his $27 million Creation Museum in rural Petersburg, Kentucky.

Ham has ruffled many feathers in the scientific and academic communities with his exhibit of Adam and Eve along side dinosaurs, featured in the museum. The 50,000-square-foot facility, complete with a 40-foot-tall depiction of Noah's Ark and roaring robotic dinosaurs opened to the public this past Memorial Day, and is expected to draw an estimated 250,000 visitors in its first year. Why such large numbers? People believe in creationism.

After Republican presidential candidates were put on the spot this past June about their views on the subject, a USA Today/Gallup poll showed two-thirds of 1,007 adults surveyed said creationism is definitely or probably true. To be clear, creationism is the idea that God created humans in their present form within the past 10,000 years (the dinosaurs you have to deal with on your own).

Another, more broad concept is revolutionizing the scientific community: Intelligent design. Mario Seiglie explains in the February 2006 article *The Intelligent Design Revolution*:

"In the 1980's, several scientists began meeting together to try to explain the incredible complexity they were witnessing inside the cell—and especially the vast amount of information in the form of a language imbedded in the DNA molecule. They began to challenge the theory of evolution within their own field of biology rather than from a religious point of view.

"One of those scientists, biochemist Charles Thaxton, coined the term 'intelligent design' to explain the need for intelligence behind the elaborate information found inside DNA. 'Just when it seemed that natural causes might suffice to account for all natural phenomenon,' he notes, 'there were breakthrough discoveries in both mathematics and biology' ('A New Design Argument:' *Cosmic Pursuit,* March 1, 1998).

"The intelligent design movement gained momentum when New Zealand molecular biologist Michael Denton, a medical doctor and agnostic, carefully examined the main arguments for Darwinian evolution and found them very deficient

"He wrote in his book *Evolution: A Theory in Crisis* that the problems with the theory of evolution 'are too severe and intractable to offer any hope of resolution in terms of the orthodox Darwinian framework' and that the accepted traditional view 'is no longer tenable' (1985, p. 16).

"He then concluded at the end of the book, 'Ultimately the Darwinian theory of evolution is no more nor less than the great cosmogenic myth of the twentieth century' (p. 358).

"In England, a University of California at Berkeley law professor on sabbatical, Philip Johnson, read *The Blind Watchmaker,* by prominent British zoologist and atheist Richard Dawkins, who advocated evolution as the real designer behind all living things.

"Professor Johnson's legal mind quickly noticed the flimsy and emotional arguments in the book, bereft of solid evidence. He wondered why a noted scientist would resort to such trickery if the theory was on such solid ground. Here was a challenge, he thought.

"Professor Johnson began a thorough investigation of the evolutionary literature and was astounded with what he found. As a famous fable says, truly the emperor wasn't wearing any clothes! He began publishing his findings about Darwinian evolution in popular books such as *Darwin on Trial* (1991) & *Defeating Darwinism by Opening Minds* (1997).

"Meanwhile, at a biology lab in a Pennsylvanian university, biochemist Michael Behe was also puzzled by the astounding complexity he found inside the cell. On reading Dr. Denton's book, he was angered about the suppression of such evidence by the scientific community. He wrote a bestseller, *Darwin's Black Box* (1996), exposing major scientific weaknesses in the theory of evolution.

"Another biologist, Jonathan Wells, also was incensed with the faulty information being perpetuated by Darwinian evolutionists in schools and universities. He wrote the book *Icons of Evolution* (2000), which exposed how some of the major 'scientific' examples used to teach Darwinian evolution are in fact fraudulent or misrepresented.

"Since then the intelligent design movement has gained notable influence on the public. A 2005 poll

USA Today/Gallup poll
People who say they believe:

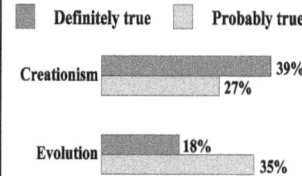

	Definitely true	Probably true
Creationism	39%	27%
Evolution	18%	35%

Source: USA Today/Gallup Poll of 1,007 adults June 1-3, Margin of error: +/- 3 percentage points.

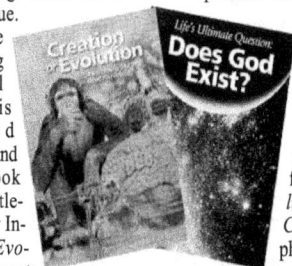

showed that a majority of Americans believe in it, and another poll of medical doctors found that 65 percent think intelligent design should be allowed or required to be taught in schools along with evolution. Now a growing number of U.S. school boards are beginning to insist that intelligent design be taught alongside evolution" (*The Good News,* p. 19).

This transition, however, has been met by staunch opposition from supporters of Darwinism. A now famous school board in Dover, Pennsylvania, attempted to mandate the inclusion of intelligent design in ninth-grade biology classes in 2005. The ACLU backed parents who sued and won a landmark decision in which a federal judge ruled intelligent design was religion, not science. That decision sent shockwaves through the educational community and quieted other efforts to bring intelligent design into school curriculums.

In the July 21, 2007, issue of *World* magazine, columnist Mark Bergin interviewed public highschool teacher, Doug Cowan, about his approach to teaching Darwinian theory within current school guidelines.

"'I don't teach alternative theories, because that's not part of the curriculum,' he explained. 'There aren't a whole lot of alternative theories other than design theory, but that's not in our curriculum. So unless a kid asks specifically about it, I don't deal with it.'

"Instead, Cowan deals more thoroughly with Darwinism than most existing biology textbooks, adding reading materials from outside the standard evolutionary syllabus: *Darwin on Trial, Icons of Evolution, Darwin's Black Box, Evolution: A Theory in Crisis.* Cowan says these extra texts engage his students, challenging their ability to analyze and discern truth from competing sides of a controversial issue.

"This fall, the 34-year teaching veteran will restructure his evenhanded presentation around a new textbook from the Seattle-based Discovery Institute. *Explore Evolution: The Arguments for and Against Neo-Darwinism* (Hill House Publishers, 2007) does not address alternative theories of origins but succinctly lays out the scientific strengths and weaknesses of the most critical elements of Darwinism. 'It's made my work a lot easier,' Cowan said.

"*Explore Evolution* encapsulates a 'teach the controversy' paradigm that the Discovery Institute has advocated for the better part of the past decade....

"State school boards in Pennsylvania, South Carolina, New Mexico, and Minnesota along with local boards in Wisconsin and Louisiana have adopted science standards that encourage critical analysis of Darwinian Theory. To date, not a single lawsuit has challenged such standards.

"'This is an approach that if I were a Darwinist I would be particularly frightened of,' said John West, associate director of the Discovery Institute's Center for Science and Culture. 'The policy that we've recommended turns out to be the precise common-ground approach we said it would be. It reduces the decibel level; you don't get sued; you get good education; and the Darwinists don't have a leg to stand on'" (P.13).

Still, with all the support mounting for creationism and intelligent design, evolution remains the dominant explanation taught in American schools and supported by the mass media for the appearance and wondrous variety of more than a million living species on planet earth.

Why is Darwin's theory, soon to be 150 years old, still so prevalent in American culture? Because it is not just a scientific theory, it has become a philosophical viewpoint. Anthropologist Ashley Mantagu claims, "Next to the Bible, no work has been quite as influential, in virtually every aspect of human thought, as *The Origin of Species*" (*The Origin of Species,* 1958, Mentor edition, quote on the back cover).

As intelligent design has been criticized by the courts as "religion, not science," Darwin's theory itself has become, for many, a belief system which promotes materialistic naturalism—the idea that all that exists in the universe is matter and its law.

As biochemist and agnostic Michael Denton says, "It is ironic to recall that it was the increasingly secular outlook in the nineteenth century which initially eased the way for the acceptance of evolution, while today it is perhaps the Darwinian view of nature more than any other that is responsible for the *agnostic* and *skeptical* outlook of the twentieth century. What was once a deduction from *materialism* has today become its foundation" (*Evolution: A Theory in Crisis,* p. 358, emphasis added).

If you would like to take a closer look at the scientific findings about evolution, please request the fascinating booklets, *Creation or Evolution: Does It Really Matter What You Believe?* and *Life's Ultimate Question: Does God Exist?* Both publications are provided free as an educational service in the public interest. Send your request to: The Good News, P.O. Box 541027, Cincinnati, OH 45254-1027.

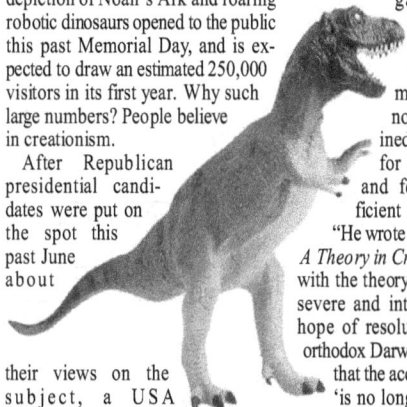

Survey: Majority of medical doctors reject strict Darwinism

In a surprising result, a majority of 1,482 physicians polled by HDC Research and the Louis Finkelstein Institute for Religious and Social Studies rejected strict Darwinism.

Strict Darwinism was defined as: "Humans evolved naturally with no supernatural involvement—no divinity played any role." Only 38% of the physicians polled accepted that belief. Other types of evolutionary explanations that can take into consideration a Creator received more support by margin of 42% to 38%.

The same poll revealed 65% of doctors surveyed believed intelligent design should be allowed or required to be taught in schools alongside evolution. In fact, although the intelligent design explanation is quite recent, a third of doctors polled favored it over evolution.

"Of course most doctors are skeptical of Darwinism," said Dr. Robert Cihak, M.D., former president of the Association of American Physicians and Surgeons and a medical columnist for JewishWorldReview.com. "An eye surgeon knows the astonishing intricacies of human vision intimately, so the vague, just-so stories about eye evolution don't fool him. And the eye is just one of the countless organs and interdependent systems in the body that defy Darwinian explanation" (Discovery Institute, *Nearly Two-Thirds of Doctors Skeptical of Darwin's Theory of Evolution,"* May 31, 2005).—Mario Seiglie

Purpose

from page 18

even some of the guards I assumed would be our biggest supporters. I was not surprised that the most retrograde among their ranks would resist anything labeled "honor" associated with prisoners, but I underestimated how many of them would resent prisoners taking control of their own lives. The guards have built a prison mind-set no less pervasive and negative than the prisoners'. Within this warped world-view, all the players have assigned roles. Prisoners are always bad, always wrong, and always suspect. Guards are always good, always right, and always justified in their actions, no matter how apparently unethical, due to the evil, incorrect, and devious nature of prisoners.

The guards' moral issue split them into warring camps; those supportive of the program, the larger but quieter group, and those opposed, the more vocal and determined. I have continued to campaign on behalf of the program, but as positions hardened, it became difficult to reach the other side. I believe the root factor of their resistance is fear. They are terrified their actions will be called into question, or even the very justification for their professional existence. The empire California prison guards created are built on a false premise, that California prisoners cannot and will not conduct themselves in a civilized fashion. At its heart, the Honor Program sets out to prove that premise inaccurate. As the years stretch out behind us, peaceful, productive, and civilized, the earth beneath their feet has been crumbling away.

Six years after conception, and almost four years after implementation, the results have been impressive. There have only been a couple of incidents when the opposition managed to slip some ringers into our midst; no guards assaulted, no mass uprisings or riots or strikes. (No small feat in a state prison system that is, literally, in a meltdown, with uprisings and riots and strikes happening daily in other prisons.) A flourishing culture of positive energy that includes lowering of racial barriers and a growing sense of ownership. New arrivals are advised by other prisoners that this is a good thing, so don't screw it up. There is even optimism; just a bit, because prisoners tend to be the most pessimistic people in the world. More fundamentally, there is a sense of possibility, of expectation.

The Honor Program has been featured in newspapers and on television. In one long piece on a local channel, I was interviewed and identified as the prisoner who came up with the idea for the program. Shortly after the segment aired, I received mail from admiring members of the public. People want to believe that prisoners, indeed everyone, are capable of good, of affecting the world in a way that results in an advance in the human condition. As sad as it has been to observe the response of too many of the guards, it has been extremely gratifying to see how others of them have risen to the challenge. Several have gone so far as to become our biggest supporters after initially doubting the Honor Program concept.

One in particular, a 25-year veteran, raised in a family of guards, has become our most effective and insistent supporter. Such is the nature of an idea, of a plan, of a worthy purpose.

For me, after these years of struggle, and a lot of bruises incurred along the way, pursuing something worthy of sacrifice has altered my sense of myself. I am reminded of the words of Feoder Dostoyevsk's Grand Inquisitor, that the secret to a life well lived is to have something to live for. I have identified my raison d' etre, taking the hard-won knowledge I have earned from a lifetime of imprisonment and putting it to good use; more specifically, reforming the world's largest prison system from within one of its cells. It has been, and will surely continue to be, a hard slog but it must be done. For some reason I am not fully sure of, luck of the draw, fate, providence, it appears to be my task.

Prisons, as institutions, have an atavistic quality. Across the American West they dot the landscape like latter day outposts, surrounded by watchtowers that face inward, designed to keep the modern savages in the compound. Serving life without the possibility of parole in one of these outposts is a terribly dispiriting experience. The most enlightened prison system is still a prison system, a place of separation and despair. Nevertheless, my experience leads me to believe prison can be a place of growth. All but the most defiant of criminals can be reformed, in the literal sense of the word, into better, more productive and useful human beings. Most radically, I know they want to be reformed; they just don't consciously know it themselves.

My crusade to alter my world, to pick up the flag of fundamental reform and push it to the crest of the hill, has affected thousands of people. Even those who oppose the concept have had their lives changed. The California prison system has a shining example of the possible. The lives of all those connected to this place, directly and indirectly, have been altered for the better. Into this alternate reality of misery and disorder, of exploding canisters of tear gas and acts of desperate meaninglessness, the honor-concept backfire has been set. It is also a challenge to the free world; honor being applied to the discourse regarding the outcasts necessarily implies the presumption of a higher standard of conduct from the rest of society. Such is the nature of purpose, of the power of a purpose-filled existence to affect change. The power of purpose can even overcome the concrete and steel hearts of a prison world. ✍

Postal offenses

Number of arrests in top postal crimes in 2005:

6,788	Mail theft
1,855	Mailing of controlled substances
1,577	Mail fraud

Source: U.S. Postal Inspection Service;
By Garry W. Johnson, MOUNTAIN REVIEW Staff

Postal rates have gone up, in more ways than one

By Jeremy Ingram
MOUNTAIN REVIEW Staff

The size of the letter you send in the mail just got important. In the past, letters were assessed postage based on the weight, not on the size. As of May 14 that has changed. Now letters are assessed postage based on both weight and size. The new price structure classifies first-class mail into four divisions: postcards, letters, large envelopes (flat) and packages (parcels). Each item has its own pricing scheme. According to the U.S. Postal Service, "The new price structure recognizes that each of these mail shapes has substantially different processing costs so each mail shape will now have separate prices."

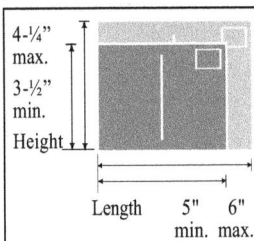

Figure 1. Dimensions of a postcard, according to the U.S. Postal Service. For domestic mail, the cost to send a postcard is 26¢, up from 24¢.

Graphics by Garry W. Johnson, MOUNTAIN REVIEW Staff

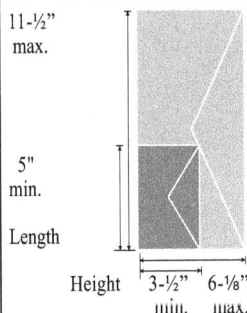

Figure 2. A U.S. letter is a machinable mailpiece with these dimensions. Letters can weigh up to 3.5 ounces.

Graphics by Garry W. Johnson, MOUNTAIN REVIEW Staff

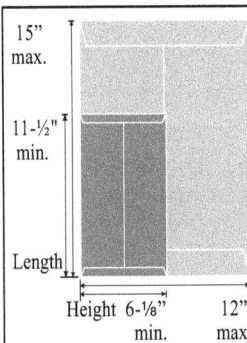

Figure 3. The dimensions of what the Postal Service calls "large envelopes (flats)." A 2-ounce letter with these characteristics cost 97¢ at the new rate. Prior to May 14, it cost 63¢.

First-class shape-based mail rates:

Letters		Large envelopes (flats)		Packages	
Weight not over (ounces)	Rate	Weight not over (ounces)	Rate	Weight not over (ounces)	Rate
1	$0.41	1	$0.80	1	$1.13
2	0.58	2	0.97	2	1.30
3	0.75	3	1.14	3	1.47
3.5	0.92	4	1.31	4	1.64
—	—	5	1.48	5	1.81
—	—	6	1.65	6	1.98
—	—	7	1.82	7	2.15
—	—	8	1.99	8	2.32
—	—	9	2.16	9	2.49
—	—	10	2.33	10	2.66
—	—	11	2.50	11	2.83
—	—	12	2.67	12	3.00
—	—	13	2.84	13	3.17

Figure 4. Chart for the new U.S. shape-based first-class mail rate structure that started May 14.

Chart by Garry W. Johnson, MOUNTAIN REVIEW Staff

POSTCARDS

The new postcard rate is 26 cents, and a postcard must fit the minimum and maximum dimensions given in Figure 1. A card's thickness can be a minimum of 0.0007 inches and a maximum of 0.016 inches. These standards are the same as under previous rates.

LETTERS

The new 1-ounce first-class letter rate is 41 cents, with each additional ounce at 17 cents. Such letters must fit the minimum and maximum dimensions shown in Figure 2. If a letter is sent that cannot pass through the Postal Service's automatic sorting machines but stays within the dimensions pictured, a nonmachinable surcharge of 17 cents is assessed. The rates for letters only go up to items weighing 3.5 ounces or less.

LARGE ENVELOPES

Any envelope weighing more than 3.5 ounces is considered to be large and falls under the rates for what the Postal Service calls "large envelope (flats)." For items that fall within the dimensions pictured in Figure 3, the base rate for a 1-ounce large envelope is 80 cents, with 17 cents assessed for each additional ounce. For example, a large 9-inch-by-12-inch envelope weighing 2 ounces would have cost 63 cents under the previous rate structure. Under the new rate structure, it will cost 97 cents because of its size. If the contents were folded and put into a standard No. 10 business envelope, the 2-ounce letter would cost 58 cents. Figure 4 shows a chart with the basic new first-class rates that became effective May 14. The Postal Service's new rate structure also says that "flat-size pieces with certain characteristics are subject to parcel rates." A large envelope (flat) must also be flexible, rectangular and uniformly flat. Figure 5 pictures a diagram showing a clerk doing a flexibility test.

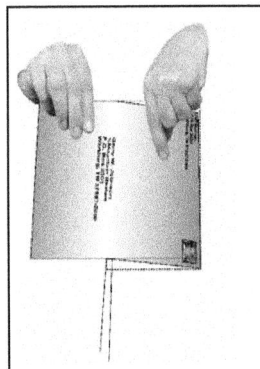

Figure 5. Reproduction of flexibility test diagram used by the Postal Service to determine if a mailpiece is a flat or a parcel.

Graphics by Garry W. Johnson, MOUNTAIN REVIEW Staff

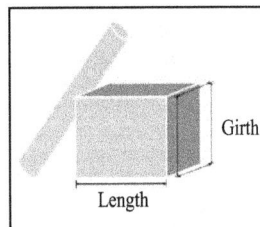

Figure 6. Parcel dimensions cannot exceed 108 inches (130 inches for parcel post). A 1-ounce parcel cost $1.13

PACKAGES

Items that fail this test or do not have the characteristics of a flat are considered to be packages and fall under the package (parcel) rates. Figure 6 pictures the critical factors for a package: length and girth. The girth is the measurement around the sides perpendicular to the length. Length plus girth cannot exceed 108 inches (130 inches for parcel post). 1-ounce parcel costs $1.13. Additional ounces are 17 cents each. For any piece of mail weighing more than 13 ounces, the Postal Service refers customers to its Priority Mail rates. ✍

Crock's Puzzle Fun

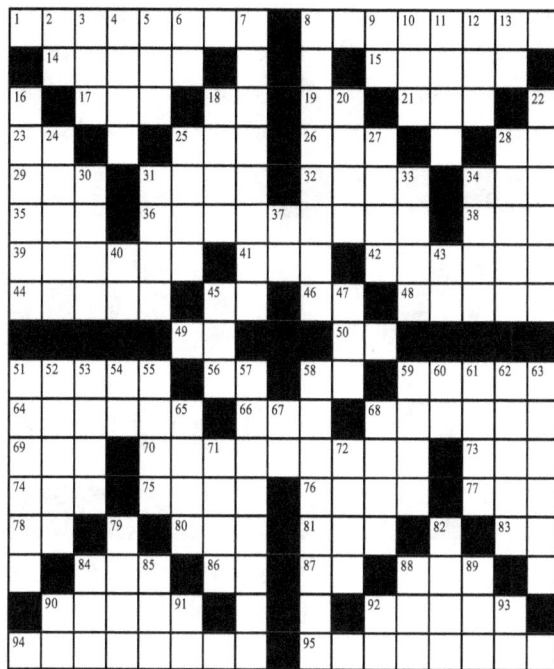

ACROSS

1. Plan of procedure
8. Horse drawn carriage
14. Snitches
15. Unpleasant sound
17. Bask in the sun
18. ___ - 549
19. UFO pilot
21. Fish catcher
23. With "coco," ornate
25. A section, a ___ment
26. Reading and Shortline
28. F___, animal hair
29. Canadian province
31. First class
32. Prompts
34. Put "der" with it and you have 8 legs
35. 19th, 3rd, 1st, of 26
36. Actress Jane
39. Sword topper?
41. Help!
42. Plumping
44. Long for
45. ___ what?
46. Popular medical drama
48. Ilks
49. Ma's mate
50. ___ if!
51. Ort
56. Jackson's St.
58. Mr. Asner
59. Type of beam
64. Puzzle
66. Consume
68. Meeting with familiar spirits
69. Dodge truck type
70. Showy trinket
73. Electrical term
74. Cleo's killer
75. Gaelic person
76. Castle protector
77. Sway
78. ___ the people ...
80. End of it (abr.)
81. Follower of
83. Under the word (Latin)
84. Pouch
86. Absolutely not
87. Concord's St.
88. Rutger's critic, ____ Imus
90. Kathmandu's country
92. Line
94. Cinemas
95. Grapefruit's cousin

DOWN

2. MD's assistant
3. Grain
4. Unit of weight
5. Royal Canadian Navy (abr.)
6. ___ the world turns
7. Gulfweed
8. Jumping jacks, e.g.
9. 7-Up, the ___-Cola
10. Charged particle
11. Type of piper?
12. One connected with (suf.)
13. They bring good things to life?
16. City NNW of Liverpool
18. Has _____, old news
20. Right
22. Squeezes, like a chicken's neck
24. As prompted
25. Go nuts
27. Ego
28. Turn over
30. Scarlett's digs
31. Arab nation
33. Pierre's St.
34. Whirl
37. Flight officer (abr.)
40. Symbol for Lawrencium
43. Symbol for Titanium
45. Likes green eggs and ham?
47. Cool!
51. Are sometimes grasped at
52. Quit
53. Access
54. Ditto 6 down
55. Nails down
57. Quadrants
58. Worsted fabrics
59. _____ we forget
60. Alcoholics Anonymous, in short
61. Winter precipitation
62. Reverberates
63. Take away
65. Author Anne
67. Little Rock's St.
68. Card game
71. Bare bottom?
72. Black jack
79. Auto parts store
82. No good
84. Spy
85. Feline
88. 4th, 16th, 4th of 26
89. Modern
90. Never hinged (abr.)
91. French article
92. Bolivia's cont.
93. Lowercase (abr.)

Edited by Garry W. Johnson, MOUNTAIN REVIEW Staff

DAVE'S CRYPTOGRAMS

Dave's Cryptograms are created from Biblical quotes.
Each letter in the puzzle stand for another.

Clue: H equals N

WFO CHWOSICWD TN WFO BEICSFW

KFZMM SBCJO WFOL: PBW WFO

EOIQOIKOHOKK TN WIZHKSIOKKTIK

KFZMM JOKWITD WFOL.

Original cryptograms produced by David Pendleton

Search the Word - Word Search

```
P S S E N D O O G A
Y B M E E K N E S S
G N T O R T O I S E
A A C A J O Y C W M
R T D E O X F A I A
G H A R E G S M N J
F A L L O W D E E R
P N G W A B W L E H
E A L N S I U T I A
E E T N L D E C G W
H L A D T P U L K K
S I O M A H C H J I
L X G M B L O V E T
T E M P E R A N C E
```

Can you find ...

12 "unclean" animals (Leviticus 11*)
9 "clean" animals (Deuteronomy 14*)
5 fruits of the Spirit (Galatians 5*)
3 disciples (John 1*)
2 nations of escape (Isaiah 66*)

* all Scriptures quoted from the King James Bible

By Garry W. Johnson, MOUNTAIN REVIEW Staff

Mouse Story ...

**Anonymous E-mail,
Contributed by Judy Johnson**

A mouse looked through the crack in the wall to see the farmer and his wife open a package. "What food might this contain?" the mouse wondered. He was devastated to discover it was a mousetrap.

Retreating to the farmyard, the mouse proclaimed the warning, "There is a mousetrap in the house! There is a mousetrap in the house!"

The chicken clucked and scratched, raised her head and said, "Mr. Mouse, I can tell this is a grave concern to you but it is of no consequence to me. I cannot be bothered by it."

The mouse turned to the pig and told him, "There is a mousetrap in the house! There is a mousetrap in the house!" The pig sympathized, but said, "I am so very sorry, Mr. Mouse, but there is nothing I can do about it but pray. Be assured you are in my prayers."

The mouse turned to the cow and said, "There is a mousetrap in the house! There is a mousetrap in the house!" The cow said, "Wow Mr. Mouse. I'm sorry for you, but it's no skin off my nose."

So, the mouse returned to the house, head down and dejected, to face the farmer's mousetrap—alone.

That very night a sound was heard throughout the house like the sound of a mousetrap catching its prey. The farmer's wife rushed to see what was caught. In the darkness she did not see it was a venomous snake whose tail the trap had caught. The snake bit the farmer's wife. The farmer rushed her to the hospital and she returned home with a fever. Everyone knows you treat a fever with fresh chicken soup, so the farmer took his hatchet to the farmyard for the soup's main ingredient. But his wife's sickness continued, so friends and neighbors came to sit with her around the clock. To feed them, the farmer butchered the pig.

The farmer's wife did not get well; she died. So many people came for her funeral, the farmer had the cow slaughtered to provide enough meat for all of them.

The mouse looked upon it all from his crack in the wall with great sadness.

So, the next time you hear someone is facing a problem and think it doesn't concern you, remember—when one of us is threatened, we are all at risk. We are all involved in this journey called life. We must keep an eye out for one another and make an extra effort to encourage one another. Each of us is a vital thread in another person's tapestry; our lives are woven together for a reason.

Answers to puzzles on page 26:

Dave's Cryptogram:

"The integrity of the upright shall guide them: But the perverseness of transgressors shall destroy them."

Search the Word:

12 unclean—1) camel, 2) hare, 3) swine, 4) eagle, 5) kite, 6) owl, 7) hawk, 8) swan, 9) bat, 10) tortoise, 11) snail, 12) mole
9 clean—1) ox, 2) sheep, 3) goat, 4) robuck, 5) fallow deer, 6) wild goat, 7) pygarg, 8) wild ox, 9) chamois
5 fruits—1) love, 2) goodness, 3) joy, 4) meekness, 5) temperance
3 disciples—1) James, 2) Peter, 3) Nathanael
2 nations—1) Pul, 2) Lud

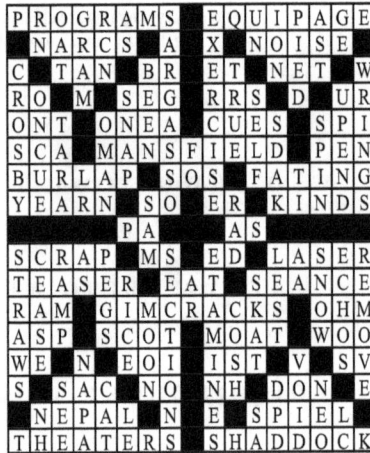

The *Mountain Review* was produced as a free government document written by prisoners at Brushy Mountain State Penitentiary and Morgan County Correctional Complex. It was sponsored by the Education Department at those facilities and was a censored publication. Permission to reprint was granted in this section of each edition. The views expressed are those of individual authors.

PRISONER Resource Guide

2021 Edition

California Lifer Newsletter
P. O. Box 277
Rancho Cordova, CA. 95741
1-916-402-3750
staff@lifesupportalliance.org

The oldest and most comprehensive publication devoted to lifers. Published bi-monthly, the 50-60 page newsletter covers current court cases and decisions affecting lifers as well as new laws and policies from CDCR. Available by paid subscription only. It is mailed directly to lifers in all California prisons. Subscription rates are as follows: Prisoners – 1 year, $35; 2 years, $60; Free Person – 1 year, $99, and "piggy back" (1 prisoner and 1 free person) 1 year, $120.

Graterfriends
c/o The Prison Society
230 South Broad Street, Suite 605
Philadelphia, PA 19102
info@prisonsociety.org
215.564.4775
Fax: 215.564.1830

Graterfriends is a publication that allows prisoners to voice their opinions and concerns about criminal justice. The newsletter strives to maintain communication between prisoners and the outside community. Prisoners have the option to submit articles or receive Graterfriends for an annual fee of $3.

The Philadelphia Trumpet
P.O. Box 3700
Edmond, OK 73083
theTrumpet.com

A surprisingly in-depth, full-color, and free world-news magazine from a Christian organization. Books by Herbert W. Armstrong offered in each issue.

The Prison Scholar Fund
1752 NW Market Street, # 953
Seattle, Washington
info@prisonscholars.org
prisonscholars.org

Provides incarcerated students the tools they need to become successful members of their communities by funding college, vocational, and technical courses, and providing mentoring and counseling services. They also advocate for reform in correctional education to increase access to all.

Asheville Prison Book Programs
Downtown Books and News
67 N. Lexington Avenue
Asheville, NC 28801
828.216.0243
prisonbooks31@hotmail.com

Sends a *National Prisoners Resource* list to those who request it. They can sometimes provide books in Spanish.

ACLU – National Prison Project
915 15th St. NW 7th Fl.
Washington D.C. 20005
aclu.org/prisons
npp@npp-aclu.org
202.393.4930

Provides advice and materials to individuals or organizations involved in prison issues. Also only handless class action suits involving prison conditions and related issues in state and federal institutions. Litigation is usually limited to cases involving major class actions challenging prison conditions or otherwise of national significance. Send SASE for information.

All Of Us Or None
℅ Legal Services for
Prisoners with Children
4400 Market Street
Oakland, CA 94608
415.255.7036
Fax: 415.552.3150
prisonerswithchildren.org

Fighting for the rights of formerly- and currently-incarcerated people and their families; fighting against the discrimination that people face every day because of arrest or conviction history. Through grassroots organizing they fight to win full restoration of human and civil rights and against all forms of discrimination.

Fall 2007 Volume 20 Number 3

MOUNTAIN REVIEW

A Morgan County Correctional Complex Publication

Death penalty under review

Just seven days after Tennessee *electrocuted* its first inmate in 47 years, a state judge declared *lethal injection* "unconstitutional." Six days later, the U.S. Supreme Court took up the issue nationally 7

This Issue Focuses On

Feature Articles

Criminal Trends

Heist on the rise

Percentage increase in robberies in the USA from the first half of 2005 to the first six months of 2006:

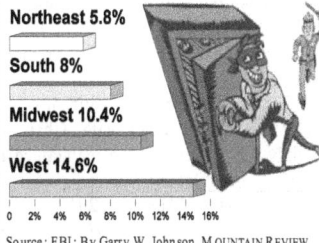

Northeast 5.8%

South 8%

Midwest 10.4%

West 14.6%

0 2% 4% 6% 8% 10% 12% 14% 16%

Source: FBI; By Garry W. Johnson, MOUNTAIN REVIEW

This year's club banquets deserve a standing ovation!

(We have photos, club news, and reporting on all the food and fun, pages 10-15)

New visitation rules at MCCX

By Garry W. Johnson
MOUNTAIN REVIEW Staff

As of August 1, several new rules went into effect statewide regarding visitations in Tennessee prisons. Sargent Bill King was nice enough to discuss some of the changes in policy with the *Mountain Review*.

According to Sgt. King, the most important thing for inmates and visitors to know is everyone must now have an approved visitation form on file. Under the old rules, children under the age of 12 were not required to apply for approval. The new policy says "a CR-2152 with a recent picture must be on file" for any child wishing to visit a TDOC inmate. Of course, children must still be accompanied by an approved adult.

The policy says specifically, "Every visitor, regardless of age, shall have an approved visitation application on file. All visitors who are currently on [an] approved list but do not have visitor applications on file, shall submit an updated application within 6 months of the effective date of this policy." If you have young children on your visitation list, please have their parent or guardian complete a visitation application for them before March 1.

The new policy also contains dress code revisions. Among the prohibited apparel are steel-toed boots and tattered clothing. Sgt. King says clothes which are ripped, torn, or worn out, fall under the category of "tattered." Arousing undergarments also made the prohibited list. Thong underwear and bust-enhancing "water brassieres" (bras lined with pouches of water to enhance bust lines) will not be permitted. Correction Commissioner George Little told *The Tennessean* that prisoners "don't need any help getting turned on."

Commissioner Little went on to say that there were no thong-detectors being installed at visitor gates, but anyone caught wearing the banned lingerie during pat downs or other inspections would not be allowed to visit. Sgt. King said there were no new inspection procedures in place at MCCX, and visitors here should expect "the same routine as before."

"Visitations are an important part of the prison experience," said Commissioner Little. "We want them to be as safe as possible and as uneventful as they can possibly be."

The former policy stated, "Persons with past criminal felony convictions may be added after one year of release from prison if no problems exist unless [that person is] an immediate family member" (*Inmate Rules and Regulations*, March 2006).

I asked Sgt. King about non-family parolees visiting friends still incarcerated. He told me that no one with an "active conviction" would be permitted to visit a non-family member in prison under the new policy. Only convictions prior to 1989 might be considered "inactive," if they do not appear on TOMIS.

For relatives recently released from

See **Policy** *on page 02*

New laws to increase prison population in Tenn., nationally

By Garry W. Johnson
MOUNTAIN REVIEW Staff

Correction Commissioner George Little told the *News Sentinel* that new laws passed during the 2007 legislative session will mean longer sentences for many convicts, especially child rapists and those using firearms in violent crimes. The preliminary estimates show the new laws will create the need for 1,000 new prison beds in 10 years.

Little said the projected need was originally 1,500 new beds by 2017, before the new laws took effect. Now, if preliminary estimates are confirmed by more detailed analysis later this fall, the state will need a total of 2,500 new beds.

As authorized by the Legislature earlier this year, Governor Phil Bredesen is soon expected to appoint a special commission to study the corrections system and eventually make recommendations on how to deal with the anticipated influx of new prisoners.

Little said some of the options include alternatives to hard-time prisons, especially for those committing "less serious" offenses.

Get tough legislation in the 90's is also catching up with the TDOC. The aging prison population is becoming more costly to care for as they serve out their lengthy sentences.

The following appeared in *USA Today*, August 14, 2007: "The state's aging prison inmate population is straining the correction budget. Tennessee's Deputy Correction Commissioner Gayle Ray said the issue is serious and could become a crushing burden. The state spent more than $1 million each for two inmates' health care last year, Ray said. Some prisons may be built as assisted living centers in the future, she said."

On the national scene, the Justice Department's Bureau of Justice Statistics reported in June that U.S. prisons and jails added more than 42,000 inmates last year, the largest increase since 2000. For the physical year ending June 30, 2006, the total number of people put in prison by federal or state authorities was roughly 1.6 million, up 2.8% from 2005.

The report says the increase is due to

See **Increase** *on page 06*

Policy

from page 01

prison, there is a new six month waiting period before they can be approved to visit family still incarcerated. Females with an active conviction who marry inmates will be considered "Immediate family," and fall under the guidelines as such (see policy excerpts below).

Other stipulations in the new policy are aimed at inappropriate liaisons between prisoners and staff, like the minimum four-year waiting period before ex-employees of the prisons can visit friends behind bars.

The old guidelines said, "If former employees are granted permission to and do marry an inmate, the person may be approved at the warden's discretion after one year. It will be 24 months if separation from employment was involuntary or criminal" (ibid.).

"One big problem we have is relationships springing up inside institutions," said Little. "We don't want to encourage someone to come to a prison to hunt for a husband or a wife." While he doesn't believe the relationships are "pervasive," Little said they can lead to security breaches and the smuggling of contraband.

According to Little, if as few as 0.5% of the 19,200 inmates and 5,300 employees of the Tennessee Department of Correction decided to hook-up, two dozen inappropriately amorous ties between staff and prisoners could result.

The following are excerpts from the new visitation policy; index #507.01; effective August 1, 2007:

DEFINITIONS:

A. Child: Anyone under the age of eighteen (18) years.

B. Contraband: Any item that is not permitted by law or is expressly prohibited by Tennessee Department of Correction (TDOC) or institutional policy.

C. Guardian: A person authorized by a child's custodial parent or legal guardian to be responsible for a child while visiting a correctional institution. This authorization shall be evidenced by a notarized statement from the custodial parent or legal guardian submitted to the institution for file.

D. Immediate Family: Mother, father, husband, wife, children, grandchildren, brother, sister, grandmother, grandfather, half-siblings, son-in-law, daughter-in-law, sister-in-law, brother-in-law, mother-in-law, father-in-law. Stepparents may be considered within this definition. Stepchildren may also be considered immediate family if the offender and his/her spouse were married prior to the current incarceration and the spouse's children were minors who resided in the home, shared by the inmate and spouse, on a regular basis at the time of incarceration.

E. Legal Guardian: A person appointed by the court to provide partial or full supervision, protection, and assistance of the person of a minor, as evidenced by a certified copy of a court order.

F. Official Visitor: Employees of the TDOC, other governmental agencies, or private sector who are conducting business at the institution.

G. Prostheses: Any artificial limbs, cardiac pacemakers or defibrillators, or any other related artificial devices intended to replace or augment a missing or impaired part of the body.

H. Transient Inmates: Inmates who are temporarily (not exceeding 60 days) in the in-house count of a receiving institution and in the assigned count of a sending institution.

I. Valid Identification (ID): Any original method of identification with photograph issued by a local, state, or federal agency by which to identify a particular individual.

J. Visitor: Person who has completed application/approval process for permission to visit an offender.

PROCEDURES:

A. Guidelines

1. Local rules pertaining to visiting shall be available to all staff, inmates, and visitors.

a. In addition to continual posting in an area accessed by visitors, a visitor's handbook shall be produced and made available for new applicants who provide a self-addressed stamped envelope with their application. Additional copies will be available at checkpoint.

b. Whenever possible, visitation policies or procedural changes should be posted on bulletin boards, announced to inmate council, and published in inmate newspapers 30 days in advance.

B. Approval and List

a. All immediate family members who apply and eight additional adults may be approved to visit an inmate upon receipt of Visitor Application, CR-2152.

b. Every visitor, regardless of age, shall have an approved visitation application on file. All visitors who are currently on approved lists but do not have visitor applications on file, shall submit an updated application within 6 months of the effective date of this policy.

c. Children age 6 and older shall have a photograph (not a photocopy) attached to their visitor application. These photographs will be updated at ages 10, 14, and 18. Updated photographs may be requested more frequently if there have been significant changes in the child's appearance.

d. Children under 18 years of age may visit provided they are accompanied by their parent, legal guardian, or guardian who is also on the inmate's approved visiting list. Identification is not required for children under the age of 16 years: however, a CR-2152 with a recent picture must be on file. The custodial parent or legal guardian must provide a completed and notarized Parental Consent/Release for Minor's Visitation Form (CR-2152, page 2), which designates permission for the assigned visitors (as guardians) to accompany the child to visit and consent for the child to be searched.

e. The requirements of (e)[sic] above do not apply if a visitor is under the age of 18 and legally married to the inmate they are visiting. Proof of marriage must be provided.

f. Members of the clergy, as recognized by the chaplain or Warden, need not be placed on the Approved Visitors List.

g. Attorneys of record need not be placed on the Approved Visitors List.

h. Persons the Warden determines could have a harmful influence on the inmate and/or may constitute a threat to the security of the institution shall not be approved for visitation. This information shall be entered on e-TOMIS screen LIML under Visitor Concerns.

i. The following will apply for persons with past criminal felony convictions:

(1) Only immediate family members with active felony conviction records may submit a visitor application for approval six months following release from incarceration or placement on probation/community corrections or parole supervision (written consent of supervising officer/counselor is required).

(2) The Warden may disapprove visitation applications of immediate family members with felony convictions if it is believed that the security of the institution or safety of individuals could be jeopardized. This information shall be entered on e-TOMIS screen LIML under Visitor Concerns.

j. The following will apply to former employees:

(1) Current or former employees of TDOC, TRICOR, or contract agencies (in Tennessee), interns, and practicum students shall not be approved unless they are immediate family members of inmate.

(a) If the person's separation from TDOC service was due to a violation of state law, e.g.; trafficking in contraband whether or not prosecution occurred, visitation requests will not be considered, even if the employee has become an immediate family member.

(b) If the person's separation from TDOC service was the result of a violation of Policy #305.03, Employee/Offender Relationships, visitation requests will not be considered, even if that individual has become an immediate family member.

(c) If the person's separation from TDOC service was voluntary and not due to the events as described in (a) and (b) above, the individual may submit an application for consideration after 48 months from the date of TDOC separation.

(d) If a person's separation from TDOC service was completely voluntary with no policy violation and the person is currently married to the inmate, visitation requests shall also not be considered for a period of 12 months from the date of the marriage to the inmate, nor for a period of 48 months from the date of TDOC separation. If the former employee worked at the facility where visitation would occur, visitation will not be allowed.

(2) Former TDOC employees, on visitation list as of October 1, 1998, shall be allowed to remain on the list.

m. Visitors may be approved for placement on only one inmate's visiting list unless there are additional incarcerated inmates who are immediate family members of the visitor and the relationships can be substantiated.

n. [see policy]

o. When a visitor has been removed from a non-immediate family inmate's visiting list due to a request from the inmate or the visitor, there shall be a one year waiting period before that visitor may be placed on another non-immediate family inmate's visiting list.

p. After inmates are released from TDOC custody or released to probation/parole, their currently approved visitors will be required to wait one year before being considered for placement on another inmate's visitation list.

M. Dress Code for Visitors, Official Visitors, and Volunteers

1. Persons entering TDOC facilities should be encouraged to dress comfortably and in casual attire; however, they shall be expected to comply with the following basic dress requirements. Wardens may further define these requirements in local policy.

a. Clothing shall fit in an appropriate manner. Clothing appearing to be too large or too small for the wearer, which creates obvious gaps or exposure, or would present a hazard to the wearer will be rejected by the shift supervisor.

b. Visitors must wear undergarments. (Samples of undergarments deemed inappropriate are thongs and water brassieres.)

c. Appropriate footwear to provide basic foot protection shall be required while on institutional grounds. Open toe shoes or sandals are permitted. Steel-toed shoes, shower shoes, and flip-flops, are prohibited.

d. Shorts or skirts are permitted provided the leg is covered, to within three inches above the knee in a standing position with the garment worn in the position in which it is intended to be worn.

2.The below listed types of clothing are specifically prohibited throughout the year:

a. Garments manufactured from spandex or spandex-type fabrics

b. Any clothing that is transparent or translucent in nature

c. Sleeveless shirts and blouses

c. [sic] Dresses or clothing exposing a bare chest or midriff

d. Camouflage attire

e. Worn or tattered clothing with holes

f. Clothing with logos that contain pictures, slogans, or vulgarity, or contain signs or symbols of security threat groups (STG), or any clothing determined by the processing officer to be associated with any STG. The association may be made by color combination, designs, or logos affixed to the clothing, or the manner in which the clothing is worn.

g. Splits in dresses or skirts that extend three inches above the knee, or slits which cause the entire dress or skirt to be above three inches above the knee, will not be permitted.

h. Bandannas

3. Visitors may not wear excessive clothing such as two pairs of pants or an extra shirt under their top layer of clothing. This is necessary to prohibit the exchange of clothing between inmates and visitors.

4. Prosthesis, artificial limbs (plastic or other substances), and cardiac pacemakers and defibrillators shall be allowed and the visitor may be required to present a doctor's note.

N. Institutions with closed circuit television, with recording capabilities, shall operate the recorders continuously during visitation hours. All recordings will be retained at least one week. If the recordings reveal criminal activities, disciplinary offenses, or activities resulting in inmate grievances, those recordings will be maintained until the resolution of the disciplinary, criminal proceeding, lawsuit, or grievance. Recordings, along with Chain of Custody, CR-3255, shall be maintained in the office of the Deputy Warden.

EXPIRATION DATE: August 1, 2010 ✍

Editor's Note: Policy # 507.01 is on file in the MCCX library.

Continuing Education While Incarcerated

Distance Learning in Prison:
Accreditation
By Jeremy Ingram,
MOUNTAIN REVIEW STAFF

This article will serve as the beginning of a series of articles on correspondence education in prison. There is an ever-increasing need for continuing education among prisoners that sadly has not been met. The United States has the greatest percentage of citizens incarcerated than any other nation in the world. Each year, more money is spent building and expanding prisons, while less and less money is used for education and rehabilitation purposes. During the 1990's, along with a "Get Tough on Crime" approach to corrections, over half the states in America cut back educational opportunities for prisoners. Along with these educational cuts, came the Omnibus Crime Bill (1994), which eliminated prisoner eligibility for Pell Grants. For most prisoners across America, this eliminated the possibility of a formal education beyond a GED or vocational certificate. It could be argued that the soaring recidivism rates and perceived need for prison expansion during the nineties was due, at least in part, to the unavailability of post-secondary education.

One common pattern of thinking among prison officials and lawmakers is that increasing the length and severity of prison time will significantly reduce the rate of crime. The idea is that the offender, due to the increased severity and length of punishment, will conclude that the cost of crime is too high and therefore live a productive life. However, it seems this thought pattern, although in some respects true, ignores the history of corrections. Never has crime been significantly deterred based solely on the increased severity and length of sentences. How can a prisoner become a productive member of society once released, when he or she has had no opportunity for education during incarceration? Instead, it is logical to conclude that the prisoner will go back to what he or she knows: a life of crime.

It is my belief that education is an essential part of rehabilitation. For many prisoners in America who have exhausted the opportunities presented to them by the Department of Corrections, a college education is the only chance left. This series of articles will take a brief look at the various aspects of pursuing a college education. This article will focus on one aspect of the pursuit of a college education behind bars: accreditation.

WHAT IS ACCREDITATION?

Accreditation is the recognition of a school by a group of experts, after a thorough investigation has been made. Simply put, accreditation is the acknowledgment that a particular school is worthy of approval.

Accreditation is primarily a concept used only in America. Most colleges and universities in other nations are operated by the government of those nations. Thus, they deem these schools worthy insofar as the government has commissioned them. This is not the case in the United States. The US federal government does not have a body of experts who investigate and approve individual schools. In fact, accreditation in the US is entirely a voluntary process. Furthermore, the government does not commission accrediting agencies; they are essentially private firms made up of experts for investigating and deeming worthy schools that are willing to be accredited.

Unfortunately, this lack of central supervision has led to the fact that not only is there good accreditation, but also there is bad accreditation. Everyone knows that the University of Tennessee is a highly accredited university; it is, in the highest sense, legitimate. However, take for example an accrediting agency that calls itself the Accrediting Commission for Specialized Colleges (ACSC). This agency accredits, among others, a school named Indiana Northern Graduate School. This sounds impressive until an inquiry was made. Investigators found that this graduate school is none other than a dairy farm in Gas City. The accrediting agency will accredit anyone willing to mail them a check for $110.

HOW DOES A SCHOOL BECOME ACCREDITED?

The process is often long and complicated. I will hash out several main details of accreditation so the reader can get a general idea of the accreditation process. Note that this process is used for legitimate accrediting agencies. As noted earlier, there are many bad accrediting agencies who will award accreditation for a small fee. This section does not include these "pseudo-accrediting" agencies.

The first step in the accrediting process is the school must be willing to undergo the process. In fact, some schools forgo accreditation entirely. Although it is rare that a legitimate school is not accredited, this possibility exists. After a school applies for accreditation from an accrediting agency, a preliminary investigation follows which will determine if the school is operating legally. This process may take anywhere from months to a couple years to finish. Afterward, they grant the school a provisional status. This status in no way means they accredit the school; it only means the school has begun the long process of accreditation.

The next step is an on-site, thorough investigation of the school. A group of experts from the accrediting agency, often composed of faculty from other accredited institutions, visits the school frequently and investigates a variety of subjects, including educational philosophy, curriculum, legitimacy of the school's faculty, financial and legal planning, and the school's plans. These are just a few of the areas covered in this investigation that often last a year or longer.

After this investigation, they observe the school for at least two years while being considered by the accreditation agency. If, after successful operation during this time, the school passes all preliminary inquiries, they give it the status of "candidate for accreditation." This status is held for several years until the final accreditation is given. Most schools that make it to the candidacy level eventually become fully accredited. Some accrediting agencies do not have this intermediate step of candidacy.

Once the school is accredited, the agency will frequently inspect the school at regular intervals. This is akin to the annual accreditation inspections at MCCX. Should any new programs or degrees be developed, the agency will oversee such improvements. If any deficiencies are found, the agency will work with the school to overcome the problems. If a problem does arise, the accrediting agency will first place a school on a "warning" and then on "probation." If the problem is not corrected within adequate time, and if the problem is severe enough, accreditation can be revoked. Normally this is the case with schools who lack financial resources.

AUTHENTIC ACCREDITATION

So, when determining which school to take courses from, what do you need to know about their accreditation? At this point, the idea of authentic accreditation needs to be explained. As noted, no national standard for accreditation exists. Since there are literally thousands of accrediting agencies, which ones are authentic? This problem is compounded with the fact that not all states recognize the accreditation that may be recognized in another state.

Before I explain what authentic accreditation means, allow me to establish why some legitimate schools forgo accreditation and why some illegitimate schools can call themselves accredited. Some good schools exist that decide not to pursue accreditation. There are many reasons for this. Perhaps the school does not have the money to pursue accreditation. The accreditation process is often a very expensive process and many small schools simply cannot afford the high cost of accreditation.

Other schools are too new or too experimental to seek accreditation. Several years ago I read an article by a highly educated, successful man who sought to recommend one school that stood out to him as the "best of the best" for the particular area in which he was involved. The school he recommended offered graduate level degrees in various disciplines. He considered this school as providing the best education in this area. However, the school had not pursued accreditation. This is an example of a good school without accreditation.

Much more often the problem is that a bad school, or more likely, a phony school, claims to be accredited. This is possible because anyone with money can set up a business and claim to be an accrediting agency. Frequently, a person will set up an accrediting agency and then set up a "school." Afterward, they will accredit themselves. As prisoners, we run across these schools occasionally. One person I knew claimed to have earned a doctorate degree from scratch in only a few weeks. When asked what kind of school would award a doctorate only after a few weeks, he replied that the school was "accredited." This goes to show that prisoners need to be careful in their educational pursuits.

Authentic accreditation is the only way of determining if a school is legitimate. Authentic accreditation is not based on financial alone; rather, it is based on the actual performance of a school. Authentic accreditation is, for the most part, the only accreditation acknowledged by employers. If you are seeking a degree or course of education for occupational opportunities once released, make sure the school you are taking classes from is authentically accredited.

HOW DO YOU KNOW IF A SCHOOL IS AUTHENTICALLY ACCREDITED?

This is not an easy question to answer. Let me give one suggestion that I found basically essential in determining if a school is legitimate: check with the Council of Higher Education Accreditation (CHEA). The CHEA is an agency that oversees all regional accrediting agencies, six national accreditation agencies, and nearly fifty professional agencies. CHEA was established in 1996, after a long debate over the "appropriate role for a national organization concerned with accreditation of higher education institutions," according to its web site. The process by which CHEA recognizes an accrediting agency as authentic is similar to the steps involved when a school seeks accreditation.

CHEA does not micro manage individual accrediting agencies; it allows a great deal of flexibility. This enables individual schools to choose accrediting agencies that suit their individual needs. However, this flexibility has its shortfalls in that various accreditation agencies may not accept the credits from other agencies. One example is that two regional accrediting agencies, WACS and MWACS do not look favorably on credit earned by correspondence. On the other hand, the NCACS is much more

The country's biggest colleges

U.S. college and universities with the largest single-campus enrollment[1]:

Arizona State University, Tempe	51,612
University of Minnesota, Twin Cities, Minneapolis	51,175
Ohio State University, Columbus	50,504
University of Texas, Austin	49,696
University of Florida, Gainesville	49,693
Michigan State University, East Lansing	45,166
Texas A&M,	44,910

1 - Data are from fall 2005, the most recent year for which national data are available
Source: Data from the National Center for Education Statistics, compiled by the American Council on Education

By Garry W. Johnson, Mountain Review Staff

*See **Accreditation** on page 04*

Accreditation
from page 03

favorable regarding distance education. This is why most WACS schools do not offer many programs through correspondence while many NCACS schools do. The lack of recognition of credits by different schools is a major problem for those in prison. Nothing guarantees credit from one school will be accepted in transfer by another school.

When you write a college and request a catalog, almost every catalog you receive will list the accreditation each college has. How do you know if that agency is authentic? As noted earlier, check with CHEA. CHEA has a database of approved schools on its web site www.chea.org/Institutions/search.cfm and it has a list of approved accreditation agencies at www.chea.org/Directories/index.cfm. If they do not list the school you are interested in on this web site, chances are high that it is not an authentically accredited school.

HOW DO YOU KNOW IF A SCHOOL IS FRAUDULENT?

Although there is not one method by which to decide if a school is a waste of time, I have found several suggestions helpful in determining if the school in question is a fraud. First, does the school claim to be "globally" accredited? Some schools claim they are accredited on a "global" scale instead of a national scale. This is not true because the CHEA does not recognize any "global" accrediting agencies. A second fraudulent method that is common is the claim that a school is not eligible for authentic accreditation because it is exclusively a correspondence school. This is not true because many authentic accrediting agencies will accredit a correspondence school given certain requirements are met and standards upheld. Another word of warning: any school claiming that it is "seeking candidacy" is lying. Schools are not allowed to divulge that information until they have been granted accreditation.

In summary, let me offer a few points about authentic accreditation that should clarify the issues. Basically, there are two levels of authentic accreditation: regional and national. The six regional accrediting agencies are, by far, the best. The names of these agencies are: Middle States Association of Colleges and Schools (MSACS), New England Association of Colleges (NEACS), North Central Association of Colleges (NCACS), Northwest Association of Colleges (NACS), Southern Association of Colleges (SACS), and Western Association of Colleges (WACS). If one of these accredits the school you are interested in, you are on the right track. Just keep in mind that credit from any of these schools is not automatically accepted by any other school. Check with individual schools if the transfer of credit is a concern. The two national accrediting agencies are Accrediting Council for Independent Colleges and Schools (ACIS) and Distance Education and Training Council (DETC). There are also close to fifty professional accrediting agencies

under CHEA.
GENERALLY ACCEPTED ACCREDITATION PRINCIPLES

The purpose of this article has been to help the prospective student differentiate between authentic accreditation and phony accreditation. In the educational world, there is a term for authentic accreditation known as Generally Accepted Accreditation Principles (GAAP). GAAP is not a policy determined by someone in particular, but rather it is a set of policies that the majority of decision makers generally accept. GAAP determines if a degree or course of study is recognized as legitimate or not. According to the *Bear's Guide*, an accrediting agency must meet one of four criteria to be deemed legitimate. Since three of these criteria concern out-of-country schools, I will list only one: "For schools based in the US, there is no disagreement: accreditation by an accrediting agency recognized either by the US Department of Education, and/or by the Council on Higher Education Accreditation." In other words, if the Department of Education or CHEA recognizes a school as legitimate, then in most cases, that school is legitimate. If not, chances are that the school is not legitimate (although there are exceptions).

NON-RECOGNIZED SCHOOLS

Many inmates choose to pursue an education at a non-recognized school. Most prisoners who choose to pursue an unaccredited degree do so for financial reasons. An unaccredited degree may cost significantly less than its counterpart. One course from the University of Tennessee can cost $684. However, one year of classes from a particular unaccredited school (eight classes) costs $690. For the cost of two classes at UT, a person can earn his Associate's degree at this college. Many people prefer to do it this way. However, this begs the question, "Is this route a waste of time?" Before I discuss this question, let it be known that I use

What colleges look for
Percent of colleges reporting that these factors were of "considerable importance" to admit a student:

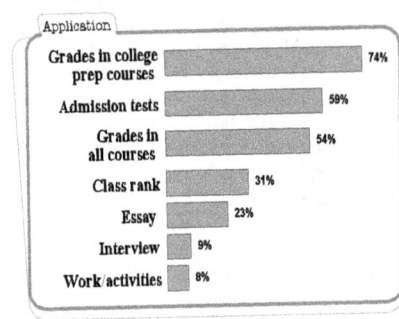

Application
- Grades in college prep courses — 74%
- Admission tests — 59%
- Grades in all courses — 54%
- Class rank — 31%
- Essay — 23%
- Interview — 9%
- Work/activities — 8%

Source: National Association Admission Counseling, 2005
By Garry W. Johnson, Mountain Review Staff

Is university prestige important when job hunting?
Financial executives are divided on whether the prestige of an entry-level job candidate's university is important:

Important 51%   Not important 49%

Source: Accountemps survey of 1,400 chief financial officers. Margin of error +/-3 percentage points.
By Garry W. Johnson, Mountain Review Staff

the word unaccredited to mean "accredited from an unrecognized accrediting agency." There are many unrecognized accredited agencies out there that are not fraudulent.

Typically, a regionally accredited degree is worth more than an unaccredited degree. More employers will recognize the accredited degree, its credits will be more easily transferable, and there is more prestige with an accredited degree. However, many people have benefitted from an unaccredited degree. Not only, as I have mentioned, are unaccredited degrees less expensive, but also an unaccredited degree may be the easiest way to earn a degree in prison. Assuming the degree is not a fraudulent degree, there are many benefits: the earning of a college education will generally improve a person's outlook on life, it will provide the parole board with evidence that the offender is committed to rehabilitation, and it may open doors for opportunities to use the knowledge the graduate has gained. Another benefit is simply the fact that a person has completed the prescribed course of study. Many employers look for someone who will be committed to his job; the completion of a college degree evidences commitment.

Although unaccredited degrees are not easily transferrable in the academic world, it seems that many employers look favorably on any degree, accredited or not. Do not expect to be able to transfer unaccredited credit to a major university once you are released. However, if you have earned an unaccredited degree, you are better off than if you did not pursue any education. Prisoners entering the work force upon release may use the degree as a marketing tool. Already the prisoner is at a disadvantage because he has served prison time and carries a felony conviction on his record. However, with a college degree on his resume, the scales of advantage are tipped in his favor. An employer might give an ex-con a second look if he or she is

made aware of the ex-con's education.

In conclusion, taking college courses through correspondence is often confusing and difficult. The concept of accreditation is not much clearer. If you stick with a regionally accredited school then you have less of a chance at going wrong. However, educational opportunities abound for those willing to do the work involved. ✍

PAST closes its doors

By Randall McPheeters

The Prisoner's Aid Society of Tennessee (PAST) has closed its books and let go it's programs. PAST held its annual meeting for 2007 as usual but it was their last meeting. They consider their goals accomplished and only one charter member, Charles Barton, remained. Rather than set new goals, they closed the doors and put their support behind another program called Victims Voices.

For those of you who do not know what PAST is, let me tell you a little of it's history. In 1971, PAST was born in Oak Ridge, Tennessee. Robert Clausing, chairman of the Social Concerns Commission of the First United Presbyterian Church of Oak Ridge called some people together to discuss the need of an organization to meet the needs of inmates at Brushy Mountain State Prison. From that meeting, the idea of PAST was born. Article II of their by-laws reads:

"The object of this society shall be to assist the rehabilitation of prisoners by collecting funds to supply needed materials and services to prisoners and to develop programs to inform the community of the ways in which it can contribute to the rehabilitation of prisoners."

The PAST organization was only about a month old when two of its members were asked to help inmates at Brushy put together a list of grievances they wished to present to TDOC Commissioner Mark Luttrell. The commissioner found many of the requests to be reasonable and instituted them at Brushy Mountain. Commissioner Luttrell also asked all of the Brushy staff to accept outsiders, specifically members of PAST, as helpers in rehabilitation.

Since then, PAST has been involved in numerous programs for inmates and their families. Their members, Claudine Norris, Joe Crichton, Charles Barton, have worked tirelessly for many years. They have been a constant force in our favor offering a voice against unfavorable legislation in the eighties and keeping programs going while the administration wasn't helpful in keeping them alive. One such program, AVP, still exists at Morgan County.

We hope to have a good relationship with the Victims Voices organization in the future. We will always remember PAST and honor them with our continued support of their new face and their new direction. ✍

Prisoner and Family Resources

Important Documents
By Jeremy Ingram,
MOUNTAIN REVIEW Staff

In this, and future editions of the *Mountain Review*, we will include a section on prisoner and family resources. This may include pre-release and post-release resources, helpful advice detailing ways to be more productive inside prison and once released, as well as other topics and addresses practical to the inmate population and their families. If you have any questions, or would like to contribute to this section, feel free to contact the *Mountain Review* staff. This edition will deal with documents needed for life in the free world.

BIRTH CERTIFICATE

Perhaps the most important certificate a person needs before he is released from prison is a birth certificate. A certified copy of a person's birth certificate is easy to obtain, and should be obtained before he is released. There are many reasons why a person needs a birth certificate. Many services in Tennessee require a person to have one.

If you were born in Tennessee, the process by which you can obtain a copy of your birth certificate is simple. The Tennessee Department of Vital Records in Nashville will send you a copy of your birth certificate through the mail if you send them a completed application and a fee.

The application requires specific information including:
- Your full name
- Date of birth
- Place of birth
- Hospital where birth occurred
- Full name of father
- Full maiden name of mother
- Information concerning siblings
- Reason for requesting birth certificate
- Signature

Copies of the application will be provided in the library upon request.

Tennessee Department of Vital Record's address is:

Tennessee Vital Records
Central Services Building, 1st Floor
421 5th Avenue North
Nashville, TN 37247

When you write the Office of Vital Records, be sure to state that the birth certificate you are requesting is your own. Most states will allow you to request only your birth certificate or a birth certificate of an immediate family member.

If you were born after 1949, you do not need to go through the Department of Vital Records; you may instead contact the health department of the county in which you were born.

Several Tennessee County Health Departments are:

Davidson County
311 23rd Ave. North,
Nashville, TN 37203

Hamilton County
921 E. Third St.
Chattanooga, TN 37404

Knox County
140 Dameron Ave.
Knoxville, TN 37902

Shelby County
814 Jefferson Ave.
Memphis, TN 38105

Washington County
415 State of Franklin Rd.
Johnson City, TN 37604

If you were born in a state other than Tennessee, contact the Department of Vital Statistics in the state in which you were born. If you need an address, contact the *Mountain Review* staff or check with the library.

If you were born on a military base outside the United States, or if you were born in a country other than the United States, and you need help obtaining a certified copy of your birth certificate, feel free to contact the *Mountain Review* staff.

SOCIAL SECURITY CARD

A Social Security card is almost as important as a birth certificate. If you have never been issued a Social Security card, need a replacement card, or have changed your name, there is a form you can fill out. The form is known as the Application for a Social Security Card SS-5. A copy of this form will be provided in the library upon request.

The Social Security card is a document you should obtain before you leave prison. You will need this card to get a job, to get your driver's licence, and to apply for various services.

A word of warning, the Social Security Administration will not process your application unless everything is filled out correctly. There are several lists of the do's and don'ts associated with filling out this application. Most of the instructions are simple; however, if you have questions, or would like a list of the do's and don'ts, contact the *Mountain Review* staff.

When you submit the application, certain documents must be included. These documents must be original, not copies. In fact, the Social Security Administration requires these documents be certified. They will return these documents to you once your application is approved.

There are three categories in which you would be requesting a Social Security card: applying for an original card, a duplicate card, or a corrected card.

If you are applying for an original card, you must submit proof of your age, identity, and US citizenship (or lawful alien status). From what I have read, if you have never been issued a Social Security card, and if you are over the age of 18, you must apply in person. If you are applying for a duplicate card, you must submit proof of identity, unless born outside the US. In that case, you must submit proof of US citizenship or lawful alien status. If you are applying for a corrected card, the same requirements for a duplicate card apply.

Listed below are valid documents that satisfy the age, identity, and citizenship requirements.

Age: Birth certificate, hospital record of birth made before the age of five, religious records made before the age of three months, or a current passport if born outside the US. If none of these documents are available, contact the Social Security Administration.

Identity: Driver's Licence, passport, employer or school ID card, marriage or divorce records, adoption records, health insurance card (not Medicare), military records, or insurance records. (Birth certificate, hospital birth records, Social Security card, or Social Security records are not acceptable.) The name on these records must be the name that will appear on the Social Security card.

Name Change: If your name now is not the name on your original Social Security card, you must submit identity documents in both your original name and the name you currently go by now.

US Citizenship: If you were born outside the US, and if you are trying to establish US citizenship, the Social Security Administration will accept the following: US Consular Report of Birth, US passport, Certificate of Citizenship, or a Certificate of Naturalization.

Alien Status: Before a legal alien can be issued a Social Security card, a person must possess the current document issued by the US Department of Immigration and Naturalization Service (INS), such as I-551, I-688B, I-94, or I-766.

If you have any questions, contact the *Mountain Review* staff or the Social Security Administration at this address:

Social Security Administration
4527 Nolensville Pike
Nashville, TN 37211
(615) 781-5800

STATE IDENTIFICATION CARD

The State of Tennessee offers a State Identification card which can be used as a proof of ID. It is easy to obtain; however, it is not permanent—it lasts for only one renewal cycle. This card does not authorize a person to operate a motor vehicle.

If you do not plan to obtain a driver's licence, you may want to obtain a State ID card. You must appear at a county Driver's Licence Examination Station (operated by the Tennessee Department of Safety). They will require both proof of identity and a $9.50 fee. (For acceptable proofs of identity, see section on identity valid for Social Security application).

TRICOR'S "DO YOU REALLY WANT TO STAY OUT OF PRISON?" TEST

With every American success story, what has been the common thread? Desire! Granted, many of these success stories had vision, talent and other personal qualities to help them succeed, but they all had desire to succeed! Do you have this desire? Do you really want to stay out of prison? Do you really want to change your life for the better? Then take the following 12-question "Yes-No" test to see if you really want to stay out of prison.

Be honest in answering the questions. You will not be "graded" by anyone except yourself. The only person you can cheat is yourself. This will be private. Only you will know the final grade.

1. Do you admit to your offense, and/or do you accept responsibility for your offense?
2. Are you willing to look deeply at the reasons for your incarceration?
3. Do you secretly wish you would not react so strongly or negatively to authority figures?
4. Do you wish that it would be as easy to function "on the streets" as it is for you to function in prison?
5. Can you imagine yourself taking instructions/direction from a supervisor on the job?
6. Are you getting tired—really tired—of the prison experience?
7. Do you find yourself wishing more and more that you could live like "straight" people on the outside?
8. Are you getting more worried about dying or being seriously hurt in prison?
9. Are you between the ages of 34 and 40?
10. Do you worry more about being able to stay out of prison this time?
11. Are you going to be paroled to a place at least 30 miles from where you lived before going to prison?
12. Have you ever been affiliated with or a member of any gang?

Rating Scale:

If you answered "Yes" on 4 questions or less, you have a minimum desire to stay out of prison. If you answered "Yes" on 5 to 7 questions, you have a medium desire to stay out of prison. If you answered "Yes" on 8 or more questions, you have a strong desire to stay out of prison.

Prison Life

AN OVERVIEW OF PRISON NEWS AND CRIME STATISTICS FROM AROUND THE U.S.A.—BY GARRY W. JOHNSON

Increase

from page 01

from page 01

people being incarcerated at a faster rate than those being released.

According to Alex Busansky, executive director of the Commission on Safety and Abuse in America's Prisons, the spike corresponds to an increased federal emphasis on anti-crime programs, from the Reagan administration's anti-drug campaign to the Clinton program that provided funding for 100,000 additional police officers.

Census data shows that since 1980 the number of people in prisons and jails has increased dramatically: from 466,371 in 1980, to slightly more than 2 million in 2006.

The Census numbers, released September 27, bolster the June report by the Justice Department, which tracked similar rates of growth during that period and put the total number of incarcerated in U.S. jails and prisons at 2.2 million. Of that number, the report showed almost six out of 10 locked up were African American or Hispanic.

In July, the Sentencing Project, a Washington-based think tank, found that African Americans in the U.S. are imprisoned at more than five times the rate, and Hispanics at twice the rate of whites.

States in the Midwest and Northeast have the greatest black-to-white disparity, according to the report. Iowa imprisons blacks at more than 13 times the rate of whites. States with the lowest black-to-white ratio included Georgia, 3.3 to one, and Hawaii, 1.9 to one.

Brushy Mountain B&B?

Brushy Mountain State Prison may be open to tourists, once it closes to inmates.

There is no definite date set for "decommissioning" the century-old prison, according to Tennessee Department of Correction Commissioner George Little. However, plans do call for transferring all inmates to the new Morgan County Regional Correction Complex by early 2009.

"We will be sealing up old buildings, taking up utilities where appropriate," Little said. "We will be working closely with local government to try and identify acceptable uses that will benefit the people in the area." He went on to say one idea that has been floated is to transform the main prison building into a "bed and breakfast."

One of the prison's most infamous prisoners, James Earl Ray, was housed at Brushy while serving a life sentence for the murder of Martin Luther King Jr. in 1968, in Memphis. Now deceased, Ray escaped from Brushy once, but was recaptured with the help of bloodhounds.

Crime doesn't pay, but it is costly

Estimated value lost by victims of property crimes[1] in 2005 (in billions):

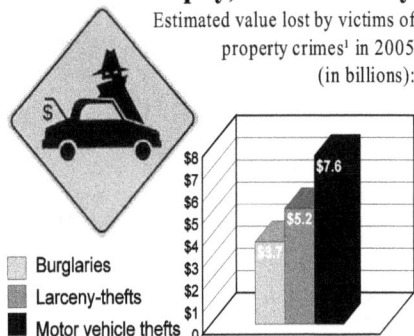

- Burglaries — $3.7
- Larceny-thefts — $5.2
- Motor vehicle thefts — $7.6

Source: U.S. Department of Justice   1 - excludes arsons

State officials order Polk County Jail closed

The State Fire Marshal's office ordered the dilapidated Polk County Jail shut down late Tuesday, August 14, one week after two Circuit Court Judges gave Sheriff Bill Davis 10 days to release many of his prisoners or move them to a new facility.

Judge John B. Hagler and Judge Carroll Ross signed the order August 8, citing a grand jury report on the "deplorable conditions" at the jail. The report said the jail is not in compliance with a federal court order and has been cited by the state fire marshal for fire hazards. It went on to report that the new $8.8 million Polk county justice center was completed several months ago and county commissioners still had no plans to move either the jail or the court system into the new building.

County commissioners said the new 150-bed facility will not be ready until early October and will cost an estimated $800,000 in operating cost for the first year. At a late-night budget meeting August 20, the commission unanimously approved a resolution to open the new jail and justice center with help from a 10-cent property tax increase.

The problems in Polk have been accumulating since July, when the commission hesitated to open the new facility because of budget constraints. Instead, they named a three-man panel to look into renovating the old jail and upgrading the courthouse.

The fire marshal's report found a lack of sprinklers, occupancy in excess of capacity, exposed wiring, combustible materials found throughout the facility, extensive use of extension cords, and a deteriorating condition of the nearly 50-year-old jail.

The jail was also investigated by the Tennessee Corrections Institute which cited a high incidence of staph infections and said there was no place to separately house sick inmates. According to Peggy Sawyer, assistant director of the institute, the last time the jail was certified was March of 1996, for 33 prisoners. It was decertified in 1997, and at the time of its closing housed about 50 inmates.

According to the judges' order, a plan of action for the jail was to be completed and sent to the fire marshal within seven days. The order also gave the commission 60 days to move the courts to the new facility or close down the courtrooms. The current courthouse has no means of enhancing security and no secure place for problem prisoners, according to the order.

About 1:00 p.m., August 15, Polk County sheriff's deputies began transporting inmates to the Bradley County Jail after officials agreed to pay Bradley County $40 a day per inmate for housing, said Sheriff Davis. "The majority of all prisoners, if not all, will be housed in Bradley County, including any new people."

Bradley County Sheriff Tim Gobble said he expected to house about 26 of Polk's inmates and release another 25 or so on their own recognizance after booking. By August 30, only 5 Polk County prisoners remained at the Bradley County Jail.

JAIL FUNDING NOT POPULAR, BUT NECESSARY

As we reported in the last issue of *Mountain Review*, the 1850's-era Bledsoe County Jail was shut down in May over similar concerns to those in Polk. Polk and Bledsoe are the only two county jails in Southeast Tennessee that have not been certified this year. Furthermore, every county in the area, except Bledsoe, has expanded, renovated, or replaced its jail in the last 15 years, according to the Tennessee Corrections Institute.

Sequatchie County, where Bledsoe County's prisoners are being housed, has the newest lockup in Southeast Tennessee. The $6.7 million, 96-bed facility opened in May 2006 and was funded by a 5-cent property tax hike, said Sequatchie County Sheriff Ronnie Hitchcock.

Hitchcock says the county saved money this year on medical and maintenance cost and liability insurance. He also noted the new justice center gives the county more options, like housing state prisoners and receiving state reimbursements.

No matter how people feel, the county must care for its inmates, Hitchcock said. "They are human."

In 2004, Bradley County built its $16 million, 408-bed facility. That same year Rhea County added 12 beds to its jail at a cost of $200,000 with no tax increases.

Rhea County Executive Billy Ray Patton said jails are a necessity, but not popular with the public. "When people move into the county, they ask what kind of schools we have and what kind of medical facilities ... They don't ask, 'What kind of jail do you have?'"

Violence up for 2nd year, Memphis tops list

The annual FBI crime report, released September 24, showed violent crime nationwide increased for the second consecutive year in 2006, an overall rate of 473.5 violent crimes per 100,000 people.

An estimated 1.4 million violent crimes—murders, rapes, robberies and aggravated assaults—occurred in 2006. Although that is an increase over 2005, it is still the third-lowest total in the past two decades. Robbery was up 7%, and murder rose by nearly 2% last year, with 17,034 murders recorded. In 1991, that figure was 24,703.

Property thefts dropped 2% nationwide for 2006, hitting their lowest level since 1987, according to the report.

Justice Department spokesman Brian Roehrkasse said, "While there's encouraging news in the latest crime rates from the (FBI), violent crime remains a challenge for some communities."

The Memphis metropolitan area topped the FBI's national ranking for violent communities. The eight-county metro area recorded 1,262.7 violent crimes per 100,000 residents in 2006.

Florence, South Carolina, topped last year's ranking, with Memphis a close second, that year reporting 1,197 per 100,000 residents.

Jackson, Tennessee found itself ranked 13th this year at 879.2, Nashville was 20th at 857.7, Chattanooga was 59th at 599.5, and Knoxville came in at 106th at 513.5. All these areas were well above the national average of 473.5.

The FBI report, among the most reliable national measures of crime, closely corresponds with a survey of 56 U.S. cities published earlier this year by the Police Executive Research Forum and reported on in the *Mountain Review* (*Studies show violent crime still going up*, Spring/Summer 2007, p. 11).

The advocacy group's survey showed a nearly 3% increase in murder and a 6.5% jump in robbery.

The recent increases in violence have prompted new efforts by the federal government to address evidence of rising gang activity and drug markets in some cities. The Justice Department requested $200 million in 2008 to assist local violent crime enforcement units.

Violence rises, after years of decline

U.S. violent crime rate for every 100,000 people:

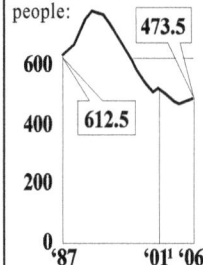

- 473.5
- 612.5
- 600
- 400
- 200
- 0

'87   '01[1]   '06

1 - Does not include murders and non-negligent homicides related to the Sept. 11, 2001 terrorist attacks.
Source: FBI

First Tennessee electrocution in 47 years

Confessed child killer Daryl Keith Holton, 45, was put to death September 12, at Riverbend Maximum Security Institution in Nashville. He was the first prisoner to die in Tennessee's electric chair since William Tines was electrocuted on November 7, 1960.

Electric chairs see little use

Since the death penalty was reinstated in 1976, 154 inmates have been executed by electrocution—about 14% of the total. Number of electrocutions by year:

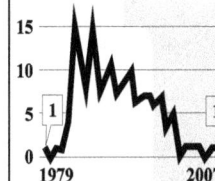

Source: Death Penalty Information Center

For the most part, Holton had fought his appointed defense attorneys for several years and had refused to speak with them or sign petitions to file appeals on his behalf.

Holton's lawyers said he had a long history of mental illness and may have suffered from post-traumatic stress disorder from his service in the Army during the Gulf War.

Kelly Gleason, a state post-conviction defender, said Holton believed he was convicted in an unconstitutional manner, but did not think an appeal on those grounds would be successful.

Before his execution, she said that she and others who had come to know and like Holton were saddened by his pending death. "Part of it for us is that he is being portrayed as a monster," she told the Associated Press. "The act itself was horrific, but he is not a monster. He snapped."

On November 30, 1997, Holton fatally

shot his three sons, Steven 12, Brent 10, and Eric 6, and his ex-wife's 4-year-old daughter, Kayla.

According to Shelbyville police, he told the children they were going Christmas shopping, took them to his uncle's auto repair garage, lined them up, and shot them with an assault rifle. Holton told police he suffered from severe depression and killed the children because his ex-wife had denied him from seeing them for several months. He said he intended to kill her and himself too, but after an unsuccessful search for his ex-wife and her boyfriend, Holton turned himself in. The whole ordeal lasted about five hours.

Because Holton committed the murders before Tennessee adopted lethal injection as its preferred method of execution in 1999, he was given the option of electrocution or lethal injection.

Holton did not say why he chose the electric chair, but his spiritual advisor, Dixie Gamble, said Holton believed he would die instantly and painlessly. The chair's builder, Fred Leuchter, did not share Holton's optimism.

Leuchter, who built the current chair in 1989, asked Governor Phil Bredesen not to use it, saying it has been modified in such a way that it would be "tantamount to torture." Leuchter said the 1,750 volts specified by the state is too low and should be at least 2,000.

Jay Wiechert, an electrical engineer from Fort Smith, Ark., made the modifications to the chair in the 1990's and said it would work as intended. Wiechert said he modified controls, increased the voltage and changed protective devices to provide steady, adequate current.

The day before Holton's execution, a group of 68 Tennessee lawyers unsuccessfully petitioned the state Supreme Court to stop the electrocution on the grounds of cruel and unusual punishment. They recom-

mended the high court follow a Georgia Supreme Court decision declaring the electric chair unconstitutional.

According to the filing, Georgia found "undisputed proof that those electrocuted are to some degree physically mutilated."

Holton requested Nashville defense attorney David Raybin to attend the execution. "He's asked me to serve as his council at the execution, and I will be present for that purpose." Neither Holton's family nor his ex-wife, Crystle Holton, were present at Riverbend.

Gamble said Holton was at peace and ready to die the day prior to his 1:00 a.m. execution. "He's not nervous," she said. "He's very clear, very focused." Holton made no special request for his last meal.

TDOC spokeswoman Dorinda Carter said Holton started to hyperventilate prior to entering the execution chamber at Riverbend and was given time to calm down. When asked by warden Ricky Bell if he had any final words, he mumbled inaudibly. When asked to repeat what he said, he replied, "Two words: I do."

The newly revised TDOC execution manual says the electric chair delivers 1,750 volts of electricity at 7 amps at contact points at the head and ankles through sponges soaked in saline.

Writer Kristin M. Hall gave the following account for the Associated Press, "A black

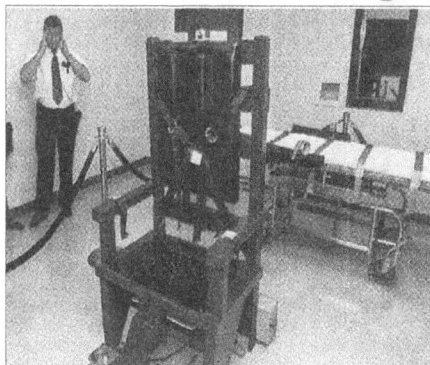

A 1999 picture of the execution chamber at Riverbend Maximum Security Institution in Nashville.

shroud was placed over Holton's head and a cable was connected to the bottom of the chair. Around 1:16 a.m. CDT, a 20-second shock was administered. Holton's back straightened and his hips moved up out of the chair

before he slumped back.

"After a 15-second pause, Holton was given a second shock that lasted 15 seconds. He was pronounced dead at 1:25 a.m."

Dr. Bruce Levy, the state's medical examiner who performed Holton's autopsy, said inmates can suffer broken bones from the violent muscle spasms associated with electrocutions. Holton had no broken bones, and Levy said he found nothing unusual about the autopsy.

According to the autopsy report, Holton suffered minor burns on his head and legs. "The electricity generates a lot of heat, and there can be very significant burns at the site of skin contact," Levy said. "Because they were using sponges soaked in saline, there was first- to low-level second-degree burns, similar to what you see with a severe sunburn."

According to the Death Penalty Information Center, eight other states allow some or all condemned inmates to choose the electric chair: Alabama, Arkansas, Illinois, Florida, Kentucky, Oklahoma, South Carolina, and Virginia. The state of Nebraska still uses the electric chair exclusively. ✍

Judge throws out lethal injections in Tennessee

A federal judge on September 19, ruled Tennessee's new lethal injection procedures are unconstitutional and halted an injection execution set for the following week.

The new protocol, released in April, "presents a substantial risk of unnecessary pain," according to U.S. District Judge Aleta Trauger. She halted the execution of inmate Edward Jerome Harbinson, scheduled for September 26, saying the protocol violates the provision against cruel and unusual punishment as provided in the Eighth Amendment.

Trauger said the protocol does not ensure that inmates are properly anesthetized before the lethal injection is administered and could "result in a terrifying, excruciating death."

Officials are reviewing the ruling and have not decided whether

to appeal, said a spokeswoman for the state attorney general's office. Governor Phil Bredesen's office had no immediate comment.

Trauger did not issue a stay or throw out the death sentence for Harbison, who was convicted of beating an elderly woman to death during a 1983 burglary. The spokeswoman said he had lost all his appeals, and Harbison can be legally executed as soon as the state adopts a valid method of execution.

Legal director for the Criminal Justice Legal Foundation, Kent Scheidegger, said the 6th Circuit Court of Appeals might reverse Trauger's ruling. "They have been fairly hostile to these sort of claims."

But the appeals court may not have much of a say. NBC Nightly News reported on September 25, that the U.S. Supreme Court may

be planning to halt executions nationwide, while it reviews lethal injection as a form of execution. The high court will hear a challenge early next year from two inmates on death row in Kentucky, a state which uses a similar protocol to Tennessee. The court has previously made it easier for death row inmates to contest lethal injections, but has passed up cases challenging the constitutionality of the drug mixture and how it is administered. Of the last 1097 executions in the U.S., 927 were by lethal injection. The report said it was hard to determine how the court will proceed, as it has not looked at anything like this since upholding the firing squad in 1879.

As we reported in the Mountain Review, Philip Workman was executed by lethal injection May 9, just seven days after the expira-

tion of a 90-day moratorium on executions in Tennessee. Bredesen, a Democrat, issued the moratorium because of several glaring problems with Tennessee's execution guidelines, including conflicting directions that mixed lethal injection instructions with those for the electric chair.

Judge Trauger said current training and medical expertise are still not sufficient to ensure a painless execution and she seemed to favor a single drug method over the standard three-drug lethal injection cocktail used by Tennessee and three dozen other states.

The three drugs—thiopental, an anesthetic; pancuronium bromide, a nerve blocker and muscle paralyzer; and potassium chloride, a drug to stop the heart—are each supposed to be capable of killing all by itself. If that does not hap-

pen, the anesthetic is suppose to render the inmate unconscious while the other two kill.

On September 26, Tennessee's Supreme Court reset Harbinson's execution for January 9, 2008. The state attorney general's office asked the state's high court to move the execution date so it could respond to Trauger's ruling. A spokeswoman for the office said two more death row inmates are scheduled to be executed before January 9, but it was unclear whether the state would ask for those dates to be reset too.

Thirty-seven states have adopted lethal injection as a cheaper and more humane alternative to electrocution, gas chambers and other execution methods. But its use has been suspended in at least 11 states after opponents alleged it is ineffective and cruel. ✍

—By Garry W. Johnson, Mountain Review Staff

Bledsoe prison gets new design, lessons learned from MCCX

On August 21, a legislative committee unanimously approved the TDOC's plan to redesign a new state prison in Bledsoe County, even though approximately $2 million had already been spent on the original design plan.

Correction Commissioner George Little told the committee that a new design could wind up saving as much as $22 million in construction costs. "Yes, we may wind up spending millions, or two million more than we had intended (on design), but we believe, with that investment, we will realize savings of $20 million to $22 million." Little added, "I would argue that is a good investment for the state of Tennessee."

Initially, the new Bledsoe prison was to be built adjacent to the existing state prison, just as it has been done here. Little said, "We were going to take what we did in Morgan, drop it down to Bledsoe and do the same thing."

The cost of the construction here in Morgan County had reached $155 million by August, and the TDOC feared the Bledsoe facility, under a similar design plan, would surpass $200 million (the original estimate when the Bledsoe project was announced in March 2004 was $102 million, Morgan County's original estimate was $80 million).

The department hired Mark Golman Associates, an Atlanta-based consulting firm, at an initial cost of $348,352, to review the plans. They recommended replacing the "cookie-cutter" approach to building prisons in Tennessee and to have architects bid on becoming the "design team" for Bledsoe. Little said the original plans failed to incorporate recent advances in security technology and take into account security issues with building in close proximity to an existing prison (those of us who work in education and at TriCor can attest to that). He hopes the "new generation" of prisons will translate into more competitive bidding for the final construction projects. Only two companies bid on the Morgan County project, with Ray Bell Construction winning the contract.

Little hopes to have new bids in on the Bledsoe prison by October 6. Recent estimates have put the total cost at around $182 million, with a tentative completion date of February 2011 (the original completion date was estimated to be June 2009).

The new Bledsoe prison, officially known as Southeast Tennessee Regional Correctional Facility, will be built as a separate facility on more level property nearby the existing prison, and will be linked to a new $20 million pipeline that will bring water from the Tennessee River to the area. Runoff from a dairy farm operated by TriCor at Bledsoe also presents environmental problems for the project. "It is far more complex than anything this department has taken on," Little said. "We learned a lot at Morgan County."

The new Morgan County Regional Correctional Complex is on track and should be in full operation next year, according to Commissioner Little. Minimum-security inmates should be moving into completed buildings (annex) this fall. Little said they will be doing the landscaping on the new prison grounds. With the closure of Brushy Mountain State Prison, the TDOC will net 838 beds from the Morgan County project. The Bledsoe project will bring that total up to almost 1,800 beds.

Little said the increase in construction cost came from corresponding increases in the cost of concrete, steel, other building materials and fuel. Chairman of the Correction Oversight Committee, Representative Bill Harmon (D), believes the costs are understandable. "That's happening in every construction job. There are astronomical increases in the cost of concrete, steel, and fuel." ✍

SOUTHEAST TENNESSEE REGIONAL CORRECTIONAL FACILITY

❖ Capacity when completed: 2,400
❖ Net new beds: 1,444
❖ Original estimated cost: $182 million
❖ Original completion estimate: Spring 2009
❖ Current completion estimate: 2010 or 2011

Source: Tennessee Department of Correction

MORGAN COUNTY REGIONAL CORRECTIONAL COMPLEX

❖ Capacity when completed: 2,441
❖ Net new beds: 838
❖ Original estimated cost: $80 million
❖ Current estimated cost: $155 million
❖ Current completion estimate: Early 2009

Source: Tennessee Department of Correction

Military paratroopers invade prison

Colorado's Fremont Correctional Institute received an unexpected visit July 12, as a unit of 25 military paratroopers landed inside the state prison's perimeter.

They where not there to quell a riot or attempt a movie-script breakout, they simply messed up.

Armed with exercise rifles that shoot rubber bullets, the paratroopers landed in a cornfield on the prison grounds, according to Colorado Department of Corrections spokeswoman, Katherine Sanguinetti. She told the *Rocky Mountain News* that guards escorted them off the property without any incidence of violence.

The newspaper reported the Army and Air Force denied knowledge of the episode, and the Colorado National Guard did not return a call seeking comment. ✍

Breaking In

Most common places that burglars enter homes:

Front door 34%
First-floor window 23%
Back door 22%
Garage 9%
Basement 4%
Unlocked entrance 4%
Storage area 2%
Second floor 2%

Source: The National Burglar & Fire Alarm Association

Prosecutors' power increased in Tennessee courts

The Tennessee Supreme Court gave state prosecutors a boost in power through a ruling handed down in January concerning two Anderson County murder cases.

The state's high court found that now-retired Anderson County Judge James "Buddy" Scott overstepped his bounds by rejecting plea deals sought by prosecutors in two homicide cases and turning aside moves to drop heftier charges.

The first case involved the killing of Ginger Powers by Melissa Ann Layman in July 2003. Powers and Layman were involved in a lesbian relationship and sharing a house in Oliver Springs when the killing occurred. Layman claimed self-defense and prosecutors at the time insisted they could not prove anything more than reckless homicide.

The second case involved a married couple. Jonathan Ray Taylor fatally shot his wife, Patricia L. Taylor, in December 2003, but insisted he did not mean to kill her. Again the prosecutor said he could not prove murder, only reckless homicide.

In both cases Scott cited the gravity of the cases involving death in rejecting prosecutors' recommendations. He also allowed Power's relatives to weigh in on Layman's proposed plea deal.

The court's opinion concluded that absent an "extraordinary" showing of "betrayal of the public interest," state judges could not overrule state prosecutors seeking to dismiss charges—even if the case involves murder.

Writing for the majority, Justice Janice M. Holder opined, "Although the trial court may disagree with the decision to terminate the prosecution, that, in and of itself, is an insufficient reason to deny an uncontested motion to (dismiss a charge)."

Weighing in on victims' rights in Tennessee, Holder wrote, "With regard to the right to be heard, crime victims may be heard at critical stages of the criminal justice process." The court further stated that "critical" hearings were limited to those specifically cited in the Victims' Bill of Right; Critical hearings are limited to bond hearings, sentencing hearings, hearings to set restitution and parole hearings.

Holder went on to point out, "Hearings concerning plea agreements (and motions to dismiss) are notably absent from the list of proceedings at which victims have a right to be heard." The court further ruled that although prosecutors must listen to victims' wishes, they do not have to honor them.

The court's lone dissenter, Judge Gary R. Wade of Sevierville, believes prosecutors need judges to keep them in check. He also disagreed with the majority's view of victims' rights. "In my view, a motion by the state to dismiss charges would also qualify as a critical stage in ordinary sense of the term," he wrote in his dissent. "Our legislature surely did not intend to deny victims the right to be heard at a proceeding where the disposition of the case is at stake." ✍

Passengers in traffic stops considered "seized"

The Supreme Court ruled June 18 that passengers stopped in cars by police are "seized" and therefore have a right to contest the legality of the stop if they are searched and arrested.

In the 9-0 ruling, the court found that "A sensible person would not expect a police officer to allow people to come and go," and stressed that the police show of authority restricts a passenger's sense of freedom.

The decision clarifies the law on traffic stops and overturns the view of state courts in California, Colorado, and Washington, which have ruled that the passenger has no constitutional right to challenge the propriety of the initial traffic stop.

In November 2001, police pulled over a Buick driven by Karen Simeroth on the suspicion of an expired registration tag, in Yuba City, California. Although the temporary tag was valid, the officer recognized her front-seat passenger as Bruce Brendlin.

After asking Brendlin to step out of the car and patting him down, the officer discovered syringes and a plastic bag containing a green leafy substance. That triggered a further search of the car. The driver was not charged, but Brendlin was arrested and later convicted of making methamphetamine. He challenged his arrest as the product of an "unconstitutional seizure" by police, but lost before the California Supreme Court. In 2006, Brendlin appealed to the U.S. Supreme Court.

In its ruling the court made clear what it had implied in the past. "When a police officer makes a traffic stop, the driver of the car is seized within the meaning of the Fourth Amendment," [which forbids "unreasonable searches and seizures"] said Justice David H. Souter. "We hold that a passenger is seized as well and so may challenge the constitutionality of the stop. ... Brendlin was seized from the moment Simeroth's car came to halt on the side of the road."

Souter's opinion dealt only with private cars and he noted that a different rule may apply to taxi cabs or buses, in which passengers may well feel free to leave if an officer stops and questions the driver. ✍

— By Garry W. Johnson, MOUNTAIN REVIEW Staff

The power of pink

By Garry W. Johnson
MOUNTAIN REVIEW Staff

Imagine if we were all dressed in pink instead of blue. Do not be too quick to laugh. The use of pink is becoming more prevalent in lockups nationwide.

The South Carolina Department of Corrections is currently being sued over its use of pink jumpsuits to punish prisoners for sexual misconduct.

Sherone Nealous is serving time at the Allendale Correctional Institution in South Carolina for assault and battery with intent to kill, aggravated assault and assault and battery on a police officer. His lawsuit claims forcing inmates to wear pink is discriminatory and makes them more likely to be assaulted by other inmates.

"When the inmate population views an inmate wearing a pink jumpsuit, it is known that the clothing was assigned by (the Department of Corrections) as punishment for sexual misconduct," says a legal memorandum filed by the department. It "conveys no suggestion that the inmate is a willing participant in homosexual activity or otherwise vulnerable to ... assault." [It begs the question, what do they consider "sexual misconduct," if not "homosexual?"]

Court documents claim pink was chosen as the identifying mark for sexually active inmates partly because other colors were taken—yellow for segregation units, dark green on death row—but also because the system's prisoners do not like wearing pink, which "contributes to its deterrent effect," the memo states. The policy applies to both male and female housing facilities.

Other institutions use pink in more creative ways. In Mason County, Texas, Sheriff Clint Low was aiming to cut down on recidivism in his small-town jail. He painted the cell walls pink and gave inmates pink jumpsuits, underwear, socks, shoes, sheets and towels—a full matching set. Afterward, Low said his return customers dropped by 68%. "It's not about trying to humiliate people. It's simply that with them not liking it, they're embarrassed by it, and they don't want to come back."

In Phoenix prisoners were smuggling out jail-issue underwear, featuring the jail logo, to sell on the black market. So Sheriff Joe Arpaio began dying them pink. "Why would I give them a color they like? They're in jail."

Alexander Schauss, senior director of natural and medicinal products research at AIBMR Life Sciences in Puyallup Washington, first documented the effect of pink jail cells in the 1970's. He says there is more to the effect of pink than outlaws not liking it.

At the U.S. Naval Correctional Center in Seattle, the facility had an average of one assault on staff per day before painting the "drunk tank" pink. Afterward, there was only one assault over the following six months, according to Schauss.

Vandalism and assaults dropped dramatically in East St. Louis, Ill., after buses were painted pink, and violent inmates at the Washington State Penitentiary in Walla Walla became less aggressive when placed in all-pink rooms, Schauss said.

So, if you see a roll of pink material roll out on a cutting-table at TriCor, do not be too upset. And if you are, just think pink ... Schauss says even the thought has a calming effect.

Science: The Theory of Evolution

By Derek Delaney

According to the theory of evolution, one of two events are believed to be the beginning of life. Both of these, however, trace the origin of life to nonliving substances.

In the first of these two theories, it is believed that living organisms evolved out of chemicals (nonliving) in a primeval "soup," some three billion years ago. The second theory says these organisms originated from clay minerals in the primeval lands. Proponents of the evolutionary theory say it is one of these two occurrences that began the evolutionary process of many species, such as fish, reptiles, mammals, etc.

Despite the many failed attempts to prove either of these theories of origin, Darwinian scientists remain optimistic. However, there have been certain findings of which other scientist dispute as evidences of evolution.

One such finding is that of fossils found in various depths of the earth. It is believed by evolutionists that fossils found in the sedimentary rocks of the earth's crust have been deposited there for more than a hundred million years. In order to identify the process of real evolution, a geologic column was made, placing the less complex life forms in the lower stratum, being considered the earliest, and the more complex forms on the top, near the surface. The problem with the geologic time scale is that no fossils have been found in any strata to resemble actual transition from one creature to another. Also, many fossils found nearest the surface have not changed at all from those of modern day species. Dr. Henry M. Morris, PhD., President of the Institute of Creation Research in San Diego, California, suggests that even more of these fossils would be considered unchanged, if it weren't for paleontologists renaming fossilized species that closely resemble modern living creatures.

Finally, most of the modern kinds of species said to have changed from earlier forms are obviously less complex than those believed to be their ancestors. Some examples are shown in both mammals and reptiles.

In an attempt to possibly sway evolution critics, fossils were presented to the public of an early stratum, half bird/half reptile (called an Archaeopteryx) which was shown to be proof of the evolutionary process. Unfortunately, in 1984, several scientists found these fossils to have been falsified or planted after Darwin published his book, *The Origin of Species*.

HOMOLOGIES AND EXPERIMENTAL DATA

As a means of experimenting with the resemblance and similarities (Homologies) of different species, scientists often compare anatomies, embryologies, behaviors, biochemistry, and many other factors to determine if evolution has actually taken place amongst the species being compared. This hypothetical analyzing is the cause of the assumption that man transcended from apelike creatures called "hominid" forms.

Because of the fact that apes and humans have similar features, many evolutionists make this assumption. But this too, in spite of its widespread speculation, has flaws and questionable attributes. The fact that only a few supposed fossils of these ape-man intermediates are found, leaves the question of why so few, especially when you compare a few fossils to the millions of apes and humans who exist in our time. The process of evolution (if any is possible) would have had to have been accelerated.

On so many other occasions, hoaxes have been revealed; individuals fabricating evidence to validate what is a clearly defined "faith," rather than science. There is the hoax of the tooth found in Nebraska, back in 1922. Promoted by Henry Fairfield Osborn as an ape-man, it was discovered two years later to be that of an extinct pig. Or how about the hoax of the Piltman, which is universally acknowledged as such, fooling a number of the world's leading anthropologists for decades.

Without true scientific proof—sufficient, unquestionable evidence—how could evolution ever be considered real science? ✍

Recommended Reading: Darwin's Black Box, *by Michael Behe*

We need your submissions!

The 2007 Veteran's Club banquet was an overwhelming success. With good food and fellowship, all attendees had an outstanding time.

Guests began arriving at 5:00 p.m. on Monday, August 27 (which turned out to be the birthday of Veteran's Club VP David "Bulldog" Presley—coincidence?). Among the invited guests were Volunteer Chaplains Donnie Moore, Herb and Pat Judkins, Randall and Kim Vespie, (who also helped with the food), Lonnie and Leda Gregg, Unit Manager Craig Williams, and many friends and family of Veteran's Club members. After a short prayer by Mr. Vespie, the servers began doling out generous size plates of Captain D's fish, shrimp, and sides, not to mention the delicious chicken picked-up from Kroger by Volunteer Chaplain David Upton.

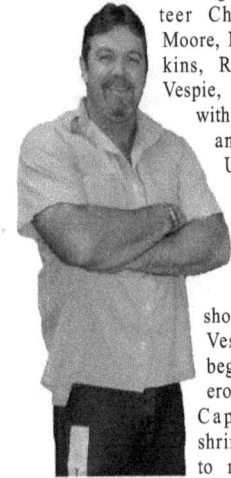

After the first course was served and the servers and guards had an opportunity to eat, deserts were made available to everyone. There were cakes, ice-cream, and toppings of all kinds thanks to the generous contributions of Bethel Presbyterian Church. The banquet came to an end around 8:00 p.m. with everyone leaving full and happy.

The board of the Veteran's Club asked that thanks be given to the administration for allowing the club banquets to continue. Also, special thanks be given to AW/PR Jennie Jobe, inside sponsor Chaplain Dean Yancey, and outside sponsors Ray and Stella Braden for their diligent support, and Randall Vespie and David Upton for filling in as sponsor for Chaplain Yancey during the banquet. Extra special thanks goes out to Lou Ann Roberts for picking up the newspaper camera, taking pictures, and making this article possible.

The Veteran's Club board consists of: President Grant Henderson, Vice President and acting Treasurer David Presley, Secretary Terrill Turpin, Sargent at Arms Howard Humphrey, and Chaplain Randall McPheeters.

The Veteran's Club meets the first Tuesday of every month in the staff dining room and would like to extend an invitation to all the veterans on the compound to join. The VA Representative, Ray Braden, is available at every meeting (you do not have to be a member to speak to him). ✍

—By Garry W. Johnson, Staff Writer

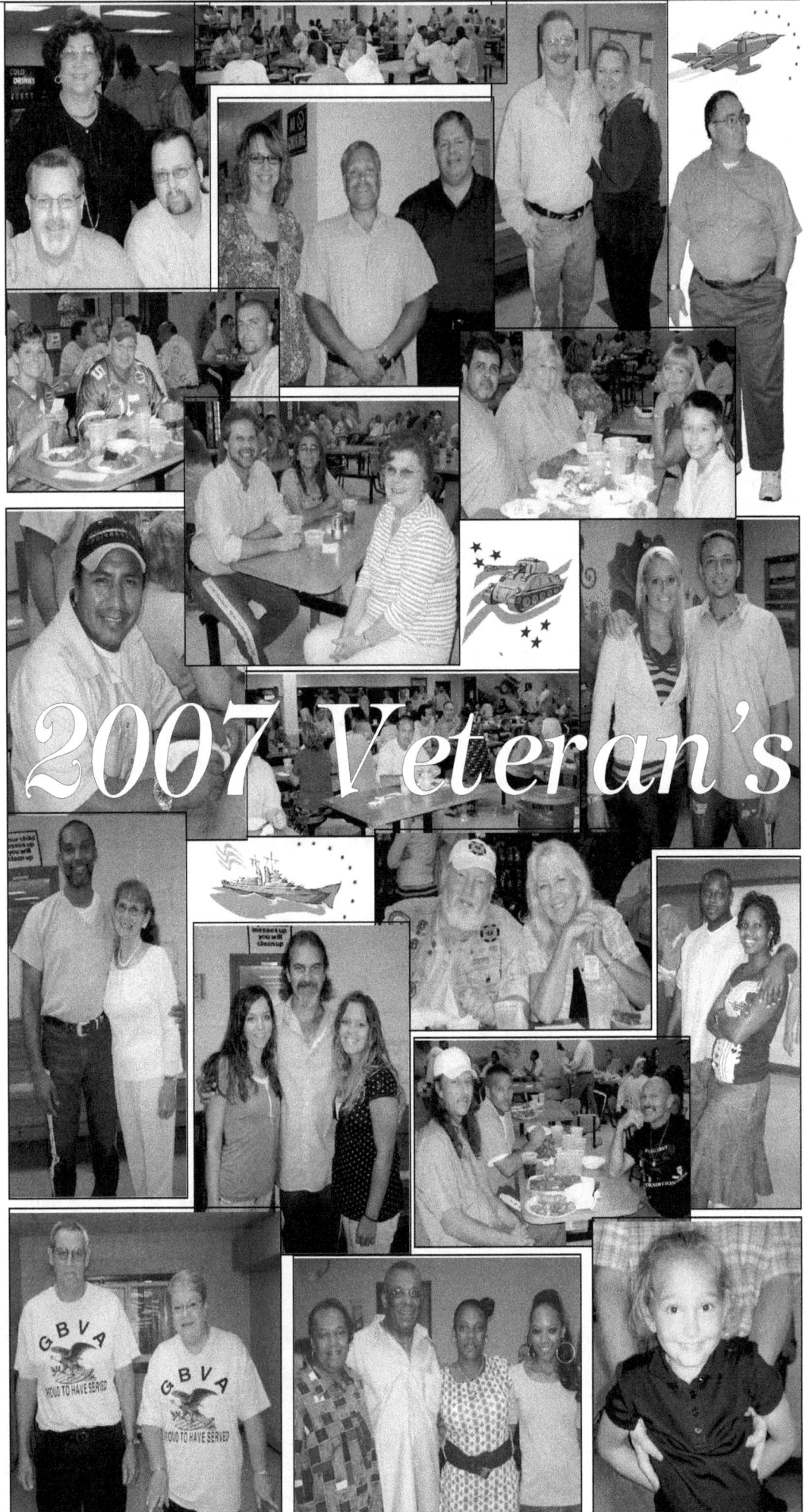

Fewer prisoners are veterans

Percent of state prisoners reporting prior service in the U.S. armed forces:

20% — 1986
12% — 1997
10% — 2004

Source: Bureau of Justice Statistic

2007 Veteran's

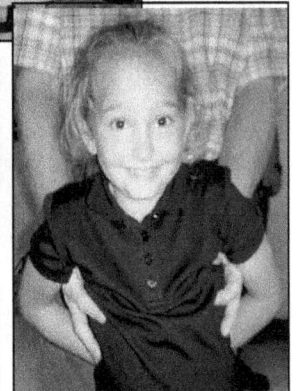

Club Banquet

Vet receives benefits while on the lam

Pierce L. Gross received treatment for addiction and mental health woes at a federal Veterans Administration facility while on the lam in a federal drug case.

In 1999 Gross failed to appear for trial in U.S. District Court on charges of selling crack cocaine and going armed while doing so in the Western Heights housing project in Knoxville. A minor auto accident earlier this year ended the federal fugitive's run.

At a hearing July 9, Gross told U.S. District Judge Leon Jordan that he "just left" the VA hospital in Kentucky after undergoing three months of treatment. Gross apparently entered the program using his real name, and it is unclear why his status as a fugitive was not realized or how he remained eligible for VA benefits.

During Gross' almost eight year flight, he was also arrested in Detroit, Michigan where he gave authorities a fake name. He was allowed to post bond and skipped town before that case was tried as well, according to Assistant Federal Defender Kim Tollison.

Gross pled guilty to both his 1999 case and the failure to appear charge with no plea agreement from Assistant U.S. Attorney Greg Weddle. Facing a minimum sentence of 10 years, Jordan will decide Gross' fate at a sentencing hearing November 7.

According to Weddle, Knoxville Police noticed Gross walking around the housing project wearing a bulletproof vest. They found crack cocaine and a gun in Gross' jacket pocket, which he admitted to owning. "He (told the officers that) he was addicted to crack cocaine and he had been selling crack cocaine to pay his bills ... and his child support." Gross is 32 years old.

—By Garry W. Johnson, Staff Writer

Crime in the military

Most common serious offenses for active-duty military prisoners in custody:

Offense	Percentage
Sexual assault	29%
Drug offense	22%
Military offense	14%

Source: Bureau of Justice Statistic

129

The best kept secret on the compound

By Jeffery Stratton & Donald Streck

Bank account forms, sample credit card applications, and driver's licence test information began surfacing in the housing unit. There was even a brochure explaining a free federal bonding service which would help me get a job. I began watching people around me who were handling these items. I intended to get to the source of this new supply chain. The inmates possessing the information were somewhat reserved, and I couldn't quite put my finger on what it was that made them different. I became instinctively jealous. The baggage these guys used to carry was gone. I was going nuts trying to figure out what their game was now. How in the heck did these guys become so focused? What possible goals could you possibly pursue in prison? What exactly were they focusing on? I want to go home but I can't. Somehow these guys had discovered another way to freedom. I wanted to know more, so I finally approached my cell partner.

"Where have you been getting all this information you have been reading?" He smiled and said he had signed up for the Pre-Release class and the contract required him to keep an open mind to new ways of dealing with aggression and problems. The program's theme is "Thinking for a Change."

Here's how I figure it: I'm locked up; I've lost my family and all my worldly belongings. I'm living in this closet size bathroom with you for company. My beliefs, attitude, and behavior got me here and I'm tired of being tired. I, too, want to go home, but when I do, I don't ever want to come back. I've wasted a lot of time blaming others for my current plight. I played the role of the victim of this merciless society. This course has taught me that I have a choice. No one made me commit my crime. More importantly, I now realize that I'm not the victim, but I darn sure created a lot of them. Sure, I may have had a rough childhood or experienced a traumatic event, but the majority of people deal with their share of pain without resorting to crime. As

our instructor, Mr. Rickey Bunch, so aptly put it: "Get over it! Life's not always fair!" This comment initially made me mad, but then I started thinking. Sounds tough, but when viewed from society's prospective, it hit the nail right on the head. After all, they are paying the cost of me being here. Do you know how many spouses and children are suffering because we are here? What did they do wrong? The answer is simple: ABSOLUTELY NOTHING! So why then do I have the right to feel victimized?

"Thinking for a Change" requires a person to take a trip directly to the source of the problem. In doing so, one ends up looking in the mirror. Mr. Bunch has been criticized by some as being too hard on the class participants. From my prospective, he hasn't been hard enough. Coddling has gotten us here. The old adage, "If it walks, talks and squawks like a duck, it ain't no swan," is apropos here. Mr. Bunch minced no words when challenging us to take a hard look at ourselves. If someone had done this fifteen years ago, just maybe there would have been another bunk available here now.

"It sounds like one of those brainwash sessions to me. These people get federal funding for pushing us through courses like that. No one is disrespecting me!"

First, no one can disrespect you but yourself. Second, you came to me with questions. I've explained to you about the Pre-Release class I'm attending. Look, I came into prison alone and soon I'll be leaving alone. The difference is that this time, I have acquired some tools to take with me to keep me out. The fact that I received the opportunity to look at myself without the rose colored glasses probably has saved my life. How did it help? It allowed me to realize that life isn't always about me. My rights stop where yours begin. My friends, family, and coworkers are suffering because of my bad choices. All I really ever wanted out of life was

a happy family, good job, and maybe some day, a nice home. All that my previous choices got me was a short high, a dozen or more victims, and a fifteen year prison term. My way isn't working! Maybe its time I stop, be quiet, and listen.

"Well, what guarantee do I have that it will work for me?"

The instructor will give you the tools and point you in the right direction. How you choose to use them will determine the outcome. Therefore, only you can write the guarantee you're looking for. Oh, by the way, you receive premium pay while attending the course and will maintain the same upon successful completion, if you are within nine months of parole or release. It's a good deal for us. What you choose to get out of it is left up to us.

"Why can't I just keep doing what I'm doing?"

That's your choice, but you should take time to review the definition of "insanity." It goes something like: "To keep performing the same acts while expecting to get different results."

"Can you apply the principles you learn while still in prison?"

Sure, and if you do, you will begin liking yourself, making better choices, and initiating positive change, which will benefit yourself and everyone around you. Keep in mind, the most permanent thing in life is change. I am now choosing to be part of the solution instead of the problem. It's hard, and some days, I catch myself slipping back to my dangerous and destructive old habits. That's okay, because at least now I'm aware of what is happening to me. That awareness will allow me to take the needed corrective action before doing something stupid or hurting another person again. If you are too busy to help yourself, then this class isn't for you. ✍

Editors Note: Anyone wishing to sign up for the Pre-Release class may submit an Information Request Form to Pre-Release Instructor Rickey

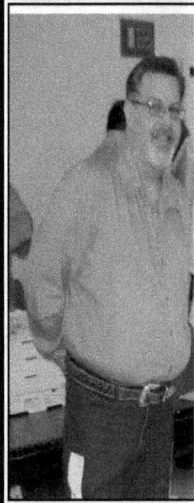

What does an inmate need to know to make it in the free world?

By Michael Gay, Jr.

In order to survive in the free world, we know we must eat, and food costs money; therefore, we must work. In order for us to get to work, the grocery store, a halfway house, the probation office, or wherever else we might need to travel, we will need to have means of transportation. Gas costs money, cabs cost, and houses cost—nothing is free. We know we must have patience to wait for the paychecks once a week or every other week. Yet one thing we do not know is exactly what type of circumstances, situations, obstacles, or opportunities we will face.

Say you just left the Bank of America with $435.75 one sunny Friday in August. Just last Saturday you were in the penitentiary, and since that Monday, you have been working twelve hour shifts on a construction site mixing and shoveling concrete. You have been working hard all week and you cannot wait to get home to your wife and kids. On the way home, you decide to stop at the corner where a guy sells brand-named women and children's clothing. Four dudes jump out of a van, rob the guy for his money and all his clothes, and get you for all your hard-earned $435.75. Now, to top it all off, when you get home and tell your wife exactly what happened, she does not believe you one bit. She tells you that you have not been working all week; instead, you have been with another woman. She proceeds to kick you out of the house. What is your next

move?

This is just something to think about, because no one knows what he will face; situations may be easier for some and harder for others. Look at me, I will be twenty-five years old, with no job, no car, no house, no wife, no kids, five years on probation, and a mandatory six-month stay at a halfway house. Now, I have an opportunity to start a whole new life however I so choose. I can enroll in school, or I can go work; contractors are always looking for strong, healthy, young men. Tattoos, skilled, or unskilled—its does not matter; there will always be a need for labor. I can accept dope from one of my ex-home boys (I know it will be given to me). Believe me, it never fails.

However, for you, your situation might be different. You may be fortunate enough to have a job, car, house, wife, and kids. Yet realize that you will be at work the very moment you step foot out of these gates. You will go from laying around in the penitentiary, to being a full-time husband and father, and working eight-hour shifts five days a week. This will take a toll on the average person. You may be tempted to quit when that burden begins to wear on you physically, mentally, and spiritually. My advice is to keep striving because it will get easier.

It is like lifting weights: if you have gone a year without lifting weights, then when you start back, you are not going to be able to lift the same weight you formerly lifted. So, you start light, and after that first workout, you are going to be sore or until you work the soreness out. Once you have worked through that soreness, you will not have to worry about being that sore again. Still, until you work through that soreness, it will be there. So, continue striving for success, even through the trials and tribulations. It will get easier.

Final thought: In order for anyone to make it in the free world, they must trust and believe that God will provide. ✍

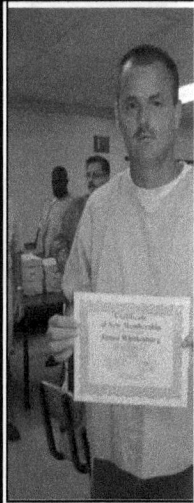

STEP FOUNDATION

Seventh Step banquet a success

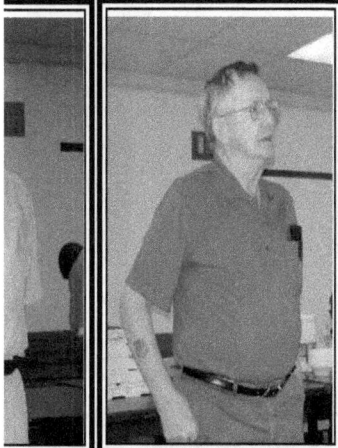

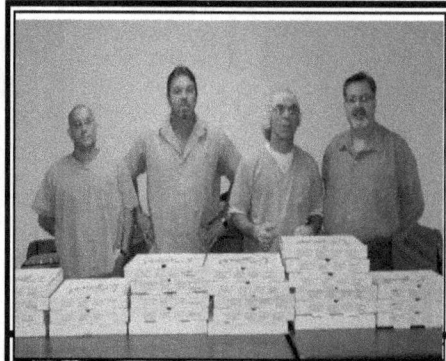

By Jeremy Ingram
MOUNTAIN REVIEW Staff

The Seventh Step Foundation held their annual banquet on September, 6, 2007. Bill Copeland, Bob Liveson, and Alice Hanks, three sponsors from Seventh Step, were in attendance. As the banquet kicked off, awards were given to several members. Bill Copeland, president of the outside chapter of Seventh Step, spoke about the purpose of the program and encouraged the membership to pursue change .

Bill Copeland has been active in Seventh Step for thirty years. He got his start at Brushy Mountain State Prison when it was a time building facility. After BMSP changed into a classification center, the Seventh Step program moved to the Morgan County Regional Correctional Facility, where it has been ever since.

Also in attendance were Alice Hanks, Secretary of Seventh Step, and Bob Liveson, Treasurer. Alice has been active in Seventh Step for thirty years while Bob began his service in 1981, when MCRCF opened. Also volunteering, although absent from the banquet, are Jessie Quarles and J.B. Mankin.

The Seventh Step program originated in the mind of an ex-con named Bill Sands. He sought a way to offer inmates, returning to society, the tools necessary for success. The Seventh Step program was born out of his effort and since then, has bloomed into an international non-profit organization.

The purpose of Seventh Step is to change the attitude of inmates by providing self-help classes on a variety of subjects. One such topic covered by the program is "How to have a pleasing personality."

Another service the Seventh Step program offers is what they call the "Hot Seat." The Hot Seat is intended for inmates who are close to going up for parole. They are placed on a seat and questioned to determine their strong and weak points. This, in effect, prepares them for a more successful parole hearing. According to Mr. Copeland, out of the 390 inmates to participate in the program and who were released from prison, only two returned.

Chris Tatrow, present at the banquet, said "We appreciate Sergeant Manis being in attendance, the wings, and the pizza. The desserts smell enticing and we are all ready to eat till we bust." With an abundance of food, most inmates came close to the point of busting. Seventh Step provided bottled cold drinks, pizza, buffalo wings, and premium ice cream. In attendance as the Newspaper Editor, I felt it my duty to sample the food to ensure its quality. On a strictly professional level, I ate several helpings of food just to make sure everything was good—it was.

Bob Liveson summed it up well in these words: "Seeing guys get out and put their lives back together is all worth it."

Seventh Step meets every Thursday at 7:00 in the Staff dining room. All are welcome. ✍

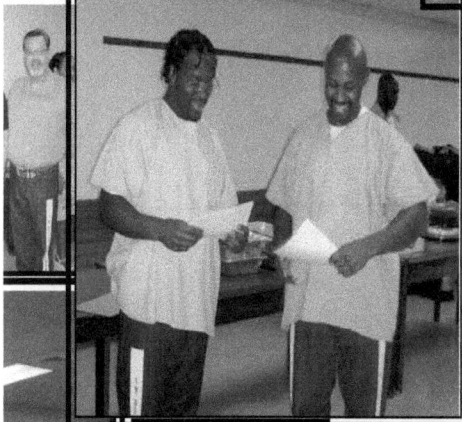

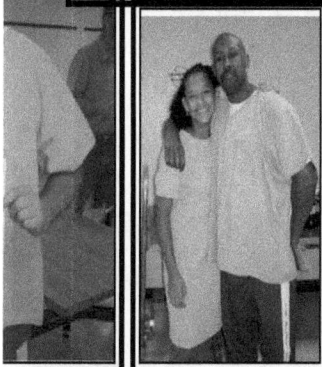

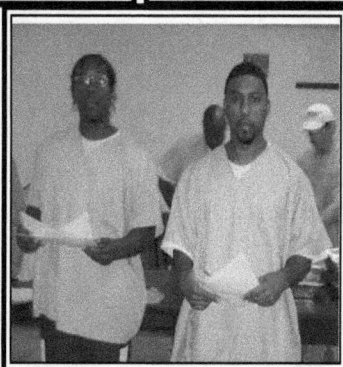

131

MCCX Varsity Club "Producing Productive Citizens Through Education"

The Varsity Club was established in 1992 to address the needs of the incarcerated student. Since its inception, the Varsity Club has done a great deal to further rehabilitative programs here at MCCX, create community awareness, and promote public support for these programs.

The results of the efforts of the Varsity Club are evident—the ideas that constitute good citizenship have been instilled, dignity, and self worth have been nurtured, and the motivation to further one's education has been fostered. Ultimately, the efforts of the Varsity Club have helped lower the recidivism rate and provided a foundation for success for inmates once they are released.

There are many programs and classes at MCCX that the Varsity Club directly aids. Because of the monthly dues by its members and donations by inmates, the Varsity Club is able to purchase supplies and provide certificates for many classes offered to inmates. Through the cooperation of the Varsity Club, the administration, and free-world volunteers, many programs that inmates have access to were created. Inmates from the Varsity Club facilitate many of these programs.

Some of the current projects the Varsity Club is involved in are:

• Alternative to Violence Project (AVP)—The Varsity Club helps pay for supplies and certificates needed for this program.

• Parenting class—The Parenting class follows the philosophy of the Cline and Fay Institute. It utilizes the materials from Love and Logic Parenting and Nurturing Parenting.

• Domestic Violence Prevention class—The Domestic Violence Prevention class uses material from Paul Kivel's Men's Work publications and selected exercises from the AVP manual.

• Anger Management—The Anger Management class, facilitated by current facilitators and AVP facilitators, utilizes material from *Cage Your Rage*.

• Sign Language class—The Sign Language class teaches American Sign Language. It is facilitated by Paul Rutherford, who was a graduate of the first sign language class. The class meets every Tuesday night at 6:00 P.M.

• GED Tutoring—Tutoring is held, as needed, by William Barney. Several others are also available for tutoring.

EDUCATION

2007 Varsity

• Writer's Workshop—Writer's Workshop meets every Thursday except the first Thursday of the month, meeting in the library classroom at 6:00 P.M. Everyone is welcome to attend. The workshop utilizes material from Long Ridge Writer's Group. The Writer's Workshop aids in editing, rewriting, and critiquing any written material by its participants. They also facilitate in the participation in writing competitions and publication markets. This workshop is not facilitated by any individual—it is a group project. Caroline Matthews, and Dick and Marge Hettrick from Bethel assisted in setting up the Writer's Workshop.

Besides these programs, the Varsity Club is involved in other activities that benefit inmates. The club helps the enrollment of inmates in various correspondence courses and recording and tracking the participation in these studies. The Varsity Club has helped aid inmates in paying for the EPA Certification Examination. It has also helped inmate students afford their academic needs.

Periodically, the Varsity Club will do special projects. In the past, the club donated money to Mr. K's Used Books in Oak Ridge to buy the library some different books. Other projects have included an Easter Egg Hunt and Christmas Stockings for children who come to visit during the holidays. Although the Varsity Club is concerned with helping the inmate population, it also has a burden for those less fortunate outside these walls. For instance, the Varsity Club has sponsored the collection of donations to be sent to the Red Cross for the victims of both the 9/11 terror attacks and the tsunami. Each month the club sends a donation to the Knoxville Area Rescue Ministry. During the Thanksgiving and Christmas season, the club donates money to the same ministry to pay for meals for the homeless.

A word should be said about the effort of one of the club's most prestigious members. Dr. Myer Pettyjohn, along with several others, created the Parenting class, the Domestic Violence Prevention class, and the Anger Management class. Several free-world people aided P.J. in the formation of these programs. Dick and Marge Hettrick, from the Bethel volunteers, Veteran's for Peace, Linda Barbier, Chaplain Dean Yancey, Claudine Norris, and the prison administration worked together to bring these classes to inmates at MCCX. P.J. passed away several years ago, but his selfless efforts live on.

If you are interested in joining the Varsity Club, we meet on the second Tuesday of every month in the library classroom at 6:00 P.M. Dues are three dollars a month and they go to help the club continue providing the valuable services mentioned in this article as well as many others. ✍

—By Jeremy Ingram, Staff Writer

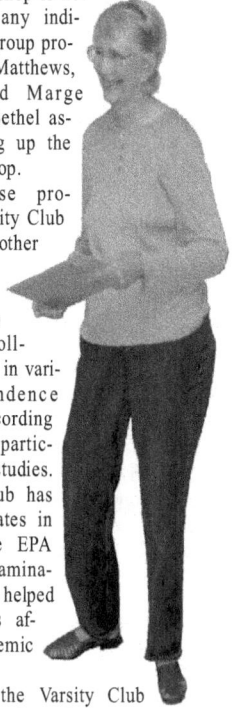

Club Banquet

EDUCATION

How To Read Music

Part Two: The Music Staff
By Jeremy Ingram,
MOUNTAIN REVIEW STAFF

In the last "How To Read Music" article, I gave a brief history of music. In this article, I will focus on one of the single most important concepts in modern music: the music staff.

The music staff should be familiar to everyone. It is the musical notation found above the words in any hymnbook. Before I explain what comprises the music staff, I will explain the history of how we came to have a music staff. In the previous article on the history of music, we saw that a scale originated by breaking an octave into twelve divisions. This division is also known as a chromatic scale. We also saw that choosing any note on a piano keyboard and playing up or down thirteen notes is a chromatic scale The first note on which you begin will be the same as the last note you play, only an octave different.

The piano was invented before the music staff. In fact, it was the piano keyboard that led, not only to the desire for written music, but also to the idea of the music staff. One note is of central importance at this point—the middle C. When you look at a piano keyboard, the middle C is the white key in the dead center of the keyboard.

Figure 1

Long ago, the middle C naturally became the note the music staff would center around. The middle C served as a reference point in the middle of two, five-line staffs. Figure 1 shows one note (middle C) and a staff above it and a staff below it. This is basically the setup of the music staff you see in most written piano music. The staff above the middle C is known as the treble clef, and the staff below middle C is known as the bass clef. As you can see in figure 1, there is a symbol at the beginning of each staff. These symbols simply show us what clef we are looking at.

So far so good. Turn your attention to the two basic components of the staffs: lines and spaces. If you count the lines of the treble clef, you will see that it is composed of five lines. In between each line is a space; hence, there are four spaces. (At this point, do not be concerned with the spaces above or below each clef.) Each line and each space of each clef have their own name. In figure two, each line and space is labeled according to their names. Notice that the letters of the alphabet, A through G, are used. After these letters have been used, they are repeated. If you read my last

article, you will remember that in each octave, there are seven white keys on a piano; hence, there are seven note names. More on that later.

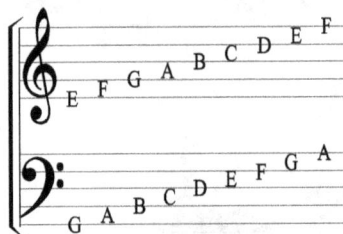

Figure 2

When I was a kid, my mother took my sister and I to piano lessons. We were taught a popular acronym so we could better remember the lines and spaces in each staff. There are four such acronyms that will help you tremendously. The first two acronyms relate to the treble clef and the last two relate to the bass clef. First, look at the treble clef. You will see, in figure 2, that the names of the five lines are E,G,B,D, and F. The acronym most students learn is, "Every Good Boy Does Fine." If you remember this acronym, you will know the names of the five lines of the treble clef (beginning with the bottom line). Next, look at the spaces between the lines of the treble clef. These are named F,A,C, and E. That is very easy to remember. All you have to do is simply remember the word "FACE."

Now turn your attention to the bass clef. The lines, according to figure 2, are G,B,D,F, and A. The acronym for these lines is, "Good Boys Do Fine Always." Next, look at the spaces between the lines of the bass clef. The names are A,C,E, and G. The acronym is "All Cows Eat Grass." Of course, in today's world, it might be easier to remember "All Cars Eat Gas."

Now comes the hard part: practice. After you commit these note names to memory, perhaps by utilizing the acronyms, you are ready to look at any piece of written music and name each note. You should practice doing this until the note names are firmly planted in your mind. Reading music is very much like reading a book. After you learn how, you should immediately be conscious of every note without thinking about it, just as you are conscious of every word in a sentence without consciously sounding it out. Furthermore, like reading a book, reading music skillfully can only come through practice.

We have used the words staff and clef without really defining them. I want to take the opportunity to define these terms and introduce two more: Grand Staff and stave.

A staff is the horizontal lines on and between which notes are written or printed. Thus, either the top set of lines we call the treble clef or the bottom set of lines called the bass clef can be referred to as a staff. The word stave is simply another word for

a staff. The joining together of these two staffs (or staves), much like what you see in piano music, is called the Grand Staff. Remember, the note in the middle of the two staffs of a Grand Staff is called the middle C.

The next word we need to define is a clef. Officially, a clef is the symbol written at the beginning of a musical staff to indicate the pitch of the notes. However, the word clef is usually used to denote a specific staff—the treble clef and the bass clef.

At this point, let me note that the treble and bass clefs are not the only clefs. If you run across a piece of music that has more than two staffs, do not be surprised. However, at this pont, it is easier to concern ourselves with the two most popular staffs, the treble and the bass.

Now we come to the music notes. If you picture the staff as the skeleton of a human body then the notes are the muscles.

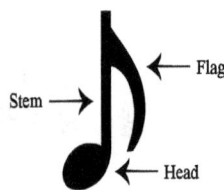

Each note has three parts: head, stem, and flag. Figure three shows a simple eighth note. Do not be concerned at this point with why this note is called an

Figure 3

eighth note. Simply learn the three parts of the note. All notes will have a head but not all notes will have a stem or a flag. For instance, a whole note has neither a stem nor a flag. A half note and a quarter note do not have a flag (See figure 4). Also notice that with some notes, the head is black and with other notes, the head is white. This will be explained later.

Figure 4

There is another way of learning note names without any knowledge of the staff. It is called tablature. Tablature is a method of notation for guitar in which vertical lines represent the strings, horizontal lines represent the frets, and dots on these lines indicate finger placement.

In Volume 18, Issue No. 2 of the *Mountain Review*, Charlie Brandler wrote an article on reading tablature and playing scales on a guitar. Even though some musicians learn tablature and neglect music theory, it is important in learning music theory not to neglect tablature. To conclude this article, I will reprint a portion of

Charlie's article:

"Being able to read tablature will make learning to play the guitar a lot easier. Tablature is an alternate form of sheet music and is very helpful in learning scales, licks, and even whole songs. It is simple to read. There are six lines—the bottom line is the top string of the guitar, and the top line is the bottom string of the guitar (see figure 5).

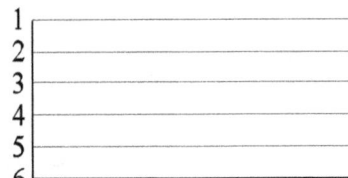

Figure 5

"Looking at the six lines on paper is like looking at your guitar lying on your lap. The number on the line tells you which fret to put your finger on that particular string. If the numbers are on top of each other or stacked, then they are played simultaneously (together).

Figure 6

"Figure 6 shows three chords as they would appear in tablature (TAB). If the string has no number on it, then it is not to be played.

"A zero indicates that a string is to be played open. If the numbers are not stacked, then you play them one at a time.

"If you want a further explanation of how to read TAB, just let me know and I will provide you with a sheet explaining all of the symbols and their meanings."

In summary, we discussed the concept of a music staff. A staff is composed of five lines and four spaces in between the five lines. A Grand Staff is composed of a treble clef and a bass clef. We discussed acronyms for the note names of both clefs. I noted that practice is the key to learning how to read music. A simple project is to find a piece of written music, possibly a hymnbook from the chapel, and figure out the names of each note. Lastly, we discussed the concept of tablature. Even though we will not dwell on tablature, it is important to know.

In the next issue of the *Mountain Review* I will continue this series on reading music with an article on musical timing and note values. ✍

Graphics by Garry W. Johnson

Nursing News

Mentally-Ill Equipped?
U.S. Prisons and Offenders With Mental Illness
By Jennifer Anderson, RN

One in six prisoners is mentally ill. Many of them suffer from serious illnesses such as schizophrenia, bipolar disorder, and major depression. There are three times as many men and women with mental illness in prison as there are in mental health hospitals. Somewhere between two and three hundred thousand men and women in U.S. prisons suffer from mental disorders. An estimated seventy thousand are psychotic on any given day. Yet across the nation, many prison's mental health services are greatly lacking. Understaffing, insufficient facilities, and limited programs all too often result in many prisoners receiving little or no meaningful treatment. Instead, they are neglected, accused of malingering, or just simply treated as disciplinary problems.

Paranoid schizophrenia is one of the most prevalent mental disorders seen in the prison system. It is defined as a form of schizophrenia in which a person suffers from delusions, hallucinations, jealousy, hostility, aggressiveness, unfocused anxiety, argumentativeness, and in some severe cases total detachment from reality. Bipolar disorder is characterized by extreme mood swings, deep depression, or a manic phase. Another serious disorder that is often not talked about is a disorder termed "Anti-social Personality Disorder." With this particular mental illness, a person is usually verbally or physically harmful to other people, animals, or property. The behavior of these individuals violates social expectations for any given environment. Causes that lead to adults with this disorder include: family problems as a child, child abuse, frequent changes in a primary caregiver or housing, and attention deficit disorder. All the illnesses listed above can be treated with a variety of anti-psychotics, mood stabilizers, and anti-depressants. The trouble comes when these medicines are not available to the prisoner suffering with the mentioned disorders.

Prisoners with mental illness are more likely to be picked on, physically or sexually abused, and manipulated by other inmates. Mentally ill prisoners find it difficult, if not impossible, to comply with prison rules, and eventually end up with higher than average rates of disciplinary infractions. Security staff, who usually lack training in mental illness, do not distinguish between the prisoner who is disruptive or fails to obey an order because of illness, and a prisoner who causes problems for other reasons.

Prisons were never intended as facilities for the mentally ill, yet that is one of their primary roles today. Without the necessary care, mentally ill prisoners suffer painful symptoms and their conditions can deteriorate. Deterioration can result in uncontrollable mood swings, debilitating fears, delusions, hallucinations, self-mutilation, and suicide. Prison time is undoubtedly hard for any person to do. Prisons are overcrowded, tense facilities in which prisoners are constantly struggling to maintain their self-respect and emotional stability. But doing time in prison is particularly difficult for prisoners with mental illness that impairs their thinking, emotional responses, and ability to cope.

Research suggests that few prisons accommodate mental health needs. Some mentally ill that are viewed as disruptive are placed in high security solitary confinement units. The lack of human interaction and mental stimuli dramatically aggravates the suffering of the mentally ill. Offenders who need psychiatric interventions for their mental illness should be held in secure facilities if they have committed serious crimes, but those facilities should be designed and operated to meet treatment needs. Society gains nothing from imprisoning offenders with disorders in a place where treatment is unavailable and dangerous to the offender's mental and physical well-being. Mental health treatment can help some recover from their illnesses, and for others

it can drastically reduce painful symptoms. It can enhance independent functioning, help a prisoner to regain health and coping skills, thus promoting community safety when the offender is released. After all, isn't the true reason for incarceration, in essence, rehabilitation? How is this at all possible when the reason for law-breaking behavior, such as mental illness, is being neglected and ignored?

Human right's standards do not allow correctional facilities to ignore or undertreat mental illness just because a person is in prison. The Eighth Amendment of the U.S. Constitution, which prohibits cruel and unusual punishment, also provides prisoners a right to humane conditions of confinement, including mental health services for serious illnesses. A Federal Advisory commission appointed by President Bush, recently reported that the U.S. mental health system was "in shambles". Prisoners are not a powerful public constituency, and often their rights are ignored. Finally, the misguided Prison Litigation Reform Act has hampered the ability of prisoners to obtain effective and timely help from the courts. The bottom line is the mentally ill that are imprisoned have the right to be diagnosed and treated.

In conclusion, I will leave you with an eloquent notation from a federal judge regarding this matter:

"All humans are composed of more than flesh and bone—even those who, because of unlawful and deviant behavior, must be locked away. Mental health, just as physical health, is a mainstay of life. Indeed, it is beyond any serious dispute that mental health is a need as essential to a meaningful human existence as other basic physical demands our bodies may make for shelter, warmth, or sanitation." ✍

Jennifer Anderson is a Registered Nurse at Parkwest Hospital in Chattanooga, TN. She is the sister of Mountain Review *editor, Jeremy Ingram. Jennifer is a regular contributor to the* Mountain Review.

Summer heat poses serious threat

This summer has seen some of the highest temperatures in recent history. With the opening of the lower yard, many inmates at MCCX have felt first hand the effects heat can have on a person. Being cautious in the heat is a given. However, not everyone is aware of the dangers the heat poses and the ways to prevent heat-related injuries.

The human body is remarkable in the way it cools itself. When the body's temperature is too high, the body perspires sweat through tiny pores in the skin. The evaporation of sweat from the skin is a mechanism in which the body is cooled.

Another way the body cools itself is through blood circulation. Tiny blood vessels near the skin's surface dissipate heat.

However, humidity and high temperatures can impede the body's ability to cool itself. Humidity, or moisture in the air, interferes with the evaporation of sweat from the body. This in turn, interferes with the body's ability to lower its own temperature. Two dangers are prevalent in high temperatures: heat exhaustion and heat stroke. It is important to be aware of the warning signs of both.

SIGNS OF HEATSTROKE

- Fever of 105 degrees or more.
- Dry, hot skin.
- Rapid heartbeat.
- Rapid and shallow breathing.
- Confusion or delirium.

HEALTHBEAT
By Jeremy Ingram,
MOUNTAIN REVIEW Staff

Physical activities and counting calories

Being active brings many benefits to your heart and your health.
About 3,500 calories are equivalent to a pound of body weight
Calories used in 30 minutes by activity and weight:

Activity	150 lb. person	200 lb. person
Playing basketball	282 calories	376 calories
Bicycling	163	217
Gardening	195	260
Hiking	204	272
Jogging at 5 miles per hour	270	360
Mowing with a light pushing mower	135	180
Playing tennis (singles)	234	310
Walking at 1 mile per hour	68	90
Walking at 5 miles per hour	225	300

Source: Kellogg's® Smart Start® cereal

By Garry W. Johnson, Mountain Review Staff

If you, or someone you know, exhibits these symptoms, get out of the sun and under shade. Heat stroke is very serious. Medical attention should be sought if someone is suspected of heat stroke. In some cases, heat stroke has led to seizures, comas, and even deaths.

Heat exhaustion is not as serious as heat stroke, but it poses a very real threat. Left untreated, it can lead to heat stroke.

SIGNS OF HEAT EXHAUSTION
- Faintness.
- Rapid heartbeat.
- Low blood pressure.
- Cold, clammy skin.
- Nausea.

If you, or someone you know, suffers from heat exhaustion, immediate help is necessary. The person should be brought to a shady or air-conditioned place, and made to lie down on his or her back. The feet should be slightly elevated. The person should be made to drink water. However, the water should not be too cold and a teaspoon of salt should be added. Clothing should be loosened or removed when appropriate. If condition worsens, medical help should be sought.

TIPS FOR KEEPING YOUR COOL IN HOT WEATHER
- Wear cool clothing
- Never wear plastic "weight loss" suits. They will increase body temperature and cause dehydration.
- Drink water before and after exercise in warm, humid weather. If you exercise for more than 30 minutes, stop and drink water every 15 to 20 minutes during the activity.
- Contrary to popular belief, it is not necessary (and may be harmful) to take salt tablets or increase salt intake in warm weather. Some salt is lost through sweating, but most Americans eat several times their required salt intake every day.
- The "heat index" is a good indicator of the severity of the heat. The heat index is the combined temperature and humidity. When the heat index exceeds 120, people should take caution when outdoors. Always think ahead when you are going to be outdoors. Proper planning and hydration go a long way in preventing these ailments ✍

MCCX vocational classes finish projects

By Jeremy Ingram,
MOUNTAIN REVIEW Staff

Commercial Food Service class

Recently, the Commercial Food Service class, taught by John Cross, finished work on a four-tier wedding cake for an officer at MCCX. The wedding cake was constructed in a traditional style, dating back to the Victorian Era. Decorated by students Robert Laffolette and Chester Williams, the cake took eight hours to complete and would retail upwards of $300 in the free world, according to John Cross.

The Commercial Food Service class offers four state certificates in Hospitality, Culinary Arts 1,2 and 3. Upon completion of all four certificates, the student will become eligible for a sixty-day sentence credit (if he meets criteria), and may earn up to an extra two dollars an hour upon release.

A federal certificate is also offered upon completion of 6,000 hours. The federal certificate will enable a student to enter the job force as an apprentice cook, possibly earning two dollars an hour more than someone who does not have this certification.

Anyone interested in the Commercial Food Service class needs to have a verified high school diploma or GED.

Building Trades class

The Building Trades class, instructed by Rusty Patterson, finished construction on a large storage building for a MCCX officer.

The building measures twelve feet wide by twenty feet long. It is eleven feet tall. This made for a challenging transport from the prison to the officer's home; a trip 35 miles long.

The building is described as an integrated workshop. It will be used for storage, as a wood shop, leather shop, and various other purposes. It was custom made by the Building Trades class according to specific requests. The inside is designed for assembly line work. There is a built-in saw, room for an air compressor, and a tool box. There is even room to plane lumber. One security device was the lack of "see-through" windows. Even though windows existed, they were made completely of wood, thus keeping curious eyes from seeing inside.

In the near future, the workshop will be used to aid in the construction of a large 2,000 square foot garage. The construction of the garage was in mind when the workshop was being built. Because doors were installed on both ends of the building, lumber can enter through one side, planed and cut inside, and tossed through the open doors on the opposite end. This will greatly assist in the assembly of the garage.

The owner of the building would like to thank Rusty Patterson, the Building Trades class, and in particular, Jerry Devereaux. Jerry helped design and draw the plans for the building. He also came up with the list of building materials that were required for construction.

New vocational programs coming to MCCX

Coming soon to MCCX are several new vocational programs that will provide inmates a chance to learn a trade that will prepare them for a job once released. Although these classes are tentative at this point, plans are underway to have a total of thirteen vocational classes (eleven on the compound and two at the annex). The compound classes include the following: Carpentry I, Carpentry II, HVAC, Small Engine Technology, Electrical (Residential) Wiring, Masonry, Computer Applications (software oriented), Computer Literacy (computing basics), Culinary Arts, Foundations of Hospitality, Core Construction, and Career Management Success. The two annex classes will be Horticulture and Advanced Carpentry. The Core Construction class will be a "feeder" class, in that, it will be required before a person can begin either HVAC, Masonry, Carpentry I, or any building maintenance job. ✍

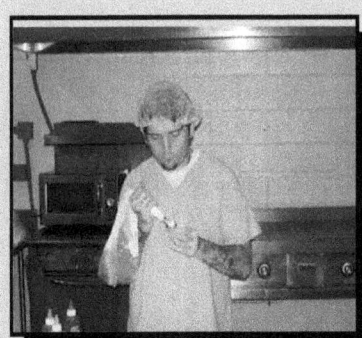

Christian Apologetics: The Defense of the Faith

By Jeremy Ingram
Mountain Review Staff

The word apologetics is derived from the Greek word *apologia*, which means to make a defense. This word is used throughout the New Testament, referring mainly to the disciples' defense of the Christian faith. A few examples will suffice to show the fact that Christians in the early church defended Christianity from religious, cultural, and often political pressures.

There are various usages of the word *apologia* in the book of Acts. Because of severe persecutions, early Christians were frequently called on to make a defense of their faith: "The Jews pushed Alexander to the front, and some of the crowd shouted instructions to him. He motioned for silence in order to make a *defense* before the people" (Acts 19:33), "Brothers and fathers, listen now to my *defense*" (Acts 22:1), and "When the governor motioned for him to speak, Paul replied: 'I know that for a number of years you have been a judge over this nation; so I gladly make my *defense*'" (Acts 24:10).

Some Christians will argue they are under no obligation to defend their faith to an unbelieving world. They say something to the effect that "God does not need defending." However, besides the many examples of those in the Bible who regularly defended their faith, (including Jesus Christ), the Bible explicitly commands Christians to be able to give a defense of their faith: "Always be prepared to give an answer to everyone who asks you to give the reason for the hope that you have. But do this with gentleness and respect, keeping a clear conscience, so that those who speak maliciously against your good behavior in Christ may be ashamed of their slander" (1 Peter 3:15-16).

Not only does the Bible command us to be able to defend our faith, but it also tells us how we are to do this task.

1. The believer does not approach the defense of the faith on neutral ground. He realizes that it is because of his faith in the gospel message that he has a hope in which to defend.

2. There is a clear implication in Scripture that the Christian message is intellectually defensible. Some people would rather divide religion from the realm of rational knowledge. They would argue that the Christian message, itself being by nature spiritual, cannot be explained or defended by appeal to intellectual exercises. However, the stance of the Bible is clearly that the gospel is intellectually defensible. Why else would the Bible command us to be able to defend something that is indefensible?

3. There is common ground on which the believer and the unbeliever can communicate. This does not mean that both the believer and unbeliever lay aside their convictions. This, in fact, is not possible. Rather it means that the believer and unbeliever arrive at a point in which rational communication is possible. Not all apologists arrive at a consensus on this point. "What is the point of common ground?" is frequently debated.

4. The Bible does not leave anyone who calls upon the name of Christ untouched by its exhortation to be prepared to give a defense for the hope that is within them. It says that *every* Christian has the obligation to make a defense *every* single time to *everyone* who asks for the reason of the hope within them.

5. The Bible explicitly tells us the attitude we are to have. Too many opportunities to share the good news of the Gospel end prematurely because of intellectual pride. However, the Bible warns Christians against intellectual pride, pointing instead to an attitude of humility, gentleness, and meekness. How can we, who believe in the sovereignty of God, expect our intellectual efforts to convince anyone of the truth of God's word? Instead, we must humbly rely on God to use our efforts for His glory.

What is the task of Christian apologetics?

1. To answer particular objections. Most apologetical encounters began as an opportunity to answer an objection to the Christian system. Sometimes these objections are directed toward the truthfulness of the Bible. Many people think the Bible contains assertions that do not line up with reality. Others think parts of the Bible contradict other parts. Still others believe the Bible is just not relevant to their life. These objections provide the Christian an opportunity to answer objections and provide a rational defense of the Christian faith.

Objections to the faith have served the Christian church for millennia by providing the context in which the church investigates, formulates, and defends truth. In the early era of the church, after Christ's resurrection, Christians were forced into considering the person and work of Jesus Christ.

Before that time, the facts of His divinity and atoning sacrifice were taken for granted by most Christians. It was not until erroneous opinions began to be propagated that Christians took to their studies. What resulted, were some of the best formulations of the doctrine of Christ that have ever been written (The Apostles' Creed and the Nicene Creed).

Likewise, God has often used objections to the Christian faith to grow individual believers in the knowledge of the truth, strengthen their faith in the immutability of His word, and answer the objections of the unbeliever.

2. The second task of apologetics is to account for the foundations of the Christian faith. Sometimes, the Christian will be called upon to make an answer for the foundations of his faith. At times, this may seem a harder task than answering the types of objections mentioned above. The foundational issues of the Christian faith are questions like: Does God exist? Can anything be known for sure? Are all religions valid, or is Christianity alone the only true religion?

These, and other questions, are considered foundational because Christians assume them in their thinking. Thus, they form a foundation for the rest of Christian theology.

Picture a pyramid. The very pinnacle of the pyramid rests upon a layer, and this layer rests upon another layer, and so forth. Eventually, if you follow the layers to the bottom, you will find there is a starting point, or ground floor, which does not depend on another layer for its existence. Such are some of the foundational truths of the Christian faith.

Yet, this does not mean that these foundational truths are irrational or indefensible. On the contrary, they are often self-evident and indisputable.

3. The third task of apologetics is to challenge erroneous opinions. As far back as the apostolic church, men of God were challenged with philosophies that contradicted clear Biblical teaching. In Scripture the apostles and other disciples of Christ challenged these false beliefs, and at the same time promoted the truthfulness of the Christian system. Today, books abound in Christian bookstores about world religions and modern cults.

It is true that the Christian who will be able to defend his faith is the Christian who is able to refute these false beliefs while clearly setting for the message of the cross. Even from within Christendom, a defense of sorts is needed against heresy that has crept in. Above all, the defense of the faith is not an attack on what is false, but an opportunity to spread what is true.

4. This leads to the fourth task of the apologist: to persuade men of the truth. This does not imply that someone can argue another person into the Kingdom of Heaven. On the contrary, all men are lost in sin and unable to come to the knowledge of the truth apart from the regenerating power of the Holy Spirit through faith in Christ. Yet, the Christian apologist always seeks to persuade men of the truth. This implies an implicit dependence on God.

In turn, the defense of the faith is very much like evangelism and can be used by God as the tool by which He draws men to Christ. To pass up an apologetical encounter solely because we think the other person will "never believe" is a reflection that we believe God is unable to save.

There are several approaches to apologetical method prevalent in the church today. The first is called Presuppositionalism. It gets its name because it "presupposes" the truthfulness of the Christian position. In other words, every person in the world builds their belief system on certain presuppositions, or beliefs that are foundational. There is no exception. Some believe they stand on neutral ground, presupposing nothing. But this is not only false, but also contrary to the Word of God. The Bible teaches that all men are by nature opposed to God and His Word. Therefore, all men, before regeneration, presuppose their ability to understand reality apart from the revelation of God. The word that describes man's supposed ability to determine truth apart from God is called autonomy, which literally means, a law unto oneself. The Presuppositional method admits this and its approach is tailored, based on this information.

The believer must not try to meet the unbeliever on "neutral ground" because there is none. Instead, he must presuppose the truthfulness of the Christian position and call upon the unbeliever to make an account of his own presuppositions. Hopefully, the unbeliever will realize that he has no justification to believe anything apart from the truth of Christianity.

This approach is likened to an unarmed man in a room with an armed assailant. The assailant has a gun in hand, ready to pull the trigger. What choice does the unarmed man have? Either he can learn to dodge the bullets, or he can disarm his opponent. This is precisely what the presuppositionalist does. When the unbeliever attacks the truthfulness of the Christian position, the believer does not "dodge bullets" but instead calls upon the unbeliever to account for their foundational assumptions. This disarms the opponent, if he is honest with himself.

Evidentialism is probably the most widely used apologetic system. With this approach, the apologist attempts to offer proofs for the truthfulness of Christianity. He may defend the virgin birth of Christ, Christ's resurrection from the dead, or the inspiration of the Scripture. He does this by asking the unbeliever to weigh the evidence, much like what a jury is called upon to do in a criminal case.

Of courses, certain assumptions are made by this approach concerning the unbeliever's ability to use his reason correctly. A downfall of this system is the unbeliever is not challenged to account for his unbelief, but rather called upon to judge whether or not Christianity is true. This is a position no person has the right to take.

Another problem with Evidentialism is the fact of the depravity of man's minds. Man, left on his own, will always suppress the truth of Christianity because it goes against his own supposed autonomy.

Apologetics is, in essence, the science of defending the faith. It is important that all Christians be able to offer a valid answer when they are questioned by an unbelieving world. Many resources are available that help equip believers to defend their faith. From a cursory glance at the most popular Christian book catalogs, the study of apologetics, world religions, and modern cults has become popular. Above all, a strong knowledge in basic Bible doctrine is essential.

However, the best textbook we have of the main lines of Christian defense is the Bible itself. F.F. Bruce wrote "Jesus remains the same, and the gospel in the twentieth century does not differ in essence from the gospel in the first century." Therefore, the need and method of apologetics need not differ essentially from that laid out in the New Testament.

Church history is another valuable tool to help Christians understand and see the outworking of apologetics. The second century, in particular, is known as the "age of the apologists" because many Christians, living during that time, were constantly confronted with contradictory claims to truth. F.F. Bruce says that above all, these early apologists remind us today that "a victory in a debate is a barren thing compared with the winning of men and women to the cause of Christ." ✍

Defeat the enemy

"To defeat the enemy you must know who he is."

By Roland Matlock

Why are believers losing so many of their spiritual battles? Why is it they so often end up fighting each other? We as Christians spend far too much time arguing about trivial matters amongst ourselves. We too often end up holding grudges against others because we've been deceived into believing just because a person has said or done something we don't like, it's this person we need to fight. Why is this?

It's because we're fighting the wrong enemy. So, who's the real enemy? Look at Ephesians 6:12: "For our struggle is not against flesh and blood, but against the rulers, against the powers of this dark world, and against the spiritual forces of evil in heavenly realms."

This Scripture shows us that we are looking at the wrong one as the cause of our problems. It clearly states that our fight is not against flesh and blood but is against the powers of this dark world—the spiritual forces of evil in heavenly realms (the spiritual realm). If you are looking at the man instead of the spirit in the man, you've already lost the battle. So how do you identify the spirit in the man?

Paul explains to us in Romans 6:16 that to whomever we yield our members to serve, that is to whom we belong. This means you either obey God Almighty and belong to Him, or disobey our Creator and belong to Satan. It's either the Holy Spirit, or the spirit of iniquity.

In writing to the Galatians, Paul also was inspired to describe the attributes, or "fruits" of the Spirit. He first described what acts follow being lead by the spirit of iniquity, or as he described the "works of the flesh." He described them as, "adultery, fornication, uncleanness, lasciviousness, idolatry, witchcraft, hatred, variance (discord), emulations (jealousy), wrath, strife, seditious (dissensions), heresies, envyings, murders, drunkenness, revellings (orgies), and such the like."

He went on to describe the attributes of the Holy Spirit. These are, "love, joy, peace, longsuffering, gentleness, goodness, faith, meekness, temperance: against such there is no law" (to practice these is not sin).

Jesus said, "Ye shall know them by their fruits," (Matthew 7:15-20). Here Jesus gives the analogy that a good tree cannot bring forth evil fruit, neither can an evil tree bring forth good fruit.

Now let's go back to Ephesians 6 and find out about your weapons and protective gear in this spiritual war. Here, starting at verse 10 and going through verse 18, we are told to put on "the whole armor of God," that we may be able to withstand all that Satan has to throw at us when the day of evil comes. With it, you will be able to stand your ground. So let us take a look at each piece of this armor.

The first is to have your loins girt about with truth. Satan fights and deceives with lies and his lies sound like truth, so only by having an intimate knowledge of God's Word can you defeat Satan's lies.

The next is the breastplate of righteousness. The breastplate covers your vital organs, most specifically the heart. The heart, as strong and as durable as it is, would be severally damaged if a blow was dealt directly to it. So in battle, this part of your body must be well protected. It is your obedience to the truth of God's Word that keeps God's hedge of protection around you. When you know the truth and live by it, you are protected by the breastplate of righteousness.

We're next told to have our feet shod with the preparation of the gospel of peace. We all, after coming into Christ, have taken on the ministry of reconciliation—that is the responsibility of bringing others to Christ. Satan does not want lives to be won over to Christ. He wants you to doubt that your labors as a soul winner will produce any fruit. So, he does not want you to focus on the best witnessing tool you have, which is the life you live. The feet are the instruments by which you walk. So if you are wearing the gospel of peace as the shoes of your spiritual walk, this means that the words you speak and the life you live are the same; therefore, your witness is true and much more effective. When you have this combination, the words you speak become powerful and effective with those to whom you speak. You will become a great soul winner for Christ, even if you never get to see the fruit of your labors.

We are next told to take the shield of faith, where with we shall be able to quench all the fiery darts of the wicked. Faith is trusting in God and believing He is real and a rewarder of them that diligently seek Him. So, when the wicked come against you with insults, making fun of what you do for Christ, trying to get you to turn from doing what you know to be right in God's sight, you will continue to obey God because you believe in God, His Word, and His promises. Therefore, your faith is able to withstand any wickedness thrown in your direction, as if you are literally protected by a shield.

The last of these pieces of armor is the helmet of salvation. The helmet protects the mind, where our thoughts originate and are processed. Romans 12:1-2 gives us insight into how to understand and use the last piece of our armor: "I beseech you therefore, brethren, by the mercies of God, that ye present your bodies a living sacrifice, holy and acceptable unto God, which is your reasonable service. And be not conformed to this world: but be ye transformed by the renewing of your mind, that ye may prove what is that good and acceptable, and perfect, will of God."

Paul is inspired to encourage us as brothers in Christ to remember we have received mercy from God and to present our bodies as living sacrifices, holy and pleasing to God, as a spiritual act of worship. He also warns us not to conform to the ways of this world, because we are new creatures in Christ, but to be transformed by the power of God's Word, by renewing our minds with it. By doing so, we will be proving all of our actions by the Word of God, thus showing what His good and perfect will is.

Jesus spoke in John 14:6, "I am the way, the truth, and the life: no man cometh to the Father, but by me." John 1:1 says, "In the beginning was the Word, and the Word was with God, and the Word was God." Verse 14 of the same chapter says, "And the Word became flesh and dwelled among us, and we beheld His glory, the glory as of the only begotten of the Father, full of grace and truth." We can be sure by what we've read that Jesus Christ is the Word of God. John 17:17 tells us God's Word is truth. Jesus is not only the Word of God, He is the truth. The helmet of salvation is the Word of God, active and alive in your mind as you live in obedience to it, under the direction and heeding of the Holy Spirit.

The last of the armor is the only weapon given to the believers in this spiritual battle. It is the Sword of the Spirit, which is the Word of God. Jesus is the Word of God, and when He was raised from the dead, He was raised with all power in heaven and earth. This makes the Word of God the most powerful thing there is. It is a spiritual weapon that cannot be defeated. "If God be for us, who can be against us?" (Romans 8:31). When Jesus Himself was being tempted by Satan, the only weapon He used against him was the Word of God and His obedience to it (See Matthew 4:1-11).

Believers, please remember every piece of this armor is spiritual, and based on your obedience to the Word of God. If your desire is to serve God, you must acquire an intimate knowledge of His Word and live in obedience to it. With this knowledge and the Holy Spirit, you will be able to try and discern the spirit in the man—and if it is not of God Almighty, you will have a competent weapon to defeat it.

If you belong to Jesus Christ, make no mistake in your thinking—Satan is angry! And he has come to make war with you (Revelation 12:17). Because of his anger, you will suffer persecution from men. This persecution is not just a manifestation of that person's hate for you. It is also a manifestation of Satan's fear of you. When Satan comes against you keep in remembrance the Word of God and resist him by obeying it, and he'll flee from you (James 4:7). He flees from you because of whom you are in Jesus Christ. I hope you now understand it's not the man who persecutes you, but the spirit in the man. The battle is not in the human realm, but in the spiritual realm. So walk in the Spirit and not in the flesh, and the battle is won! ✍

Editor's note: Roland Matlock is a member of God's Church and an inmate minister here at MCCX. He and other inmate ministers conduct a service every Saturday in the chapel, at 11:00. All are welcome to attend the service and join in the discussion and fellowship that follows.

Friendships of life

By Ruth L. Overby

God gave us an incredible gift of the beautiful world in which we live. We share this planet with so many others, and the risk of seeing its beauty diminish is greater with each generation, but it is our responsibility to respect the earth and preserve its resources for future generations. What you are is God's gift to you; what you make of yourself is your gift to God.

As we travel down the road of this earthly journey, the people we meet and the friendships we have are also very important, and each should be preserved with dignity and respect.

This earthly journey will lead us down many paths and our footsteps will go in many different directions. We will meet and greet many, only soon to be forgotten. Some others will find a pathway into our life and heart. They will stay a short while and then move on, leaving behind many pleasant memories. Then there are a "special few" who will enter our life and touch both our life and heart in a very special way. They will move into our heart and find a loving home there.

These special people's footsteps are on the same road as yours, and that is "the highway of holiness" that leads to heaven! They have the love of God in their heart and it shows on their face as they bring joy into the lives of others. These people are kind, loving, and giving. They give from the heart of their time, energy, and often times, money. I like to think of these special people as "God's earthly angels."

We all know life can be fragile and sometimes can become almost as fragile as a snowflake. It is in these times when words of love and encouragement from a friend can make all the difference in the world. I've often heard that the love and understanding of a friend is sometimes more healing than a doctor's prescription.

This poem, *The Miracle of Friendship*, is by an unknown author, but the words touched my heart and maybe yours too.

THE MIRACLE OF FRIENDSHIP
There is a miracle called friendship that dwells within the heart, and you don't know how it happens or where it even starts. But the happiness it brings you always gives a special lift and you realize that friendship is God's most precious gift!

Yes, it's true! We all travel different paths, but one day our footsteps will lead us to heaven's gate and we will hear "Welcome home my child." Then we will know it was worth all earth's trials to live in heaven through all eternity.

So when we show God's love and kindness here on our earthly journey, isn't that the way God in heaven would like us all to be? For in serving those around us, we serve Him too.

So as you travel life's weary road, let Jesus and friendships lift your heavy load. ✍ *Editor's note: The preceding was adapted from an article printed in the Dunlap Tribune. Ruth Overby is a family friend of inmate Danny J. Johnson.*

It has weighed on my mind for sometime to present a lesson on Biblical instruction for dealing with different individuals. The Bible is full of practical advice on how to handle scorners, brawlers, busybodies, fools—a panorama of human dispositions. Yet I have found in my personal dealings with other professing Christians, most want to handle every situation under the guidelines given for a "brother" in Christ (e.g., Matthew 18:15-17), or, otherwise, in a manner completely inconsistent with Scripture all together. It is the purpose of this article to identify the authentic Christian and better equip the reader to apply Biblical mandates.

WHO IS MY BROTHER?

There are several authenticating marks of God's people given throughout the Scriptures, but the most striking and fundamental is love. "He that loveth not knoweth not God; for God is love," (1 John 4:8). "Love is patient, love is kind, and is not jealous; love does not brag and is not arrogant, does not seek its own, is not provoked, does not rejoice in unrighteousness, but rejoices with the truth; bears all things, believes all things, hopes all things, endures all things. Love never fails ..." (1 Corinthians 13:4-8a NASV).

Love believes all things, and those who present themselves to us as our brothers should be accepted as such, but not blindly. "For there are certain men crept in unawares, who were before of old ordained to this condemnation, ungodly men, turning the grace of our God into lasciviousness, and denying the only Lord God, and our Lord Jesus Christ" (Jude 1:4). Some who profess Christianity are intentionally deceitful, turning the grace of God into a license to sin. Others believe they are doing the work of God and simply cannot tell the difference.

Christ said the words He spoke to us "are spirit, and they are life" (John 6:63). In other words, the Bible describes essential values and spiritual forces that operate automatically in many cases. This can be confusing to the unconverted. As they apply various principles outlined in Scripture, they experience the power of these spiritual laws and misconstrue that power as justification of their beliefs. "Many will say to me in that day, Lord, Lord, have we not prophesied in thy name? and in thy name have cast out devils? and in thy name done many wonderful works? And then will I profess unto them, I never knew you: depart from me, ye that work iniquity" (Matthew 7:22). The distinguishing mark of both the deceived and the deceiver, is sin.

"Everyone who practices sin also practices lawlessness; and sin is lawlessness. And you know that He appeared in order to take away sins; and in Him there is no sin. No one who abides in Him sins; no one who sins has seen Him or knows Him. Little children, let no one deceive you; the one who practices righteousness is righteous, just as He is righteous; the one who practices sin is of the devil; for the devil has sinned from the beginning ..." (1 John 3:4-8a; NASV).

Sin is the transgression of the law. "... [T]he wages of sin is death; but the gift of God is eternal life through Jesus Christ our Lord" (Romans 6:23). Christ made it possible for us to be reconciled to God by grace (Romans 3:24,25), but it is the *life of Christ* which saves us, not His death. "For if, when we were enemies, we were reconciled to God by the death of his Son, much more, being reconciled, we shall be saved *by his life*" (Romans 5:10, emphasis mine throughout).

True Christianity is *a way of life,* not a philosophy or an academic endeavor. It is based on the doctrine of Christ (1 John 1:9), who lived His life as a model for us to follow. "He that saith he abideth in Him ought himself also so to walk, *even as He walked*" (1 John 2:6). Paul wrote, "I am crucified with Christ: nevertheless I live; yet not I, but Christ liveth in me: and the life which I now live in the flesh I live by the faith of the Son of God, who loved me, and gave himself for me" (Galatians 2:20). That is true Christianity.

If you have the Son of God living in you, by the power of the Holy Spirit, then you are a child of God. "For as many as are led by the Spirit of God, they are the sons of God" (Romans 8:14). But if this is true, you must be striving to do what Christ did, overcome the wickedness of this present evil world: "To him that overcometh will I grant to sit with me in my throne, even as I also overcame, and am set down with my Father in his throne" (Revelation 3:21). "Be not overcome of evil, but overcome evil with good" (Romans 12:21).

Our chapel is open to everyone, as it should be. And everyone has the opportunity to participate in any worship service held there. But we cannot, and should not expect everyone to be what they claim to be. Not even ministers, preachers or leaders in the congregation are above reproach, if their deeds betray them: "For such are false apostles, deceitful workers, transforming themselves into the apostles of Christ. And no marvel; for Satan himself is transformed into an angel of light. Therefore it is no great thing if his ministers also be transformed as the ministers of righteousness; whose end shall be according to their works" (2 Corinthians 11:13-15). As in the examples above, these "transformed" ministers still show that identifying mark of sin: "Beware of false prophets, which come to you in sheep's clothing, but inwardly they are ravening wolves. Ye shall know them by their fruits" (Matthew 7:15-16a).

Your brother is the one who walks in the truth, if, and only if, you walk in the truth. "Know ye not, that to whom ye yield yourselves servants to obey, his servants ye are to whom ye obey; whether of sin unto death, or of obedience unto righteousness?" (Romans 6:16). Jesus answered our question this way, "For whosoever shall do the will of my Father which is in heaven, the same is my brother, and sister, and mother" (i.e., His family; Matthew 12:50).

WHAT IS THE CHURCH?

The Church of God is a spiritual organism, not a physical organization. The word *church* is translated from the Greek word *ekklesia,* meaning *a calling out* (Strong's #1577). "But ye are a chosen generation, a royal priesthood, an holy nation, a peculiar people; that ye should shew forth the praises of him who hath *called you out* of darkness into his marvelous light: (1 Peter 2:9). This calling out of God began on the Day of Pentecost following the ascension of Jesus Christ. God poured out His Spirit on the disciples, and over the next several days He "added to the church daily those who were being saved" (Acts 2:47). These were repentant people who "gladly received" the truth of God and were baptized —symbolizing their acceptance of the sacrificial death of Christ for forgiveness of their sins and burial of their old sinful ways.

Believers cannot simply "join" the Church the way you might a local congregation, members are placed by God into His Church. Jesus said, "No man can come to me, except the Father which hath sent me draw him ..." (John 6:44), and "... unless it has been granted him from the Father" (v. 65). God initiates the calling and leads a person to repentance and baptism.

Christ is the Head of the Church, and all of its members are His begotten family. "Blessed be the God and Father of our Lord Jesus Christ, which according to his abundant mercy hath *begotten us again* unto a lively hope by the resurrection of Jesus Christ from the dead" (1 Peter 1:3). "And hath put all things under his feet, and gave him to be the head over all things to the church, Which is his body, the fulness of him that filleth all in all" (Ephesians 1:22-23). These brothers in Christ make up "the body of Christ."

It is the mission of the Church to preach the gospel (good news) of the coming Kingdom of God to all nations as a witness (Matthew 24:14), and help reconcile to God such people as are now being called. The Church does not make financial gain of the gospel, its outreach to the world is free of charge, "freely ye have received, freely give" (Matthew 10:8). The Church also has the responsibility to strengthen, edify, and nurture the children of God in the love and admonition of Jesus Christ.

The Church provides a powerful message of hope through its preaching work coupled with the combined testimony of the individual lives of its members. "Let your light so shine before men, that they may see your good works, and glorify your Father which is in heaven" (Matthew 5:16).

God gives each member of the Church spiritual gifts for the edification of the body. "Now there are diversities of gifts, but the same Spirit. And there are differences of administrations, but the same Lord. And there are diversities of operations, but it is the same God which worketh all in all. But the manifestation of the Spirit is given to every man to profit withal" (1 Corinthians 12:4-7). The Church also provides a haven for fellowship (Acts 2:42; 1 John 1:7), encouragement (Hebrews 3:13; 10:24), and spiritual nourishment (Ephesians 5:29; Colossians 2:19).

Members of God's Church are His "special people" (Titus 2:14; 1 Peter 2:9), transformed by the renewing of their minds through the power of God's Holy Spirit (Romans 12:2). Loving one another establishes their credibility as disciples of Jesus Christ. "A new commandment I give unto you, That ye love one another; as I have loved you, that ye also love one another. By this shall all men know that ye are my disciples, *if ye have love one to another*" (John 13:34-35).

Christ promised His Church would never die (Matthew 16:18) and that He would never leave nor forsake His true followers (Hebrews 13:5). He promised to be with His people "even to the end of the age" (Matthew 28:19-20), empowering them to do His work. When Jesus returns to this earth to establish the Kingdom of God, His Church will rule with Him (Revelation 2:26; 3:21; 5:10; Daniel 7:22, 26-27), having become teachers and judges (I Corinthians 6:1-3).

ARE YOU CALLED?

"[M]any are called, but few are chosen" (Matthew 22:14). If the issues discussed in this article have struck a nerve with you, it is possible God is calling you into a deeper understanding of His will. If you see the corruption in today's religious organizations and in the actions of many professing Christians on this compound, know that you are not alone.

There will continue to be many among the Church who do not know God, all the way up to the return of Christ (Matthew 13:25-40). These are the ones that the world focuses on, "And many shall follow their pernicious ways; by reason of whom *the way of truth* shall be evil spoken of" (Peter 2:2).

Not everyone who says they are your brother, nor every organization who claims to be the Church, is what they say. If you have attempted to apply Scriptural remedies to your problems with other professing Christians to no avail, the problem *is not* with the Scriptures.

Examine your heart today (2 Corinthians 13:5-8). Consider the actions of those you associate with (Luke 6:22; 1 Corinthians 5:11), as well as others who take to themselves the name of Christ. Can you see Him in them? Are they showing forth the fruits of His Spirit? (Galatians 5:19-23). Are you? ✍

If you are interested in learning more about the *way of life* that is Christianity, and the Church as it is described in the Bible, please request a free copy of *The Ten Commandments* and *The Church Jesus Built*. Both booklets will be sent to you absolutely free of charge, when you write to:

United Church of God
P.O. Box 541027
Cincinnati, OH 45254-
1027.

Authenticity

By Garry W. Johnson
MOUNTAIN REVIEW Staff

Chaplain's Corner

By Chaplain Dean Yancey
"Communicating With God" (Part 1)

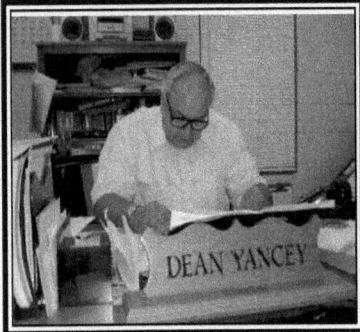

The vital and blessed fellowship of the believer with the Father and the Son is the unfailing evidence of having experienced the saving grace of God. Without being saved, you cannot communicate with God except to pray the prayer of repentance. Jesus tells His disciples, "Now we know that God heareth not sinners: but if any man be a worshiper of God, and doeth his will, him he heareth" (John 9:31). The redemptive purpose of God is fulfilled in the communion of the redeemed soul with God.

Prayer, in the highest sense, is the communion of the believer with God, in which the believer speaks to God and God, in turn, speaks to the believer. Even before time as we know it, God communicated with Himself. All through the creation we find that "God said." We even find in the very beginning of time that God communicated with man. He actually walked and talked with Adam and Eve.

We can see through Scripture that praying is more than supplicating to God for our needs, but that it is God revealing Himself to the one who prays. As we communicate with God, He will reveal himself through an intimate relationship. Therefore, the better the communication with God, the better the relationship with God.

The prayer life of many is unsatisfactory because there is a lack of understanding as to the conditions governing prayer. In order to get your prayers answered, you must have a forgiving spirit. Jesus tells us, "And when ye stand praying, forgive, if ye have ought against any, that your Father also which is in heaven may forgive you your trespasses" (Mark 11:25). Some do not get their prayers answered simply because they lack a proper motive. James tells us, "Ye ask, and receive not, because ye ask amiss, that ye may consume it upon your lusts" (James 4:3).

Also, we must be persistent in our asking. Some, today, believe that it is a lack of faith to ask more than once for your needs. Not so, to ask more than once is to show dependence on God for your needs. Do you remember when you were a child and you asked your parents for a dollar to spend? If you will remember, you kept asking until you saw them start to respond. Then you became quiet and waited with anticipation. I believe we do God the same way. Keep asking until He starts to respond, then be still and watch God work. Jesus tells us, "And I say unto you, Ask, and it shall be given you; seek, and ye shall find; knock, and it shall be opened unto you" (Luke 11:9). The words "ask, seek, knock" are present imperative in the Greek language which means, "keep asking, keep seeking, and keep knocking."

When we ask, we should ask in faith. Jesus instructs us to pray in faith, believing. "Therefore I say unto you, What things soever ye desire, when ye pray, believe that ye receive them, and ye shall have them" (Mark 11:24). You can have all the faith that you need, but if your prayer is not in accordance with God's will, it will not happen. John tells us, "And this is the confidence that we have in him, that, if we ask any thing according to his will, he heareth us: And if we know that he hears us, whatsoever we ask, we know that we have the petitions that we desired of him" (1 John 5:14-15). God wants all that we do to be in His will for our life. If He gives us the things that we want outside His will, He will be fighting against Himself. Our will should be inside His will for our life. This shows that you are obedient to his divine commands and if you are, you can have what you ask. "And whatsoever we ask,

we receive of him, because we keep his commandments, and do those things that are pleasing in his sight" (1 John 3:22).

Being obedient to God is abiding in Christ, and when we abide in Christ, we will get our prayers answered. "If ye abide in me, and my words abide in you, ye shall ask what ye will, and it shall be done unto you" (John 15:7). Jesus says, "If you abide in me," (that means be saved), "My words abide in you," (that means live it), "Ask what you will and it shall be done unto you," (He will answer your prayers). Knowing that Jesus said this, we should pray everything in His name. He tells us in John 16:23 "And in that day ye shall ask me nothing. Verily, verily, I say unto you, Whatsoever ye shall ask the Father in my name, he will give it you."

I have been asked numerous times about to whom we are to pray. Should we pray to God, should we pray to Jesus, or is it OK to pray to the Holy Spirit? It is OK to pray to God. Luke tells us, "Peter therefore was kept in prison: but prayer was made without ceasing of the church unto God for him" (Acts 12:5). Luke also tells us when Stephen was stoned to death, that he called out to Jesus. "And they stoned Stephen, calling upon God, and saying, Lord Jesus, receive my spirit" (Acts 7:59).

There is no scriptural precedent for praying to the Holy Spirit, but we are urged to pray in the Spirit. "Praying always with all prayer and supplication in the Spirit, and watching thereunto with all perseverance and supplication for all saints" (Eph. 6:18). My opinion is that we should pray to the Father, by the authority of Jesus Christ, in the power of the Holy Spirit.

If we can pray and get our prayers answered, the question asked is: For whom should we pray? First of all, we are to pray for ourselves. Jesus prayed for himself. "These words spake Jesus, and lifted up his eyes to heaven, and said, Father, the hour is come; glorify thy Son, that thy Son also may glorify thee" (John 17:1). I am sure that there are times when every one of us needs to pray for himself. I know that for me I have to pray for myself on a daily basis. I pray for safety, for healing, for forgiveness, just to name a few. I believe that praying for ourselves daily helps us to be dependent on God for the things that we as individuals need.

Secondly, we should pray for one another. The love that we have for our fellow Christian brothers and sisters, family, and friends should compel us to pray for them. Being that we can communicate with God and know that He hears us is not only a privilege but a responsibility that we have to stand in the gap for those who cannot reach God. James tells us, "Confess your faults one to another, and pray one for another, that ye may be healed. The effectual fervent prayer of a righteous man availeth much" (James 5:16).

The Bible teaches us to pray for ministers also. I realize with all the bad publicity the media is giving ministers these days, not all ministers are out to get your money. The Word tells us to pray that the ministers will have freedom to preach the Word. "Praying always with all prayer and supplication in the Spirit, and watching thereunto with all perseverance and supplication for all saints; And for me, that utterance may be given unto me, that I may open my mouth boldly, to make known the mystery of the gospel, For which I am an ambassador in bonds: that therein I may

speak boldly, as I ought to speak" (Eph. 6:18-20). Paul also tells us to pray that the ministers will receive the word to preach. "Withal praying also for us, that God would open unto us a door of utterance, to speak the mystery of Christ, for which I am also in bonds" (Col. 4:3).

Quite naturally we should pray for the sick. We will always have the sick with us. Sometimes we get sick and it is always good knowing that someone who loves us is praying for you. James tells us how we are to pray for the sick when we are at church. "Is any sick among you? let him call for the elders of the church; and let them pray over him, anointing him with oil in the name of the Lord: And the prayer of faith shall save the sick, and the Lord shall raise him up; and if he have committed sins, they shall be forgiven him" (James 5:14-15).

Not only should we pray for our loved ones and fellow Christians, but we should also pray for our enemies. Jesus tells us, "Bless them that curse you, and pray for them which despitefully use you" (Luke 6:28). I believe that praying for your enemies cause them to become your friends. Years ago, when I worked as a firefighter, one of the Captains disliked me. He knew that he could not fire me because of Civil Service, but he would try to make me miserable enough to quit. I started praying for him every night. Each morning it seemed that he would be even harder on me, but I continued to pray. During this time, I went up for promotion to pumper operator. When I went before the fire commission, there he stood. As they started interviewing me, he told them that I was the best fireman that he had and I got the promotion. I believe it was because of prayer that changed his heart. Since then, we have been good friends. Prayer can change your enemy's heart.

We should also pray for Israel. The people of Israel are God's chosen people and He told them hundreds of years ago that those who blessed Israel would be blessed and those that cursed Israel would be cursed. I think I would rather be blessed by God than to be cursed. Paul even stated, "Brethren, my heart's desire and prayer to God for Israel is, that they might be saved" (Romans 10:1).

Lastly, we should pray for our rulers. We need to pray that they will make decisions according to the will of God. Paul tells Timothy, "I exhort therefore, that, first of all, supplications, prayers, intercessions, and giving of thanks, be made for all men; For kings, and for all that are in authority; that we may lead a quiet and peaceable life in all godliness and honesty. For this is good and acceptable in the sight of God our Saviour" (1 Timothy 2:1-3).

"Chaplain's Corner" will be a regular feature in the **Mountain Review** written by MCCX Chaplain, Dean Yancey. In the first series of articles, Chaplain Yancey will be explaining the Christian practice of prayer, taken from his book, *Communicating With God.*

Crock's Puzzle Fun

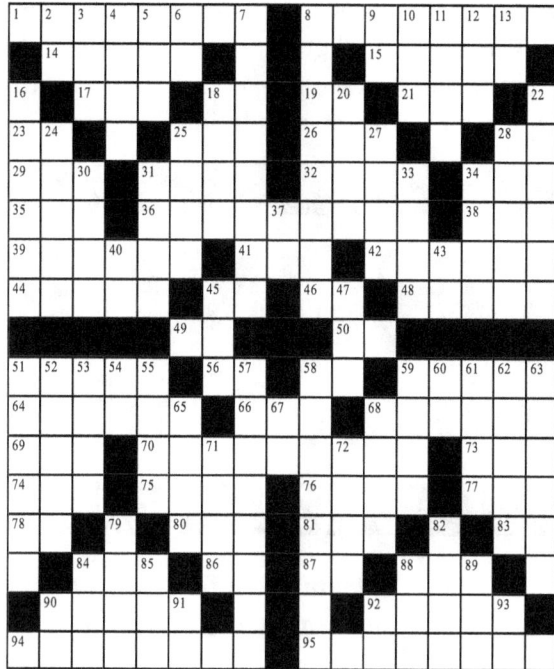

ACROSS

1. Grooming aid
8. Grocer
14. Arise
15. He said "Nevermore"
17. Transgression of the law
18. Mr. Bundy
19. For example
21. Rec room
23. News service
25. French friend
26. Stir-fry cooker
28. Morning
29. With "ble," three fold
31. Garry & Jeremy do
32. Agog
34. Page (abr.)
35. The ___-squad
36. T.B.S. founder
38. In the manner of
39. Canadian peninsula
41. Mind-altering drug
42. Trimmer
44. ___ ___ is an island
45. NBC's parent company
46. And?
48. Section of L.A.
49. Penn's state
50. 7-up, the ___-cola
51. Bend low
56. Prosecutor
58. Vols' college
59. Armor plates
64. With "off," wanes
66. Heavy weight
68. Separated
69. 18th, 23rd, 5th of 26
70. Tina's ex
73. Yes, in Paris
74. Ms. Landers
75. Iron ___ Tyson
76. Snaky fish
77. 16th, 4th, 3rd of 26
78. With "ro," fireworks
80. Can beat a sword?
81. Consumed
83. "Phone home"
84. Year of birth (abr.)
86. Pierre's state
87. Gilligan's ship, ___ Minnow
88. Mr. Flemming
90. Ran
92. Intended
94. French gold coin
95. One's in the running?

DOWN

2. Disclaimer, "___ is"
3. ___ a good thing
4. Precipitation
5. News network
6. Overdose
7. Disparage
8. Managers
9. Oak Ridge (abr.)
10. Groovy
11. "What ____"
12. Guys
13. ___ apple a day ...
16. Robin's pal
18. In the thick of
20. Long dress
22. Smudges
24. City in Utah
25. Port in Yemen
27. 21.2 long tons
28. Clothing ornament
30. Yellow Dutch cheese
31. Town in Berkshire
33. Sketched
34. Breathe heavily
37. We
40. I love __
43. Alcoholics Anonymous, in short
45. Just on the go
47. Down and ___
51. Whips
52. Brownish orange
53. Not closed
54. Old English (abr.)
55. Proper
57. Goer
58. Madness
59. Prepares for paving
60. Little Rock's state
61. Quit
62. Blue ____ shoes
63. Orders
65. Omit
67. Letters on Sooner's helmet
68. Soccer legend
71. Gets by
72. Fish catchers
79. Arizona Indian
82. To Condemn
84. Just ___ and I ...
85. It ___ like that sometimes
88. Roman 3
89. Born
90. __ and behold
91. Ike's first 2 initials
92. What kind of fool __ I?
93. Delaware

Edited by Garry W. Johnson, MOUNTAIN REVIEW Staff

Dave's Cryptograms

Dave's Cryptograms are created from Biblical quotes. Each letter in the puzzle stand for another.

Clue: Y equals U

C XCBNFNCTNT TNANCBNXE INDTNXI:

FYX EN XECX ZI JG C GCZXEGYB

IHZTZX DJKDNCBNXE XEN LCXXNT.

Original cryptograms produced by David Pendleton

Search the World - Word Search

```
L A G U T R O P Q K
U P D T E X A S D V
X S A S N A K F N I
E F R A N C E I A R
M A I N E E A O L G
B Z A K S P V W O I
O E D N S R T A P N
U C I R E L A N D I
R E R X E P B H G A
G E O R G I A A T S
A R L H Y W L T K U
R G F Z I T A L Y R
N O G E R O S A F P
D E N M A R K M R Y
M R G E R M A N Y C
```

Words may appear forwards or backwards, straight or diagonally.

Can you find ...

12 of the 25 EU member nations? & 12 of the 50 U.S. States?

By Garry W. Johnson, Staff Writer

Submitted by Judy Johnson from internet e-mail

This will boggle your mind, I know it did mine! The year is 1906; one hundred and one years ago. What a difference a century makes!

Here are some of the U.S. statistics for the year 1906:

The average life expectancy in the U.S. was 47 years.

Only 14% of the homes in the U.S. had a bathtub. Only 8% of the homes had a telephone. A three-minute call from Denver to New York City cost eleven dollars.

There were only 8,000 cars in the U.S., and only 144 miles of paved roads. The maximum speed limit in most cities was 10 mph.

Alabama, Mississippi, Iowa, and Tennessee were each more heavily populated than California. With a mere 1.4 million people, California was only the 21st most populous state in the Union.

The tallest structure in the world was the Eiffel Tower!

The average wage in the U.S. was 22 cents per hour. The average U.S. worker made between $200 and $400 per year. A competent accountant could expect to earn $2,000 per year, a dentist $2,500 per year, a veterinarian between $1,500 and $4,000 per year, and a mechanical engineer about $5,000 per year.

More than 95% of all births in the U.S. took place at home. Ninety percent of all U.S. doctors had no college education. Instead, they attended so-called medical schools, many of which were

The year 1906

condemned in the press and by the government as "substandard."

Sugar cost four cents a pound. Eggs were fourteen cents a dozen. Coffee was fifteen cents a pound.

Most women only washed their hair once a month and used borax or egg yolks for shampoo.

Canada passed a law that prohibited poor people from entering into their country for any reason.

The five leading causes of death in the U.S. were: 1. Pneumonia and influenza; 2. Tuberculosis; 3. Diarrhea; 4. Heart disease; 5. Stroke.

The American flag had 45 stars. Arizona, Oklahoma, New Mexico, Hawaii, and Alaska hadn't been admitted to the Union yet. The population of Las Vegas, Nevada, was only 30!

Crossword puzzles, canned beer, and ice tea hadn't been invented yet. There was no Mother's Day or Father's Day.

Two out of every 10 U.S. adults couldn't read or write. Only 6% of all Americans had graduated from high school. Marijuana, heroin, and morphine were all available over the counter at the local corner drugstores. Back then, pharmacists said, "Heroin clears the complexion, gives buoyancy to the mind, regulates the stomach and bowels, and is, in fact, a perfect guardian of health."

Eighteen percent of households in the U.S. had at least one full-time servant or domestic help.

There were about 230 reported murders in the entire U.S.

Try to imagine what it may be like in another 100 years. ✍

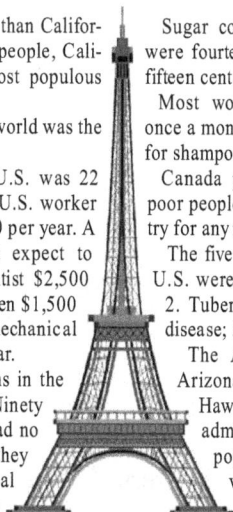

141

Answers to puzzles on page 26:

Dave's Cryptogram:

"A talebearer revealeth secrets: But he that is of a faithful spirit concealeth the matter."

Search the World:

12 of the 25 EU nations—
1) Cyprus, 2) Denmark, 3) France, 4) Germany, 5) Greece, 6) Ireland, 7) Italy, 8) Luxembourg, 9) Malta, 10) Poland, 11) Portugal, 12) Spain

12 of the 50 U.S. states—
1) Alaska, 2) Florida, 3) Georgia, 4) Iowa, 5) Kansas, 6) Maine, 7) Nevada, 8) Ohio, 9) Oregon, 10) Tennessee, 11) Texas, 12) Virginia

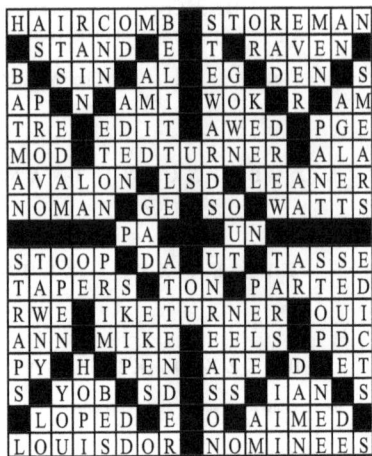

The *Mountain Review* was produced as a free government document written by prisoners at Brushy Mountain State Penitentiary and Morgan County Correctional Complex. It was sponsored by the Education Department at those facilities and was a censored publication. Permission to reprint was granted in this section of each edition. The views expressed are those of individual authors.

PRISONER Resource Guide
2021 Edition

American Bible Society
101 N Independence Mall East, Floor 8
Philadelphia, PA 19106-2155
americanbible.org
215.309.0900
Free Bibles, including large print and study guides. They can arrange with a chaplain to have books sent if necessary. Will send books in Spanish upon requests.

American Psychological Association
750 First St. NE
Washington DC 20002
apa.org
800.374.2721
Education, information, and publications.

A.R. Simmons Jacobs McNamee (SMJ) Family Preservation Campus, Inc.
4130-4150 Farm Market Road 123, Box 163
Deberry, Texas 75639
thesjmgroup.com
214.699.8973
Formerly the SMJ Family Foundation, they oversee several organizations. Their website links to several free resources and downloadable publications for prisoners.

Church of God, A Worldwide Association
P.O. Box 731480
Dallas, TX 75373-1480
cogwa.org
LifeHopeandTruth.com
Publishers of a free Christian magazine, booklets, and a plethora of online materials through there expansive websites.

Art of Prison Survival
Prison Foundation
2512 Virginia Ave, NW #58043
Washington, DC 20037
prisonsfounfation.org
202.383.1511
A bimonthly publication including profiles of prison artists, previews of prison art to be exhibited at upcoming Prison Foundation shows news of prisoners, staff, activists and programs that are improving the prison environment. Available to prisoners for a $2 donation (postage stamps accepted) and to non prisoner for a donation of $25.

Center for Constitutional Rights
666 Broadway, 7th Fl.
New York, NY 10012
ccrjustice.org
Offers publications including the Jailhouse Lawyers Handbook.

Campaign for the Fair Sentencing of Youth
℅ Community Organizer
1090 Vermont Ave. NW, Ste. 400
Washington, DC 20005
fairsentencingofyouth.org
202.289.4673
A national coalition and clearinghouse that coordinates, develops and supports efforts to implement just alternatives to the extreme sentencing of America's youth with a focus on abolishing life without parole sentences for all youths. The campaign does not provide direct legal representation.

Centurion Ministries
221 Witherspoon St.
Princeton, NJ 08542
Legal assistance only for those convicted of murder or rape and sentenced to death or life without parole; only for those who have hard evidence of actual innocence.

Coalition of Prison Evangelist (COPE)
2400 Ludelle St. #400
Ft. Worth, TX 76105
817.535.1218
Provides a national referral network for visitation/emergency needs. Links families with local churches.

Winter 2007/2008
Volume 20, Number 4

MOUNTAIN REVIEW

A Morgan County Correctional Complex Publication

MCCX honors its volunteers
This year's Volunteer Banquet expressed the gratitude and appreciation we all feel for those who give of their time and energy to help us overcome and succeed 11

This Issue Focuses On

Criminal Trends

Corporate crime and punishment

Should corporate officers and members of boards of directors who are convicted of practices harmful to employees, investors and the public be sent to jail?

Yes 89%
Don't know 4%
No 7%

10

10

Source: Pepperdine University Graziadio School of Business and Management Corporate Board survey of 482 adults 18 and older. Margin of error +/- 5 percentage points.

—By Garry W. Johnson, MOUNTAIN REVIEW

Christmas Banquets have huge impact on inmates

By Jeremy Ingram
MOUNTAIN REVIEW Staff

For those of you not familiar with David "Bulldog" Presley, you can see how impoverished he was. But thanks to East Tennessee churches, who came to his rescue, Bulldog was able to put on some much needed weight. Over a dozen churches and ministries graciously donated their time and money to feed the entire population of Morgan County Correctional Complex and provide treat bags for every inmate. Check out the center page layout for pictures, recognitions, and thanks for their dedication and service. One more thing, is it just me, or did anyone else notice Bulldog's weight gain happened when his cellie became missing? Coincidence? On behalf of the population of Morgan County Correctional Complex, we wish to sincerely thank all the people that helped make this Christmas a little more like home. ✍

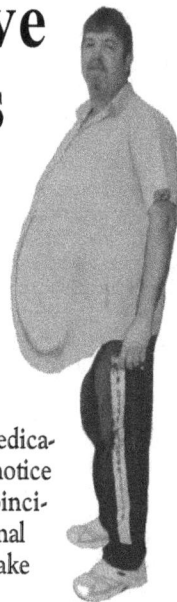

Punishment for ex-cons does not always end after prison

By Garry W. Johnson
MOUNTAIN REVIEW Staff

Prison life is not any fun. Being denied our freedom, an endless list of personal choices, and the comforts of life most U.S. citizens take for granted is just part of the price we pay for violating the laws of this country. Most of us, however, will not realize the full extent of our sentences until we are released from prison, back into what we now remember as "the free world."

A hodgepodge of state laws around the country can spell big problems for an ex-con trying to rebuild a shattered life. Some ex-convicts in New Jersey cannot get a driver's license, while Alabama bans anyone with a misdemeanor drug conviction from adopting a child. Former felons in 12 states are ineligible for food stamps, and convicted sex-offenders are finding it hard to live, well, anywhere.

These extra sanctions are known as "collateral punishment," and states across the country write them into a variety of laws. Increasingly, lawmakers are pushing to standardize these sanctions which are creating an underclass of people living and working in the United States. Stephen Saltzburg, a law professor at George Washington University and chairman-elect of the American Bar Association's criminal justice section puts it this way: "What we're seeing around the country is prosecutors, defense lawyers, [and] judges all coming to an understanding that just because someone has committed a crime and

had to pay a price for it, doesn't mean they should be relegated forever to second-class citizenship."

The Bureau of Justice Statistics reported in June that the number of people released from prisons and jails has increased 16% since 2000. With record numbers of people leaving prison, thousands of ex-criminals are finding that their convictions bar them from many jobs, state and federal aid, some types of housing and living in many communities. "We've created a class of people who essentially don't fit in," says Marc Mauer of the Sentencing Project, a criminal justice think tank in Washington.

A study released in July by the Marijuana Policy Project, a group that seeks to decriminalize marijuana, found that punishments triggered by a marijuana conviction include restrictions on professional licenses, ineligiblity for many jobs, loss of financial aid for education, housing and food, driver's license suspension, bars on adoption and bans on voting and jury service. "With marijuana offenses, it's common thought that it's a slap on the wrist," says Richard Boire, who conducted the analysis. "But it's not just 30 days in

jail. The unseen part is the sanctions that in some cases can last a lifetime."

Leaving prison
Number of prisoners who have been released from state and federal custody:

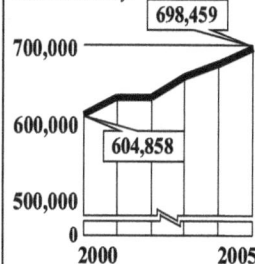

698,459
700,000
600,000
604,858
500,000
0
2000   2005

Note: 2005 is latest year statistics are available
Source: Bureau of Justice Statistics

Nearly one in six Americans, some 48 million of us who have a record, are permanently shut out of many jobs and other opportunities needed to build productive, law-abiding lives. "We're supposed to live in a society where if a person does the crime, they do the time. That's not the reality. You do the crime, but you continue to do the time, sometimes for the rest of your life," says Jesselyn McCurdy, legislative counsel with the American Civil Liberties Union.

Recently released sex-offenders pose special problems in the collateral punishment debate. Residency restrictions and social stigma in many states are creating a growing number of homeless sex-offenders, according to an analysis released in November by *USA Today*. "As sex offenders are more and more in the media, people are starting to think twice before renting to them," says Patty Morris, supervisor of sex-offender compliance at the Arizona Department of Public Safety.

See Released on page 06

Economic independence—the ability to provide for your economic needs —is a major hurdle to overcome for many people. Inmates who return to society unprepared to support themselves and their dependents will, in all probability, cause problems for the community and eventually return to prison. Furthermore, if you find yourself unable to stay free of debt while in prison, (unless you are financing an education) you are definitely unprepared for the free world. [Please take the *TRICOR Economic Independence Survey* below.]

WHAT WE ARE OWED

American society in general has developed an entitlement mentality. Advertisers tell us we "deserve" their new and improved products, and most of us willingly believe them. Yesterday's luxuries are increasingly becoming today's necessities.

Coupled with the ever growing list of things we "need," credit in the recent past was ridiculously easy to come by. Credit card companies went wild, upping limits on cards by more than a third in the 90's alone. Banks shamelessly peddled plastic as the way for those left behind to live the good life. They promoted the idea of "post-saving"—buying on credit and paying over time—as opposed to the idea of saving money until one could actually afford a big purchase.

The result of these and other predatory lending practices has turned the U.S. into a nation of debtors. In July, the average U.S. credit card holder owed $8,400! That figure is up $900 from last February's average of $7,500. The average card holder in 1995 owed $1,300, in 1983 it was $700, and in 1970 the average was only $185. Today, the average American household carries a total debt worth 118% of its annual income.

TIME TO TAKE ACTION

Although credit and credit cards are widely abused, they can be and often are essential tools to financial success—*when used properly*.

Credit cards can be a wonderful convenience and a good way to develop new credit. They eliminate the need to carry cash and make distant transactions possible by means of the telephone and Internet. They should be used, however, only when the cardholder is capable of completely paying off his balance at the end of each month.

Before applying for a credit card, you will want to check your credit history. Do not contact the credit bureaus directly for this. Free annual credit reports are now available by visiting the website www.annualcreditreport.com, calling 887-322-8228, or writing to:

Annual Credit Report Request Service
P.O. Box 105283
Atlanta, GA 30348

Once you have obtained a copy of your credit report, review it closely. If you find any fraudulently opened accounts or other suspicious activity, you may be the victim of identity theft.

While I was in the county jail, I learned of a guy who was giving his girlfriend names and Social Security numbers from inmate commissary forms. Through seemingly casual conversation he would inquire about a potential mark's date of birth. If successful in obtaining this information, he would then have everything she needed to open utility and charge accounts in the inmate's name. Just because you are locked up, does not mean someone else is not using your credit.

Money matters: Self analysis
By Garry W. Johnson
MOUNTAIN REVIEW Staff

If you think you have become a victim of identity theft or fraud, take action immediately.

Contact one of the three major credit bureaus to have them place a fraud alert in your file. This will require that creditors contact you before opening new accounts in your name or changing information on existing accounts. Once the alert is activated, the other two credit bureaus will be notified. If you are still incarcerated, you may want to consider having your credit frozen until you get out.

The credit freeze is a new service which went into effect nationwide in November. Once a freeze has been placed on your credit reports, credit card issuers, lenders and others cannot review the summary of loans and payments that makes up your credit history. Without that information, lenders will not issue credit in your name.

Unlike the free fraud alert, the credit freeze will cost you. At the time of this writing, Equifax had not provided details on their fees, but Trans Union and Experian set the rate at $10 each. Assuming Equifax follows suit, a freeze on your credit files will run you $30 (the service is free to victims of identity theft).

If you are not incarcerated and are actively using your credit, you might want to think twice about freezing your files. Each time you apply for a mortgage, car loan or other type of credit you will have to temporarily suspend the freeze, which will cost you another $30. You might also need to suspend the freeze to get an insurance policy, utility service, an apartment, activate a cell phone, or even get a job. Many people are unaware of just how often their credit histories are reviewed and just how important their credit is. In the next edition of *Money Matters,* we will be looking at how to build and repair damaged and nonexistent credit.

In the mean time, if you would like to further analyze your financial situation or begin planning for your future, you can obtain the free booklet *Managing Your Finances,* by mailing a request to the Christian living magazine:

The Good News
P.O. Box 541027
Cincinnati, OH 45254-1027

In this booklet you will find a form for determining your net worth, a monthly income and expense worksheet, a buying self-test, and contact information for the Consumer Credit Counseling Service. The booklet is provided as a free educational service in the public interest and is yours for the asking. ✍

CREDIT BUREAU CONTACTS:

Equifax
P.O. Box 740241
Atlanta, GA 30374-0241
Reports: 800-685-1111
Fraud alerts: 800-525-6285
www.equifax.com

Experian (formerly TRW)
P.O. Box 2002
Allen, TX 75013
Reports and fraud alerts:
888-EXPERIAN
www.experian.com

Trans Union
Reports: P.O. Box 1000
Chester, PA 19022
800-888-4213
Fraud alerts: P.O. Box 6790
Fullerton, CA 92834
www.transunion.com

To determine your economic independence, circle the number beside the statement that best describes you. After indicating your answers for each question, add up the circled numbers and compare the total with the "Scoring." (Some questions will require basing your answers upon your lifestyle just before you entered prison).

1. 0 I didn't miss any days from school or work during the last two weeks.
    1 I missed one day from school or work during the last two weeks.
    2 I missed several days from school or work in the last two weeks.
    3 I didn't go to work or school during the last two weeks.

2. 0 I do my work well.
    1 I do my work well, but have minor problems.
    2 I need help with work.
    3 I do my work poorly most of the time.

3. 0 I don't have arguments at school or work.
    1 I usually get along well at school or work.
    2 I have had more than one argument in the last two weeks.
    3 I have many arguments at school or work.

4. 0 I never feel upset at work.
    1 Once or twice a week, I feel upset at work.
    2 I feel upset most of the time at work.
    3 I feel upset all of the time at work.

5. 0 My work is always interesting.
    1 Occasionally, my work is not interesting.
    2 My work is usually boring.
    3 My work is always boring.

6. 0 I'm not afraid to take risks in my work.
    1 I'm usually not afraid to take risks in my work.
    2 I'm sometimes afraid to take risks in my work.
    3 I'm very afraid to take risks in my work.

7. 0 I don't explain myself or my points too much at work.
    1 I sometimes explain myself or my points too much at work.
    2 I often explain myself or my points at work.
    3 I over explain myself and my points at work.

8. 0 I'm not excessively worried about money.
    1 I worry about money occasionally.
    2 I worry about money frequently.
    3 I worry excessively about money.

9. 0 I pay my bills on time as soon as I can.
    1 I sometimes pay my bills late.
    2 I often pay my bills late.
    3 I always pay my bills late.

10. 0 I keep track of my financial records.
    1 My financial records are pretty much up to date.
    2 I am behind in my financial records.
    3 My financial records are hopelessly incomplete.

11. 0 I eventually pay all my bills.
    1 I usually pay all of my bills.
    2 I occasionally don't pay a bill.
    3 I don't pay my bills.

12. 0 I don't buy things for status.
    1 I sometimes buy things for status.
    2 I usually buy things for status.
    3 I always buy things for status.

13. 0 I'm employed at my level of training and education.
    1 I'm employed slightly below my level of education and training.
    2 I'm employed below my level of education and training.
    3 I'm employed very much below my level of education and training.

14. 0 I don't rely on others for money.
    1 I sometimes rely on others for money.
    2 I often rely on others for money.
    3 I always rely on others for money.

15. 0 I don't spend more than I make.
    1 I sometimes spend more than I make.
    2 I often spend more than I make.
    3 I spend more money than I make.

16. 0 I have made financial plans for the future.
    1 I have made most of my financial plans for the future.
    2 I have made some of my financial plans for the future.
    3 I am unable to make financial plans for the future.

17. 0 I am not a compulsive spender.
    1 I occasionally spend compulsively.
    2 I often spend compulsively.
    3 I always spend compulsively.

18. 0 I am not in debt.
    1 I am slightly in debt.
    2 I am somewhat in debt.
    3 I am heavily in debt.

19. 0 I do not rely on others to know how to invest my money.
    1 I sometimes rely on others to know how to invest my money.
    2 I usually rely on others to know how to invest my money.
    3 I always rely on others to know how to invest my money.

20. 0 I have an employable job skill.
    1 I have some employable job skills.
    2 I have few employable job skills.
    3 I have no employable job skills.

21. 0 I am always upgrading my (employable) skills.
    1 I frequently upgrade my skills.
    2 I seldom upgrade my skills.
    3 I never upgrade my employable skills.

22. 0 I pay my bills on time.
    1 I have some trouble paying my bills on time.
    2 I have a great deal of trouble paying my bills on time.
    3 I can't seem to pay my bills on time.

23. 0 I'm able to balance the money coming in with the money going out.
    1 I have some trouble balancing the money coming in with the money going out.
    2 I have a great deal of trouble balancing the money coming in with the money going out.
    3 I can't seem to balance the money coming in with the money going out.

24. 0 I have my own source of money.
    1 I provide most of my money.
    2 I provide some of my own money.
    3 I count upon others for all my money.

25. 0 I can manage my money independently.
    1 I can manage my money, but have occasionally forgotten to pay a bill or overdrew my checking acct.
    2 I manage day-to-day purchases, but need help with banking or major purchases.
    3 I can't handle my money.

26. 0 My future financial picture is in order.
    1 My future financial picture is untidy.
    2 My future financial picture is a mess.
    3 My future financial picture is a disaster.

27. 0 I am not in debt.
    1 I am mildly in debt.
    2 I am heavily in debt.
    3 I am bankrupt or nearly bankrupt.

—————————SCORING:—————————

0 to 6:	High level of economic independence
7 to 17:	Moderate level of economic independence
18 to 25:	Low level of economic independence
25 or Above:	A severe problem with economic independence

On September 13, 2007, Verna Wyatt, Executive Director of "You Have the Power," talked with the Pre-Release class and other invited guests about her experience as a victim of violent crime. What follows is a summation of what she said.

Martha was a funny, smart teacher. She had previously earned two degrees, one from the University of Tennessee and the other from Vanderbilt. She was in the process of earning her doctorate when she became missing. Martha was not your traditional teacher. She traveled to students' homes, because the students she taught were too sick to go to a regular school.

The night that Martha failed to come home, her husband and two boys knew something was wrong. Being out late without calling was unusual for Martha. Eventually, her family filed a missing person's report with the police, but there was no follow up. The next day, Martha's family and friends searched for her. This search lasted for days. Eventually, one of Martha's students told Martha's husband that he had seen her car outside his home all day long. In fact, Martha's books had been laid on the kitchen table—the place where she normally puts her books when she tutors a student. Still, the student had not seen Martha all day. Mysteriously, there was no sign of her keys. Three nights of cold weather passed without one word of Martha's whereabouts.

News of Martha's death was first reported on television, as images of her lifeless body being pulled from the Cumberland River filtered into the living rooms of her family. Martha had been stripped from the waist up, tied with an electrical cord around her ankles and a belt around her neck, and wrapped in a dirty bed linen. One of her earlobes had been ripped off. Apparently, it was determined that Martha was alive but unconscious when she was thrown into the river—awakened by the sharp coldness of the water, only to die by drowning.

An investigation linked the items found on Martha's body with the aforementioned student's house. Remarkably, a woman watching the news report recognized the house. Weeks earlier, a man had offered her a ride. The man, being well-dressed and nice, did not seem to be a threat. He took this woman to his house and raped her at gunpoint. This woman later escaped. Consequently, the man turned out to be the student's mom's live-in boyfriend. Apparently, he found out that Martha had rescheduled her tutoring session for the day, and he arranged for them to be alone. Martha's keys were eventually found under a couch in the student's home, explained by a struggle and a wise choice to "hide" the keys, so the live-in boyfriend could not move her car. This was the pivotal piece of evidence that led to his conviction.

During the criminal proceedings in court, they offered the defendant a deal of life plus thirty for both crimes. In a later Post-Conviction hearing, he told the victim's family, "I feel like a victim," because he thought he had ineffective counsel.

Verna Wyatt, Executive Director of "You Have the Power," was the sister-in-law and best friend of Martha. Martha's murder devastated Ms. Wyatt. She described violent thoughts directed toward Martha's killer following the crime. Ms. Wyatt was spiritually devastated—it took her a long time to recover from the loss she was forced to endure. However, she admits that amid the darkness of the circumstances, God brought her blessings. She eventually found a different attitude about life, a true knowledge of God, and a stronger faith. However, immediately following the crime, she possessed no answers.

Describing her feelings of being a victim, Ms. Wyatt says that it is like being cut really deep. At first, moving without the cut hurting is hard. However, once the wound heals, the scar is always there. "You just have to learn to live with it," she said. Learning to live with it was not easy for Ms. Wyatt. A particular instance recounted by Ms. Wyatt illustrates the pain through which she went. At the Post Conviction hearing, she heard Martha's killer describe himself as a victim. Ms. Wyatt admits being furious when she heard this. After the hearing, she realized that she could not live with the anger and bitterness any longer.

Ms. Wyatt eventually reached out to others for help. One of the many people she wrote was Andrea Conté, the Governor of Tennessee's wife. Mrs. Conté, herself a victim of a violent crime, along with Ms. Wyatt, convened a meeting that included many people (police, lawyers, and victims). From this meeting, the organization "You Have the Power" was formed. Some purposes of "You Have the Power" are to inform the public about crime, provide resources for victims, and to facilitate Victim's Impact classes. Ms. Wyatt herself helps facilitate these programs in four prisons in the state of Tennessee. Ms. Wyatt is optimistic about helping inmates. She says that people can change and take responsibility for their lives and move on. She has met many inspiring inmates, but warns that change "has to be something you want."

Just what do victims want? They want the one who committed the crime to take responsibility for his action and admit that he has caused much pain. Ms. Wyatt admitted that some victims want to hear an apology, while others do not. In the end, victims mostly want a changed life—no more victims.

Ms. Wyatt illustrated her thoughts on her attitude toward inmates. She asked the group, "If I offered you a twenty-dollar bill, would anyone want it?" She then asked, "If I wad the bill into a ball, throw it on the floor, and stomp on it, would you still want it?" Of course the answer was affirmative. Her point was that, even amid a life wadded up and thrown to the ground, inmates are still inherently worth something. Just like the twenty-dollar bill, you do not lose your value simply because you came to prison.

Ms. Wyatt works with offenders in more than one capacity. Besides her work in Victim's Impact classes, she is involved in the Genesis Program. This is an intensive twelve-week program. She also works with Men of Faith, a nonprofit, faith-based ministry for inmates in Nashville and some CCA prisons. In this program, each inmate has his own mentor.

In Ms. Wyatt's experience, she understands that the choice to commit a crime usually comes after a lifetime of violence, drug addiction, and alcohol abuse. These, according to Ms. Wyatt, are sometimes symptoms of child abuse. She maintains that growing up in an environment where these symptoms are prevalent, and where domestic abuse is common, often victimize children. Frequently, these children become criminals. Still, people in these situations are presented with a choice.

What is that choice? Ms. Wyatt responds that it is simply the choice to be a survivor, rather than a criminal. Victims do not have a choice concerning what happened to them. However, they do have a choice in how to respond. She mentioned Martha's killer again. During sentencing, they had revealed that he was a victim of domestic violence. Early in his life, at six years old, he witnessed his mother's murder in a drug deal gone bad. Yet, instead of choosing to be a survivor, he chose, instead, to be a criminal.

Ms. Wyatt encouraged everyone present with one last story of an inmate's willingness to be a survivor. This inmate served his time and was released from prison. He had absolutely nothing, except a desire to survive apart from the criminal lifestyle that had characterized his life so far. With twenty-five dollars he had saved from prison, he bought a bike and became a worker at a restaurant near where he lived. With the money he saved from the restaurant, he put himself through college. Still, he had a need for restitution. On his way to work, he always passed a domestic violence center. One day he stopped and told the person in charge that he had been released from prison, he still felt the need to pay back society and the least he could do was mow their grass—this he did. Eventually, he put himself through law school and found himself working as a clerk for a judge. The judge, recognizing this former inmate's drive to change, worked for his eventual pardon.

It has been a common conception among inmates that victims of crime simply do not care whether an inmate changes or not. In many cases, it seems people in the free-world do not think that an inmate can change. Unfortunately, it has been the fault of those who consistently re-offend after being released who give credibility to what many in the free-world believe.

Yet, in the past few years, it seems there are an increasing number of free-world people willing to take the risk and believe there is hope for those who are locked up. It is only when prisoners are given a chance to change—an opportunity to prove to society that they will no longer create victims—will the fruits of people like Ms. Wyatt be justified. On behalf of the group who listened to Ms. Wyatt, I would like to say thank you for your dedication ✐

MCCX hosts "You Have The Power" Executive Director
By Jeremy Ingram
MOUNTAIN REVIEW Staff

Jennie Jobe, Associate Warden of Programs & Rehabilitation, and Verna Wyatt, Executive Director of "You Have the Power."

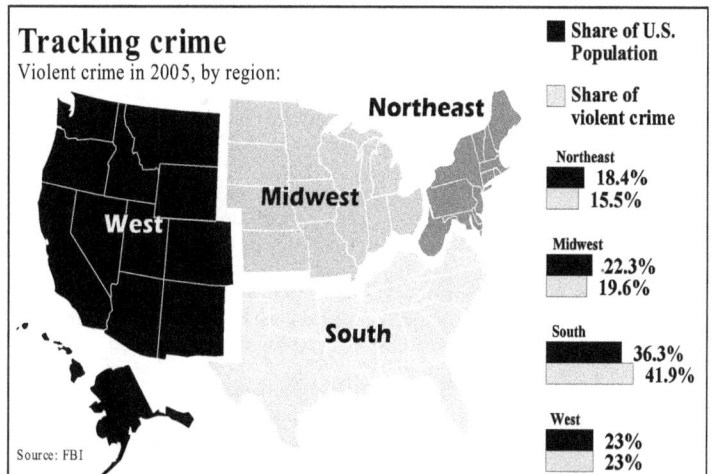

Tracking crime
Violent crime in 2005, by region:

	■ Share of U.S. Population	□ Share of violent crime
Northeast	18.4%	15.5%
Midwest	22.3%	19.6%
South	36.3%	41.9%
West	23%	23%

Source: FBI

The Transitional Assessment Program's purpose is "to establish a component of the classification process that will assist in determining an inmate's transition assessment plan (TAP) at intake and annual updates." According to policy, *all* TDOC inmates housed in state facilities or privately managed facilities shall have a documented assessment plan. The only exception are inmates who receive a death sentence or life without parole. However, if an inmate is sentenced to death or life without parole and their sentence is overturned and a new sentence imposed, a TAP will be created.

Unless you are one of the people noted above, you will have a TAP. This is done at your annual reclassification hearing, or as part of the initial classification process, if you are new to the system. The TAP will include two things: program recommendations and classification action. I will explain each in its turn.

PROGRAM RECOMMENDATIONS

First, when you are reclassified, or as part of your initial classification process, you will be required to sign a Program Recommendation Guide (PRG) (CR-3683). This consists of two pages. Your counselor will explain the PRG using the first page. You can read both pages as part of Policy #513.04. This paper explains that the purpose of a PRG is to "identify the criminogenic needs of offenders during prison intake." The reason someone wants to identify your criminogenic needs is to prioritize which program you should be involved in, improve the decisions at your classification/reclassification hearings, and improve your participation in these programs. The idea is to reduce your chances of re-offending once you get out, making sure there is an improved selection of programs for you, and making sure you participate in these programs. This, in essence, is what TAP is all about—getting you to take programs.

The second page of the PRG is what you will sign at your classification hearing. If you have already been reclassified after March 2007, you have already signed this page. The second page of PRG lists six categories:

1. *Mental Health—Case Management*: This is done by a certified professional. If you are one who needs psychiatric medicine, this will be considered a top priority.

2. *Substance Abuse*: If you tested positive at intake, it will be noted on the PRG. Your score for the substance abuse category is determined by your TCUDS score. If your TCUDS score is high, indicating an identified substance abuse issue, a substance-abuse

class will be among the top program recommendations on your TAP. In fact, if you do not need case-managed mental health treatment, then substance-abuse treatment will be at the top of your priorities.

3. *Mental Health—All other Mental Health Excluding Case Management*: This category is an either/or—either you need a mental health program or you do not.

4. *Education*: If you have a high school diploma or verified GED, then you will score a zero in this category. If, however, you need a GED, your education score will be based on your WRAT score. If you do not have a GED, then this is considered a high priority.

5. *Vocation/Job*: If you need a vocational class, this will be noted here. However, if a vocational class is recommended, this need will be addressed closer to your RED or expiration date.

6. *Special Programs*: These may include STG, Pre-Release, Transition Center, Victim Impact, or any other program recommended by the TDOC.

Each category has a number (anywhere from zero to three), that is chosen based on your perceived needs. These numbers prioritize what areas you most need help with. For instance, if you do not have a high school diploma or a GED, then you will score a three in that category and probably wind up in an academic class. However, if you have a GED or high school diploma, then you will score a zero in the education category, and this will not be a priority during your incarceration.

CLASSIFICATION ACTION

The second part of the TAP is the Transition Assessment Action Plan (TAAP). This is where you get to speak up on what you plan to do about all these recommendations. The TAAP is divided into three parts. The first part is a prioritized listing of the programs you are recommended to take. This comes directly from the PRG. The second part of the TAAP is a section where you are asked how you plan to meet the recommendations. For example, say that I am recommended the Alcohol and Drug Program. I would tell the reclassification panel that I plan to sign up for the class that week, and take the class whenever it is my turn. Then, I would plan on meeting the next program recommendation. The reclassification panel would then set a date to review my progress to ensure I am sticking to my plans. The last part of the TAAP

is where the staff writes down their plans on how you will meet the recommendations.

Both staff and inmates are required to sign these forms at the reclassification hearing. Make sure you read and understand what these two forms say before you sign them. Once you sign them, they will be documented in your file and on TOMIS. If, during your annual reclassification hearing, a program was recommended that would require you to be placed on a register (i.e., Drug and Alcohol Program), then the job coordinator will be notified within seven days of your hearing.

For anyone at a TDOC classification center, once the initial TAP is done, that inmate's institutional assignment will be made based on the first and/or second recommended program.

AT ANNUAL RECLASSIFICATION HEARING:

During your annual reclassification hearing, the reclassification panel will review your progress in the TAP program and update your program recommendations. The two times your program recommendations will be updated are when you are annually reclassified and when you finish a program. TAP reviews, and program recommendation updates, will be entered on TOMIS. Also, the counselor will e-mail the job coordinator within seven working days with any new program recommendations.

A few months ago, a questionnaire was made available to the compound pertaining to the TAP program. Several inmates took the opportunity to complete the questionnaire. Below are listed the questions inmates at MCCX had about the TAP program. Associate Warden Jennie Jobe met with Jim Cosby, Assistant Commissioner of Rehabilitative Services, and RaeAnn Cauglin, Executive Assistant to Mr. Cosby, about the questions raised. Hopefully, these answers will further dispel the mystery surrounding the Transitional Assessment Plan.

QUESTIONS AND ANSWERS ABOUT THE TAP

From this point, to the end of this article, I have simply reprinted what I received from the administration in response to the questions turned in:

Transitional Assessment Plan (TAP)

By Jeremy Ingram
MOUNTAIN REVIEW Staff

1. In Policy 513.04 it states there is an appeals process regarding the TAP recommendations. What is involved in this process?

Ans. The appeals process for TAP recommendations is exactly the same as the appeals process for any classification or re-classification issues. The same forms and process are used.

2. What happens once your TAP recommendations are completed?

Ans. If you are still incarcerated at that time, then you would be assigned to a regular job placement. Please note: if you have other issues arise during your incarceration (i.e. you produce a dirty drug screen or you become physically assaultive), issues that were not present when your TAP was created, then items can be added to the TAP recommendations.

3. After TAP classification recommends programs, will these programs be mandatory?

Ans. That is the goal the entire TAP process is working toward.

4. Will everyone be part of the TAP process?

Ans. Everyone is part of the process except for inmates on death row or those inmates who are sentenced to life without parole.

5. How will the TAP program benefit me?

Ans. The TAP program is intended to point out those areas in which each individual in the Department of Correction needs additional help. An attempt will be made to meet those needs (i.e. provide more educational opportunities, increase the level of social and psychological programs, etc.). It is obvious that there are behaviors that have to change if any inmate in TDOC custody is going to make a positive change in their life that will allow them to remain out of prison once released. The goal of TAP is to pinpoint those needs and to provide services to meet those needs.

6. Am I going to have to give up my job just to go to a program? Can I put the program off? Will I get my job back after the program?

Ans. Yes, you will have to give up your job to go to a program. No, you cannot put off program attendance. But, when you finish the treatment program you will be placed on the top of the job register for the job you previously held.

7. Will I ever be shipped to a different prison just to go thru a program that this prison does not offer?

Ans. Yes, you can be shipped for program purposes.

8. Can I refuse the TAP program?

Ans. No, you cannot refuse. There are things in your life that led you to prison, whether it was drug addiction, poor impulse control, violence, etc. Until you learn new ways of living your life you will keep doing the same things. It is your responsibility to your family to learn better ways of coping so that you never come back into TDOC custody. Participating in programs is one way to turn your life around.

9. I have heard that for new inmates the TAP program will function like contract parole. Is this true? What about those who came into the system before TAP?

Ans. No, the TAP program is not an automatic contract for parole for anyone. However, you need to address your completion of the TAP recommendations when you talk to the parole hearing officer as it can effect the recommendation for parole.

10. When will I become a part of TAP?

Ans. During your annual reclassification process. From April of 2007 forward, those of you in time building situations will become part of TAP. For new people entering TDOC at the reception centers, the TAP is completed upon intake classification.

11. Will TAP help a person make parole?

Ans. Refer to answer for # 9. Plus, it is important that your behavior changes as you participate in programs. If you go to A & D treatment and continue to get dirty drug screens then it won't help. If you go to treatment and actually change your behavior—not just your verbal understanding of any program—but change your behavior, then it will help. It is not a guarantee—but it is one positive thing you can do for yourself.

"The bottom line is this: it is incredibly important that you take an interest in changing your behavior. Not your words—your behavior. There are ways you can help yourself—you can go to programs, you can learn new ways of living, you can be consistent in doing the things you need to do to be able to go home, you can ask questions, and you can be a success. There are also ways you can hurt yourself—you can hang out with the same people you got in trouble with, you can change nothing about yourself, you can get out of prison and come back again and again, and you can blame everyone around you for causing your problems. Which way are you going to choose to live your life? The only proof of what works is if you get out of prison and stay out." ✍

Seventh Step Foundation
By William Foret

The 7th Step Foundation once again has a newsletter! Within this newsletter, we will start a new era of expressing the programs, goals, objectives, and news of the organization.

We want to encourage you to contact William Foret (Unit 3), if you have any questions or articles you wish to share with the rest of the members.

So far, we feel the program has done a great job in helping the men learn more things about themselves and others. A majority of the men openly participated, giving great answers to the questions asked.

We all have a great time sharing our ideas and experiences with one another. We hope you will continue to be a part of the program, continue to learn—not only how to help yourself be a better person, but also how to help someone else realize they can be a better person too.

New members are always welcome, so invite your friends or anyone you feel our program will benefit. Remember: freedom is for everyone!!

On July 26, 2007, William Foret was elected as our new newsletter editor.

For me, one of the best parts about this program is being able to help others better prepare themselves to go out into the world to start a new life with a better understanding of themselves.

We, on the Board, would like to see the men take an honest look at themselves and know that they really need to put effort into doing what they need to do in the program to go out into the real world and make a difference, not only for themselves, but others also.

I am honored to be a part of this program. I hope to help with the best of my ability and to learn from others as others have learned.

What we try to offer the members of the 7th Step group here at Morgan County Correctional Complex, is a three-point application toward parole.

We offer those coming up for parole, counseling, based on what is best for the individual. We also offer help with halfway houses (the starting point where parolees enter society), thus increasing their chance of successfully staying out of prison.

We also help them with outside agencies such as N.A., A.A., treatment centers, and

```
+-------------------------------------------------+
| REVISED 7TH STEP BOARD MEMBERS                  |
| Kenneth Greene     Chapter Coordinator          |
| Lewis Thompson     Assistant Chapter Coordinator|
| Gregory Gregg      Parole Counselor             |
| Buddy Coward       Secretary                    |
| Jerry Patton       Assistant Secretary          |
| Christopher Gause  Treasurer                     |
| Seth Mitchell      Sergeant-At-Arms             |
| Steve Bright       Assistant Sergeant-At-Arms   |
| William Foret      Editor                       |
+-------------------------------------------------+
```

health care service. We work with T.C.C., a state agency that offers jobs listings for those who need employment. T.C.C. has offices in all the major cities in Tennessee.

Also, we help with a parole petition. This shows that staff members feel the inmate is ready to return to his community and has worked hard toward his freedom.

In conclusion, concerning the role the 7th Step program takes toward helping parolees, we try to do our best to offer inmates a plan for parole, as well as every possible solution to help them be prepared for the outside world—always maintaining our freedom in here, as well as out there!

GOING UP FOR PAROLE

Anyone that is going up for parole in the future, be sure to see the 7th Step Parole Counselor; Gregory Gregg, approximately one or two months ahead of time.

Gregory will give you some help with information concerning halfway houses, the Tennessee Career Center (T.C.C), and a parole petition. If you have any questions, we encourage you to ask any of the board members. We will find the answers for you . Good luck and stand firm.

OUR INSIDE SPONSOR

As with all programs in the TDOC, there has always been an inside sponsor, someone to make sure things are going according to the guidelines—the 7th Step program is no exception. We are lucky and blessed to have Chaplain Dean Yancey as our inside sponsor. Chaplain Dean Yancey has volunteered to sponsor this program. We gratefully thank Dean Yancey for all the help and guidance he has provided this program and prayers for all the men.

OUR OUTSIDE SPONSORS

Bill Copeland, Bob Livesey, and Mrs. Alice Hanks are our outside sponsors.

Mrs. Alice Hanks is secretary of the outside chapter of the 7th Step Foundation. She has been an active member for thirty years.

We thank these sponsors deeply for their time and energy they give to us each week. God blessed us with them. God blesses them also. Thank you once again.

EDITOR'S NOTES

Be the best we can be! The future is ours for the taking. We can't do anything about our past. We don't know what the future holds for us.

Today is the only day we have. Make the best of the present moment, thereby enhancing our future!

No matter where we are, or what challenges we are facing, don't go through life with low self-esteem—focusing on the negative, or dwelling on some reason why we can't be happy.

Enlarge your vision, choose to be happy, and what we keep before our eyes will affect us.

Develop an image of victory, success, health, and happiness. Nothing will keep us from holding on to these things.

To experience this, we must rid ourselves of that small-minded thinking, and start anticipating good things. Let's change our attitudes. If we can conceive it in our minds first, then and only then will we receive it. ✍

Varsity Club
By Randall McPheeters & Jeremy Ingram

As 2007 closes, the Varsity Club is thankful for another year of service. This has been a busy year for the club, and we would like to take this opportunity to sum up several activities we have been able to offer. Hopefully, by calling attention to these opportunities, many inmates will be better informed and take advantage of programs offered at MCCX.

Earlier this year, the Varsity Club, together with Bethel Presbyterian Church, offered the opportunity for the awarding of an educational grant. The grant grew out of a desire to memorialize former MCCX resident, Myer Pettyjohn. PJ, as he was affectionately known, was instrumental in founding many programs offered at this prison. These programs included the Alternative to Violence Project, Anger Management, Domestic Violence Prevention, and the Parenting class. PJ worked hard during his incarceration to improve himself academically. Before his death, he earned his Doctorate degree.

The Myer Pettyjohn Memorial Grant was awarded to Dan Hunley and Chris Russell. Both men received a $300 scholarship toward their educational pursuits. They were chosen from among nine applicants by a board of five from the Bethel Presbyterian Church prison volunteers. Dan is studying at the Blackstone School of Law and Chris is taking courses from Ohio University. The Myer Pettyjohn Memorial Grant is awarded each year. Watch your bulletin boards for information on the next opportunity to apply for this grant.

The Varsity Club's Arts and Crafts Workshop has enjoyed an increase in participation during the holiday

season. We are very pleased to offer the opportunity for men to make their own cards to send their families. The Arts and Crafts Workshop is held every Sunday morning at 8:00 a.m. in the Library Classroom. The club has been blessed with extraordinary support for this project in the form of donations and participation. We hope to continue the Arts program well into the future.

The Varsity Club's Writers' Workshop (pictured above) meets on Thursday nights in the Library Classroom at 6:00 p.m. We try to meet every week, but the availability of a chaplain to open the classroom is key. Writers come to the workshop to present their articles, stories, and poems. Other writers in the workshop comment on the pieces and help the writers edit their material and prepare them for submission and publication.

The Varsity Club's Sign Language class continues to meet on Tuesday nights in the Library Classroom at 6:00 p.m. The class works with American Sign Language and has a dedicated core group who are willing to help newcomers with whatever they need. Sign language is an excellent form of communication to learn, and if you already know it, you can practice it here.

In addition to these programs, the Varsity Club routinely involves itself in charity causes. Knox Area Rescue

William Barney, Richard Peters, Randall McPheeters, and Paul Rutherford discuss and review writings at the Writer's Workshop.

Ministries, a Knoxville-area shelter for the homeless, receives a donation monthly from the Varsity Club. During the holiday seasons, the club sends an extra donation to help KARM buy food for the homeless for Thanksgiving and Christmas meals.

The Varsity Club, in conjunction with visitation Sergeant Bill King, purchase various items to help the visitation experience become more enjoyable.

On Easter, the club hosted an Easter egg hunt and passed out bags of candy for children who visit on this day. On Christmas, the club set up a tree it purchased for visit.

All activities and purchases by the club are done directly from monthly membership dues by the club's members. If you want to have a positive effect on your environment, the Varsity Club provides many opportunities to allow you to help those around you and others in need. Please consider joining the club, or donating money for future projects.

The Varsity Club meets on the second Tuesday of every month at 6:00 p.m. in the library classroom—everyone is welcome. We encourage anyone wishing to be a part of the Varsity Club to attend the next meeting. Dues are $3.00 a month and are used to support the programs listed in this article, as well as others. We look forward to seeing you at our next meeting. ✍

Prison Life

AN OVERVIEW OF PRISON NEWS AND CRIME STATISTICS FROM AROUND THE U.S.A.—BY GARRY W. JOHNSON

A look at the future, one year out?

In April, the Urban Institute's Justice Policy Center released the final report on its study of 300 former prisoners living in Cleveland, Ohio, entitled *One Year Out*. The report compiled statistics about the lives of these ex-cons one year after their release from prison.

As with most studies of this nature, family and friends were vitally important to the released prisoners. Most (79%) were living with family members one year after leaving prison. The men in the study identified family support as the most important factor in their staying out of prison. Of course, this is a two-edged sword in some cases, as 49% said drug dealing was a major problem in their neighborhood and 23% lived with drug users or serious alcohol drinkers. Of those who were rearrested, 21% identified their failure to avoid certain people or situations as the reason for their reincarceration.

Employment was also a big issue with ex-cons. Even after a full year on the streets, 65% reported having difficulties finding a job, and 56% said they had trouble making enough money to support themselves. This could be related to the fact that 23% reported being depressed and 20% suffered from symptoms of post-traumatic stress syndrome related to their incarceration experiences. More than half of the men reported chronic medical conditions such as hypertension, asthma, arthritis, or high cholesterol, yet only a third were receiving treatment.

The report showed that drug and alcohol addiction still played a predominate role in the lives of these men. Before their incarceration, 72% used drugs and 60% drank to intoxication. One year after release, 35% reported drinking to intoxication or using drugs in the month prior to the survey. Most reported remaining crime-free after release, with only 24% saying they committed another crime, usually drug possession (51%) or drug dealing (32%). Only 15% were returned to prison within the first year, 81% of those for a new crime. ✍

DEA says drug prices are up

The Drug Enforcement Administration reported in November that prices for cocaine and methamphetamine have risen for the fourth quarter in a row, indicating that the supply has dropped. "I don't think anyone is prepared to declare victory, but this is certainly encouraging news," said Scott Burns of the Office of National Drug Control Policy.

According to a DEA database, a gram of pure cocaine cost about $137 in September 2007, up from $93 in October 2006. A gram of pure methamphetamine went up from $133 in October 2006, to $245 in September. ✍

Cocaine flow interrupted

Kilograms of cocaine lost or seized in transit toward the USA:

Year	Kilograms
2000	117,000
2001	141,000
2002	143,000
2003	157,000
2004	197,000
2005	234,000

Source: Department of Justice

Law enforcement eyeing iris scans

The technology of tomorrow is here today. Iris scans are being used by a growing number law enforcement agencies to identify sex-offenders, runaways, abducted children, and wandering Alzheimer's patients.

Sean Mullin, president of BI² Technologies, says that more than 2,100 sheriff's departments in 27 states are taking digital pictures of eyes and storing the information in databases that can be searched later to identify a criminal or missing person. "It's evolving quickly," says Mullin, whose company sells the devices which make the scans.

Iris scans of children and senior citizens are being done voluntarily by most of the sheriffs, and at least 10 metro areas are scanning criminals to insure the right inmates are released and for identifying repeat offenders.

Sheriff Greg Solano of Santa Fe County, N.M. began scanning the irises of convicted sex-offenders in November. He says with the central database and the level of detail provided by the scans, matches can be made in seconds, as opposed to DNA which takes months and finger prints which can take weeks.

Airports and the government have been using iris recognition technology to expedite security checks of low-risk travelers and track possible terrorists. When the patent expired in 2006, other companies rushed to expand its uses.

Mullin says the camera, laptop and software his company sells cost $10,000 and uses harmless infrared light to record the iris' minute ridges and valleys. His product can detect 235 unique details and differentiate between left and right eyes and those of identical twins. Fingerprints have only about 70 details.

Barry Morse, CEO of Retica Systems, says his company is seeing tremendous growth due to concerns about terrorism and identity theft. His company will deliver test devices to the Defense Department in 2008 which are able to scan crowds and store iris data for many people at once.

Iris scans are here to stay, as irises are not affected by age, Lasik eye surgery or disease. Mullins says the data base is gaining more than 2,000 scans every week. ✍

The eyes have it

The iris' hundreds of markings help law enforcement make identifications. Three examples:

Furrow — Crypt   Freckles

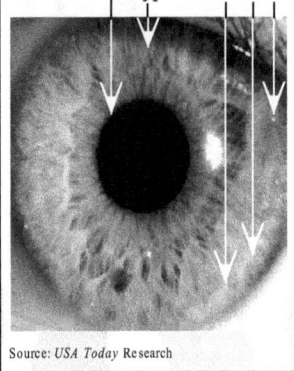

Source: *USA Today* Research

Robbery in Nashville rises, despite drop in crime

Nashville is on track this year to have the most robberies since 2001, in spite of beefed-up efforts by Metro police in crime hotspots.

Even with surveillance cameras and more patrols in troubled areas, street-level robberies have jumped 8.1% and overall robberies have increased 3.1% this year to 1,695 as of September 6, according to Metro police statistics.

With most other types of crime on the decline in Nashville, robberies are defying the trend.

Metro Police Chief Ronal Serpas puts the blame on the state's juvenile justice system, which he has criticized for years as a revolving door that allows children to continue to commit violent crimes without facing harsh punishments.

"The police department is doing more and more and more, to arrest these kids, but arrest isn't our solution," said Serpas. "We have to find a way to teach children not to rob. As a community, we need to help find that way." ✍

Robberies in Nashville

Following are the number of robberies in Nashville through September 6:

	2006	2007
East Precinct	310	298
West Precinct	225	203
North Precinct	364	379
South Precinct	397	477
Central Precinct	130	97
Hermitage Precinct	218	241
Total	**1,644**	**1,695**

Released

from page 01

At least 27 states and hundreds of cities have passed laws in the past decade to restrict where sex-offenders live. Landlords in unrestricted areas often reject renters after background checks reveal their criminal record. As a result, thousands of convicted sex-offenders are reporting to police that they are homeless, raising concerns that their lack of a permanent address could make them harder to track.

The National Association of Attorneys General urge caution in efforts to standardize state laws, pushing to allow states to keep sex-offender registries and restrictions on ex-offenders that have clear public safety benefits. The association believes that some collateral sanctions are an "important element in protecting the public," and that "ex-offenders must be held accountable and accept that in addition to incarceration that their illegal behavior may cause other ramifications."

Richard Cassidy, an attorney in Burlington, Vermont, who supports efforts to uniform state laws, says the goal is not to endanger public safety but to guarantee that the sanctions relate to the crime. He comments that a pedophile should not be allowed to work at a day care center, or an embezzler at a bank. Cassidy goes on to say, "If you look at the numbers of people who have some sort of criminal history in the United States, it's huge. ...We're creating an underclass of citizens, and that's probably not in our best long-term interest." ✍

Sex-offenders by state

Number of registered sex-offenders per 100,000 residents:

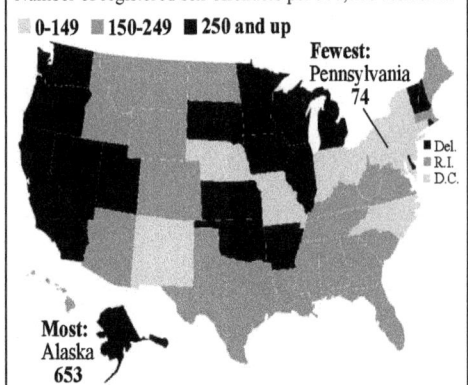

■ 0-149   ■ 150-249   ■ 250 and up

Fewest: Pennsylvania 74

■ Del.
■ R.I.
■ D.C.

Most: Alaska 653

Source: National Center for Missing & Exploited Children

County jails still pushing for more money

By Garry W. Johnson
MOUNTAIN REVIEW Staff

County officials in Tennessee plan to ask the General Assembly again this year for more money to cover the cost of housing felons in local jails. Legislation earlier in 2007 failed to raise the reimbursement rate from $35 per day for each state inmate held in county custody to the desired $50. The cap has remained unchanged since 1994, according to an October report by the *Chattanooga Times Free Press*.

"We've lost thousands of dollars in revenue because of their not paying us the right price," said Hamilton County Sheriff Billy Long. "We're going to talk a lot about that in the upcoming session here in January. And hopefully we can get the support of the state to go ahead and start paying us the right (amount), what our jail cost is." The Tennessee County Services Association also plans to make the payment increase a top priority in 2008.

Governor Phil Bredesen believes the issue is not as simple as it seems. He said some jails are getting paid over and above the $35 cap, and others have much lower cost.

"It's a complicated process because in many cases they're being paid well over their cost for keeping (inmates), for example, in older jails," Bredesen remarked. "In other cases, where someone has built a new jail, they may be being paid under their cost."

The issue of state reimbursements has recently become a hot-button political topic. In October, the Nashville newspaper, *The Tennessean*, ran a full page of articles devoted to the subject. The paper found that about 65 local jails have cost above the cap, while 38 have cost below. According to the report, jails which run at cost below the cap are reimbursed only for their actual reported cost.

Nashville-based Corrections Corporation of America (CCA) has also been drawn into the debate, as their reimbursement rates for South Central Correctional Facility have increased 22.8% since 1998, and Hardeman County Correctional Facility has seen an increase of 29.1% over the same time period.

The company's CEO, John Ferguson, had this to say: "Though many people commonly use the words 'prison' and 'jail' interchangeably, they are in fact very different entities. The duration of an inmate's stay, the amount of inmate programming, and a host of other factors all mean that budgets at state prisons will normally be higher than those at local jails. ...

"While our contracts for operating prisons have provisions that allow our per diem reimbursement to go up when cost go up, those contracts also require that our reimbursement go down if cost go down" (*Privately run prisons are money-savers for state*, October 31, 2007, *The Tennessean*).

The paper also requested comment from TDOC Commissioner George Little, who submitted the article on this page: *Prison-jail resources, populations vary.* ✍

Prison-jail resources, populations vary

By George Little

Attention has focused recently on differences between state of Tennessee payments for housing state felons in privately managed prisons and the county jails.

The Tennessee Department of Correction has well-established partnerships with county jails and, since 1992, has contracted with privately managed prisons for this purpose. These unique partnerships both serve Tennessee public safety.

Commissioner George Little

Fundamentally, jails and prisons serve distinct felon populations. In the mid-'80s, when I first began work with TDOC, about 70% of offenders housed in state prisons were nonviolent or property offenders. Today, about 60% of offenders in state and privately managed facilities are violent offenders. On the other hand, many of the less serious offenders are housed in county jails, and others are served by community-based alternative sentencing programs.

The need for these partnerships rises and falls with the number of state prison beds available. Since no new prisons were built for eight years, the state acquired additional capacity through contracting. Our prisons are among the best in the nation, with both state and privately managed facilities being accredited by the American Correctional Association and offering a wide range of educational, substance abuse, mental health and other programs to reduce recidivism.

Capacities and capabilities of jails across the state vary widely, with few jails having the resources to offer programming. Very few jails are accredited; health and mental health services are often basic. Yet the amount of money appropriated and expended for reimbursements to counties has continued to grow. The state reimburses Corrections Corporation of America an average of $46 per day per inmate; jail reimbursement, set by the legislature, is generally capped at $35 per day. However, actual jail costs and reimbursements vary significantly. The custody level of inmates and the programming available also vary significantly.

RAISE JAIL ALTERNATIVES

In this analysis and as incarceration costs rise, I think an examination of the entire range of sanctions is in order.

The state may want to increase its alternatives to incarceration for appropriate offenders. Probation costs of $2.78 per day and community-correction costs of $4.59 per day are cost-effective and may produce better results for some offenders.

We should examine the outcomes of all available sanctions to find the best fit in terms of public safety and the cost benefit to taxpayers. But we cannot afford to be shortsighted and fail to offer adequate programs and services to address risks and needs posed by felony offenders. The cost of continuing to pay for the revolving door of offenders is tremendous.

Jails serve our less serious offenders and can help with successful re-entry of offenders to the community. Probation and community corrections allow offenders to continue to work while getting needed services and treatment.

Our challenge is to determine what best promotes public safety and wisely expends scarce taxpayer dollars. Every dollar saved in corrections is a dollar more to spend on schools or health care for Tennesseans. ✍

The preceding appeared in the October 31, 2007 issue of The Tennessean.

Tennessee State Penitentiary may get restoration

By Garry W. Johnson
MOUNTAIN REVIEW Staff

Opened in 1898, the menacing structure known to many of us as simply "The Walls," has recently become the focus of a TDOC rehabilitation project.

Correction Commissioner George Little revealed plans to rehab the century-old structure to lawmakers in December's meeting of the Select Oversight Committee on Corrections.

Forced to close in 1992 due to inhumane conditions, the Tennessee State Penitentiary still sports the foundation for a hangman's noose, the state's method of execution prior to 1913. There is also still standing a pedestal where the Tennessee's electric chair once rested.

The 120-acre campus on the banks of the Cumberland River includes a hospital, mess hall, chapel and gymnasium, and has been the location for many blockbuster Hollywood movies. But film makers have recently rejected the site because its buildings are falling apart.

Nathan Lux, spokesman for the Tennessee Film, Entertainment and Music Commission said that "The state now requires anyone who enters to sign a liability waiver. ... Just a few years ago, that wasn't necessary."

The state allows production companies to film free at the prison, which has seen more than 2,000 hours of production time in the past two years, according to Lux.

The TDOC plans, however, may make the location less attractive to Hollywood film makers, as they include turning the cellblocks into an atrium with modern office spaces for the department. An architect's rendering of the possible transformation also includes the addition of exterior glass stairwells.

Commissioner Little said the department is taking into consideration the site's importance as a popular film setting—easily the state's most-requested location. "The yard will still be there, and there's still one smaller cellblock building that potentially could be rehabbed" for interior filming, Little said. (In the past, the state has enjoyed the large Hollywood productions boosting the economy by spending on services like hotels, rental cars and restaurants.)

"As the state copes with the need for expanding office space, we have to look into this type of thing," said Finance Department spokeswoman Lola Potter. "The availability of downtown office space is pretty sparse, and the cost is high."

The rehabilitation is estimated to run $27.8 million and would need to be included in the governor's budget and approved by the Legislature, she said. ✍

MARK HUMPHREY/ASSOCIATED PRESS

The Walls, as shown in this 2001 photo, is the state's most requested film location, but has become increasingly rejected by movie companies because of its unsafe condition.

STATE PEN MOVIES

The following are films that have been shot on location at the Tennessee State Penitentiary:

▶ "The Furnace," 2006, Melee Entertainment
▶ "Walk The Line," 2004, 20th Century Fox
▶ "Civil Brand," 2001, Lions Gate
▶ "The Last Castle," 2001, DreamWorks Production
▶ "The Green Mile," 1998, Castle Rock Entertainment
▶ "Letters from Death Row," 1997, Sheen/Michaels Entertainment
▶ "Last Dance," 1996, Touchstone Pictures
▶ "Against the Wall" (TV), 1994, Araba Films for HBO
▶ "Marie," 1984, De Laurentiis Entertainment/MGM/UM

149

Commissioner pushes for more funding to pursue escaped Tennessee felons

By Garry W. Johnson
Mountain Review Staff

Corrections Commissioner George Little says Tennessee needs help tracking criminals who have managed to escape custody.

In 2006 the Commissioner asked for more funding to add three officers to the department's internal affairs unit, which handles, among other things, escapes. His request that year was cut out of the final state budget.

Little has also advocated a statewide criminal justice database that allows law enforcement officials throughout the state to share critical information.

A pilot program for the database was set up in 2006 and law enforcement agencies across the state have been signing up for the service. The state Administrative Office of the Courts administers the criminal justice portal which cost about $198,000 to set up and, according to officials, is common in other states.

Little said, "I recognize we're in competition (for tax dollars) with a whole lot of things that probably are a whole lot more appealing to folks than what we do every day."

In the past the TDOC relied on other law enforcement agencies to find escapees, primarily through active warrants.

"If they do escape or walk away, I think it's better to use existing police law enforcement resources to try to recapture them, instead of having Department of Correction task forces going all over the state and into other jurisdictions. ... It's more than resources. It's philosophy and policy," said former correction commissioner W. Jeff Reynolds, who worked under Governor Ned Ray McWherter in the late 1980s and early '90s.

Unfortunately, Tennessee escape warrants have not always stuck around in the past. Prison officials said that in some old cases warrants became inactive when the system under which they were issued became outdated.

One such case, that of Billy Wayne Hayes, sparked an investigation by *The Tennessean* in December of 2006 after his arrest on charges of walking away from a Nashville work release program in 1972. A tip to federal authorities led to his arrest outside an Alabama gas station.

The newspaper investigated more than 200 men and women who escaped from the state prison system since the 1930s.

Commissioner Little told the paper the state should have more of a role in pursuing fugitives, although it is the county's job first, if the escape occurred at a county facility.

"I would say it's our responsibility to make every reasonable effort to identify these individuals, work ourselves to get these individuals back into custody, or at least provide the information to other law enforcement agencies so that they can bring these individuals back into custody as quickly as possible before something happens to anyone," Little said.

Only California and New York have more unsolved escapes than Tennessee, which counts 156 fugitives (see sidebar).

"I think it clearly points out an area where we need to make greater efforts for improvement," Little told the paper.

Prison officials have put together a partial list of escapees who do not have active warrants and plan to turn it over to prosecutors once they feel they have a complete list.

Once officials are notified of an escapee's arrest through the warrant, jurisdictions can decide whether to spend the required money to bring the escapee back to Tennessee to stand trial, which can add as much as 5 years to the fugitive's original sentence.

"I can say for this commissioner, if they're brought back into custody (in another state) they will come back to do the balance of their sentences," Little said.

The state said it has captured 89 escapees since 1997, which includes all 68 people who escaped from state prison during that period. However, 35 state inmates who escaped from county jails during that time are still on the run. ✍

Tennessee's 156 escapees as released to *The Tennessean* by the Tennessee Department of Correction

Nabiel David Akhdary, Escaped from Sumner County Jail, 3/23/2005
Peggy Ann Barton, Escaped from Nashville Community Service Center, 10/17/1980
Jeffrey Lynn Beach, Escaped from Shelby County Correction Center, 12/11/1987
Jesse Lee Bishop, Escaped from Shelby County Correction Center, 11/7/1988
Thomas G. Bogdanovich, Escaped from Knox County Penal Farm, 4/10/1987
Ricky A. Bowman, Escaped from Greene County Jail, 5/1/1991
Gary L. Brooks, Escaped from Tennessee State Penitentiary, 4/6/1976
Terry S. Bullard, Escaped from Knox County Penal Farm, 6/5/1990
Doyle Ray Bullock, Escaped from Luttrell Correctional Center, 12/12/1983
Louis Cameron, Escaped from Fort Pillow, 2/9/1976
Ronald B. Campbell, Escaped from Hamilton Co. Workhouse Silverdale, 10/13/1988
Paul Carr, Escaped from Knox County Community Service Center, 9/24/1990
William Carson, Escaped from Rutherford County Workhouse, 1/23/1996
John H. Carter, Escaped from Turney Center, 7/30/1975
Craig L. Caslin, Escaped from Hamilton County Workhouse Silverdale, 6/9/1991
Oscar Castenda, Escaped from Overton County Jail, 12/20/2004
Antonio A. Castro, Escaped from Nashville Community Service Center, 2/22/1992
Robert M. Chapman, Escaped from Knox County Penal Farm, 1/5/1990
Larry P. Chism, Escaped from Turney Center, 9/13/1978
Michael E. Christian, Escaped from Dyer County Jail, 9/17/2006
Michael Cisewski, Escaped from Nashville Community Service Center, 7/31/1982
Terry Baxter Coker, Escaped from Macon County Jail, 3/24/1988
J.B. Cole, Escaped from Middle Tennessee Correctional Complex, 6/4/01
James R. Collard, Escaped from Rutherford County Workhouse, 3/29/1993
Terry R. Collins, Escaped from Lincoln County Jail, 11/6/2004
Milton J. Cook, Escaped from Washington County Jail, 11/30/2002
Michael Corey, Escaped from Knox County Community Service Center, 10/9/1982
Fydias Correa, Escaped from Tipton County Jail, 8/4/1990
Jerry W. Culver, Escaped from Nashville Community Service Center, 6/19/1987
Robert J. Damron, Escaped from Knox County Penal Farm, 11/3/1987
James C. Day, Escaped from Davidson County Detention Center, 8/25/1999
Paul Driggers, Escaped from Obion County Jail, 7/4/1989
Johnny M. Duck, Escaped from Nashville Community Service Center, 4/21/1983
Michael J. Dunn, Escaped from Knox County Jail, 10/22/1981
Francisco Espinosa, Escaped from Shelby County Correction Center, 5/19/1994
Jamie P. Evans, Escaped from Fayette County Jail, 6/18/1992
Booker J. Farr, Escaped from Middle Tennessee Reception Center, 7/5/1977
George W. Fedick, Escaped from Nashville Community Service Center, 3/3/1983
Ramon Felix, Escaped from Shelby County Correction Center, 10/1/2003
Clay Anthony Ford, Escaped during transport, 7/22/1980
Greg Foster, Escaped from Middle Tennessee Reception Center, 7/10/1976
Bradley S. Foulks, Escaped from Greene County Jail, 8/1/2002
Luther R. Freeman, Escaped from Fort Pillow, 2/16/1979
Thomas N. Furgason, Jr., Escaped from Rutherford County Workhouse, 4/12/1996
Pachino Gant, Escaped from Shelby County Criminal Justice Center, 12/13/1985
Douglas G. Giles, Escaped from Hamilton County Workhouse Silverdale, 7/15/1987
Barry A. Gray, Escaped from Riverbend, 10/28/1995
Edward H. Gray, Escaped from Fort Pillow, 8/28/1980
Freddie Green, Escaped from Tennessee State Penitentiary Stockade, 7/4/1980
Gerald Green, Escaped from Chattanooga Community Service Center, 12/15/1980
Phillip Griggs, Escaped Crockett County Jail, 8/2/1990
Jerry Gullett, Escaped from Jefferson County Jail, 11/16/2000
Terry Haley, Escaped from Tipton County Jail, 10/10/1988
Melvin C. Harrell, Escaped from Carter County Jail, 1/28/1989
Warren D. Harris, Escaped from Memphis Cor. Rehabilitation Center, 4/3/1975
Debbie Havner, Escaped from Chattanooga Community Service Center, 7/25/1982
Gerald L. Hemp, Escaped from Tennessee State Penitentiary, 7/10/1984
Robert T. Henry, Escaped from Davidson CJ2, 6/10/1980
Donald W. Hignite, Escaped from Nashville Community Service Center, 5/28/1992
Michael L. Hines, Escaped from Hamilton County Workhouse Silverdale, 5/19/2003
John W. Howell, Escaped from Shelby County Correction Center, 12/15/1992
Phillip Huddleston, Escaped from Nashville Community Service Center, 2/16/1983
Timothy R. Hughett, Escaped from Montgomery County Workhouse, 9/6/2003
Dennis R. Hutchinson, Escaped from Shelby County Correction Center, 3/15/1988
Glenn L. Inman, Escaped from Knox County Penal Farm, 6/1/1987
Paul N. Jefferson, Escaped from Knox Co. Community Service Center, 6/29/1979
Jimmy Jennette, Jr., Escaped from Nashville Community Service Center, 5/16/1982
Keith A Jerrell, Escaped from Davidson CJ2, 7/16/1989
Neal Johnson, Escaped from Hamilton County Workhouse Silverdale, 11/4/1988
John L. Jones, Escaped from Tennessee State Penitentiary, 5/2/1975
John R. Jones, Escaped from Tennessee State Penitentiary, 8/30/1988
Steven D. Jones, Escaped from Davidson CJ2, 7/20/1997
Guy T. Kennison, 51, Escaped from Davidson, 7/27/1980 [CAPTURED 10/30/2007]
Ronald L. Kimmel, Escaped from Nashville Community Service Center, 1/31/1989
Robert L. Knight, Escaped from Hamilton County Workhouse Silverdale, 1/9/1991
Charles T. Kolb III, Escaped from Sullivan County Jail, 11/25/1981
Andreas Kutzner, Escaped from Shelby County Correction Center, 11/9/1992
Helen Lawler, 71, Escaped during transport, 12/13/1981 . [CAPTURED 10/30/2007]
Christopher S. Lawrence, Escaped from Davidson Co. Detention Center, 8/3/1999
Robert M. Ledford, Escaped from Hamilton Co. Workhouse Silverdale, 5/22/1989
Eunie Lee Lindsey, Escaped from Hamilton Co. Workhouse Silverdale, 6/26/1991
Linda A. Long, Escaped from Tennessee State Penitentiary, 8/30/1988
Guillermo Lopez, Escaped from Shelby County Correction Center, 9/5/1997
Billy Lovingood, 51, Escaped from Knox Co, 2/6/1984 . .[CAPTURED 10/30/2007]
William C. Lowe, Escaped from Tennessee State Penitentiary, 11/19/1979
Terry Luckett, Escaped from Shelby County Correction Center, 8/6/1996
Eddie Maddle, Escaped from Jackson County Jail, 6/2/2000
Tommy A. Martin, Escaped from Shelby County Correction Center, 11/4/1993
Lohman R. Mays, Escaped from Turney Center, 7/1/1984
Brett A. McCarthy, Escaped from DeBerry, 1/5/1983
Randall McCarty, Escaped from Cock County Jail, 5/15/2001
Wesley D. McClure, Escaped from Lake County Jail, 4/1/1988
James S. Miller, Escaped from Tennessee State Penitentiary, 11/4/1976
Michael A. Miner, Escaped from Montgomery County Workhouse, 6/11/2001
Bobby Mitchell, Escaped from Riverbend, 10/28/1995
Donald R. Mitchell, Escaped from Middle Tennessee Reception Center, 2/4/1978
Robert L. Moone, Jr., Escaped from S.E. Tenn. St. Regional Prison, 1/17/1984
James E. Moore, Escaped from Chattanooga Community Service Center, 2/5/1982
Tommy L. Morris, Escaped from Lauderdale County Jail, 3/21/2002
Estill L. Murray, Escaped during transport, 3/6/1981
Henry L. Newman, Escaped from Monroe County Jail, 1/1/1994
Brenda F. Ogle, Escaped from Sevier County Jail, 2/23/1993
Robert L. Palmer, Escaped from Cheatham County Jail, 2/6/1997
Rowland W. Patrick, Escaped from Davidson Criminal Justice Center, 4/4/1999
Larry E. Payne, 60, Escaped from Nashville, 7/18/1981 . .[CAPTURED 10/30/2007]
Donald Peden, Escaped from Giles County Jail, 10/21/2004
Donald Peeler, Escaped from Fort Pillow, 11/20/1981
Jackie Lee Permenter, Escaped from Dyer County Jail, 2/2/2005
Gail B. Phillips, Escaped from Tennessee State Penitentiary, 8/30/1988
Donald R. Pitts, Escaped from Morgan County Regional, 2/3/1990
Robert Poteat, Escaped from Tennessee State Penitentiary, 8/30/1988
Larry A. Ray, Escaped from Sequatchie County Jail, 7/29/2004
Ron L. Ray, Escaped from Davidson CJ2, 6/29/1991
William R. Reegen, Escaped from Middle Tennessee Reception Center, 10/24/1977
Robert S. Riley, Jr., Escaped from Knox County Jail, 11/4/1980
Grover Roberts, Escaped from Shelby County Correction Center, 11/28/1987
Jason M. Roberts, Escaped from Rutherford County Workhouse, 3/10/1993
Michael Rodgers, Escaped from Shelby County Correction Center, 7/6/1986
Phillip A. Rollins, Escaped from Sequatchie County Jail, 5/29/1993
John D. Rowlette, Escaped from Knox Co. Community Service Center, 6/16/1981
Wendy N. Russell, Escaped from Henderson County Jail, 3/13/2003
Robert H. Sanders, Escaped from Tennessee State Penitentiary, 4/20/1990
Wesley Sawchuck, Escaped from Tennessee State Penitentiary, 5/30/1980
Robert Sayler, Escaped from Middle Tennessee Reception Center, 8/6/1975
John Scott, Escaped from Hamilton County Jail, 11/17/1995
Maurice H. Shaw, Escaped from Tennessee State Penitentiary, 8/30/1988
Roger W. Sheets, Escaped from Cocke County Jail, 6/11/1993
Michael Silvers, Escaped from Unicoi County Jail, 10/27/1997
Richard Simmons, Escaped from Nashville Community Service Center, 11/18/1981
Barbara S. Sloan, Escaped from Nashville Community Service Center, 9/2/1979
Allen Smith, Escaped from Polk County Jail, 5/14/1999
Daniel Smith, Escaped from Montgomery County Jail, 4/9/1999
Raymond Smith, Escaped from Fort Pillow, 7/15/1977
Samuel H. Smith, Escaped from Davidson Criminal Justice Center, 8/3/2000
Vanessa D. Smith, Escaped during transport, 10/11/1980
James I. Sowell, Escaped from Knox County Community Service Center, 7/21/1977
Patricia A. Stone, Escaped from Tennessee Prison for Women, 6/24/1980
Floyd J. Swayney, Escaped from Knox Co. Community Service Center, 4/22/1994
Arthur B. Taylor, Escaped from Tennessee State Penitentiary, 8/30/1988
Johnny Thomas, Escaped from Tennessee State Penitentiary, 8/30/1988
Bramlett Walker, 64, Escaped during transport, 8/23/1980 .[CAPTURED 10/30/2007]
William J. Ward, Escaped from Washington County Jail, 7/8/1999
James E. Ware, Escaped from Tennessee State Penitentiary Stockade, 7/15/1980
Kenneth M. Warren, Escaped from Robertson County Jail, 9/24/2002
Kevin D. Washington, Escaped from Luttrell, 7/3/1989
Ronald D. Welch, Escaped from Middle Tennessee Reception Center, 6/21/1975
William T. West, Escaped from Brushy Mountain, 2/22/2000
Jimmy D. Wheeler, Escaped from Nashville Community Service Center, 5/7/1982
Howard L. White, Escaped from Tennessee State Penitentiary, 9/2/1988
Darin Wilbanks, Escaped from Claiborne County Jail, 4/1/1990
Thomas W. Williams, Escaped from Davidson CJ2, 6/15/1987
Raymon D. Wyant, Escaped from Cheatham County Jail, 8/27/1994
Terry L. Wynne, Escaped from Brushy Mountain, 11/17/1985
Raymond A. Young, Escaped from Nashville Community Service Center, 6/14/1982
Roosevelt Young, Escaped from Shelby County Correction Center, 10/23/1987
William E. Zumbado, Escaped from Tenn. State Penitentiary Stockade, 3/13/1980

$101.7M awarded for false convictions

In July a federal judge in Boston heard the case of four men who spent decades in prison after the FBI withheld evidence of their innocence to protect a mob informant. The malicious prosecution case was brought by Peter Limone, Joseph Salvati, and the families of two other men who died in prison after being falsely convicted. Their lawyers claimed that Boston FBI agents knew a mob hit man lied when he linked the four men to the 1965 death of Edward Deegan, and that the men were "acceptable collateral damage" in the FBI's priority at the time: taking down the mob. The judge ordered the government to pay $101.7 million to the plaintiffs. ✍

New study to begin of the "criminal mind"

In October a $10 million grant was announced by the John D. And Catherine T. MacArthur Foundation, to launch a three-year study of the link between the brain and criminal behavior. The grant will be used to review new brain research related to addiction, brain abnormalities and decision-making to help policymakers in the legal system. Based at the University of California-Santa Barbara, the project will involve scientists and scholars from more than a dozen universities. ✍

Many deaths during arrest tied to drugs

In October a new analysis by the Justice Department found that one in eight people who die while being arrested succumbs to alcohol or drug intoxication.

Forty-seven states provided the data which covers the 2,002 people who died during the arrest process between 2003 and 2005. The report is the first of its kind to provide causes of death for suspects beyond those resulting from law enforcement officer's use of force (1,095 of the total deaths).

The new information was provided by the Justice report to account for additional fatalities during often tense encounters between suspects and law enforcement. ✍

Prison stocks rising, despite new census numbers

Barron's reported in its October 8, 2007 edition that prison stocks are expected to rise despite a U.S. Census report pointing to a lower-than-expected increase in the prison population. The census numbers were in contrast to a February report by the Pew Charitable Trusts, which we covered in the Spring/Summer 2007 issue of *Mountain Review* (*Inmate population to continue rising*, page 8). The Pew forecast predicted a 13% annual rise in the prison population, whereas the census report said the population was only growing by 4% annually. The Pew report is likely a more accurate assessment, according to *Barron's*, as the government report only polled 37 states, compared to Pews data from 42 states and estimates from the other eight. *Barron's* went on to say that Corrections Corporation of America (CCA), which trades at about $27, is likely to see its profit rise 20%. ✍

TDOC gets $ to help kick habit

Despite Tennessee prisons going smoke-free in March, officials are still seeing tobacco-related contraband coming into the system regularly.

As a result, the TDOC is using $10,000 of tobacco settlement money to pay the American Lung Association of Tennessee to implement a systemwide smoking cessation program.

Corrections Commissioner George Little says, "It's the right thing to do for the taxpayers, for quality of life for staff and the inmates."

According to the Associated Press, "The program will offer classes in behavior modification for inmates and prison staff. Partici- pants will have access to education materials at prison libraries and online."

Margaret Smith, director of lung health programs for the American Lung Association of Tennessee, says the program recommends coupling those resources with pharmaceutical assistance, so medicated lozenges will be provided.

Little says he is committed to finding a way to fund the program after the initial grant money runs out, as it will likely take years to assess the program's effect.

The TDOC spends just under $59 million each year on health care for the department's 19,500 prisoners. That's about $4,000 per inmate. ✍

Death row inmate acquitted in retrial

A jury in Tennessee acquitted a man who spent more than 15 years on Tennessee's death row for the fatal shooting of a woman. Jurors in the retrial of Michael McCormick, 55, agreed with defense lawyers who said McCormick was lying when police secretly recorded his confession. His retrial came after an appeals court ruled he had inadequate defense counsel at the 1987 trial where a jury sentenced him to death.

DNA test results in 2001 showed that a hair used to place him at the scene of the killing could not be his. McCormick's attorney, Michael Richardson, argued [December 4] that the only evidence was the confession secretly obtained by police who "set up a man they knew to be an alcoholic and a notorious liar." ✍ —*USA Today*, December 6, 2007

Mexican prisons packed

Prison overcrowding in Mexico is the highest it has been in over a decade, with nearly 217,000 inmates jammed into prisons built for 164,000, according to Mexican government figures. New attention has been focused on the prison system since the U.S. government promised a $1.4 million aid package to Mexico to crackdown on drug trafficking. Experts say the dangerous and overcrowded prisons could make it difficult for Mexico to lock-up more narcotics smugglers.

According to inmates and activist groups, corruption among guards, violence and drug dealing are rampant. Alberto Orozco, 25, described the six weeks he spent in a Mexico City prison for robbery as, "Nothing but shouting and beatings." He was housed in a 20 by 26 foot cell with 9 other inmates and only six bunks. "And that was the VIP room," Orozco said.

In its March 2006 Report on Human Rights Practices in Mexico, the U.S. State Department singled out the prison system saying, "Poorly trained, underpaid and corrupt guards staffed most prisons," and that "health and sanitary conditions were poor."

Shortages of supplies inside the prisons mean inmates must buy medicine, blankets, beds and food on the black market. A study by the Center for Economic Research and Education found that a quarter of all bribes paid in the prisons were to bring in food and clothing. "You have to buy everything," said Orozco. "If you want to shower with hot water, you have to pay 10 pesos." ✍

U.K. prison workers strike

In a pay dispute last August, thousands of British prison officers walked out of more than 140 jails in England and Wales, challenging Prime Minister Gordon Brown's government. "This government has failed to deliver promise after promise," said Brian Caton, general secretary of the Prison Officer's Association.

A main issue of contention was over a review board's recommendation that officers' receive a 2.5% pay increase this year. The government decided to reduce the value of the raise by paying the increase in stages, which prompted the strike.

The planned 24-hour walkout—the first in the union's 68 year history—ended immediately after the government won a court injunction and agreed to hold talks with the union. Under British law, prison staffers are not legally allowed to strike. ✍

Federal judges balk at sentencing guidelines

A 52-year-old woman diagnosed with a mental illness was convicted two years ago as an accomplice after her live-in boyfriend plead guilty to a series of armed robberies in Billings, Montana. The federal judge in her case said sentencing rules gave him no choice but to sentence Marion Hungerford to 159 years in federal prison.

In May the U.S. Supreme Court agreed, and backed the U.S. Court of Appeals in denying Hungerford's claim that the sentence was unconstitutional.

Legal activists and judges, both conservative and liberal, are increasingly pointing to cases like this one in saying that the federal sentencing system is out of wack. They hope to move Congress or the Supreme Court to give judges more leeway to impose shorter and, they say, fairer sentences.

The system is a holdover of the mid-1980's and the so-called "war on drugs," when Congress set fixed prison terms for crimes involving guns and drugs and adopted set sentencing guidelines for all other federal crimes, including white-collar offenses. Those laws also eliminated parole in the federal system.

U.S. District Judge Paul G. Cassell, a Bush appointee from Utah, said, "the worst aspect is the utter irrationality of the system. ... When I have to sentence a mid-level drug dealer to more time than a murderer, something is wrong."

In recent congressional testimony, Cassell cited the case of Weldon Angelos, whom he was forced three years ago, by federal mandatory minimum sentences, to send to prison for 59 years because of three $350 marijuana sales. In each instance, Angelos had a gun with him in the car. As a comparison, Cassell offered the following list of maximum federal sentences for other crimes:

♦ Hijacking an aircraft: 24 years, five months
♦ Terrorism-related bombing in a public place: 19 years, six months
♦ Second-degree murder: 14 years
♦ Rape of a 10-year-old child: 11 years, three months
♦ Providing weapons to support a foreign terrorist organization: 8 years, one month

The new U.S. attorney general also supports a change in the federal sentencing system. Before he took the oath of office on November 9, Michael Mukasey spoke out against the sentencing laws from the federal bench. He was among several judges who thought the limits the guidelines placed on courts violated the principle of separation of powers under the Constitution.

The conservative Washington Legal Foundation has also chimed in on "the unduly harsh sentences" imposed by the federal rules, saying too many business owners and white-collar defendants are given long prison terms for violating regulatory laws. "We have clients who are serving eight years for importing seafood packed in the wrong containers," said Paul Kamenar, an attorney for the group.

Harlan Protass, a New York lawyer, points out that defendants can also be given extra time for charges on which they were acquitted. This "goes against virtually everything we know and respect about the American criminal justice system," he said.

At this point, the sentencing laws are still in flux. The "mandatory minimum" sentences that are put in place by Congress cannot be changed by the high court. It did rule recently, however, that the sentencing guidelines are not legal mandates. The court must now decide when judges can ignore the guidelines. ✍

—**Garry W. Johnson**, MOUNTAIN REVIEW Staff

New crack cocaine sentencing guidelines made retroactive in Federal system

Beginning March 3, sentencing guidelines put in place by the U.S. Sentencing Commission in November will become retroactive, making nearly 20,000 federal inmates eligible for early release—3,804 in the first year alone.

On Monday, December 10, the U.S. Supreme Court gave judges more leeway to impose shorter sentences for crack cocaine offenses. The next day, the seven-member commission voted unanimously to make their new sentencing guideline apply to past convictions.

A survey by the Commission found that just in Tennessee, 497 prisoners could be eligible for release or reduced sentences—59 in Middle Tennessee, 289 in East Tennessee and 149 in West Tennessee. The decision, however, affects only those in federal prison and not state prisoners, who make up the vast majority of convicted drug offenders.

Federal prisoners who are eligible for sentence reductions would have to apply to a judge and could see their sentences reduced an average of 27 months, according to estimates by the Sentencing Commission. The releases would occur over the next 30 years, but "not every crack cocaine offender will be eligible for a lower sentence under the decision," said the commission in a statement. "A federal sentencing judge will make the final determination."

The new guidelines reduce, but do not eliminate, the difference in mandatory sentences between crack and powder cocaine offenses. Previous guidelines directed judges to impose much stiffer sentences on people convicted for crimes involving crack cocaine, a disparity long criticized by civil liberty and legal groups such as the American Civil Liberties Union and the American Bar Association.

Of the 19,500 federal prisoners serving time for crack offenses, 86% are black, fewer than 6% are white and 94% are men, according to U.S. Sentencing Commission data. In 2006, crack cocaine offenders were sentenced to an average of 122 months in prison, while powder cocaine offenders received only 85 months. The commission's decision does not change sentencing recommendations for powder cocaine.

Neither the Supreme Court decision nor the commission's new sentencing guidelines change the federal law's minimum sentences of five and 10 years for crack cocaine offenses. Only Congress can change the law which was established in 1986, and mandates the same five-year minimum sentence for dealing 5 grams of crack cocaine or dealing 500 grams of powdered cocaine. There are currently several bills up for consideration which would reduce or eliminate the disparities. ✍

New Jersey bans death penalty

On December 17, New Jersey became the first state to legislatively ban the death sentence since the U.S. Supreme Court allowed states to restore capital punishment in 1976.

Governor Jon Corzine signed the legislation which replaces the death penalty with life in prison without parole. The new law "best captures our state's highest values and reflects our best efforts to search for true justice rather than state-endorsed killing," he said.

In January, the New Jersey Death Penalty Study Commission issued a report which concluded the death penalty did not meet the evolving standards of decency and the state could not guarantee an innocent person would not be put to death.

According to Gannett News Service, "Republican Assembly Leader Alex DeCroce called the bill's signing a week before Christmas 'a cause for shame.'" ✍

Legal News was written and edited by Garry W. Johnson, MOUNTAIN REVIEW Staff

Police testing new meth detector

A new handheld device developed by an Arizona company will potentially provide police with a new investigative tool to detect methamphetamine with the click of a button, but some lawyers are already raising concerns.

Law enforcement agencies in Missouri and Arizona are evaluating the meth scanner, which was manufactured by the Tucson-based CDEX. The company planned to test the device on different types of meth over the month of November. The device emits ultraviolet light to scan skin, clothes, or other surfaces for traces of meth, according to the company's CEO, Malcolm Philips. He says the device will detect as little as one microgram of meth (one millionth of a gram), an amount so small it can only be seen under a microscope.

Philips says meth gives off a telltale signature that differs from other chemicals, even the drug pseudoephedrine (one of meth's key ingredients that can be found in many over-the-counter medications). "We tested pseudoephedrine, and it's going to give a different chemical signature than meth."

The technology used in the scanner is not new, says Greg Story, a professor of atomic physics at the University of Missouri-Rolla. "I can't speculate on (the scanner's) accuracy, but yes, in principle, it's absolutely possible." According to Story, energized by ultraviolet light, molecules emit a unique color spectrum that can be measured.

The scanner was initially field-tested by the Missouri State Highway Patrol in Joplin, Springfield, and Willow Springs in 2006. Philips said troopers found it difficult to know if they were aiming the device properly. CDEX responded by installing a laser pointer to guide targeting and has done its own testing on police-supplied samples of meth. The company has not reported on any independent verification of the test, which causes concern by defense attorneys and civil rights activists.

"Anytime you have testing of a device by someone who stands to make a lot of money off of it, I am always suspect of that," said Springfield defense attorney Stacie Bilyeu. "If the testing was done by unbiased, nonpartisan groups, the results would be more reliable." The American Civil Liberties Union agrees, according to Barry Steinhardt, director of the group's Technology and Liberty Program in Washington, D.C. They feel that the technology needs to be independently tested before a court can admit results from the scanner in court, he said.

According to Eric Sterling, president of the Washington, D.C.-based Criminal Justice Policy Foundation, the use of the scanner by law enforcement agencies falls into a legal grey area. He poses two possible scenarios with pertinent legal questions: First, if police use the scanner to detect meth on the door of a house which is suspected of being a meth lab, is that enough for a judge to issue a warrant? And second, is a search warrant required for police to use the scanner during a routine vehicle search on car surfaces or the hands and face of the driver, or does this meet the standard of plain view?

Sterling notes that on the door of a house the scanner would only show that someone who handled meth had touched the door and that it could have been anyone. He further notes that police are restricted by the U.S. Supreme Court from using thermal-imaging devices to detect the presence of marijuana growing inside a home without a search warrant, but the same search of a vehicle might result in a different ruling. A further concern would be the trace amounts of illicit drugs that show up on paper money and other everyday items. "This scanner only detects chemicals, not criminal conduct," attorney Bilyeu said.

CDEX is not expected to wait to see how the legal questions play out before putting the scanner on the market. Their product, which cost between $2,500-$5,500 depending on the sensitivity level, will be available by February. ✍

Gunning for meth
Police are testing a new methamphetamine detection device. How the "meth gun" works:

2 An optical "signature" of area scanned is sent back to the gun

3 If the scans match meth chemistry, the handler is alerted

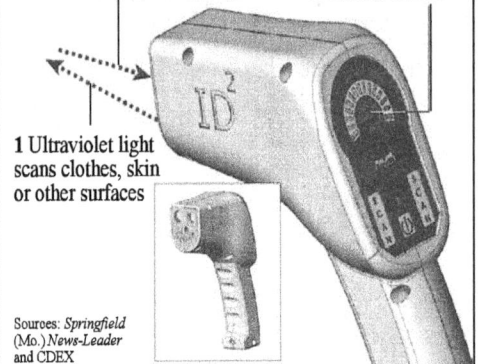

1 Ultraviolet light scans clothes, skin or other surfaces

ID²

Sources: *Springfield (Mo.) News-Leader* and CDEX

TENNESSEE: Nashville—A special legislative committee on the death penalty heard a former U.S. attorney say police should record interrogations. Thomas Sullivan chaired a commission that reviewed Illinois' capital punishment statute after several death row inmates were exonerated. Sullivan said recordings also can reduce appeals based on allegations of false confessions.—*USA Today*, 12-7-2007

Mental retardation claims restricted

Claims of mental retardation to avoid the death penalty have gotten harder in Tennessee. In the recent case of *Tennessee v. Danny Strode*, the Tennessee Supreme Court handed down a ruling which bars reliance on adult testing for the disorder.

In a unanimous decision the high court found that Danny Strode is eligible for the death penalty in the beating death of a Bledsoe County store owner during a 2001 robbery, because intelligence tests taken when he was a juvenile did not show signs of retardation, even though later testing did.

The court ruling will likely limit defense attempts to use mental retardation to fight a capital sentence, death penalty experts say. The state will still prohibit executing inmates who showed signs of mental retardation before adulthood.

In its opinion the court noted that Tennessee law prohibits executing "any defendant with mental retardation at the time of committing first-degree murder," which coincides with the U.S. Supreme Court ban on executing the mentally retarded.

The state Supreme Court, however, relied further on a Tennessee statue that requires "mental retardation must have been manifested during the developmental period, or by 18 years old."

At the age of 20, police say Strode beat to death Harvey J. Brown during an aggravated robbery December 17, 2001. IQ testing before his 18th birthday showed Strode in a range between 75 to 88. According to state law, 70 or less constitutes mental retardation.

The high court looked at the legislative history of the statute and reviewed recordings in which lawmakers discussed the legislation before ruling in favor of the state and affirming the appeals court decision.

Justice Cornelia A. Clark wrote, "The proof in the record is that although the defendant had his IQ tested at least four times before reaching the age of 18, he never scored 70 or below on any of those occasions." ✍

The spirit of giving remembered

By Garry W. Johnson
MOUNTAIN REVIEW Staff

This year's annual Volunteer Appreciation Banquet was outstanding.

On October 18, 2007, at 5:30 p.m., the visiting gallery began to fill with prison volunteers from across East Tennessee. These guests were treated to hors d'oeuvres of chicken wings, deviled eggs, grapes, pears, apples, peanuts, pickled peppers, and some of the best cheese balls I can ever remember eating.

The visiting gallery was decorated in a fall theme, with a woven-wood basket centerpiece on the hor d'oeuvre's table and ceramic pumpkins on each guest table. There were also many fall decorations produced by the MCCX Art Shop.

A little after 6:00 p.m., Chaplain Dean Yancey introduced Warden David Mills. Warden Mills welcomed the guests and thanked them for their diligent efforts over the years. He spoke about the new construction taking place here at MCCX, and acknowledged the pivotal role volunteers play in the prison experience. That role, Warden Mills said, will become increasingly more important over the next year and a half as the new prison comes online.

At 6:15 p.m., Chaplain Yancey offered a prayer of thanksgiving, and the volunteers were invited to dinner. Food Service Manager Carey Newberry and his inmate staff of food service workers provided a delectable spread: Turkey and dressing, pork loin, sourdough rolls, squash, garden peas, cranberries, pecan and pumpkin pies, etc. It was truly a great meal.

During the event, everyone was treated to music by the Fellowship Chapel Choir and musicians. At 7:40 p.m., Chaplain Yancey began drawing numbers for door prizes which were produced by the Upholstery and Building Trades classes, and the MCCX Art Shop. A special honor was awarded to Ms. Claudine Norris for a lifetime of volunteer service.

Jeremy Ingram interviewed several of the guests and reported that Kim Miller, Program Director for Avalon Domestic Abuse Center, and Veronica Wright, Morgan Country Court Advocate, are active volunteers at MCCX. Both women offer to speak to both Alcohol and Drug classes and Pre-Release classes about domestic abuse issues. They have been active in volunteer services for several years.

Deacon Norm is a volunteer chaplain. Representing the Roman Catholic Church, he and Mike Sweeney see to it that a Catholic service is held every other Monday night in the chapel. In addition to his services on Monday night, Deacon Norm also assists with the Catechism of the Catholic Church class.

We at the *Mountain Review* would like to thank all of the folks who willingly give of their time, energy, and finances to volunteer here at MCCX. Your efforts are greatly appreciated by both the staff and inmates. You touch more lives than you will ever know. THANK YOU!

Photos by...

153

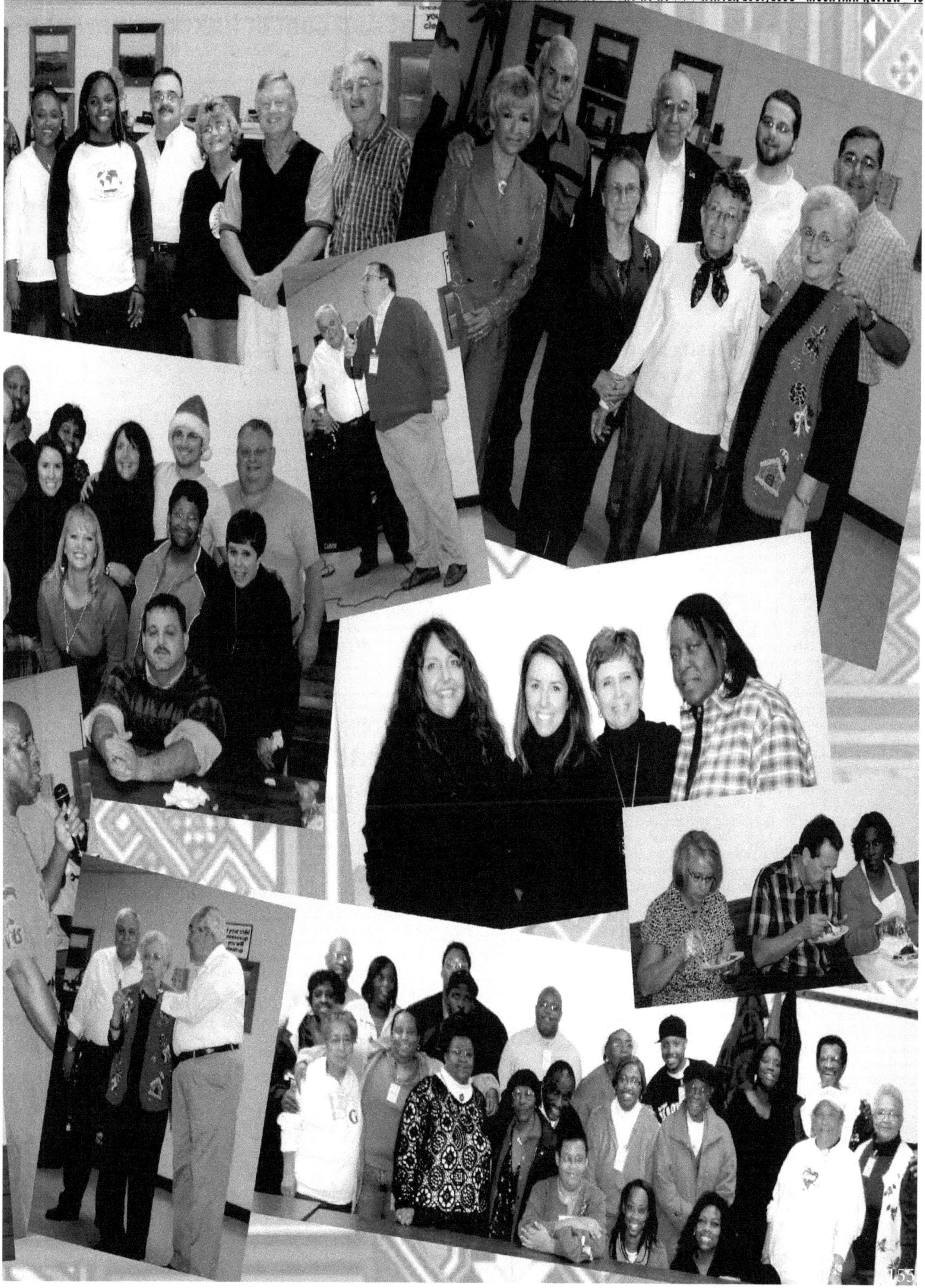

NURSING NEWS: PNEUMONIA 101

By Jennifer Anderson, RN

Get ready to learn any and everything you ever wanted to know about pneumonia. This infection could quite possibly be the single most common complication in hospitalized patients, but even if you are not in the hospital, you are still at great risk. Pneumonia has claimed many lives, but just to throw out some famous names: Fred Astaire, James Brown "The Godfather of Soul," Jim Henson "Creator of the Muppets," and Harriet Tubman, just to name a few of the people that succumbed to this infection. So let's get down to the basics and find out how you can ward off this potentially fatal infection.

Pneumonia is an inflammatory illness of the lungs that can result from a variety of causes including: infection with bacteria, viruses, fungi, or parasites, and chemical or physical injury to the lungs. Pneumonia is a common illness which occurs in all age groups, and is the leading cause of death among the elderly and people who are chronically or terminally ill. Vaccines for certain types of pneumonia are available. The prognosis depends on the type of pneumonia, the appropriate treatment, any complications, and the person's underlying health.

So let's focus now on recognizing the symptoms of pneumonia. I know everyone has heard the term "walking pneumonia," and as far as any physician I have talked to, there is no such thing as this. If you are truly stricken with pneumonia you don't just walk around as usual and carry out your everyday activities. Symptoms of infectious pneumonia include a cough that produces greenish or yellowish sputum, high fever, shaking chills, shortness of breath, chest pain, sharp pain upon taking deep breaths, clammy skin, loss of appetite, fatigue, nausea, vomiting, mood swings and muscle aches. In the elderly, manifestations of pneumonia may not be typical. They may develop worsening confusion or may experience unsteadiness on their feet leading to more frequent falls.

Don't think for a minute you're exempt from pneumonia if you are in the hospital. As hard as we health care professionals try, even we can't totally protect our patients from this. Hospital acquired pneumonia is termed as pneumonia that is acquired during or after hospitalization for another illness or procedure with onset at least 72 hours after admission. Hospitalized patients may have many risk factors for pneumonia, including mechanical ventilation, prolonged malnutri-

tion, underlying heart and lung disease, decreased amount of stomach acids, and immune disturbances. Because individuals with hospital acquired pneumonia usually have underlying illnesses and are exposed to more dangerous bacteria, it tends to be more deadly than community-acquired pneumonia.

So, maybe you think you are having some pneumonia-like symptoms—how can one get a diagnosis? To properly diagnose pneumonia, healthcare professionals rely on patient's symptoms and findings from a physical examination. Information from a chest X-ray, blood tests, and sputum cultures are used to make a diagnosis. Chest X-rays can reveal an area of opacity (seen as white) which represents consolidation. Pneumonia is not always seen on X-rays, either because it is in its initial stages, or because it involves a part of the lung that is not easily seen on an X-ray.

Once diagnosed, let's delve into how we can go about treating this infection. In most cases, pneumonia can be treated without hospitalization. Typically, oral antibiotics, rest, fluids, and home care are sufficient for complete resolution. Antibiotics are the main treatment, but as with any illness, staying hydrated is of vital importance.

Just so none of us have to worry about all of this, let's just prevent it, right? Well, to be educated on all the facts of pneumonia is extremely important. Recognizing symptoms early can save one a lot of headaches. The good news is there are several ways to prevent pneumonia. First, appropriately treating underlying illnesses (such as AIDS) can decrease a person's risk of pneumonia. Smoking cessation is important not only because it helps limit lung damage, but also because smoke interferes with many of the body's natural defenses against pneumonia. Vaccines are now available for preventing pneumonia in both adults and children. Because pneumonia bacteria enter through inhalation, be aware of sick individuals that you are around. And yes, I know I harp on this every time, but I just can't say it enough —wash, wash, wash your hands.

This concludes my crash course in pneumonia. It's basically everything you need to know about pneumonia. After all, isn't knowing half the battle? ✍

Editor's note: Jennifer Anderson is an employee of Parkwest Hospital in Chattanooga. She is a regular contributor and sister of Mountain Review editor Jeremy Ingram.

Pneumonia as seen on chest x-ray

A- normal; B- abnormal (There is a large area of white in the lower picture):

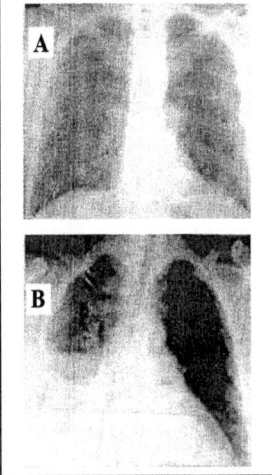

Fat and cancer linked in new study

By Garry W. Johnson
MOUNTAIN REVIEW Staff

Evidence is piling up that those who weigh too much are more likely to develop cancer, according to a landmark report in November.

The analysis from the American Institute for Cancer Research and the World Cancer Research Fund also found that no amount of processed meat is considered completely safe, specifically mentioning bacon, sausage and lunch meat.

The report (www.dietandcancerreport.org), was developed by an international panel of experts who reviewed more than 7,000 large-scale studies over a five year period. They found that excess body fat increases the risk of cancer of the colon, kidney, pancreas, esophagus and uterus, as well as postmenopausal breast cancer.

Karen Collins, a cancer institute nutrition adviser, says, "People forget fat is not an inert glob that we are carrying around on the waistline and thighs. It's a metabolically active tissue that produces substances in the body that promote cancer risk." The report also found:

➤ The risk of colorectal cancer is increased by 21% for every 1.7 ounces of processed meat consumed a day.

"This is a wake-up call for people who eat hot dogs or pepperoni pizza regularly," Collins says. She also notes that smoked meats have been linked to carcinogens, and processed meats contain high levels of salt and nitrates.

➤ The report says the evidence linking red meat intake to colorectal cancer is more convincing than it was a decade ago. It suggests limiting weekly intake of cooked red meat to 18 ounces. Collins says the risk is minimal for people who consume that amount, but beyond that the risk rises.

➤ An increased risk of cancer of the mouth, throat, larynx, esophagus, breast, colon and liver are linked to alcohol consumption.

Also released in November, a separate survey of 1,022 adults by the cancer institute showed that 39% say cancer is their top health concern and 49% say it's highly unlikely they can do anything to prevent cancer. "Let's not be afraid anymore," Collins says. "There is something you can do about it." ✍

How to cut your cancer risk

The American Institute for Cancer Research and the World Cancer Research Fund recommend:

➤ Maintain a healthy body mass index of 18.5 to 24.9.

➤ Limiting consumption of red meat to no more than 18 ounces (cooked) a week.

➤ Eliminating processed meats such as bacon, ham, sausage and lunch meat.

➤ Eating five servings or more of fruit and vegetables a day.

➤ Limiting consumption of alcohol to no more than two drinks a day for men and one for women.

➤ Exercising at least 30 minutes a day.

➤ Limiting consumption of salt.

➤ Limiting processed foods high in added sugar and fat.

Heart disease risk may be lowered by fasting

Doctors have long thought that Mormons have less heart disease due to the religion's ban on smoking, but new research suggest that another of their "clean living" habits may also be helping their hearts: Fasting.

The study was conducted in Utah, where the Mormon church is based, and found that those who regularly took breaks from food (Mormons and non-Mormons alike) were less likely to be diagnosed with clogged arteries than those who did not regularly fast.

The Church of Jesus Christ of Latter-

Day Saints advises abstaining from food the first Sunday of each month, which lowers their risk of heart disease by 40%, according to Benjamin Horne, a heart disease researcher from Intermountain Medical Center and the University of Utah in Salt Lake City.

Horne, who led the study, says that of the 515 people surveyed, only fasting made any significant difference in heart disease: 59% of periodic meal skippers were diagnosed with heart disease verses 67% of the others. The results persisted even when researchers took into account weight, age, and other maladies. ✍

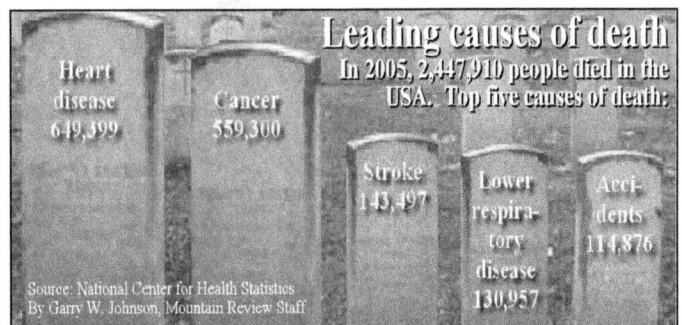

Leading causes of death
In 2005, 2,447,910 people died in the USA. Top five causes of death:

Heart disease 649,399
Cancer 559,300
Stroke 143,497
Lower respiratory disease 130,957
Accidents 114,876

Source: National Center for Health Statistics
By Garry W. Johnson, Mountain Review Staff

Anger Management back after brief respite

By Jeremy Ingram
MOUNTAIN REVIEW Staff

The Anger Management class is back after a brief break. Originally designed years ago by a collaboration between Myer Pettyjohn and others, this class is suited for inmates who have a problem managing their anger.

Anger can be defined as a whole-personed response to a negative moral judgement. This complex definition contains all the essential components that describe anger's source. First, anger is a "whole-personed response." Anger is not simply an emotional response that is not controlled by an individual. Rather, anger is a choice one makes. This implies that when you get angry, you can be in control of your anger. The frequent saying in Anger Management class is "Own your anger!"

Another implication in the above definition is that the source of our anger is based on how we perceive the world. If anger is either increased or decreased by how we view the world around us, then we must be careful to analyze the causes, sources and functions of our anger.

Take, for example, an annoying habit the person you are living with may have. The way you perceive this particular situation can be the difference between a serious anger issue on the one hand and a simple solution on the other. If a person interprets this habit as blatant disrespect, then anger is sure to follow. However, if it is interpreted as simply an annoying habit, then anger is greatly reduced.

The Anger Management class will not make you quit being angry, but it will provide the tools needed to better manage anger and use anger in a constructive way.

If you wish to sign up for the class, please fill out an information request form, explaining your desire to sign up for Anger Management. Forward this form to Jeff Bemesderfer in the clinic. Your name will be added to the waiting list.

The program is fourteen sessions long and meets on Tuesdays and Thursdays from 3:00 to 4:30 in the library. Everyone is welcome and encouraged to sign up. Although, this program will not fulfill any recommendation by the parole board, it is a good way to show initiative. ✍

Pre Release class twelve graduation

By Jeremy Ingram
MOUNTAIN REVIEW Staff

After a ten week intense course, Pre-Release class twelve graduated on September 20, 2007. Students, aides, instructor, and other invited guests gathered in the outside visitation area to commemorate the completion of the Pre-Release program. Instructor Rickey Bunch began the graduation by commenting that this class was a "tough class." He explained that some students really had a desire to go home while others were happy to be in prison. The later students are ones who like who they are and who they have been. Mr. Bunch, quoting Dr. Phil asked, "How's that working for you?"

Everyone has made mistakes, no one in life is perfect. But the mistakes we have made have cost our family and friends dearly. Mr. Bunch told the graduating class that his goal was to see every one on the street living a productive life. He said that he would be happy to see one of his students making more money than him, married, and with children.

Mr. Bunch stressed accountability for one's actions. He frequently referred to society as a playing field. He said, "This is their playing field, their rules, and their referees. Winning on someone else's field is hard." His point was that a well-managed life involves discipline, and discipline involves playing by the rules. Just as a sports hero disciplines himself through constant practice, and knows what the rules are and how to play by the rules, the ex-con must do the same.

Mr. Bunch talked about growing up on a farm. He spoke about driving a tractor through a muddy field one day and getting the tires stuck in some deep mud. The rut that was created by the tractor made it very hard to get out of the mess he had gotten himself into. When he tried to dig the tractor out of the mud, he got dirty in the process. After calling one of his friends to help him get unstuck, his friend became stuck in the process. Mr. Bunch commented that if he would have listened to what his father had told him in the first place he never would have been stuck. He turned this experience around and asked each graduate if they had been told what to do. Then he asked how many people did they drag down with them financially, emotionally, and spiritually. Lastly, he asked, "If you get stuck again and ask for help, then how many times are you going to hurt your family, yourself, and society?"

Mr. Bunch finished his address with the thought that if a person did wrong without knowing it was wrong, then that is one thing. But if a person does wrong while knowing it is wrong, then that is altogether different. He remarked that some in his class had evaluated him as having said the same things over and over again. "Still," Mr. Bunch said, "at least you've been told." He concluded with this: "Can you do all you have learned? Will you remember all you have learned? Will you apply what you have been taught to your family and society? Is the ability to manage your own life worth it? There comes a time in a man's life when enough is enough. Have you come to the point where you can say, 'I've had enough. It's time to change?'"

Associate Warden Jennie Jobe was in attendance. She asked everyone present how many had family they love, to which everyone raised their hand. Then she asked how many have criminal behaviors they love, to which many raised their hand. Dr. Jobe explained that a person could not love both his family and his criminal behavior. If he loves criminal behavior, then it is evident that he does not love his family. Dr. Jobe challenged everyone to choose which one they love the most.

Steve Schrimsher, recently released after serving over two decades behind bars, said, "The Pre-Release class was an excellent tool for me. After twenty-five years, it prepared me for the possibility of being released into society. The class made me aware of the changes, and what will be expected of me for this to work. It increased my vocabulary about my feelings and taught me how to talk to people better. I would advise all old-timers to look into this class before meeting the parole board."

Shane Barber said, "Pre-Release has been very insightful and I believe anyone could benefit from the class. I encourage anyone that can get into the class to take the opportunity." ✍

This photo shows just some of the handy work of the MCCX building trades class.

New life for old books

By Jeremy Ingram
MOUNTAIN REVIEW Staff

Irwin Herman, your average retiree, moved from Chicago to San Diego to get away from the harsh coldness of the Chicago winters. Little did he know, that this was the beginning of a new career as the "Bookman."

Not long after moving to San Diego, a friend of his mentioned to him that inmates in the jail needed books to read. So, Mr. Herman donated some used books he had lying around.

Soon afterward, the inmates who had received the books invited Mr. Herman to their GED graduation. He took them up on the offer and was surprised that these inmates were more than the traditional "prison number" some people make them out to be. In his words "These were real people, not numbers. They told me I helped change their lives."

The inmates affectionately named Mr. Herman the "Bookman" for his generosity. So, he started buying more books to donate to inmates in the area. This began a booming business and the Bookman's exit from retirement.

The Bookman's warehouse is filled with books of all kinds, available to anyone who wants them.

At first, Mr. Herman worked out of his garage with a few other men. Very soon, all their garages were full of books and the operation needed somewhere to move. After an article about Mr. Herman ran in a San Diego newspaper, the daughter of a local building owner offered him a 5,000 foot warehouse he could use free.

What is more, is this building owner offered to pay all the rent and utilities free, and match contributions toward buying books up to $3,000.

Along with the increased space came increased numbers of volunteers. Men, calling themselves "Elves," help Mr. Herman collect, sort, and distribute books to inmates and prisons.

What started as a small, personal gift, turned into a $60,000 business. Mr. Herman is now able to help people in addition to inmates. He frequently donates books to teachers, students, and anyone else who needs books. His motto is "Providing books to anyone who wants to read and learn." ✍

This is a story about a young man's journey in life. It covers his childhood and ends when he finally wakes up to life and becomes a man who accepts responsibility for his actions.

He grew up seeing some of the adults in his life drink alcohol and use different types of drugs. They always seemed to be laughing and having fun, but occasionally they would argue and fight. So, he started thinking that was how you lived life and had fun.

He started by experimenting with weed and alcohol. His first time was not a very pleasant experience. He got caught trying to smoke pot at school during recess in the third grade. This scared him enough to keep him away from trying it for awhile, but not for very long. Fear wore off and curiosity took over once more and he tried it again about a year later. This time he got away with getting high by smoking some marijuana. This drug made him feel like he was on a roller coaster, a fun ride like he had never before experienced in life. He was experiencing what he thought was the key to happiness. From that day on, the thrill of chasing that feeling was forever in his system and his journey down the "Fast Lane" of life began.

He was a young boy around the age of ten. Small and skinny for his age. He grew up in a large city going to public schools. He was picked on because of his size and he looked like he was a welfare kid wearing second hand clothes. His father and mother separated when he was ten years old. That loss played a role in his attraction to drugs, because he needed something to fill the void left by his father. Growing up, he was the oldest of three kids living in a single parent home with his mother. She was falling apart at the seams and using various drugs to try and cope with her emotional problems, as well as everyday life. Marijuana was a way for him to escape his childhood troubles and feel more like a grown up. Never did he think that this one decision in life would have such a lasting affect and would later in life help lead him to much stronger drugs.

From the time he started using drugs, life was a total waste because he spent all his time chasing after and doing different types of drugs. He was learning to live a life of criminal and addictive behavior and the attraction of it at first was to feel more grown up than he was. The list of drugs he tried the first couple of years was long and it is a wonder he didn't die from using the type of drugs he was experimenting with.

The next couple of years were a blur to him and the only thing he really can remember is that he was high during them. Life at home was an everyday party and he was enjoying every bit of it that he could. Little did he know that he would pay a price later in life for the very things he was learning to do. Childhood was slipping away. He was making the same mistakes that grownups were making, but he was doing them at the age of ten—learning poor coping skills, criminal behavior, and acquiring an ever growing habit of wanting to get high and do more drugs.

From the age of twelve to fourteen, he lived at so many different places that he can't even recall them all. The different schools he went to meant always being the new kid on the block. Feeling like an outcast was a common feeling for him. It was like he accepted the part about his life that he was not like the other kids, that he was always going to be different and a failure.

He always seemed to excel at whatever he was doing when someone payed attention to him or encouraged him. But most of the time it was not the right people he got encouragement from or for the right things he was learning and doing. The life he was learning how to live was a life of drugs, alcohol, and crime. He always wanted to be different, he just didn't realize how much power a decision he made a few years before would have in his life or the impact it would make on the people who cared the most about him.

By the time he was sixteen, his habit had leveled off and he was basically sticking to marijuana with occasional use of various pills. The mistakes and poor decisions that he was making at this point in life didn't come to mind as being associated with his drug use and the way he learned to use drugs to cope with life. The influence that drugs had on the decisions he was making in his life was incomprehensible to his young and immature mind. Drugs were influencing almost every decision he was making in life. When he woke up in the morning, he was thinking about how he was going to get high. When he went to sleep, he was doing the same. This child was becoming selfish, with the desire to only please himself.

Drugs were consuming his life and would continue to do so for many years to come. He started drinking alcohol when he was eighteen and life really started going by even faster than it was before, now that he had another drug in his life. Thinking back over the years, he remembered nothing that didn't involve drugs or alcohol in some way or another. His days consisted of "How am I going to get high today?" not "How am I going to provide for my needs today?" As you can guess, life only became more difficult for him. He kept repeating mistakes in life; lying, stealing, and hurting others who cared about him by doing these things. He damaged relationships with the people who had taken care of him and gave him what love he had received in life. They had tried every way they knew how at that time to try and get him to wake up and see the damage he was doing to himself and the people around him, but he was blinded by his addiction and could not see past it. Anytime someone tried to talk to him about his problem with drugs and alcohol, he felt attacked and threatened because they were attacking the one thing in life that he felt was comforting him. The real comfort was right in front of him, it was the people who loved him dearly and cried many tears over his actions. He continued to get worse, and the grip his addiction had on him was getting tighter and tighter.

He used and abused all who tried to help him. He lost every legal paying job he ever had because of his selfish habit. He had let his addiction get so deeply ingrained into his character that it became his identity. Any attack on his addiction was an attack against him. Drugs and alcohol had became his security, his mother, his father, his best friend, and his escape from reality; drugs were his life.

He was doing every kind of drug he could get his hands on to try and cope with the life that he thought was so terrible. He had let the drugs and alcohol blind him to the fact that life is not easy for anyone, and that it can be really hard on some until they do something to make it better. Instead, he just continued his life doing drugs and alcohol, and feeling like he was a victim of a terrible life, creating carnage and wreaking havoc upon the lives of all who cared about him.

Most of the victims he created throughout his life would be there for him when he turned his life around, but some of them would not. Some had passed away while he was still living a life consumed by his desire for drugs. The guilt, shame, and regret over the pain he had caused these people would be in his heart forever. He used this as fuel to repair the damaged relationships and as a reminder of what he was capable of doing while he was using drugs and alcohol.

After he realized all these things about himself and what he had let drugs and alcohol do to his life, he started his journey along the road to sobriety. The road of sobriety was a road that traveled back the same road as he had been running wide open on for many years, but it was going the opposite direction. The road was filled with many regrets due to the wrongs he had done to others, some were people he knew; some were just innocent victims. Seeing these people and putting himself in the spot to face his victims, to make the wrongs in his life right, and to repair what relationships he could with the people who were still alive and in his life, was going to be a lifelong job.

There is still the regret of the hurt and pain that he has to deal with over the people who are no longer in his life because they had passed away. Those are the problems of real life and he is dealing with them the way a real responsible man is suppose to—sober and straight forward.

Life doesn't get easier when you stop using drugs, it just gets simpler. The problems that you had before you started using drugs and alcohol are still going to occur, but the problems that drugs caused will not. I heard a man say one time that if you stop and think before you act or speak, half of the problems in your life will disappear or never materialize.

Life is not easy by a long shot, but using drugs and alcohol will only complicate things. You will be amazed at how much easier things go for you when you don't rely on drugs and alcohol to deal with them. Drugs and alcohol are the biggest illusions in this world because they only disguise the problems we seek to fix. They don't fix them or help them get better.

The role that drugs and alcohol play in people coming to prison, breaking homes up, and tearing marriages apart is astounding.

God played a big part in this person's life. Even when this man gave up on life, himself, and others, God never gave up on him. He knew there was a plan for him that involved him helping others to change. He was going to be a tool in His plan. He had some people who believed in him and he was tired of letting people down and being a failure in life. He used that as fuel to become a better person.

I hope that anyone reading this who does drugs, alcohol, or practices criminal behavior will reevaluate his life and take a step toward changing. Life is too precious to waste on drugs and throw away committing crimes. Help yourself to be what you once dreamed you wanted to be, then help someone else to do the same. Just think, if every person in this country would do their part to make it a better place, how great would this country be? Remember, it is our responsibility to do something that will improve our environment. You owe the world whatever you can do to make it better, not make it worse. Please do your part in helping to make it better.

Life in the Fast Lane

Anonymous Contribution

High numbers
More than 19 million Americans 12 years and older are users of an illicit drug. Past-month users (in millions):

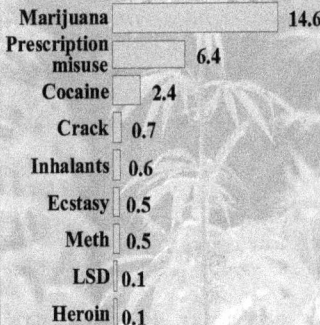

Drug	Users (millions)
Marijuana	14.6
Prescription misuse	6.4
Cocaine	2.4
Crack	0.7
Inhalants	0.6
Ecstasy	0.5
Meth	0.5
LSD	0.1
Heroin	0.1

Source: 2005 National Survey on Drugs Use and Health

By Garry W. Johnson, Mountain Review

Underage alcohol danger
Rates of emergency room visits among people ages 12-20 involving alcohol or alcohol combined with other drugs (per 100,000 population):

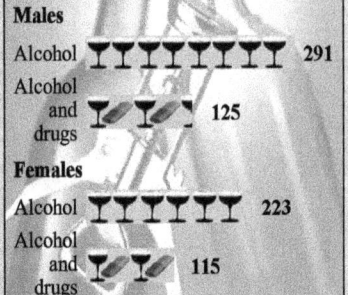

Males

Alcohol — 291

Alcohol and drugs — 125

Females

Alcohol — 223

Alcohol and drugs — 115

Source: Drug Abuse Warning Network

By Garry W. Johnson, Mountain Review

American Addiction

By Garry W. Johnson
MOUNTAIN REVIEW Staff

Drug and alcohol addiction is endemic in American families. A USA Today/HBO nationwide poll conducted April 27-May 31 2006, found one in five adults said they had an immediate relative who at some point had been addicted to alcohol or drugs. That comes out to roughly 40 million American adults with a spouse, parent, sibling or child battling addiction—not to mention the millions of children living with an addicted parent.

Psychiatrist and lawyer H. Westley Clark said he was not surprised at the 20% response to the poll's question about addicted family members. "I don't think that's particularly high," said Clark, who is director of the Center for Substance Abuse Treatment at the Substance Abuse and Mental Health Service Administration (SAMHSA). "Roughly half of American adults drink alcohol. You're dealing with a large number here."

FAMILIES SUFFER

The poll, which was conducted by Gallup, showed women who had an addicted relative mentioned their spouse 31% of the time, compared with only 12% of men. Women were also significantly more likely than men to say that a family member's addiction had hurt their mental and physical health and their marriage. Three out of four respondents with addicted close relatives said they thought their family member could make a full recovery. Yet two-thirds of them believed that recovery was only possible with professional help.

A nationwide household survey in 2003 found that six million children in the USA lived with at least one parent who abused or was addicted to alcohol or drugs during the previous year, according to the SAMHSA director. "Children who are in critical developmental phases, who are quite young, can be profoundly impacted."

In a study conducted by the University at Buffalo, researchers found that among fathers of 12-month-olds, those who abused alcohol spoke less to their children and expressed less positive involvement. When it came to their kids, they also felt more negative emotions and aggravation.

The study showed that by 18 months of age, children of fathers who abused alcohol had more symptoms of anxiety and depression than their peers. According to

The Negatives

A USA Today/HBO poll found U.S. women bear the brunt of the problems caused by relatives' drug and alcohol addiction. Percentage who suffered major negative effects on their:

Emotional or Mental health	Women 35% Men 23%	Physical health	Women 18% Men 8%
Relationship with other family members	Women 22% Men 19%	Personal financial situation	Women 19% Men 12%
		Relationship with friends	Women 14% Men 10%
		Job	Men 9% Women 6%
		Marriage	Women 21% Men 11%

theNational Association for Children of Alcoholics (NACA), about one in four kids of an alcoholic will become alcoholics themselves, if no one intervenes.

"There's a very disproportionate number of people growing up in those families who end up with addiction or abuse," said an NACA representative. "These children are so good at looking OK that they fool their parents." Sherri Fisher, co-author of a study exploring the usefulness of consultations with parents about their children's drug and alcohol use agrees. "Our conclusion is that parents do not provide valuable information (to researchers) about their children's use of alcohol and drugs because they simply don't know about it."

Further complicating the situation is an increasing number of teens getting high with legal drugs like painkillers, mood stimulants, and even cough syrup. The annual study by the National Institute on Drug Abuse released in December of 2006, found a small but growing number of teens were popping prescription painkillers like OxyContin and Vicodin and stimulants like Ritalin. As many as one in every 14 highschool seniors said they used cold medicine "fairly recently" to get high. Researchers found that marijuana re-

mained the single most abused drug among teens. Nearly 12% of 8th graders reported using it, compared to 25% of 10th graders and 31% of highschool seniors. Alcohol consumption was reported by one-third of 8th graders, more than half of 10th graders and two-thirds of the seniors surveyed.

Though still small by comparison, the number of teens who got high from medications is on the rise. Nearly 10% of highschool seniors admitted to using excessive dosages of Vicodin, and 3.6% of 10th grades got high off Ritalin. Experts say that teens turning to cough syrup to get high is particularly alarming, because the medicine is cheap and easy to get.

The study also found teens abusing inhalants had dropped slightly, with 9% of 8th graders reporting sniffing glue, spray paints, cleaning fluids or other inhalants to get high.

SOCIETY SUFFERS

As research shows, drug addicted and alcoholic parents often raise drug addicted and alcoholic children. These children grow into drug addicted and alcoholic adults —adults which are steadily pouring into the prison system.

In October of 2006, the Bureau of Justice Statistics released a report on prior drug use among state and federal prisoners which

compared the years 1997 and 2004.

The 1997 numbers showed 45% of federal and 57% of state prisoners had admitted to using drugs in the month prior to their offenses. When they committed their crimes, 33% of state and 22% of federal prisoners said they were high. By 2004 the number of federal prisoners reported using drugs the month before their crimes was up to 50%, and 26% reported using drugs during the commission of their offence. The state numbers for 2004 remained roughly the same, dropping one percentage point in both categories to 56% and 32% respectively.

Extensive criminal histories were also found to be prevalent among prisoners reporting a recent drug dependence prior to their crime. Fifty-three percent of state prisoners who were dependent or using drugs had at least three prior sentences to probation or incarceration, compared to 32% of other prisoners. They also were more likely (48%) to be on probation or parole at the time of their arrest compared to other prisoners (37%).

STOP THE CYCLE

If you find yourself in these statistics, or you know drugs and/or alcohol has played (or is playing) a role in destroying your life and family, get help now. This institution offers several programs to help you overcome your addiction. The Alcohol and Drug (A&D) program, Celebrate Recovery, and Alcoholics Anonymous (AA), all have proven track records of helping addicts get control of their lives.

One favorable finding to come from the Justice Department report involved those who said they used drugs the month before committing their crime. The percentage of prisoners in that group receiving treatment in both state and federal custody has gone up. The state percentage rose from 34% to 39% between 1997 and 2004, while the federal numbers went up from 39% to 45% over the same span of time.

Stop the vicious cycle of addiction today, and put yourself in a better statistical category: Sign up for the A&D program with the counselors in unit 5, attend AA Tuesday nights at 7:00 p.m. in the inmate dining room, and/or Celebrate Recovery on Wednesday nights at 6:00 p.m. in the library classroom. All you have to do is show up, and be ready to change your life. ✍

Methadone-related deaths rising

As methadone is being used for pain relief, more people are dying from it:

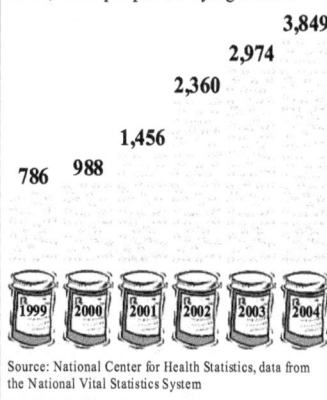

786 988 1,456 2,360 2,974 3,849
1999 2000 2001 2002 2003 2004

Source: National Center for Health Statistics, data from the National Vital Statistics System

High arrest

Federal prisoners who reported use of drugs the month before their arrest, by drugs used:

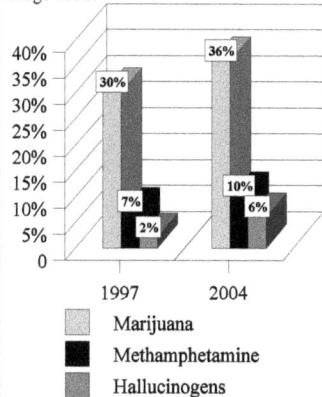

	1997	2004
Marijuana	30%	36%
Methamphetamine	2%	6%
Hallucinogens	7%	10%

Source: Justice Department Report, 2006

Contact information

ALCOHOLICS ANONYMOUS:
AA World Services, Inc.
P.O. Box 459
New York, NY 10163
www.alcoholics-anonymous.org
(212) 870-3400

NARCOTICS ANONYMOUS:
Narcotics Anonymous World Services
P.O. Box 9999
VanNuys, CA 91409
www.na.org
(818) 773-9999

CELEBRATE RECOVERY:
Cokesbury United Methodist Center
9915 Kingston Pike
Knoxville, TN 37922
www.cokesburychurch.org
(865) 693-0353

Deaths during arrest

From 2003 to 2005, 47 states and the District of Columbia reported more than 2,000 arrest-related deaths. Top causes of such deaths:

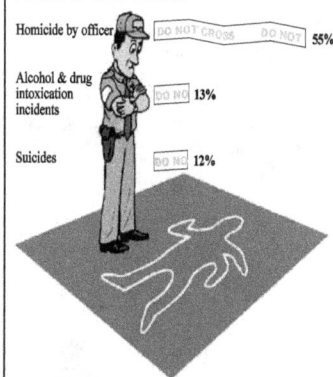

Homicide by officer ... 55%
Alcohol & drug intoxication incidents ... 13%
Suicides ... 12%

Source: Department of Justice

KAIROS ELEVEN

God's Special Time

By Jeremy Ingram
MOUNTAIN REVIEW Staff

Kairos is an interdenominational Christian ministry established to bring God's love and forgiveness to all incarcerated individuals, their families, and those who work with them, and to assist in the transition of becoming a productive citizen. Kairos begins when a volunteer team of men from East Tennessee present a three-day introductory course, described as a "short course in Christianity." After the three-day weekend, a monthly reunion is held to encourage inmates to pursue the truths introduced to them during the weekend.

What happens at a Kairos weekend is not often spoken of in detail so the experience will be new for those who have never been a part of Kairos. Yet, many know that the weekend is filled with music, cookies, prayer, cookies, talks by free world men who share their life experiences, cookies, and overall fun activities (did I mention cookies?) The weekend is Christian in nature, but no religious affiliation is necessary to attend. The only thing expected of inmate participants is attendance the entire weekend and an open mind.

Kairos Prison Ministry got its start in Raiford State Prison in 1976. From earlier attempts to develop a three-day weekend for prisoners, similar to other programs vying for acceptance, a program was developed that could be taken into any correctional institute across the world. The name of the new program was called "Kairos." What set this program apart from others, was that it was specifically designed for the prison environment.

There are two Greek words for time. One of

them, with which we are all familiar, is "kronos," meaning linear time. The other is "kairos," used in the sense of a time set by God for a particular occurrence. In prison, the idea of time can carry many different connotations. Hence, the use of Kairos is significant to those serving time.

Anyone who has not already attended a Kairos weekend may sign up by filling out an application in the chapel. Spaces are limited, so sign up now. Once your application is turned in, you will be put on a waiting list until the next available spot opens.

Albert W. Holmes, former Regional Chaplaincy Coordinator of Texas Department of Criminal Justice, said, "Kairos is the most consistent and effective ministry I experienced in the Texas Criminal Justice System. The format of Kairos aids in a practical presentation of the gospel message which reaches 'residents' where they are. It impacts every facet of their lives: emotional, physical, social and spiritual. The philosophy of this program focuses on residents of all races and personalities in an intense setting and lays a foundation for them to begin communicating, relating and working with each other harmoniously in an environment that usually breeds hostility, prejudice and racism. This ministry permeates both residents and staff."

A participant in a past Kairos weekend had this to say about the experience: "Kairos gave me a reason to live. I believe that, had I not come to know God's love, I probably would not be here today. . . all things are possible with God. "

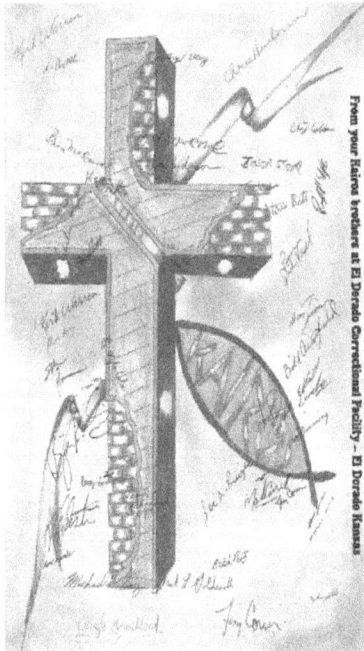

Piece of "Agape"—a letter of encouragement from Kairos graduates at El Dorado Correctional Facility in El Dorado, Kansas.

Kairos 11 Participants

Boyd Adkins
Jim Bailes
Terry Barr
James Carmichael
Ron Conley
Chuck Dugger
David Elkins
Lawrence Grob
Gregory Hoffman
Spencer Hudson
David Jackson
Gary Johnson
Dennis Jones
James Jordan, Jr.
Thurman Kinnebrew
Thurman Kinnebrew, Jr.
Bob Lambert
Merle Larson
Rollin McKean
Joe Melia
Wally Moore
Joe Pace
Patrick Rowan
Jason Taylor
David Vick
Robert Walsh
Wilber Wilson
Bill Wolff
Joanne Beckley
Gwendolyn Carmichael
Bonnie Conley
April Dugger
Rebecca Kinnebrew
Shirley Lundy
Johnny Lundy
Janet Moore
Crystal Schrof
Lillian Mae Shultz
Wilma Walden
Barbara Wolff
Michael Siler
James Ownby
Secdrick Booker
Kris Jackson
Marcus White
Orville Buford
Robert Roddy
William Barney
Charles Russell
Jeff Johnson
Jerry Williams
Gerald Conrad
Hobert Price
Seyed Bagheri
Shrone Hill
Charles Lane
Harold Sharkley
Stanley Decker
Wallace Hann
Mike Hedrick
Doug Duncan
James White
Joey Garrison
Joel Pemberton
David Presley
Richard Vowell
Johnny Hines
Donald Blair
Danny Furr
George Burkett
Michael Gay
Bobby Tate
Charles Brandler
Terrell Turpin
William Vaughn
Randall McPheeters
Joe Baker
Paul Rutherford
Cory Millikin
Jeremy Ingram

Comfort Ministries visits Morgan County

By Jeremy Ingram,
MOUNTAIN REVIEW Staff

Comfort Ministries is a Christian ministry established in Kentucky over fifteen years ago. Hillus and Dottie Pardue, its co-founders, along with Marvey and Frances Wood, annually set up their large tent and host a revival on the compound of MCCX.

The Pardues got their start in prison ministry over fifteen years ago. Hillus Pardue, prior to going into prison ministry, owned and operated his own NAPA auto-parts store. However, when God called him to prison ministry, he gave up everything and heeded the call.

The Pardues frequently work in other prisons across the state of Tennessee and Kentucky. Both Hillus and Dottie, are regular volunteer chaplains at Turney Center, located in Only, Tennessee.

Their work in correctional institutes has not gone unnoticed. Both Tennessee and Kentucky have recognized their selfless efforts and have bestowed on them the prestigious Volunteer of the Year award. In fact, Hillus was given this award twice, in 2000 and 2002, in the state of Kentucky.

The Comfort Ministries tent revival is not unique to Morgan County. The Pardues travel to other correctional institutes during the year and host a tent revival. Turney Center and Morgan County, as well as Special Needs and Green River Correctional Center in Kentucky are fortunate to have Comfort Ministry visit their institutions. The Pardues do not stop there, six other prisons also partake in the Pardue's generous week of revival and praise.

Dottie and Hillus Pardue reside in Kentucky. They are the proud parents of one child and grandparents to two boys. They live with their dog, Toby.

On behalf of the inmate population at Morgan County, I would like to thank the Pardues and the Woods, together with all who allow the tent revival to take place. We appreciate your time and effort and look forward to next summer's revival. ✍

TDOC hires state's first Director of Religious Services

By Jeremy Ingram
MOUNTAIN REVIEW Staff

Ron Turner, 59 years old and a devout Unitarian, was recently appointed as the state's first Director of Religious Services. This new position oversees the state's 18 chaplains in 16 prisons.

Turner comes from a diverse background. He has been a lawyer, poet, and college professor before coming to work for the Department of Corrections. He was first introduced to corrections as a graduate student at Vanderbilt University's divinity school. As part of his program of education, he was assigned to work at Riverbend Maximum Security Institute. There he served in a capacity in which he met all the duties a full-time chaplain might encounter—coordination of religious programming, one-on-one counseling with inmates, and death notifications.

Perhaps drawing on the words of Jesus in Matthew 25:36, "I needed clothes and you clothed me, I was sick and you looked after me, I was in prison and you came to visit me," Turner says that "Jesus said 'visit,' not 'evangelize.' It's a ministry of presence."

With the power to rewrite religious policy for the DOC, it is good news to hear that Turner is sympathetic toward the needs of prisoners. "I'd love to see 19,000 volunteers working one-on-one—mentoring, treating [inmates] as human beings with dignity, an hour a week helping with reading and writing and other needs," says Turner.

With growing concerns for rehabilitation, Turner seems suited for the job. ✍

Percentage of TDOC inmates according to religious belief

100%		
80%		
60%		
40%		
20%		
0%		
Christian	No Religious Belief	Islam or one of 13 other faiths

Federal court rules against state funding for Prison Fellowship

By Jeremy Ingram
MOUNTAIN REVIEW Staff

Charles Colson is one of the few who left prison and followed through with his promise to help prisoners. Founder and chairman of Prison Fellowship, Colson has arguably done more to help prisoners and their families than any other person who has served time. Yet his efforts could not keep a federal appeals court from ruling that state funding for Prison Fellowship's programs is unconstitutional.

Prison Fellowship has been running a faith-based program in Newton Correctional Facility in Iowa. The program is a strict, 18-month voluntary program. Inmates live in their own unit, do Bible studies, and take other classes. The program's success is undeniable. In it's six-year history, only twenty percent of it's graduates have returned to prison (compare with the 65% national average).

Obviously success of this magnitude is not as important as ensuring public funds are not used for faith-based initiatives. This, according to Americans United for Separation of Church and Sate was the reason they brought this lawsuit against Prison Fellowship. Yet, even amid their seeming victory, Prison Fellowship will be allowed to operate this program and nine other programs in six states. The only difference, is that the programs will be funded privately.

Is opposition against the cooperation of church and state, at the expense of a sizably lower recidivism rate, worth the overall cost to taxpayers? For some, the only answer is yes. ✍

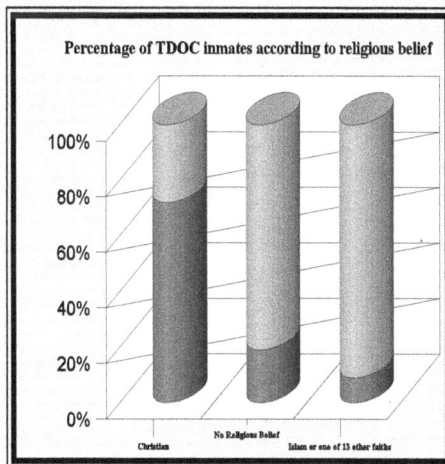

161

The Lord's Prayer
By Jeremy Ingram

The occasion on which Jesus taught His disciples to pray was the Sermon on the Mount recorded in the fifth chapter of Matthew. In chapter five, Jesus warns his followers against the corrupt practices of the scribes and Pharisees: the religious leaders of that time. These religious leaders pretended to be obeying God's commandments, but were in reality distorting His Word to suit their own fancies. In chapter six, Jesus seems to turn his attention toward a more personal temptation—the temptation of hypocrisy. After warning his listeners against hypocrisy in their prayers, he sets forth the true form of prayer so they may be guided in their devotions.

The "Lord's Prayer," as it is traditionally known, says a lot in a very little space. Man's whole duty in prayer is summarized in five verses (Matthew 6:7-13). Matthew Henry, commenting on the Lord's Prayer, says, ". . . it is of his composing, of his appointing; it is very compendious, yet very comprehensive, in compassion to our infirmities in praying. The matter is choice and necessary, the method instructive, and the expression very concise. It has much in a little, and it is requisite that we acquaint ourselves with the sense and meaning of it, for it is used acceptably no further than it is used with understanding and without vain repetition."

The prayer is traditionally divided into a preface, six petitions, and a conclusion. We will examine each in its turn.

The preface to the Lord's Prayer is "Our Father, which art in heaven" (v. 9). The preface to the Lord's Prayer implies two things: that we are to pray, not only for ourselves, but also for others; and we are to pray to our Father in Heaven.

There are two senses in which God is our Father. God is the Father of all mankind in that He created and preserves all mankind by His sovereign power. Yet there is another sense in which He is the Father of those He has adopted into His family. It is to these that this prayer is given.

Next, let us turn our attention to the six petitions. The first three petitions seem to refer mainly to God, His honor and glory. The last three seem to deal mainly with our concerns and needs.

"The petitions, and those are six; the three first relating more immediately to God and his honour, the three last to our own concerns, both temporal and spiritual; as in the ten commandments, the four first teach us our duty toward God, and the last six our duty toward our neighbour. The method of this prayer teaches us to seek first the kingdom of God and his righteousness, and then to hope that other things shall be added" (Matthew Henry's Commentary).

The first petition of the Lord's Prayer is "Hallowed be thy name" (v. 9). The name of God can signify two things: His essence or His character. By His essence I mean who God essentially is. However, as God is incomprehensible (the finite cannot comprehend the infinite), He has made Himself known by His attributes. Thomas Watson explains that, "As a man is known by his name; so by his attributes of wisdom, power, holiness, and goodness, God is known as by his name."

To hallow God's name means to sanctify it, or set it apart from all that is evil. As the temple and the priesthood were set apart in the Old Testament, likewise God's name should be set apart as sacred. This does not mean that anything can be added to God's name. Rather, it means that God's name appears more honorable and glorious in the eyes of others.

Watson mentions sixteen times when it can be said that we hallow and sanctify God's name. Among these are when we profess His name, when we esteem Him highly in our thoughts, when we give Him holy and spiritual worship, when we ascribe the honor of all we do to Him, when we obey Him, when we grieve when His name suffers, when we give the same honor to God the Son that we give to God the Father, when we prefer the honor of His name before the dearest things, and when we hallow and sanctify God's name by a holy conversation.

Watson concludes that we can hallow God's name by gaining a sound knowledge of Him and a growing love for Him.

The second petition of the Lord's Prayer is "Thy kingdom come" (v. 10). In the Gospels alone, the Kingdom of God is referred to more than a hundred times. It was the subject of John the Baptist's preaching, Christ's words, and the commission by which the apostles were sent to preach. Still, what is meant by this petition?

There are two things it does not mean. It does not mean that we are to pray for an earthly, physical kingdom. The people of Jesus' day sought a king who would establish a physical kingdom. Yet Christ explained to Pilate, "My kingdom is not of this world: if my kingdom were of this world, then would my servants fight, that I should not be delivered to the Jews: but now is my kingdom not from hence" (John 18:36). This petition does not mean that we pray God would begin to exercise His providence over creation. He does indeed rule all of creation by His most holy and wise will. Not one thing exists that is outside his control.

Still, what is meant by "Thy kingdom come?" Essentially it means that we pray for God's kingdom to be established in our hearts and that He hasten the coming Kingdom of Glory. Dr. Whitby, quoted by Matthew Henry, writes, "Let thy kingdom come, let the gospel be preached to all and embraced by all; let all be brought to subscribe to the record God has given in his word concerning his Son, and to embrace him as their Saviour and Sovereign. Let the bounds of the gospel-church be enlarged, the kingdom of the world be made Christ's kingdom, and all men become subjects to it, and live as becomes their character."

The third petition of the Lord's Prayer is "Thy will be done in earth, as it is in heaven" (v. 10). In this petition we pray for God's will to be done, essentially that He does what He pleases and we in turn are enabled to obey Him. No better example of this prayer in use is seen than Jesus in the garden. Facing the horrendous death looming over him, he lifted his voice to the heavens and uttered these words: "May your will be done." Matthew records that Jesus prayed this prayer three times during the course of that night. That Christ would tell his disciples to pray that God's will be done "on earth" seems to signify that in this present evil world, so full of disappointments and afflictions, God has a purpose. It is as if Christ was bidding His followers to look behind the visible realm and trust that God's purpose, even amid trials, be done.

The fourth petition of the Lord's Prayer is "Give us this day our daily bread" (v. 11). One of the first things to note is that this petition comes *after* we have prayed "Thy kingdom come. Thy will be done in earth, as it is in heaven." The order is significant because we should always prefer God's glory over our own desires.

Matthew Henry, commenting on this verse, draws six lessons from the words in this petition: "We ask for bread; that teaches us sobriety and temperance; we ask for bread, not dainties, not superfluities; that which is wholesome, though it be not nice. We ask for our bread; that teaches us honesty and industry: we do not ask for the bread out of other people's mouths, not the bread of deceit (Prov. 20:17), not the bread of idleness (Prov. 31:27), but the bread honestly gotten. We ask for our daily bread; which teaches us not to take thought for the morrow (v. 34), but constantly to depend upon divine Providence, as those that live from hand to mouth. We beg of God to give it us, not sell it us, nor lend it us, but give it. The greatest of men must be beholden to the mercy of God for their daily bread. We pray, "Give it to us; not to me only, but to others in common with me." This teaches us charity, and a compassionate concern for the poor and needy. It intimates also, that we ought to pray with our families; we and our households eat together, and therefore ought to pray together. We pray that God would give us this day; which teaches us to renew the desire of our souls toward God, as the wants of our bodies are renewed; as duly as the day comes, we must pray to our Heavenly Father, and reckon we could as well go a day without meat, as without prayer."

The fifth petition of the Lord's Prayer is "And forgive us our debts, as we forgive our debtors" (v. 12). The word, debt, is here used fitly because it is a debt we owe God for failure to preform our duty. This debt is of the most horrible kind because not only have we wronged an infinite God, but also we have wronged him an innumerable amount of times. G. I. Williamson observes that "... for every sin [we commit], there is a debt to pay."

Yet, we are here provided with a solution to the problem: God's forgiveness. All men are guilty before God in a real way. Everyone, save God's grace, deserves eternal damnation. Sometimes we hear from popular psychologists that we should get rid of our feelings of guilt. This is often done through therapy, medication, and other methods. However, the source of this feeling is a very real guilt. There is an infinite debt we owe to our creator. Yet, when God forgives, this guilt is taken away forever by the atoning sacrifice of Jesus Christ.

Some have objected to the use of this prayer by Christians in today's world because of the statement "as we forgive others." They argue that this phrase is works-based righteousness, and as so, belongs to the Old Testament era. However, they misunderstand the intent of this phrase. It is not a supplication for merit, but rather a call for imitation. Christians, having understood God's forgiving grace, ought to be the most forgiving people. Sadly, how often we fail in this regard, Yet, whenever the Lord's Prayer is prayed, the duty of the Christian to forgive as God has forgiven is called to mind. Watson comments: "It is not a cause of God's forgiving us, but a sign. We need not climb up into heaven to see whether our sins are forgiven: let us look into our hearts, and see if we can forgive others. If we can, we need not doubt but God has forgiven us."

The sixth petition of the Lord's Prayer is "And lead us not into temptation, but deliver us from evil" (v. 13). God does not tempt any man. Temptations can come from within ourselves or from outside ourselves. Although our hearts are great tempters, deceitful and wicked; Satan is a much more powerful enemy. He is called a strong man, and as a spirit he can tempt the mind by placing evil thoughts in it. He can stir up the natural corruptions that remain in each of us. He has thousands of years experience in this deceitful craft. Who are we to contend with him?

Yet there is one rock of support God's children can lean on: that God would deliver us from being drawn into the power of temptation and save us from Satan's powerful attacks. We have, in the Bible, a promise that God has made provision for a way out of temptation: "There hath no temptation taken you but such as is common to man: but God is faithful, who will not suffer you to be tempted above that ye are able; but will with the temptation also make a way to escape, that ye may be able to bear it" (1 Cor. 10:13).

The second part of this petition enjoins us to plead to God to deliver us from evil. There are three sources of evil: ourselves, Satan, and the world. The overwhelming number of our foes should cause every Christian to look to God, who alone is able to deliver.

The conclusion to the Lord's Prayer is "For thine is the kingdom, and the power, and the glory, for ever. Amen" (v. 13). There is a problem with the conclusion as found in the reading in Matthew. It is this: many ancient manuscripts of Matthew do not include the conclusion. Probably, sometime in early church history these words were used whenever the Lord's Prayer was prayed. Since these words express a very biblical idea, it is fitting they should be prayed at the conclusion of the Lord's Prayer.

The sovereignty of God is what is in view in these concluding words. There are many ways in which God can be seen as Sovereign. For one, He alone has created the heavens and earth and He alone preserves the universe. A second way that we see the sovereignty of God is in His redemptive work. All men, being by nature dead in their sins and utterly helpless to convert themselves, are in a most dreadful condition. Yet it is in the fact of this "field of bones" that we see God sovereignly renewing the hearts of sinful men, irresistibly drawing them into His grace, and preserving them until the end.

It is only when we grasp the magnitude of God's sovereignty will we find true joy and peace in life. This felicity and God's glory are what is in mind when we pray this conclusion to the Lord's Prayer.

In conclusion there are countless number of ways the Lord's Prayer benefits God's children. But perhaps the greatest way we use this prayer is when our prayers are characterized by Christ's instruction and glorify God in heaven. "For from Him and through Him and to Him are all things. To Him be the glory forever! Amen." ✍

The warfare against one's *self* is the greatest battle ever fought. The yielding of *self*—surrendering one's all to the will of God—is a mighty struggle; but the soul must submit to God before it can be renewed in holiness.

How shall a man be just with God? How shall the sinner be made righteous? It is only through Jesus Christ that we can be brought into harmony with God, with holiness; but how are we to come to Jesus Christ?

True repentance is a sincere sorrowfulness for one's sin and a turning away from it. We shall not renounce sin unless we see its sinfulness; until we turn away from it in our hearts, there will be no real repentance or change in our lives.

But when the heart yields to the influence of the Spirit of God, the conscience will be quickened, and the sinner will discern something of the depth and sacredness of God's holy laws—the foundation of His government in heaven and on earth. Conviction takes hold upon the mind and heart.

The prayer of David, after his fall, illustrates the nature of true sorrow for sin. His repentance was sincere and deep. There was no effort to hide his guilt; no desire to escape the judgment threatened. David saw the enormity of his transgression; he saw the defilement of his soul; he loathed his sin. It was not for pardon only that he prayed, but for purity of heart. He longed for the joy of holiness, to be restored to harmony and communion with God. A repentance such as this is beyond the reach of our own power to accomplish; it is obtained only through Jesus Christ.

The whole heart must be yielded, or the change can never be wrought in us by which we are to be restored to His likeness.

Jesus Christ is ready to set us free from sin, but He does not force the will. Study God's Word prayerfully. As you see the enormity of your sin, as you see yourself as you really are, do not give up in despair. It was sinners that Jesus Christ came to save. When Satan comes to tell you that you are a great sinner, look to your redeemer and speak of His merits. Acknowledge your sins, but tell the enemy that Jesus Christ came into the world to save sinners like you, and therefore you too may be saved.

All too many of us have grown up in some mainstream church and taken our religious beliefs for granted. We have simply assumed that all would be well if we just went along with the crowd, blended into this world, and lived reasonably decent and respectable lives. That is precisely how most of us have been terribly deceived (as I was in the years past) and have unwittingly come to believe in a false gospel, a wrong way of life and a different teaching. This false teaching is opposed to what Jesus Christ really came to reveal to us: God's way of life and His true gospel.

What is the major deception that Satan has palmed off on mainstream Christianity? The doctrine of antichrist. Yet this widespread antichrist doctrine is only the "tip of the iceberg" in the vast religious deception being carried out in the name of Christianity. In fact, this deception is so thorough that thousands of professing Christian ministers and priests are themselves deceived and therefore do not even realize that they are perpetuating a lie! Jesus Christ similarly described the false religious leaders of his day: "let them alone. They are blind leaders of the blind. And if the blind leads the blind, both will fall into a ditch" (Matthew 15:14).

Satan is content to let us believe in God and Jesus Christ as long as he can still control us—making us

Don't be deceived
By David Skipper

miss the true instruction of Jesus Christ, the Word of God, and His laws and commandments. Satan's goal is to keep you out of the coming Kingdom of God. There have been in the past, and are now, many antichrists! And underlying all of their deception is the spirit of antichrist— the wrong approaches and false doctrines which have blinded billions of human beings from understanding God's truth. The doctrine of antichrist is not understood by most of the world's religious leaders, nevertheless, there is a very real Satan. Jesus Christ twice called him the ruler of this world (John 12:31; 14:30). Satan is the great deceiver and so will be the soon coming antichrist. The apostle John made it very clear that Satan deceives the vast majority of mankind: "So the great dragon was cast out, that serpent of old, called the devil and Satan, who deceives the whole world; he was cast to the earth, and his angels were cast out with him" (Revelation 12:9).

James explains how the true Christian must not merely believe in God, but must surrender to God's will and do what He says (James 2:17-26). James writes: "You see then that a man is justified by works, and not by faith only" (v.24).

"Justified by works?" Yes—along with faith! It should be very clear that true Christianity involves more than just accepting, in faith, Jesus' death as full payment for our sins. When we accept His sacrifice, we must also make a true covenant with our Creator to *quit sinning*, to truly surrender and let Christ Jesus live His obedient life in us through the Holy Spirit! So we must repent of our sins, repent of breaking God's spiritual laws, which are founded on the Ten Commandments. This involves a life of humble obedience—the spiritual work of keeping God's laws and commandments.

Make no mistake, and let us understand, that no one can ever earn salvation—it is God's gift! The true grace of God leads to the gift of salvation through our Lord Jesus Christ (Ephesians 2:8-10; Romans 6:23). Those willing to obey God (Acts 5:29, 32), and who are under true grace, will be His workmanship, created in Christ Jesus for good works (Ephesians 2:10). God's grace does not eliminate the need for obedience, good works, and keeping God's commandments. The apostle Paul warned that one could "receive the grace of God in vain" (2 Corinthians 6:1), and while the apostle Peter exhorted Christians to "rest your hope fully upon the grace that is to be brought to you at the revelation of Jesus Christ" (1 Peter 1:13), he continues with the expectation that we do so as obedient children (v.14; cf. v.2).

When men cleverly misuse grace—teaching cheap grace, without real repentance from sin—it is the very essence of the doctrine of antichrist! This false concept has allowed millions of professing Christians to go through life regularly and habitually disobeying the Ten Commandments—yet assuming they are living a good Christians life by grace through Jesus Christ (1 John 2:3-7; 1 John 3:4, 7, 22, 24; 1 John 5:1-4; 2 John 1-6).

In his epistle, Jude was inspired to warn us of this very deception. "Beloved, while I was very diligent to write to you concerning our common salvation, I found it necessary to write to you exhorting you to contend earnestly for the faith which was once for all delivered to the saints. For certain men have crept in unnoticed, who long ago were marked out for this condemnation, ungodly men, who turn the grace of our God into licentiousness and deny the only Lord God and our Lord Jesus Christ" (Jude 3-4).

Jude warns of false teachers using the idea of grace as a vehicle for *licentiousness*—license to disobey the very laws of God! Why is this such a serious matter? Because it creates a lawless society—a society cut off from God, since the Ten Commandments actually portray His character. God's awesome purpose involves our going through a process of spiritual growth and overcoming to reflect the very character of God and be made fit to rule with Jesus Christ in His soon-coming Kingdom. Jesus directly states: "And he who *overcomes*, and *keeps my works until the end*, to him I will give power over the nation—he shall rule them with a rod of iron; as the potter's vessels shall be broken to pieces —as I also have received from my Father " (Revelation 2:7, 26-27; 14:12-13; 22:14). The antichrist will be coming, and he is coming to pursecute the saints who abideth in the Ten Commandments, and overcometh, and walks as Jesus Christ did—in His Father's Commandments (Revelation 12:17). ✍

U.S. lawmakers turn to prayer
By Garry W. Johnson, MOUNTAIN REVIEW Staff

This year some politicians have decided to turn to the Almighty for help with the drastic situations this country finds itself in.

In November, Georgia Governor Sonny Perdue and 250 others prayed for rain outside the state Capitol in Atlanta, in hopes of ending the epic drought that state is experiencing.

"We haven't done all that we should have done (to conserve water), and I think we all acknowledge that," Perdue said. "But we're doing better, and once we began to do better, I thought it was time to acknowledge that to the Creator. ... We ask God to shower our state, our region, our nation with the blessings of water."

Alabama Governor Bob Riley began asking his state's citizens to join him in praying for rain this past June. As an exceptional drought began baring down on Alabama, Riley issued a proclamation declaring June 30 through July 7 as "Days of Prayer for Rain." He asked residents to pray individually and in their houses of worship.

Riley said that, "Throughout history, Alabamians have turned in prayer to God, to humbly ask for His blessings and to hold us steady in times of difficulty. This drought is without question a time of great difficulty for our farmers and for communities across our state."

Most of north Alabama had been placed under the worst classification of "exceptional drought," by the U.S. Drought Monitor. The next category of "extreme drought," covered much of the rest of the state, with the exception of the coast which was under "moderate drought" conditions.

As drought condition persisted all over the U.S., a bipartisan congressional group began encouraging Americans to spend five minutes a week praying for the nation. Volunteers are asked to sign up for specific time periods at the website www.prayercauces.org, so that someone is praying for the nation every moment. Virginia House Representative J. Randy Forbes (R) who heads the Congressional Prayer Caucus Foundation said the idea is to "build a spiritual prayer wall around America."

These lawmakers are on the right track, but they seem to be missing a key factor to God's ever enduring mercy—**true repentance**. In Isaiah 59:1-2 God tells His children, "Behold, the LORD'S hand is not shortened, that it cannot save; neither his ear heavy, that it cannot hear: But your iniquities have separated between you and your God, and your sins have hid his face from you, that he will not hear." Only true heartfelt repentance will remove our past sins and take away the barrier between our people and the Living God. As the Psalmist reminds us, "Righteousness exalteth a nation: but sin is a reproach to any people" Proverbs 14:34. ✍

If you want lean vital tools to securing your petitions with God, please request the free booklet *Twelve Keys to Answered Prayers*. This booklet, and many others, are available upon request at no cost to you, when you write to:

The Living Church of God
P.O. Box 3810
Charlotte, NC 28227-8010.

God wants us to talk to Him, to praise Him, and even to petition Him with our requests. But we cannot assume just because we talk to Him that He hears us. God did say through David, "If I regard iniquity in my heart, the Lord will not hear me" (Psalms 66:16). Jesus also tells us, "Now we know that God heareth not sinners: but if any man be a worshipper of God, and doeth his will, him he heareth" (John 9:31).

We must first live in a way that honors Him and follows His standards. When we do that, we are assured that He will hear our prayers. Although God knows our every thought, He may disregard our prayers and petitions if we have allowed sin to destroy our fellowship with Him. I want us to look in this article at the things we may do that hinders us in our prayers.

One of the things that causes God to turn His ear away is disregarding the Word of God. The writer of Proverbs tells us, "He that turneth away his ear from hearing the law, even his prayer shall be abomination" (Proverbs 28:9). Today there seems to be so many people who want to do things their way and not even hear what God has to say about it. How can we expect God to listen to us when we do not listen to Him. I believe that God is more concerned with our eternal things than with our temporary things. All that God wants to hear from a sinner is the prayer of repentance.

Another area that will hinder your prayer life is having unforgiveness in your heart. Jesus tells us, "And when ye stand praying, forgive, if ye have ought against any: that your Father also which is in heaven may forgive you your trespasses" (Mark 11:25).

I realize that in our world today we have so many Christians that have gone through divorce or separation. I am sure that they feel betrayed and rejected and have deep hurts from their ex-spouse. I have counseled with some and they are having a hard time forgiving them. I believe that if you will call on God with an honest heart and ask Him to forgive you for your bitterness and then start praying for your ex, you will see the animosity melt away. God wants to help you but you must let Him.

Another barrier for answered prayers is having your heart cherish some sin. When we were in sin, sin was fun and exciting for a time. Possibly you may have treasured memories of some sin that you committed and every now and then just relive them. Be careful, know that sin separates man from God and this sin can become a barrier. Jesus tells us, "He who puts his hand to the plow and looks back is not fit for the kingdom of God." David tells us, "If I regard iniquity in my heart, the Lord will not hear me" (Psalms 66:18). God is more interested in your soul than in your desires.

If we ignore the pleas of the poor, God will not hear us. There are churches today who do not want the poor around them. Probably, if a street person should come into their church, I feel sure they would ask them to leave. It is our responsibility to take care of the poor. I am reminded of the parable of the marriage supper. If you will remember, the master asked the servants to go and invite the people to come to the marriage supper that the master was preparing. They invited them, but they made their excuses of why they could not come. When the servants told the master, he became angry and told them to go to the "poor, lame, and the halt." The servants said, "We have done that and there is still room." The master then told them to go to the "highways and hedges" and compel them to come. We know that the first group were the Jews. When they were invited they rejected the groom, Jesus Christ. The second group is you and me. There have been many invitations (revivals) to the Gentiles and a lot have accepted the invitation. But there is still room. So they have gone to the highways and hedges. The highways represents the homeless and the hedges represents the institutions. The word hedge in the Greek means: "walled up places." How much like God is it to have the last revival before He comes reach out to the poor who cannot afford the hot-shot preachers?

Solomon writes, "Whoso stoppeth his ears at the cry of the poor, he also shall cry himself, but shall not be heard" (Proverbs 21:13). God wants us to help the helpless, care for the homeless, and lift up the down trodden. He didn't just save us to give us fire insurance. When we are born again we become servants of God to be servants of those in need. James tells us, "What doth it profit, my brethren, though a man say he hath faith, and have not works? can faith save him? If a brother or sister be naked, and destitute of daily food, And one of you say unto them, Depart in peace, be ye warmed and filled; not withstanding ye give them not those things which are needful to the body; what doth it profit? Even so faith, if it hath not works, is dead, being alone" (James 2:14-17).

If you really want to have true religion and know that you are doing what God wants you to do, then obey James 1:27: "Pure religion and undefiled before God and the Father is this, To visit the fatherless and widows in their affliction, and to keep himself unspotted from the world."

Living in sinfulness will also hinder your prayers. God spoke to the children of Israel through Isaiah because of this problem. God said, "Behold, the Lord's hand is not shortened, that it cannot save; neither his ear heavy, that it cannot hear: But your iniquities have separated between you and your God, and your sins have hid his face from you, that he will not hear" (Isaiah 59:1-2).

It seems that Satan has deceived sinners into believing that it's OK to pray to God and He will hear you. I remember a time when I was witnessing to one of my brothers and he stated, "Dean, you would be surprised if you knew how much I prayed." I told him, "No I wouldn't, because when I was lost I prayed every night." I remember praying each night was like a ritual. When I would go to bed and the lights were off and everything was quite, that small voice would speak to me and say, "Where would you go if you died tonight?" Each night I would pray, "Oh, God, forgive me of my sins." Knowing that when I woke up the next morning I would be right back into what I was in the day before. I wasn't being saved, I was just deceived. The writer of Proverbs tells us, "He that covereth his sins shall not prosper, but he who confesseth and forsaketh his sins shall have mercy."

The only prayer that God wants to hear from a sinner is the prayer of repentance. Jesus told his disciples this in John 9:31, "Now we know that God heareth not sinners: but if any man be a worshipper of God, and doeth his will, him he heareth."

Another hindrance to your prayers is having discord in the home. Today with all of the divorces taking place no wonder people can't get through to God. Peter warns us of this in 1 Peter 3:7, "Likewise, ye husbands, dwell with them according to knowledge, giving honour unto the wife, as unto the weaker vessel, and as being heirs together of the grace of life; that your prayers be not hindered." Peter is writing to Christians who apparently are having problems in their marriage. I believe that if we give honor to our wife and treat her as your equal in your walk together in the grace of life you will not have to worry about your wife causing problems in the marriage. Sometimes the problem with men is that we think our wife is not our equal. In fact, some treat their wives as though they were the family slave. Men, we don't need to fool ourselves. Without the wife, you and I would only be a shell of who we are with our wives.

Some Christians do not get their prayers answered because of doubting God's ability to answer them. We use the excuse, "Well, if its God's will." This tends to let God off the hook. Let me tell you, God doesn't want off the hook. He wants to answer our prayers. God wants our family saved. He also wants to heal us and to help us in our every day life experience. We just need to believe and call on Him. James tells us in James 1:6-7: "But let him ask in faith, nothing wavering. For he that wavereth is like a wave of the sea driven with the wind and tossed. For let not that man think that he shall receive any thing of the Lord."

On the other hand, our requests may be self-centered and this will hinder our prayers also. So many times we go overboard in asking God for what, we want and our prayer requests become self-centered and not considering other people. God is not Santa Claus who will give us all we want. Neither is God a bull dog that we can sic on those that we don't like or who do us wrong. I remember counseling with a former pastor who had left his wife and had run off with a member of his church. He had moved to another town and was working and living with this girl, but he was miserable. He told me that sometimes he could not even sleep because of the guilt and conviction that God was putting him under.

After living with her for six months, her father found out where they were and went to see them. When the father knocked on the door, and when my friend answered the door, the father immediately started praying, "God, send fire from heaven and devour this man." My friend cried out, "Instead of praying for God to kill me, why don't you pray that your daughter will repent and go back to her husband." You see, the father was so angry that he wanted him dead. To me, that is a selfish prayer. Later on the daughter did repent and went back to her husband, and my friend repented and went back to his wife. Thank God.

Remember, James tells us that it's the prayer of the righteous man that is effective. I believe that is the key to getting your prayers answered. James 5:16 says, "Confess your faults one to another, and pray one for another, that ye may be healed. The effectual fervent prayer of a righteous man availeth much." ✍

"When God Doesn't Hear Our Prayer"
By Chaplain Dean Yancey

Our views respecting prayer need to be revised and brought into harmony with the teaching of Scripture on the subject. The prevailing idea seems to be that I come to God and ask Him for something that I want, and that I expect Him to give me that which I have asked. But this is a most dishonoring and degrading conception. The popular belief reduces God to a servant, our servant: doing our bidding, performing our pleasure, granting our desires. No; prayer is a coming to God, telling Him my need, committing my way unto the Lord, and leaving Him to deal with it as it seemeth Him best. This makes my will subject to His, instead of, as in the former case, seeking to bring His will into subjection to mine. No prayer is pleasing to God unless the spirit actuating it is "not my will, but Thine be done." "When God bestows blessings on a praying people, it is not for the sake of their prayers, as if He was inclined and turned by them; but it is for His own sake, and of His own Sovereign will and pleasure. Should it be said, to what purpose then is prayer? it is answered, This is the way and means God has appointed for the communication of the blessing of His goodness to His people. For though He has purposed, provided, and promised them, yet He will be sought unto, to give them, and it is a duty and privilege to ask. When they are blessed with a spirit of prayer it forebodes well, and looks as if God intended to bestow the good things asked, which should be asked always with submission to the will of God, saying, Not my will but Thine be done" (John Gill). —Excerpt from: *The Sovereignty of God*, By Arthur W. Pink (1886-1952)

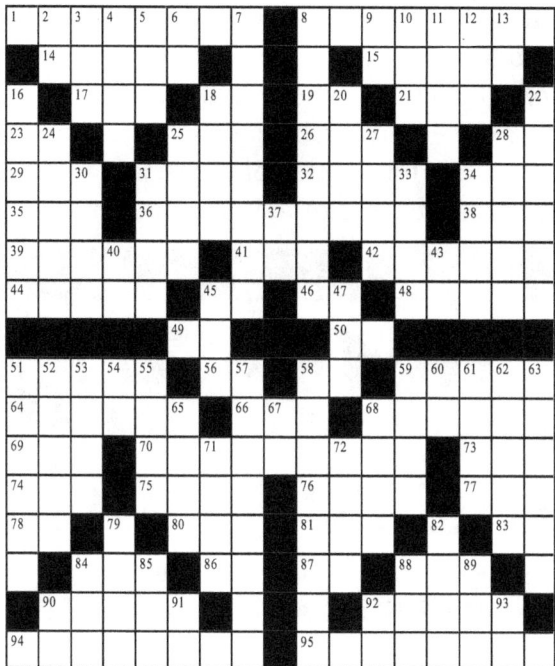

Crock's Puzzle Fun

31. Quaker William
32. ____ Gin Fiz
34. G.W.'s bro
35. Robert E. ___
36. Type of ladder or cord
38. Neighbor of Mexico
39. Noah's parking mount
41. Kanga's kid
42. Harken
44. Not as common
45. Jackson's state
46. Egyptian sun god
48. Dry and dirty
49. State's lawyer
50. Trenton's state
51. With "net," percussion instrument
56. Penn's state
58. Pierre's state
59. Make clear
64. Confidence
66. Favorite
68. Whip
69. Wade's opponent
70. Finished
73. Emmet
74. Translated (abr.)
75. Organic compound
76. Hence
77. Snitch
78. UFO pilot?
80. Nickname for Andy's son?
81. Address (abr.)

83. Sea level
84. Booster
86. VCR setting
87. Juneau's state
88. Followers of Dees?
90. With "sone," arthritis treatment
92. English navigator and explorer
94. Big squirter
95. Going into

DOWN
2. Letters on electrical appliances
3. Male offspring
4. Little horse
5. Opposite of WSW
6. 22 down's state
7. Mule drivers
8. Like a rat on a sinking ship
9. Trustee (abr.)
10. Hearing organ
11. Prepare for publication
12. Pop's mate
13. Prefix with chant or drive
16. Nab
18. ½ quart
20. 1,151 in Roman times
22. Capitol of 6 down
24. Singing play
25. Words in print
27. Swimming hole?
28. Return to ready
30. Close by
31. Fruit
33. City in Oklahoma

34. Protrudes
37. Absolutely not
40. Symbol for Rhenium
43. T separates them
45. Survey
47. Plus
51. 38th U.S. President
52. Left side
53. Snow slider
54. __ be, or not ...
55. 1st, 13th, 3rd, 5th of 26
57. As American as _____ ___
58. Cheap berths
59. Rover's pal
60. The Wizard of __
61. Russian ruler
62. Arm bones
63. Colonize
65. U-2's singer
67. Elevated railway, for short
68. Cribbage needs
71. Brood
72. Star-____
79. Goods
82. Ursa
84. ___ he's a jolly ...
85. ___ degree
88. Before
89. Slide around
90. Cast iron (abr.)
91. Zeus made a cow of her
92. Double Time (abr.)
93. Ditto 13 down

ACROSS
1. Hangs
8. Respected
14. Crazy
15. Radioactive gaseous element
17. Opposite Of SSW
18. Magnum __
19. Room (abr.)
21. Edge
23. Pool filler?
25. Container
26. Electroconvulsive pulse (abr.)
28. Radial length (abr.)
29. RN's helper

—Edited by Garry W. Johnson, MOUNTAIN REVIEW Staff

Life in the 1500's

Contributed by Judy Johnson, from Internet email

The next time you are washing your hands and complain because the water temperature isn't just how you like it, think about how things used to be. Here are some pretty interesting facts about the 1500's:

Most people got married in June because they took their yearly bath in May and still smelled pretty good by June. However, they were starting to smell, so brides carried a bouquet of flowers to hide the body odor. Hence the custom today of carrying a bouquet when getting married.

Baths consisted of a big tub filled with hot water. The man of the house had the privilege of the nice clean water, then all the other sons and men, and then the women, and finally the children—last of all the babies. By then the water was so dirty you could actually lose someone in it. Hence the saying, "Don't throw the baby out with the bath water."

Houses had thatched roofs—thick straw-piled high, with no wood underneath. It was the only place for animals to get warm, so all the cats, dogs, and other small animals (mice, bugs, etc.) lived in the roof. When it rained it became slippery and sometimes the animals would slip and fall off the roof. Hence the saying "It's raining cats and dogs!"

There was nothing to stop things from falling into the house. This posed a real problem in the bedroom where bugs and other droppings could mess up your nice clean bed. Hence, a bed with big posts and a sheet hung over the top afforded some protection. That's how canopy beds came into existence.

The floor was dirt. Only the wealthy had something other than dirt. Hence the saying "dirt poor."

The wealthy had slate floors that would get slippery in the winter when wet, so they spread thresh (straw) on the floor to help keep their footing. As the winter wore on, they added more thresh until when you opened the door it would all start slipping outside. A piece of wood was placed in the entrance-way. Hence the saying a "thresh hold." (Getting quite an education, aren't you?)

In those old days, they cooked in the kitchen with a big kettle that always hung over the fire. Every day they lit the fire and added things to the pot. They ate mostly vegetables and did not get much meat. They would eat the stew for dinner, leaving leftovers in the pot to get cold overnight and then start over the next day. Sometimes stew had food in it that had been there for quite a while. Hence the rhyme, "Peas porridge hot, peas porridge cold, peas porridge in the pot nine days old."

Sometimes they could obtain pork, which made them feel quite special. When visitors came over, they would hang up their bacon to show off. It was a sign of wealth that a man could "bring home the bacon." They would cut off a little to share with guests and would all sit around and "chew the fat."

Those with money had plates made of pewter. Food with high acid content caused some of the lead to leach onto the food, causing lead poisoning death. This happened most often with tomatoes, so for the next 400 years or so, tomatoes were considered poisonous.

Bread was divided according to status. Workers got the burnt bottom of the loaf, the family got the middle, and guests got the top, or "upper crust."

Lead cups were used to drink ale or whisky. The combination would sometimes knock the imbibers out for a couple of days. Someone walking along the road would take them for dead and prepare them for burial. They were laid out on the kitchen table for a couple of days and the family would gather around and eat and drink and wait and see if they would wake up. Hence the custom of holding a "wake."

England is old and small and the local folks started running out of places to bury people. So they would dig up coffins and would take the bones to a "bone-house" and reuse the grave. When reopening these coffins, 1 out of 25 coffins were found to have scratch marks on the inside and they realized they had been burying people alive. So they would tie a string on the wrist of the corpse, lead it through the coffin and up through the ground and tie it to a bell. Someone would have to sit out in the graveyard all night (the "graveyard shift") to listen for the bell; thus, someone could be "saved by the bell" or was considered a "dead ringer."

And that's the truth ... Now, who ever said that History was boring!!! Educate someone ... share these facts with a friend. ☺

Answers to puzzle on page 23:

Editor's note: The MOUNTAIN REVIEW *is an* INMATE NEWSPAPER, *and we need your help!*

If you have information on prisoner resources, opinions on improving living conditions, advice on surviving the prison system—anything useful to the rehabilitation, education, or entertainment of the inmate population, please submit your articles to Jeremy Ingram in unit 4, or Garry Johnson in unit 14, or by mail to the address on the right.

The deadline for submissions for the Spring paper is February 28, the cutoff for the Summer issue is May 31, so please send in your articles today!

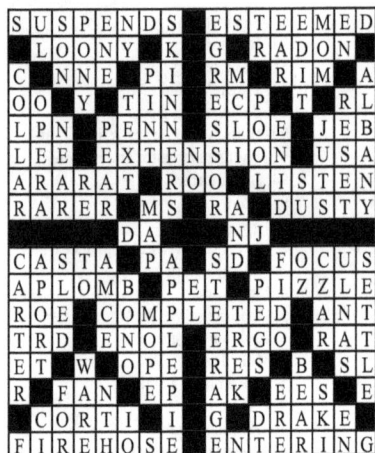

The *Mountain Review* was produced as a free government document written by prisoners at Brushy Mountain State Penitentiary and Morgan County Correctional Complex. It was sponsored by the Education Department at those facilities and was a censored publication. Permission to reprint was granted in this section of each edition. The views expressed are those of individual authors.

PRISONER Resource Guide

2021 Edition

Chapel Library
2603 West Wright St.
Pensacola, Florida 32505
chapellibrary.org
chapel@mountzion.org
850.438.6666

They sell quality reference books (lexicons, Bible dictionaries, and concordances) at wholesale prices. Ask for an Inmate Order Form, to receive directly over 100 free literature titles or the Inmate MZBI Application Form to enroll in their correspondence courses.

Ohio University Correctional Education
Haning Hall 102
1 Ohio University
Athens OH 45701
correctional@ohio.edu
800.444.2420

Since 1974 Ohio University's Correctional Education has provided an opportunity for incarcerated students to study through print-based courses, to earn college credit, and work toward an Ohio University degree. Ohio University is accredited by the Higher Learning Commission. Students who want to learn but aren't interested in a degree can take a few courses or complete a legal studies certificate.

United Church of God, an International Association
P.O. Box 541027
Cincinnati, OH 45254-1027
ucg.org

Publishes Christian literature (booklets on numerous subjects), books, Bible studies, and a bimonthly magazine, all offered free as an educational service in the public interest. Ministers are available to counsel, answer questions, and explain the Bible through correspondence.

Correctional Education Association
P.O. Box 3430
Laurel, MD 20709
ceanational.org
443.459.3080

A professional association serving educators and administrators around the world, committed to educating individuals in correctional settings.

CURE
National Capital Station
P.O. Box 2310
Washington, DC 20013
curenational.org

Providing rehabilitative opportunities to turn lives around. Prisoners may request their newsletter or for further information.

The Center for Children of Incarcerated Parents (CCIP)
P.O. Box 41286
Eagle Rock, CA 90041
e-ccip.org
ccip@earthlink.net
626.449.2470

Correspondence centers are available to prisoners nationwide. Courses taught by CCIP staff are offered regionally. They also train instructors to teach CCIP curricula; the clearinghouse project offers a collection of over 3,500 documentary and audiovisual items that can be purchased on line or by mail through two catalogs. By mail, through the catalog for Incarcerated Parents, they offer more than 200 items free of charge to prisoners and their families. Their mission is the prevention of intergenerational crime and incarceration.

Compassion
140 W. Boundary St.
Perrysburg, OH 43551
compassionondealthrow.net

Newsletter written by death row prisoners, free to people on death row, $25 for other prisoners, $50 for people outside of prison. Half of the subscription money given in scholarships to family members of murder victims.

Dedication: In most books you'll find this right after the title page, but this isn't like most books. *A Prison Anthology, Bushy Mountain 2005-2007* is dedicated to the handful of solid dudes I spent my 18 years of incarceration with. And "handful" isn't simply an expression. At any given time you could count the number of folks I associated with on one hand – not those I came in contact with (in prison you're in constant contact with all kinds) but those I shared ideas and experiences with. They know who they are, and you know the kind of folks I'm talking about – the kind that aren't blowing smoke but telling you the honest truth. There are still a few, but the number seems to be shrinking as time goes on. One of the markers of a "solid dude" is that he does the right thing even when he has nothing to gain from it, just because it's right. He is the type of man who donate his time, energy, and finances into prisoner clubs, prisoner ministries, and legal assistance (really, assistance of any kind). So if some guy is tutoring you through the GED, or helping you with your case, or walking a blind guy to chow, cut him some slack. He is one of the ones making your environment better, and he could use your help. Many of these type people are listed below.

Index By Contributor:

Index By Subject and/or Title

Covenant Concepts
A Church of God Prison Outreach

P.O. Box 12
Eidson, TN 37731

Established in 2019 by a former state prisoner of 18 years, our organization is a nonprofit dedicated to providing free educational materials to the incarcerated worldwide. We provide one new or used educational book every six months, free of charge. We request that you send us three areas of interest, preferably one from each field we cover (academic/vocational, self-help, and spiritual). To each inquiry we will respond with acknowledgment of your request, receipt for the book we purchased, a free magazine from one of our affiliate Church organizations, and any additional information we believe helpful. We do not provide any fiction materials and we work from donations, so please be patient. The following form should be used when requesting books, or requests should include the following information:

Full Legal Name: _____

Prison ID Number: _____

Name of Institution: _____

Mailing Address: _____

_____

Earliest Possible Release Date: _____

Areas of Interest –

    Academic/Vocational: _____

    Self-Help: _____

    Spiritual: _____

Special Mailing Instructions: _____
(e.g.: hardcover/paperback only; restricted distributors/suppliers)

Thank you for your efforts to make the most of this time. There are people out here pulling for you.